Integrated Buildings

THE SYSTEMS BASIS OF ARCHITECTURE

LEONARD R. BACHMAN

JOHN WILEY & SONS, INC.

Published by John Wiley & Sons, Inc., Hoboken, New Jersey

Published simultaneously in Canada

For general information on our other products and services or for technical support, please contact our Customer Care Department within the United States at (800) 762-2974, outside the United States at (317) 572-3993 or fax (317) 572-4002.

Wiley also publishes its books in a variety of electronic formats. Some content that appears in print may not be available in electronic books. For more information about Wiley products, visit our web site at www.wiley.com.

Library of Congress Cataloging-in-Publication Data:

Bachman, Leonard R.
    Integrated buildings: the systems basis of architecture / Leonard R. Bachman
       p. cm.
    Includes bibliographical references and index.
    ISBN 0-471-38827-0
       1. Architecture and technology. 2. Architectural design — Case studies.
    3. Architectural engineering. I. Title
    NA2543.T43 B33 2003
    729—dc21   2002015346

Printed in Mexico

10 9 8 7 6 5

Integrated Buildings

Contents

Preface

The idea for this book originated at the University of Houston, Gerald D. Hines College of Architecture. Our technology faculty met in the spring of 1986 to discuss course revisions and curriculum coordination. The pressing needs we saw at that time were twofold. First, our research methods class needed to be reconfigured. Second, we wanted to provide more opportunities for students to assimilate technology course topics in the studio setting. We settled on a new textbook, *The Building Systems Integration Handbook* (Rush, et al., 1986), as the solution to both problems.

The course remains a capstone technology class in the college today. It is a case study seminar class of about 25 upper-level undergraduate students and a few graduates who take the class as an elective. Anatomical studies are made of the systems used in landmark buildings as if we were in a biology laboratory. Students ponder over the component systems, deduce how the design and the technology came to fit, and propose how that fit enables the design's architectural success. David Thaddeus, our structures curriculum leader, later joined the faculty at the University of North Carolina at Charlotte and initiated a similar course there. Meanwhile, a growing number of integration courses are offered at architecture schools around the world.

The inclusion of integrated systems design in our increasingly complex and technically sophisticated architecture seems like an obvious idea. It seems so obvious, in fact, that the counter-position of seeing *integration* as "just another word for design" is worth pondering. Isn't architecture already among the most inclusive of all disciplines? Are architects not truly the "last of the Renaissance professionals"? What is so new about integration that distinguishes it from what architects have always done?

The answer to these questions requires preliminary inquiry. First, "What is integration?" and "How do architects manage it?" The answers are illustrated by a push-pull dynamic. Integration is specifically concerned with that aspect of architecture in which technology constantly pushes design possibilities expansively while design assimilation continuously pulls them inward toward a final solution. As part of the design process, integration activity follows a path paved by the architect's philosophy of appropriate judgment. Technical requirements restrict the subjective freedom of such judgments and set up a series of integration challenges for the architect to solve. There is nothing new about "integration" per se. It is not a stylistic or comprehensive design approach, and the discussions in this book are not a critique of present practice or a new historical perspective. Integration is, however, an emergent and increasingly critical focus of architectural design. This book is about that emergence and focus.

> First, the medium of architecture must be re-examined if the increased scope of our architecture as well as the complexity of its goals [are] to be expressed. Simplified or superficially complex forms will not work....Second, the growing complexities of our functional problems must be acknowledged."
>
> *Robert Venturi, Complexity and Contradiction in Architecture (1966, p. 19).*

Focus on integration as a discipline arises from the sudden injection and rapid advancement of technical systems since the Second World War. Change has since occurred at a revolutionary pace, far outstripping the advances of design accommodation and the technical education of architects. And revolutionary change has never been the mode of mainstream architectural thinking. Creative risk taking for architects is usually confined to elements of style, formal expression, and contextual relevance. Experimental building systems are seldom selected over proven ones (except for world's fair pavilions, where dramatic and usually temporary solutions are expected). An example of risk-taking failure might be the early shortcomings of "solar architecture" in achieving mainstream status in the eyes of the profession or in the dreams of a large public audience.

This book puts integration into what could be called the mediating or middle ground between design and technology. The middle ground has previously fallen primarily to a few works that chronicle the advent of building technology. Peter Reyner Banham, James Marston Fitch, and Martin Prawley were among the first to give integration issues a voice. David Guise, Carl Bovil, and Richard Rush (et al.) are among later contributors. Buckminster Fuller's special contributions are covered in Chapter 2 of this book. Along the way there have also been a number of architect/engineers whose individual design work and architectural collaborations qualify as purely integrative: Luigi Nervi, Felix Candela, Frei Otto, and Peter Rice, to mention some prominent individuals.

Integration as an independent topic came to the foreground in 1986 when Richard Rush and an impressive team of investigators researched and wrote the *Building Systems Integration Handbook* (Rush, 1986). *The BSI Handbook* was still in popular use in its sixth unrevised printing. This present text will, it is hoped, find an audience with continuing interest in integration topics. The author gratefully acknowledges a debt to those who pioneered the field.

This present textbook assumes that the reader has some preparation in architectural design, technology, and history. It is not a primer, and there is no easy substitute for the background that this book presumes. The novice will do well to use a good number of the cited references as companion reading. The conceptual overviews offered in this text are probably not adequate for the beginning student.

Methods of integration make up Part I of this book. This part is broken into four chapter-length topics. The first of these presents a rationale and overview of integration topics. Chapter 2 describes "Systems Thinking" from the time of the Crystal Palace forward. Chapter 3 looks at different modes of integration activity and overviews the integration potential of building systems. The final chapter on methods, Chapter 4, presents an analytical model for tracing integration through any work of architecture, as well as an expanded case study of Ibsen Nelsen's design for the Pacific Museum of Flight as an example analysis.

The sole intent of methods section is to illustrate a procedure for analyzing building integration. No attempt is made to imitate the holistic complexity of design; the integration paradigm in this Part necessarily portrays design activities in a simplified step-by-step fashion. The value of this limited perspective is, of course, that it allows isolation of topics so that they can be digested piece by piece. Analytical exercise of the paradigm should ultimately lead to a greater ability to define and synthesize one's own design ambitions.

The case studies selected for inclusion in Part II illustrate how systems technology and integration thinking have been championed and advanced. The grouping of the example buildings by type and chronology provides a matrix of works that are widely accepted as significant buildings. Critical evaluation of these buildings is not vitally important in this text; the buildings were selected primarily for ease of unfolding their integration lessons. Nonetheless, most of the buildings chosen are well recognized in the mainstream and easily accessible through numerous publications. It is hoped that their inclusion here helps to illustrate integration in clear and relevant ways.

Please send feedback to the author's attention at:

LEONARD R. BACHMAN
University of Houston
College of Architecture 4431
Houston, Texas 77204-4431

or

LBachman@UH.edu

Acknowledgments

First comes love, then comes courage,
then comes truth.

Richard Rush, February 21, 2001, in an
E-mail of encouragement

A colleague and mentor, Bruce Webb, suggested that a meta-book, or at least a story about how this book unfolded, might be worthwhile. It struck me later that perhaps something of that account could serve as an acknowledgment of the many people and institutions that contributed to its cause.

First I want to recognize the University of Houston College of Architecture and students who participated directly by producing material for the book. Aside from course participation, there were some special contributions. Rich Kaul completed the lion's share of the graphics and did considerable work on the manuscript for workshop credit. He also generated the PA Technology Laboratory case study in Chapter 5. Andrew Lewis worked on the graphics for no reason other than his sincere interest in the topic. Both Rich and Andy are graduate students. Travis Hughs, a fifth-year senior in our undergraduate program, constructed the 3-D CAD models used as illustrations of some buildings.

My longtime friend and grandly popular peer, David Thaddeus, was first to suggest publication of the coursework and case studies being developed in the Building Systems Integration class. In late June of 1999 he and I met John Wiley & Sons editor Amanda Miller at the American Collegiate Schools of Architecture (ACSA) conference in Montreal, and the three of us discussed a book proposal. David had just joined the faculty at the University of North Carolina–Charlotte, however, and ongoing demands of moving his career and family there from Houston eventually kept him from collaborating. David worked on the formative concepts and some of the case study material. He will see his own hand in many parts of this book.

Richard Rush endorsed the notion of a successor to the *Building Systems Integration Handbook* and provided mounds of wisdom and support for this project. Several members of the Society of Building Science Educators (SBSE) offered direction and comments on the proposal. Other members contributed photographs in response to a single posting on the (SBSE) server. G. Z. Brown mentored early ideas at the Montreal ACSA conference. Murray Milne was there with encouragement and direction and also helped plan a California case study expedition. John Reynolds provided the workings of the Emerald Peoples Utility District case study (Chapter 11). As always, the best advice provides some of the highlights of this book, but the author is to blame for the remaining blemishes. SBSE can be found at http://www.sbse.org. Alternately, send SBSE inquiries to Walter Grondzik / Department of Architecture, University of Oregon / School of Architecture / Florida A&M University / Tallahassee, FL 32307-4200.

In December 2000, I received an invitation from Chris Luebkeman on behalf of Ove Arup & Partners to research eight of the case study buildings that had passed through their offices. The offer included mention of searching Arup archives, so I quickly booked a flight to London. An internal grant from the University of Houston's Office of Sponsored Programs and support from the UH College of Architecture actually got me off the ground. The eight busy days I spent in southeast England were vital to everything in this book.

During the London stay, Luebkeman and colleagues were profoundly generous with their time and resources. Maureen Gil arranged building tours; Pauline Shirley opened the Arup photo library. Robert Lang and Jo

DaSilva granted interviews and offered insights on how integration happens in an Arup project. Peter Warburton of Arup Associates spent a day of his time with me at Briarcliff House, introduced me to Briarcliff teammate Terry Raggett, and also toured me around his own office group. Everyone at both Arup organizations was an intrepid listener, and I will never overcome the fascination I felt while talking with them. It inspires one to say things worth listening to.

John Jacobson patiently ushered me through the confines and corners of Lloyd's of London, as did Ken Osborne at Schlumberger in Cambridge. Both took an obvious and possessive pride in their respective buildings and also went to great lengths to make sure I didn't miss any of the high points. Some of their firsthand knowledge may be apparent in the case studies. An intimate working relationship with an architecturally successful building is a profound matter.

Everywhere, the book made friends. Queries and requests for information always seemed to broaden the alliances. Thanks go to Kay Poludniowski at the Sainsbury Center for Visual Arts and to several people at Deere & Company for sending comments and photographs. Burns and McDonald Engineering even mailed its 50th Anniversary book publication and put me in touch with associates who had worked with Eero Saarinen on the Deere Headquarters and Dulles Airport.

On the home front, many thanks to my dean, Joe Mashburn, for the resources and support of the University of Houston College of Architecture. Kudos to the entire staff at the William R. Jenkins Art and Architecture Library (you can have your books back now), starting with our head librarian, Margaret Culbertson. Bruce Webb reviewed several draft versions of the manuscript. Rives Taylor, who already splits time between our college and duty as campus architect for M. D. Anderson Hospital, still had the patience to read and comment on drafts. Some of the visiting lecturers at the college also contributed important ideas: Bernard Plattner from the Renzo Piano Workshop and Alistair McGregor from the San Francisco office of Ove Arup & Partners, to name just a couple. Peter Wood, my former dean now serving at Prairie View A&M, helped with formative ideas and recommended Daniel Willis's *Emerald City.*

Portions of this book were written while visiting my wife's family, the Kellers, in Bulle, Switzerland, and their parents' house was the base camp for several case study expeditions. The Kellers' hospitality and encouragement are with me still, not to mention my memories of the coffee, wine, and seemingly continuous banquet at their lively dinner table.

Finally, no book should ever be written without mentioning the people who suffered its tribulations in their own daily lives. Fortunately, my friend, lover, and partner, Christine, finished her master's thesis and began her doctorate work through the same time frame of this book's story. Of course, the background research, the building visits, and the obsessive stack of photographs were acquired over several years and Christine was there for all that too. She just finished one of many readings of yet another draft. We have had a great deal to talk about these last few years — whenever we looked up from our computers.

LEONARD BACHMAN

Integrated Buildings

PART I Methods

The Idea of Integration

CHAPTER 1 TOPICS

- Hardware: Integration Among Building Systems
- Software: Integration in the Design Process
- Philosophical Digression: Integration and the Progress of Technology
- Framework of Discussion

Discussion about the architecture of integrated buildings systems begins with a few basic questions. These fundamental questions underlie the four "methods" chapters of Part I. The seven succeeding chapters of Part II explore how these questions relate to several works of architecture. Taken as a whole, then, this book shows how case studies can be used to understand the integration of building systems and how inquiry into integration contributes to architectural success.

- What are integrated buildings?
- How does design for integration impact architectural thinking?
- Is integration the architect's responsibility?
- How does the notion of "building system" tie in with the idea of "systems thinking"?
- What benefits does integration provide?

Hardware: Integration Among Building Systems

In theory, it is entirely possible to design and construct a building made of totally independent components. The separate pieces of such a building could be designed in isolation, each part having an autonomous role to play. Someone who proposes this idea may note that a beam is a beam and a duct is a duct, after all, and there is no need to confuse one for the other. For every function or role to be performed in a building, there are a host of competing and individualized products to choose from. As long as the final assembly has already been worked out, the independent pieces can fulfill their single-purpose roles simply by fitting in place and not interfering with other pieces.

Most architects would quickly denounce this isolationist approach to design. Where, they would ask, is the harmony, the beauty, or even the practicality in such an absurdly fragmented method? Surely there is some sympathy and order among the parts that lead to a comprehensive whole?

Architects are, in fact, inherently prone to take exactly the opposite approach: Starting with carefully considered ideas about the complete and constructed building, they would then explore inward, working through intricate relationships between all the parts and functions. But how far does this concern for relationships go, and how inclusive is the complete idea? Equally important, what sort of thinking is required to comprehend and resolve all the issues that arise in the process? This is where the topic and discipline of integration fits in—providing an explicit framework for selecting and combining building components in purposeful and intentional ways.

Integration among the hardware components of building systems is approached with three distinct goals: Components have to share space, their arrangement has to be aesthetically resolved, and at some level, they have to work together or at least not defeat each other. These three goals are physical, visual, and performance integration. The following sections serve as a brief overview of how these goals are attained.

PHYSICAL INTEGRATION

Building components have to fit. They share space and volume in a building, and they connect in specific ways. CAD drawing layers offer a useful way to think about how complicated these networks of shared space and connected pieces can become. Superimposing structure and HVAC (heating, ventilating, and air-conditioning) layers provides an example: Are there problems where large ducts pass under beams? Do the reflected ceiling plan and furniture layouts put light fixtures where they belong?

Physical integration is fundamentally about how components and systems share space, how they fit together. In standard practice, for example, the floor-ceiling section of many buildings is often subdivided into separate zones: recessed lighting in the lowest zone, space for ducts next, and then a zone for the depth of structure to support the floor above. These segregated volumes prevent "interference" between systems by providing adequate space for each individually remote system. Meshing the systems together, say, by running the ducts between light fixtures, requires careful physical integration. Unifying the systems by using the ceiling cavity as a return air plenum and extracting return air through the light fixtures further compresses the depth of physical space required. If the structure consists of open web joists, trusses, or a space frame, then it is possible that all three systems may be phys-

ically integrated into a single zone by carefully interspersing ducts and light fixtures within the structure.

Connections between components and among systems in general constitute another aspect of physical integration. This is also where architectural details are generated. The structural, thermal, and physical integrity of the joints between different materials must be carefully considered. How they meet is just as important as how they are separated in space.

VISUAL INTEGRATION

Exposed and formally expressive components of a building combine to create its image. This is true of the overall visual idea of the building as well as of the character of rooms and of individual elements, down to the smallest details. The manner in which components share in a cumulative image is decided through acts of visual integration. Color, size, shape, and placement are common factors that can be manipulated in order to achieve the desired effect, so knowledge of the various components' visual character is essential to integrating them.

Visual harmony among the many parts of a building and their agreement with the intended visual effects of design often provide some opportunities for combining technical requirements with aesthetic goals. Light fixtures, air-conditioning, plumbing fixtures, and a host of other elements are going to have a presence in the building anyway. Ignoring them or trying to cover them with finishes or decoration is futile. Technical criteria and the systems that satisfy those functional demands require large shares of the resources that go into a building. It follows that architects should be able to select, configure, and deploy building elements in ways that satisfy both visual and functional objectives.

PERFORMANCE INTEGRATION

If physical integration is "shared space" and visual integration is "shared image," then performance integration must have something to do with shared functions. A load-bearing wall, for example, is both envelope and structure, so it unifies two functions into one element by replacing two columns, a beam, and the exterior wall. This approach can save cost and reduce complexity if it is appropriate to the task at hand.

Performance integration is also served by meshing or overlapping the functions of two components, even without actually combining the pieces. This may be called "shared mandates." In a direct-gain passive solar heating

Figure 1.1 The Kimbell Art Museum, Louis Kahn, Fort Worth, Texas, 1966 to 1972. *(Photo by Kristopher L. Liles.)*

system, for example, the floor of the sunlit space is sharing in the thermal work of the envelope and the mechanical heating system by providing thermal storage in its massive heat capacity, which limits indoor temperature swings from sunlit day to cold starry night. The envelope, structure, interior, and services are integrated by the shared thermal mandate of maintaining comfortable temperatures.

INTEGRATING INTEGRATIONS: LOUIS KAHN AND THE KIMBALL ART MUSEUM

The three modes of integration among systems are frequently interwoven, so it is difficult and probably unnecessary to label every act of integration as either physical, visual, or functional. The previous example of physical integration in a floor-to-ceiling section among lighting, ductwork, and structure also has important performance benefits if the lighting fixtures are used as return air registers and the plenum is used as a return air path. In addi-

tion, combining the lighting and return air register functions within the light fixtures simplifies the aesthetic of the room's ceiling. Most components of a building have physical, visual, and functional impacts; it is likely that one sort of integration will involve other sorts.

For an example of how these forms of integration can be combined, consider Louis Kahn's design for the Kimbell Art Museum. The synthesis of major systems is characterized by unification and meshing among structure, envelope, services, and interior systems and is embodied by the repeated use of an elegant concrete vault. This one element is both structural support and envelope enclosure. It also forms the interior space. Finally, by virtue of its cycloid ceiling shape and skylit ridge, its functions are meshed with the important services mandate of lighting a space for artwork. The physical, visual, and performance benefits are complete and convincing. The systems go beyond being minimally resolved; they are synergistic to the point of being provocatively elegant. It would be trivial to worry about their exact classification.

Software: Integration in the Design Process

For integration issues to surpass the technology-for-its-own-sake aspect and become celebrated in the design process, they must transcend the nuts-and-bolts of hardware integration and engage basic architectural ambition. Resolving the physical, visual, and functional fit among building systems is well and good. All buildings have to achieve these basic levels of integration to some degree before they can be built and occupied. It is also obvious that different levels of integration among the systems is possible and that a more highly integrated building is more likely to enjoy better degrees of fit, image, and function. But although these aspects contribute toward a better building, they do not inherently satisfy the notion of architecture.

If building components are the hardware of integration, then design can be thought of as the software complement. Design establishes the major architectural goals of a project and then directs the process of attaining them. The major goals can be described as the "architectural intention," and the management objectives as explorative work toward its realization. Constant human evaluation and the lens of subjective judgment prevent this from becoming a literal sort of design computation. Like the "if X then Y else Z" logic of software computation, however, design is the comparable rational process by which architects manage the process.

UNIFYING ART AND SCIENCE

Design and technology, if considered separately, present opposing priorities and agendas for architects. Fortunately, their complementary nature allows for an endless variety of starting places and any number of resolutions. At one pole of thinking, for example, there is the architect-as-artist, for whom technology is a means to the higher ends of aesthetic and formal ideals. At the other pole, for the architect-as-scientist, design is largely the result of technically optimized and honestly expressed solutions. Pure examples of these two poles would be hard to find, however, because successful buildings usually have some flavor of both aspects.

In modern architecture, the tensions between these two poles, and their resolution, form an often-overlooked aspect of successful buildings—overlooked despite how they typify sound architectural practice. The marriage of design ideals and technical innovation has become a strong and prevailing generative device. This is especially true since the postwar popularization of mechanical systems and the resulting complexity of interwoven building systems.

Integration topics were born of these new complexities, and the struggle to incorporate large and expensive new systems into buildings continued. But architects would not be forever content to simply fit new systems into old ways of thinking about buildings. Accommodation of technology changed architectural practice in more than an additive way. Physically incorporating the machines of industry and the magic of science into the bowels of their buildings led many architects to think of new and dynamic approaches to design. Here was the opportunity of an expanded vocabulary of parts and an almost magic essence of technical wizardry. In general terms, air-conditioning, lighting design, vertical transportation, and information systems became integral parts of more and more buildings. At the same time, scientific advances in structural materials and envelope components led to other equally intriguing possibilities. Exponentially expanded dimensions of design followed as serviceability joined constructability in the domain of architectural thinking. It was also at this juncture, of course, that the two polar approaches to the marriage of design and technology split apart.

INTEGRATION AS A TEAM APPROACH

Architects have a unique role in the business and culture of society, for no other profession is charged with a scope as broad as that of the architect. Neither artist, scientist, engineer, nor craftsman, the architect is simultaneously a little of each and something different altogether. Making architecture brings together those diverse broad concerns with several other demands, such as marketing, code compliance, budgeting, building climatology, human behavior, ergonomics, cultural history, urban planning, and so forth. No wonder it has been said that architecture is the only profession capable of equal concern for world hunger and door closers. On the basis of knowledge alone, architecture is perhaps the ultimate profession of integration. Artists may make better sculptures. Engineers may make better machines. Psychologists may prescribe superior environments. Only the architect is charged with bringing all of that together in a resolved, artful, and commodious final product that will serve for generations.

The increasing technical complexity of these fields and the implications of legal liability quickly led to the development of specializations. Mechanical engineering was founded by doctors, interior design by cabinetmakers, and so on. No one person can competently perform all of the responsibilities of designing a public building, and no one person should be responsible for all of the required expertise, background experience, or knowledgeable insights. Architects consequently work with many sorts of engineers, a host of project-specific types of consultants, and any number of product suppliers and fabricators. Large and complex buildings require teamwork, collaboration and coordination from the very inception of the project. The architect is almost always the team leader, however, and orchestration of the team happens only when the architect is a competent conductor.

Through the years of preindustrial society there was little distinction between the architect's roles of creative spirit and master builder. The Michelangelos and Brunelleschis of their era were artist, engineer, and architect. Over time, our culture and our use of buildings became more sophisticated, crowded, and mechanized. Inevitably, responsibility for buildings separated into specializations under the architect's direction and supervision. As individual buildings became more functionally unique and less repetitive of simple design programs, architects increasingly relied on the critical input of allied professions. What first evolved as a hierarchal organization with the architect at the top has become a deeply interwoven network of information feedback and shared decisions.

THE ACCUMULATED WISDOM OF ARCHITECTURE

Borrowing from Walter Gropius, a work of architecture can be operationally distinguished from mere buildings as something that adds to the "accumulated wisdom of architectural thought." Obviously, not all works of architecture can be monumental icons of civilization; most good architecture remains in the background. These less assuming works must meet the same criterion, however: If something is to be built, the opportunity should be maximized and only the highest results expected. Technical and design innovations have no merit if they are only fanciful. Architecture expects rigor and ambition. Nothing less will be recognized.

A metaphor to explain this expectation and the emerging role of integration within it is helpful here. Suppose a mythical architecture library full of splendid volumes and the "accumulated wisdom of architectural thought." Many shelves in this library hold books and journals covering theories of critical design significance and the exemplary buildings that have achieved it. An equal number of works (the dustier ones) in another wing of the library illustrate robust building technologies and acclaim the technical mastery of architects who so ably

employ them. Alas, precious few of these volumes in either wing categorically address how creative design thinking and technical wizardry ever come together in these marvelous works of architecture — and this despite the mysterious fact that the same buildings are frequently acclaimed in both sets of texts. Design and theory writers are often keen to acknowledge the enabling technologies. Authors of environmental and construction texts are similarly appreciative of innovative and appropriate design expressions. But neither set of books has set out to bridge the middle ground between their respective wings of the library.

The fledgling small body of literature of the middle ground today would hardly constitute the beginnings of a third wing in our allegorical library. It currently exists only as a curious and dimly illuminated corner between the two giant wings. The peculiar books in these corner stacks do not fit comfortably in either primary classification. The few shelves allocated for them inhabit a narrow passageway between the twin bodies of knowledge that anchor the library. Lodged between the two main wings, the middle ground is largely transitional, and patrons pass through without much notice. But pass through they must.

There is another way to catalog the design creativity and the rationalist technology wings of this library: internally stimulated and externally stimulated. Internally ordered design books convey ideas, discoveries, and inventions — these convey implicit knowledge of the sort that can neither be categorically proven nor refuted. Technology, on the other hand, is the external, explicit order of architecture made of facts and figures that have been demonstrated empirically.

In his description of creative flow, psychologist Mihaly Csikszentmihalyi (1996) uses similar terms to discuss *domain* and *realm*. Externalities can be thought of as the *domain* of architecture. These are the rules to which building design must conform in order to be safe and functional. The internal orders of *realm*, as it may be defined in architecture, is the continuity of past architectural accomplishments against which the contribution of a new work will be judged. David Bohm (1917–92) summarized in his studies of the implicate order and undivided wholeness: "The universe enfolds an 'implicate order' (the ultimate, connected reality behind things) and unfolds the 'explicate order' that we see — a continuous double process" (see especially *Wholeness and the Implicate Order*, 1980). Think of these two aspects as the domain and the realm of architecture and compare them to the two "wings of the library."

Structural equilibrium and air-conditioning system performance are examples of external order. External technical orders like these are initially isolated and disconnected from meaning. In design practice, external order comes to architects as independent and loosely related items on a series of separate lists: programs, space requirements, codes, and specifications. These are usually described by numbers that are more in the form of raw data than of usable information. To derive meaning from them, we must study principles and rules that are external to our perceptions and sensibilities.

Design creativity, in contrast, is internally generated order. With only a blank piece of paper and a sharpened pencil we can sketch the kinships between external givens, such as those we intuitively grasp in a building program, like the adjacency of spaces and their placement on the site. This differs sharply with details of external facts that are initially unimportant to our ability to imagine possible solutions and poetic places. Architects find the internal, innate, implicit order of these relationships within themselves without having to know the laws of physics. Of course, internal order is neither communicated nor acquired in the same way that external knowledge is. Exposure and practice are the only ways to develop skill at internal ordering. Design creativity comes from within, from an internal sense of arranging the puzzle pieces into poetic unity. Architects imagine that the whole and complete picture will convey their internal sense of poetry to others. They believe that the final product will prove to be consistent with external determinants in an elegant way. They also imagine that the pragmatic solutions will be ennobled in the poetic statement. The final "poetic" product will, if all goes well, synthesize internal and external order as complementary states in harmony rather than as separate elements of a sorry compromise.

Architects seek to unify the external technics with the internal poetry. For example, daylighting, structural expression, and shading strategies are some of the more ennobled external orders of technology that are often thought of as part of design creativity. All three of these examples are evident in Le Corbusier's famous description of architecture as "the magnificent play of mass in light and shadow" and are embodied in the idea of his *brise soleil* shading compositions. Of course, Corbusier's long struggle with the underlying external principles of these technical ordering principles is usually ignored along with the inappropriateness of some of his solutions. What matters to architecture is that he pioneered the fit between the technical and the poetic ordering principles, between internal and the external realities.

Integration reveals the fit between these external and internal orders, between explicit facts we know to be true and implicit truths we desire to realize. It resolves the dissonance between their separate realities. It also separates imagination from whim by the discipline of making good connections—not just between one fact and another, but also between the facts in isolation and the design ideal of a whole truth. In more practical terms, integration resolves building program and technical constraints with the ultimate design objectives. Learning about integration has a great deal to do with realizing how these internal and external orders complement each other. For now, it is obvious that design is unfinished until the two ordering forces are in harmony. Integration is the dynamic that aligns them.

Philosophical Digression: Integration and the Progress of Technology

Integration can be considered in separate stages of cultural and architectural significance across three ages of civilization: preindustrial, industrial, and postindustrial. Each of these eras is associated with different prevailing philosophies that defined and redefined the overlapping missions of art, science, nature, and culture. Many respected thinkers have considered these evolutions, and some of their thoughts are incorporated in the following discussion.

INDUSTRIALIZED SYSTEMS AND THE MATHEMATIZATION OF ARCHITECTURE

The beginning of a middle ground between creative design and rational technology dates to the end of World War II. The postwar economies produced a flood of new materials, industrialized building systems, and a worldwide construction boom. Integration issues emerged with the advent of practical air-conditioning, new structural and envelope material systems, and eventually with the promise and threat of computer optimization. All of these influences led to a technical revolution in architecture. It was the beginning of an architecture that was both enabled and inspired by technical building systems. In short, critical integration issues are co-evolutionary with the "systemization" of architecture. Chapter 2 is dedicated to articulating various meanings of "systems" and tracing several trends toward the systems view of architecture. For now, it is important to acknowledge how systems thinking directly transformed the design of buildings in that most prolific period of the industrial era.

This transformation into systems-based design hinges on the native qualities of building systems themselves. Each industrially mass-produced system comes with a particular set of requirements and an immutable internal logic, hence "techno-logical." The act of choosing one of these preconfigured systems correspondingly decides material quality, performance factors, finished appearance, dimensional characteristics, space requirements, and the details of connection to other systems. This techno-logic encompasses all building systems: site, structure, envelope, servicing, and interior.

It is exceedingly difficult, expensive, and rare for architects to have made-to-order control of the systems they select. The Hong Kong and Shanghai Bank Building by Sir Norman Foster (see case study #25) is a lucid example of how elaborate and infrequent such total control presently is. Instead of custom configuration like that of the Hong Kong Bank, the predominant model of design has become the innovative selection and interfacing of off-the-shelf building systems. With each system or subsystem selection, internal logics must be coordinated with the workings and connection points of other systems. The architect is continually manipulating the physical fit, visual effect, and functional relationships between multiple systems and subsystems. The preconfigured qualities and numerical characteristics of these systems must now be considered in all phases of design thought. They cannot be relegated to programming or research activities. Nor can their manipulation be dealt to project engineers or other consultants without forsaking the central design activity. In standardized practice of days gone by, systems were detailed in the design development "phase" after conceptual design had been formulated independently. Now the selection of systems has become so critical that phases of design are less distinct, more overlapping.

This first aspect of industrialized systems can be summarized as the concern for relationships between building components. Design, to some degree, is a calculated juggling act between the requirements of major systems and subsystems. Difficulties arise when the juggling exceeds the architect's technical training. Problems of another sort occur when the designer's focus on juggling overwhelms the original visionary goals. Christopher Alexander (1964) writes, "Efforts to deal with the increasing cognitive burden actually make it harder and harder for the real causal structure of the problem to express itself."

Another description of the differences between the architecture of industrialized systems and the handmade architecture it replaces is what High Tech architects have termed "wet" versus "dry" building construction. The wet systems, like concrete, wood, and plaster, have a plastic quality that lends itself to the architect's fancy—if you can draw it, the material can be molded accordingly. They can be formed, cut, or crafted to any shape and dimension, detailed and connected in many different ways. Within the characteristics and limits of a given material, the designer

employs a wet system rather freely. Dry systems, on the other hand, are largely preconfigured, so what you pick is what you get. These include any prefabricated or preengineered component system—meaning they are essentially not of the architect's design. Dry-type systems now dominate building design and construction. This fact compels architects to substitute a large measure of creative selection and coordination of dry systems for the age-old wet plastic imagery of their formal imagination. Martin Prawley (1990) sees a dark side to this transformation of the Second Machine Age, referring to the danger of architects becoming a profession of "licensed specifiers."

Other disciplines related to the arts have experienced a parallel metamorphosis from the purely intuitive into the overlapping technological and scientific realms. The mathematization of music, to choose an example with architectural consequence, begins with the abstraction of written musical notation. The process progresses through discoveries in the physics of sound, is consummated by Wallace Clement Sabin's description of sound absorption in rooms, and continues through Leo L. Beranek's (1962) total quantification of the subjective listening experience. Music is now so thoroughly understood in quantifiable terms that it has been called "the math of time." It is recorded, manipulated, and even synthesized with great accuracy, and such accuracy itself is scientifically described by frequency, amplitude, reverberation time, bass ratio, and a host of other acoustical measures. Music is still music, however, and our ability to enjoy it is in no way diminished by its measurement. Similarly, most events and artifacts of our physical world are well understood in numerical terms. Like music, they are certainly no less significant for our greater understanding. Graphic arts, photography, lighting design, virtually everything around and in buildings, have succumbed to numerical portrayal and manipulation. Mathematical certainty and empirical measurement are the agents of this information culture.

Most professions have long ago settled into operational modes in which the enigmas of abundant data and statistical information reflect the empirical certainty of industrial culture. When architects are too slow or unwilling to put numbers to their ideas, they are often questioned by a host of complementary professions whose specialties are to provide optimization. Value engineers, efficiency experts, construction consultants, loan officers, and the like have all arisen from industrial inclinations toward expediency and the use of information to minimize depletion of capital resources.

Notions of order and relation are familiar enough to designers. Abstraction of relationships and representation in form are also the architect's everyday tools. The adaptation of undigested numerical data, however, calls for new tools and therefore for new understanding. Buildings are vast mounds of empirical accuracy, and their accounting has many ledgers. Program, budget, code, climate, structure, site—all these items have numbers to be tallied and balanced against one another. This is not the sort of technical coordination one automatically gets from project engineers; it is too project-specific and too widely interconnected among different engineering specialties. Consequently, as buildings became more technically sophisticated, situation-specific criteria replaced generalized design guidelines and standardized practice. The training and continuing education of architects will have to respond to this new mandate. As John Tillman Lyle (1994) predicts, observation, knowledge, and participation will replace the "large safety factors" of standardized practice.

The "large safety factors" that Lyle correctly blames on standardized practice is a measure of how empirically correct we expect buildings to be. This is partly due to new business practice and astute clients who have in-house expertise to weigh their architects' judgment against their own criteria. It is also partly due to the expectation of computer precision in technical decision making. Finally, it is a translation of Buckminster Fuller's idea of "ephemeralization," whereby it becomes increasingly possible to get more building with fewer resources. Expressed in an equivalent business culture paradigm, this may be stated as follows: "By making more intelligent design decisions, architects are expected to produce economically elegant buildings that perform optimally and at very close margins of error." Consumer culture believes that contradictions can be solved without compromise: taller buildings with lighter structure, more glass with less energy consumption—in short, better design for less cost.

Fortunately, there is some significance in measured information beyond the industrial age mentality of bean counting and economic optimization. Some architects, like Edward Mazria (1992), have revived the medieval spirit of sacred geometry and number magic. These ideas reveal the significance and meaning of numbers and data by examining the relationships and patterns that they depict. Gary Stevens (1990) even sees mathematics as the underlying source of beauty in architecture and "the most long-lived notion in architectural theory." Christopher Alexander (1964) concludes that "modern mathematics deals at least as much with questions of order and relation as with questions of magnitude."

The second aspect of industrialized architectural design can be summarized as the progressively finer measurement of project conditions and more critical specification of performance factors. It is the mathematization of architecture.

POSTINDUSTRIAL PARADOX AND ECOLOGICAL DESIGN

Our world perspective has changed radically since the industrial activity following the Second World War. Industrial progress has proven to be a double-edged sword. We have endured tragedy at Hiroshima and Chernobyl; continual pollution of our air, land, and water; dangerous depletion of natural resources; and accumulations of toxic waste we have no place to safely dump. Entering the postindustrial era, we seek a deeper consciousness and renewed sensibilities.

The *preindustrial* romance of a mysterious universe was replaced with verifiable fact and calculated number. Now, the industrial certainty of a machinelike universe has faltered. In its place, culture faces a *postindustrial* paradox of information versus meaning. The smokestack is out and the World Wide Web is in. We have replaced the machinelike numerical model of reality with probability and complex relationships among the data. Historically, preindustrial beliefs featured intuition, superstition, and mystery. *Industrial* thought, beginning with René Descartes in the seventeenth century, replaced medieval romance with machined certainty and viewed the universe as a great extension of the machine. The postindustrial mindset collapses mechanistic certainty and substitutes new understanding about the complex and deep interrelationships of the universe as a vast single ecology and interdependent organic network.

Integration was unimportant in preindustrial architecture. The ages before Cartesian mechanics knew no difference between significant building and wonder for nature's law. To varying degrees, science was magic, buildings were ritual places, and their form was indistinguishable from their meaning. With no differentiation between symbolic form and functional form, between nature and technology, or between science and art, there were no cultural constructs to bridge and no concept of integrating them. Today the study of this preindustrial belief system has created the field of archeoastronomy, which investigates how ancient and indigenous buildings were oriented and aligned with the cosmos. The Anasazi culture of Chaco Canyon, for example, near what is now Albuquerque, New Mexico, subsisted on corn that took 100 days to maturity. The average frost-free growing season at the 7500-foot altitude was about 150 days. This left little leeway for error in their annual calendar. The Great Kiva at Chaco Canyon's Casa Rinconada (constructed at about A.D. 1070–1110) exemplifies their architecture as a point of contact with the cosmos. Its circular perimeter wall surrounds the space like an artificial horizon and contains 28 niches illuminated by low sun angles at the solstices and other specific times of the year. Researchers deduce that the Anasazi used these celestial events to time their crop planting or at least to celebrate their spiritual alignment with the cosmos. The building is a cosmic clock, a place of ritual, a calendar, and perhaps was a key to their survival. The Anasazi, like other preindustrial peoples, clearly had less need for conscious acts of integration precisely because there was no distinction between the meaning of form and the magical technology it embraced.

Progression in our scientific understanding of the cosmos eventually displaced the sense of magic once attributed to natural events. Physics and chemistry replaced alchemy just as astronomy replaced astrology. Consequently, the empirical certainty and mechanistic reasoning of the industrial age separated both technology and nature from their earlier symbolism. We were spared the tyranny of naturalistic superstition, but significance then had to be supplied by human intention rather than by a sense of wonder. Design and technology disconnected into the agent of meaning on one hand and the resources used to accomplish it on the other. Integration arose to heal this rift when industrialization and systems building inundated architecture in the postwar era. But society now seeks a broader consciousness to temper our industrial prowess with environmental sensitivity. The pioneering spirit of man-over-nature has lost its gloss and relevance. Architecture in turn searches for poetic expression of the complex patterns of our greater understanding. The integration challenge of postindustrial architecture will be to combine the technical sophistication of industrial progress with sensibilities reminiscent of the Anasazi kiva.

Postindustrial culture manifests the shifts from labor to leisure, from goods to services, from energy to control, and from factual data to manipulated possibilities. Of these transitions, the emergence from an information culture is most important to architecture. Daniel Bell (1973) describes industrial information technology as the linear prediction of results by projecting past trends into the future. He compares this to postindustrial occupations in which data is used to understand possibilities, to shape them, and to choose selectively from various potential futures. Where industrial thought reacted to the past in hindsight, postindustrial thinking shapes the future proactively. Industrial-era design took information literally. It was the bottom line of the *local scale* of perception. As long as no one looks beyond the immediate and obvious impacts of local scale decisions, industrial bottom line reasoning appears to model reality quite well. The shortcomings of this narrow view seem obvious in retrospect. Bottom line decision making leads to short-term profits and sacrifices long-term sustainability. Today, to use a popular quip by Albert Einstein, "The mentality that will save us from our present predicament is necessarily different from the one that got us here." Postindustrial insights are inclusive of broader values and wider impacts than the local scale of industrial thought. For architects, "broader value" suggests an accounting that extends further into the future than did industrial decision making. This implies that architects will preserve the quality of life that we enjoy

Figure 1.2 The Great Kiva of Casa Rinconada, Chaco Canyon, New Mexico.

for the benefit of future generations—a basic principle of ecological design. "Wider impact" implies that architects will weigh how their design decisions interact with present context and future circumstances, and that they will look beyond the bottom line.

Postindustrial challenges are clearly a call to an expanded scope of professional thinking. Sustainability is characteristic of these challenges. This ecological approach to design, to parallel the Anasazi example, translates long-term weather data into patterns of climate. Through responsive design, the patterns of sun and wind give form to passive thermal building components and deployment of systems. Passive design commodifies and interprets the geometries of sun path and wind vectors into the human experience of comfort by capturing their patterns. Similar logic can be applied to air-conditioning systems, interior circulation patterns, structural loads, daylighting, and all the attendant building systems and subsystems. Application of this reasoning requires only that we first apply the larger scope and broader scale of postindustrial consciousness.

The same challenges support Fritjof Capra's (1988) assertions of a pivotal turning point. His holistic approach to postindustrial problem solving closely resembles the ecological example of integrated systems design. Capra sees holistic solutions in thinking outside the "box" of mechanistic cognition in much the same fashion that architects find design resolution in the and/both "likeness" of conflicting design criteria. In both cases, the larger truth is served by initially excluding the local scale of what appear "on the surface" to be conflicting truths. This truism illustrates the important distinction between symptomatic methods and systemic ones and embodies an important aspect of postindustrial thinking. We associate symptomatic methods with industrial era mechanics and systemic ones with expanded postindustrial consciousness. The symptomatic cure for a headache is to take an aspirin for pain relief. Using reading glasses to relieve headache-causing eyestrain would be a systemic cure. Clearly, the systemic cure requires a different kind of doctor. An architectural example might substitute window shading in favor of larger air-conditioning capacity (note that shading devices have more architectural potential than bloated air-conditioning systems).

Finding the systemic deeper cause, in the case of architecture, requires an understanding of the interrelationships of a building's many systems and their context. This entails a definition of the building as a system itself, a topic that is covered in the opening section of Chapter 2. Looking beyond the local scale to the deeper cause in turn requires insight beyond the everyday impressions of a casual observer. This is especially relevant because architecture generally rejects the mechanical perception of buildings as functional assemblies responding to Cartesian deterministic constraints. Instead, buildings are considered as organic entities involved in complex interactions with their occupants, their context, their environment, and even within their own systems. The architecture of such buildings, particularly in the postindustrial era, must occur through insights and inspirations outside the simple cause-and-effect local scale of normal perception. Table 1.1 describes the imperceptible macro- and microscales of reality that make up the complex broader insights and lists their architectural significance.

Architectural design, in this post-Cartesian sense of complexity, resembles what modern science terms "nonlinear." The parallels between complexity science and integrated buildings will help explain the postindustrial paradox that confronts architects today.

The science of nonlinear dynamics, which has been confusingly called "chaos theory," and is referred to here instead as "complexity science" in order to differentiate it from popular misconceptions about chaos and images of fractal patterns. Complexity science probes the deep interrelatedness of natural events that cannot be explained by linear cause-and-effect thinking. Weather patterns, snowflake crystals, the self-organizing flow of boiling water, and cloud shapes are common examples of nonlinear behavior in nature. Their forms appear to be spontaneous because the natural forces that shape them are so unimaginably complex and intricately interdependent. But "chaos," as it were, is not chaotic in the common sense of the word. Chance and confusion play no role in the weather, in the irregular pattern of the earth's orbit, in the growth pattern of a tree, or in the population limits of

TABLE 1.1 Macro-, Local, and Microscales of Influence

Macroscales	
Cosmos	Solar and lunar influences
Ecology	Sustainable design
Climate	Environmental influences, regional context
Local Scales	
Site	Setting and surroundings
Envelope	Intervention: filters, barriers, and switches
Interior	Comfort
Microscales	
Bacterial	Indoor air quality
Chemical	Fire, material aging, toxicity
Molecular	Properties of materials, elasticity, thermodynamics
Subatomic	Light, electricity, heat, radiation

wild species—these are all nonlinear systems. Within the seemingly random and erratic behaviors of these everyday phenomena, complexity science reveals deep order and patterns of relationships. Even the most irregular and seemingly nondeterministic cycles of nature actually oscillate around "strange attractors" that divulge the general trends of such dynamic systems. Even more astounding, these complex systems resist disturbance to the point of being self-correcting. If the earth's orbit were simply deterministic, the slightest perturbation could throw us out of orbit and crashing into the sun. Instead, its complex dynamics constantly maintain periodic behavior, mystically returning to patterns close to the strange attractor that keeps us safely spinning through space. We find such nonlinear complexity anywhere in nature we care to look. Complexity, in fact, proves to be the prevailing condition, not the rare exception. The work of the twentieth century's greatest scientists, from Bohr to Heisenberg to Einstein, and contemporary researchers has deeply altered our perception of cosmic truth in this way. Today we see how these perceptions parallel society's rejection of Cartesian mechanics and the dead end of industrial resource depletion, thus fueling the postindustrial quest for deeper meaning. The cosmos is not a maze of deterministic machines whose gears grind on to a simple cadence; it is a single probabilistic system of interrelationships that connect the visible and invisible scales of reality, the local and the most remote events.

Ecological design provides a salient example of deep interrelatedness and nonlinear behavior in buildings. The links between macroscale site characteristics, regional resources, and global sustainability exemplify interrelatedness, as does the microscale biological codependence of native species and human habitation. The complexity of these relationships obscures the predictability of flows from site, to regional, to global-scale events. Nonlinear relationships such as these are visible only as bifurcation diagrams that illustrate the splitting and resplitting of possible combinations. By the same logic, ecology also illustrates our insight and sensibilities beyond the visible local scale into invisible levels of complexity. Charles Jencks (1995), discussing the possibilities of nonlinear order, concludes that "architecture must look to science, especially contemporary sciences, for disclosure of the Cosmic Code."

Jencks' Cosmic Code, or the nonlinear, nonintuitive, and nonlocal scale of perception, is a postindustrial cue to meaningful form. It is a way of reconciling complexity, meaning, and beauty in sympathy with D'Arcy Thompson's description of morphological form giving in *On Growth and Form* (1945). This new set of perceptions is, in turn, a postindustrial equivalent of transcendental

experience that has always been a source of design inspiration (See, in Chapter 4, a discussion of Mihaly Csikszentmihalyi's transcendent flow). Architects will identify with the spontaneity of nonlinear dynamics in nature. They may even adopt it as a nonmechanistic path toward resolving demands of an expanded professional scope. Faced with parallel upheavals in world culture, the only alternatives to confronting this postindustrial paradox are to continue standardized practices or to surrender ever-larger shares of building design to other more qualified professions.

An impressive roster of postindustrial professions has already adopted nonlinear complexity models. Engineers study nonlinear dynamics, especially in the convective behavior of fluid motion. Economists, yielding to Oscar Wilde's quip that "a cynic is someone who knows the price of everything and the value of nothing," move beyond supply-and-demand mechanics to inclusive models of worth and life cycle accounting. Medicine forsakes the simplistic treating of symptoms and adopts holistic health and alternative medicine. Agriculture no longer relies on fertilizer and pesticide for complete control of production, turning instead to organic farming and beneficial insects. In each of these instances, the result has been the adoption of more inclusive, broader-scaled views of how outcomes are interrelated and how measures of success are balanced.

TABLE 1.2 Postindustrial Professions

Physics	Quantum mechanics and the Unified Field Theory (Bohr, Heisenberg, Einstein)
Engineering	Nonlinear and chaotic systems
Psychology	Self-actualization and psychosynthesis (Maslow, Graf)
Sociology	Knowledge-based culture (Kuhn)
Business	Industrial Organization Psychology
Medicine	Holistic health and mind/body healing (Capra)
Agriculture	Organic gardening and beneficial insects (Rodale)
Economics	Life-cycle costs and externalized accounting (Henderson)

Architects lag behind the postindustrial revolution of other professions. Their coattails seem to be stuck in the exit door from the smokestack age. Architecture still aspires to the technological possibilities signaled by Banham's *Theory and Design in the First Machine Age* (1960), but our buildings lag a generation behind available technology. Architects may still revere Buckminster Fuller's holistic concepts of synergy, tensegrity, and ephemeralization from decades earlier, but design generally proceeds according to accepted practice and standardized assumptions. Compared to other professions, architecture seems to tick along like a wind-up clock in a chronograph world.

These shortcomings are, however, more a combination of choice, professional liability, and the heritage of design tradition than of procrastination or intellectual unwillingness. Architecture is judiciously slow to change and remains poorly suited to more than an occasional radical experiment. The inevitable transformations signaled by Alexander, Lyle, and Capra, as well as by Bell, Kuhn, and the other apostles of postindustrial change, will change architecture no faster than the deliberate pace of continual refinement allows.

CONCLUSION

Preindustrial civilization was couched in the mystical romance of nature's capricious bounty and awesome power. Industrial culture derived methods of controlling limited ranges of nature and categorized the techniques into isolated packages of knowledge and generalized trends of behavior. Postindustrial culture merges a broader appreciation of relationships between complex systems with the possibility of beneficial interaction. Perhaps the most remarkable transformation from industrial to postindustrial thinking is the inevitable surrender of absolute technical control and the acceptance of this more organic beneficial interaction.

Integration provides a link between the familiar history of industrialized architecture and the increasingly complex world of postindustrial advancement. This linking role of integration helps us understand design and technology as complementary opportunities rather than conflicting values. Buildings of critical design merit will continue to be examples of well-considered technology, no matter how preconfigured, ephemeral, or ecologically camouflaged the packaging. By focusing on the act of integration, we can improve the selection of appropriate systems, their integrated fit to comprehensive buildings, and their faithful service to our guiding design intentions.

The systems management view of architecture furnishes a complementary illustration to that of integration. It demonstrates the empirical demands of design and the increasing complexity of buildings. "Systems thinking" encourages innovative selection and interfacing of industrialized building components and their preconfigured attributes. Most important, the systems view provides postindustrial clues to the coexistence of rationalism and spontaneity as implicate and explicate orders.

Framework of Discussion

The everyday experience of buildings is fragmented into glimpses. Customers seldom see the bank vault, the retail office area, or the restaurant kitchen. Even in the buildings where people live and work, they may never think of mechanical rooms, interstitial levels, or basement foundations. The general population experiences buildings in piecemeal encounters, not as integrated wholes. Architects, of course, have a different responsibility toward wholeness. They cannot leave out the restaurant kitchens, the ducts above the ceilings, or the basement foundations simply because the general public never sees the machines or thinks much about how the building stands up. Architects must be intimate with all building systems and their interworkings.

An architect's academic education seldom conveys this sense of intimacy. A history lecture may include ten buildings of Frank Lloyd Wright and focus on their contrast with those of other masters; a structures class may use a more complete building example or two, but never discuss anything except tributary loads. An environmental lab looks at sun angles. A theory seminar discusses Foucault. The assimilation of all these topics into an inclusive and coherent paradigm is usually left to the student. Even in the studio, where educational institutions imagine that all this comes together in some vague way, learning is frequently limited to the discovery of meaningful approaches to formal and organizational issues. It is difficult for one student working alone for one semester to move a project much beyond that, especially with structures, environmental systems, history, theory, and core classes demanding separate attention. There is usually not enough time in a design studio or a specialized topic class for a fertility to develop, which is created in professional practice through interactive feedback among the disciplines, especially while students are focusing on their basic creative, analytical, and synthetic skills. In architectural practice it can take a team of experienced professionals years to arrive at a comprehensive solution. There are no grounds for expecting complete assimilation in a six-week studio project.

It is equally difficult to form a holistic view of architecture, or of any one building, through architectural literature. Journal articles usually contain short overviews and repeat similar comments and graphics. Architecture books are generally preoccupied with one or two of the special topics of design. Occasionally, an entire volume is devoted to a seminal work of architecture, but such works are rare and often consist more of detailed anecdotal information than of connective ideas. It takes a large collection of publications and a bit of insight to decipher the underlying picture from the frequently repeated highlights and scattered details. The metaphor of the library earlier in this chapter illustrates the myopic view that results from the basic division of architecture and its literature into separate wings of design and technology.

Another shortcoming of the commonly fragmented view of architecture has to do with the idea of design as a strategic planning activity. Strategic design refers to the methods for "delivering" buildings and incorporating these strategies into architectural meaning. This relates to a host of project management issues: special site conditions, construction methods and sequencing, building material selections, fabrication versus prefabrication, delivery and storage during construction, phased occupancy, future expansion, flexibility of use, technology uptake, and myriad associated concerns. Architects have always had to design around the constructability of their solutions and, more recently, for serviceability. Good design has also always been measured in part by its internal plan for delivery and occupancy. These are not just Modernist functional dogma; they are fundamentals. The expansion of technical possibilities, the demise of generic templates for any building type, and the mounting expectation of optimized performance solutions ensure a continual escalation in delivery issues. As an aspect of integrated design, strategic planning is engaged throughout this text, both in the chapters that discuss methods and in the building examples.

GOALS AND OBJECTIVES

Ultimately, attaining an intimate or comprehensive understanding of any one building requires either designing and building it personally, or reconstructing a case study that fully considers what was required to perform that design and construction. This book offers something of the latter in the hope of advancing the causes of the former. The primary goal is to dissect good examples of architecture in order to show how they work as integral buildings, what went in to their consideration, why they differ from comparable buildings, and what they add to the accumulated wisdom of architecture. Working with good examples saves the overhead of iteration that design from scratch requires; there is no need to retrace anything but the fruitful decisions. It also avoids the necessity of extensive technical research—much easier to examine a difficult or novel problem that has already been splendidly solved. Presumably, the outcome of these analytical exercises will be an enhanced ability to synthesize a personally considered design process from first principles.

The tools for resolving this goal are a dissection kit and some anatomical illustrations. The scalpel and tweezers are provided in the four chapters of Part I, "Methods":

- Chapter 1 (this chapter), "The Idea of Integration."
- Chapter 2, "The Systems Basis of Architecture." What a system is: kit, prototype, relationships, and species. A brief history of trends toward systems building and systems thinking in architecture.
- Chapter 3, "Integrated Building Systems." Three nonexclusive notions of integration: physical, visual, and performance. Shared space, shared image, and shared mandates. Classification of primary building systems: site, structure, envelope, services, and interior. The integration potential of systems and subsystems.
- Chapter 4, "The Architecture of Integration." The integration paradigm and how to apply it: program, intention, critical issues, appropriate systems, and beneficial integrations. The importance and use of precedents. The example of the Pacific Museum of Flight.

Part II of this book comprises seven sets of case studies. These fulfill the objective of anatomical illustration. Case study chapters begin with an overview of the inherent qualities and technical issues that shape the topic building type. The succeeding building studies, arranged chronologically, begin with an early precedent example of integration in the particular building type.

- Chapter 5, "Laboratories." The technical transition from structural to environment-dominated issues. Louis Kahn's served and servant spaces.
- Chapter 6, "Offices." Designing for the workplace as well as the corporate image: productivity, energy, and health; flexibility, adaptability, technology uptake.
- Chapter 7, "Airport Terminals." Terminal buildings and their infrastructure; transit, ecology, noise, and traffic.
- Chapter 8, "Pavilions." Prototyping new technologies. Exhibitions and world's fairs as experimental architecture.
- Chapter 9, "Residential Architecture." Artful living in industrial society: smaller, lighter, cheaper, and faster. Hosting technology in the background.
- Chapter 10, "High Tech Architecture." Commodifying technology to human experience. Serviceability meets constructability. Function expressed as a visual dynamic.
- Chapter 11, "Green Architecture." Shades of green in the sustainable ethic. The model of science. Shallow versus deep ecology.

Each of the 29 case studies in these seven chapters follows a format established in the methods of Part I. They contain similar components:

- Description of the building and its parameters
- Basic documentation: plan, section, elevation, and site
- Fact sheet with project highlights and systems descriptions
- Anatomical section showing the interworking of the systems
- Climate data and analysis of relevance to the project
- Discussion of intention, issues, precedents, systems and integrations

DESIGN, TECHNOLOGY, AND INTEGRATION

Every act of architectural design requires the appropriate selection, configuration, and combination of architectural technologies. The dual activities of design synthesis and technological accommodation are so interwoven in architecture that distinguishing between them can be difficult.

Design, for discussion's sake, is defined here as an activity toward architecturally worthy goals. Technology, on the other hand, can be thought of as pathfinding through the realm of possibilities within which design is realized. Every decision about function, aesthetics, or cost is both a decision about technological means and a decision about design results. An integrated decision satisfies both aspects.

Integration can be a dangerously all-inclusive term, and something of a disclaimer should be made. Once the idea of integration is announced, any conversation on how to attain it can easily become unduly elaborate and all-encompassing. The problem is one of scope: Integration is about bringing all of the building components together in a sympathetic way and emphasizing the synergy of the parts without compromising the integrity of the pieces. An inherent danger is that a comprehensive discussion of integration can sound like an overwhelming Theory of Everything. Focusing on the particulars of integration and treating it as a specific discipline avoids this problem. The focus includes a host of terms that apply to integration: *inclusive, assimilative, whole, complement, fit, appropriate, multipurpose, adaptable, flexible, comprehensive,* and so on.

2

The Systems Basis of Architecture

CHAPTER 2 TOPICS

- Systems Thinking
- Architectural Systems
- Levels of System Organization in Architecture: Hardware, Prototype, Grammar, and Species
- Developments in Systems Architecture: Precepts and Trends

Systems Thinking

The significance of seeking a scientific basis for design does not lie in the likelihood of reducing design to one or another of the sciences.... Rather, it lies in a concern to connect and integrate useful knowledge from the arts and sciences alike.

Richard Buchanan, "Wicked Problems in Design Thinking," in Margolin and Buchanan, eds., The Idea of Design, *1995.*

The world is animated by flows of information, energy, and material. Any network of structured relationships defining these flows forms a system. Systems are so common that their inherent levels of

sophistication are often forgotten and the word *system* seemingly designates a single object rather than a web of functional, organizational, or regulatory networks. In everyday life there are justice systems to resolve complaints; library systems to catalog documents; construction systems comprising building kits. Our own bodies function through self-regulating systems of respiration, circulation, digestion, perception, and so on. Buildings contain structural, lighting, electrical, plumbing, mechanical, and many other systems. Urban environments are similarly made up of transportation systems, park systems, zoning systems, and a host of other infrastructure networks. Ultimately, of course, all these systems operate within the largest of all systems, our ecosystem.

Corresponding to the preceding examples—justice, library, construction, and ecology—the various applications can be generalized as systems of control, classification, planning, and biology. Buildings manifest all of these forms of systems. The sophistication of building components and of the design process long ago achieved the level of *system*. This fulfills the scientific and classical definition of a system as a cluster of interrelationships with internal flows of information, forces, or material. Classical systems are categorized as simple or complex, like a fulcrum or a combustion engine; and as either deterministic or probabilistic, like gravity or a coin toss. As a science, the idea of systems, systems thinking, systems theory, and so forth, is described as cybernetics. This is an effort to gain understanding into how flows of information or material become networked and how decision making about the systems can affect outcomes. The study of systems is concerned with models of optimization, control, information structure, numerical analysis, and simulation.

The common architectural mention of structural, mechanical, and other building elements uses the term *system* rather differently from its scientific meaning to distinguish and classify sets of elements from one another and inclusively suggest their many individual parts and functions. A structural system, for example, would nominally consist of a network of columns and beams that transfer gravity, wind, and occupant loads from the top of a building through its network of supports to a supporting foundation. Load-bearing masonry is a structural system in this context, as is steel frame or heavy timber. Again, the designation of *system* indicates that the components form an interrelated group connected by flows of force, material, or information.

The notion of *systems* as an approach to architectural design begins with the recognition of the interrelated flows of material, forces, and information in buildings. Widespread use of industrialized building components led to similar systems nomenclature as a shorthand for how functional mandates of a building would be satisfied. Envelope systems function as separation of the inside from the out, structural systems keep buildings stable, environmental systems keep occupants comfortable, and so on. Familiar use of this shorthand, however, has corrupted *systems* into a form of hardware classification—it captures the idea of functional mandates but often overlooks the underlying complexity of internal relationships.

The methods of science, engineering, and technology are commonly understood to use a more systematic approach to problem solving than architecture. But these analytical disciplines have always influenced architectural thinking because of their inherently honest logic and explicit means of achieving well-defined goals. This influence emerged in the late 1960s and 1970s along with the study of environmental behaviorism and systems management. This *systems theory* or *systems thinking* can be briefly described as the management of complex problems through rigorously detailed descriptions of the problem, the establishment of project goals and objectives, and the recognition of dynamically interconnected elements of the solution.

Much of the research into architectural design as a disciplined method and teachable activity refers to the application of systems thinking to buildings. This is also the source of division between two philosophical positions: design as structured methodology and design as free creative exploration. If, to take an extremely skeptical and methodological view, design is principally the result of genius and refined taste, then architectural education is largely an ordeal by fire to identify the most gifted candidates. This first position argues that some collection of structured thoughts on design processes can be assembled and discussed, refined, and translated. Otherwise, design is a haphazard and unreliable pursuit that has more to do with fancy than with creative imagination. This perspective holds that systems thinking is directly applicable to what an architect does. The second, conflicting point of view, taken to its similar extreme, sees design as a creative exploration that is antithetical to the notion of a deterministic or functionalist process. It holds that architectural design is indeterminate, a forest through which no methodological map can be systematically plotted. Although a design can be good or bad, for example, it is not absolutely right or wrong. There is no single solution for any given architectural problem, no limits on how broadly it is formulated, no conclusive test of how well it has been solved; and, finally, the built solution will be unique and nonreplicable.

Richard Buchanan summarizes this "wicked problem" of design as a "fundamental issue that lies behind practice: the relationship between *determinacy* and *indeterminacy* in design thinking." Discussions about the appropriate balance between determinant and indeterminant approaches to design are important to architectural education and practice. The resolution of the question is largely a matter of personal philosophy; any number of credible arguments can be made and several parallels to the arts and sciences can be drawn. They are, after all, two different perspectives of the same activity, and it is possible that they are two complementary views of the same coin: heads and tails. Perhaps they can even be compared to the explicit and implicit wings of the hypothetical library in Chapter 1.

Determinant and indeterminant views obviously differ in the detail to which design activity could or should be considered an objective investigation. They do, however, share an appreciation of the overwhelming complexity of design thinking and of architectural design tasks. The complexity of design is so deeply rooted in both arguments that it moves the discussion closer to a common and widely accepted meaning of *system* in architecture—namely, as a discrete assembly of building components collectively satisfying a particular set of requirements. The primary architectural systems, for example, are site, structure, envelope, services, and interior. A discussion of what makes each of them a system is presented in the next section.

Architectural Systems

The building is served and manifestly seen to be served. The act of the servicing is seen to be within the architect's control, even if the details of the servicing are not completely of his design.

Peter Reyner Banham, describing Marco Zanusi's 1959–1964 Olivetti factory in Argentina, in The Architecture of the Well-Tempered Environment, *1969.*

Since the industrial age began in 1830, buildings have changed from hulking monolithic structures with marginally controlled passive environments to glass-covered space frames with intelligent robotic servicing. The proliferation of mechanical, electrical, and plumbing systems since 1940 had a great deal to do with this change, and the underlying technical evolution is evident in every aspect of building. Structure, envelope, interior, and site systems are all equally affected by the sweeping advances in building technology.

First, the most obvious influence of industrialization is the progression of advanced materials that performed better and lasted longer. There were also more choices between alternate materials. Second, building components were standardized into parts that could be efficiently produced by machines. Then the meta-technology began: the technology of the technology. Advances in industrial production affected what industry could produce, and progress in engineering influenced what industry should supply. Efficiency, economy, and quality were all enhanced in a spiraling cycle of production.

Modern technical solutions now come as well-ordered or totally preconfigured systems designed by other professionals. A curtain wall system, for example, can be used only within the limitations of its matched components; a steel building kit is preengineered and packaged for delivery. Particulars of these solutions are not open to the architect's design manipulations. The designer must instead assume the role of field marshal to coordinate and integrate the decisions made, along with input from engineers and other consulting specialists on the design team.

From time to time through modern history, especially since the advent of air-conditioning, various movements of architectural practice have alternately embraced or rejected an inclusive and formative attitude toward technical systems as an organizing idea. Bauhaus, High-Tech, and Sustainable Design are different modes of utilizing an overt systems approach to the broad framework of conceptualizing and realizing works of architecture. The International Style and Postmodernism illustrate design approaches that tend to reduce technology to a necessary means of achieving a higher end. Both frameworks of design-and-technology have, of course, created noteworthy architecture in their time; certainly both employ technical systems in constructing and servicing. The difference lies in whether systems are seen as ennobled participants in the conception of building form or rather as liberating machines whose workings are separate from the significance of the buildings they enable. These approaches also differ as to whether the image of technology is allowed to express its inherent logic or whether its workings are subjugated to other design ideals. The common grounds on which both approaches must stand are the ever increasingly technical complexity of building programs and the sophistication of the finished building product.

Later sections of this chapter explore several shifts in architectural practice from formal and structure-dominated thinking toward more performance- and systems-based concerns. Before progressing, though, it is useful to elaborate on some various meanings of systems design as they pertain to architecture.

LEVELS OF SYSTEM ORGANIZATION IN ARCHITECTURE

Several questions about the idea of integration were posed at the beginning of Chapter 1, and most of them have been subsequently discussed as an overview of integrated buildings. The first sections of the discussion in the present chapter concern the question of connections between *systems thinking* and *building systems*. In summary, the term *system* has evolved into twin descriptions, concerning both the complexity of the design task and the complexity of building components. These two concerns, part method and part product, constantly antagonize and inspire each other in the architect's quest to resolve design. They are also, of course, connected by the sophistication and technical expectations of modern society and enlightened clients.

What follows next is an exploration of different levels of system organization that can be achieved in architecture through design and technical integration. In these examples, the last two questions posed at the beginning of Chapter 1 are addressed: "What benefits does integration provide?" and "How do we recognize or measure relative levels of integration?"

System as Hardware

Sir Joseph Paxton transformed his experience with railroad and greenhouse construction into a radical solution for London's Crystal Palace. Faced with a challenge that 233 architects had failed to meet during a design competition for the Great Exhibition of 1851, the self-taught railroad engineer Paxton set out to satisfy the requirements of a project that had been put in motion by Prince Albert, consort to Queen Victoria. The Palace was needed to house more than 13,000 exhibits and serve 6 million visitors. It would cover about 700,000 ft^2, the biggest building in the world at that time. Most critically, it was to be produced for £230,000, completed in ten months over the winter, and would outshine any of the 11 previous large exhibitions sponsored by England's rivals in France.

Paxton, with the firm of Fox, Henderson & Company, completed the design and construction drawings in ten days. The Crystal Palace was erected in 17 weeks between September 1850 and January 1851 and opened on time, May 1, 1851. Based on a module of 49 in. glass and bay sizes of 24 ft, the building was framed in 3500 tons of cast iron members and 202 miles of wood glazing bars. It measured an enormous 1848 by 408 ft and reached 108 ft high at its transept. Including its upper level mezzanine, the palace provided more than a million square feet of space and 33 million cubic feet of volume. It was four times bigger than St Peter's in Rome and six times larger than London's own St. Paul's Cathedral.

The Crystal Palace was the first kit-of-parts systems building. Rapid construction was followed by a successful exhibition. Dismantled shortly afterward, Paxton's huge invention was moved to south London and rebuilt to its original form with the same pieces. It was part of a Victorian theme park until a fire destroyed it in 1936. As a nuts-and-bolts or system-as-hardware assembly, the Crystal Palace proved the worthiness of industrial application of prefabricated components to architectural design. Utilizing standard parts, modular bays, mass production, and lightweight construction allowed the grand structure to be realized quickly, inexpensively, and with impressive results.

All of the strategies and construction components of the Crystal Palace were interrelated in such a way that each made the others possible and successful. These relationships were intentional and planned. Not only did Paxton's design of the Palace embrace these new ideas, they were the essence of the idea and of the building. This dynamic between program, creativity, method, and technology is precisely what defines the Crystal Palace a systems building. Its innovations have inspired every generation of architects since the birth of the industrial age.

System as Prototype

William Le Baron Jenny is credited with the invention of the high-rise building in his 1884 Home Insurance Building in Chicago. By bringing together the fireproofed and riveted steel frame, the elevator, and the curtain wall, Jenny composed a method of systems that together constituted a new building type. Jenny's high-rise surpasses the Crystal Palace kit-of-parts or systems-as-hardware definition. Not only did the nine-story steel frame manage to free the skin of the building from carrying loads, it also avoided the problem of constructing thick load-bearing masonry walls on Chicago's unstable soils. Jenny's window wall in an open lattice of structure was followed by the projecting Chicago bay window in Burnham and Root's 1894 Reliance Building. The Chicago school of architecture emerged, and high-rise construction as we know it today gave birth to the commercial high-rise style or "capitalist vernacular."

The term *high-rise* may suggest a building defined by its structural system, but the Home Insurance Building was not much of a structural invention inasmuch as steel framing had already been devised. What is defined by Jenny's high-rise is the building as a particular combination of systems or, in other words, an ordered collection of systems combining to make a prototypical description of a building type. High-rise is just one of the prototypical approaches to design that deal with appropriate sets of systems that are matched to make a whole: steel frame and elevator, plus window wall, equals a generic or standard solution set. This is perhaps what Christian Norberg-Schultz (1965) was referring to in defining architectural systems as "a characteristic way of organizing architectural totalities." Other system-as-prototype buildings included as case studies in Part II of this text include laboratories, offices, airports, and pavilions.

System as Grammar

A significant shortcoming of early modernist architecture is identified with the failure of the postwar generation of architects to incorporate the advances in material and environmental technology to match the capabilities of mechanized society. Instead of accommodating the new vocabulary to meet new challenges, industrial materials and techniques were disappointingly used to create a visu-

Figure 2.1 Centre Georges Pompidou, Paris, France. *(Architects Piano + Rogers.)*

al style of formal expression. The great increase in architectural activity and the number of its practitioners after World War II simply overwhelmed the ability of technically unprepared architects to cope with the shift from formalist composition of building-as-object to the already emerging unity of industry and craft.

In hindsight, it is clear that the modern movement missed the opportunity to continue the sophistication of innovations in architecture to which more technically advanced architects have since returned. Postwar design, despite its rationalist origins in movements like the Bauhaus, aimed at expressing the visual glamour of industrial civilization. The suggestive forms of trains and ocean-liners were widely imitated. Contemporary practice has turned decidedly more toward translating those same technical possibilities into performance benefits that are simultaneously desirable architectural features.

Seeking and expressing technical relationships in building systems required a level of technical and scientific interest more reminiscent of Renaissance architects than of Beaux-Arts and Victorian designers. It also required a period of design freedom when buildings could shed their historical significance and representational value. This period reached public consciousness with Renzo Piano and Richard Rogers and their 1972–1975 design for Centre Georges Pompidou in central Paris, a building that Piano's on-site architect Bernard Plattner still calls " a provocation" (see case study #22). The High Tech Style follows in this genre of exploration. Its characteristics are discussed in Chapter 10, but it can be described briefly here as the quest for an architecture that expresses its dedication to technical servicing.

This system-as-grammar approach is predominantly concerned with coordinated interactions among the components and criteria of a building. It reflects the general term now in use that refers to functional categories of buildings as individual *systems:* site, structure, envelope, services, and interior. Through fundamental scientific insight, the designer manages and configures these workings and interworkings of building elements and then brings them into the architectural vocabulary. The expanded palette of High Tech design does this explicitly by incorporating exposed elements of structure and mechanical systems to functionally define and visually

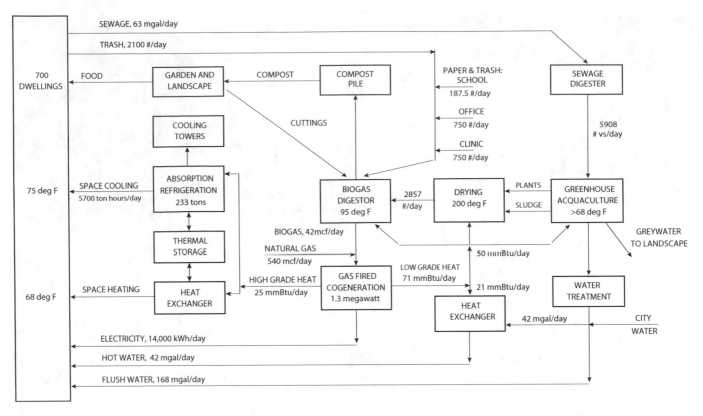

Figure 2.2 Example flow diagram for proposed Allen Parkway Village redevelopment. (*From a study by the author for the International Center for the Solution of Environmental Problems, with The Studio of Robert Morris, Architect, and James Burnett and Associates, Houston, July 1996.*)

express the building. The architectural systems grammar of High Tech's best practitioners surpasses the glamorized machine aesthetic of the early modernist by including the complex dynamic of the machine into the essence of the building.

System as Species

In the anatomical and biological sense, buildings can be considered as organisms that function as interrelated systems. A sectional slice of a building becomes the anatomical "vivisection" of a complex organism. As an equivalent sectional diagram of an animal can tell us about the relationships between skeletal, respiratory, muscular, nervous, and digestive systems, the anatomical section of a building explores how structure, cladding, HVAC (heating, ventilating, and air-conditioning), wiring, and plumbing systems combine in cooperative ways to produce an organism we may call architecture. Interestingly, there is even some anatomical correspondence: skeletal system to structural, respiratory to ventilation, epidermal to envelope, nervous system to electrical, and so forth.

How do buildings acquire a living, organic quality beyond diagrammatic complexity? A dominant characteristic of the biological model of architecture is evident in the tracing of interactive processes, as exemplified by the

energy and waste flows in sustainable design. These processes are concerned with cycles of flow within a system of designed interactions. Process interaction is manifested in buildings as "filters, barriers and switches," as Christian Norberg-Schultz first put it. Steven Groák (1992) said it another way, describing a building as a series of "conduits, reservoirs, and capacitors of flow." Throughput diagrams illustrating flows of energy, information, and material frequently accompany the plans and sections of biological buildings. Usually the flow diagrams contain much more information about the system dynamics of the building than do the typical architectural depictions.

John Tillman Lyle was the project director of an interdisciplinary team of designers responsible for the Center for Regenerative Studies at California State Polytechnic University in Pomona. In his book, *Regenerative Design for Sustainable Development,* Lyle distinguishes the "paleotechnic" mechanistic views of design in the industrial age from the "neotechnic" post-fossil-fuel era we are entering by relating the work of Scottish biologist, urban planner, and ecologist Patrick Geddes (1854–1932). Geddes coined those terms in his 1915 publication of *Cities in Evolution* to distinguish between industrial society and what he envisioned as its more organic successor. He saw the existing urban patterns as a linear mechanistic mode of industry and consumerism that continually converts natural resources to waste and proposed in its place a cyclical and biological model of city and regional planning. Lewis Mumford (1926) saw Geddes as a father figure, compared him to Frank Lloyd Wright, and described his work: "It is not as a bold innovator in urban planning, but as an ecologist, the patient investigator of historic filiations and dynamic biological and social relationships that Geddes's most important work in cities was done."

Geddes's neotechnic ideals are gaining recognition in the wake of postindustrial evolutions and popular disenchantment with the same industrial schemes of production that he denounced almost a hundred years ago. Anatomical and biological approaches to architecture capture neotechnic ideals by using design knowledge to harness and manage cyclical flows in building systems.

Developments in Systems Architecture

The current market of preconfigured and standardized building components implies that manufacturers' catalog information is an important basis of product selection and specification. For work to proceed expediently, design choices must fit what is readily available from suppliers. The year 2000 on-line compilation of *Sweet's Catalog,* for example, claims 59,600 products from 10,200 manufacturers. These items are searchable by specification and come with downloadable text files and drawing details. A product representative can be summoned directly from your keyboard.

This information marketing relationship works as it should, breaking down the barriers between design and accurate specification. But it also poses the possibility of replacing design decision making with the easy expediency of window-shopping. When sales representatives arrive, it is not unusual for them to serve as consultants for detailed product selection. These informal consultants usually provide guidance or even engineered specifications at no charge on the basis of making a sale. The architect can be tempted to specify a suggested product in return for the free and timesaving technical assistance. Consequently, questions about self-interest arise in this relationship. A sales representative wants to promote his or her own product, despite its potential shortcomings and a lack of interest in similar products from competing manufacturers. The architect must treat this relationship as a biased one and constantly filter through the representative's claims for neutral information. The danger is that

architects may become, as Martin Prawley (1990) feared, professional specifiers without sufficient control over the fundamental design of what they are selecting.

At a sufficiently high level of professional candor, the designer can exploit a mutually rewarding affiliation with manufacturers and their representatives in the field. Naturally, the architect is also guided by the work of professional engineers in some or all of the final decision-making. But unless the architect understands the precepts and trends that shape the selection and deployment of building systems, there is little hope of realizing design aspirations.

PRECEPTS

Before examining the trends that have promoted the integrated systems perspective in contemporary building design, a few of the architectural concepts that paved the way for integration in the first place are discussed.

Bauhaus

The idea of industrial mass-production building systems as a basis of design has origins in the 1920s with Walter Gropius and the New Architecture of the Bauhaus. For the progressive Bauhaus spirit this meant closing the gap between craft and art, as well as between functionalism and pure form. Two aspects of this idea did a great deal to further the systems basis of architecture: function as the foundation of design and industrial standardization as the basis of construction.

The Bauhaus sought to close the gap between the progress of industry and architecture by adopting factory techniques to building components. The materials and components of construction were to accommodate the use of mass manufacturing techniques, rather than as architects generally desired, for components to be custom-made from raw materials to the specification of unique designs. Ultimately, in the Bauhaus ideal, buildings would be constructed of high-quality components that were efficiently produced at a low cost. Further, these components would be of the most modern and advanced technologies available, not just to an elite few, but democratically to all.

The complementary aspect of this vision involved the art and craft of production. Mechanized civilization was believed by many people at that time to be vacant of human spirit, so for production to be meaningful to a New Architecture it would have to be given a soul. Artists would become educated in the exact science of materials and the methods of industrial manufacture. With this palette, enlightened designers would marry productivity to human spirit through art.

Underlying the reeducation of the artist and the vitalization of industry with human spirit was the Bauhaus notion of functionalism. For architecture to be new, it would have to be unencumbered by the weight of history. This meant a return to first principles of shelter and functional commodity in everything that could be designed. It also entailed the stripping away of ornament, to be replaced with a freedom to express function and the means of production.

Brutalism

Ideas toward the evolution of systems-based architecture and the freedom to exploit the industrial character it implied were further necessitated by the devastation of the Second World War. Much of Europe would be rebuilt; the postwar population and industrial expansions would be provided for. This required a rationally refined, rapidly constructed, and materially conservative series of buildings. Le Corbusier's 1946–1952 housing project, Unité d'Habitation at Marseilles, was the first major work of postwar architecture to fit this prescription.

Severe housing shortages meant that residences were often built as efficient superclusters. Building at this heroic scale also held the potential to establish new urban patterns. But construction materials, especially steel, were in short supply and the building trades were in hectic disarray. Eventually, only one of the three complexes planned for Unité could be constructed. There would be no fine finishes, not even a cover coat of plaster. Inspired by these constraints rather than daunted by them, Corbusier allowed raw concrete from crude formwork to be expressed as a finished surface. He did so in an intentional and controlled way, setting the formwork planking in directional patterns of alternating squares and allowing rough carpentry and board texture to create jagged rustications. He termed his technique *béton brut,* and it gave rise to what Reyner Banham (1966) captioned as "the New Brutalism."

Among the more enthusiastic advocates of brutalism, Peter and Alison Smithson were probably the most widely published (see case study #18 for more on the Smithsons). Their own work was categorized as belonging to the group of modern buildings that adopted honest exposure of materials to the point of sensual expression. This group was also understood to include exposed materials other than concrete, such as the bold structural steel of Mies van der Rohe. The Smithsons' work, particularly their 1949 Secondary School at Hunstanton in Norfolk, England, is structurally Miesian but more Corbu-like in its services and interior fittings.

The Smithsons' descriptions of brutalism popularized its reverence for honesty in material expression and sever-al of the style's characteristic methods. It was known as a-formal and a-proportional in attitude, forsaking geometric discipline in favor of modern functionalist expression. It was also characterized by Banham in articles in two periodicals, *L'Architecttura* (February 1959) and *L'Espresso* (March 1958):

- Visual articulation and affirmation of structure
- Romantic esteem for raw, untreated, virgin materials
- Exposed services
- Noble regard of mass production
- Strong moral chastity and social goals

Brutalism continued many of the systems-friendly ideas of the Bauhaus. Legitimacy and ennoblement of industrial components were forwarded. Exposed structure, visible servicing, and raw materials were acceptable. Industry had already been given a soul, and the allied arts of industrial design, automobile manufacture, and commercial advertising were exploring its poesy. Architecture was beginning to embrace the technical aspects of its component systems in the same way. The freedom to do so had been established.

TRENDS

The precepts of systems thinking as can be traced through its industrial, Bauhaus, and brutalist forbears, now set the stage for several links between integrated systems and design. These trends, as discussed in the following sections, cover current issues more than historical evolution.

Trend One: From Handmade Buildings to Kit of Parts

The Sydney Opera House (1956–1973) and the Kimbell Art Museum (1964–1972) mark the end of an architecture dominated by handcrafted buildings. Obviously, there is still a great deal of manual work and craft to be done on any construction site and many small buildings are still made largely by hand, but the trend is to use more components bought off the shelf and fewer that are custom-made from raw materials. The economies of factory mass production, the ease and speed of construction from prefabricated components, and the reliability of industrial-quality parts all contributed to this transition.

In keeping with this trend, intensive field labor has been replaced to a large degree by factory working conditions. The factory automates and mechanizes much of the work previously done on-site. Factory fabrication is faster, less expensive, more accurate, and less subject to weather conditions than on-site construction. Machines replace arduous manual labor, and calibrated accuracy replaces the rusty tape measure. Although the relative benefits vary with the scale of construction and other conditions, economy usually dictates the use of prefabricated components wherever possible. IKOY Architects have even renamed their construction sites *assembly sites* to better describe the actual distribution of labor embodied in their prefabricated building designs (see case study# 5).

The kit-of-parts era of building is blessed with an endless number of products to choose from. Manufacturers compete within limits of standardization, and those standards are based on conventional building practice. Custom sizes, finishes, and colors are also available for a premium price and delivery time. Light fixtures, cabinetry, hardware, and furniture systems arrive in boxes. Structural components, windows, door frames, and most other bought elements are available in standard sizes with pre-fitted connections. Some assemblies like wood trusses are custom-prefabricated for delivery. In the end, there are simply fewer things to actually design and more connections to coordinate between the ready-made pieces. This kit-of-parts consideration is one of the roots of integration activity in systems-based design.

It is increasingly less feasible today to construct hand-crafted buildings, such as the masterpieces realized by Jorn Utzon and Louis Kahn a few decades ago. Labor is too expensive and craftsmen are too rare. Furthermore, construction economy is based increasingly on the lightweight structure and rapid assembly of industrialized products. But if architecture has lost some of the freedoms of custom design, at least it has gained the new vocabulary of the Machine Age.

What does architecture gain from this transition? Aside from the inherent differences between handmade and machine-fabricated construction palettes, there are some changes fundamental to design thinking. Most of these changes, which should be accepted as opportunities, are demonstrated historically by the precepts of industrial, Bauhaus, and brutalist design.

Visually, the expression of technical systems offers a language that has been adopted under the banner of High Tech. As Richard Rogers (*Serving the World*, 1986) describes the Lloyd's building, the visual integration of systems provides "scale and legibility." How a building resists gravity and how it maintains comfort inside can be readable, if not always perfectly intelligible, by merely looking at the building. At the opposite extreme, the same technical advances allow technical systems to be hidden neatly away and act invisibly subservient to both the image of the building and the activities it contains. There are appropriate and inappropriate applications of both approaches and lots of room for argument between.

Functionally, buildings have virtually become machines. Mechanical, electrical, and plumbing systems (MEP) easily occupy 20 to 50 percent of any typical building type by size, volume, weight, and total first cost. The lifetime cost of operation, maintenance, and replacement of this machinery is of even greater proportion. For perspective, consider that half the electricity in the United States is consumed in buildings and that half of that is for electrical lighting alone. It is not possible to design a building without fundamental consideration of these practicalities. It would be reasonable to expect the magnitude of their impact to be reflected in the architecture they serve. Learning how to convert this challenge into an opportunity is a still-evolving transition.

Morally, functionalism and industry have always assumed the honorable high ground of service to humanity. The means to a solution, however, are also part of the problem. High standards of living brought about through technology have also resulted in resource depletion, pollution, and unmanageable piles of waste beyond the environment's capacity to absorb. Finding the appropriate balance between natural and mechanized living is a design problem in and of itself. Further, the problems of technology are compounded by the high density of living conditions it promotes. Architecture confronts this third aspect of transition in the pursuit of sustainable design.

Trend Two: From Formal to Technical Constraints

Innovative technical systems have added invisible and dynamic dimensions to architecture. These new dimensions shifted the focus of design from predominately visually ordered solutions to forms that also embody invisible and imperceptible forces. Visual ordering produces forms and volumes that are experienced personally and immediately. Moreover, a greater understanding of building science and improved technologies for the manipulation of building physics have added thermal form, acoustic form, solar form, and aerodynamic form, to mention just a few considerations. Most of these invisible ordering principles have been developed in the last 100 years and have impacted critical decisions about building form only in the last 50 years. The science of architectural acoustics, for example, did not exist until the turn of the century, and practical auditorium acoustics were not well understood until about 1960.

Science and Technology. The advent and evolution of building sciences and their incorporation into building technologies transformed the means of evaluating architecture. Suddenly, many of the qualitative aspects of built form were measurable in quantitative terms. Comfort, music, light, color, and all means of spatial experience were no longer left to intuition, conventional practice, or homogenous engineering standards. Objective goals could be established to ensure qualitative results, and architects could work backward from the goals to derive and refine verifiable solutions. Experiment was moved from the trials of building failure to the imagination of the sketchpad.

Stephen Groák, in *The Idea of Building* (1992), observed that new building technologies produced constant pressures for change in design. The first of these has to do with the advent of new building systems waiting to be commodified into architectural application and human benefit. New and better products enhance possible solutions, producing new economies and new design configurations. The second issue relates to radical new programs for emerging building types. Laboratories, clean rooms, and computing centers do not fit into conventional building shells. In both cases, Groák proclaimed the loss of "robust solutions" and the "decline of technical precedent." Each and every building thus becomes both a specific application of appropriate technology and a unique configuration of responses to program, site, climate, and context.

The Worship and Loathing of Technology. Prospect or portent? The two poles of acceptance of science and technology have been labeled technophilia and technophobia. The first of these, technophilia, is about a faith in technical advancement as the solution to today's problems with an assurance of continued success and increasingly spectacular triumphs to come. Technophobia, on the other hand, is the fear that an unduly avid reliance on technology will dehumanize society and ravish our natural resources. The technophobic extreme is linked to the notion of technostress, the malaise of constantly coping with unwanted technical change and related pressures. A chronic level of technostress can also result from what psychologists term "cognitive dissonance," whereby differences between how we think of our environment and the way we actually live in it produce a subconscious state of mental confusion.

As society and its built environment become increasingly complex and dominated by technical demands, these two perspectives portray part of the transition from formal to technically dominated ways of considering design. Technophilia is epitomized by Buckminster Fuller's term "ephemeralization," an idea he coined in 1922 to describe the accelerating pace at which we accomplish more and more with less and less. Fuller believed that design should constantly strive to achieve higher levels of performance with decreasing amounts of time, material, and energy. By this route, he reasoned, humanity would be freed of its burdens. Technophobia, on the other hand, is dramatically illustrated by Mary Shelley's 1817 novel, *Frankenstein.* Shelley, only 19 years old at the time and writing in the dawning age of industrial revolution, was fearful of a walking, talking technology that had no soul. In light of civilization's evolving disenchantment with the perils of paleotechnic industrial progress, her haunting reflections are as poignant now as they have ever been.

Like many polar arguments about architecture, the extreme positions of technophobia and technophilia provide a useful dichotomy that animates and propels design thinking. The dynamic of resolving an appropriate middle ground between them should be continually reexamined with each building project and each new application of technology. Ian McHarg (personal correspondence) used Louis Sullivan's duality "form follows function" to describe these oppositions as "a dance, not one following another, but part of the conversation that makes architecture." Good architects may not always make for good dancers, but they have to learn the two-step of technophilia/technophobia.

Architecture-as-art versus architecture-as-science forms another part of this particular dichotomy. The rational and functional aspects of design cannot be forsaken, but neither should fancy and style replace imagination and intuition. Likewise, the wonders of architecture cannot be replaced by fine-tuned problem solving, but civilization's technological artifacts can scarcely be eliminated from the essence of artful building. Looking again at these two positions as opposite sides of the same coin, consider these thoughts on the matter:

> Science is true or false; art is meaningful or insignificant. . . . Science constantly compares the guesses that the mind makes with the reality it tries to probe; art builds new ideas on old ones without rejecting them.
>
> *Robert Mueller,* The Science of Art: The Cybernetics of Creative Communication, *1967.*

> That was a hundred years ago: science then was the manipulation of exact measurements. . . . The aim of science we now see, is to find the relations which give order to the raw material, the shapes and structures into which the measurements fit. . . the relations which the facts have with one another—the whole they form and fill, not with their parts. In place of the arithmetic of nature, we now look for her geometry: the architecture of nature.
>
> *Jacob Bronowski, "The Discovery of Form," in Gyorgy Kepes,* Structure in Art and in Science, *1965.*

Condensation of Technical Time Frame in Building. A final note on the evolution of technical dominance in architectural design concerns the ever-accelerating pace of technical change. For perspective on the subject, consider the Florence Cathedral, which took 140 years to complete (1296 to 1436); Brunelleschi's ingenious dome alone comprises the bulk of the work done after 1420. In contrast to those quieter times, current generations have witnessed the evolution of many different and completely new building types and the demise of several others. Any building older than ourselves is nowadays considered dated enough to be obsolete because it does not contain the technical advances of newer and seemingly more innovative buildings.

The construction of great Gothic cathedrals in a revolutionary quest for spiritual light commenced with the abbey church of St. Denis in 1144. The Gothic cathedrals were each built over periods of multiple construction campaigns spanning several decades. By today's standards, however, the technology they embodied changed little during their lengthy design and construction. The principal innovation of Gothic architecture, for example, was the use of external buttressing to relieve structural loading of the walls where stained glass windows could be inserted to tell the story of the Scriptures to illiterate masses. The notion of load-bearing masonry construction was supplemented in the Renaissance by the use of chains to contain the spreading thrusts of domes. Little else changed in building technology until the industrial revolution. In contrast to that technical constancy, today's era of rapid advancement may force any number of technical adaptations into the realization of a building project. This modern scenario results in a condensation of technical time frame and dictates that today's architect be constantly attuned to new and developing systems.

Chartres Cathedral, for example, was constructed between 858 and 1220. The first four attempts to complete it collapsed and the fifth burned. A fire on the night of June 10, 1194, destroyed much of the town but miraculously spared a sacred icon of the church, a tunic worn by the Virgin Mary at the Nativity. On finding the tunic safe in the crypt, construction of a new cathedral began in earnest on the remains of the old. It was completed around the time of the Fourth Crusade.

Compare the technically uneventful 400-year time frame of Chartres to that of Richard Rogers and Partners' project for Lloyd's of London (see case study #24). The Lloyd's design competition was awarded to Rogers in 1977, and the building was constructed from 1979 to 1986. When the project was initiated, Lloyd's owned four small computers used exclusively for storing data files. At the conclusion of construction, every broker at Lloyd's was working on a personal computer connected to a local area network. In addition, the insurance syndicate had developed an in-house cable television network for viewing throughout the building. This means that during the ten years of design, development, and construction there were radical adaptations to new technologies. The entire information infrastructure of the facility had to be rethought and the architecture made to accommodate the changes.

Of course, change was not new to an institution such as Lloyd's. The insurance syndicate was formed by a collection of underwriters at Edward Lloyd's Coffee House at 16 Lombard Street in the seventeenth century. Since 1927, Lloyd's had outgrown its offices three times and specified that the new facility should accommodate floor space for another 50 years of further growth. Rogers's response to the challenges of the Lloyd's project was geared to these problems of expansion and technology uptake from its very inception. The design competition was won not with the finished design of a stellar corporate facility, but with the designation of a *system* of solutions. In the end, Rogers had to convince the client that the designers understood the nature of the Lloyd's building problem better than the client itself.

Trend Three: From Structural to Environmental Issues

The lineage of structural dominance through the history of architecture was documented by Lance Levin and Steven Weeks some years ago for a presentation to the American Collegiate Schools of Architecture (ACSA) summer program on energy in Seattle, Washington. The line they traced runs basically from temple to castle, to cathedral, palace, factory, and high-rise. In each of these building types the predominant technical challenge was an issue of structure. After the high-rise, the shift to environmental domination of technical issues has been thorough and complete. At the same ACSA event, Donald Prowler presented a paper on the ascendance of the laboratory as a predominant building type and the parallel transition from alchemy to science. Prowler included a study of Louis Kahn's Biological Laboratory at the Salk Institute (see case study #2). It was a fitting coincidence that placed these presentations back to back: the last of the structural eras and the first of the environmental ones.

The changing of the guard officially occurred in the early 1970s and was emphatically announced by the 1973 OPEC cartel oil embargo. Background rumblings had been going on for several years: Pollution, acid rain, toxic wastes, and global warming were already issues. Rachel Carson published *Silent Spring* in 1962, and Earth Day celebrations began around the world in tandem with Vietnam War protests in 1970.

Architecturally, the changes first began with the practical advent of mechanical space cooling. For commercial buildings this started in the 1920s and reached residential-scale construction in the late 1950s. Energy was relatively inexpensive at the time, so cooling systems were applied broadly and naively. The always-experimenting Le Corbusier seems to have thought, for example, that chilled air flowing between sheets of window glass would intercept solar radiation. Regional and vernacular design suffered from these early viewpoints because climatically responsive forms could be borrowed and used stylistically in unfriendly climates. And dramatic glass-clad buildings could be built anywhere; they only needed larger cooling systems to match the climate.

Once the initial backlash to these mistakes was appreciated, responsible designers, including Le Corbusier, moved on to integrating the new mechanical and advanced envelope systems into the arena of design, physically incorporating their components into the schemes of new types of buildings. Two important books chronicle the early years of this integration: James Marston Fitch's (1966) *American Building: The Environmental Forces That Shape It* and Reyner Banham's (1969) *The Architecture of the Well-Tempered Environment.* Readers are referred to their authoritative histories.

The intersection of mechanical systems integration with the accompanying ecological crisis of the early 1970s culminates with the laboratory building as a defining prototype of late-twentieth-century building. The laboratory as a systems integration model is discussed in Chapter 5. The broader implications of environmental systems are discussed here as a transformation in the systems approach to buildings in general.

From the beginning of architectural history, all rooms were given access to light and air. Buildings were extroverted, opening out with extended forms and vented domes or wrapped around central courtyards. With the advent of electrical lighting and mechanical ventilation plus the stimulus of urban crowding, buildings relied more on introverted strategies powered by technology. Passive connections to the outdoors remained, but these were generally designed around view and access; light, sun, and air were only incidental. As long as energy was believed to be cheap and the effects on the ecology considered benign, formal and structural problems were of greater interest.

Structural invention and the expression of tectonic strategies, meanwhile, had been neatly integrated into architectural significance by centuries of formal experiment. Coupled with the mandate of static equilibrium against gravity and wind, structural considerations were easily the most critical and empirical technical influences on design. Buildings had to stand up, and demonstrating how this was accomplished led to a lofty central role of structure in design. The only environmental concern to reach this ennobled standing until recently was addressed by the time-honored art of daylighting.

The Sydney Opera House design competition illustrates the role of critical structural issues in the early 1960s. The competition was won by Jorn Utzon on the basis of drawings indicating a series of huge shells spanning over the auditoriums and other main spaces of the proposed complex. There was a great deal of affection at that time for thin shell structures. Eero Saarinen, one of the Opera House jurors, was in fact working on thin shell buildings of his own at the time. But no one knew how Utzon's shells could be constructed. They were almost freehand in form, perhaps drawn with curves borrowed from Utzon's father, a boat builder. The opera house's sail-like shapes were classified as structurally indeterminate because their profile could not be described by a formula and therefore the forces produced could not be easily calculated. It took Peter Rice and his engineering team of Arup & Partners a great many man-hours working on the best room-sized computers of the day to approach a solution. Utzon, in the end, converted the shells to regular spherical sections based on the diameter of a uniform circle.

Today the critical mathematical aspect of structural problems has been, in a word, ephemeralized. Indeterminate structures can be solved on a laptop computer with validated simulations. Alternate schemes can be analyzed, and the structural components can be optimized. Removing the issue of calculation means that more options can be explored and solutions can be more thoroughly refined.

As issues of calculation, structures are basically static responses to static conditions. Gravity is constant, and other loads are assumed to act always at their peak magnitude. The resolved structure is permanent and fixed. Oversizing for safety factors may be uneconomical, but it does not adversely affect the performance of the structural system. Environmental design is, conversely, a dynamic response to dynamic forces. Several states of environmental control may be active at different times of the day and seasons of the year in response to varying outdoor and indoor conditions. Either oversizing or undersizing environmental systems will have serious negative impacts on performance, operational economy, and comfort levels. Environmental control is also complicated by the simultaneous and interrelated requirements of thermal, lighting, and acoustical criteria. The only thing simpler about environmental design than structural design is that a small miscalculation results only in slight discomfort—it will not make the building fall down.

Many modernist architects have used the dynamic nature of environmental servicing and the visual vocabulary of mechanical equipment as explicit design elements.

High Tech design is particularly given to this idea. Reasoning that environmental hardware is as much a vital part of building as structural or envelope systems, and allowing that ducts and pipes constitute so much of the total design solution, High Tech gives these elements an appropriate place and expression. Louis Kahn, who hated ducts and pipes, was the first to formalize this attitude by recognizing the overwhelming scope of servicing required for the 1959–1961 Richards Medical Research Laboratories at the University of Pennsylvania (see case study #1). He set up his solution to the new building type by separating "served and servant spaces" and articulating their differing characters.

With constant reference to Kahn's innovation, succeeding generations have developed an architecture of served and servant relationships whereby the servicing of the building is ennobled to a level once reserved for structure. It is now possible to say that environmental concerns and the presence of servicing systems have influences on design that are equal if not superior to those of structure. There are still different avenues for expressing these influences, even among High Tech practitioners. Exposure of mechanical systems is, for example, one of the distinctions between Richard Rogers and Norman Foster. Rogers often uses an exuberant display of ducts and pipes, whereas Foster favors a more classical treatment of space that expresses servicing but keeps its visceral extremities contained.

Serviceability now equals constructability. This is true at both the visual and the performance level of integration. The performance mandates and physical impacts of heating, ventilating, and air-conditioning (HVAC) systems in particular are too large to be pushed to the basement and left to the attention of engineering consultants. Lighting, electrical, plumbing, and even acoustical concerns have all proven to be rich sources of architectural inspiration. Although structure will always retain its own important influences, it is also true that buildings may become "the optimized system[s] surrounded by six inches of architecture." At any rate, per Banham's (1969) observation, the Olivetti Factory's servicing is now "manifestly seen to be…within the architect's control."

Trend Four: From Intuitive to Optimized

The technical requirements generated by complex building design problems have overcome the architect's ability to deal with them intuitively. Christopher Alexander sounded the first siren in his 1964 book, *Notes on the Synthesis of Form,* warning that complexities can overwhelm the original design intentions.

In a world of computer accuracy and virtual simulation, clients have come to anticipate that design professionals will optimize their building project resources. This is simply part of their expectation of the value an architect provides and a cultural consequence of the insidious computer. A corresponding shift in the modern business world has produced a postindustrial generation of accountants and managers who specialize in overseeing these client expectations. Value engineering, life cycle cost, risk analysis, and budget control are brought to bear. The focus is increasingly on performance: worker productivity, indoor air quality, flexibility of use, adaptation, and future expansion. Tools and measurements are numerical and objective. Architects should expect that their ideas will be put to numbers and that they must be able to argue for their design intentions within a numerical framework. Developments in emerging professions such as industrial organization, human resources, and health psychology will continue this trend.

Working in this postindustrial mindscape of optimization will require a redistribution of the architectural services involved in a building project. Several mobilizing factors of this redistribution are being put in place by the use of computers. The Renaissance and Beaux-Arts tradition of graphic presentation, for example, is already being transformed into animated virtual reality. Computer-driven plotterlike cutters that stencil detailed drawings from wood or metal are being used to produce scale models. Aspects of design development and construction document services are being shortcut by CAD drawings and digitized detail libraries from the manufacturers. Finally, the sharing of drawing files on the Internet allows architect, consultant, and fabricator to work on drawings simultaneously and to better coordinate their efforts. These aspects of computer use in production enable the design team to spend less time on drawing documents and more resources on exploration and optimization.

Another factor introduced by computers is the use of digital drawings to generate numerical modeling and performance simulation. Simple examples of this application include area take-offs and material quantities. Midlevel computer tools can simulate sunshade performance and artificial lighting illumination levels directly from design drawings. High-level applications will likely incorporate *expert engine* tools that provide rule-based feedback as design work progresses, rather than after the fact. Then, after the building is constructed, the architect's as-built digital drawings can provide the framework for an automated building management system. At some level of this change in the distribution of services, the computer will increasingly become a design thinking tool and graduate from its current status as a kind of graphic word processor used primarily for documentation. The ultimate goal, whether technological pressures demand it or not, should be to utilize computers for the true purpose of architecture, namely, the exploration and refinement of well-developed design intentions.

Trend Five: From Monumental to Sustainable

The systems concept of architecture from an ecological perspective is that of organic systems. *Organic* in this sense implies that buildings are participants in the biological cycles and processes of nature. Sustainable buildings are not intended to simply *look* organic and visually represent a harmony of nature and human habitation; they must actually provide a functional harmony by participating in natural processes. Hence, a sustainable building is thought of as a complex web of dynamic biology, rather than a distinct assemblage of machinery that possesses and occupies a small site.

Passive solar architecture, as it was called in the 1960s and 1970s, referred to building system interaction with processes of climate: sun, wind, rain, and daylight. It featured a number of technologies for converting sunlight directly into winter heat gain. Most of its cooling strategies consisted of means of heat gain avoidance, but some work was done with earth sheltering, external mass, and night sky radiation cooling. Greenhouses, Trombe walls, and direct-gain heating strategies were most popular. Taking cues from indigenous and vernacular architecture, the components of passive environmental servicing were integrated directly into the envelope and structure of the building. This integration is part of what distinguishes passive architecture from active solar systems. Active systems are independent mechanical devices for converting sunshine, wind or other diffuse natural energies into usable concentrations of energy like heat or electricity. They include solar water heating, photovoltaic electric cells, and wind turbines. Active systems can power any building regardless of whether they are integrated into its construction, added on the roof, or in a remote location. Passive systems have a more powerful impact on building design than add-on active systems, precisely because the architecture itself is the passive system. This first phase of ecological architecture was very much about harnessing benign and renewable sources of energy that coexisted with the building on the site.

Passive design (which was always a poor choice of terminology for a dynamic energy system) was soon supplanted by a more broad-based ecological approach termed "sustainable." More than just providing "free" energy to tightly constructed and carefully oriented passive buildings, the sustainable ethic embraced the ecology of the total life cycle of buildings. It proponents deemed that living on the interest of nature was superior to harvesting its current capital. Design externalities like protection of habitat, embodied energy of building materials, and carbon dioxide pollution debt were among the many issues of this second phase of ecological architecture. *Sustainability* is a broad term for the healthy habitation of nature. The systems mode of sustainability addresses biological patterns as well as the physics of building energy use.

The twentieth century, as James Gleick (1988) has noted, will be remembered for three scientific advances: quantum mechanics, relativity, and chaos. First, Heisenberg and Bohr reveal the uncertain, probabilistic, and interactive dynamic of nature and thoroughly dispel Descartes's view of the universe as a clockwork machine. Then Einstein unveils the relative nature of mass, energy, and time and places our worldview on an even less machinelike footing. The final revelation, chaos, is still unfolding in studies of synergistic systems, fuzzy logic, nonlinear dynamics, and patterns of interrelated complexity. It seems obvious, however, that chaos theory will finally exorcise the reductive and deterministic demons of classical physics. For general discussion here, the unity of these ideas is called *complexity science*.

Chaotic patterns of intricate organization are present in most every formal arrangement of nature, including the human body. Blood vessels, for example, are about 10,000 miles long stretched end to end and reach, within two or three cells, everywhere in the human body, yet they make up less than 5 percent of total body weight. At this high order of complexity, patterns of self-organization occur that cannot be explained by mechanistic cause and effect. These emergent patterns are evident in everything from the organized flow of boiling water, to cycles of rabbit population, to how the brain organ achieves the level of mind. Complexity science tells us that nature has the following attributes:

- Chaotic form that is spontaneous, self-organizing, and self-regulating, like the shape of a cloud or a snowflake, the path of a river, the population of a wild species, or the pattern of convection in boiling water.

- Deep interrelationships to the extent that all events everywhere are connected, so a fluttering butterfly in Texas can set up a chain of events leading to a storm in Asia.

- Nondeterministic and nonlinear systems of unpredictable behavior whose final state is heavily determined by small differences in its initial condition. The weather makes a good example.

To paraphrase John Barrow in *The Artful Universe* (1995), chaos is how the universe moves from order to entropy and simplicity to complexity: "It is why we can talk of finding a Theory of Everything, yet fail to understand a snowflake." Chaos, finally, is how we understand that nature can be composed of self-organizing patterns and successful acts of morphogenesis. This new organizing principle is so pervasive that linear ordering is now thought to be the rare exception to how the universe negotiates reality. The mathematician Stanislaw Ulam has even remarked that calling the study of chaos *nonlinear science* was akin to calling "zoology the study of nonelephant animals."

Naturally emergent patterns of self-organization are one link between architectural form-finding and complexity science. D'Arcy Wentworth Thompson documented naturally emerging paths to form in his 1917 landmark *On Growth and Form.* The relationships he discovered between natural forces, form, and function deal with the science of *morphology,* concerning the natural and evolutionary shaping of organisms by their habitat so that form is seen as a revealed manifestation of process. Sustainable design, morphology, complexity science, growth, and form—taken together, they describe the same realities.

The cosmology of complexity science and deep interrelatedness is sympathetic to architecture's quest for meaningful expression. *Chaoplexity,* as science journalist John Horgan (Papakakis, 1998) has termed it, meshes resolved functional order with spontaneous and imaginative forms and spaces—a reasonable description of the passion of architecture. It is both nondeterministic and unselfconscious. But there are difficulties as well: Any mention that nature is not simple and deterministic and not responsive to anthropocentric control is often met with resistance. Despite architecture's disdain for mechanistic reductionism, the prevailing cultural attitude is that nature is subject to simple, local manipulation and can be harvested to serve some higher intent. This view paradoxically argues that architecture should not be reduced to the machine but that nature somehow must be.

CHAPTER

3

Integrated Building Systems

CHAPTER 3 TOPICS

- Modes of Integration: Physical, Visual, and Performance
- Building Systems: Envelope, Structural, Mechanical, Interior, and Site
- Integration Potentials

This chapter proposes a framework for the integration of building systems by identifying different modes of integration and delineating a classification of major building systems. These taxonomies are supplemented in Chapter 4 with an overview and example of how integration thinking is included in design activity.

Integration can be described by its intended result as effecting physical, visual, or performance benefits. Frequently, any combination of these three methods is employed to achieve compound results. The classification is nonetheless helpful in understanding the various approaches and outcomes.

The major designations of building systems are site, structure, envelope, mechanical, and interior. Within each of these macrosystems are subsystems. A forced-air

ductwork distribution is a subsystem of the mechanical system; doors are a subsystem of the envelope, and so forth. Integrations occur with equal ease between major systems, between subsystems within major systems, and between subsystems of different major systems.

Modes of Integration: Physical, Visual, and Performance

The most fundamental goal of integrated building systems design is the elimination of redundant resources, usually achieved through strategic combinations of the systems that are deployed in concert with their shared mandates of space, image, or function. It is important that integration measures provide these and sufficient other tangible benefits to justify the effort involved. Exposing structure or mechanical systems components, for example, is a popular and often highly visible aspect of integration. But exposure itself is not inherently good, no matter what level of integration is attained. Some design intention or programmatic goal must actually be served.

PHYSICAL INTEGRATION

Physical integration occurs wherever systems share architectural space by occupying a common area or volume. This is the most fundamental of integration activities and must be considered for practically all building components. For an air-conditioning duct to pass through a steel bar joist system, for example, the structural system and the mechanical system must be physically integrated. This can be accomplished by comparing the size of the duct to the space available in the web of the joist. If the optimal size and shape of the duct is greater than the available space in the optimal joist, then one of the systems will have to be modified if physical integration is to occur. This specific modification would more likely involve the duct system inasmuch as its dimensional characteristics are less critical than those of the structural supports. But because the air-conditioning duct has its own criteria of cross-sectional area for the volume and velocity of air it carries, the modification to achieve physical integration would be limited to shape.

An interesting application of computer-aided design (CAD) drawing is its use in identifying physical integration problems and opportunities. By its organizational nature, CAD separates different systems of a building into distinct layers of the drawing. Turning various layers of the drawing on and off allows the designer to examine the physical intersections of different systems and identify specific integration tasks. In the ductwork-to-structure example it may be found that the duct indeed does fit through the truss but will not pass under the solid steel beam located at the end of the structural bay. The same method can apply to lighting and air diffuser arrangements above furniture layouts, interference between lighting and ductwork, and so forth.

Physical integration is also accomplished by the meshing, layering, and folding together of space taken up by building systems. The aforementioned exercise of placing ductwork in the structural voids is only a crude example of meshed space. A more refined example can be seen in IKOY Architects' design of the interior street of the Wallace Building in Winnipeg (see case study #5). Here, the corridor is left wide enough to double as a gathering place for class discussions, social meetings, and geology displays. Collecting the building's four levels of circulation together in a central axis also forms an interior street that serves as the entryway from major parking lots to the central campus. Similar examples of physical integration of space are found at different scales in many buildings: Storage systems fold space into itself compactly; open rooms expand into one another, making small houses feel big; and so on.

Another mode of physical integration commonly occurs in every building wherever two systems or different materials connect; that is, in the details. The proper detailing of these connections assures permanence and security through the integrity of the joint as well as the intended finish condition of adjoining materials. Water- and airtightness, water drainage, thermal expansion and contraction cycles, differential movement, structural deflection, dissimilar metal separation, and a host of other pragmatic factors have a part in the physical integration of the joint. These joints are most pronounced where two macrosystems intersect, such as where structure and envelope systems meet, but they occur as well at the level of subsystem or material interface. Detailing is also important to visual integration because it expresses design intentions, or at least an attitude about how a particular detail expresses the larger design concept.

VISUAL INTEGRATION

The expression of a system or combination of systems as a visual design element constitutes an act of visual integration. For systems to be visually integrated, they must be either exposed and ordered in some compositional way or concealed behind layers of finish materials. Compositional techniques used in visual integration include modifications of the color, size, shape, and placement of systems and their component pieces.

Exposure of commonly hidden structural or mechanical systems is an integration strategy that relies heavily on such visual modifications. This strategy of exposure can be traced to the precedent of Brutalism in the works of Le Corbusier or Alison and Peter Smithson. The concrete structure at Corbusier's Unité d'Habitation in Marseilles is left exposed and unfinished to express the wooden formwork of fabrication, for example. As a design method, the notion of exposure has opened the architectural palette of materials to include the visual potential of previously foreign and characteristically industrial elements. And as these elements are exposed, the essential nature of their function, materials, and detail connections necessarily become part of the architect's concern and enthusiastic attention.

Separation of systems by the layering of materials is also a method of visual integration. This strategy commonly employs a layer of finish material to cover and segregate unwanted systems from exterior or interior view. This is something of a negative approach to integration as compared with the gesture of exposure but is often an effective and economical way of solving the problems caused by the distribution of services and structural systems in a building. Finish layers are often helpful, if not particularly inventive means of dealing with the problems of dirt accumulation and noisy equipment. They also can perform critical functions: sound-absorbent ceiling tiles in offices, acoustically reflective panels in auditoriums, light-reflective surfaces for daylighting, and so forth.

PERFORMANCE INTEGRATION

Whenever building systems share functional mandates, performance integration is accomplished. In the case of Louis Kahn's Kimbell Art Museum, the cycloidal vault of the concrete structure also forms the container of the building envelope and defines the interior space. Further, in concert with the narrow skylight and perforated reflector at the ceiling level, the vault becomes an integral part of the daylighting system by washing the galleries with diffused and comfortably graduated levels of light.

A second mode of performance integration deals with the adaptive response of buildings to fluctuating demands. The ability to adjust and regulate building response to changing conditions through intelligent use of design elements constitutes "dynamic integration." This sort of integrative and comprehensive design is what allows a building to respond appropriately to daily and seasonal changes in temperature, wind patterns, solar geometry and other environmental variations. Dynamic systems are integrative in the same multifunctional and shared mandate ways that hardware systems are integrative. Passive and sustainable buildings are generally good examples of integration through dynamic response. A basic example of dynamic integration is a roof overhang that allows sunlight to penetrate a window during underheated seasons of the year when the sun is low and then provides shade from high sun in overheated periods. The overhang shading device is bimodal in that it differentiates according to the thermal needs of the building, even though it has no moving parts.

Bimodal sorts of dynamic integration are typical of buildings where aerodynamic response is tuned to winter winds versus summer breezes, or day versus night thermal response is controlled by the heat capacity of structural mass. Designs for adaptation to summer versus winter, day versus night, empty versus occupied are all examples of bimodal response. Such responses can be associated with factors of the thermal environment or any other performance function based on changing conditions. Norman Foster's headquarters for Willis Faber Dumas in Ipswich, England, changes from dark glass, reflecting its historic surroundings by day, to an illuminated interior showcase at night (see case study #7). In this instance, the change in envelope mode is accomplished by employing the luminous properties of glass that make it reflective to the bright side and transparent from the dark side.

Automation technologies advance performance integration as well. Computerized control systems have transformed buildings into intelligent robots that not only respond to changes and schedules, but actually anticipate, measure and learn from them. Replacing resources with measured responses provides such benefits as improved comfort, operational economy, and reduced capacity of servicing equipment. In other words, automation replaces brute strength with intelligence.

The Example of Exposed Ductwork

Consider an example of exposed ductwork in a building interior. This common treatment can be used to illustrate the thinking associated with all three modes of systems integration. First, of course, the motivation for visually exposing ductwork to occupied interior spaces must be considered. Such motivations may relate to the architectural character of the design in general or may simply be dictated by physically restricted space as in a low floor-to-ceiling height that makes a dropped ceiling undesirable. The results of these motivations become the initial benefits of the integration. Other consequences of the integration may provide additional positive results. In the final analysis, cumulative benefits will have to outweigh both the extra resources required and the negative trade-offs of the decision to expose the ductwork. In this example there are several compromises to consider, such as mechanical system noise and additional cleaning maintenance.

In terms of physical integration, exposed ductwork provides additional volume to the occupied space by eliminating the ceiling layer and meshing the structural void of the space between the ceiling and the floor or roof above. These are issues of shared space that define physical integration. Visual integration of the ducts is more complicated, as the design will be exposing a hardware component that is normally configured and installed to maximize performance and economy without regard to visual appeal. The designer may take care to arrange the horizontal duct routing in overhead patterns that reinforce the order of the space, perhaps following the circulation paths between workstations, without sacrificing the ability of the duct system to deliver air efficiently to where it is needed. Other compositional techniques may then be applied through the material and finish selections for the ductwork. Consideration can also be given as to how the ductwork is supported by the structure, its connection to air register devices, and all manner of detailing.

Performance integration of ductwork adds considerable sophistication to the idea. Ducts not only provide temperature relief and air motion in a space, they also play a role in the acoustical environment, specifically in the background noise level. Performance benefits may include energy savings by removing cooling air at 55°F from a nonconditioned attic at 140°F and thereby eliminating thermal duct losses. Acoustically, however, it may be necessary to use internally insulated ductwork with thicker wall construction to provide adequate noise isolation from air friction noise in the duct and low-frequency reflected fan rumble from the air handler.

When Louis Kahn decided to expose the mechanical systems at the Richards Medical Research Laboratory, he planned on weaving ducts and pipes into the open webbed concrete trusses of the floor-ceiling layer and maintaining a low 8 ft clear ceiling height below the trusses (see case study #1). Initially, this proved to be a problem of coordination with building trades, which failed to realize that the systems would be left exposed and so installed them in the usual messy but convenient functional arrangements. Much of the initial work had to be redone. Eventually, Kahn realized that the exposed ducts, conduits, and pipes merely provided excessive areas for dust to collect and would thus be impractical in a biological research setting. Kahn used this experience at the Richards laboratories by providing 7 ft deep interstitial attics for all the mechanical services above each of the three laboratory floors of the Salk Institute for Biological Studies (see case study #2). The interstitial spaces at Salk are connected to the lab spaces via stainless steel access slots. This ensures complete freedom and flexibility of services, in keeping with the requirements of laboratory spaces. After Richards Medical, Kahn never employed exposed ductwork again.

A positive example of ductwork integration is found in IKOY Architects' Wallace Earth Sciences Laboratory in Winnipeg (see case study #5). Ducts are painted in the color scheme of the interior street and provide scale and visual interest to the long corridor.

Integrated Systems

This section describes the component elements, performance mandates, and relationships of the five fundamental systems of a building. These systems are categorized as follows:

- Envelope—the separation of indoor and outdoor conditions
- Services—HVAC, electrical, plumbing, vertical transportation, and life safety systems
- Structural—elements providing static equilibrium against gravity and dynamic loads
- Interior—occupied space encompassing partitions, finishes, lighting, acoustics, furniture, and so forth
- Site—landscape and support systems for the building, including parking, drainage, vegetation, utilities, and the like

Any attempt to analyze or synthesize the integration potential of building systems must be based on a sound understanding of how each system and its subsystems satisfy their roles in the total design package. The following descriptions establish a very general and necessarily incomplete framework for the systems approach to integration. Encyclopedic knowledge of building systems is not the goal here, and much of this framework should be general knowledge to the readers of this text. There are a virtually infinite number of systems that can be combined in a possibly infinite number of ways, and no one text can do much more than graze the surface. Further, the particulars of each building design form a shifting picture in these times of what Forrest Wilson (1987) has called "relentless technological change." Moreover, each building design presents its own unique context for selecting building elements and methods of assembly. The ability to deal with this complexity and shifting variability in design requires considered reasoning more than it does practical knowledge. In other words, systems integration has a great deal more to do with the relationships between systems than with the particulars of any one technology.

An obvious subplot to the theme of integration involves the relationship between natural systems and building systems. Most building systems entail some level of environmental performance, so the pragmatic theme of natural systems is largely self-evident. Ethical concerns for the environment that confront the practice of modern architecture are equally compelling. From energy conservation to land conservation, from worker productivity to indoor air quality, and from construction waste management to sustainable design, the relationship between buildings and nature has become an integral part of the practice of architecture.

What follows, then, is a conceptual framework for facilitating the appropriate integration of systems and subsystems. A basic understanding of design and technology is assumed to be at hand or easily acquired from reference sources.

As an example of what is being addressed here, consider the case of a hypothetical passive cooling system that offsets all the heat transferred through the building envelope as well as from internal gains. This may, on the surface, seem to be a satisfactory replacement for mechanical cooling. In fact, mechanical systems provide far more than the sensible heat relief of passive cooling. Omitting a mechanical system would ignore other needs. The problem of humidity control, which most passive cooling systems cannot address, is only the most prominent oversight. This error in judgment also overlooks mechanically provided benefits of air motion, air filtration, and ventilation air—a package of requirements that passive cooling does not reliably deliver. So what at first appear to be redundant passive and active systems that the designer can choose between actually offer an opportunity to examine how the two might work together to satisfy building comfort requirements more comprehensively and elegantly. It is fundamental considerations of this sort that an outline for the integration of systems must address.

This review of the five major building systems, their elements, and functional mandates, is ordered by general familiarity with their integration issues. Different approaches are taken with each system to broaden the scope of how each component can be thought of in the context of the complete building. Envelope systems are discussed first because the envelope forms the most obvious part of any building as its outside skin and container of space. Structural systems follow, as the traditionally ennobled framework of form and space. The discussions of physical, visual, and performance integration of structural systems will be familiar to most readers. Mechanical services are third, with an emphasis on how extensively air-conditioning impacts today's highly serviced buildings. The ensuing discussion of interior systems focuses on functional, thermal, luminous, and acoustical zoning as both ordering concepts and integration opportunities. Finally, the site is presented in special terms of the architecture's microclimatic response and the ongoing interface with natural forces.

ENVELOPE SYSTEMS

Building envelope systems separate the indoors from the outdoors—they provide the "skin" of architecture. For this reason, they become the fundamental interpretation between the interior and the site condition. This interpretation sets in motion a large number of modulating functions of the envelope system—thermal, solar, acoustic, aerodynamic, and other forces largely invisible to direct observation but highly significant to human occupation.

The envelope is also the most visible element of the building and must respond to our appreciation of image, form, and orientation to the building. These dual roles of invisible forces and visible mandates are repeated to a lesser degree in other major building systems, but the envelope is the most obvious point of their resolution.

Elements

- Walls
- Fenestration
- Roofs

Mandates

Separation/Connection. The distinction between indoors and outdoors is not always an exclusive one. There are often ambient conditions that benefit the interior environment and can be employed passively to condition occupied space. The dynamic relation of these indoor and outdoor conditions leads to an interactive definition of the envelope system. As discussed in the previous chapter, the ability of designers to respond to this interaction is one of the important trends in the systems view of architecture. Reynolds and Stein (2000) (after Christian Norberg-Schultz, 1965) describe this concept as "filters, barriers and switches" or as Stephen Groák says in discussing flows of matter and energy, "The building forms a system of barriers, filters, containers—sometimes condensers—for an enormous collection of materials and energies."

Control over levels of connection and separation to the outdoors plays a direct role in the comfort of occupants. Weather has to be excluded so that the indoor environment can be controlled. But rooms allowing visual contact with the natural environment are more restful than windowless rooms. Workers with a view, for example, are more productive, and hospital patients in windowed wards heal faster. On the other hand, people require various degrees of separation from the outdoors for privacy, security, and control of indoor conditions.

Because the envelope must satisfy both the barrier and the filter roles, switches have to be provided. Window blinds are a good example of switches; they allow the window glazing to be effectively turned off, along with view, light, and sun. Operable shading devices such as movable awnings, movable insulation like window shutters, and operable windows for ventilation are further examples.

Weathering. Upon the completion of a finished exterior envelope surface, there begins a continuous relationship with the elements of weather. Sun and wind, moisture and ice, dust and decay all tend to age the building, diminishing its pristine newness. Erosive elements like acid rain, ultraviolet radiation, and chemical interactions with building components accelerate this process. Either the building will require continual renovation to maintain its newness, or it will be, to some extent, reclaimed by the site. The former choice results in a building that has been "stained" by time and the elements; the later can produce a building that acquires a graceful "patina" (see Mostafavi and Leatherbarrow, 1993).

Structural Form. The structural possibilities of envelope systems range from Louis Kahn's cycloidal vaults of concrete at the Kimbel Art Museum in Fort Worth, Texas, to Philip Johnson's transparent space frame structure at the Crystal Cathedral in Garden Grove, California.

Thermal Form. The thermal form of a building refers to its level of exposure between inside and out. For heat transfer by temperature difference, this exposure is a product of the area of exterior skin and its thermal conductance. From a purely geometric view, an efficient form has a low surface-to-volume ratio, enclosing the maximum amount of interior space with the minimum of skin exposure, and will also have a low heat transfer conductance. An inefficient form, conversely, will has a high surface-to-volume ratio and high-conductance envelope assemblies.

In actual practice, of course, as compared with a purely geometric view, the envelope becomes more efficient if it is shaped to maximize good exposures. Although a sphere would be the most efficient thermal container of space, a long rectangle stretched from east to west offers better opportunity for collecting low winter sun and avoiding harsh summer solar impacts. For this reason, various ratios of length-to-width can be considered before determining an appropriate aspect ratio (see Olgyay, 1963).

Thermal form is a way of talking about the "leakiness" of the envelope. This encompasses not only heat transfer by temperature difference, it also includes the consideration of accidental air change by infiltration and exfiltration as well as the migration of moisture into and out of the building.

Solar Form. Solar impacts on a building are determined less by its overall shape as considered in thermal form than they are by the placement and distribution of glazing and the use of shading devices to protect them. So solar form results primarily from window size and orientation.

Mitigating factors can also play a large role: appropriate use of external shading devices, both fixed and operable; the selection of glazings with differing ratios of visible light transmission versus total solar transmission; the slope of window glazings toward the sky or the ground. Even the configuration of the building envelope into self-shading forms such as courtyards and setback stories makes a significant difference.

Unlike thermal form, solar form is bimodal. In small surface-load-dominated buildings in particular, the need for solar gain in colder months will be replaced by a need for defensive shade in comfortable and warm seasons. Because every latitude has its own schedule of solar geometry and every building a particular set of sun-to-shade requirements, the interplay of these factors is one of the enduring truths to which a designer must respond.

Luminous Form. In terms of daylighting, the luminous form of an envelope is bound up in the solar form. Because most building spaces are occupied for daytime activity, daylight through the envelope is generally a desirable resource. In fact, the abundance of available natural light is usually much less of a resource problem than the difficulty of distributing daylight any distance away from a glazed aperture.

Separating natural light from the heat it eventually becomes is possible, to a limited extent, by admitting light in measured portions and avoiding the Promethean overheating that usually accompanies daylight saturation. Because daylight is generally useful year-round, it is not a bimodal condition as found in solar form, which confronts sun versus shade. But because available daylight levels vary with sky condition, time of day, and season of the year, it is no less a dynamic condition than solar geometry.

The envelope glazing is the lens of a daylighting system and functions just as the cover lens of an artificial lighting fixture does. Additional envelope components, such as reflectors and baffles, can also serve as artificial lighting fixture equivalents. These components bounce the light deeper into a room or modulate its penetration in other ways. When total control of natural light is important, such as in theaters and auditoriums, the envelope must function as a switch by means of daylight-control curtains or blinds, to close out the sky. Switchable glazing that employs laminated glass with an electrically excited diode layer of mylar to change from opaque to clear will be an option when the technology matures. Phototropic and thermotropic glass that darkens in response to high light levels and warmer temperatures (like darkening sunglasses), are technically proven but have not yet demonstrated economic practicality.

Aerodynamic Form. Wind is both a structural and a comfort factor in envelope design. The magnitude of uplift and surface wind loads are the important structural considerations. Cross-ventilation and buffering of cold winds are prime environmental concerns. The environmental aspects qualify as bimodal dynamics because of the changing seasonal patterns of prevailing winds and the alternating needs of a building for opening to ventilation versus closing for heating or cooling.

Computational fluid dynamics (CFD) is the science of predicting airflow in closed spaces and around freestanding obstructions. Recent advances in computing power have made CFD an important tool in studying the complexities of convective air currents. Three-dimensional modeling is accomplished in carefully constructed wind tunnel tests. Two-dimensional modeling can be performed on fluid mapping tables by standing a scale profile section of the building in a moving horizontal film of water.

Acoustical Form. The acoustical form of an exterior envelope is primarily related to site noise control. Self-sheltering forms include courtyard and atrium plans. Because mass is the primary source of noise attenuation, the solid, heavy elements of the envelope can be directed to reflect unwanted sounds away from occupied spaces.

Hydrological Form. The rainscreen functions of an envelope mandate the routing of precipitation away from the structure to the storm drainage system. In many cases this integrates the form of the roof into the topography of the site. Other factors, such as the need to provide a dry cover for entry to the building, may also be considered.

STRUCTURAL SYSTEMS

Conceptually, structural systems comprise the following functional elements:

- Bearing—transfers loads to stable supporting grade, generally made up of foundations, footings, grade beams, piers
- Lifting—columns, load bearing walls, arches and other members providing vertical support
- Spanning—horizontal support of beams, girders, trusses, purlins, slabs, arches, vaults, coffers, domes, space frames, and the like; also includes roof structures of cable and membrane or pneumatically supported envelopes
- Bracing—diagonal bracing and diaphragm resistance to racking and lateral loads

Structure is fundamentally intended to provide static equilibrium, just as mechanical systems are meant to supply thermal equilibrium. Where heating, ventilating, and air-conditioning (HVAC) work to maintain a constant indoor temperature by equalizing heat losses and heat gains, structure works to transfer physical forces to supporting foundations and into supporting grade. There are some important conceptual differences of course—thermal loads are dynamic and heat flow changes direction with changes in the climate. HVAC systems use a constant source of energy to balance thermal loads and are controlled to operate in response to climatic change. Structural loads are generally static rather than dynamic; they result primarily from the uniform and unchanging force of gravity. Gravity loads consist of the dead load of the structure itself and uniformly distributed live loads imposed by the interior furnishing and occupants on the floors as well as snow loads on the roof.

There are some dynamic forces that influence structural design: wind and seismic lateral loads, for example, and imbalanced loads incurred during construction. From a systems perspective, it is interesting to note that structure must be designed for the worst set of loads that code can dictate and then left to operate at full load conditions forever, whereas HVAC capacity is designed for the 95 percent worst condition and operates at partial load in all but the worst of weather. Further, because building structure is permanent and difficult to modify, and because the structural loads are only estimates, structural systems must have large safety factors built into them. They must respond statically and continuously, even to dynamic events like hurricanes and earthquakes that may never occur. This precaution is based on the fact that failure in a structural system is potentially sudden, catastrophic, and disastrous. Failure in an HVAC system may be equally dangerous, such as involving an outbreak of Legionnaires' disease or other indoor air quality hazards, but air-conditioning disaster is usually prevented by proper maintenance. Ongoing HVAC failures are easily remedied by modifying or replacing the system. Not so with structure, which is never bimodal and seldom dynamic. Earthquake design has opened a few possibilities for dynamic dampening of seismic loads, but these are rare exceptions (study the John Hancock Building for an example of seismic dampening).

Another issue of physical integrity that structural systems must address is fire safety. Here, the selection of wood, masonry, concrete, or steel construction must be weighed against the presence of fire suppression sprinklers or the need to protect the structural members with another layer of noncombustible material. These decisions have significant first-cost impacts and thus can reduce the amount of resources available for other design features. They also, however, involve ongoing costs associated with insurance premiums. Sometimes a more expensive structural system pays for itself in the reduction of insurance costs.

Visual Integration

Structural systems selection, then, generally involves the choice of the lightest-weight members of the most economical-grade material, allowing the most efficient configuration that is appropriate to the anticipated loads. Taken in isolation, there is nothing architectural about this procedure; it is pure engineering. In concert with other systems, however, structure acts in visually expressive ways. It creates a grid and rhythm with the envelope system, for example, through modular repetition of horizontal and vertical supports. It creates an open frame or a closed shell for the envelope to infill. Exposed to the interior, it modulates space and orders the plan. Left clear, structure contains and organizes service elements such as ductwork and lighting.

In all, the visual expression of building structure and its intentional integration with other major systems is part of what Kenneth Frampton (1995) calls the "tectonic order." This ordering is primarily an ennoblement of how architects think about and through the construction of a building while fully considering the methods and materials to be employed. It arises from a long tradition of the challenge of structural problems before the advent of numerical method. Structure, as a means of architectural clarity, is also associated with the human sense of stability that comes from the everyday experiences of gravity: remaining upright on a top-heavy two-legged base and walking around by continually falling forward. This lifelong experience of gravity gives the structural expression of buildings an easy communication with our intuitive senses—if it looks as though it will stand up, it probably will. Comparing this to HVAC systems again, it is clear that we have no such intuitive sense about systems of thermal equilibrium. It is hard to intuitively judge the adequacy of a mechanical system by the physical size of its components.

Another visually accessible aspect of structural systems is the graphic depiction of loads, vectors, and the resultant forces in members. These diagrams take the familiar form of free-body moment and reaction, shear and funicular diagrams. At the scale of a building they become tributary load diagrams that can be used to generate the basic geometry of the structure. These graphic illustrations connect the visible geometry of structure to the invisible geometry of imposed forces. Because the illustrations are literal, they give the structure its necessary

geometry. Antonio Gaudi (1865–1934) used graphic methods like these to work out the form of the huge dome over the Segrada Familia in Barcelona, Spain (begun in 1884 and still in progress). An upside-down, three-dimensional model of the dome was constructed to scale in his workshop. Small bags of lead weights were then attached to the load points to reveal the regular parabolic curves of the structure. Later, however, when Jorn Utzon proposed the irregularly curved form of roofs in his competition scheme for the Sydney Opera House (1957–1973), there was no similar empirical method for resolving the indeterminate loads. Ove Arup and his team of engineers in London, including Peter Rice, had to write massive computer programs to resolve the transfer of loads through irregular shapes. In the end, Utzon found it preferable to base all the shells at Sydney on a radius of 246 ft (75 m).

Because gravity is static, uniform, and constant, and because the dynamic forces acting on buildings are assumed to act uniformly on any surface with equal probability, certain consistencies are manifested in structural design. The first of these, hierarchical consistency, results from the cumulative transfer of loads from top to bottom of a building and from intermediate members to primary members. In terms of a tributary load diagram, horizontal structure grows larger from purlin to joist to beam. Vertical structure grows in size as loads from above accumulate in columns and load-bearing walls transferring loads to grade. The second result of the uniformity of loads is consistency of pattern. Uniform loads dictate uniform member size and uniform spacing. Uniform member size and spacing in turn creates patterns within the hierarchies: purlin spacing, joist spacing, beam grids, column modules, and so forth.

Physical Integration

From the perspective of physical integration, structure is often made to contain the service systems. At one scale, the interstitial space between floor and ceiling layers in a building normally carry the horizontal distribution of services: HVAC ducts, electrical wiring, and recessed lighting systems. Similar but usually smaller voids in walls can carry services as well. At another scale, hollow structural members are stronger in bending than solid members of the same diameter. This allows the voids in individual members to be used for the distribution of services. Shaped steel beams, box beams, tubular frames, and hollow-core slabs are all appropriate conduits for the distribution of service elements.

Performance Integration

Functionally, structure can often lend its massive materials or its void interstitial spaces to the mandates of other systems. Return or supply air plenums are easy examples. This is an elaboration of physically integrated ducts to the extent of structure's actually becoming a duct rather than just housing it. Such plenums are now frequently found in ceiling or floor voids and occasionally in wall cavities.

A more dynamic example of performance integration in structural systems is the use of structural mass as thermal heat capacity. Passive heating systems normally use floor slabs as thermal batteries to store absorbed solar energy and limit interior temperature swings. In hot, arid climates, external envelope building mass is used for its flywheel effect to effectively balance the impacts of hot days followed by cool nights. Night ventilation cooling is also used in both surface-load-dominated and internal-load-dominated buildings to provide a passive cooling heat sink for daytime heat gains. In some instances, internal thermal mass in a supply air plenum is cooled continuously by the HVAC system in order to lower the peak cooling load.

MECHANICAL SYSTEMS

Mechanical systems, for the purposes of this discussion of integration, are limited here to HVAC and related thermal comfort components. The other "mechanical" aspects of buildings such as lighting and plumbing are considered in the discussion of interior systems later in this chapter.

Mandates
There are eight fundamental requirements of mechanical air-conditioning, the last three of which are predominantly for public buildings:

- Temperature control by heating or cooling
- Humidity control by cooling air below its dew point for dehumidification, or by evaporatively adding moisture when humidification is required
- Air motion to occupants by forced air circulation
- Air filtration to remove some level of particulates
- Exhaust of polluted air from indoor sources of heat, odor, moisture, or chemical concentration, such as found in toilet rooms, laboratory vent hoods, and kitchens
- Air change for ventilation, economizer cooling, and nighttime flush cooling
- Air balance for positive indoor pressure to avoid infiltration of untreated outdoor air, dust, and moisture
- Smoke exhaust and fire safety control of indoor air pressure by compartmentalization

Elements
Conceptually, the mechanical systems of a building consist of the following functional components:

- Thermal plant where heating and cooling energy are generated
- Distribution of thermal energy to individual zones of the building
- Delivery of comfort to occupants by forced air or radiant temperatures
- Control of mechanical equipment to match HVAC operation to thermal loads
- Thermal energy storage (TES) as an optional HVAC operating scheme

The Thermal Plant
Every mechanical system has at its heart a mechanism whereby source energy is converted into comfort energy. This thermal plant can also be the connection between the building's indoor conditions and the environment serving as a source of thermal energy or a thermal "sink" for heat being rejected from the building. At the largest scale, a campus of buildings would have a central plant where boilers and chillers produce hot and cold water. This requires the use of utility-provided energy, normally in the form of electricity and natural gas. The hot and cold water is sent from the plant to individual buildings where fans blow room air across coils of circulating water, much like what occurs in the radiator of automobiles. Cooling towers in the central plant reject the space heat captured in chilled water return lines back to the environment by evaporation. This evaporative effect is used to cool the condensing side of the central plant chillers, thus moving the heat from occupied space back to the central plant and then into the environment. Besides using outside air to reject heat, cooling systems can be designed to use below-grade soil as geothermal heat sinks or to reject building heat to large bodies of water such as cooling ponds or even seawater.

The most common sort of thermal plant is the conventional split-system direct-expansion freon cycle machine, which works for one single individual thermal zone of the building. In this arrangement, the outdoor unit of compressor and condensing coil make up the cooling plant and a gas furnace or electrical resistance heat strip is located in the indoor half of the system to provide heating energy. The outdoor compressor and condensing coil are connected by refrigerant lines to the indoor evaporator coil. Heat collected at the evaporator coil is thus rejected to the environment by outdoor air blowing across the evaporator. Split-system heat pumps use a reversing valve to get double-duty cooling and heating from the outdoor unit. They employ a valve to reverse the flow of refrigerant between the indoor and outdoor coils. This allows the unit to either "pump" heat from indoors to out, or from outdoors to in; a feat conventional direct expansion systems can perform only in one direction.

At the smallest scale the thermal plant can be part of a compact package of equipment that contains all the elements of mechanical servicing. A wall unit heat pump, a package rooftop unit, or a window unit air conditioner are examples of systems that not only produce comfort energy by converting source electricity, but also deliver it directly to the occupants.

Integration concerns for incorporating thermal plants into design schemes, or simply in accommodating their functional requirements, entail several givens. The first is that utility services have to be routed to the central plant as a large portion of the building's power and energy requirements. Second, thermal energy has to be delivered from the plant to the zones in some form. Generally, there is also the necessity of dealing with exhaust flues from combustion equipment and similar functional requirements. Finally, in the vast majority of systems, there must be some outdoor component where heat is rejected to the environment (water source heat pumps are an important exception to this arrangement).

Distribution of Thermal Energy to Zones. In large heating and cooling systems, the distribution of energy from the plant to the fan/coil systems located in zones of a building is a distinct part of the system. These distribution systems are usually composed of all-water systems (also called hydronic systems) in which two, three, or four pipes are used to convey thermal energy from the plant to the individual thermal zones. In medium-sized systems, where direct expansion air-conditioning prevails, delivery from the plant is made by the freon loop between the condenser and evaporator coils.

Once thermal energy is delivered to a zone, there are a host of choices as to how the system will distribute comfort to individual areas of the zone or to separately controlled subzones. Aside from the common "single zone, single duct" system, there are variable air volume, multizone, and dual duct options.

Delivery of Comfort to Occupants. Delivery of comfort to the occupant of each space is generally accomplished by forcing supply air through a tapering network of insulated ducts. Air delivery registers then direct the air into rooms to promote complete circulation. A return-air system serves the complementary function of extracting the room's thermal load and excess humidity by recycling room air though ducts or open plenums and removing it. Air is returned to the distribution fan for filtering and reconditioning, and the cycle is repeated. Exhaust fans are located in kitchens and toilet rooms and other sources of air pollution and excess humidity. Outdoor air is provided in public buildings to mechanically replace the polluted air and keep buildings positively pressured relative to the outdoor environment. The prime components of the delivery system are ducts, registers, and grilles.

Aside from air delivery systems, the designer can use radiant systems to provide or ensure thermal comfort. The mean radiant temperature of surrounding surfaces is some 10 percent more important to comfort than air temperature at normal room and activity conditions. Controlling surface temperatures is sometimes accomplished by artificially heating an overhead "radiant panel" or a floor slab with hot water or electricity. Frank Lloyd Wright used hot water coils in the floor slab of the Solar Hemicycle Jacobs House (Madison, Wisconsin, 1944) to replace upright radiators hidden behind intricate wood grilles of his earlier Prairie Houses. This was one of many innovations that defined the course of his Usonian Houses.

Passive solar heating of the thermal mass of a floor, Trombe wall, or other interior room surface is another way of accomplishing the radiant effect. Passive systems are slower and rely on subtle temperature differences than does active radiant heating. Further, passive systems use greater mass and therefore have greater thermal inertia, resistance to temperature swings, and are more difficult to control as compared with the on/off of active heating. Recently "air walls" have been used to circulate return air from a room through a glass cavity exterior wall as part of the return air path. This eliminates the effects of cold window walls during cold weather. Richard Rogers and Partners' headquarters for Lloyd's of London is an early example of this comfort delivery strategy (see case study #24).

Control of Mechanical System to Match Thermal Load. Thermal loads in a building vary both in magnitude of heat transfer and in mode of operation between heating and cooling. The match between thermal loads and mechanical systems operation is intentionally controlled to maintain a fairly constant indoor condition. This is accomplished by modulating the heating and cooling energy expended to offset thermal loads. Better controls mean both lower energy consumption and superior comfort conditions, because controls replace indiscriminate energy use with some level of building intelligence. Each 1°F of error in a cooling thermostat, for example, results in about a 5 percent error in energy use.

This match between the operation of mechanical equipment and the opposing variations in environmental conditions amounts to what has been termed "using information to replace power" (Lyle, 1994). More exact information about needs and conditions always allows for better design and operation of systems. Basic control strategies can vary from on/off switching to one-way sensing like that found in a thermostat. More sophisticated systems include feedback loops of two-way sensing, whereby mechanical equipment can provide operating information back to the controls. At the extreme, computerized controls result in intelligent building systems that can anticipate indoor and outdoor environmental changes and learn to accommodate such things as the building's thermal response time.

Control strategies are often used in combination to fit the required degree of critical control to the appropriate sophistication of hardware. The most common of these are as follows:

- On/off switching—such as may be used on a ceiling fan
- Clock timer—providing a daily or weekly on/off equipment schedule
- Thermostat—sensing the dry-bulb temperature of the return air stream
- Humidistat—sensing the moisture content of the return air stream
- Setback thermostat—a programmable thermostat with a schedule of selectable temperature setpoints
- Occupant sensor—motion or infrared detection of the presence of room occupants
- Direct digital control—automated control of mechanical systems by computer program and potential integration of controls with lighting, security, fire safety, and other systems
- Intelligent buildings—robotic intelligence of building control decisions; sensing of outdoor, indoor, and mechanical systems conditions; may incorporate the ability to learn and anticipate changes; may integrate control of all building systems; can interface with building management personnel

For hardware controls to be most effective, it is essential that the thermal scheming that underlies the design of a building's mechanical system be integrated with the interior systems. These schematic strategies include the following:

- Zoning of interior into distinct areas of servicing, usually under the control of an individual thermostat;

divisions are made according to exposure, orientation, occupancy type, and use schedule.
- Staging of successive levels of cooling capacity to accommodate different modes of occupancy (such as entertaining large crowds) or environmental loads (such as morning versus afternoon).
- Diversity of independent package units for individual zones versus economy of central plant, which can shift capacity from zone to zone.
- Modulation of cooling capacity in very large buildings or campus central plants by use of variable speed equipment.
- Thermal energy storage systems (TES).

Because most mechanical cooling systems are sized to the peak hourly load of a building, their full capacity is utilized only about 5 percent of the year. And because heating systems operate at a much higher temperature difference from room air than do cooling systems, the need for air circulation in heating is much less than that for cooling. Consequently, heating is generally sized to match the fan and delivery systems required for the cooling system. Heating systems usually use the same fan and ducts as the cooling system by operating less frequently and more intermittently than the cooling. At any rate, most of the heating and cooling capacity of a conventional system is greatly underutilized.

The economics of this oversizing does not end with the excessive capacity of the cooling equipment that must be installed and maintained to meet infrequent peak conditions. The real penalty comes in the way large buildings pay for electrical power to operate their cooling systems. Not only do they pay for energy in kilowatt hours (kWh), they also pay for their peak demand in watts, or in utility engineering language, in kilovolt-amperes (kva). This is where thermal energy storage can be beneficial.

TES systems use smaller cooling plants that run continuously under full load to produce the same amount of ton-hours of cooling that a peak-load-sized plant would produce running intermittently at part load, or on/off cycling, over the same period of time. Instead of providing cooling energy directly to the building load, however, TES systems produce chilled water or ice and store it for later use. The building then draws from the thermal storage as needed. The time period for equalizing the storage capacity and the fluctuating building load may be as short as a day, but the aim is frequently a one-week interval in order to save up cooling energy over the weekend when the building is used more sparingly. Thus, instead of operating a large cooling plant to relieve small off-peak cooling loads, TES systems use smaller plants to produce ice or chilled water for later use.

TES systems require less peak power (kva) at any one given time than conventional systems because they are significantly smaller in cooling capacity. They do use about the same amount of total energy (kWh) over the course of a month as conventional systems, as they ultimately produce the same amount of cooling. Because the constant power load of TES matches the way utility companies have to continuously produce power in case it is needed by a customer somewhere on their electrical grid, there are significant savings in avoiding the cost of having to construct new generating capacity. The utility companies can pass these savings on to the consumer in the form of lower demand charges as an incentive to control peak loads. Many utilities even rebate some portion of the initial cost of TES installations.

The designer should remember that TES requires a significant increase in equipment and physical storage area for ice or chilled water, as compared with conventional systems. The first costs of a conventional system and a thermal energy storage system are frequently about the same. The benefit of thermal energy storage results from the savings in peak load demand from the utility, measured as the highest power requirement at the building meter for any one time during a month.

Another consideration in favor of TES, more specifically for ice storage systems, is the ability to supply conditioned air at very low temperatures. Whereas conventional systems deliver cooling at about 55°F supply air temperature, ice storage systems can approach 35°F. This enables the use of much smaller, high-velocity duct systems for delivering the cooling energy to occupied spaces. The smaller ducts require less space and allow for lower floor-to-floor heights.

Mandates

- Basic controls—temperature, humidity, air motion, air filtration, ventilation.
- Size and placement—HVAC requirements range from 10 to 50% of a building's area, volume, and cost.
- First cost—capacity in installed tons and associated distribution, delivery, and control. There is also an associated cost in size of required electrical service.
- Energy and power—efficiency in Seasonal Energy Efficiency Ratio (SEER) and Coefficient of Performance (COP), energy use (kWh), and power demand (kva).
- Servicing—maintenance, replacement, and repair of equipment.

INTERIOR SYSTEMS

Occupied space reflects a basic principle of architecture by serving the many aspects of human comfort and security. Beyond this overriding goal, interior spaces are usually individually arranged to facilitate a particular set of uses and are optimized accordingly. Flexibility is often an issue, as the use of the space and the people in it will change over time. In many cases, rapid technical advances change the way a space is used and the services needed. The advent of the desktop computer is a prime example. Architects frequently must anticipate future interior conditions as well as addressing current ones.

Elements

- Lighting—ambient and task lighting fixtures, as well as display, accent, and emergency light
- Acoustics—sound absorption, reflection, reverberation time control, room acoustics, noise control, and privacy
- Circulation—communication between spaces, emergency egress, security, signage
- Furniture—fixed and movable elements
- Finishes—floor and wall coverings, hardware and trim, paints and stains
- Specialties—equipment

Mandates

Zoning for Function. The grouping of building spaces together to best serve their various common needs is the act of zoning. Zoning provides for intelligent marshalling of resources, ease of control, and articulation of the inherent order of the building's character. Such groupings into separate zones are fundamental to organization of the building problem and are performed separately for different aspects of the design. Resolving the discrepancies between the various organizing forces requires work of informed inspiration.

Functional zoning is best recognized in the bubble diagrams of adjacency relationships common to conceptual design thinking. These clustering relationships may reveal the organization of a complete plan or suggest component modules that are repeated to fulfill the design. The number of potential zoning principles that should be overlaid on a plan varies from project to project according to the critical issues to be addressed. But even restricting these overlays to the most basic ones can create a complex organizing scheme. Arriving at an integrated scheme requires attention to each and the ability to synthesize the requirements of each into an overall plan.

Thermal Zoning. *Thermal zoning* is common parlance for the grouping of different rooms into distinct areas serviced by HVAC systems. Each distinct area is typically under the control of one thermostat. Common residential zoning strategy separates the day-use public spaces from the night-use bedroom spaces and places them on different HVAC systems. Note that this typically reflects the functional organization scheme of locating bedrooms upstairs or in a separate wing of the residence.

In order for thermal zoning to satisfy thermal loads and times of peak gain in all rooms in a zone with any degree of uniformity, the rooms must share five characteristics:

- Similar solar exposure and orientation: East-facing rooms and west-facing rooms will have vastly different schedules of thermal needs, just as rooms with large window areas will have different needs than rooms with smaller windows.

- Similar envelope exposure: Perimeter rooms with exposure to the outdoor environment through the exterior envelope will have different needs than rooms in the core of the building, which always need cooling because they have no means of heat loss.

- Similar occupancy type and density: Libraries and auditoriums should be grouped in different zones. Likewise, private offices and large classrooms should also not share a thermostat.

- Similar schedule: The weekday classrooms of a church school should not be in the same zone as the Sunday congregational assembly space. Weekend-use offices where cooling systems may be activated for the comfort of a few workers should not be zoned together with large lobby spaces.

- Shared incremental capacity: Where multiple modular HVAC systems are used, it is common engineering practice to select small package units and distribute them as needed across the different zones of the building. Retail buildings typically use rooftop units of about 8 to 10 tons cooling capacity and divide the retail floor area into zones of appropriate size.

Luminous Zoning. Luminous zoning is primarily determined by the availability of daylight and its depth of penetration into interior spaces. Typical approaches consider perimeter, interior, and core areas of a plan. Supplemental artificial lighting must be planned for each of these zones individually, to account for the amount of fill light required to reach desired illumination levels.

More recent and enlightened luminous zoning strategies reverse the typical uses of these zones—clerical areas are placed close to windows, where demanding visual tasks receive high-quality and abundant natural light. Executive offices and conference rooms in this scheme are placed to the interior of the plan, where fewer critical demands are made on illumination. Finally, core areas, elevators, stairs, and the like are positioned on east and west walls so that no windows are exposed to the worst solar orientations. Norman Foster's Hong Kong Bank, Leo Daly's Lockheed Building in Sunnyvale, California, and the Farmers Credit Bank Building in Spokane, Washington, are all examples of this luminous and solar zoning scheme (see case studies #25 and #9).

Acoustical Zoning for Noise Control and Privacy. Noise is unwanted sound. The discomfort it causes is of concern to designers of buildings. Privacy is a complementary concern, related to matters such as confidential conversation. Both of these issues require planning for sound separation between the sound source and the listener. Neglecting acoustical issues in the early stages of design may dictate very-high-performance walls and door separation (Transmission Loss, TL, or Sound Transmission Class, STC) between occupancies, as well as increased levels of background masking sound (Noise Criteria, NC, or Room Criteria, RC) in the final solution (see Stein and Reynolds, 2000).

In terms of basic acoustical zoning, spaces can be classified as noisy, quiet, silent, or buffer areas, depending on the noise level generated by activities they house. Rooms for mechanical equipment, copy machines, toilets, and so forth, are noisy. Conference rooms, study carrels, and sleeping rooms are examples of silent spaces. Good acoustical arrangement isolates noisy areas and separates them from silent rooms with buffer spaces such as storage rooms and closets.

Using just these four fundamental principles of functional, thermal, luminous, and acoustical zoning, it is easy to imagine the complexities encountered when all four are being considered simultaneously. Any multiuse building program will have areas with distinct thermal, luminous, and acoustic needs. Even a residence will require different thermal zones based on schedule, different luminous zones based on activity, and different acoustical zones based on noise and privacy. Consider how an overlay of these zoning considerations would affect the interior systems of a hotel, office, or school.

Circulation, Egress, and Life Safety. There are many systems of flow within building interiors. Air circulation, electrical power, daylight penetration and diffusion, paperwork and supplies, and so forth. The most important flow in a building, however, is the circulation of the occupants. Individuals and groups of people need easy access to each other, to the facilities of the building, and to its exitways. In the case of fire or other emergency these circulation flows become highly critical matters of life or death. Even in normal operation the flow rates and resulting density of people requiring open routes can be very high. Lunchtime at the Lloyd's of London building, for example, leads to increased usage of the escalators, elevators, and toilet room arrangements of the office building as 8000 people leave the market floor and surrounding offices, only to storm back in at the end of their break (see case study #24). Other buildings, such as airports and classroom buildings, have similar critical issues related to circulation.

Life safety codes dictate organizational design responses to circulation in all public buildings. The minimum number of exits and minimum width of corridors, as well as the maximum distances to exits, are just some of the basic form regulating design considerations. The construction assembly fire rating and the corresponding fire rating of doors and mechanical penetrations are also specified by code.

Aside from the convenience and safety factors, horizontal and vertical circulation strategies are also connective elements of space planning. To use the example of Lloyd's of London again, the market trading floor, or The Room, as it is called, is the focus of the building, much like the trading floor of the New York Stock Exchange. Richard Rogers and his team enhanced the level of face-to-face communication among the traders by folding five floor levels of The Room back onto themselves around an open atrium and connecting the vertically layered floors with open escalators. This greatly reduces the walking distance from the most remote desks as compared with the situation that would have been produced by a larger floor plate and fewer stories. It also reduces the distance to exitways and the required width of the circulation paths. Rogers then used the site area preserved by the smaller floor plate for towers containing the elevators, toilet rooms, and stairs and located them in six residual corners of the site. Norman Foster used a similar strategy at the much larger Hong Kong and Shanghai Bank (see case study #25) to organize the 43-floor bank into seven distinct vertical villages with interconnecting escalators but only one elevator stop per village.

SITE SYSTEMS

Systems integration at the site level deals with issues of context: environmental, social, urban, cultural, and whatever special conditions are presented by the exact situation of the building project and its neighboring surroundings. Site systems are the first level of interface between the building solution and the site context.

Elements

- Topography—building set on, above, or into differing grade levels; retaining walls and modifications to natural grade
- Surrounding structures—shade, wind, and view determined by immediate surroundings
- Footprint—orientation, elongation, and massing of the building
- Perimeter—defining the boundaries of the site with fences, gates, walls, hedges, and/or landscaping
- Landscape—vegetation, bodies of water, and other natural features
- Paving—parking, access, driveways, pedestrian paths, terraces, patios
- Storm water—rainwater drainage, detention ponds, swales, gutters and downspouts, area drains, curbs, and gutters
- Utilities—service connections, transformers, meters, waste disposal
- Site lighting—general illumination, façade lighting, lighting for pathways, security, signage
- Appurtenances—gazebos, porte-cocheres, arbors, fences

Microclimates and Environmental Site Design

From the environmental perspective, the site forms microclimatic conditions by modifying the regional climate. Then the relationship of a building to its site begins as a series of formal responses: thermal, aerodynamic, solar, luminous, and so on. For example, a building on the north side of a hill is in a very different microclimate than a building on the south side of the same hill; a building surrounded by asphalt is in a very different condition than one surrounded by trees. To a large degree, these microclimatic modifications can be controlled by careful design and deployment of the site systems. This means that the site can be treated as an outer layer beyond the envelope and act to interpret environmental conditions favorably.

The integration of site systems should maximize the results of these modifications. Trees established for shade also affect wind patterns and views into and out of the building. Paving is used to drain storm water from parking and surrounding areas. Solar orientation and the placement of glazing impact the availability of lighting and the issues of view and privacy. Natural bodies of water and storm water detention ponds can work as cooling towers for the HVAC system. This list can be elaborated at length, as can be seen in the next section of this chapter, but bear in mind that potential benefits depend heavily on the particulars of the building program.

Architecture as an Armature for Nature

Ultimately, site design determines a building's place in nature. As soon as the building is completed, nature begins to reclaim it by acts of weathering, erosion, and chemical and biological change. High levels of maintenance will be required if the building and site elements are to resist nature's reclamation. Without continuing maintenance, nature will mark the building with its weathering processes. The architect has to design according to assumptions about ongoing maintenance over the building's lifetime to accommodate this aging. Durable materials that defy the weather are more expensive than those with shorter lives; exposed materials require more detailing than painted ones.

Mostafavi and Leatherbarrow (1993) have characterized two opposing perspectives in their book, *On Weathering*. They portray the maintenance of a building's original condition as resistance to *stain* and the planned aging of a building into its surroundings as a graceful *patina*. On another level, this opposition can be seen as a more philosophical distinction between the entropy of nature and the organizational work of industrial society. Nature works toward diffuse homogeneity as wet moves to dry, hot moves to cold, high pressure moves to low, mountains erode to fill the valleys. The laws of physics move our environment toward homogenous conditions, higher states of entropy. Any potential for movement, any difference in energy levels, drives the work of nature. In nature's pristine state, all of these motions are present. The works of an industrial society, on the other hand, are directed against natural entropic decay. In the pristine state of industry, everything is clean and gleaming. Civilization to date has been the history of this pioneering against entropy, moving instead toward organization, focus, and concentration. The pioneer mentality that generated the rise of industrial society was always aligned against the erosion of nature; stain was a symptom of failure to hold back its forces.

Accepting the inevitability of weathering embraces the opposite perspective: a graceful patina acquired as nature reclaims a built work and its setting. This attitude is more evident in Eastern civilization and in organic and naturalistic approaches to architecture. Certain aspects of it have crept into Western thinking as economic pressures make submission to entropy more practical than resistance: xeroscape and native landscapes, organic gardening, passive solar design, and the selection of natural materials, to mention a few.

Many attitudes about design are prone to regard the site as a resource for the building. The imposition of the architectural footprint on the land is given dominance over the condition of the site in terms of everything from orthogonal geometries to border plantings. The counterposition asks about the notion of buildings as systems that will gradually be reclaimed by nature anyway. It proposes that a building is, in fact, an armature for nature and so replaces industrial mechanics with natural ones wherever feasible:

- Paving blocks or stones replace concrete and asphalt paving
- Water gardens replace runoff and storm water retention ponds
- Hedgerows replace border plantings and fences
- Natural landscaping is used in favor of pesticides, fertilizers, watering, mowing and raking
- Earth-integrated buildings are designed in underground, earth-covered, or earth-bermed configurations instead of on graded sites
- Habitats for native species are incorporated in favor of exterminated lawns.

Conclusion: Integration Potentials

There are an infinite number of possible integrations between the five major building systems, between the subsystems of each, and among subsystems of different major systems. There can be no exhaustive list, and, more important, developing the correct list for each building project is a matter of careful decision making in design. It is quite possible, however, to generate a beginning list based on what has been defined here as shared mandates between the major systems. Examples of the integration potential of overlapping shared space, shared image, and shared function among the ten possible pairs of major building systems are outlined in Table 3.1.

TABLE 3.1   Some Integration Opportunities as Shared Mandates Between the Ten Possible Pairings of Five Major Systems

	Site	Structure	Envelope	Services
Interior	Indoor/out relationships	Exposed structure Integrated lighting	Daylighting	Exposed ducts Masking background Air-handling luminaries
Services	Cooling ponds Earth tube cooling	Duct routes Interstitial mechanical Plenums	Passive design Solar roofs Vented skin Double envelope	
Envelope	Earth shelter Natural habitat Noise barriers Storm water	Building shell Shading Light diffusing		
Structure	Underground Terraced			

The Architecture of Integration

This chapter applies the rationale of systems integration, as disussed in the preceding chapters, to a working method for examining levels of integration in architectural design. The method gives equal weight to programmatic constraints and architectural intention in the determination of critical technical issues. Technical issues, in turn, drive the selection of appropriate systems that satisfy both program and intention.

Finally, the happy marriage of component systems in beneficial integration is shown to be essential to achieving unified and successful results. The discussion centers on a developmental example, the Pacific Museum of Flight (PMF) in Seattle, Washington, by architect Ibsen Nelsen, with references to Johnson & Burgee's design of the Crystal Cathedral in Garden Grove, California, as its design precedent.

THE PACIFIC MUSEUM OF FLIGHT

The Pacific Museum of Flight provides an excellent example of building systems integration and the use of architectural precedent. It also serves as an analytical model and framework for the building studies in Part II, where the same format will be repeated.

Figure 4.1   General view of the museum.

TABLE 4.1 Fact Sheet

Project	**Building name**	The Pacific Museum of Flight (PMF)
	Client	Museum of Flight Foundation, Howard Lovering, Executive Director
	City	Seattle, Washington, USA
	Lat/Long/Elev	47.5N 122.3W, 20 ft (6.1 m)
Team	**Design**	Ibsen Nelsen and Associates, Architect, with Robinson, Mills & Williams Architects
	Structural	Jack Christiansen of Skilling, Ward, Ragers, Berkshire, Inc.
	Mechanical	Carl W. Miskimen of Miskimen/Associates
	Electrical	Gerald Fitzmaurice of Travis Fitzmaurice and Associates, Inc.
	Energy	Vladimir Bazjanac
	Landscape	Richard Haag & Associates, Landscape Architects
	Exhibit Lighting	Frank A. Florentine, National Air and Space Museum
	Exhibits Design	Aldrich/Pears
General	**Time Line**	Design began in 1979. Construction 1984 to 1987. Vice President George Bush cut the ribbon on July 11, 1987.
	Floor Area	142,816 ft^2, of which the Main Gallery is 47,213 ft^2
	Occupants	5863 rated occupancy load, 3147 of which is calculated for the Gallery.
	Cost	$26.4 million.
	Cost in 1995 US $	$35.4 million, or $248/ft^2.
	Stories	Auditorium, library, offices, and viewing mezzanine over full basement in two-story wing attached to open Gallery space that slopes to 75 ft high ridge.
	Plan	Gallery is a clear span trapezoid of 385 ft base and 173 ft top with 239 ft sides. The height of the trapezoid across the Gallery is 165 ft. Support spaces extend this shape at its base by an additional 74 ft along the sides to 496 ft across the base.
Site	**Site Description**	Industrial area located on busy six-lane roadway. Land adjacent to Boeing Field where air shows are performed. Poor load-bearing soil and tidal flooding characterize the subsoil conditions.
	Parking, Cars	306 surface spaces.
Structure	**Foundation**	Slab on pads on driven pilings.
	Vertical Members	Exoskeletal space frame of white painted metal pipe and connector plates. Frame is 9.5 ft deep at SW street elevation and 6.0 ft deep on the S and NW sides.
	Horizontal Spans	Space truss of similar construction to wall frame, custom fabricated, 17 ft deep. Based on an equilateral triangle of 19.4 ft with 20 chords on the long base, 9 chords at the narrow top, and 11 chords on each side of the plan.
	Special Features	Extensive numbers of driven pilings are used to support lightweight and transparent steel frame.
Envelope	**Glass and Glazing**	Heat mirror glazing on vertical surfaces, clear at ground level and increasingly darker tint at higher divisions of Gallery wall.
	Skylights	Roof glass in Gallery rated at 25 lb/ft^2.
	Cladding	Insulated glass plus a Mylar inner membrane with low-emissivity coating.
	Roof	Roof is triple glazed and reflective coated with inner lite being ½ in. thick laminated glass.
	Special Features	Operable doors in south wall for delivery of aircraft. Operable vent windows for mechanical ventilation cooling. This is an early application of spectrally selective glazing for heat gain control, daylighting, and ultraviolet radiation protection.
HVAC	**Equipment**	One 350 ton centrifugal chiller with a 1050 gpm cooling tower and a 54 horsepower boiler in basement.
	Cooling Type	Direct expansion.
	Distribution	Comfort is distributed by ten fan coil systems.
	Duct Type	Fan coils and variable-air-volume air terminal multizone system.
	Vertical Chases	Below-grade ducts, exposed ducts on interior.
	Special Features	Ventilation cooling is provided by 100% outside air flushing of Gallery via two 36,000 cfm variable air-volume fans and mechanically operated vent windows high in the Gallery walls.
Interior	**Partitions**	Open Gallery space. Administrative wing has metal stud partitions with gypsum wallboard.
	Finishes	Primarily glass envelope with exposed structure and carpeted floors.
	Vertical Circulation	Observation elevators at Gallery. Several open stairs and fire egress stairs are provided in administrative wing.
	Lighting	Metal halide 400 W fixtures provide ambient light but are seldom needed during daylight hours. An automatic three-step dimming system was provided to modulate artificial lighting in response to available daylight. Some accent lighting and display lighting fixtures.
	Special Features	Areas include a 268 seat auditorium.

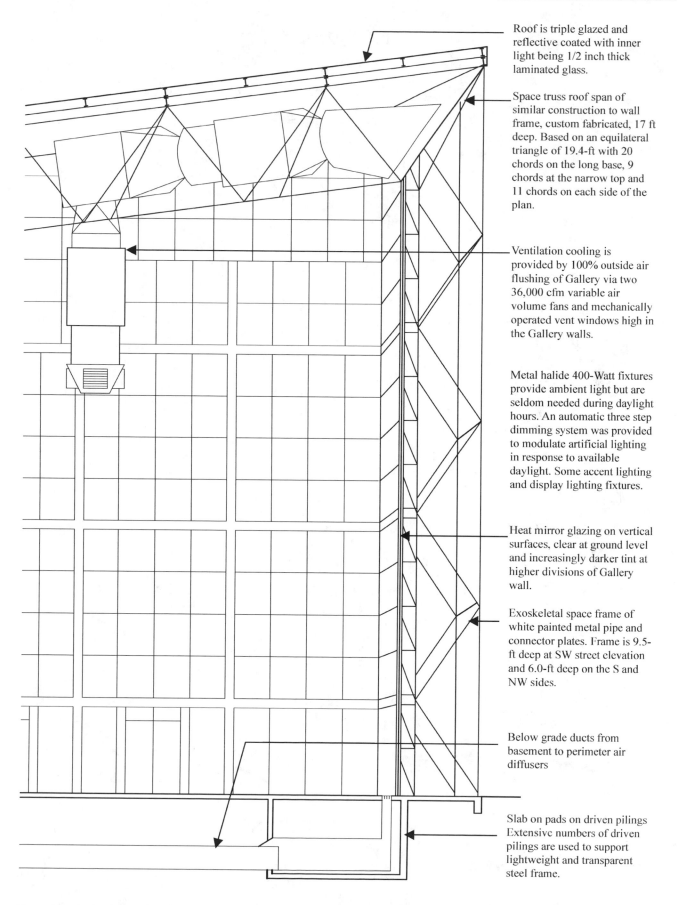

Roof is triple glazed and reflective coated with inner light being 1/2 inch thick laminated glass.

Space truss roof span of similar construction to wall frame, custom fabricated, 17 ft deep. Based on an equilateral triangle of 19.4-ft with 20 chords on the long base, 9 chords at the narrow top and 11 chords on each side of the plan.

Ventilation cooling is provided by 100% outside air flushing of Gallery via two 36,000 cfm variable air volume fans and mechanically operated vent windows high in the Gallery walls.

Metal halide 400-Watt fixtures provide ambient light but are seldom needed during daylight hours. An automatic three step dimming system was provided to modulate artificial lighting in response to available daylight. Some accent lighting and display lighting fixtures.

Heat mirror glazing on vertical surfaces, clear at ground level and increasingly darker tint at higher divisions of Gallery wall.

Exoskeletal space frame of white painted metal pipe and connector plates. Frame is 9.5-ft deep at SW street elevation and 6.0-ft deep on the S and NW sides.

Below grade ducts from basement to perimeter air diffusers

Slab on pads on driven pilings Extensive numbers of driven pilings are used to support lightweight and transparent steel frame.

Figure 4.2   Anatomical section of the Pacific Museum of Flight.

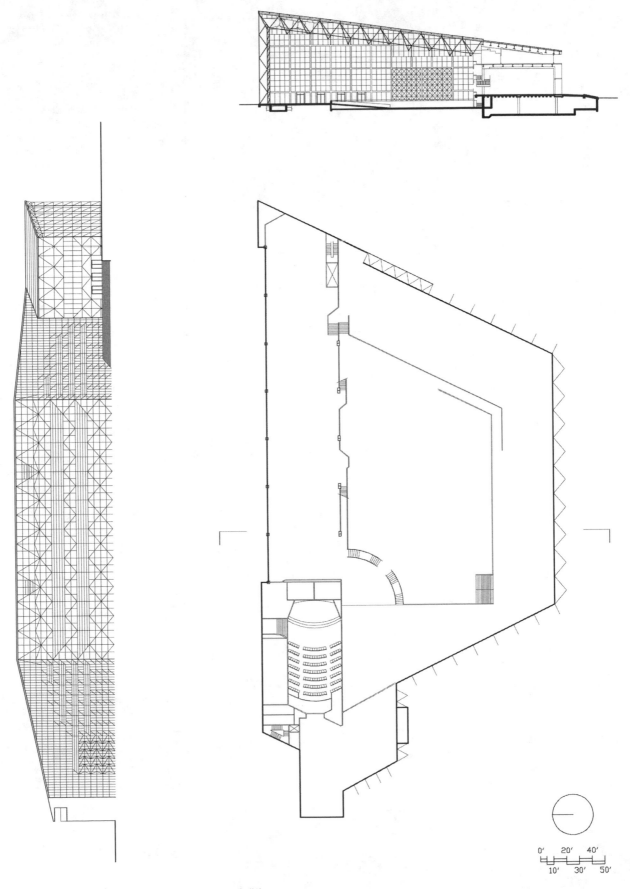

Figure 4.3 Drawings of the Pacific Museum of Flight.

0' 20' 40'
10' 30' 50'

Program

Program, in the context of integration, is the total problem set. It consists fundamentally of four criteria: client, code and other constraints, climate, and site.

CLIENT

Client criteria are generally taken as the project "brief." The brief communicates the client's mission in terms of their wants, needs, and project resources as a guide for the architect's design work. It may include a preliminary room inventory, floor areas, cost and time budgets, level of finish quality, anticipated lifetime use of the building, desired image, and other criteria for the architect to satisfy.

For the Pacific Museum of Flight (PMF), the client was collectively a small group of aviation enthusiasts who banded together in 1964 to form the Pacific Northwest Aviation Historical Foundation. They were acting on their individual interests (though most of them seem to have been Boeing employees) to preserve a collection of aircraft and memorabilia associated with the history of flight in general and Boeing aircraft specifically. Moving the original Boeing factory building to the site and restoring it as a walk-through display had already completed Phase One of the project. The small wood building was appropriately renamed the Red Barn. Phase Two (1979–1987) was to be the Great Gallery for the display of the aircraft collection as well as administrative and library functions. Successful fund-raising collected the $26.4 million budget for Phase Two construction.

PMF, like any other museum, set the highest priority on maintenance of the collection. This imposed considerations of flexibility for rearranging aircraft displays, as well as the protection of the airplanes from damage or ultraviolet degradation from the sun. Ibsen Nelson, a Seattle architect, was selected to design the Great Gallery in 1979. Vice President George Bush cut the ribbon to commemorate the opening of the Gallery on July 11, 1987.

Clients generally provide their architect a brief that describes their own understanding of the project in terms of their goals. At a general level of detail, the brief or other client-generated description of the building problem gives the architect insights as to priorities of size, quality, and budgeted cost of the project. The brief is then further developed interactively with the architect in a process William Pena (1969) described as *problem seeking*. The term *brief* is used here instead of the usual and more inclusive label *program*. *Brief* describes what the client provides, and *program* is reserved to distinguish the architect's developmental interpretation and expansion of the client brief.

CODE

Within the broad context of the items that are generally included in a brief, several constraints serve to shape appropriate responses to the project. Building codes are the best example of these constraints. Typically, however, there are special issues related to each project that are factored into the problem.

For PMF there was the special matter of the King County energy code. This was primarily a prescriptive code rather than a performance code, meaning that items such as insulation levels, glazing percentages, and equipment efficiencies were dictated to the designer. The code did provide an alternative performance option for satisfying energy efficiency requirements. This optional compliance mode dictates an allowable level of annual energy consumption per square foot, based on the predicted performance of the proposed design. The Gallery did not meet the prescriptive code option on glazing area alone, so the performance budget was the only hope of energy code compliance. The prescriptive code did not, however, have specific provisions for the sort of museum Nelsen was proposing, nor did it recognize sophisticated trade-offs achieved by daylighting strategies. The actual energy use allowance had to be negotiated with code officials. Eventually, a budget of 60,000 Btu/ft^2 (189 kWh/m^2) per year was established. Vladimir Bazjanac, who had worked in a similar role on the Garden Grove Crystal Palace with Johnson and Burgee, was hired as the energy consultant on the building.

CLIMATE

The architect must understand and interpret, as part of the context of the project, the regional climatic characteristics. These influences can be summarized as temperature distribution, humidity, cloudiness and sunshine, wind or breezes, and length of daylight hours. All these parameters must be initially compared with the building's own thermal metabolism by identifying the degree to which the building is internally heated by people, lights and indoor equipment. Buildings with relatively low levels of internal heat gain and large areas of skin exposure will be surface load dominated. These surface, or "envelope," load dominated buildings have needs closely corresponding to the outside weather. When it is warm outside, the surface load–dominated building will be overheated, and cool weather will drive a corresponding interior need for heating. Internally load dominated buildings, on the other hand, are almost always in the cooling mode because of high levels of internal heat gain. Differentiating between surface load dominated and internal load dominated buildings is fundamental to understanding the character of a building. Completely different thermal strategies will be selected for each and then be prioritized according to the metabolism of the building and the regional character of the climate. Surface load dominated buildings will often emphasize winter sun and summer shade as well as summer ventilation and winter sheltering. Internal load dominated buildings are usually good candidates for daylighting or other methods of reducing internal heat gain.

The Seattle climate is temperate, cool, and frequently overcast. As the notion of a museum developed, it was decided to employ daylighting in the Gallery. This decision capitalized on the regional climate and began some consideration of how to deal with energy codes. Had the museum been in a desert climate rather than in Seattle, then daylighting would have had very different influences on the design. The mild temperatures for much of the year were also considered as a possible asset to ventilating the museum.

Climate Data Sets: Normal, Typical, and Design

Several classifications of climate have been developed for various specialized purposes. These range from classification by latitude (equatorial, tropical, temperate, polar) to Köppen's scientific classification of five main climates and numerous second- and third-order divisions. In between there are typologies based on continental versus maritime location (proximity to large bodies of water), vegetation, geographic elevation, and topographical features. Although all of these classifications are useful for undertakings like agriculture, they fail to satisfy the architectural imagination and concern as to how a specific building will interact with its climatic context.

Certain sets of regional climate data must be familiarized before considering even the most conceptual idea of a building. Normal, or "average," conditions for each month have been used to generalize the climate type because of the readily availability of this data from government agencies. More recently, Typical Meteorological Year (TMY) data has been published for ease of in-depth analysis and

TABLE 4.2 Normal Climate Data for Seattle International Airport

		Jan.	Feb.	Mar.	Apr.	May	June	July	Aug.	Sept.	Oct.	Nov.	Dec.	Year
Temperature	Degree-Days	783	618	612	468	299	152	60	58	151	385	595	749	4931
	Degree-Days	0	0	0	0	6	21	59	54	17	0	0	0	158
	Extreme High	64	70	75	85	93	96	100	99	98	89	74	64	100
	Normal High	45	49	52	57	64	70	75	75	69	60	50	45	59
	Normal Average	40	43	45	49	56	61	65	65	61	53	45	41	52
	Normal Low	35	37	38	41	46	51	54	55	51	45	39	36	44
	Extreme Low	0	1	11	29	28	38	43	44	35	28	6	6	0
	Dew Point	33	35	36	39	44	48	52	53	50	45	39	35	43
Humidity	Max. %RH	83	83	84	83	80	79	79	83	88	88	86	85	83
	Min. %RH	75	69	63	57	54	53	49	51	56	68	76	79	62
	% Days with Rain	66	67	67	64	53	49	32	35	42	56	73	72	56
	Rain Inches	6	4	4	3	2	2	1	1	2	3	6	6	38
Sky	% Overcast Days	81	79	71	67	55	57	32	42	47	67	77	84	63
	% Clear Days	9	11	11	11	13	15	32	29	28	15	8	8	16
Wind	Prevailing Direction	S	S	SSW	SSW	SSW	SSW	SW	SSW	N	S	S	S	SSW
	Speed, Knots	10	9	11	10	9	8	8	8	8	9	10	10	9
	Percent Calm	6	6	4	4	4	4	4	5	6	6	6	5	5
Days Observed	Rain	20	20	20	19	16	15	10	11	13	17	22	22	204
	Fog	18	16	13	10	8	8	8	11	16	19	19	19	166
	Haze	5	5	4	3	3	2	3	6	9	10	6	4	61
	Snow	7	4	3	1	0	0	0	0	0	0	2	5	22
	Hail	0	0	0	0	0	0	0	0	0	0	0	0	1
	Freezing Rain	0	0	0	0	0	0	0	0	0	0	0	0	0
	Blowing Sand	0	0	0	0	0	0	0	0	0	0	0	0	0

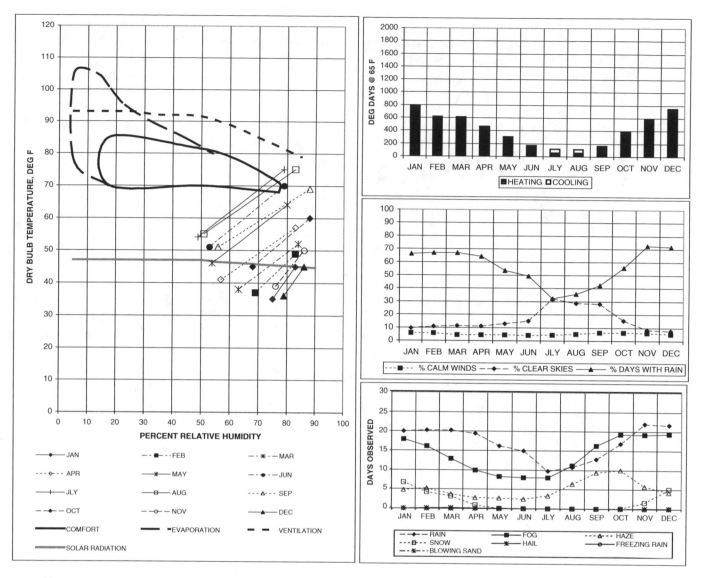

Figure 4.4 Climate analysis graphics.

hourly heat transfer simulation. This data is constructed from actual weather history over periods that best match the long-term averages. Additional data, like solar radiation, which is not available for many locations, is statistically modeled into the TMY. This detailed data set not only lists hourly readings for many weather measurements, it also eliminates the errors of averaging that disguise the variability every climate exhibits.

Victor Olgyay (1963) presented a simplified method for analyzing climates based on monthly normals. His "Bioclimatic Chart" depicts dry-bulb temperature as the vertical axis and relative humidity as the horizontal x axis. Comfortable conditions are represented in a kidney-shaped area of the chart, and thermal responses to restore comfort are plotted around it. By using average daily low temperature and high relative humidity as the morning condition and average daily high temperature and low rel-

ative humidity as the afternoon condition, the two extremes of daily weather for each month can be represented on the chart. By connecting the two extremes with a straight line, the regime of each month's climate can be generalized. Thus, with only 48 numbers, a very descriptive picture of the entire year's worth of climate is generated.

To apply generalized climate data to a building design, a background idea of the thermal character of the proposed building is essential. The foremost indicator of what the thermal needs of a building may be is related to the level of internal heat gain from people, lights, and equipment. All equipment, lights, and miscellaneous electrical loads in a building convert energy directly into room heat. If these internal heat gains are high, relative to the volume of the building and its external skin exposure to climate, the indoor environment will be internally load dominated. Buildings generally fitting this description include large office buildings and brightly lit retail stores. These buildings provide a great deal of their own heat and require cooling for an extended part of the year. Surface load dominated buildings, on the other hand, respond more directly to the climate. A house or most any small building fits this surface load (sometimes called "skin" or "envelope" load) dominated category. Whenever the outdoor temperature is above about 65°F, a surface load dominated building is considered to be in the cooling mode. Whenever conditions outside are below 65°F, the same building is in the heating mode. In this case, the 65°F outdoor condition is the assumed "balance point temperature" of the building. It can also be thought of as the equilibrium temperature of a building, because it is at this outdoor temperature at which internal heat gains are equal to and offset by heat loss to the colder outdoors.

Large internally load dominated buildings can have balance point temperatures below freezing. Obviously, different areas of a building will have different thermal characteristics, but the overall balance point temperature is a good planning benchmark. Rough calculations of the balance point can be approximated with only a few assumptions of surface area, insulation levels, and internal heat gains. Whenever outdoor temperatures exceed a building's balance point, shading and ventilation become important design elements. Conversely, whenever it is colder outside than the building's balance point temperature, solar heat gain and draft-free conditions are to be promoted. Because internally load dominated buildings have lower balance points than surface load dominated ones, they will require less heating and more cooling. Fundamental questions of sun versus shade and breeze versus still air begin to set the correct response in balancing the context of climate and the thermal metabolism of the building.

Correlated Data

Aside from the general character of the regional weather patterns, it is also necessary to study several sets of relationships between individual measures of climate data. When it is cold enough for a building to require some source of heat, how much sunshine is typically available? Where are the breezes coming from when ventilation would be an asset? These and a host of other critical questions are addressed in correlated climate data sets.

Degree-Days. The 65°F balance point temperature used in the discussion of balance point temperature happens to be the criterion on which degree-day data is based. Degree-days describe the severity of heating and cooling seasons in a climate by comparing the average daily temperature with an assumed balance point. The 65°F standard was

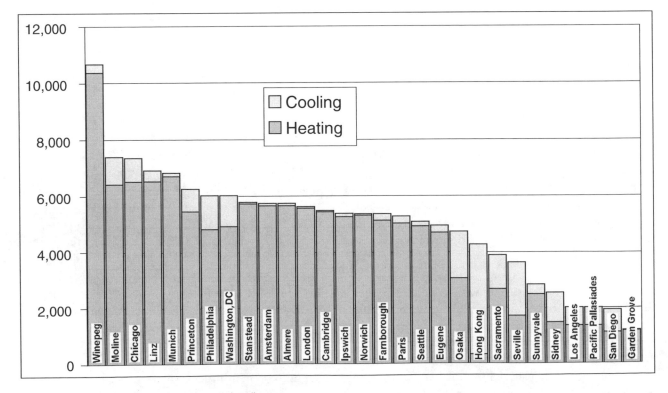

Figure 4.5 Annual degree-days for representative climates.

established before high levels of insulation in construction were common. Despite the fact that most new buildings and even most newer houses have balance points lower than 65°F, degree-days are still a good means of evaluating the general severity of the climate, looking at the ratio of heating degree-days to cooling degree-days as a means of prioritizing building thermal response and comparing its seasonal character with that of a more familiar climate. Degree-days are also good predictors of annual heat loss because 65°F is so close to indoor winter temperatures. Standard degree-days at the 65°F base temperature or special data sets of degree-days adjusted to different balance points are also used to perform monthly and annual heat transfer calculations based on temperature difference between inside and outside climates.

Bin Data. Another adjunct to utilizing building balance point is the use of bin data. This data set was first collected at military installations around the world and published in the United States Navy and Air Force *Engineering Weather Data Manual* (1994). Bin data tabulates the number of hours per year dry-bulb temperatures will fall into each five degree Fahrenheit "bin" range and the coincident wet-bulb temperature that can be expected at the same hours. The data is also presented in eight-hour ranges for morning, afternoon, night, and total hours for each month of the year. It is the annual hours of occurrence, though, that are most useful during conceptual and schematic design.

By comparing the balance point of a building to the bin data for the city in question, several environmental planning strategies can be prioritized. The hours of annual occurrence above and below the building's calculated balance point predict how often heating and cooling will be required. Hours of shading and hours of solar heat gain can be ranked. Likewise, the relative duration of ventilation versus the buffering of winds can be compared. These clues work to reveal the duration of heating and cooling seasons in much the same way degree-days indicate the severity of the seasons.

A great deal more can be learned about the relation of the building's thermal metabolism to the host climate by pairing the annual hours of occurrence for each dry-bulb bin range with the correlated "mean coincident wet-bulb" numbers. A graphic tool developed by Givoni and Milne allows the plotting of the paired dry-bulb to wet-bulb data on a modified psychrometric chart. This "bioclimatic" chart is divided into regions of outdoor conditions to represent the potential of various passive heating and cooling strategies. Tabulating hours for each of the strategies allows a detailed prioritizing of thermal design strategies. It must be remembered, however, that the divisions of this

TABLE 4.3 Bin Data Distribution for Seattle

Conventional bins are given in 5°F dry-bulb (DB) ranges with the mean coincident wet-bulb (MCWB) temperature for each range. This data was first collected and published by the U.S. military from sites around the world as "Engineering Weather Data." The bin data distribution graphics in this text were generated with more detailed 1°F level bin data to help in visualizing the distribution of temperature and humidity conditions in the case study climates.

Data sources: Engineering Weather Data, typical meteorological year (TMY) data, from the National Climatic Data Center, and the *ASHRAE Weather Data Viewer* from the American Society of Heating, Refrigerating, and Air-Conditioning Engineers.

DB (F)	Hours/yr	MCWB (F)
95 to 100	4	67.2
90 to 95	4	67.2
85 to 90	4	66.3
80 to 85	78	64.2
75 to 80	137	62.3
70 to 75	348	59.9
65 to 70	406	57.6
60 to 65	1018	55.3
55 to 60	1379	52.7
50 to 55	1335	48.9
45 to 50	1450	43.8
40 to 45	1175	39.5
35 to 40	1098	35.3
30 to 35	280	30.5
25 to 30	40	26.0
20 to 25	4	22.1

bioclimatic tool, somewhat similar to Victor Olgyay's comfort chart, are based on a balance point close to human thermal comfort, thus approximating a surface load dominated building. Application of prioritized strategies to internally load dominated buildings should be evaluated carefully, particularly those priorities indicating the need for passive solar heating.

Bin data plots in Figures 4.6 and 4.7 graph the temperature and humidity characteristics of Seattle. Similar plots are given with each of the case studies in Part II for comparison and to illustrate the discussions of climatic influence on each building design.

Solar Geometry

The sun is a perpetual and undeniable factor in all building environments. Aside from the question of sun-versus-shade in response to a building's thermal metabolism, there is the architecturally ennobled and infinitely useful employment of daylight to consider. Le Corbusier's *brise*

Figures 4.6 and 4.7 Bin data distribution for Seattle. These graphics show how two different data sets are used to create bin data illustrations. Figure 4.6 shows a plot of dry-bulb and mean coincident wet-bulb temperature data from Table 4.3 but does not convey frequency of occurrence. Figure 4.7 shows a detailed contour plot based on hourly occurrences in a typical year from TMY data. Concentric areas of Figure 4.6 indicate the frequency of hours per year that weather conditions normally occur in this climate. Similar to elevation readings on topographic maps, highest frequency occurrences of weather are at the center peaks of the graph. (Data sources: *Engineering Weather Data, typical meteorological year (TMY) data from the National Climatic Data Center, and the* ASHRAE Weather Data Viewer *from the American Society of Heating and Refrigeration Engineers.)*

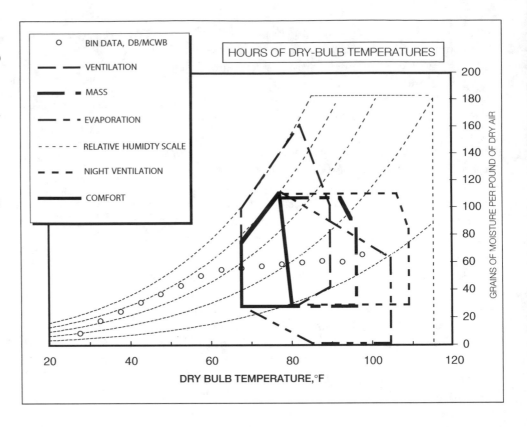

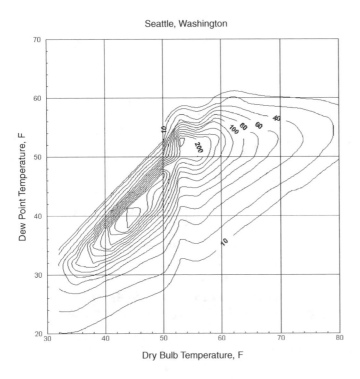

soleil, used as the "sun breaker" elements of his modular proportioning system, is the best-known example of an architectural strategy for shading devices. But Corbusier's *brise soleil* is not always based on sound solar rationale—he frequently used same shading device on multiple elevations of the same building with more regard to proportion than to orientation. There is little evidence that Corbusier used a technically correct shading methodology at all; as Harris Sobin (1980) chronicles, the design strategy seems to have sprung almost apologetically out of his experiences in the Algerian desert and with the initial environmental failure of the 1930 Salvation Army Hospital in Paris. But it should not be overlooked that Corbusier pioneered what is thought of today as the architecturally considered shading strategy, even if he did not invent or perfect it. Despite technical shortcomings, the *brise soleil* serves as a splendid example of how technology and design can be considered as opposite sides of the same coin.

Given the precedent of the *brise soleil* and a battery of new tools devoted to the interactions of solar geometry and building surfaces, it follows that current architectural design should be informed and inspired by a correlation of building needs and solar position. This need was first filled by another of Victor Olgyay's developments, described in *Design with Climate* (1963), and a collaboration with his brother, Aladar Olgyay, in another book, *Sun Control and Shading Devices* (1957). The Olgyay method begins with a horizontal equidistance graphic projection of the sun's daily paths onto an imaginary horizontal ground plane, with an outer circle representing the horizon. The graphic forms a slide rule by which the sun's azimuth and altitude polar coordinates relative to a specific location at the appropriate latitude can be read for the desired time of the solar day. This is the same chart popularized as the LOF Sun Angle Calculator, published in slide rule form and generally referenced in textbooks on environmental control. What Olgyay adds to the chart for shading design is the color coding of outdoor temperatures overlaid on the solar calendar to identify the sun's position when temperatures are overheated, underheated, or comfortable. This correlates outdoor temperatures with solar position for an entire year on one graphic. Again, the use of human thermal comfort levels as the criteria for sun versus shade should be weighed against the building's balance point temperature. Internally load dominated buildings generally require more shading than those that are surface load dominated.

Regional Character

Despite the technical overtones of weather data and building dynamics, the impact of climate-responsive design is not relegated to the mere functional issues of building performance. The innate qualities of place engendered by regional character and vernacular tradition are respected for reflecting local building traditions, and capturing the *genus loci* spirit of place. Response to climate produces a unifying aspect of regionalism similar to that which Amos Rappaport (1969) distinguishes as physical and cultural determinism. Response to climate is a fundamental bridge between rational and emotive design motivations. And unlike the unimaginative mimicking of established local styles, climate-responsive buildings are authentic in the real sense of belonging to the site and recognizing the significance of local context.

The elements of regional character are most evident in smaller buildings because physical characteristics of climate have a dominant role in their overall character. Residential and small commercial buildings usually employ characteristics reminiscent of indigenous buildings of their particular climate. The adobe style of southwestern American domestic architecture is a well-known example. Of course, it is necessary to distinguish between buildings with fine-tuned high thermal mass and their synthetic stucco impersonators.

Larger buildings, on the other hand, may at first seem to be more generally dominated by economy of construction than by climatic dictates. The economies of lightweight steel frames and curtain wall systems are wedded to the adoption of mass-produced components and speed of field assembly. The whole idea of modernity, as postulated by the International Style, was the universal application of similar industrialized building products. But climate considerations have returned to the design of larger buildings. In recent years, the density of internal heat gains in many occupancy types has grown enough to prioritize efficient interior design practices. Comfort and energy are now understood to go hand in hand with productivity and the bottom line.

As a response to climate, the Museum of Flight exemplifies many of these design principles. Clearly, the Great Gallery of the museum is a surface-load dominated environment, with its glazed walls and roof, its low internal heat gains, and its almost total reliance on daylighting. The selection of the different glass products and their solar properties are critical factors that are discussed later in this chapter.

SITE

Site is context. It informs the building by influences of view, orientation, access, surrounding structures, and microclimate. The site itself is composed of elements of topography, vegetation, soil conditions, and microclimate. Into this matrix the designer imposes interventions of massing and fenestration, circulation, parking, landscape, drainage, and a host of structural and environmental responses.

The PMF site was donated by King County. It adjoins the Boeing factory and airfield (also known as the King County International Airport) just off the freeway about six miles south of central Seattle. The museum occupies a site with the Boeing airstrip, where flight shows are performed on one side and a there is busy industrial thoroughfare on the other. The original Boeing factory building, the "Red Barn," was donated to the museum by the Port of Seattle in 1975. The barn was moved to the present site in 1980 for restoration, and the public opening was held in 1983. The Concorde supersonic airliner made its first West Coast appearance in November 1984, right in the museum's backyard, before the Great Gallery was constructed.

Because of flight safety standards on the adjacent airfield, limitations were set on the height of the museum Gallery. An even greater restriction is that the property rests on poor load-bearing soil that is subject to tidal flooding below grade level.

Intention

Architectural intention, for the purpose of this discussion, is defined as the particular aspirations of the designer or

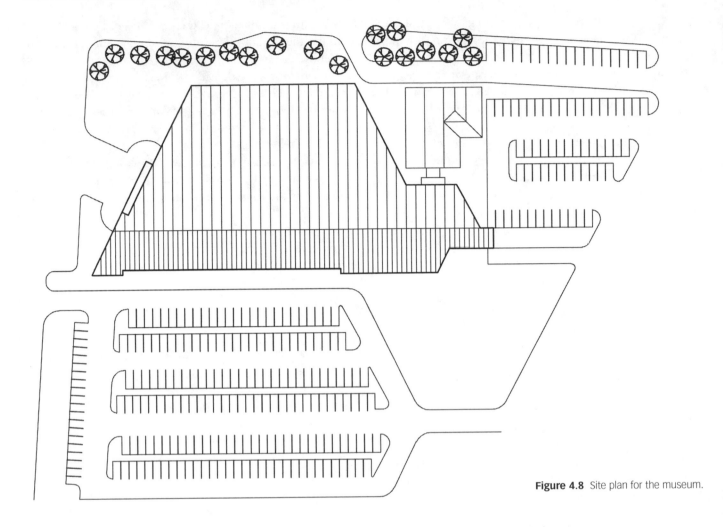

Figure 4.8 Site plan for the museum.

design team that lends a unique character or set of qualities to a building. The intention is usually a formative rule established early in design thinking. Based on a literal or symbolic interpretation of the problem, it takes the shape of a value statement about the essential nature of the design solution.

Karsten Harries, in his essay "Thoughts On a Non-Arbitrary Architecture" (1983), identifies several notions of how architectural intentions are founded. The philosophical foundations he discusses include the primitive but noble basis of shelter, the resolution of art and science, the ethical duty of providing a meaningful world order, and the goal of articulating beauty as an essence. Christian Norberg-Schultz writes of similar motivations in his book *Intentions in Architecture* (1965). These two works convey a sense of how critically acknowledged architecture is differentiated from the functional commodity of commonplace buildings. Successful architecture has historically come from individual assertions and the built manifestations of personal philosophies, not from standardized practices, geometric formulas, or stylistic fancy.

Authenticity implies that each designer must find and sincerely act upon his or her personal belief system. It is for time and culture to decide how appropriate the vision was to the problems addressed.

As a method of delving into the philosophical basis of architectural intention, consider some of the dualities with which architects deal and how individual ideas will result in a comfort level at some position between the two poles of the conversation. The most familiar of these discussions is of the paired determinants "form" versus "function." Rather than seeing the two as opposing forces, where "form follows function" or vice versa, consider instead that they "dance together." Imagine that this dance is a generative conversation in which an appropriate balance must be struck. It is from such conversations about the determinant forces of architectural solutions that unique, creative, and responsive resolutions arise.

These dualities, these generative conversations between poles are everywhere to be discussed in architectural thinking. Consider the following list, based loosely on Karsten Harries's essay:

- The urge to beauty
- Oneness with nature
- To dwell (after Martin Heideger, 1949)
- Complexity of inclusive whole (after Robert Venturi, 1966)
- To create meaning from order
- To establish order from chaos
- To articulate a binding worldview
- To heal the rift between science and art
- To heal the rift between craft and industry
- Sustainability
- Distrust of technological solutions
- To express the view of an ideal way of life

Each of these items represents a philosophical position that can be thought of as a basis for architectural intention. Each is a generative issue from which arise design ambitions. And each item also represents a range of possible positions between two polar ends of the same notion. A considered system of beliefs will articulate the means of establishing a balance between these and doubtless other dualities. The significance of these operational beliefs clearly delineates the distinction between architectural accomplishment and commodity building.

It is clear from a historical perspective that significant examples of good architecture are not likely to result from whim, fancy, personal taste, or a bag of design tricks. Experience has proven that it is essential for architects to articulate a set of ideas that act as the binding glue and unifying agent for both their collective works and for individual buildings. This "binding glue" also acts as means by which, as Harries and Norberg-Schultz have shown, technology and design are integrated into architectural expression.

Intentions for individual buildings are often expressed as philosophical statements, geometric parti, or pattern-making rules of form. They serve an adductive purpose, a template for testing alternate possibilities for the design solution. This is the corollary to deductive reasoning that scientific thought uses to reduce possibilities through logical clues to correct answers. Unlike a scientific or engineering solution, architectural intention is not a rational deduction from the constraints as much as an empirical attempt to make design problems fit into a well-considered but idealized template.

Architectural intention cannot always be summed up in short, pithy sentences. This is naturally because good buildings are seldom composed of one simple idea. And intention is not always explicitly stated as an element of the design process. An analytical look at examples of widely recognized architecture, however, reveals strong organizing concepts with a basis in sound statements of value. It is these organizing concepts that express the architect's interpretation of the essential design problem and thus form the intention.

Intention must be distinguished from programmatic criteria. A fundamental failure is virtually ensured by confusing the goals of ambitious design intention with the checklist objectives of programmatic needs. Making the Pacific Museum of Flight a daylit museum, for example, only summarizes a programmatic decision and would be just one of several on a long list of design objectives. Ibsen Nelsen (1991) looked for the ambitious intention that would order his work on the museum. He sized up the PMF by touring other museums of flight around the country to gain a sense of precedent. He was disappointed to see most collections sitting in hangarlike buildings and displayed rather plainly. The guiding architectural intention that Nelsen finally used to formulate the design of the Gallery was "to display the airplanes as if they were in flight."

DIFFERENTIATING CRITICAL ARCHITECTURE FROM COMMODITY BUILDING

In his book *The Emerald City and Other Essays on the Architectural Imagination* (1999), Daniel Willis describes the difference between lowly "labor" and meritorious "work." Labor, he points out, exhibits an absence of human imagination and does not result in a product. Labor is best done by machines. Sufficiently enlightened work, meanwhile, becomes analogous to play. Poetic works, by Willis's analogy, can be taken to be those products of endeavor that appeal to significant human experience by evoking imaginative response. This distinction is in close agreement with Mihaly Csikszentmihalyi's investigation into the imagination of especially creative people. In his book *Creativity: Flow and the Psychology of Discovery and Invention* (1996), he interviewed 91 exceptional individuals collectively sharing 14 Nobel prizes, among countless other significant accomplishments. The common ground of their experience was what Csikszentmihalyi terms "flow." The elements of this transcendent experience will be familiar to most readers: "Always knowing what needs to be done, a merging of action and awareness, intense focus without fear of failure, disappearance of self-consciousness, and a total distortion of time [sic]."

The description of this working flow as "transcendent" is a logical extension of the psychologist Abraham Maslow's (1954) study of "peak experiences." Maslow

Figure 4.9 The Pyramids of Maslow and Vitruvius.

believed that these nonordinary experiences were essential to "self-actualization." With Karlfeid Graf Dürckheim (1967), Maslow pioneered the term *transpersonal psychology* and outlined the parameters of transcendent experiences and the barriers to encountering them.

The link between architectural intention and "flow" leads, it is hoped, to poetic and "actualized" works of architecture. It is the portrayal of this personal transcendent experience that architects wish to convey in built environmental form. A simplification of this conveyance may use the Vitruvian maxim "Commodity, firmness, and delight" as a three-tiered pyramid of "architectural needs" (Figure 4.9). As in Maslow's pyramid of human needs (1954), a building must first satisfy our basic requirements for safety, shelter, and space. Thereafter, its lasting qualities and endurance can be ensured. Then, we find refreshment for the human spirit in the delight of our surroundings. Finally, adding a layer to the Vitruvian maxim, the crowning tier of the architect's pyramid is the nonordinary and transcendent aspect of critical architectural intention. Successful realization of inspired intention is what separates the splendor of architecture from the merely satisfactory buildings of everyday experience.

FORMATIVE INTENTIONS AS THE ADDUCTIVE BASIS OF DESIGN

Because building design is such a large task influenced by so many factors, architects tend to think in adductive and synthetic rather than deductive and analytical terms. Adductive logic differs from inductive and deductive logic by starting with an idea and then testing it against the facts. In mathematics a theorem may be proven through

adductive reasoning that begins with the statement of an equality and then produces transformations that give proof of an identity, like $1 = 1$. Inductive reasoning, on the other hand, builds truths from observed facts, and deductive reasoning uses chains of logic to analytically reduce what is known to a final conclusion.

The very nature of their inherently integrative thinking means that architects seldom engage in design as an inductive or analytical process. Their approach is necessarily more inclusive, less mechanistic, and therefore more systems oriented than any linear procedures can describe. So unlike the deductive reasoning a scientist or engineer is classically believed to employ, architectural reasoning is better described as adductive. Analytical deductive processes work by optimizing single factors in isolation and constructing a whole from sound elements. Adductive, integrative thinking conceives the complex whole and explores the proper fit of different subunits into the superlative value or truth of the whole, the gestalt. This is part of what Christian Norberg-Schultz refers to in his definitive *Intentions in Architecture* (1965) as "the integration of the problem into a larger whole." It is worth noting that many other disciplines are moving toward this holistic approach to the design of solutions for everything from agriculture to particle physics.

Somewhere in the architectural process of design, the activity moves from research and shaping of the building problem into a graphic organization of response. This diagram or parti (to use the Beaux-Arts root) seeks to give form to architectural intention and to engender a solution to the building program. The diagram is not itself the solution, but it does present a framework within which ideas will be tried for logical fit and compliance with design intention.

Critical Technical Issues

Once the broad organizing architectural intention has been established, it becomes evident that a series of elemental technical problems must be addressed in order for design to proceed. These focal and critical technical issues become the basis for selecting appropriate building systems. To be appropriate, such systems must both satisfy the program requirements and fulfill architectural intentions. The dictates and frequently differing demands of these essential problems create a series of generative tensions and enliven the design process. Resolution of these key ideas is often the most complex and problematic task of architectural design; they often seem as contradictory as they are essential.

Inevitably, conflicts and contradictions arise between and among the critical technical criteria. These oppositions may arise in any of several contexts: between the program and the site, between the code and the architectural intention, between the program and the budget, or any combination of the possible design elements. As conflicts, these challenges are frequently what become the generative tensions that evoke the most imaginative design innovations. For organizational purposes, critical technical issues can be discussed in three categories:

- Inherent issues arising from building use
- Contextual issues generated by technical situations surrounding the project
- Intentional issues evolving from the architect's ambition for the project

At the Museum of Flight, the architectural intention became the largest driver of critical technical issues. For the aircraft collection to appear to hover in flight, it would have to be suspended from the roof structure by steel cables. For the planes to be presented against the sky, the roof itself, as well as most of the walls, would have to be glass. Consequently, Nelsen was faced with the selection of a structural system to carry large dead loads over long spans without obscuring the view. He also required an envelope system capable of providing views and admitting daylight but resistant to solar heat gain and to ultraviolet degradation of the entire collection. In the echo of these issues were secondary questions: How would the mechanical systems fit in, and what would be left of the interior for displays?

INHERENT ISSUES

Inherent, or built-in, issues always arise from a basic investigation of the building type at hand and knowledge about its typical use. Libraries need diffuse natural light and the ability to carry heavy book stacks, airports need well-defined circulation patterns and a great variety of services, and museums need flexible display space and protection for the collection. Whatever the building type, there is always a set of related critical technical issues that fundamentally define the problem and are thus part of the rational component of the built solution.

The inherent issues of the Pacific Museum of Flight differed somewhat from those of the usual museum. The large size of aircraft objects in the collection changed the normal relationship between viewer and display case, for example, and the air shows held periodically on the adjoining Boeing Field runway added another dimension. Storing and rotating the collection of exhibits was also a

unique problem. Other challenges were more typical of museums in general—lighting, circulation, egress, and security.

CONTEXTUAL ISSUES

Every project is affected by specific and special technical circumstances of its context. Identifying these circumstances is essential to satisfying the critical technical issues. Special circumstances can include site conditions, code requirements, highly critical programmatic constraints, harsh climatic environment, or any other factors unique to the project.

Code requirements were among the critical contextual issues for the Pacific Museum of Flight. The building code of the local jurisdiction, King County, included an energy code specifying allowable annual energy use per square foot of building. To obtain a construction permit, the architect would have to certify that the actual energy use of the building would fall within the budget. County officials used annual audits to validate compliance, and fines would be imposed for violations. In the end, this matter had to be negotiated because the code had no good provision for a building use that matched the museum and made little allowance for daylighting. Nonetheless, a strict energy use budget was established and the design was expected to deliver a suitably energy-conserving building.

A second contextual technical consideration was the poor soil conditions of the site. Load-bearing capacity was very low, and the site was subject to tidal flooding that inundated the subsoil periodically, effectively giving the site a very high water table. Although these contextual circumstances were not as formative as the energy code requirements, they did suggest a lightweight structure.

ISSUES OF INTENTION

The third and most significant source of critical technical issues is the tension between architectural intent and the project program. Difficult building programs often require that the architectural intention encompass a strategy for meeting the client's basic objectives. Norman Foster's design of suspended floors hung from double height trusses at the Hong Kong and Shanghai Bank is discussed as one such example of the alignment between strategy and intention (see case study #25). In other cases, such as the Museum of Flight, complex requirements are generated primarily by the architect's intention.

Nelsen's "as if in flight" ambition for the museum was clearly the springboard for everything that followed. Transparent structure and envelope are the most direct consequences, but all other decisions can be shown to align with this starting point. The one grand intention became the genesis, protagonist, and binding agent of all the systems in the Great Gallery. Simplicity may have dictated a less complicated approach; the collection could have been displayed in a hangar, for example. But this straightforward solution would have led to only a marginally satisfactory and everyday sort of building. The difference between the two results illustrates how important integrated systems are to cohesive architectural solutions. It also illustrates how the nonordinary aspect of architecture arises from ambitious and well-founded intentions.

Appropriate Systems

Appropriate building systems activate and materialize design by giving it substance and energetics. Systems selection and deployment are therefore as basic to the making of architecture as formal and spatial composition. Historical progress of architectural expertise illustrates that these systems-based activities can no longer be regarded as the simplistic "how-to" realization of artful design—their animating features are too fundamentally empowering and their machinations have become part of the architect's dream. An emphasis should be repeated here—the definition of what is appropriate about a set of chosen systems still balances between pyrotechnic flamboyance and elegant simplicity, between enhanced technology and ecological ethics, and finally, between the ephemeralization of technophilia and the technophobia of Frankenstein.

Catalogs of building products available for the architect's selection fill large office libraries of printed and electronic media. Mating these systems with the building program, the critical technical issues, and the architectural intention happens in the early conceptual stages of design. Matching these selections to design requirements, adapting them to the project specifics, and detailing their connections with other systems are integral parts of the subsequent design development process.

PERFORMANCE SPECIFICATIONS

One manner of system selection is generated by numerical performance specifications. The selection of appropriate systems is achieved by matching desired performance rat-ings against the corresponding numerical characteristics of the systems being considered. The desired target numbers may come from consultants' technical input, such as the minimal light transmission required to maintain visual transparency, or the preferred sound transmission class of wall separation between two occupancies. They may come from code requirements, such as fire rating. Just as likely, the desired performance rating can come from the architect's scheme for the dimensions of a structural bay to accommodate a modular room size.

The most important aspect of performance specifications is their objective numerical designation. Most of these ratings are arrived at through independent tests done under laboratory conditions. Although these ratings do not always reflect the performance of a product in the field, no more than the miles-per-gallon rating of new automobiles, they do provide a levelized standard. As such, they offer a beginning point for comparison and selection of systems and components.

The interconnectedness of systems, as it relatees to performance-based systems selection, is illustrated in the following list showing how a window assembly would be rated:

- Glass R-value or u-value
- Center of window R-value or u-value
- Visible light transmittance (VLT)
- Solar transmittance or shading coefficient (SC)
- Ratio of visible to infrared transmission
- Sound transmission loss (TL)
- Sound transmission class (STC)
- Percent operable opening area for ventilation
- Air infiltration rating
- Fire rating
- Security rating for breakage

This list shows how alternative window choices may be objectively filtered through a list of objective performance standards to arrive at a shorter list of acceptable selections. The procedure is biased, of course, by the critical technical issues of the project. An urban situation may emphasize noise control, for example, whereas a desert climate may stress solar reflection. Some characteristics may not be important at all, and their standards may be reduced in order to select the most cost-effective window system. Qualitative decisions will also be made, parallel to this process, by first eliminating categories of products that do not meet the architectural intention, but no selection can be made from choices that do not meet the minimum required performance standards.

PRECEDENT

When approaching an architectural project, it is normal for the designer to explore several architecturally recognized and definitive examples of the same building type or other relevant works. These definitive examples, or "precedents," serve as authoritative guides to the general character of a building type and as orientation to successful design approaches. Copying is not the intent; rather, the idea is not to reinvent work that the progress of architecture has already addressed, but to start instead from state-of-the-art and then add something to it. There are several motives for adopting a particular precedent, the most common being parallel organizational strategies, appropriate technical systems, historical model, and formal interpretation. In simpler terms, these are organizational precedents, technical, historical, and formal ones. Precedent is a major reason we study architectural history and read architectural journals. Precedent also establishes the continuum of design as a steady refinement rather than a series of spontaneous inventions of genius.

Designers use precedent derived from their preliminary project research or from their knowledge of history and professional experience to aid in identifying what they deem to be a "correct" path to developing built solutions. In addition, they seek to reduce risk taking and to avoid unproductive trial-and-error design exploration by identifying opportunities and pitfalls in the early stages of work. Eventual adoption of particular elements or design ideas from these precedents depends on how accurately the examples correspond to the designer's notions about the problem at hand. In other words, precedent is applied by analogy or an appropriately considered "likeness" between proven works of architecture and the work now being undertaken.

Peter Collins (1971) has aptly compared the use of precedent in architecture to that in legal judgments by noting that both disciplines rely on recognition of the cumulative experience of the past and what Walter Gropius termed "the impersonal accumulations of successive generations." In the legal system, precedent applied to an analogous court decision is absolute and binding unless overturned by a higher court. In architectural decision making, the use of precedent is largely subjective and can be applied more creatively. Even at the most subjective level, however, ideas adopted to inform and inspire a correct design approach must be melded with the unique particulars of the specific client and program presently being served. Whatever levels of precedent the designer chooses to recognize, it is certainly more feasible to rely on "accumulations of judgment" than to totally reinvent the whole body of architectural thought for each new project.

The lessons and inspirations to be gained from adopted precedents must be thoroughly understood before the accumulated experience they represent can be harvested. Simply incorporating a few intuitively favorable elements would amount to insensitive copying and be a disservice to both the designer's client and the integrity of the precedent building. To employ a precedent correctly, designers must recognize what does fit appropriately into the unique situation presented by the client, site, climate, and context they are seeking to satisfy. Creative judgment must be exercised. In addition, and especially if a substantial amount of time has passed since the precedent building was completed, it is necessary to examine the opportunities presented by advances in technology—both those in the building construction industry and those presently employed by the client.

Originality is another strong motive for the tailoring of a precedent to a proper fit of the architectural problem. Various levels of uniqueness may be desired, depending on architectural intention. The Louvre was expanded several times by different architects between 1625 and 1750 without much deviation from the first design by Pierre Lescot. In this example, the existing context and stable state of construction technology dictated conformity of style to achieve a harmonious complex of buildings around a single courtyard. In other eras it has become more fashionable to build in contrasting ways that reflect current culture and technology. I. M. Pei's polished glass pyramid entry to the museum under the courtyard of the Louvre is a poignant example of the latter strategy.

Occasionally, of course, new buildings emerge as unique architectural icons and establish new design precedent. The Crystal Palace (Joseph Paxton, 1851) is often cited as such an icon because of its utilization of innovative construction technology and unprecedented success as an international exhibit hall. Eero Saarinen's 1961 airport for the federal government at Dulles may be another landmark example because of its being the first facility designed exclusively for jet airliners and because of Saarinen's use of mobile transport lounges rather than lobbies and jet ways. But however definitive and original these and other examples may appear to be, they too were predicated on earlier proven work. For instance, Paxton's previous designs of large conservatories and his experience with railroad construction were fundamental to the technique and successes of the Crystal Palace. In the case of Dulles airport, Saarinen had teams working in association with his office. They performed surveys, measurements, and even timed the pedestrian walking distances through many airports before eventually adopting the European model of carrying passengers to their waiting airplanes in buses.

Figure 4.10 The Glass Pyramid at the Louvre, by I. M. Pei. After centuries of additions that followed Lescot's historical precedent, Pei updated the Louvre with a contrasting edifice.

In addition to the legal parallel in precedent seeking, it is useful to consider that the evolutionary progression of successful design solutions through adoption of proven built works is equally similar to scientific methods. The scientist, like the attorney and the architect, sees him- or herself as a contributing link in the continuum of progress in the respective discipline. Robert Mueller (1967) describes the process thus: "Science constantly compares the guesses that the mind makes with the reality it tries to probe; art builds new ideas on old ones without rejecting them." A scientific model of architecture is, of course, in some conflict with the idea of architect as artist. Art, however, seldom repeats successful propositions once they have already been proven significant or meaningful. There are many "glass box" successors to Paxton's Crystal Palace, but no prominent artist has painted a can of peaches to build on the contributions of Andy Warhol's portrait of a soup can. Use of precedent is one aspect of architectural endeavor we can see as being strongly aligned with rational scientific methods.

Precedent is not intended here as an argument for total conversion to scientific reasoning in architectural design—quite the contrary. Design by adductive logic is simply an additive form of rational thought used in architecture to explore possibilities of what a building *could* be. Deductive logic, on the other hand, is usually considered to be a subtractive or reductionist means of eliminating design possibilities until we are left with only what a building *should* be. The point is that art and science, as well as architecture and engineering, are all disciplines that demand generous portions of both rational and intuitive thinking. *The creative and practical success of any pursuit is attained by willingness and capacity to employ whichever processes are appropriate at different stages of the work.* Walter Gropius (1935) has said, "Rationalism, which many people imagine to be the cardinal principle of the New Architecture, is really only its purifying agency.... The other, the aesthetic satisfaction of the human soul, is just as important as the material."

The precedents selected by architects are sometimes widely known and published. Many architects still refer to Paxton's Crystal Palace, for example. In these cases, some of the inspirations and organizational thinking that went into a building design can be understood through their architectural references. In other instances, such as the Museum of Flight, for which no explicit precedents are disclosed by the architect, they can be deduced or at least speculated on through an understanding of the project and its context.

Ibsen Nelsen seems to have used the Crystal Cathedral in Garden Grove, California, just outside Los Angeles, for his technical precedent. Similarities between the two buildings as technical solutions are compelling: Space frame construction and high-performance glass envelopes

	TABLE 4.4 Fact Sheet	
Project	**Building name**	Crystal Cathedral
	Client	The Reverend Dr. Robert Schuller, Garden Grove Community Church
	City	Garden Grove, California, USA
	Lat/Long/Elev	33.8 N 118.0 W, 135 ft (41 m)
Team	**Architect**	Johnson / Burgee Architects
	Structural	Severud-Perrone-Szegezdy-Sturm
	Mechanical	Cosentini Associates
	Energy	Vladimir Bazjanac
	Acoustics	Klepper-Marshall-King Associates, Ltd.
	Curtain Wall	Eugene Tofflemire
	Lighting	Claude R. Engle
	Fire-Safety	Rolf Jensen
	Organ	Virgil Fox
	Construction	C. I. Peck; Morse / Diesel, Inc; Koll Co.
General	**Time Line**	October 1977 to September 1980
	Floor Area	40,000 ft2 (3,714 m2)
	Occupants	2890 seats: 1778 on main floor, 403 east balcony, 403 west balcony, 306 south balcony
	Cost	$18 million or $450/ft^2
	Cost, 1995 US$	$33.3 million or $832/ft^2
	Stories	One plus balconies
	Plan	Four-pointed star footprint—length 417 ft, width 207 ft, height 128 ft (127.1 m x 63.1 m x 39.0 m).
Site	**Site Description**	Located 35 miles southeast of Los Angeles International Airport on the 22 acre site of a church complex and arboretum designed for Dr. Schuller by Richard Neutra, beginning about 1959.
	Parking, Cars	Large, open paved parking lots.
Structure	**Foundation**	N/A
	Vertical Members	Tubular steel space frame of 2 in. to 5 in. members joined by gusset plates and cast connectors.
	Horizontal Spans	Same as vertical frame.
	Special Features	Operable doors measuring 90 ft high, one 15 ft wide and one 11 ft wide operated by a garage door opener.
Envelope	**Glass and Glazing**	A total of 10,661 lites of glass, each 2 ft x 5 ft or 2 ft x 6 ft, silver reflective coated to 8% visible light and 10% total solar transmission.
	Cladding	Annealed fixed glass flush mounted with structural silicone sealant to neoprene seals, 550 tempered glass operable windows for ventilation cooling.
	Roof	Tempered glass flush mounted with structural silicone sealant to neoprene seals.
	Special Features	Glass is approximately 50% 1/4 in. thick and 50% 3/8 in. thick in a random distribution to prevent coincidence dip of critical frequencies of sound.
HVAC	**Equipment**	Forced-air heating only.
	Cooling Type	No mechanical cooling equipment is provided. Passive ventilation is attained by operable doors and windows with an assist from the stack effect of the 128 ft high space.
	Distribution	None.
	Duct Type	None.
	Vertical Chases	None.
Interior	**Partitions**	None.
	Finishes	Carpeted floors.
	Vertical Circulation	Stairs to balconies, one elevator in gallery.
	Furniture	Exhibits.
	Lighting	Not determined.
	Special Features	Mid-frequency reverberation time is 3 to 4 secs.

Figure 4.11 Crystal Cathedral, Garden Grove, California, by Johnson/Burgee Architects, 1980.

dominate both buildings, and daylight saturation of the museum Gallery posed issues already explored in sunny and temperate Los Angeles. The cathedral was completed in 1980, and design work on the Museum of Flight began in 1979 and its construction occupied the period from 1984 to 1987. The final link between the two projects is in the person of Vladimir Bazjanac, who worked on energy and daylighting aspects with both building teams. The suitability of the cathedral's solutions to the museum program merits some exploration, particularly because of the climatic differences between Seattle and Los Angeles. It is worth noting, for example, that the museum is mechanically heated and cooled whereas the cathedral uses stack-effect ventilation through its 128 ft height in lieu of mechanical systems.

STRUCTURE

For Ibsen Nelsen, the critical issues of the museum made the selection of structure and envelope glazing most important. Few structural systems would be able to carry the suspended weight of fully restored aircraft some 75 ft above the gallery floor, span 180 ft, cover 47,000 ft² of

uninterrupted space, and still admit enough sky and horizon to convey the intention of "planes in flight." By elimination, the choice was to use a three-dimensional, 17 ft deep space truss. This system would provide a basically transparent structure and could be engineered to span the gallery while carrying the suspended aircraft aloft. It also provided room overhead for the distribution of lighting and mechanical services. To maintain the transparency of the glass envelope, a vertical truss structure was used for the exterior gallery walls, repeating the vocabulary of the roof frame.

ENVELOPE

Selection of the glazing material for the envelope system was not as clear-cut. Here it was necessary to control the sun's damaging ultraviolet radiation and to balance an abundance of daylight with some control of solar gain. Even in the cloudy, diffuse skies of temperate Seattle, there is ample solar energy available to turn the glass-enclosed gallery into a smoldering greenhouse much of the year. The energy consultant, Vladimir Bazjanac, sought to "avoid summer solar heat gain, reduce winter heat loss

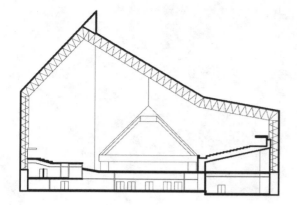

Figure 4.12 Plan and section drawings of the Garden Grove Crystal Cathedral.

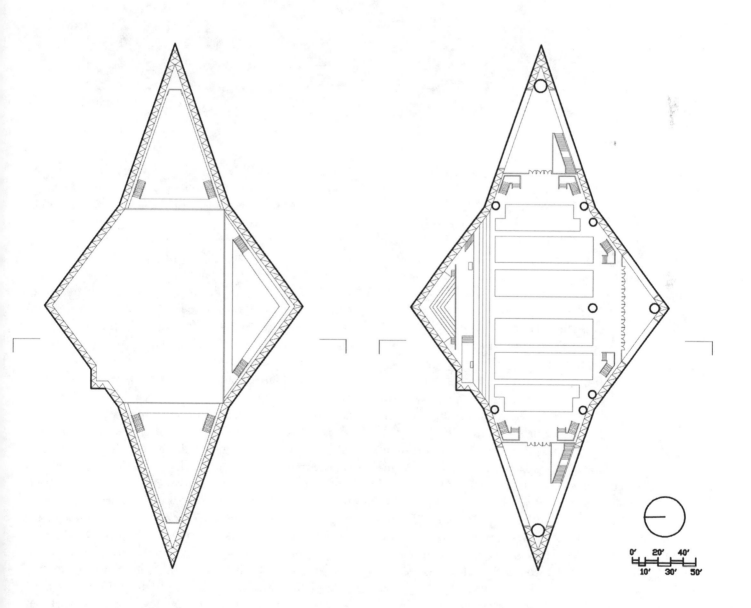

Figure 4.13 View of the museum interior.

and, at the same time, provide enough natural light to significantly reduce electric lighting loads" (Bazjanac and Winkelmann, 1989). He also recognized the need for the gallery exhibits to be visible through the glazing from the street. Optimizing these parameters required detailed computer simulation of every plausible combination of glazing selections. Not only were the results unpredictable from any previous experience, they were vital even to obtaining a building permit.

Nelsen had preliminarily specified three different glazings for the walls of the gallery. They were to be graduated in darkness of tint starting with the clearest 25 percent at street level to maintain view, then the 50 percent middle value at the middle of the walls, and finally the darkest 25 percent and most defensive tint at the top of the walls. The use of low-e glazing with three different levels of tint proved to give the optimal combination of light transmission, solar control, and low transmission of ultraviolet energy. Further solar control for the wall is achieved with exterior shading devices set in the wall trusses. The low-e glass type selected for the walls includes an inner membrane of mylar with a low-emissivity coating, thus providing two trapped air spaces and higher thermal insulation R-values than regular double-pane low-e glass.

The unshaded roof required a glazing with lower shading coefficients to provide less solar energy in all bands of the visible and thermal spectrum. Here the prime factor was visual—providing just enough transmission of

daylight to retain a convincing view of the sky while excluding as much heat as possible. The additional consideration of safety glazing in the roof (as required for all sloped and horizontal glass in the Uniform Building Code) had to be factored in. The wall glazing was ruled out for the roof because of the belief that horizontal sections of the mylar film would deflect and degrade its low-e coating. Experience with later buildings proved this to be a mistaken assumption, but the technology was deemed to be too new for certainty. In the end, triple glazing was used with a top pane of reflective tempered glass and a bottom pane of laminated safety glass.

The qualitative issue of glare in the daylight-saturated gallery was still in doubt. With so much daylight filling the exhibits, there was great concern for the excessive contrast ratios between sky and window brightness as compared with that in the foreground exhibits. Numerical modeling of brightness levels was prevented by the complexity of the roof structure and the lattice of open shading devices used on the exterior structure of the walls. Empirically, however, the museum gallery was deemed similar enough to Johnson/Burgee's Crystal Cathedral to invite qualitative comparison of the natural lighting. Because Bazjanac was also the energy consultant for Johnson/Burgee, his insights were invaluable. The Crystal Cathedral had not presented any glare problems, and it was assumed that the museum would be visually comfortable as well. Nelsen's choice of a universally white painted finish on the structural members, set against the glazing areas, provided a critical reduction of contrast. White colored structure was also used at the Crystal Cathedral precedent building. In addition, the thinness of the truss members diffused glare by feathering the brightness ratios around their rounded surfaces. Further study by Bazjanac showed that an additional 50 percent reduction in visible light transmittance would only save about 1 percent of total annual energy. And that small energy savings would result in glass that blocked the view of the exhibits from outside.

The comparison of daylighting quality in the museum with that in the Crystal Cathedral represents a common practice of inferring aspects of performance from similar buildings. Before Wallace Clement Sabine (1922) derived his equation for reverberation time, for example, concert halls were designed by copying proven configurations. The "shoebox" auditorium was a favorite and often imitated theme precisely because it had worked in previous examples. Charles Garnier (Athanasopulos, 1983), architect of the Paris Opera, stated, "I must explain that I have adopted no principle, that my plan has been based on no theory, and that I leave success or failure to chance alone." This sort of empirical precedent gave some certainty to how a room would sound before the behavior of room acoustics was properly understood. Copying did give rise to multiple and conflicting sets of design guidelines for auditoriums—length:width:height proportions for proper sound were idealized variously at 2:3:5, 1:1:2, or even 2:3:4. But even these crude guides were superior to the earlier necessity of writing "chamber music" to accommodate the acoustics of an existing room rather than the other way

around. After Sabine experimented with the Fogg Lecture Hall at Harvard and Sanders Theater in Cambridge, Massachusetts, he determined a method of predicting reverberation time by a simple equation based on the amount of sound absorption present and the volume of the room. He was subsequently commissioned to act as acoustical consultant to the Boston Music Hall in 1898—the first scientifically considered auditorium. The Music Hall opened in 1900 to broad acclaim and is still regarded as one of the musically finest concert halls in the world.

Just as in determining acoustics in pre-Sabine concert halls, using the Crystal Cathedral as a model for anticipating daylight quantity in the museum gallery was necessitated by the difficulty of numerical modeling. Even with large computer models (by 1987 standards) the detailed simulation of complex rooms with daylighting contrast levels were not reliably or practically predicted. Still today, testing of photorealistic scale models is usually superior to numerical simulation for qualitative issues in daylighting.

It is necessary to examine the details of both the museum design in Seattle and the Johnson/Burgees church outside Los Angeles to verify that the conditions are similar enough to validate any useful comparison. Although what Ibsen Nelsen gained on his visits to other air flight museums was certainly useful in informing and inspiring the design of the Great Gallery at the schematic level, its applicability to design development performance considerations is less sure. Is the Crystal Cathedral a valid technical precedent? Despite the apparent similarities of design schemes and the common challenge of daylight saturation, several differences had to be considered before

Figure 4.14 Space frame and envelope glazing of the Crystal Cathedral.

TABLE 4.5 Normal Climate Data for Garden Grove, California

		Jan.	Feb.	Mar.	Apr.	May	June	July	Aug.	Sept.	Oct.	Nov.	Dec.	Year
Temperature	Degree-Days heating	241	187	189	135	58	30	0	0	9	19	117	253	1238
	Degree-Days Cooling	5	8	13	42	55	132	238	279	237	134	27	5	1175
	Extreme High	89	89	97	108	102	107	112	104	112	105	95	93	112
	Normal High	68	69	68	72	73	77	82	83	83	79	73	68	75
	Normal Average	56	57	58	61	64	68	72	73	72	67	61	56	64
	Normal Low	44	46	47	50	55	59	62	63	61	56	47	43	53
	Extreme Low	28	29	31	34	38	42	45	48	44	30	32	25	25
Humidity	Dew Point	42	45	47	49	53	57	60	61	60	54	47	42	51
	Max %RH	79	81	82	79	77	79	81	81	81	80	79	78	80
	Min %RH	56	57	57	55	58	59	57	57	56	57	56	56	57
	% Days with Rain	7	7	8	5	2	1	0	0	1	2	5	7	45
	Rain Inches	2.4	2.4	2.1	0.8	0.2	0.1	0	0.1	0.4	0.3	1.3	1.5	11.6
Sky	% Overcast Days	35	36	36	27	22	13	6	6	10	16	27	32	27
	% Clear Days	42	43	39	13	47	53	55	55	53	55	50	45	44
Wind	Prevailing Direction	WSW	WSW	WSW	WSW	WSW	WSW	WSW	WSW	WSW	WSW	WSW	W	WSW
	Speed, Knots	6	6	7	8	7	7	7	7	7	7	7	6	5	7
	Percent Calm	39.7	35.3	29.7	25.2	21.8	22.3	22.7	26.5	32.1	36.5	40.1	45.2	31.3
Days Observed	Rain	6	6	7	4	2	1	0	1	2	2	4	5	40
	Fog	14	13	13	11	13	15	17	16	16	17	14	14	173
	Haze	12	11	11	12	15	19	23	23	20	19	14	13	192
	Snow	0	0	0	0	0	0	0	0	0	0	0	0	0
	Hail	0	0	0	0	0	0	0	0	0	0	0	0	1
	Freezing Rain	0	0	0	0	0	0	0	0	0	0	0	0	0
	Blowing Sand	0	0	0	0	0	0	0	0	0	0	0	0	1

adopting the Crystal Cathedral as the assumed guarantee of success. Three differences shed some doubt on the transfer of empirical results from the cathedral to the museum: climate, glazing types, and shading.

Comparing climate conditions and daylight availability in Seattle, Los Angeles, and Long Beach does favor applying the Cathedral model to the museum (Figure 4.17). The typical Seattle daylighting condition is more diffuse than that of Los Angeles, so direct glare from the sun is less likely in Seattle than in Los Angeles for similar schemes. A bright summer day defining the worst condition is about the same for both locations. Oddly enough, the glass used for the church structure transmits only 8% of the available visible light and only 10% of the total solar spectrum, whereas the museum used wall glass with visible light transmissions ranging from 54 percent at the lower band, 47 percent across the middle half, and 22 percent at the upper levels. Even the Gallery's reflective triple glazing on the roof is 25 percent transmitting. The differences in climate do not seem as dramatic as the glazing selections would indicate, especially with the worst-condition glare under a clear sky. The structural wall frame at the Cathedral is contained within the glass wall plane, as opposed to the more efficient external wall shading by structure at the museum, but both roofs are unshaded from above. The bands of exterior wall-shading devices at the museum are of some help with solar shade and diffusion of visual brightness patterns, but they are staggered only intermittently across the truss frames of the external walls.

The fact that the comparison is so complex establishes the need and value of qualified consultants. An erroneously adopted technical precedent, however similar it may appear, would have been disastrous. Like the room acoustics of a large auditorium, the daylighting quality of the Great Gallery would have been nearly impossible to correct. [insert Fig. 4.17]

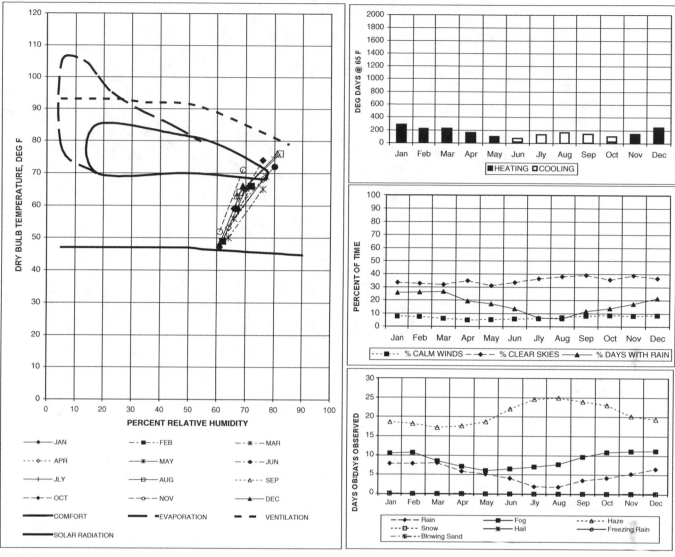

Figure 4.15 Climate graphics for Garden Grove, California.

Figure 4.16 Bin data distribution plot for Garden Grove, California. Concentric areas of graph indicate the number of hours per year that weather conditions normally occur in this climate. Similar to elevation readings on topographic maps, highest frequency occurrences of weather are at the center peaks of the graph. (Data sources: *Engineering Weather Data, typical meteorological year (TMY) data from the National Climatic Data Center, and the ASHRAE Weather Data Viewer from the American Society of Heating, Refrigerating, and Air-Conditioning Engineers.)*

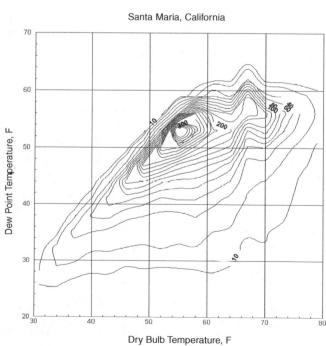

Santa Maria, California

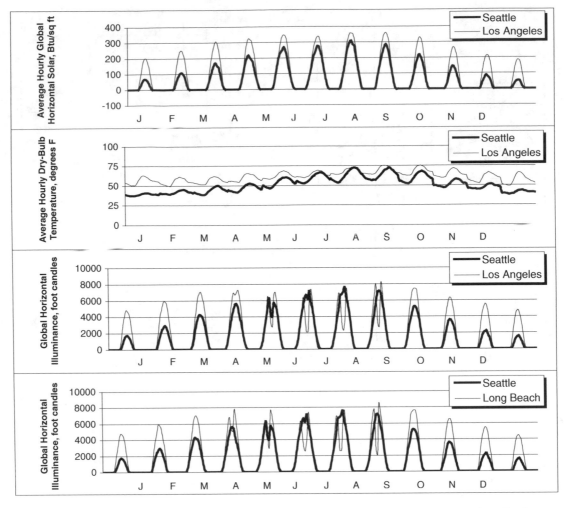

Figure 4.17 Solar radiation, temperature, and daylight in Seattle, Washington, Los Angeles, and Long Beach, California.

MECHANICAL

The majority of the PMF's mechanical systems are located in the basement area, just below the level of the lowest gallery floor. This room contains the chillers and the 530 kW boiler, which constitute the "thermal plant" where fuel energy is converted into comfort energy. A cooling tower to reject heat from the chiller plant to the environment is located at the back of the loading dock area and covered with a metal grill to allow air circulation through the cooling tower. This placement of the cooling tower conserves the view and prevents serious acoustical disruption of the gallery and balcony spaces with views toward the airfield. Sprinkler water connections for fire safety are also centralized in the basement, along with computerized controls and monitoring equipment for many of the building-servicing systems. Two underground water tanks provide thermal storage for the gallery. One tank stores heat reclaimed from the cooling system for use on chilly nights; the other

stores off-peak cooling for use in shaving the highest loads of the warmest days.

Some heating-only supply air ducts run under the gallery floor and ring the exterior wall to provide heat along the exterior glazing. Heating energy is delivered from these ducts through louvers at the base of the wall where radiant temperature effects of cold glass would be encountered. The initial waterproofing of the underground ducts against the seasonal tidal flooding of the site failed and required a number of repairs.

INTERIOR

Exhibits and lighting make up the bulk of interior systems in the gallery. Aside from the full-scale aircraft, some smaller displays contain graphic and text information. These kiosk-style exhibits use adjustable task lighting fixtures to emphasize their contents.

Figure 4.18 The museum at night. *(Photograph courtesy of Nancy Routh.)*

The ambient lighting system in the Great Gallery uses four zones of 400 W metal halide lamps in open downlight pendant fixtures. To integrate daylighting and artificial lamps, the metal halide zones were designed to be switchable in steps of one-third. One-third of the fixtures in each zone come on, but only to a preset dimming level to extend lamp life. As daylight availability decreases, photocells strike the second set of the lamps, and finally the third set. The fixtures of each third are scattered uniformly throughout the zone to ensure even illumination levels.

In practice, the metal halide fixtures are seldom required during daylight hours. In the first six years of operation at least, they were never used during daylight. The kiosk exhibit lighting is totally washed out by daylight even on the most overcast of days but probably provides some accent in morning and evening hours of the short days of winter. The metal halide general lighting is put to best effect at night when the building "turns inside out" in dramatic fashion.

SITE

The adjacency of the museum to the airfield was incorporated into the scheme of the building for air shows. The long axis of the gallery was stretched across the east to provide the greatest viewing platform. This east end of the building is divided into two levels — one to furnish a lower viewing area adjacent to the Great Gallery and the other to provide an upper level of VIP rooms with covered outdoor balconies for museum patrons. The setback distance from the airstrip is used for general parking and additional displays. The street elevation of the building is thus freed to provide an uncluttered formal entry plaza and a glazed lobby between the Red Barn and the entrance to the gallery. Delivery and utility service is via a depressed drive to the basement level at the south of the building. The south elevation also contains a huge pair of motorized doors for moving aircraft in and out of the gallery. Surrounding the building with lawns on both street elevations helped to ensure a public view into the collection.

Beneficial Integrations

To bring the various systems selected for a building into concert, they must be brought together and detailed in meaningful ways. This harmony is shaped to some extent by the nature of the systems themselves. Primarily, though, the architect works the components of the building into a complex whole — a whole that is inclusive of program and intention. As a further mandate, the final built product must achieve a resolved composition. The task of integration is to bring elements together so that everything shares space and has integral connections, then to satisfy the function of the systems without surpassing the budget, and finally to achieve a visually expressive product. To accomplish these three levels of integration (physical, functional, and aesthetic), the designer must consider how decisions about each system affect the mandates of other systems and subsystems. To achieve high levels of success, these decisions should be considered as design opportunities.

Figure 4.19 The Great Gallery on a late summer evening.

Nelsen's solutions are highly integrated. The space truss resolves the dominant challenge of the roof structure and transparent wall frame and is also elemental to daylighting and display of the airplanes. The lattice frame structure rests lightly on the poor soil supporting the building. The structural tube wall frame is adapted to a lacey but effective external solar shade. The very nature of the round tubes used in the frame provides a softened graduation of brightness at its edges. The envelope maintains adequate daylighting without ultraviolet damage to the museum collection and without excessive solar gain. The energy code issue was also resolved by the same appropriate selection and optimization of systems.

The intention of "planes in flight" is realized without compromise. The presence of the sky is clearly perceptible through the roof glazing on overcast as well as sunny days. Furthermore, the roof truss structure becomes an intentional part of the daylighting system without being visually distracting. And when the sun is low enough in the sky to peek under the exterior wall shades with a touch of horizontal light, the geometry of truss bracing provides a spectacular rhythm of light and structure.

Combinations of the systems, subsystems, and individual components reveal how well-thought-out their integrations had to be. If the space truss were any color other than matte white, for example, the gallery would be filled with sharp contrasts between the bright sky and the silhouetted frame members.

Integration of the mechanical system and the envelope provides direct space ventilation through motor-operable awning windows set high into the south and northwest glass walls. During temperate parts of the year the gallery is warmed by solar energy during all daylight hours, result-ing in interior overheating even when outdoor temperatures are quite moderate. In these situations, the two 36,000 cfm fan units nestled into the space truss at the east end of the gallery quit returning air from the space and switch to 100 percent outdoor air. The outdoor ventilation air is drawn through louvers at the top of the west wall. This temperate air is substituted for mechanically cooled air and introduced directly into the gallery. The high awning windows on the side walls simultaneously open to exhaust the stratified warm air from the top of the space. This mechanical ventilation mode of "economizer cooling" is not uncommon in internally load dominated buildings. Appropriate use of ventilation cooling in the gallery is a necessary adjunct to the glass enclosure and open sky intentions of the architect. Even though the gallery is surface-load dominated, the saturation of daylight in the space means that solar gain will often cause overheating during cool and comfortable parts of the year. This is when the mechanical ventilation mode is triggered. In Seattle, bin data indicates that there are normally 1314 daylight hours per year when the outdoor temperature is between 45°F and 60°F. This translates to roughly 30 percent of the annual hours between 9:00 A.M. and 4:00 P.M. when ventilation can be substituted for mechanical cooling during periods of solar overheating. To protect the collection from excessive moisture and retain indoor comfort levels, the ventilation mode is disabled when outdoor humidity is high. But this is most likely to occur during humid overcast or rainy days when solar gain may not drive the gallery into the cooling mode anyway. The benefits of daylighting and vision glass are therefore comfortably integrated with the mechanical system through ventilation strategies.

Conclusion

From its program and intention alone, the PMF's Great Gallery configuration could have been predicted with fair accuracy. Ibsen Nelsen's intention of displaying the aircraft collection "as if in flight" guides all the successive systems integration activities. The selection of the space frame structure and the glass envelope follows the desire for daylight and the required roof spans. Mechanical and interior systems fit cleanly into the overall scheme. The resulting building can be readily reconstructed by tracing the logic of its design.

Figure 4.20 summarizes the process by which the PMF design was analyzed in this chapter. This is the format of analysis that will be applied to all the case studies in Part II. From the client's brief and the general context of the project, the architect develops a program and intention.

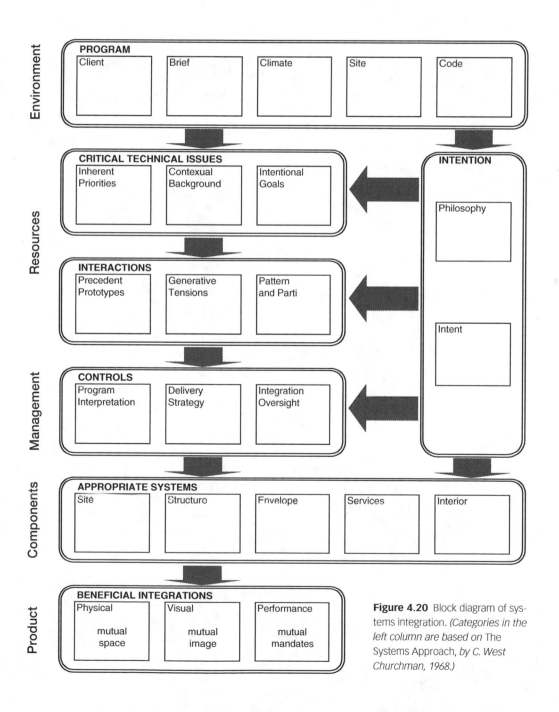

Figure 4.20 Block diagram of systems integration. *(Categories in the left column are based on* The Systems Approach, *by C. West Churchman, 1968.)*

Critical technical issues then arise from inherent, contextual, and intentional factors. Appropriate systems are selected and deployed to match objective and subjective criteria. Beneficial integrations are formed to provide physical, visual, and performance enhancements through sympathetic cooperation of the systems and subsystems via their shared mandates. The architect's thinking is shown to incorporate the management of this process, the project resources, and the desired outcome. The accumulated wisdom of architecture is applied through the use of formal, technical, and organizational approaches and consideration of historic and other precedent works.

There are limitations to this analytical method. In practice, the synthetic design process is seldom reduced to the simple model suggested by Figure 4.20. Likewise, an analytical case study can only retrace the fruitful efforts in the development of real-world projects; very few of the alternative or unproductive explorations are revealed. The time lines of the case studies plotted in the introduction to Part II indicate the long years of work and intensely collaborative teamwork that make up most architectural projects. No block diagram or process flowchart can serve as a recipe or other linear substitute for the exploratory work of design. We can probably map the flows of design information, but the dynamics of design thinking are less easily captured with boxes and arrows.

Despite these limitations, case studies provide insights into the role of systems thinking and systems integration in architecture. They are intended to distill completed works of architecture into instructive lessons. Many of the techniques they illustrate can then be replicated in practice.

The final seven chapters of this text consist of building case studies. Each chapter focuses on a particular building use or a specific design approach. Collectively, the case studies represent a matrix of projects spanning different regions, climates, and architects. The most restricted attribute of the sample is time—all of the projects were developed after World War II. Together they represent the transition to systems-based architecture since that time.

Each set of case studies (Table II.1) begins with a precedent building for integrated design in its topic area. The other case studies fall chronologically within each chapter. Organizationally, this sequence illustrates the trends and developments that have advanced integrated systems design into current and standard design approaches. The progression from precedent building to newest example should therefore be closely examined as a subplot. Among the seven chapter topics, there is a great deal of overlap and some possible cross grouping, but each case study is relevant to the chapter focus and no hard classification is intended. Further, although the building types and individual examples hardly represent a complete picture of architecture, they do provide a useful sketch of the discussion at hand.

At the beginning of each case study chapter is an overview introducing the general nature and critical issues characterizing a particular building type or design approach. These central points, in turn, frame the individual case study discussions of appropriate systems and help to outline their beneficial integrations.

Each individual case study follows the integration framework set forth in Chapter 4: program, intention, critical issues, appropriate systems, and beneficial integration. Accompanying this discussion is a condensed fact sheet, climate analysis data and graphics, and an anatomical drawing of important building system relationships. All of these elements are introduced in Chapter 4 as a means of examining integrated systems design in any building.

PART II Case Studies

TABLE II.1 Case Study Building Database

	Case Study # / Building	City	Date	Architect or Engineer	Latitude, North Is Positive	Longitude, East is Positive	Degree-Days Heating	Degree-Days Cooling	Cost, Millions of Dollars	Cost In 1995 Millions of Dollars	Floor Area In 1000 Ft^2	Cost/Ft^2 1995 Dollars
Laboratory	1 Richards	Philadelphia, PA	1961	Louis Kahn	39.95	-75.18	4824	1204	3.0	33.0	109.0	174
	2 Salk	San Diego, CA	1965	Louis Kahn	32.88	-117.22	1115	821	11.4	56.2	411.6	137
	3 Schlumberger	Cambridge, UK	1985	Michael Hopkins	52.21	0.08	5726	60	7.2	10.2	110.0	168
	4 PAT	Princeton, NJ	1986	Richard Rogers	40.17	-74.37	4982	1073	4.7	6.5	42.6	153
	5 Wallace	Winnepeg, Canada	1988	IKOY	49.90	-97.10	10363	304	9.0	11.6	110.0	105
Office	6 Deere	Moline, IL	1963	Eero Saarinen	41.47	-90.45	6413	977	10.0	49.8	350.4	142
	7 Willis Faber Dumas	Ipswich, UK	1973	Norman Foster	52.06	1.15	5319	46	11.4	32.2	226.0	142
	8 Briarcliff House	Farnborough, UK	1983	Arup Associates	51.29	-0.76	5433	44	11.3	18.0	101.4	178
	9 Lockheed	Sunnyvale, CA	1983	Leo Daly	37.41	-122.03	2488	346	50.0	76.5	585.0	127
Airport	10 Dulles	Washington, DC	1962	Eero Saarinen	38.95	-77.45	4927	1097	108.3	547.0	362.4	1509
	11 Stansted	Stansted, UK	1991	Norman Foster	51.88	0.23	5726	60	196.7	220.1	922.4	239
	12 O'Hare	Chicago, IL	1992	Helmut Jahn	41.97	-87.90	6511	839	200.0	217.2	1300.0	167
	13 Kansai	Osaka, Japan	1994	Renzo Piano	34.00	130.00	3065	1667	2000.0	2330.0	3168.0	735
Pavillion	14 Munich	Munich	1972	Behnisch/Otto	48.17	11.56	6701	130	69.9	255.1	915.0	279
	15 Arab Institute	Paris	1988	Jean Nouvell	48.85	2.36	5028	253	77.9	100.4	269.1	350
	16 Linz Design Center	Linz, Austria	1994	Thomas Herzog	48.23	14.18	6396	184	643.7	790.8	333.7	2369
	17 British Pavillion	Seville, Spain	1992	Nicholas Grimshaw	37.40	-6.00	1712	1915	27.2	29.5	75.3	391
Residence	18 Eames	Santa Monica, CA	1949	Charles and Ray Eames	34.03	-118.53	1355	656			3.0	
	19 Magney	Moruya, Australia	1984	Glenn Murcutt	-36.02	150.17	1913	667			1.9	
	20 Experimental	Almere, Holland	1984	Benthem Crouwel	52.38	5.22	5663	83			0.7	
	21 Two-Family House	Pullach, Germany	1989	Thomas Herzog	48.13	11.70	6701	130			2.5	
High Tech	22 Pompidou	Paris	1975	Piano and Rogers	48.85	2.36	5028	253	75.9	260.8	692.1	377
	23 Sainsbury	Norwich, UK	1977	Norman Foster	52.62	1.24	5319	46	4.0	10.5	66.6	152
	24 Lloyd's	London	1984	Richard Rogers	51.51	-0.08	5570	62	135.0	197.9	52.0	381
	25 Hong Kong	Hong Kong	1985	Norman Foster	22.30	114.20	319	3949	670.1	949.2	1067.0	890
Green	26 Bateson	Sacramento, CA	1981	Sim Van der Ryn	38.58	-121.50	2679	1213	20.0	47.6	267.0	175
	27 NMB	Amsterdam, Holland	1987	Alberts & Van Huut	52.30	4.77	5663	83	63.2	61.4	538.0	114
	28 EPUD	Eugene, OR	1988	John Reynolds	44.01	-123.02	4701	249	4.1	5.3	24.3	218
	29 Oberlin	Oberlin, OH	2000	William McDonough	41.29	-82.23	6059	755	6.0	5.7	14.6	441
	MOF	Seattle, WA	1987	Ibsen Nelsen	47.50	-122.29	4931	158	26.4	35.4	142.8	248
	Crystal Cathedral	Garden Grove, CA	1980	Johnson / Burgee	33.80	-118.00	1238	1175	18.0	33.3	40.0	832

Timeline of the Case Study Buildings

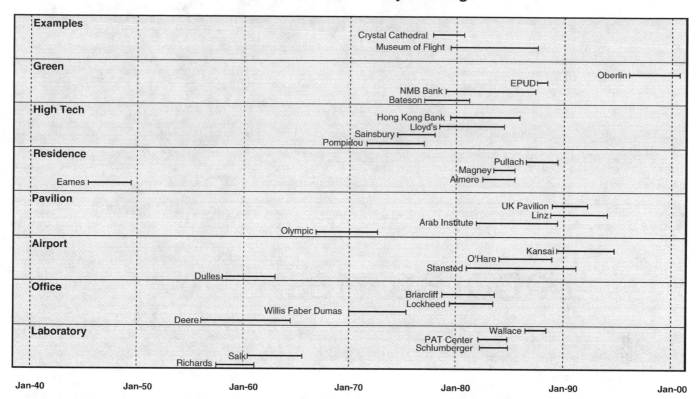

Figure II.1 Timeline of the case study buildings.

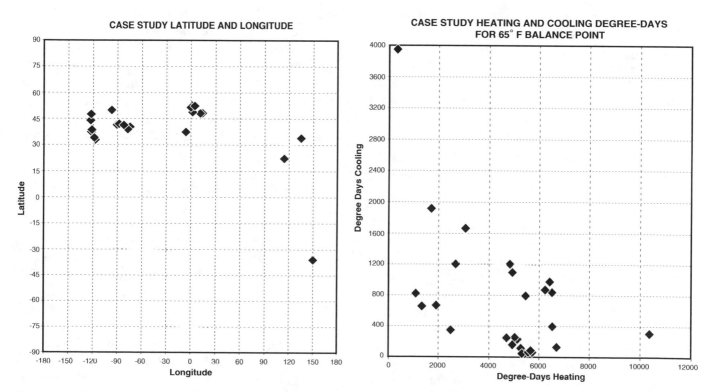

Figure II.2 Latitude and longitude of the case study buildings.

Figure II.3 Degree-days heating and cooling for the case study buildings.

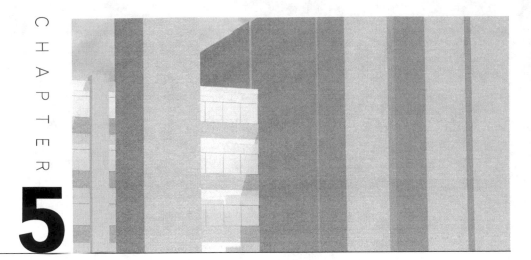

5

Laboratories

Research laboratories were the first building type to be architecturally dominated by environmental criteria. This follows the many epochs of progress during which structural integrity and construction ingenuity were the primary technical concerns of building design. Elegant solutions to gravity and span in the era of castles and cathedrals, and then in the time of high-rise buildings, perpetuated an architectural fascination and ennoblement of structural expression. We still call buildings "structures" as if that function characterized their entire purpose. Since the 1960s, however, environmental challenges such as energy conservation, indoor air quality, and the need for flexibly serviced space have combined to push the servicing of buildings to the forefront. Laboratories are inherently the most critical building type of this new focus.

Careful control of interior environmental conditions in laboratories illustrates the newer focus quite clearly. In biology and medical labs, for instance, so much air is exhausted and constantly replenished that the interior can be thought of as an occupied air-conditioning duct. In microchip research and manufacturing, "clean room" requirements dictate air that is virtually free of all particles of dust. Clean room workers have to don lintfree lab suits in air-lock-type vestibules. Indeed, many of the "dirty" industry products that once came from factory assembly lines are being replaced by manufacturing techniques that

require critical control of humidity, temperature, and indoor air quality. Further, increased technology in everyday culture creates new building uses that qualify as laboratories on the scale of environmental purpose: medical clinics, microchip manufacturing plants, teaching laboratories, surgery suites, and the like.

The high levels of environmental control associated with laboratories also pose new questions about the lifetime scenario of a building. Unlike the final consequences of structural decisions, environmental servicing requires ongoing energy, maintenance, and replacement (heating, cooling, ventilating, lighting). Eventually, technical obsolescence must be confronted. Shifts in the critical technical issues of buildings are then frequently accompanied by redistribution of construction budgets and by the flexibility of systems. The architecture of the laboratory echoes these environmental transformations.

To best appreciate the emergence of the laboratory as a symbol of environmental dominance, it is necessary to relate the other facets of environmental awareness that arose at the same time. Laboratories as a distinct building type emerged at about the same time Rachel Carson was writing *Silent Spring* (1962), a call to arms against toxic waste dumping. Soon after came air pollution, acid rain, and ozone depletion. Then, by 1973, the world was experiencing an energy crisis that added personal economic immediacy to all the detached social issues.

"Served and Servant Spaces": Richards Medical Research Building and the Salk Institute of Biological Studies

Louis Kahn's laboratory designs for Richards Medical Research and the Salk Institute are dramatic events in the evolution of building systems integration. They mark the transition from an architecture of structurally dominated criteria to a new era governed by environmental mandates. To find the essence of these new building types, designers had to augment the timeless issues of constructability with new and dynamic notions about serviceability. The ways in which building systems were considered, chosen, and deployed were altered in a positive and progressive way. As leading examples, Kahn's two laboratories are pivotal. But their importance lies in more than their being products of an inevitable transformation dictated by increasingly complex building problems— these two buildings established new fundamental parameters for architecture. They did so by employing diverse expertise and knowledge from the entire design team, by showing how masterly design can assimilate scientific complexity into provocative inspiration, and by ennobling the interaction of building systems. In short, they helped introduce the generative synergy of building systems integration.

Kahn's introduction of the laboratory as the first prototype of this environmentally dominated era is successful partly because of his career-long relationships with two world-class engineers: Fred Dubin (mechanical) and August Komendant (structural). Not only were these relationships formative in the way Kahn developed his architectural intentions, they also provided a historical perspective from the viewpoint of his collaborators. Komendant's book, *18 Years with Architect Louis I. Kahn*, is especially valuable in this regard.

The clarity and expressiveness of Kahn's basic concept for these two laboratories mark their special place in the precedent of systems integration. He was the first to deal with the technical sophistication of laboratories as an architectural challenge and to recognize the potential of their technically dominated elements. His thinking foreshadowed the still emerging challenge of accommodating environmental technology and human factors into architectural opportunity.

Kahn recognized the overwhelming role that utility services would play in the design of laboratories. They would not only impose essential practical demands but, he feared, the machines might even take over and "invade" the building. Using a common grammar to unite them, he resolved to distinguish between the occupied laboratories with one language and the mechanical spaces with another. He would give them each a separate identity and let the resulting dynamic between them express "what they wanted to be."

Kahn's concept foretells Reyner Banham's (1969) description of Marco Zanuso's 1964 factory for Olivetti in Merlo, Argentina, as served and "manifestly seen to be served." Since the advent of mechanical cooling, architects have dealt with increasingly complex demands for the servicing of buildings. The *served and servant* expression is still used repeatedly to give content and validity to built form. Articulation of mechanical, electrical, and plumbing "service" elements is now frequently as integral to the image of a building as are the structural methods of erecting it. "Served and servant" is today a well-practiced art.

Kahn was successful not only in expressing the laboratory as an architecturally worthy building type, but also in the broader context of assimilating his patent architectural features—daylighting as a means of humanizing a building, his care for materials, the notion of connection, and a sense of the room. Nonetheless, his architectural intention of distinguishing served and servant spaces is what marks these two labs as more than mere buildings.

It should be noted that Kahn worked closely with his team of consultants to develop these valid expressions. Komendant had to persuade him that the towers at Richards Medical should be "brainless" in order to avoid the structural problem of fitting them with fluted caps. And when Kahn entertained the use of spiral-shaped buildings to capture the San Diego sea breezes, Dubin had to convince him that the Salk Institute could not be naturally ventilated. These technical oversights are to be taken with a grain of salt—Kahn was pushing the edge of what could be done at that time, which is never accomplished without an occasional missed step. It was not so many years before, after all, that Le Corbusier was making the same halting sort of progressions that led him to the *brise soleil*.

1

ALFRED NEWTON RICHARDS MEDICAL RESEARCH BUILDING

Philadelphia, Pennsylvania
LOUIS KAHN

DESCRIPTION

The first of Louis Kahn's "studios for science" was built on the University of Pennsylvania campus in Philadelphia. Based on a vertical scheme of four connected towers, it consists of three seven-story stacks of biology laboratories, each surrounded by small utility shafts on three sides and connected to a central service tower on the fourth side. The laboratories are open-plan spaces and the service tower is divided into utility spaces, offices, and animal kennels.

Richards Medical is an early architectural example of precast posttensioned concrete construction, a strategy necessitated in part by the restricted site. The concrete frame is fully expressed on the exterior and in-filled with brick and glass. Inside, the open-web concrete frame is used for overhead services distribution.

Figure 5.1 Rendering of Richards Medical. (*3D rendering by Travis Hughs.*)

TABLE 5.1 Fact Sheet

Project		
Building name	Alfred Newton Richards Medical Research Laboratories	
Client	University of Pennsylvania	
City	3700 Hamilton Walk, Philadelphia, Pennsylvania, USA	
Lat/Long/Elev	39.95 N 75.18 W, 80 feet (24 m)	

Team		
Architect	Louis Kahn	
Structural Engineer	August Kommendant	
Mechanical Engineer	Cronheim & Weger, Fred S. Dubin Associates (Biology Building)	
Landscape	Ian L. McHarg	
Consulting Engineers	Keast and Hood	
General Contractor	Joseph R. Farrell, Inc.	

General		
Timeline	1959-1961	
Floor Area	109,000-ft^2 (10,121-m^2)	
Stories	7 floors plus basement, reaching 96.0-ft (29.3-m) at top roof beam, 121-ft (36.9-m) at the top of the service towers.	
Plan	Four towers measuring 47.3-ft (14.4-m) on each side, connected by a common core of ten stories	
Occupants	1500	
Cost	$3 million or $33.33/ft^2	
1995 Cost in US $	$15.7 million or $174.44/ft^2	

Site		
Site Description	Urban campus setting. Building site is on pedestrian street separating student residences from botanical gardens.	
Parking, Cars	None	

Structure		
Foundation	Not published	
Vertical Members	Precast 2.8-ft (86.4-mm) concrete "H" columns forming a typical framing bay spanning 47.3-ft x 47.3-ft (14.4-m)	
Horizontal Spans	Precast, prestressed concrete Vierendeel truss frame, 3.2-ft (1.0-m) deep spanning 45.0-ft (13.7-m) at 16.2-ft (4.9-m) spacing, frame is post-tensioned before grouting joints. Floors are two way concrete slabs supporting design load of 100 psf.	

Envelope		
Glass and Glazing	0.25-in (0.64-mm) glass covering 35% of exterior. Progression from clear to increasingly darker blue tint from first floor to top floor. 12-gauge stainless steel frames.	
Cladding	4-in (10.2-mm) concrete block with 4-in brick with insulated cavity and metal wall ties	
Roof	Tar and gravel	

HVAC		
Equipment	Central plant campus system	
Cooling Type	Variable air volume fans in penthouse with supplemental hot water radiators at perimeter zones.	
Distribution	Variable-air-volume, VAV. Fans are in roof penthouse.	
Duct Type	Exposed in ceiling	
Vertical Chases	Servant towers for fume exhaust air and some conditioned air ducting surround the three lab towers and similar towers for outside air stand to the north of the animal quarters tower. Main HVAC airshafts run through the core tower.	

Interior		
Partitions	Minimal partitions, concrete block to bottom of vierendeel beams.	
Finishes	Marble window sills	
Vertical Circulation	External stair shafts with one freight and two passenger elevators in central core.	
Furniture	Window height laboratory benches.	

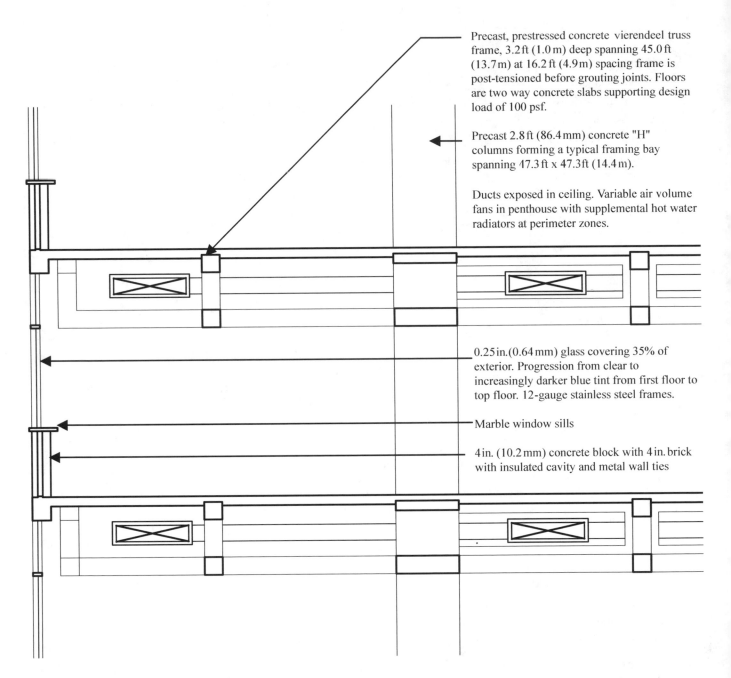

Precast, prestressed concrete vierendeel truss frame, 3.2 ft (1.0 m) deep spanning 45.0 ft (13.7 m) at 16.2 ft (4.9 m) spacing frame is post-tensioned before grouting joints. Floors are two way concrete slabs supporting design load of 100 psf.

Precast 2.8 ft (86.4 mm) concrete "H" columns forming a typical framing bay spanning 47.3 ft x 47.3 ft (14.4 m).

Ducts exposed in ceiling. Variable air volume fans in penthouse with supplemental hot water radiators at perimeter zones.

0.25 in. (0.64 mm) glass covering 35% of exterior. Progression from clear to increasingly darker blue tint from first floor to top floor. 12-gauge stainless steel frames.

Marble window sills

4 in. (10.2 mm) concrete block with 4 in. brick with insulated cavity and metal wall ties

Figure 5.2 Anatomical section.

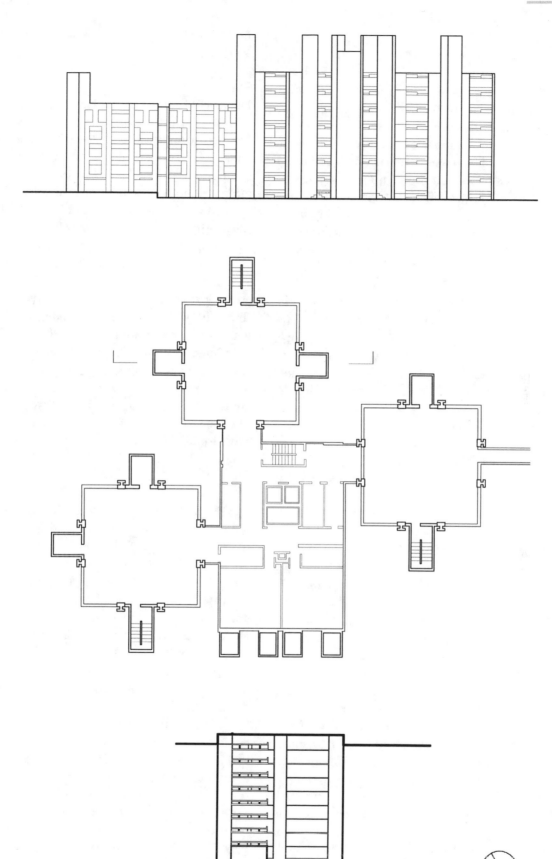

Figure 5.3 Plan, section, and elevation.

PROGRAM

Client

Benjamin Franklin was the first advocate of a public academy in Philadelphia. His 1749 pamphlet, *Proposals for the Education of Youth in Pensilvania,* targeted the creation of the first secular school and first liberal arts program in the country. Harvard, William and Mary, Yale, and Princeton were all seminary schools at the time. In 1765 a young surgeon named John Morgan organized the country's first medical school on the University of Pennsylvania campus.

In the late nineteenth century, American medical education was stimulated by the scientific activities in Europe. Although the work of Pasteur, Koch, and Ehrlich inaugurated modern medicine, teaching methods in American medical schools were still largely tied to eighteenth-century practices. The new era called for full-time teachers and research in the developing sciences such as bacteriology, biochemistry, and pharmacology. A new program of study in scientific medicine was developed that required additional years of training and higher academic standards. One of the university's decisions was to have a bedside teaching program conducted by clinical academic faculty. The University of Pennsylvania played a role in promoting this aspect of medical education.

During the early twentieth century, the School of Medicine was one of the first to encourage development of emerging medical specialties like neurosurgery, ophthalmology, dermatology, and radiology. Within the three decades that preceded World War II, American medicine caught up with European medicine and was making impressive contributions in the biomedical sciences.

One of the most important figures in the development of Penn as a center of medical science was Alfred Newton Richards. Richards had come to the University of Pennsylvania Medical School in 1910 to chair the pharmacology department and in 1939 was named vice president in charge of medical affairs at the university, a position he held until 1948. Meanwhile, in 1946, he became professor emeritus. In 1941 he was named chairman of the Committee on Medical Research of the Office of Scientific Research and Development, an office founded by President Roosevelt. In 1948, former president Herbert Hoover appointed Richards to the Medical Affairs Task Force of the Commission on the Organization of the Executive Branch of the Government. Also in 1948, Richards became a member of the board of directors of pharmaceutical giant Merck & Company. He had been a consultant to the company since 1931, and between 1953 and 1955 had served as chairman of the Scientific Committee of the board of directors. In 1948, Richards also became an associate trustee of the University of Pennsylvania.

Brief

The new Richards Medical labs were to become part of a large and busy research complex on the south side of the university campus. The building would be surrounded by several predecessors. The 211,140 ft^2 Medical Laboratories building was commissioned in 1904 as a response to the medical school's need for instructional and laboratory space. It was renamed the John Morgan Building in 1987. Construction of the Zoological Laboratory (now the Leidy Laboratory of Biology) added 67,000 ft^2 in 1910, completed by Cope & Stewardson. The 1928 anatomy-chemistry wing added more laboratory facilities to the Morgan building as the campus started to fall behind its research competitors. This phase was funded by the Rockefeller Foundation, which was then headed by former Penn medical professor Simon Flexner.

By the late 1950s the university determined that it was again behind on research space and commissioned Louis Kahn to design the Richards Medical Laboratory. The departments of genetics, physiology, microbiology, and surgical research were the original occupants of the building.

Site

The 262 acre University of Pennsylvania campus is located in the western edge of urban Philadelphia. The laboratory site is part of the medical complex on the south side of the campus. It is bordered to the north by student housing in the 512,000 ft^2 quadrangle, to the east by the 1904 John Morgan Laboratories Building, to the west by smaller laboratories, and to the south by botanical gardens and greenhouses. The Morgan building stretching 337 ft along Hamilton Walk is 192 ft deep and two stories high. The 1928 extension to the Morgan labs added a diagonal wing to the west. Most of these surrounding buildings were designed between 1892 and 1928 by the firm of Cope & Stewardson, a Philadelphia office credited with the proliferation of Campus Gothic style. This series of buildings with their hard burnt brick and Indiana limestone quoins and lintels unified the architectural ambience of Penn's turn-of-the-century growth. A stroll down Hamilton Walk, with sprawling dormitories along its north side and the medical and science buildings on the south, reveals a textbook display of "collegiate Gothic."

To the south of the Richards site is a large botanical garden with a small pond and several acres of green space. Farther to the south is an access road that loops into the university medical complex.

Climate

Philadelphia lies on the Atlantic Coastal Plain about 60 miles inland of the ocean and an equal distance from the Piedmont foothills of the Appalachian mountain range. Both of these geographic features have a moderating effect on the climate, with the ocean providing a general tempering effect and the mountains fending off the flow of continental air from the west. Consequently, long periods of extreme hot or cold weather are unusual. Temperatures above 100°F or below 0°F are rare. The hottest summer days normally range from a low of 68°F to a high of 87°F, and the coldest winter days average correspondingly between 24°F and 39°F. Normal heating degree-days outweigh cooling degree-days by a factor of 4:1 (4824 to 1204).

Bin data for Philadelphia indicates that 16 percent of the annual hours are warm, 19 percent are comfortable, 24 percent cool, 31 percent cold, and 9 percent freezing.

Summer conditions are moderate but on the humid side, with design conditions of 87°F dry bulb and 73°F wet bulb, corresponding to 52 percent relative humidity. Winter design conditions are more severe, with design conditions of 15°F dry bulb and 12°F wet bulb. Snow falls an average of 32 days per year from November to March. Measurable rainfall occurs on 200 days of a normal year, with no dry season and the highest frequency in late summer. Overcast skies dominate 38 percent of all annual hours.

Any medical or biological research lab will have a substantial ventilation requirement and therefore a sizeable thermal load attributable to the constant introduction of outside air. Most conditioned inside air will be exhausted from the building either by fume exhaust hoods at the experiment stations or by the heating, ventilating, and air-conditioning (HVAC) system when it is returned to the air handler.

TABLE 5.2 Normal Climate Data and Graphics for Philadelphia

		Jan.	Feb.	Mar.	Apr.	May	June	July	Aug.	Sept.	Oct.	Nov.	Dec.	Year
Temperature	Degree-Days Heating	1020	863	699	362	118	11	0	2	46	263	550	889	4824
	Degree-Days Cooling	0	0	1	11	68	232	385	337	147	22	2	0	1204
	Extreme High	74	74	85	94	97	100	104	101	100	89	84	72	104
	Normal High	39	42	51	63	73	82	87	85	78	67	55	44	64
	Normal Average	32	34	42	53	63	72	77	76	68	57	47	36	55
	Normal Low	24	26	33	43	53	62	68	66	59	47	38	29	46
	Extreme Low	-7	-4	7	19	28	44	51	44	35	25	15	1	-7
Humidity	Dew Point	22	22	29	38	50	59	65	64	57	46	36	26	43
	Max %RH	74	73	73	72	75	77	79	82	83	83	79	75	77
	Min %RH	59	55	51	48	51	52	54	55	55	54	57	60	54
	% Days with Rain	34	35	44	53	55	48	46	43	39	38	43	40	43
	Rain Inches	3	3	4	3	4	3	4	4	3	3	3	3	41
Sky	% Overcast Days	52	50	48	47	48	40	39	39	37	39	47	48	44
	% Clear Days	22	25	24	21	17	17	13	19	24	30	23	23	22
Wind	Prevailing Direction	WNW	WNW	WNW	WNW	SW	SW	SW	SW	SW	WSW	WNW	WNW	SW
	Speed, Knots	11	12	12	11	9	8	8	7	8	7	10	11	10
	Percent Calm	3	3	2	2	2	2	3	3	3	4	4	3	3
Days	Rain	10	11	13	16	17	15	14	13	12	11	13	12	157
	Fog	13	12	12	12	14	15	16	16	16	15	13	13	168
	Haze	14	13	13	14	18	21	23	22	19	17	14	13	200
	Snow	0	8	5	1	0	0	0	0	0	0	2	6	32
	Hail	0	0	0	0	0	0	0	0	0	0	0	0	1
	Freezing Rain	0	0	0	0	0	0	0	0	0	0	0	0	1
	Blowing Sand	0	0	0	0	0	0	0	0	0	0	0	0	0

INTENTION

Design Team

Louis Kahn (1901–1974) was born on the Russian island of Osel (now Saaremaa, a territory of Estonia) in the Gulf of Riga in the Baltic Sea. His father, a paymaster of the Russian army, and his Lithuanian-born mother were from large Jewish families. They emigrated to the United States a few years after they were married. The family settled in Philadelphia when Louis was five.

Kahn's artistic talent as a youth brought encouragement to pursue painting, and his self-taught piano skills earned him a scholarship at the conservatory. He refused that opportunity to pursue the study of architecture, but played organ music for silent movies to finance his educa-

tion. He entered the University of Pennsylvania in 1920 and studied under the Beaux-Arts French architect Paul Cret (1876–1945). He later worked in Cret's office (1929). In 1930, Kahn married Esther Israeli, a research assistant at the University of Pennsylvania's Department of Neurosurgery.

After his partnerships with George Howe until 1942 and Oscar Stonorov until 1947, Kahn was elected president of the American Society of Planners and Architects. He then set up his own practice and began teaching at Yale University, where he met the art historian Vincent Scully and humanist city planner Lewis Mumford (1895–1990). Both Scully and Mumford championed Kahn's career.

August Komendant met Louis Kahn at the architect's New York office in 1956. Kahn was preparing a complicat-

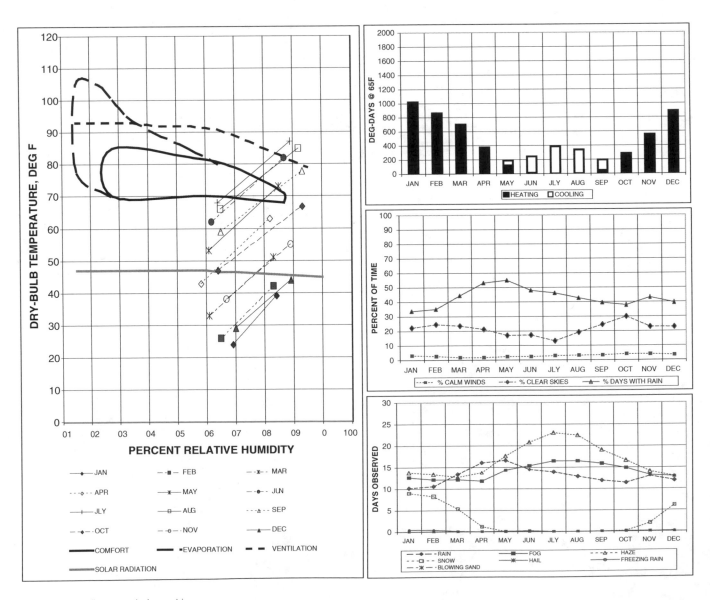

Figure 5.4 Climate analysis graphics.

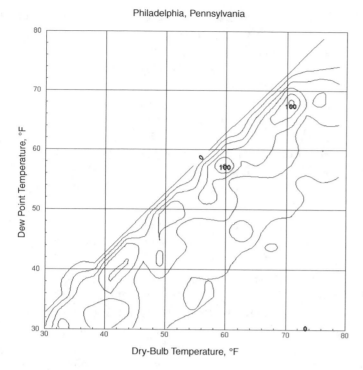

Philadelphia, Pennsylvania

Figure 5.5 Bin data distribution for Philadelphia. Concentric areas of graph indicate the number of hours per year that weather conditions normally occur in this climate. Similar to elevation readings on topographic maps, highest frequency occurrences of weather are at the center peaks of the graph. *(Data sources: Engineering Weather Data, typical meteorological year (TMY) data from the National Climatic Data Center, and the ASHRAE Weather Data Viewer from the American Society of Heating, Refrigerating and Air-Conditioning Engineers.)*

ed entry for a competition, and Komendant was recommended to him by his local engineers, Keast & Hood. Komendant had published a book on advanced engineering and was well known for his prowess at calculations as well as a talent for precast and concrete shell structures. In further conversation Kahn and Komendant discovered that they were both born Estonians.

In the fall of the same year Kahn and a group of his students from Penn visited a concrete precasting plant that Komendant had built and was a consultant for. A couple of weeks later Kahn informed him that he had been commissioned to design a medical research laboratory on the Penn campus and asked Komendant to be his consulting engineer. This began a professional and personal relationship that lasted 18 years. Komendant also joined Kahn at Penn as a teaching professor of architecture (1959–1974).

Rounding out the team were two other notable members. Ian McHarg (*Design with Nature*, 1969) was responsible for landscape design. Fred Dubin, the renowned engineer, consulted on the mechanical systems. Dubin would work with Kahn and Komendant for many years.

Philosophy

Louis Kahn's engineer and fellow Estonian, August Komendant, relates Kahn's reflections on a philosophy of aesthetic realism described by Arthur Schopenhauer (1788–1860). Schopenhauer made beauty and aesthetics a central tenet of philosophical thought and proposed that beauty is manifest in art and nature. For Kahn, this translated into a rationale: Form was the answer to "what," technology was the answer to "how." Image was the creative act and required great intuition. Design was the assimilative work of intellectual analysis, the real "how" that explains the imagination of architecture. Underlying all of this was Schopenhauer's "will to exist" as a driving essential force and the ultimate reality of things. For Kahn, finding the right questions always channeled architecture into the correct path of existence will: "what it wanted to be."

Schopenhauer was one of the first philosophers to study translations of philosophical material from India, and he was greatly influenced by the Upanishads and Buddhism. This interest, coupled with his simple and intelligible writing, made him quite influential outside the realms of philosophy. Louis Kahn enjoyed similar success with his teaching and professional lectures.

Intent

Although Kahn had designed a few projects for medical-related use before Richards, he had no experience with laboratory research facilities. His immediate reaction to the problems presented by the building's functional requirements seems to have been the basis of everything that came after. More than anything else he had encountered, the labs fit into the duality he had perceived as "served and servant." He saw that making this opposition into a monumental work of architecture that expressed the needs of the research institution required two basic remedies.

First, Kahn wished to express clearly the vital role of each element in the life of the building. To achieve this, he would give separate vocabularies to different components: glass to the offices, brick to the services, and concrete to the structure. Second, he would manifest the flow of air through the building, vertically separating outside air inlets from exhaust fumes as a formal statement. He believed that the ventilation systems would be overwhelming in size and too big to conceal; more important, he decided that the control of airflow should be used to express the critical functioning of this new building type.

CRITICAL TECHNICAL ISSUES

Inherent

- Well-diffused ventilation and isolated exhaust of polluted air
- Flexibility of space to meet changing floor area requirements
- Flexibility of services to meet unexpected and evolving needs of different experiments

Contextual

- Relationship to Campus Gothic architecture and pedestrian environment
- Tight site and narrow access, complicating construction
- Small site, dictating a vertically stacked building to satisfy floor space needs

Intentional

- Examination of the new problems confronting architecture as posed by the institutions of science
- Vertical separation of ventilation air and exhaust flues
- Crafting of manufactured components to satisfy desired level of finish
- Innovative precast concrete system posing problem of finding a suitable contractor

APPROPRIATE SYSTEMS

Precedents

An architecture of exposed mechanical elements, and thus of ennobled servicing, was rationalized through the success of Brutalist expressionism. Le Corbusier and Alison and Peter Smithson were perhaps the two most direct antecedents in this line. As technical precedent, Brutalist works introduced the expression of how a building is serviced as a part of its architectural essence and meaning. What Richards Medical wanted to be, in Kahn's mind, was a building manifestly serviced.

Historical and formal precedent for the soaring towers at Richards Medical was drawn from Kahn's three visits to the Mediterranean—in 1928–29, 1950–51, and 1959. The medieval towers at San Gimignano (eleventh to thirteenth century) appear in his 1928 sketchbooks. This small Tuscan hill town once featured 72 such towers, which served as status symbols and fortifications for the clustered palaces of wealthy families. Boiling oil poured from the towers onto invading armies set the town on fire many times. Some of the San Gimignano towers reached 50 m; the Tower of Bologna rises to a grand 96.5 m. These are repeated at Richards Medical as 37 m tall servants hovering 8 m higher than their seated masters in the laboratory blocks.

Kahn's own work before Richards Medical laboratories was limited to smaller projects, and, as happened to many architects of his day, his career was interrupted by the economic depressions of 1929–33 and 1937–38 and then World War II. The Yale Art Gallery (1952–1954) had been the only grand-scale commission before Richards Medical, and Kahn was 50 years old when the Yale project began. The Yale galleries, with their flexible partitions and complex tetrahedral coffered ceiling structure, debuted his modernist ideas of served and servant spaces by exposing air ducts and lighting fixtures. Along the way Kahn had designed some buildings relating to the Richards program: the Radbill Psychiatric Hospital (Philadelphia, Stonorov and Kahn, 1944) with its intriguing stepped shading devices, an occupational therapy building expansion to the Radbill (1950), the Medical Center Building in Philadelphia (1956), complete with portentous concrete vierendeel beams, and the unbuilt Research Institute for Advanced Science (Baltimore, 1956–58).

Kahn's ascent to fame after the laboratories at Richards and Salk was mercurial; it concluded with the National Capital of Bangladesh Assembly Hall (1966–1983, completed by D. Wisdom & Associates) and the Kimbell Art Museum (1966–1972). Louis Kahn died March 17, 1974, in New York City.

Site

Situated between the quadrangle residences and the Hamilton Walk pathway to north and the biological gardens to south, the site offered a natural connection between the two open spaces. On either side, however, were the existing laboratories. The two Goddard biology labs were completed on the west half of the site by Kahn later. The Richards complex is placed against the Morgan Laboratory building with the service tower anchoring its south end. An interior access road serves the southeast corner of the Richards site from the south, with a delivery area and parking lot connecting to a service drive south of the gardens.

Given the small site, a vertical building solution was necessary to achieve the target program floor area. Cramped construction space also dictated that precast concrete components would be erected from trucks. This avoided the need for lay-down space on the site, but it also necessitated a well-coordinated delivery schedule from the concrete plant 40 miles away. Each of the three laboratory towers is connected to the central service tower along one of its center bays, the center bays of the other three façades connect to a service shaft, a stair tower, or a passageway to the next building. This leaves the cantilevered corners floating out from behind the brick-clad servants. The ground floor of the north laboratory tower was left open as an entryway to the complex from Hamilton Walk.

The service tower is treated quite differently, relegated much as the service shafts are to a lesser supporting role. The heights of the small service shafts and the central service tower are even set equal at 121 ft (36.9 m) to mark the similarity of their functions. On the south side of the service tower are four brick air shafts, each of the same proportions as the servant shafts around the laboratory towers. These air shafts cover the only visible façade of the service tower; laboratory towers cover the other three sides. Visually, they seem to be another historical reference, this time to the rhythm of buttressing across the outer walls at the Acropolis, as shown in Kahn's 1951 travel sketches drawn from the Theater of Dionysos in Athens. Beside these shafts, the small empty corner at the southeast side of the complex is where parking and service access are located for both the Richards laboratories and the Morgan Building.

Structure

Richards Medical is one of the first precast concrete buildings in America. Uncertain of whether this innovation would entail slipshod factory components or highly precise industrial pieces, Kahn made a special priority of ensuring well-crafted components with finely detailed connections. His attention paid off. The interlocking concrete beams, the vierendeel beam components, and their posttensioning scheme were strictly of Komendant's expertise and showcased his skills of calculation.

The building frame is prestressed and posttensioned. Three laboratory towers measuring 47.3 ft × 47.3 ft (14.4 m) in plan are seven stories high above grade. Floor-to-floor heights are uniform at 12.0 ft (3.7 m), with 8.5 ft (2.6 m) open height and 3.5 ft (1.1 m) of exposed horizontal structure. These laboratories spin off the eight-story service tower of similar construction. Exterior service shafts of concrete block and brick cladding attach to the open sides of all four towers.

The laboratory towers are framed by eight precast, prestressed concrete columns. These are set at third points of the span, leaving the corners of the frame cantilevered and dividing the bays into nine squares. Two primary vierendeel trusses spanning the 47.3 ft dimension are of precast concrete, with twelve 0.375 in. (9.5 mm) prestressing strands in the top flange and twenty-eight more in the bottom flange. These are crossed by two similar precast trusses made in three parts each, which are posttensioned together between the main trusses to the other four

columns. These members appear identical to the primary trusses and are posttensioned together with three 1.25 in. (32 mm) steel rods. Precast prestressed edge trusses make the outside perimeter. These edge trusses have the same profile as the main trusses but are much thinner in section. Openings at the middle of the edge beams connect to the servant shafts and allow passage of ducts, pipes, and conduits into the ceiling layer.

Each of the nine resulting squares of the laboratory floors are further subdivided into four smaller squares of about 6.0 ft (1.8 m) by precast nonstructural concrete ladder frames. These secondary ladders provide support for service elements routed through the open webs of the frame. Two biology laboratories repeated the same structural scheme to complete the complex over the next two years. These later towers omitted the secondary ladders. Cast-in-place slabs, 4 in. thick and designed for 100 lb/ft^2 loads, made up the supporting floors. After posttensioning, the joints between various precast elements were grouted smooth.

The central service tower was unsuited to precast construction—it was constructed instead of poured-in-place concrete. Keast & Hood engineered this part of the complex along with the servant stacks, basements, and foundations. Komendant was responsible for the precast construction, erection, prestressing, and general supervision.

Because of the congested site conditions with little or no material lay-down area, precast structural pieces were erected directly from delivery trailers. All of the columns and trusses were precast with notches to receive connecting members and to accept posttensioning rods. Construction proceeded at a pace of up to three floors per week.

Envelope

Exposure of the concrete frame with its tapering edge trusses and smoothly grouted connections ensured the visual expression of the structural system. Its actions were made clear and legible. The trusses also supported the brick infill without the use of lintels. Closure to the truss above from the bench height infill wall is made with 0.25 in. monolithic glass set in stainless steel framework. As the trusses taper to the corners of the towers, larger transoms are used to fill the void above the regular-height band of windows resting on the brick. The whole affair—truss, brick, and glass—is set flush in the same vertical plane, smooth and unbroken across the exposed corner of each tower, interrupted only by the protruding column thickness and stainless steel windowsills at the top of the wall and the bottom of the transom. The coordination of material connections was so accurate that inserts to receive the transom glass and the stainless steel window frames were inserted into the concrete columns and edge trusses as they were being precast at the fabrication yard.

Behind the 4 in. brick exterior is a thin insulation cavity and then a 4 in. concrete block wall. A 1 in. thick marble sill caps the masonry and meets the windowsill. The servant tower shafts are clad completely in brick.

Glazing selections for the project consisted of clear glass at the lower levels, changing to progressively darker blue glass at the higher floors. There was no allowance for differences in solar orientation; all walls were treated identically.

Mechanical

Paralleling the strategy of exposing the structural frame, mechanical ducts pipes and conduits in the laboratories were exposed in the ceiling layer between the top and bottom chords of the vierendeel frame. This was intended to have the dual effect of expressing the technical function of the systems and the space they serve, as well as providing access and flexibility. The air-handling plant for the entire building was located on the roof of the service tower and enclosed in a penthouse. Most conditioned supply air and return air from here are distributed down through vertical chases in the main tower.

One of Kahn's programmatic intentions was to separate the polluted exhaust air stream from the fresh air supply. This is accomplished by vertical distance—exhaust plumes are collected vertically at each floor and exit at the top of the servant shafts. Outdoor air, meanwhile, is taken from the bottom of the four large air shafts on the south of the service tower up to the penthouse air handlers. This separation is used to justify the dramatic formal manipulations of the architecture and clarify the distinction between served and servant spaces. Most buildings, including laboratories, accomplish this feat with much simpler means, of course, but Kahn believed that the essence of the building's life, its "existence will," should be expressed in this powerful and exciting way.

Interior

Prior to Richards Medical, laboratory design was generally based on a simple rectangular plan with daylit offices at the perimeter and a separating hallway to the central laboratory spaces and its core of services. Kahn undoubtedly visited Johnson Burgee's Kline Biology Tower at Yale University (1962–1965) and certainly saw Frank Lloyd Wright's 1944 Johnson Wax research tower in Racine, Wisconsin.

Kahn intended each of the spaces in the building to have its own distinct identity, rather than being a repetition of similarly divided rooms within a larger system. He thought that the indeterminate nature of identical rooms off a common corridor violated the nature of space. Consequently, Kahn devoted an entire 2200 ft^2 (204 m^2) floor plate to each lab space and left the circulation to be adapted to the furniture and equipment required in different areas. This decision also reflects his familiarity with architectural studio spaces—the labs are arranged as open studios for science.

Economic restraint exerted greater control on interior finishes than on the general scheme of the building. The concrete structure and floor, as well as the concrete block exterior wall surfaces, were left exposed.

The open floor decision, fundamental as it was to the architectural scheme, proved to be a poor fit with user preferences. Kahn envisioned an integral open space, full of natural light, easily ventilated, flexibly serviced, and without defined circulation. Scientists working in the labs, on the other hand, preferred private spaces, controlled light, dust-free surfaces, and defined paths. Kahn arrived one day and began removing paper that the researchers had taped over the windows, lecturing to anyone who would listen on how the space was to be used. As a compromise, small-scale metal blinds were installed inside the windows to deal with glare. Eventually, however, the floors were partitioned, suspended ceilings were installed, and the mechanical ductwork systems were reworked to suit divided spaces.

TECHNICAL INTEGRATION HIGHLIGHTS

Physical

- Mechanical: Interior—Integration of the service layer into the laboratory ceiling became Kahn's fear of "invasion" by pipes and ducts made real. Coordination of this sort was relatively new with trades and contractors at the time, but eventually the architectural ideas were communicated to the builders.

Visual

- Structure: Envelope—The exposed concrete frame illustrated the life of the structural system, not only by making it part of the envelope, but also by clarifying how its size responded to different loads as it cantilevered out from the columns.

- Mechanical: Envelope—The brick-clad air shafts are far more dramatic than function required, but combined with the stair towers they make for visually convincing service elements. Exposing raw ductwork of any size outside a building would have been too great a leap for one building in this context to make in 1960.

Performance

- Site: Mechanical — The served and serviced aspects of the architectural intention are visually well served by the formal arrangement of building masses.
- Mechanical: Interior — Flexibility was initially provided by the open floor plan and the accessible ceiling service layer.
- Site: Mechanical — Low inlet and high exhaust air streams are separated by the exaggerated vent stacks to prevent cross-pollution of fresh air.

DISCUSSION

The problems encountered at Richards with visually tangled ceiling services, excessive dust-collecting surfaces, poor flexibility, and inattention to issues of light and sun indicate that this laboratory was just the first halting step.

Kahn had found the architectural kernel of mechanical systems in the articulation of served and servant aspects of modern buildings. He was able to convey this concept into a prominent visual and formal statement. Servicing had been ennobled. The functional problems at the labs, however, stemmed from a lack of technical accommodation. Systems aspects were employed at Richards only as formal ploys; their true essence had yet to be conveyed. Commodification of technical systems into the new invisible realities of modern architecture would require further exploration and refinement.

Footnote: the Cornell Agronomy Labs (Ulrich Franzen and Associates, 1968) and Roche Dinkerloo's headquarters for the Knights of Columbus (1969) were two prominent buildings that could be called antecedents to the Richards Medical Laboratories. Both followed Kahn's example of segregating the service systems into external towers and expressing them as distinct formal elements.

2

SALK INSTITUTE FOR BIOLOGICAL STUDIES, 1960–1965

La Jolla, California
LOUIS KAHN

DESCRIPTION

Looking west from the stone-paved courtyard, one sees a patch of ocean framed between the two laboratory wings of the Salk Institute. Sky, water, and stone seamlessly flow together in classic one-point perspective. It is difficult to tell exactly where substance changes phase from solid to liquid to vapor. Even the building looks outward as if its gaze could discern ocean horizon from cloud line. For someone surveying the dividing ribbon of water toward the vanishing point, the surreal silence of empty smooth surface is disrupted when the canyon comes into view below the high bluff. Finally, there are the lower court and the splashing fountain.

It is difficult to avoid the use of mysticism in describing this venerated place. The Salk Institute has had a dazzling effect on architects and architecture since before its completion. It has even been called a dangerous building, in the sense of its assuming more importance than the activity for which it was built.

Comparison of Kahn's landmark building with his Richards Medical is inevitable. His second laboratory revisits many of the concepts he devised for his first "studio of science" in Philadelphia. The personal themes of light, space, and essence are here. His modernist approach to materiality and construction are here. The articulation of served and servant spaces is here. But Salk is quite different from Richards. The first laboratory was remarkable in its interpretation of science into architectural strategies, and it managed to fulfill both the programmatic needs and the design ambitions. These victories made Richards Medical a landmark of transformation; it bridged a gap that had never been engaged so directly before. The second laboratory in La Jolla continues from there and shows how the "accumulated wisdom" of Kahn's contribution to architecture grew from one project to the next, even though they overlapped very closely in time. The Salk Institute is the only building that Kahn claims to have exceeded his own expectations.

Figure 5.6 View toward the Pacific Ocean across the Salk Institute courtyard.

TABLE 5.3 Fact Sheet

Project	**Building Name**	The Salk Institute of Biological Studies
	Client	Jonas Salk, the March of Dimes, and the Kennedy Administration
	City	La Jolla, California (San Diego)
	Lat/Long/Elev	32.88N 117.22W, 360 ft (110 m)
Team	**Architect**	Louis I. Kahn
	Structural Engineer	August E. Komendant and Fervor Dorland & Associates (associated structural engineers)
	Mechanical Engineer	Fred Dubin Associates
	Site Engineers	Rich Engineering Company
	Landscape Architect	Roland S. Hoyt
	General Contractor	George A. Fuller Company
General	**Time Line**	1959–July 1965.
	Floor Area	411,580 ft^2 (38,217 m^2) gross total area; each lab building is 260 ft × 65 ft (79.2 m x 19.8 m); open courtyard is 270 ft by 90 ft (82.3 m x 27.4 m).
	Occupants	Not determined.
	Cost	$11,415,000 or $27.73/ft^2
	Cost in 1995 US$	$56, 231,527 or $136.62/ft^2
	Stories	Three laboratory levels, each surmounted by a 9 ft (2.7 m) interstitial mechanical space. Surrounding office and mechanical wings are six occupied levels, with two of the levels being basements at the east end and all six levels exposed above grade to the western side of the sloping site.
	Plan	Two long laboratory wings divided by an open courtyard. Uninterrupted laboratory floors measuring 65 ft × 245 ft (19.8 m x 74.7 m).
Site	**Site Description**	Occupying 27 acres (10.8 hectares) on a bluff overlooking a deep ravine running to the Pacific Ocean some 350 ft (106 m) below and west of the laboratory.
	Parking, Cars	Open surface lots to south of complex. Visitor lots to east on the street.
Structure	**Foundation**	Basement walls and footings.
	Vertical Members	Concrete walls with color admixture.
	Horizontal Spans	Vierendeel trusses at 20 ft (6.1 m) on center spanning 65 ft (19.8 m) occupy full 9 ft (2.7 m) height of interstitial spaces.
Envelope	**Glass and Glazing**	Laboratory floors are continuously glazed.
	Skylights	None.
	Cladding	Exterior is poured-in-place "pazalonic" concrete formed against polyurethane-coated plywood with champhered joints. Form-tie voids are exposed and plugged with lead.
	Roof	Built-up tar and gravel roof.
	Special Features	Lightwells between labs and surrounding tower structures, 40 ft long and 25 ft deep (12.2 m × 7.6 m) in plan.
HVAC	**Equipment**	Absorption chillers: 233 ton unit for most of the year. Two additional 750 ton units are available for peak summer weather.
	Cooling Type	Chilled water.
	Distribution	Dual duct system in North Building with multiple zone mixing boxes controlled by area thermostats, single duct with local reheat coils controlled by multiple zone local thermostats in South Building.
	Duct Type	Rigid metal.
	Vertical Chases	All duct runs are made in interstitial spaces. Air is distributed to spaces below through aluminum covered slots left in the lab ceilings.
	Special Features	Ventilation of lab spaces requires 100% fresh air and a minimum of 12 air changes per hour.
Interior	**Partitions**	None in laboratories.
	Finishes	Teak shutters used in exterior and interior conditions.
	Vertical Circulation	Courtyard stairs in office carrels. Elevators and fire stairs at perimeter servant towers.
	Furniture	Various.
	Lighting	Fluorescent downlighting.

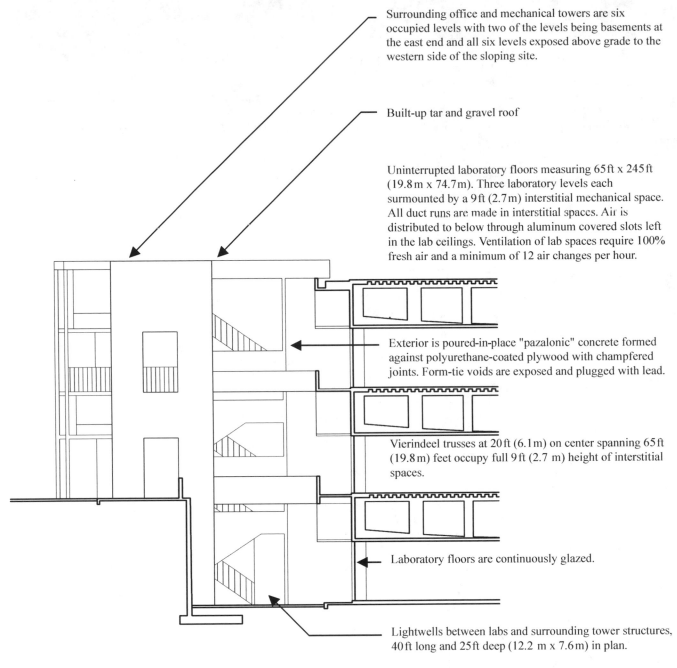

Surrounding office and mechanical towers are six occupied levels with two of the levels being basements at the east end and all six levels exposed above grade to the western side of the sloping site.

Built-up tar and gravel roof

Uninterrupted laboratory floors measuring 65 ft x 245 ft (19.8 m x 74.7 m). Three laboratory levels each surmounted by a 9 ft (2.7 m) interstitial mechanical space. All duct runs are made in interstitial spaces. Air is distributed to below through aluminum covered slots left in the lab ceilings. Ventilation of lab spaces require 100% fresh air and a minimum of 12 air changes per hour.

Exterior is poured-in-place "pazalonic" concrete formed against polyurethane-coated plywood with champfered joints. Form-tie voids are exposed and plugged with lead.

Vierindeel trusses at 20 ft (6.1 m) on center spanning 65 ft (19.8 m) feet occupy full 9 ft (2.7 m) height of interstitial spaces.

Laboratory floors are continuously glazed.

Lightwells between labs and surrounding tower structures, 40 ft long and 25 ft deep (12.2 m x 7.6 m) in plan.

Absorption chillers: 233 ton unit for most of the year. Two additional 750 ton units are available for peak summer weather.

Dual duct system in North Building with multiple zone mixing boxes controlled by area thermostats, single duct with local reheat coils controlled by multiple zone local thermostats in South Building.

Figure 5.7 Anatomical section.

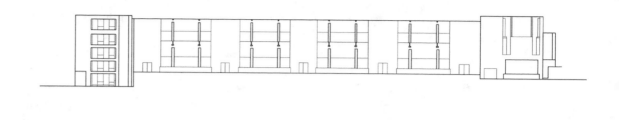

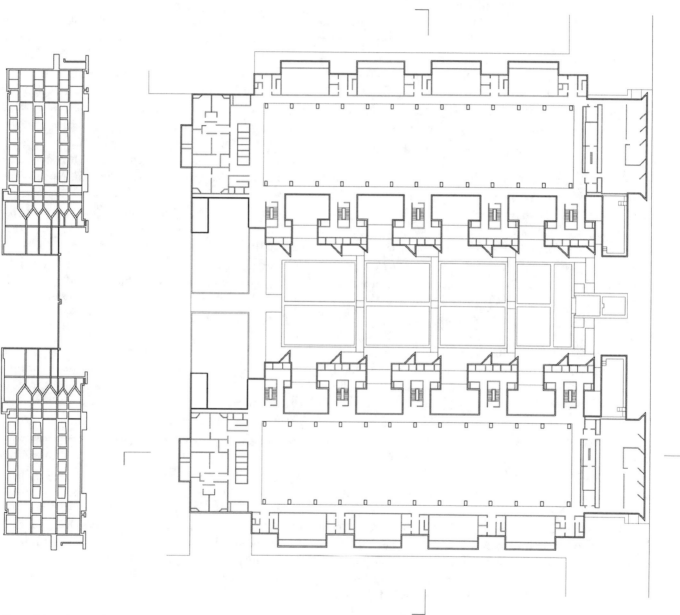

Figure 5.8 Plan, section, and elevation.

0'   20'   40'

10'   30'   50'

PROGRAM

Client

In 1959, Dr. Jonas Salk was working at the University of Pittsburgh Medical School, where he had been director of the viral research lab since 1947. It was here that Salk had developed the first polio vaccine. Rivalry and jealousy over his work was high, and some researchers thought that Salk's success had been too easily gained. Robert Oppenheimer, then director of the Institute for Advanced Studies at Princeton, convinced him that he should start a new institute and move to the West Coast. Later that year, Salk moved ahead with a plan. He secured funding from his longtime ally Basil O'Connor, head of the National Foundation for Infantile Paralysis, which was later renamed the March of Dimes. O'Connor had been appointed by President Roosevelt, who was himself a polio patient. Salk also acquired a gift of 70 acres of land from the city of La Jolla at the urging of their mayor, another polio patient.

Although funding for the Salk Institute came from the March of Dimes, Dr. Salk, by all accounts, filled the role of client alone. His visionary ideals of research activity and human community were the founding principles of the Institute. When Jonas Salk died in La Jolla of congestive heart failure on June 23, 1995, he was working toward a treatment for the disease caused by the human immunodeficiency virus (HIV). He was then 80 years old. Dr. Salk never patented the polio vaccine, and he never profited directly from it.

A friend of Salk's had heard a Louis Kahn lecture, "Order for Science and Art," related to the Richards Medical Laboratory, and suggested that Salk and Kahn meet. In December 1959, Salk interviewed Kahn in Philadelphia, intending only to query him about the best way to select an architect. While touring the Richards Medical Laboratory construction site that same day, however, he was taken with Kahn's enthusiasm and insight. Salk decided to offer him the commission for the new facility.

The story that unfolded is a tale of great success and the interaction of formidable thinkers. For Jonas Salk, the Institute was a "community of mind," where intuition and reason would merge, where the cultures of science and art would harmonize, and where work and spirituality would fuse. Louis Kahn, of course, shared these notions and had complementary motives of his own.

Brief

Having a client of Salk's intellect and visionary drive was of immense benefit to Louis Kahn's work for the Institute. There were some of the normal quantitative stipulations of course, such as a space to be about the same as Richards Medical or roughly 100,000 ft^2 (9,286 m^2). But there was no formal building program given, and Kahn was charged with working one out. There were, however, definite ideas about the qualitative aspects of the Institute. It would have to be a lab worthy, in Salk's words, of "inviting Picasso." Incidentally, this comment seemed especially poignant because Dr. Salk was married to Picasso's second wife, Françoise Gilot, herself an internationally recognized artist, author, and lecturer who had spent ten years with Picasso.

The program and concept of the Institute took form from there. Salk alluded to the cloistered courtyard at St. Francis of Assisi in Italy (1228–1253), where he had stayed briefly in the 1950s and experienced a sudden revelation concerning the polio vaccine. Kahn worked at shaping the requirements for the Institute into an objective program. Salk appointed an advisory committee. Kahn sought strategies for overcoming the problems scientists complained about at Richards. Eventually, Kahn devised a program in three parts: laboratories for eight Nobel-winning scientists, a meeting house to seat 500, and a researchers' community with living quarters and recreation facilities.

The laboratories were to occupy the central position, up on the bluff and set parallel with the ocean. There would be four clear-span laboratories of two stories each so that each researcher would have an entire floor. These independent laboratory spaces are an obvious carryover from Richards Medical, where each floor plate was conceived as one "studio."

The project underwent a series of bad turns about two years into the design work when the Kennedy administration took office in January 1961. Funding for the Institute was drastically reduced from the $20 million initially promised. Further troubles surfaced when the general contractor, George Fuller, complained about Komendant's design for the unfamiliar concrete construction across the long-span laboratories and persuaded Salk's advisory committee to force a redesign. Komendant disputed Fuller's ability to judge the structural design and refused to do further work. Eventually, the laboratory was reduced to two 3-story buildings. The meeting hall and the living community were completely eliminated. The team, fortunately, was reunited.

Site

The Institute sits on 27 acres of ground overlooking the Pacific Ocean, 1360 feet below. It is located across Torrey Pines Road from the University of California at San Diego. A deep, winding dry ravine, eroded into the low scrub brush, runs from the high ground down to the shoreline some 400 yards away.

TABLE 5.4   Normal Climate Data for San Diego

		Jan.	Feb.	Mar.	Apr.	May	June	July	Aug.	Sept.	Oct.	Nov.	Dec.	Year
Temperature	Degree-Days Heating	248	186	176	102	53	12	0	0	0	15	104	230	1115
	Degree-Days Cooling	2	4	5	14	24	67	178	224	187	90	19	2	821
	Extreme High	88	90	93	98	96	101	95	98	111	107	97	88	111
	Normal High	65	66	66	68	69	72	76	77	77	74	71	66	71
	Normal Average	57	58	59	62	64	67	71	72	71	67	62	58	64
	Normal Low	48	50	52	55	58	61	65	66	65	60	53	49	57
	Extreme Low	29	36	39	44	48	51	55	58	51	43	38	34	29
Humidity	Dew Point	43	45	47	50	53	57	61	62	61	56	48	43	52
	Max % RH	70	72	73	72	74	78	80	79	78	75	69	68	74
	Min % RH	58	58	59	60	64	66	66	66	65	64	60	58	62
	% Days with Rain	30	29	31	25	22	17	8	7	12	15	21	24	20
	Rain Inches	2	2	2	1	0	0	T	0	0	0	1	1	10
Sky	% Overcast Days	35	36	32	33	35	30	16	13	20	23	23	32	27
	% Clear Days	34	32	28	28	21	24	28	31	36	34	40	37	31
Wind	Prevailing Direction	NW	WNW	WNW	WNW	WNW	WNW	WNW	WNW	WNW	WNW	WNW	NW	WNW
	Speed, Knots	7	8	9	9	8	8	8	8	8	8	8	7	8
	Percent Calm	12	10	7	5	2	2	1	2	4	7	12	15	6
Days Observed	Rain	9	9	10	8	7	5	3	2	4	4	6	7	73
	Fog	11	10	8	7	6	8	6	7	9	11	11	11	104
	Haze	11	11	9	9	10	14	16	16	17	16	13	12	152
	Snow	0	0	0	0	0	0	0	0	0	0	0	0	0
	Hail	0	0	0	0	0	0	0	0	0	0	0	0	0
	Freezing Rain	0	0	0	0	0	0	0	0	0	0	0	0	0
	Blowing Sand	0	0	0	0	0	0	0	0	0	0	0	0	0

Climate

The La Jolla/San Diego climate is friendly and mild, and the microclimate of the Torrey Pines bluff is little different. Normal temperatures are comfortable and with little variation through the day. The climate is Mediterranean, sunny and dry with less than 10 inches of rain per year. Breezes are steady off the Pacific. Morning fog is frequent. The arid sands sometimes create dusty conditions.

INTENTION

Design Team

Dr. Salk selected a world-famous American architect, Louis Kahn, to design the Institute and worked closely with him to make the building function well for scientific research. Kahn was joined on this project by his trusted consultants, August Komendant and Fred Dubin. This time Kahn's fellow Estonian, Komendant, was in complete charge of the structural design and acted for him in coordinating much of the mechanical work from Dubin's office.

Philosophy

Dr. Salk's ideas about the laboratory as a community of research, and Kahn's ambition to humanize the spaces with silence and light, forged a strong ideological basis for the design. It is fitting that humanist and mathematician Jacob Bronowski (1908–1974) was linked to early conversations on forming the Institute, became one of the first Institute fellows, and remained there for more than 20 years. Bronowski's wife, Rita, was, like Salk's wife Françoise, an artist. Molecular biologist Leo Szilard (1898–1964) was another original Salk fellow and human-

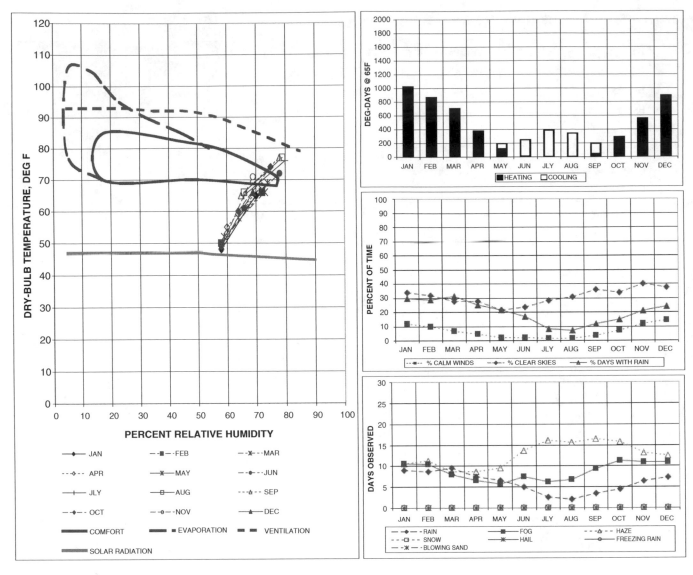

Figure 5.9   Climate analysis graphics.

ist who spent years at Salk. A common thread among these individuals and others in the group was a vital concern for the rift between science and art that C. P. Snow (1959) termed "The Two Cultures." Jonas Salk, in specifically describing why he sought out Jacob Bronowski, stated directly that healing this rift was an explicit intent toward which he would direct the Institute.

The Salk Institute was officially founded in 1964. Salk carefully selected the first group of scientists whom he would invite to work for him. The original fellows of the Institute included mathematician Jacob Bronowski, biophysicist and immunochemist Melvin Cohn, physicist, chemist, and molecular biologist Francis Crick, physician, bacteriologist, virologist, and physicist Renato Duilbecco, physicist Edwin Lennox, biochemist Jacques Monot, physicist and biologist Leo Szilard, and Warren Weaver, engineer, mathematician and physicist. Weaver also served

as chairman of the board of trustees. Charles Wilson began work as the first general manager before the Institute began in La Jolla, and William Glazier continued in the post after 1963. Dr. Salk himself served as the Institute's director until 1975, followed by Augustus Kinzel and, later, Fredric de Hoffman.

Intent

Kahn established four principles to guide the design: flexibility, silence, light, and privacy. Flexibility would be served by open-floor laboratories and independent mechanical spaces. Silence, light, and privacy took the idea of courtyard and translated it into what Kahn called "a jewel surrounded by ruins." The jewel was to be the laboratory space. The ruins were provided by study carrels and stairways that broke the southern California sun and screened the laboratories behind them. The "jewel and ruins" is also a poetic metaphor for the now familiar "served and servant." But the Salk Institute merged these concepts in a more refined way than was managed or probably even imagined at Richards Medical.

CRITICAL TECHNICAL ISSUES

Inherent

- Flexibility of services and floor space
- Air supply and mechanical cooling in the warm temperate climate

Contextual

- Strict structural requirements imposed by earthquake codes
- Capturing views to the ocean and the arroyo
- Lack of room on the site for a crane large enough to handle prefabricated concrete parts for a building complex of this size

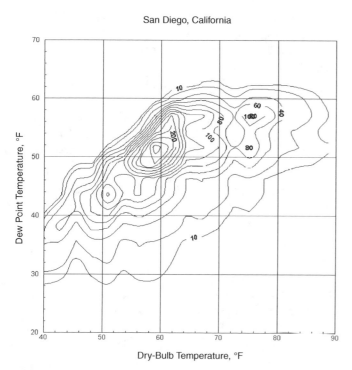

San Diego, California

Figure 5.10 Bin data distribution for San Diego. Concentric areas of graph indicate the number of hours per year that weather conditions normally occur in this climate. Similar to elevation readings on topographic maps, the highest frequency occurrences of weather are at the center peaks of the graph. *(Data sources: Engineering Weather Data, typical meteorological year (TMY) data from the National Climatic Data Center, and the* ASHRAE *Weather Data Viewer from the American Society of Heating, Refrigerating and Air-Conditioning Engineers.)*

Intentional

- Finishing of concrete to the character and color of natural stone
- View and light versus solar heat gain and glare

APPROPRIATE SYSTEMS

Precedent

The Richards Medical Laboratory is the obvious precedent in terms of functional and technical requirements as well as in representing a continuum of the architect's work. The formal precedent was drawn in some part from the monastery at St. Francis in Assisi but is likely related to other influences. Kahn and his team looked at other laboratories, but biological research was still a new field. What they saw were only old buildings with new equipment and lots of exposed rewiring.

Site

The arrangement of the site makes maximum use of its natural slope and open views toward the west. The heavy equipment for mechanical systems is buried in a basement level at the eastern end of the site, and services are distributed vertically through the six levels above it, branching horizontally into the service layer above each laboratory. The east wings also contain exhaust stack vents, and the southeast corner of the complex is used as a service court for deliveries, waste, and heavy equipment maintenance. Parking is along Torrey Pines on the eastern edge of the site and along the southern property line from the service court down the length of the laboratory building.

Structure

The lower-level laboratory rests at what is basement level to the east and terrain level to the west. Rather than having this space buried in darkness, lightwells are pushed 40 ft long by 25 ft deep between the towers on both the courtyard and perimeter sides of the laboratory wings.

The great central courtyard is a story in itself. All through the design, Kahn drew halfhearted schemes for making this into a lush garden. He never quite convinced himself. At one point, he flew Louis Barragan to La Jolla and asked his opinion. Barragan would have nothing planted there and convinced both Kahn and Salk that it should be a "façade to the sky." Kahn later flew to Mexico to visit with Barragan again and consult about details of the travertine landscape.

The key to Salk's open-plan laboratories and tall interstitial spaces is the design of a 9 ft high vierendeel beam that spans 65 ft clear across the laboratories and cantilevers out to support walkways on both sides. The over-all length of the posttensioned beams is 80 ft. Thirteen of them are used at 20 ft centers to support each lab floor above and suspend each mechanical access ceiling below. To meet earthquake requirements for ductile construction, the beams are joined to the supporting columns with lead-zinc plates at every level. Although both Komendant and Kahn would have preferred precast concrete construction, excavation for the lower levels made poured-in-place the only practical solution in concrete.

Envelope

Using the modernism of concrete, as opposed to Mies van der Rohe's modernism of glass and steel, Kahn pushed the material to its limits. Rather than the raw color of *beton brut* construction, he chose to use a pozzolana additive for a warmer tint. Pozzolana is a sandy volcanic ash, available in black, white, gray, and red. It was originally used by the Romans at Puteoli (modern Pozzuoli), near Naples in the region around Vesuvius, but later mined at a number of other sites. In addition, instead of striping off rough concrete forms, Kahn devised and tested methods for ensuring a smooth water-resistant finish with controlled joints and regularly spaced form ties. There was to be no filling, grinding, or painting.

After some experimenting, 0.75 in. plywood form boards were filled, sanded, and finished with six coats of polyurethane. Chamfered edges on each board produced a raised "V" shape at formwork joints. Finally, lead plugs were used to fill each of the form tie holes left in the concrete.

With the long axis of the laboratories stretched east to west, Kahn's surrounding ruins of study carrels and perimeter service towers offer more than adequate protection from direct sun. The overhanging walkways resting on the cantilevered vierendeel beams provide even more shade. The laboratories are thus completely sheltered, and their walls of double-strength glass are liberated to provide what light and view remain. The study carrels are located only at alternating levels of the stair towers within the bands of the vierendeels. This helps to keep some view open from the laboratory levels and makes for a deep, sheltering overhang into the courtyard from each side.

The western views from other spaces are less protected. This creates a conflict between the open views from the site and the unfavorable solar heat gain on this orientation. Kahn used a series of interior teak shutters to match the exterior teak wood infill on western exposures. This affords private views for quiet contemplation in the study carrels and wide vistas from the shared administrative areas while still providing protection from glare, if not

from heat gain. West-facing walls on the first three levels above the lower garden are treated differently—they are held back from the structural edge of the building and protected behind deep porches. At the lowest level, at grade, looking into the ravine, is a continuous *brise soleil* angled at 45 degrees and reminiscent of Corbusier's Carpenter Center in Boston (1961–1964) or the Mill Owners Association in Ahmedabad (1953–1957). This finned shading structure rests its feet in the terminating reservoir of an open-trough drainage system, where it collects what rain does fall in La Jolla. This one formal resolution of structure, guttering, and shading adds an extra dimension to the building's elements and typifies the level of detail found throughout the complex.

Mechanical

The distribution of services in both horizontal and vertical directions is fundamental to the design scheme. Rather than risk the "invasion" of pipes and ducts into the space, Kahn gives them their place in thick layers sandwiched between the labs.

The energy plant for this highly serviced program is set under the entry, beneath the orange grove. The central plant contains a 233 ton absorption chiller, which is sufficient for most of the year, and two 750 ton absorption chillers for peak cooling. The north building is operated with dual-duct distribution heating and cooling, and the south wing uses single-duct cooling with local reheat coils.

Distribution of air to the labs is based on 100 percent outside air 24 hours per day to offset the potential air contamination hazards of working in a biology lab. Each building has three supply fans and two exhaust fans, most of which operate constantly. There is a minimum of 12 air changes per hour. Air and all other services are delivered from the interstitial spaces to the lab benches below via removable aluminum boxes cast into the floor. The service slots are 4.7 ft long by 0.8 ft wide and spaced 5.0 ft apart.

The Institute has two independent sources of power from the local utility company. In addition, the Salk Institute cogenerates its own power with two 650 kW units, each driven by a 950 horsepower engine. In the unlikely event that these three sources fail at the same time, there are two smaller emergency generators to supply power for exit lighting and critical refrigeration.

Interior

Use of interior spaces is separated into three distinct occupancies. The laboratories are group workspaces with views into the gardens, the study carrels are isolated for private contemplation and views to nature, and the shared

Figure 5.11 View toward the courtyard.

administrative areas are given broad vistas to the ocean. The spaces are neatly planned according to this zoning and in harmony with the four principles of intention: flexibility, light, silence, and privacy. The laboratory floors are, of course, left barren for scientific apparatus.

TECHNICAL INTEGRATION HIGHLIGHTS

Physical

- Vierendeel beams form the interstitial cavity for distribution and maintenance of services
- The building is folded into the sloped site to maximize views to ocean

Visual

- An arcaded courtyard aesthetic is achieved by placing the study carrels and their stairs to the garden side of the laboratories and separating these stair towers with lightwells that illuminate the lower-level spaces.

- Placing the study carrels at interstitial levels outside the labs allowed for views across the courtyard. Combining them with the stair towers fulfills the "jewel surrounded by ruins" intention of screening the laboratories from sun and noise. Placing elevator and service towers to the outside perimeter of the labs accomplishes the same purpose.

- Articulation of the joints between the 29 separate structures of the complex into reveals large enough to serve as rainwater gutters forms a system of small troughs that delineate building connections.

- Placing mechanical and storage spaces on the east end of the laboratories reinforces the monumental emptiness as one approaches the courtyard. At the same time, locating conference, library, and offices on the west end allows for views to the ravine and the ocean.

Performance

- The free span of laboratory floors and their large open areas permit flexibility of experiment stations.

- Deep interstitial structural spaces are used for utilities to achieve separation, cleanliness, and flexibility of services.
- Cantilevering the vierendeels allowed greater span, removed circulation space from the valuable area of the laboratory floor, and provided shade to the fully glazed laboratory walls.
- Separation of the complex into 29 structurally independent buildings adds structural ductility and earthquake resistance.
- The large panes of glass used in laboratory and mechanical spaces are easily removed for movement of large pieces of equipment.

Figure 5.12 Dr. Jonas Salk (1914–1995), relating the story of his Institute and his work with Louis Kahn to the Society of Building Science Educators, February 1992.

DISCUSSION

Like that of Richards Medical, the systems perspective at Salk is a direct outgrowth of the size of the mechanical systems and their critical functions. Equally important is the demand for flexibility of services and the number of provisions in each lab space: water, salt water, distilled water, gas, carbon dioxide, propane, and electricity, among others. On the cusp of an age when technical considerations would dictate the fundamental premise of design, the Salk Institute illustrated how architecture can seize technical challenges and interpret them as design opportunities.

Integration logic between the structural and service systems recognizes the demands for free-span flexibility in the laboratory. This is a horizontal reinterpretation of the vertical air stacks at Richards Medical. Because the structure is made 9 ft deep to keep the labs open, the interstitial layers are deep enough to carry mechanical, electrical, and plumbing systems. This also allows ducts, pipes, and wires to be arranged and rearranged according to their own logic rather than made to fit other systems.

Vertical servicing at Salk is largely given over to Kahn's quest for silence and light; both the study towers on the courtyard side and the larger service towers on the perimeter are filters of light and sun. Their strict symmetrical deployment is more monumental than functional-north and south orientations are given the same treatment of overhanging walkways and interposing towers. But the forms certainly modulate the California skies more effectively than they would be if the laboratories were exposed.

3

SCHLUMBERGER RESEARCH LABORATORY, PHASE I, 1985

Cambridge, United Kingdom
MICHAEL HOPKINS & PARTNERS

The Schlumberger Research Laboratory encloses an oil exploration test facility with four noisy experiment stations for drilling equipment and drilling fluids. The program also includes clean research offices and related support spaces. Keeping these antagonistic but programmatically related functions in the same enclosure led Michael Hopkins and his team to design a two-part building scheme with careful connections between them.

Two bays of a large tensile structure (78.7 ft × 59.1 ft, or 24 m × 18 m each) enclose the test stations. A south-facing Winter Garden housing the entrance lobby, cafeteria, and library occupies a third bay. Together they make a 14,000 ft² (1,300 m²) voluminous tent of fiberglass membrane and natural light. At its peak, the tensile enclosure reaches about 40 ft (12 m) above the test bay floor. To each side of the canopied space, and within its superstructure of masts and cables, are lightweight construction office spaces of double-loaded corridors, based on Hopkins's own Patera modular building system.

Figure 5.13   Overview of the Schlumberger Laboratory.

TABLE 5.5 Fact Sheet

Project	**Building Name**	Schlumberger Research Laboratory
	Client	Schlumberger Cambridge Research Ltd.
	City	High Cross Research Park, Madingley Road, Cambridge
	Lat/Long/Elev	52.21°N 0.08°E, about 39 ft (12 m)
Team	**Architect**	Michael Hopkins and Partners
	Structure	Anthony Hunt Associates, structures; Ove Arup Lightweight Structures, membrane
	Quantity Surveyors	White and Turner
	Acoustics	Tim Smith Acoustics
	Services	YRM Engineers
	Construction	Bovis Construction Limited
General	**Time Line**	Commissioned in 1982; construction begun August 1983; 1985 completion; Phase II addition in 1992.
	Floor Area	60,816 ft^2 (5650 m^2).
	Occupants	100.
	Cost	$7,200,000 (£5 million) or $118/ft^2.
	Cost in 1995 US$	$10,198,300 or $168/ft^2.
	Stories	Garden: 55.8 ft (17.0 m) high gallery space.
	Plan	Rectangular, long wings flanking central garden structure.
Site	**Site Description**	A 7 acre (2.8 hectare) site in High Cross Research Park that is owned by Cambridge University.
	Parking, Cars	Surface lot.
Structure	**Foundation**	Garden: Close to 300 pilings of 18 in. (450 mm) diameter were placed 25 to 50 ft (8 to 15 m) deep.
	Vertical Members	Garden: External steel frame. Tubular steel frame towers spaced in 59.1 ft × 78.7 ft (18 × 24 m) bays. Wings: Hollow steel columns at 11.8 ft (3.6 m) centers.
	Horizontal Spans	Garden: Tubular steel trusses 4.9 ft (1.5 m) deep, spanning 78.7 ft (24 m) bays and a superstructure of masts, rods, and cables supporting the fabric roof. Wings: External trusses spanning 43.3 ft (13.2 m) supporting 4.5 in. (114 mm) steel purlins at 3.9 ft (1.2 m) centers.
Envelope	**Glass and Glazing**	21 mm (0.83 in.) thick laminated glass between test station and office. Insulated glass to exterior.
	Cladding	Glass.
	Roof	Garden: Teflon-coated fiberglass fabric membrane with 13% daylight transmission and 20 mm galvanized steel cables sewn into seams to form gridded ribbing. Wings: 1.0 in. (25 mm) galvanized steel roof deck, with single layer polymeric membrane
HVAC	**Equipment**	Central plant located in service yard.
	Cooling Type	Direct expansion chiller
	Distribution	Equipment space routed under the office wings at the edges of the laboratory floor. Office areas have perimeter hot water convection heating coils.
	Duct Type	Rectangular metal ducts below office floors
	Vertical Chases	None.
Interior	**Partitions**	Garden and wings are separated by 0.83 in. (21 mm) laminated glass.
	Finishes	The partitions include white boards in every office.
	Vertical Circulation	None.
	Furniture	Various.
	Lighting	Fluorescent troffers.

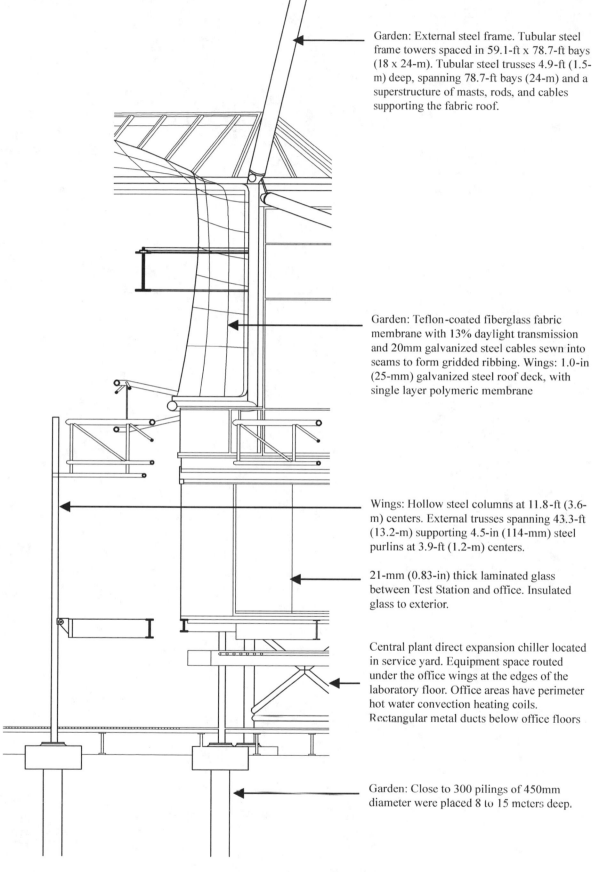

Garden: External steel frame. Tubular steel frame towers spaced in 59.1-ft x 78.7-ft bays (18 x 24-m). Tubular steel trusses 4.9-ft (1.5-m) deep, spanning 78.7-ft bays (24-m) and a superstructure of masts, rods, and cables supporting the fabric roof.

Garden: Teflon-coated fiberglass fabric membrane with 13% daylight transmission and 20mm galvanized steel cables sewn into seams to form gridded ribbing. Wings: 1.0-in (25-mm) galvanized steel roof deck, with single layer polymeric membrane

Wings: Hollow steel columns at 11.8-ft (3.6-m) centers. External trusses spanning 43.3-ft (13.2-m) supporting 4.5-in (114-mm) steel purlins at 3.9-ft (1.2-m) centers.

21-mm (0.83-in) thick laminated glass between Test Station and office. Insulated glass to exterior.

Central plant direct expansion chiller located in service yard. Equipment space routed under the office wings at the edges of the laboratory floor. Office areas have perimeter hot water convection heating coils. Rectangular metal ducts below office floors

Garden: Close to 300 pilings of 450mm diameter were placed 8 to 15 meters deep.

Figure 5.14 Anatomical section.

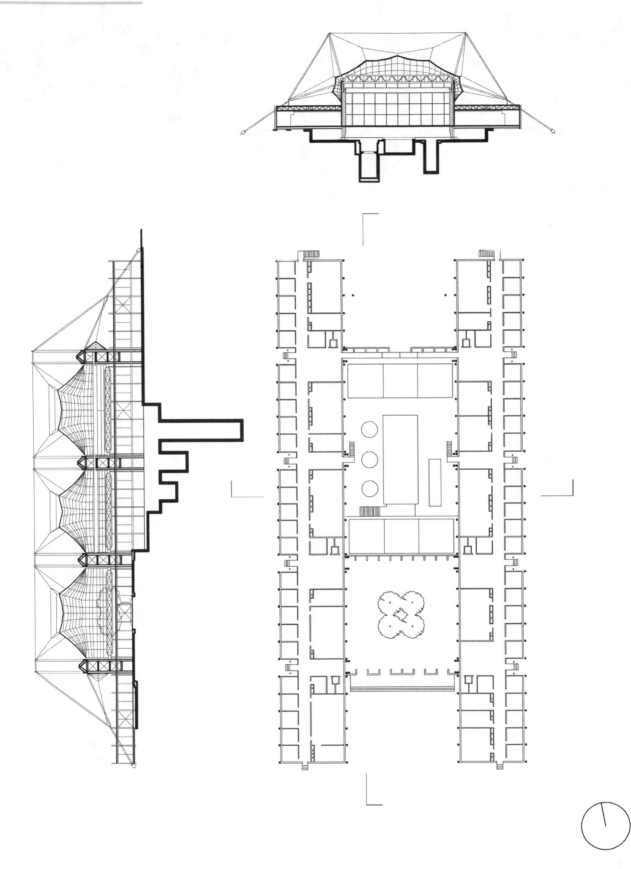

Figure 5.15 Plan and section.

PROGRAM

Client

Schlumberger Oilfield Services provides a variety of technical services and products to the petroleum energy industry. Globally, Schlumberger has more than 50,000 employees and operations in more than 100 countries. Over the years the company has gained recognition for its high-technology approach to oil exploration by advancing scientific methods for finding, proving, and extracting resources. In keeping with this image, Schlumberger has patronized modernist architects: Philip Johnson and Howard Barnstone (1953 headquarters in Ridgefield, Connecticut), Renzo Piano (1981 renovation of engineering works in Paris), and Emilio Ambaz (1984 design for an unbuilt laboratory in Austin, Texas).

The Cambridge facility was the second Schlumberger laboratory for energy research and development. The Schlumberger-Doll Research complex in Ridgefield, Connecticut, had been in operation since the 1940s. The Cambridge facility was expanded in 1992, and Schlumberger Stavanger Research was established in 1999 to conduct studies at strategic worldwide locations. Currently, the Cambridge location is moving toward a large expansion to the east of the existing structures.

Brief

Schlumberger's brief to Michael Hopkins and Partners stipulated a balanced solution—it must be "creative yet functional, attractive but not flashy." This was to be a building that impressed without "later disappointment" and where "quiet professionalism" was revealed by famil-

TABLE 5.6 Normal Climate Data for Cambridge, UK

		Jan.	Feb.	Mar.	Apr.	May	June	July	Aug.	Sept.	Oct.	Nov.	Dec.	Year
Temperature	Degree-Days Heating	814	738	709	575	397	225	122	119	231	433	635	746	5726
	Degree-Days Cooling	0	0	0	0	1	10	26	24	2	0	0	0	60
	Extreme High	57	63	69	72	82	91	91	93	84	79	63	61	93
	Normal High	43	43	48	53	60	65	70	70	64	57	49	45	56
	Normal Average	39	39	42	46	52	58	62	62	57	51	44	41	49
	Normal Low	34	33	36	38	44	50	54	53	50	45	39	36	43
	Extreme Low	12	10	22	25	30	36	41	41	34	28	21	7	7
Humidity	Dew Point	35	34	36	38	44	50	53	53	50	46	40	38	43
	Max % RH	90	90	91	90	90	90	90	92	92	93	91	91	91
	Min % RH	82	77	70	61	62	62	59	57	62	73	80	84	69
	% Days with Rain	50	40	36	43	36	36	36	40	36	43	46	46	41
	Rain Inches	2	1	1	2	2	2	2	2	2	2	2	2	22
Sky	% Overcast Days	37	34	33	24	21	19	16	16	19	25	29	33	26
	% Clear Days	6	7	6	7	6	4	6	7	6	6	7	5	6
Wind	Prevailing Direction	SW	E	W	N	N	N	W	SW	SW	SW	SW	SW	SW
	Speed, Knots	9	10	11	9	9	8	8	8	8	9	9	9	9
	Percent Calm	3	3	3	3	3	3	3	4	3	5	3	2	3
Days Observed	Rain	15	12	11	13	11	11	11	12	11	13	14	14	148
	Fog	16	14	14	12	14	14	11	15	14	17	16	17	174
	Haze	16	17	18	18	18	18	16	19	17	18	17	17	209
	Snow	8	6	5	3	#	#	0	0	0	#	2	4	28
	Hail	#	0	#	#	#	#	0	0	0	#	#	0	1
	Freezing Rain	#	1	0	0	0	0	0	0	0	0	0	0	1
	Blowing Sand	0	0	#	#	#	#	#	0	#	#	#	#	1

iarity. The client's more objective concerns emphasized cross-contact between the testing area and adjacent departments in the laboratory. A significant 50 percent expansion capability also had to be programmed into the solution.

Physical specifications for the testing area were dominated by a 10 ton gantry crane with tracks running the length of the test floor and complete freedom to move from side to side. Below the gantry crane, the test area was to shelter four experimental drilling pits, an underground high-pressure pump chamber for drilling fluids, and the all-important drilling Test Station.

Site

The Cambridge laboratory is constructed on a clear, featureless, and nearly level plot of 17.5 acres (7 hectares) east of the city. The site is rectangular, with its long axis run-

ning north to south. It is on the eastern edge of Cambridge University's High Cross Research Park. This association contributes to Schlumberger's close ties with the knowledge base of university research in oil exploration and recovery.

High grade elevations relative to surrounding sites favor good views to the east toward the rooftops of Cambridge building monuments and to the southeast countryside. The openness of the site contributes to frequently windy conditions.

Climate

Cambridge, with Stansted airport to the immediate south, shares the general characteristics of southern England climates and is typified by cool air and gray skies. Frontal movements from the north frequently produce rapid changes in daily weather.

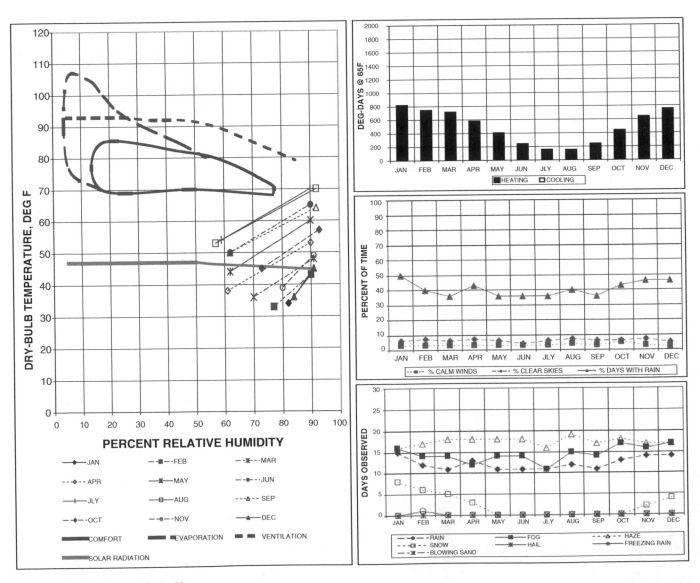

Figure 5.16   Climate analysis graphics.

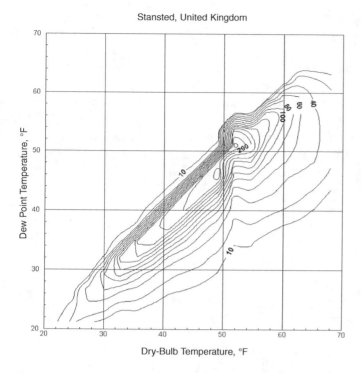

Stansted, United Kingdom

Figure 5.17 Bin data distribution for Cambridge, United Kingdom. Concentric areas of graph indicate the number of hours per year that weather conditions normally occur in this climate. Similar to elevation readings on topographic maps, highest frequency occurrences of weather are at the center peaks of the graph. *(Data sources: Engineering Weather Data, typical meteorological year (TMY) data from the National Climatic Data Center, and the* ASHRAE *Weather Data Viewer from the American Society of Heating, Refrigerating and Air-Conditioning Engineers.)*

The overcast sky at this 52°N latitude location will exceed 750 footcandles on horizontal surfaces for more than 80 percent of annual daylight hours. Because the fiberglass canopy of the central space is about 13 percent transmitting of visual light, the envelope will glow at a minimum brightness of about 100 footlamberts throughout most days. This is ample for interior lighting and diffusion into the adjacent office spaces but controlled enough to prevent glare. The design team estimated that a minimum 23 footcandles (250 lux) of natural illumination would be available at task height in the Test Station during daytime work hours.

INTENTION

Design Team

During his early career, Michael Hopkins worked in partnership for eight years with Norman Foster, from about 1969 to 1975. The two met right after the Team 4 partnership of Norman and Wendy Foster plus Richard and Su Rogers had broken up. Initially, Foster and Hopkins worked on a project Hopkins brought in for the planning of an industrial complex in Yorkshire. The two worked together on Foster's project for IBM in Cosham and incorporated ideas they shared based on the Eames House and the Californian School Construction System. They worked with component catalogs and dry construction techniques. After the Willis Faber Dumas Insurance Headquarters (see case study #7) project in Ipswich, however, Hopkins had enough ideas and business contacts to develop in partnership with his wife, Patty. Michael Hopkins & Partners was formed in 1976 with five founding partners: Michael Hopkins, Patty Hopkins, John Pringle, Ian Sharratt, and Bill Taylor. Their first project seems to have been a London office for Willis Faber Dumas in Trinity Square. The Hopkins residence, an Eames-like manifesto, was built in London in 1976, and in 1984 the firm built its offices in the Marylebone section of London, just west of Regents Park.

Philosophy

The work of Michael Hopkins & Partners is known for its pragmatic directness, lightweight structure, and Miesian detail. Hopkins calls himself "an engineering architect." The firm's subjective notions have shown a fondness for Frei Otto, Buckminster Fuller, Paxton's Crystal Palace, the Eames House (see case studies #14 and #18) and the tension between nature and artifice. The association with Frei Otto makes for a particularly interesting set of connections. Hopkins has had a long association with engineers Buro Happold, which was founded by Ted Happold, formerly of Arup & Partners. Happold in turn is a collaborator and friend of Frei Otto. Buro Happold and Otto jointly received the 1996 Aga Khan Award for Architecture in recognition of their joint venture project at Tuwaiq Palace, Riyadh, Saudi Arabia, completed in 1985. Ted Happold is, coincidentally, the Arup contact who involved Piano + Rogers in the Centre Pompidou competition of 1971 (see case study #22).

Much of Hopkins's early work was greenfield, rural, and devoted to technical exploration. More recent projects have addressed urban environments and adapted more to context. At this writing, all of the firm's work has been in the United Kingdom.

Intent

The large clear-span space for unobstructed operation of the 10 ton gantry crane seems to have fueled Hopkins's determination to cover the space with an externally stressed fabric skin. Likewise, the programmatic requirement for close communication between Test Station and laboratories provoked the decision to cluster all four elements of the complex into one building: testing, laboratories, offices, and recreation.

CRITICAL TECHNICAL ISSUES

Inherent

- Noise isolation between the Test Station and the laboratories. Generated sound levels in the drilling pits can reach 120 dBA and sporadic noise on the test bay floor area can exceed 90 dBA.
- Reverberant noise control in the Test Station area.
- Danger of explosion in the Test Station due to high-pressure and high-temperature fluids.
- Expansion of the facility at a future date to accommodate change and growth.

Contextual

- Research park setting, connections to university and site.

Intentional

- Daylighting and solar heat gain in the Test Station.
- Stability of fabric structure in windstorms.

APPROPRIATE SYSTEMS

Precedent

The Schlumberger fabric roof was the first major Teflon-coated fiberglass membrane project in the United Kingdom. The use of tensile fabric membranes had been more popular outside Britain. In 1980, for example, SOM architects used a fabric roof to cover the immense 5.4 million ft^2 (500,000 m^2) roof of the Haj Terminal at Jeddah. Hopkins took his clients to the United States to visit fabric roofs at two Bullocks department stores that were already more than ten years old before the Schlumberger scheme was decided. On the same trip they also saw a pneumatically supported fabric roof at the University of Santa Clara sports facility.

Frei Otto's fabric structures were more free-form. Hopkins showed how tensile membrane construction like Otto's could be combined with conventional frame building. He had done a few fabric structures before, including a converted parking garage for Willis Faber Dumas (now Willis Coroon) and Mound Stand Lord's Cricket Ground (1985–1987).

Site

The Winter Garden sits on the highest point of the site, and natural grade elevation on the site falls gently to the north end. Hopkins cut the lower area for the two testing bays down 7.8 ft (2.5 m) below the office wing floor to provide more overhead clearance for movement of drilling equipment. This lower level also undercuts the laboratory wings to create continuous mechanical service cores along both sides of the Test Station. A service road and parking area separate the building from the north end of the site. Chiller plant, boilers, and a service loading area are located on the north end of the testing area in a courtyard formed between the extended office/lab wings.

The undercroft mechanical basement is set level with the test area floor slab and undercuts the inside half of the office/lab wings. These mechanical rooms run along the two test bays but terminate before crossing into the Winter Garden. The excavation material was used to berm under the office/lab floors. The embankment produces an artificially level grade along the building perimeter from the high south to north.

Rainwater from the fabric roof flows across the flat office area roofs, where it is collected in roof drains. Site drainage runs from higher elevations to the south and down across the north utility drive and parking areas. Eventually, all storm water is collected in a holding pond at the northern low end of the site close to the main road.

Parking for about 100 cars is available at the southern main entry to the site, where the Phase 2 addition sits. More parking is provided off the service road on the opposite end of the property. Recently, the Madingly Road park-and-ride began operation just across the road, with frequent bus service to downtown Cambridge. There is also a network of bicycle paths connecting the research park and the city.

Structure

The laboratory's two structural systems operate independently. They have no common-load resisting elements and are coupled only by weatherproof connections and sound-isolation barrier walls.

Construction of the sophisticated fabric roof covers three independent bays of structure measuring 78.7 ft wide × 59.1 ft deep (24 m × 18 m) each. The bays are arrayed in a line stretching from north to south across the site. Four portal frames of 7.8 ft (2.4 m) wide prismatic girders divide the three separate canopies by spanning the test area and resting on vertical trusses at both ends. The top corners of each portal frame establish support points for long steel tube booms that resemble masts of a sailing ship and serve as primary external supports for the fabric roof. These corner points each support a pair of outward-sloping booms rising above the girders and a lower pair of outrigger booms. The upper boom is 12.9 in. (328 mm) in diameter, and the lower boom measures 10.75 in. (273 mm) in diameter. Both booms are hollow-section tubes with 0.31 in. (8 mm) walls. Solid steel 2 in. (50 mm) tension rods connect the ends of the upper booms across the roof, then down above the office wings to the lower outrigger booms, and finally to the ground, where they tie to 17.7 in. (450 mm) diameter pilings driven 25 to 50 ft (8 to 15 m) deep. All of the perimeter pilings that carry the loads of the fabric roof are raked inward to resist the upward lift of the tensioned steel frame superstructure.

The tension rods stabilize the frame in cross section from ground to lower boom, then to upper boom, across the roof, and back down to grade again. A similar set of tension rods runs perpendicularly across the bays, tying the upper booms into pairs and the boom pairs together and back to pilings in the long plan axis. Together, the booms, rods, and pilings make a tension-braced structure from which the three fabric roof membranes are stretched.

The three structurally separate bays of roof fabric are installed identically. Each is continuously clamped along its four edges to the building frame just above the exposed roof joists of the laboratory office wings. Cables attached at five lifting points across the membrane span suspend the fabric from the upper booms, making for ten lift points for each bay. The dome of the completed tensile roof describes an arch of about 62 ft (20 m) radius.

The Teflon-coated fiberglass membranes are factory prefabricated from flat strips calculated by the engineers at Arup's Lightweight Structures division to form double curved surfaces when tensioned into place. Fabric strips are bound together by heat welding the seams under intense pressure for several minutes. This welding process can be performed only in factory conditions before the membrane comes to the construction site. Integrity of the seam is produced by melting the Teflon coating until the surfaces fuse. The fabric assembly is reinforced on its perimeter by an 0.8 in. (20 mm) galvanized stranded steel cable that secures its edge to the building frame. An additional network of 1.4 in. (36 mm) stranded steel ridge cable was fixed to the fabric on-site via membrane fixing clamps to provide cable lifting points and resistance to the required surface stresses imposed to keep the membrane taut. Electric wenches were used to lift the fabric canopies into place during construction.

For the long office wings flanking both sides of the fabric-roofed center bays, Hopkins used an adaptation of his Patera modular building system. This example is a refinement of the 1976 design for the Hopkins residence and the 1982 version of the prefabricated kit building system. It consists of a simple but elegantly refined metal framing system with glass and insulated metal sandwich infill panels and fulfills some of the ambitions of the Eames House (see case study #18). The envelope hangs behind a steel framing system with a 5.5 in. × 0.3 in.

(139 × 8 mm) circular hollow section supporting the outer extent of roof and floor framing. A roof truss of 4.5 in. × 0.2 in. (114 × 5 mm) top chord and 3.0 in. × 0.2 in. (76 × 4 mm) bottom chord are pin connected to lugs welded on the exterior column. Floors are formed over a 16.0 in. × 7.0 in. × 49.7 lb/ft (406 × 178 mm × 74 kg/m) galvanized steel beam bolted to another column flange. A 10 in. × 5.7 in. × 20.8 lb/ft (254 × 146 mm × 31 kg/m) galvanized steel edge beam is bolted between the floor beams. Identical attachments are made at the inside wall where the structure remains independent of the canopy's steel superstructure.

Office floors are insulated sandwich panels of 24 in. (60 mm) polystyrene between 0.9 in. (22 mm) chipboard surfaces. These are laid over 2.8 in. (70 mm) deep profiled steel decking. Flooring panels are interrupted at the perimeter by convection heaters laid directly on the decking and sit flush with the finished floor. The roof is suspended from the overhead truss via 1.0 in. (25 mm) profiled steel deck resting on 4.5 in. × 2.9 in. (114 × 73 mm) galvanized purlins carried below the truss. The edge thickness of polystyrene insulation above the deck and 4.6 in. (100 mm) mineral wool insulation under the deck are concealed behind an aluminum fascia panel.

Envelope

Complete physical integration achieved by the stressed fabric roof and its supporting tensioned steel frame makes it difficult to address the envelope system as a separate entity from the structural system. Their symbiotic components, the visual distinction of one system versus the other, and even their respective functional mandates are inextricable. Rather than divide the discussion into remote categories, a description of the roof canopy portion of the envelope has been included with details of the basic structure.

At each end of the fabric roof and between each of the three bays, the steel prismatic girder is capped by a continuous triangle section skylight of clear insulated glass. These four steel-frame and glass-clad interruptions provide a view of the sky from the membrane-covered floor areas. They also include pneumatically operable panels for natural ventilation in warm weather. More glass is used to cap the ends of the prismatic girders and is carried down as vertical view glass to the top edge of roof trusses over the office/lab wing.

At both the south Winter Garden façade and the north Test Area elevation of the structure, closure is finished by glass panels set in aluminum frames and several matching sets of glass doorways. To visually emphasize the dominant fabric membrane roof enclosure, sections of the same fabric construction are stretched laterally in front of the upper glass panels.

Figure 5.18   Interior view.

Clerestory windows of 0.31 in. (8 mm) float glass are used above the office wings and below the fabric roof, in the space behind the trusses supporting the office roofs. These windows provide a greater view of the unobstructed sky, connect the two structures, allow for differential thermal movement between them, and complete the envelope enclosure.

Single-story lab/office wings make up the east and west elevations. These are fully glazed with floor-to-ceiling 9.5 ft (2.9 m) 1.0 in (24 mm) thick insulated units of .24 in (6 mm) tempered clear glass, providing u = 0.5-Btu/hr ft^2 °F (2.8 W/m^2°C). These units are operable so that each scientist can open his or her space to the outdoors in lieu of mechanical cooling. Roof and floor insulation levels are as described in the section on structure and provide u = 0.04 Btu/hr ft^2 °F (0.22 W/m^2 °C) and 0.08 Btu/hr ft^2 °F (0.45 W/m^2°C), respectively. Shading, privacy, and glare control are provided by retractable sunscreen louvers fitted outside the exterior columns. These consist of 3.1 in. (80 mm) wide aluminum louvers on 0.16 in. (4 mm) stainless steel cables fixed between an aluminum head box and a lower bracket. The 11.8 ft (3.6 m) wide shading assembly is mounted on lugs welded to the column at the same level as the floor beam and roof truss lower chord supports.

Electronic controls operate the shades in response to temperature and wind. Manual overrides allow occupants to choose their own settings spontaneously.

The office/laboratory bays are left open every sixth bay for egress stairs. These four stairs adjoin the discussion areas on each side of the building and coincide with the divisions of the center tensile structure where the portal frames cross.

Mechanical

The cool temperate climate permits a passive approach to controlling comfort levels in the testing bay and Winter Garden. These spaces are tempered by mechanical heating in severe winter weather. Because the Test Station is insulated by the fabric roof to only u = 1.0 Btu/hr ft^2 °F (5.7 W/m^2°C) construction, the building code allows only partial heating. Convection heaters in the space are thus limited to 8.0 Btu/ft^2 (25 W/m^2). Some additional heat in the test bays is gained from the warmer laboratory spaces through the uninsulated glass walls separating the two spaces. Programming of the Winter Garden space to include reception and library spaces as well as the dining and lounge areas led to provision of eight 94,000 Btuh (30 kW) space heaters. These units represent 50 percent of the total heating capacity for the entire building. The south-facing Winter Garden also benefits from direct solar gain. Passive summer ventilation of the Test Station draws outside air under the office wings, across the undercroft, and then exhausts air through operable sections of the skylights above the portal frames.

Central plant chillers and boilers are enclosed in modular buildings sitting north of the laboratory wings, where they help to enclose the service yard. These separate enclosures are moveable should the research facility be extended to the north. Laboratories are mechanically heated and cooled year-round. Offices are heated only by means of convection coils and are ventilated naturally by provision of the operable glass walls—at 9.5 ft (2.9 m) high they can hardly be called doors. Air-handling units are placed in the undercroft alongside the Test Station floor, and ducts are routed under the laboratory floors. Primary electrical, plumbing, gas, compressed air, storage tanks, and other services are organized in this undercroft as well. At the south end of the Test Station the undercroft crosses from east to west to form a perimeter service belt on three sides of the Test Station. This arrangement keeps mechanical systems off the roof, which in this case is rather limited as to space anyway. An aluminum grate deck across the Test Station serves as a raised floor, separates the drilling equipment below from the walking space above, and allows services to cross from one side of the building to the other unhindered. The design essentially places all the building service elements in the same concentrated engineering space as the drilling test equipment.

Interior

The four portal frames that define the bays of the building also punctuate its interior. Entry through the south portal into the Winter Garden reception area opens beneath the billowing luminous canopy that undulates over the three center bays. The size and brightness of the fabric surface dominates the interior as much as it does the exterior and the site perspectives of the building. Views from the Winter Garden are dominated by the overhead canopy. Surrounding spaces are screened—the Test Station floor is a level below the Winter Garden; the library limits sight lines to the west, and the kitchen wall blocks the right. Discussion areas flank the sides of the Winter Garden and are connected to it through opening glass walls. Outer wings of the office/laboratory spaces are similar to one-another, with laboratories and workshops occupying the inside half, then a corridor and small perimeter offices completing their width. The wings extend four bays past the Winter Garden and five bays past the Test Station to create an entry court and a service court (each bay is 11.5 ft, or 3.6 m, wide).

The Winter Garden is flanked by the kitchen to the east and a library to the west. Various laboratories and workshops make up the rest of the rooms that face in from the wings: fluid mechanics, rock physics, wellborne physics, and drilling mechanics. These all look down 8.2 ft (2.5 m) into the Test Station. At the north end of the wide center bay is a bridge from the east wing to the west connecting two discussion areas without interrupting the north wall service access doors. There are two stairs down along the center of the Test Station's length, one from each wing.

Finishes in the office and laboratories is generally of studded rubber or carpet tile flooring and 23.6 in. × 23.6 in. (600 × 600 mm) perforated steel acoustical ceilings. Glazing separations between the laboratories and the Test Station are 0.8 in. (21 mm) thick laminated clear glass, providing about 40 dB of noise isolation, about the practical limit of monolithic glass. Lighting fixtures are recessed into the 6.0 in. (150 mm) deep ceiling insulation.

TECHNICAL INTEGRATION HIGHLIGHTS

Physical

- Cut-and-fill earthwork took full advantage of existing grade elevations to lower the test area floor level, provide an undercroft mechanical basement, level the office wing terrain, and promote drainage to the storm water pond at the north end of the site. This was accomplished with a minimum of imported fill.

- Structure, envelope, and interior are unified in the tensile fabric enclosure.

- Separation of people spaces from equipment areas is attained by setting the office, laboratory, and Winter Garden 8 ft (2.4 m) above the level for the Test Station and mechanical equipment.

Visual

- Expression of the structural systems as an external frame gives the building legibility and expresses the theme of natural versus man-made.

- Transparent walls and the translucent roof provide light and views to the interior.

Performance

- The fabric structure and its external tension frame allow for a long span across the heavy equipment test area and unobstructed movement of the 10 ton (9 tonne) gantry crane.

Figure 5.19   Schlumberger by night.

- The fabric membrane incorporates daylighting into both the test area and the adjacent lab/office spaces while limiting glare from the unobstructed sky.

- The fabric membrane is non-sound reflective, helping to quiet noise levels inside the Test Station.

- Thick laminated glass divisions between test areas and adjoining spaces provide both acoustical control and explosion protection to the office/lab wings.

- Incorporating mechanical spaces into the undercroft of the office/lab wings grouped all of the heavy equipment together in a single zone. Maintenance can be performed from the service yard at the lower north end of the building without interrupting the quieter office and laboratory wings.

- Lightweight modular enclosure of the main mechanical plant allows for future extension to the north.

DISCUSSION

Fifteen years after its completion, Schlumberger was satisfied enough with the Phase I building and the addition to propose repeating the same scheme for an adjoining facility. Hopkins & Partners, meanwhile, went on to design other tension fabric structures:

- Willis Faber Dumas Computer and Service Center, Ipswich (conversion of parking garage adjoining the WFD headquarters), 1982–1985

- Mound Stand, Lord's Cricket Ground, Westminster, London, 1984–1987

- Younger Universe Pavilion, Edinburgh, Scotland, 1990

- Inland Revenue Center, Nottingham, 1992–1994

4

PA TECHNOLOGY LABORATORY, 1982–1984

Hightstown, New Jersey
RICHARD ROGERS PARTNERSHIP LTD.

DESCRIPTION

The Richard Rogers Partnership's first work in the United States was for an old client, PA Technology (presently PA Consulting Group). The client asked for a highly visible building that would express the technological and innovative character of the company. The solution is an industrial building on an open landscape resembling an ocean liner or transport on a sea of poppies. In contrast to the red masts of the exposed structure and silver ventilation systems above, the hull of the building is clad with a visually simple envelope of translucent wall panels and a strip of clear glazing.

Figure 5.20   Overview of the laboratory. *(3-D rendering by Travis Hughs.)*

TABLE 5.7   Fact Sheet

Project		
	Building Name	PA Technology Laboratory
	Client	PA Technology
	City	Hightstown, New Jersey
	Lat/Long/Elev	40.17 N 74.37 W, 105 ft (32 m)

Team		
	Architect	Richard Rogers Partnership
	Structure	Ove Arup & Partners, Peter Rice
	Services	Ove Arup & Partners
	Associate Architects	Kelbaugh and Lee
	Construction	John W. Ryan Construction
	Cost Management	Hanscomb Associates

General		
	Time Line	Early 1982 to October 1984.
	Floor Area	41,849 ft² (3886 m²).
	Occupants	Not determined.
	Cost	$4.7 million or $112/ft².
	Cost in 1995 US$	$6.7 million or $159/ft².
	Stories	One 12 ft (3.7 m) ceiling interior space under a 14.8 ft (4.5 m) roof.
	Plan	Rectangular, 236 ft × 172 ft (72 m × 52.5 m). The nine bays are 29.5 ft (9 m) wide and span 75 ft (22.5 m) to each side of the 25 ft (7.6 m) wide center spine. Planning grid of the interior is divided into 29.5 ft × 14.75 ft (9.0 m × 4.5 m) zones.

Site		
	Site Description	10 acre (25 ha) level grassland tract in 100 acre (250 ha) research office park 8 miles southeast of Princeton, New Jersey.
	Parking, Cars	Surface parking at building.

Structure		
	Foundation	Concrete slab on grade with pad footings.
	Vertical Members	Nine 24.6 ft (7.5 m) wide A-frame bipod masts of 12 in. steel pipe on 14 in. I-section columns along spine, spaced at 29.5 ft (9 m) centers and reaching 48 ft (15 m) above roof. Total steel is 9.2 lb/ft² (45 kg/m²).
	Horizontal Spans	Roof beams spanning 75 ft (22.5 m) suspended from A-frames.

Envelope		
	Glass and Glazing	20% of wall area is clear glass.
	Cladding	2.75 in. (70 mm) fiberglass reinforced plastic bonded on metal frame with internal translucent insulation, 17% light transmission and 0.23 Btu/ft² °F (1.3 W/m² °C) thermal conductance.
	Roof	Built-up felt on rigid polystyrene and isocyanurate insulation.
	Skylights	Double acrylic 5 ft × 5 ft domes along central spine.

HVAC		
	Equipment	Roof package units, central plant boiler and perimeter baseboard heating.
	Cooling Type	Two package direct expansion units above roof on exposed catwalk.
	Distribution	Variable volume with one terminal unit for each pair of 29.5 ft × 14.8 ft (9.0 m × 4.5 m) interior zones.
	Duct Type	48 in. (1219 mm) primary ducts exposed on roof.
	Vertical Chases	None.

Interior		
	Partitions	Open plan with demountable partitions around laboratories.
	Finishes	Various.
	Vertical Circulation	None.
	Furniture	Off-the-shelf.
	Lighting	Fluorescent.

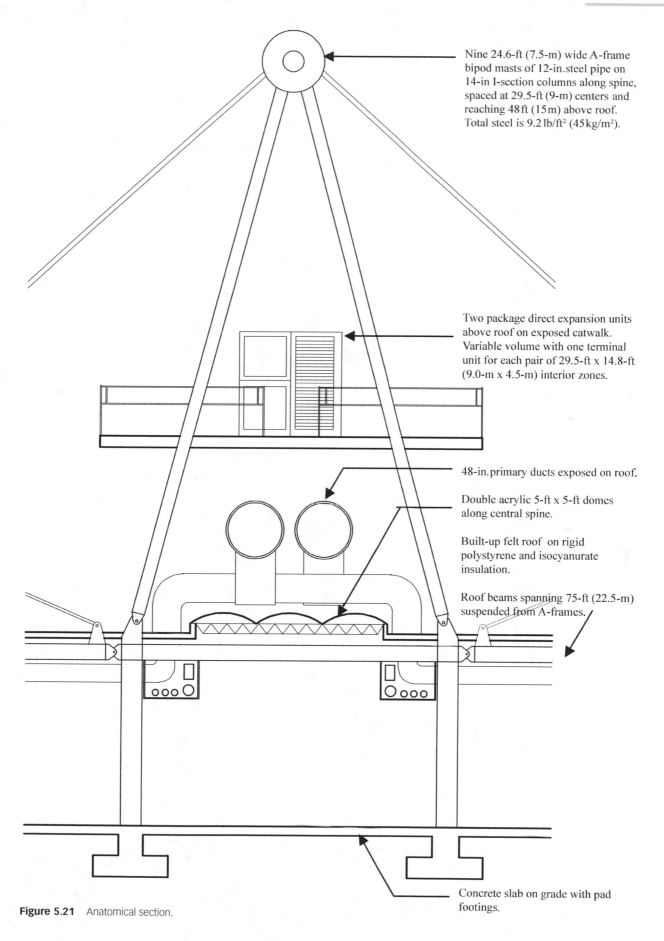

Nine 24.6-ft (7.5-m) wide A-frame bipod masts of 12-in.steel pipe on 14-in I-section columns along spine, spaced at 29.5-ft (9-m) centers and reaching 48ft (15m) above roof. Total steel is 9.2 lb/ft² (45kg/m²).

Two package direct expansion units above roof on exposed catwalk. Variable volume with one terminal unit for each pair of 29.5-ft x 14.8-ft (9.0-m x 4.5-m) interior zones.

48-in.primary ducts exposed on roof.

Double acrylic 5-ft x 5-ft domes along central spine.

Built-up felt roof on rigid polystyrene and isocyanurate insulation.

Roof beams spanning 75-ft (22.5-m) suspended from A-frames.

Concrete slab on grade with pad footings.

Figure 5.21 Anatomical section.

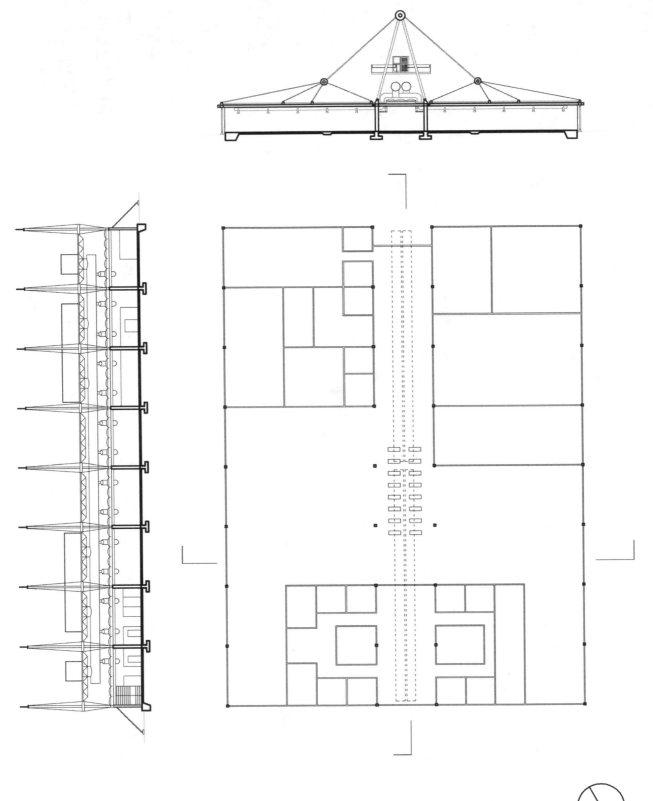

Figure 5.22 Plan and section.

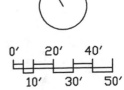

0'   20'   40'

10'   30'   50'

PROGRAM

Client

PA Technology specializes in management, research, and the manufacturing of computer microchips, and has two other facilities in England previously designed by Rogers. The 1982 project for the PA Technology Laboratory near Hightstown, New Jersey, is a management and research facility with offices, conventional laboratory space, and small clean rooms for the development of microchip prototypes.

Brief

The building entrance, conference rooms, and administrative offices make up the office/administration portion of the client brief. As a management facility, these spaces are much more important than they would be in a typical laboratory facility and constitute a considerable portion of the program.

Most of the open floor plan is made up of workspaces for research laboratories, offices, workshops, clean rooms, a dark room, and optics labs. These are the spaces that define the work of the research laboratory and with the office/administration spaces constitute the "served" spaces. The "servant" spaces of the facility are the reception area, a space for filing and a small library, primary circulation, and an employee cafeteria/lounge.

The clients made it clear in their brief that they required a plan that would accommodate workspace flexibility and future expansion. The company had experienced tremendous growth over the previous decade, and it was important that future expansion would not interrupt ongoing work and that any addition would appear to be

TABLE 5.8 Normal Climate Data for Princeton, New Jersey

		Jan.	Feb.	Mar.	Apr.	May	June	July	Aug.	Sept.	Oct.	Nov.	Dec.	Year
Temperature	Degree-Days Heating	1051	909	707	389	141	16	1	2	54	279	549	890	4982
	Degree-Days Cooling	0	0	1	8	56	207	346	314	129	13	2	0	1073
	Extreme High	70	69	83	93	94	98	102	98	96	86	81	72	102
	Normal High	37	40	50	61	71	80	85	83	76	65	54	42	62
	Normal Average	31	33	42	52	62	71	76	75	67	56	47	36	54
	Normal Low	24	25	34	43	53	62	67	66	59	48	39	30	46
	Extreme Low	-4	-2	8	24	35	43	53	48	37	28	15	1	-4
Humidity	Dew Point	22	22	29	38	49	58	65	63	57	45	37	26	43
	Max % RH	75	71	70	72	75	75	79	82	84	81	78	75	76
	Min % RH	57	53	49	50	51	51	55	56	57	52	57	56	54
	% Days with Rain	10	7	30	36	33	30	26	40	43	13	36	23	24
	Rain Inches	3	3	4	3	4	4	5	4	4	3	3	4	42
Sky	% Overcast Days	48	43	45	43	42	40	35	35	37	35	43	45	41
	% Clear Days	15	17	17	13	10	9	7	10	14	21	13	13	13
Wind	Prevailing Direction	WNW	WNW	NNW	WSW	WSW	WSW	SSW	SSW	SSW	WNW	WNW	WNW	WNW
	Speed, Knots	7	7	8	7	6	5	4	4	5	5	7	7	6
	Percent Calm	15	11	12	11	14	15	17	21	17	18	13	12	15
Days Observed	Rain	3	2	9	11	10	9	8	12	13	4	11	7	89
	Fog	13	12	14	14	17	18	20	22	19	17	14	14	194
	Haze	1	0	0	1	0	0	0	0	1	1	1	2	7
	Snow	3	3	2	0	0	0	0	0	0	0	2	10	20
	Hail	0	0	0	0	0	0	0	0	0	0	0	0	0
	Freezing Rain	0	0	0	0	0	0	0	0	0	0	0	0	0
	Blowing Sand	0	0	0	0	0	0	0	0	0	0	0	0	0

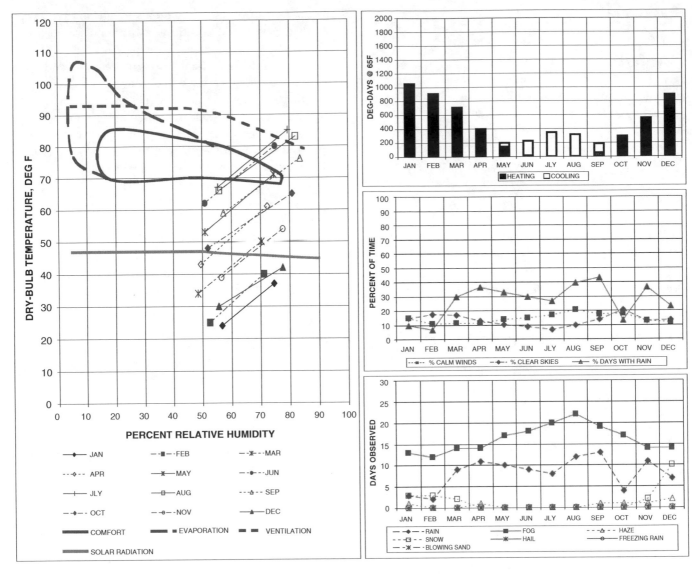

Figure 5.23 Climate analysis graphics.

seamless in transition. The solution was to build up a linear system of bays flanking both sides of the spine. The first phase of the building was to consist of eight bays; plans for future expansion would call for the construction of seven additional bays along the northern end of the building. Part of this expansion would provide an outdoor patio at the primary entrance located on the west edge of the building.

Site

Located halfway between Philadelphia and New York City, the PA Technology Laboratory is about 8 miles southeast of Princeton, New Jersey. It is sited in a technology park also planned by Richard Rogers and Partners. The rural setting is of very flat land, a few trees, and an overgrowth of wild grasses and poppies. The immediate area is home to many other research and development facilities, such as RCA, Johnson & Johnson, Squibb, Exxon, and Siemens.

Climate

Princeton, New Jersey, is located in a temperate climate with an average high temperature in July of 81°F, and an average low temperature in January of 37°F. Relative humidity ranges from a high in September of 81 percent to a low of 72 percent in the months of February, March, and April. Bin data reveals that 24.4 percent of annual hours are in the comfort zone. For two-thirds of the year solar gain should be encouraged, while wind should be discouraged. During the 7.6 percent of the year that is overheated a thermal mass strategy is effective; ventilation and evaporative cooling would also provide comfort for nearly as many hours.

The PA Technology Laboratory is cooling-load dominated because of its internal heat generation. The combined presence of the staff, lighting requirements, and extensive equipment required to operate the facility create substantial internal heat gain, making the building's balance point very low. In the long, cold winter months this situation is not a difficult one, because the balance point is very close to the outdoor temperatures (the average daily temperature in January is 30°F) and cooling can be provided by mechanical ventilation. The summer months are more problematic, as the difference between the balance point and the outdoor temperature increases (the average daily temperature in July is 74°F). It is likely that the labs are in the cooling mode most of the year, but the amount of cooling required in the winter months is considerably lower than in the warmer summer months. This situation leads to a desire for the use of daylighting in order to reduce internal heat gain and minimize cooling energy.

Intention

The architectural philosophy of Richard Rogers is grounded in his Modernist beliefs and the influence of Louis Kahn (see case studies #1 and #2). Architecture that has a "legibility of the parts" and emphasizes "the process

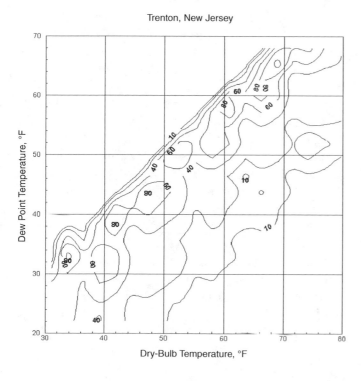

Trenton, New Jersey

Figure 5.24 Bin data distribution for Princeton, New Jersey. Concentric areas of graph indicate the number of hours per year that weather conditions normally occur in this climate. Similar to elevation readings on topographic maps, highest frequency occurrences of weather are at the center peaks of the graph. (Data sources: *Engineering Weather Data, typical meteorological year (TMY) data from the National Climatic Data Center, and the* ASHRAE *Weather Data Viewer from the American Society of Heating, Refrigerating and Air-Conditioning Engineers).*

of building" reflects two philosophies of Kahn. Rogers designs each of his buildings so that they can be broken down into elements and subelements, hierarchically organized so as to give a clearly legible order. The structural system for the PA Technology Center is what Kenneth Frampton would call "structurally honest." The members are expressive, not hidden, and even painted red to say, "Here I am and this is what I do." Other elements on the exterior of the building, including the envelope, as well as the HVAC systems and the interior systems, are similarly expressive. The intention is for the elements to clearly express their roles within the whole of the building.

In addition, Rogers was influenced by Kahn's formal distinction of servant and served spaces, especially in reference to the Richards Medical Laboratory in Philadelphia. One of the continuous themes in Rogers's work is the distinction between the workspaces and the spaces that support them. At the Centre Pompidou, for example (see case study #22), the servant spaces do double duty as the building envelope and the served spaces are entirely free-plan. In the PA Technology Center a similar scheme is followed: The served spaces are the offices, labs, and clean rooms, and the support spaces are in the clearly identified spine containing the library, circulation, cafeteria, entry/reception, and the external superstructure with its embraced mechanical systems.

CRITICAL TECHNICAL ISSUES

Inherent

Ventilation requirements for laboratories tend to dominate the technical issues of their programs. Because of the cleanliness required in laboratories and the toxic fumes they produce, the primary issue is air handling. In the case of microchip manufacture, some work is performed in "clean rooms," requiring the removal of nearly all dust and other particulates in the air. A minimum allowable particle filtering efficiency of 99.97% for a 0.3 micron particle is typical, and this requires special air handlers and filters, control of dust accumulation, and even air-lock entries. The question of where to place this very large equipment is an important design issue.

Laboratories like PA Technology also need interior flexibility and a design that provides for easy future expansion. Interior arrangements change as needs vary, both for experiment setups and for new equipment. The opportunity to expand the facility without interruption to the existing workspace was explicitly requested in the client's brief.

Contextual

Because of the climate's mostly cloudy skies (clear days are measured 21.8 percent of the year), effective daylighting strategies to provide ambient lighting levels are difficult to achieve, yet important to combat interior heat gain. Because the PA Technology Laboratory is an interior load dominated building, direct sun daylighting would be problematic, while indirect light that does not add greatly to the air-conditioning load would be more beneficial. The situation was complicated somewhat by compliance to the ASHRAE 90/75 building energy code, which stipulates minimum levels of envelope insulation.

Partly to minimize expense and partly to expedite construction, the client required that Richard Rogers use only readily available building materials in the construction of this facility.

Intentional

Richard Rogers has expressed on numerous occasions that the life expectancy of buildings, especially laboratories, is about 75 years, whereas the life expectancy or obsolescence of the all-important air-handling equipment is more like 25 years. Because of this uneven life span, Rogers thinks it necessary to provide for easy access to heating, ventilating, and air-conditioning (HVAC) systems so that they can be changed without serious disruption to the rest of the building. These systems must also be designed and arranged to balance the delivery of services while separating servant from served spaces.

External structure and mechanical systems components did present critical roof design issues. Every supporting member or duct penetration of the membrane would have to be reliably waterproofed. In the final design there are 90 structural and 16 duct penetrations through the roof.

APPROPRIATE SYSTEMS

Precedent

Two precedents seem to have influenced Rogers's design of the PA Technology Laboratory. The first is Louis Kahn's 1961 Richards Medical Research Laboratory in Philadelphia, 50 miles southwest of the PA Technology site. This was one of the first architecturally considered laboratory buildings, and it set a precedent in the typology. In addition, Rogers adopted Kahn's philosophy of a clear division of "servant" and "served" spaces. Kahn's influence on Rogers is discussed in more detail in case study #22 on the Centre Pompidou.

The second precedent, in the progression of Rogers's own work, is his 1982 design for the INMOS Microprocessor Factory in Newport, Gwent, South Wales.

In addition to both facilities being used for microprocessor research and manufacturing, an obvious characteristic of these buildings is the central spine. In both buildings the spine contains the servant spaces and articulates the visual integration of exposed structure and ventilation systems. The PA Technology Laboratory and the INMOS Factory are also both one-story structures designed as an extensible system of bays. This strategy facilitates construction, allows for future expansion, and provides a flexible open plan.

Site

Rogers's proposal for the technology park development site consisted of a ring of buildings surrounding a parklike inner circle with a pond and various park amenities. Each of the structures was to be linked together by a pedestrian corridor. Parking was planned to be located in a ring around these buildings. A landscaped buffer zone surrounded the perimeter of the property. PA Technology sits at the northern boundary of the site.

Structure

Eight central bays of the building's long axis form a portal frame with W14 × 99 columns at 29.5 ft (9.0 m) centers on spread footings. This square bay, 29.5 ft wide spine is the circulation and services core of the building. Longitudinal connections between bays are made by extra strong 6.0 in. (152 mm) steel pipe. Above the 12.0 ft (3.7 m) roof level of the spine are nine 49.2 ft (15 m) high A-frame masts of 12 in. (305 mm) extra-strong steel pipe weighing 65.4 lb/ft (97.4 kg/m) that rest on the portal frame columns. These masts form the armature for both a suspended roof structure and an air-handling systems scaffold. Large column-free office/laboratory spaces are enclosed under roof bays extending 75 ft (22.9 m) outward from the either side of the spine. The roof is supported from the masts on a solid 3.5 in. (89 mm) steel tension bar connected to a subassembly of 1.5 and 2 in. (38 and 51 mm) solid bar and extra-strong 4 in. (102 mm) diameter pipe with 0.75 in. (19 mm) steel flange plates. Each 4 in. (102 mm) pipe member weighs 15lb/ft (22 kg/m). The 75 ft (22.9 m) span W14 × 74 roof beams are lifted from above at four points.

At the top of each mast is a signature 5 ft (1.5 m) diameter connecting-ring made from 1.5 in. (38 mm) thick steel plates. Each mast is topped with a lightning rod. Where suspension subassembly members intersect, the smaller ring is 3.5 ft (1.1 m) in diameter and also made of 1.5 in. (38 mm) plate steel. All connections are clevis pinned with stainless steel hardware.

The building's perimeter columns at the end of the beams thus have to act both in compression and in tension, resisting the roof's weight as well as the uplift from wind loads. A 5 in. (127 mm) deep metal roof deck bears on secondary W14 beams at 14.8 ft (4.5 m) centers and works with the main roof beams as a diaphragm.

Envelope

Richard Rogers was intent on using a large portion of the cladding system to provide daylighting, but was confronted with the needs of insulating in the cool New Jersey climate. The solution uses a translucent cladding system of fiberglass-reinforced plastic. This 2.75 in. (70 mm) thick prefabricated system is made up of two panels of light-transmitting fiberglass sandwiching a light-transmitting insulation and fitted with an aluminum framework (see case study #21 for a similar application). It yields an R-value of 4.5 (0.22 Btu/hr ft^2 °F or 1.26 W/cm^2 °C) and transmits about 17 percent of incident light, scattering it diffusely into the space. The envelope also has a clear double glazed strip window on all four façades. In addition, a continuous band of three 5 ft × 5 ft (1.5 m × 1.5 m) double acrylic domed skylights runs along the length of the spine, protected from direct sun by the mechanical system on its scaffold above.

Mechanical

Air-handling units and primary ventilation equipment are located on the roof of the building within the A-frame of the structural masts, though the weight of the equipment and its walkway are actually carried by the columns below and not by the masts. Exterior 48 in. (1219 mm) diameter primary ducts flank the masts and penetrate the roof on both sides of the spine at each structural bay. Air is distributed through each 75 ft (22.9 m) deep zone by variable air volume (VAV) fans, with one VAV fan terminal unit covering two of the 29.5 ft × 14.75 ft (9.0 m × 4.5 m) zones of the interior system, or about 870 ft^2 (80.8 m^2) each.

Each air-handling unit receives chilled and hot water from the central plant's 400 ton chillers. Mechanical rooms below contain electrical services, air compressors, air driers, vacuum pumps, and a deionization plant producing high-purity water. Clean rooms are supplied by separate air-handling units, each producing 33,000 ft^3/min. The clean room service chase receives about 2,800 ft^3/min, and 14,400 ft^3/min are handled by vertical laminar flow (VLF) hoods. Perimeter hydronic heating coils provide supplemental warmth along the lightly insulated exterior wall.

Electrical distribution lines, along with other services —telecommunications, hot and chilled water, deionized water, and pressured air for the laboratories—are lined along the spine below the main beams of the roof cladding and are supported by cradles with bracing running at right angles to the beams. High-voltage electrical gear is housed in a remote building, and building voltage is brought in underground to avoid disrupting magnetically sensitive laboratory equipment. Perimeter and interior gutters are also provided in the concrete slab for distribution of services to the floor areas.

Interior

The spine of the building includes its circulation corridor, lobby, library, and offices. It is also a technically intense space with services run in yellow trays of 1.5 in. bent pipe along the upper corners, an exposed grid of red structure, and a view through the skylights to the mechanical systems scaffold.

A demountable partition system is used in the main wings to separate some spaces, such as laboratory and administrative areas. These partitions can be rearranged as needed. Fluorescent lighting is provided in all spaces and is supplemented by individual task lights. Continuous linear troffers are used in the open spaces where there are no dropped ceilings.

TECHNICAL INTEGRATION HIGHLIGHTS

Integration of all types—visual, physical and performance—is concentrated in the spine of the building. This servant space, both inside and outside the building envelope, serves as the arteries of the building and the focus of its integration.

Rogers's solution is flexible, expandable, serviceable, brightly daylit, energy-efficient by code, and highly serviced. PA Technology is both an inventive solution and an architectural expression of its logic. The client requirements are met with modular structure and column-free spaces, and the architectural program is developed with exoskeletal structure and exposed servicing.

Physical

- The open interior floor plan is a direct result of the assisted span structural system.
- The yellow-colored secondary structural system above the building roof doubles as a catwalk for servicing the ventilation equipment.
- Placement of the major ventilation equipment on the roof greatly reduces the amount of interior floor space needed.

Visual

- The HVAC system is embraced by the exterior structure, thus expressing the dominance of the technical systems of the laboratory building.

- A technical aesthetic is achieved through the use of exposed systems and expressing the construction of the parts.
- Exposed structure helps to visually balance the mass of the exposed ventilation system within the A-frame primary structural system.
- The dynamics of the exposed exterior structure and ventilation systems are grounded by the base of the building, clad with a visually simple envelope of translucent wall panels and a strip of clear glazing.
- The exposing of the services along the interior spine reinforces this as a space "serving" the rest of the building.
- The "A" shape of the structure, with the contained HVAC system, visually reinforces the line and function of the spine as the center of the building.

Performance

- The primary ducts above the building envelope shade the domed skylights in the central spine of the research laboratory.
- The nature of the insulated sandwich panels allows one building material to serve both the envelope and the daylighting systems, acting as an insulated skin for the building while admitting diffuse daylight to the interior labs and offices. The same technology is revisited in Thomas Herzog's design of a house near Munich (see case study #21).
- Exposed services within the central spine allow for ease in servicing.
- The extensive use of daylighting reduces the interior load of the building.

DISCUSSION

Microchip production is a cross between factory and laboratory processes. Clean room areas are examples of this breeding that may seem particularly "alien," with air lock entries, air filtering workbenches, and workers in what look like lightweight spacesuits. From the small laboratory area at PA Technology to the huge wafer fabrication facility at its precedent INMOS Factory, these and similar laboratory buildings for advanced technology research and clean industry applications are definitive examples of the evolution from structural dominance to environmental and service-dominated design. This is not the kind of architecture that fits the category of decorated sheds.

As a species, the laboratory building is typical of the technology-driven requirements for highly serviced flexible space, and the same advances in technical requirements that led to its ascendance are also infiltrating other buildings. Recurring demands for technology uptake and reconfiguration of floor space are evident even in the common office building. Stringent considerations of comfort levels, indoor air quality, energy standards, and environmental preservation are equally influential in the trend toward highly and critically serviced buildings. As discussed in Part I, for example, the music recording industry changed from records to eight-track to cassette to compact disk to DVD and MP3 in a space of about 20 years. That is the equivalent of six technology conversions in what is usually thought of as a very short lifetime for the buildings that host these activities. The once insidious computer room is another such casualty, already lost in a parallel 20-year transition from mainframe to desktop to laptop to handheld wireless personal data appliance.

The inside-out configuration of PA Technology is Rogers's response to the fluctuating use of served space coupled with the upgradeable hardware of servant mechanisms. The building binds together the architectural intention, an essence of its program, and its corporate image with exuberant structure and mechanical systems. The separation of served and servant spaces is the glue of this binding, for although they are functionally independent in the sense of occupied space versus maintained equipment, they are also integrated by physical, visual, and functional dynamics that are experienced everywhere in the building and on its site.

The initial form and content of this case study were contributed by Rich Kaul and were generated during his graduate studies at the University of Houston.

5

ROBERT C. WALLACE EARTH SCIENCES LABORATORY, 1986–1988

Winnipeg, Manitoba
IKOY ARCHITECTS

DESCRIPTION

The Robert C. Wallace Earth Sciences Laboratory building on the University of Manitoba campus combines true kit-of-parts design with bare-bones high-tech expressionism. The motives behind this approach stem overtly from both the typical laboratory concerns for functional flexibility and from the harsh constraints of the Winnipeg climate on construction activities. More to the point, however, IKOY's design philosophy embraces industrialized building components and prefabricated construction. The Wallace building vindicates the architects' beliefs by demonstrating a great deal of technical exuberance and plug-in flexibility—all at a completed cost 10 percent below budget.

From the outside, the laboratory and classroom building is wrapped in a skin of black glass and black anodized aluminum. It sits alone outside the perimeter road of the campus, adjacent to the main parking area to the immediate west. North of the building is the Red River, which surrounds the campus; to the south is the core of early-twentieth-century brick and limestone buildings, surrounded by a less appealing group of 1960s academic and service buildings. The classroom/laboratory is situated as a gateway between the car park and the central campus, linking them with its central corridor and a strategic connection to the campus pedestrian tunnel system.

The most striking feature of the structure is the 18 ft wide central street corridor running full length and full height through the long two- and three-story building. Here, in the most public part of the building, all of the systems are brought to play. Structure, HVAC, electrical, and interior systems are articulated in a busy gallery for walk-through traffic and a generous gathering place for the earth science occupants.

Figure 5.25 Overview of Earth Sciences Library. *(Photograph courtesy of Ron Keenberg, IKOY Architects.)*

TABLE 5.9 Fact Sheet

Project	**Building Name**	Wallace Earth Sciences Building
	Client	University of Manitoba
	City	Winnepeg (Fort Gary campus), Manitoba, Canada
	Lat/Long/Elev	49.9 N 97.1 W, 230 ft (70 m)
Team	**Architect**	IKOY Architects
	Engineer	Not determined
General	**Time Line**	1986 to 1988.
	Floor Area	110,000 ft^2 (10,214 m^2)
	Stories	Three.
	Plan	Long rectangular plan,396 ft × 118 ft (120.7 m × 36.0 m) with long axis facing directly south.
	Occupants	Not determined.
	Cost	$9 million US, $1.5 million under budget ($10.5 million Canadian, about $1.6 million under budget).
	Cost in 1995 US$	$11.6 million or $105/ft^2.
Site	**Site Description**	One acre situated near the campus entrance on the outside of a perimeter loop road. To the west is a large parking lot, and to the immediate north is the Red River.
	Parking, Cars	Adjoining surface lot is the main parking area for the campus.
Structure	**Foundation**	Precast driven pilings through clay soil.
	Vertical Members	Exposed precast concrete columns full height of building, sandblast finish.
	Horizontal Spans	Precast concrete beams, sandblasted and exposed, carrying precast 12 in. deep hollow-core concrete planks.
Envelope	**Glass and Glazing**	Insulated.
	Skylights	None.
	Cladding	Steel studs and extruded aluminum grid with 20-gauge anodized aluminum panels and double glazing.
	Roof	Not published.
HVAC	**Equipment**	Heat pumps.
	Distribution	Zoned heat pumps.
	Duct Type	Factory-finished 9 in. diameter ducts run in cores of hollow concrete floor planks and exposed in central "street."
	Vertical Chases	None.
Interior	**Partitions**	Demountable.
	Finishes	Rubber tile floors, exposed concrete and services, painted metal hardware.
	Circulation	18 ft wide central hall extends as a street to all three levels.
	Furniture	Fabricated from readily available hardware.
	Lighting	Bare industrial fluorescent strip with hardware screens.

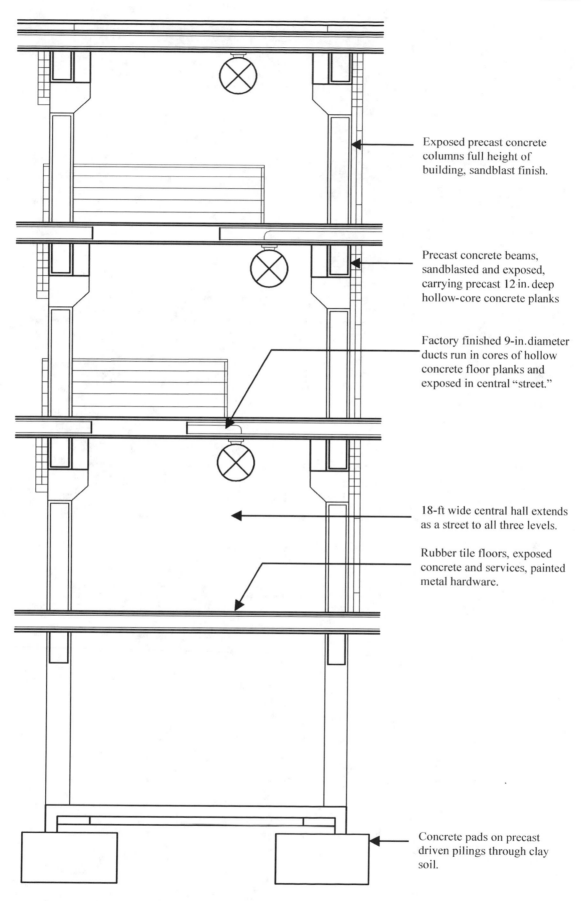

Exposed precast concrete columns full height of building, sandblast finish.

Precast concrete beams, sandblasted and exposed, carrying precast 12 in. deep hollow-core concrete planks

Factory finished 9-in. diameter ducts run in cores of hollow concrete floor planks and exposed in central "street."

18-ft wide central hall extends as a street to all three levels.

Rubber tile floors, exposed concrete and services, painted metal hardware.

Concrete pads on precast driven pilings through clay soil.

Figure 5.26 Anatomical section.

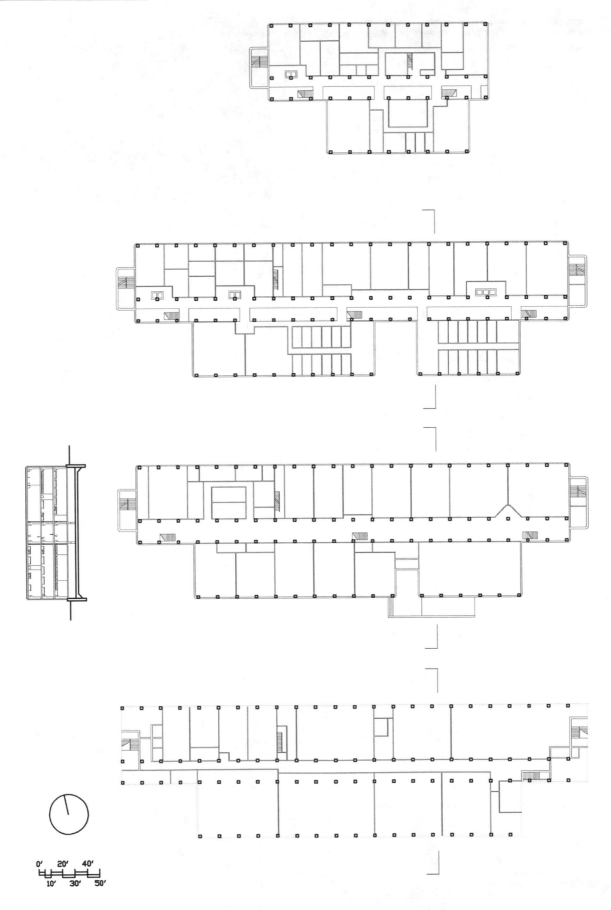

0'   20'   40'

10'   30'   50'

Figure 5.27   Plan and section.

PROGRAM

Client

The University of Manitoba is a government-supported institution offering graduate and undergraduate degrees in the humanities, social sciences, natural sciences, the arts, and major professions. Established in 1877, it is the oldest institution of higher learning in western Canada. The university approached IKOY to design a replacement for its aging earth sciences facility, to be dedicated to the memory of the university's first professor of geology and mineralogy, Robert Charles Wallace (1881–1955).

Brief

The building program was developed to specify an 80,160 ft^2 (7,447 m^2) building with a budget of $13.2 million Canadian in 1982. Space allocations were divided into seven groups, or "design blocks," representing the required functions (Table 5.10). A generous allowance was also made for circulation to accommodate the gateway function of the building for public access to the tunnel system. In the end, IKOY's design provided sufficient budget savings to greatly expand the storage design block by building a full basement. This additional storage space accounts for the difference between the building program requirement and the final 110,000 ft^2 (10,214 m^2) completed building.

Technical requirements for the Earth Sciences Building included a calculated energy consumption budget not to exceed 18.1 kWh/ft^2 per year, based on an assumed 2500 operating hours per year. Calculations were to exclude the special ventilation exhaust requirements of the laboratories where such loads were incurred for scientific purposes and not part of the building's normal thermal loads. Several other energy-efficiency standards were set forth, such as minimum acceptable insulation R-values and the mandatory use of double glazing. Interior relative humidity levels were specified at very low levels, to be maintained during cold winter conditions to avoid condensation.

The space inventory included:

- Electron Microbeam and Image Analysis Laboratory
- Geochemistry Laboratory
- X-Ray Diffraction Laboratory
- Earth Science Information, Integration, and Imaging Laboratory
- Technical Support Group

Site

The architects looked at four different site options surrounding the existing Earth Sciences Center before choosing the area between the main parking lot and the perimeter road. IKOY intended to place the building here to form a gateway to the campus. The 1 acre (4000 m^2) site is shifted about 40 degrees off the main campus grid and forms a triangle between two legs of the campus perimeter road and the river. The 436 ft (132.9 m) long river side of the site faces directly north.

Climate

Of all the case study locations considered in this book, Winnipeg has the coldest climate, with more than 10,000 F degree-days heating. The region experiences freezing

TABLE 5.10 Wallace Earth Sciences Building Program

Design Block	Description	Net ft^2	Net m^2	Percent of Gross
1	Classrooms—2 @ 1500 ft^2, 2 @ 3000 ft^2	9,000	835.7	12%
2	Teaching Laboratories—9 student labs, photography lab, computer room, 5 preparation/storage areas	15,365	1,426.7	21%
3	Student Services—100 lockers and 50 study carrels	1,650	153.2	2%
4	Administration—26 staff offices, 2 support offices, large general office area, 1 lounge/conference/seminar room	6,266	581.8	8%
5	Museum—public display and collection storage areas	1,700	157.9	2%
6	Graduate and Research—dry, wet, dirty, and electrical labs, 36 graduate student offices	22,090	2,051.2	30%
7	Storage—secondary storage for large rocks and heavy equipment adjacent to loading dock	6,300	585.0	9%
	Total Net Area	56,131	5,210.0	76%
	Allowance for building systems, circulation, and toilets	17,790	1,651.9	24%
	Total Building Gross Area	73,921	6,862.0	

TABLE 5.11   Normal Climate Data for Winnipeg

		Jan.	Feb.	Mar.	Apr.	May	June	July	Aug.	Sept.	Oct.	Nov.	Dec.	Year
Temperature	Degree-Days Heating	1943	1604	1352	750	358	137	36	89	342	727	1254	1812	10363
	Degree-Days Cooling	0	0	0	2	28	57	117	90	13	0	0	0	304
	Extreme High	43	45	61	93	99	97	95	100	100	87	75	48	100
	Normal High	10	16	29	50	66	72	78	75	64	51	30	14	47
	Normal Average	2	8	21	40	54	62	68	65	54	42	23	7	37
	Normal Low	-6	0	13	29	42	52	57	54	44	32	16	-1	28
	Extreme Low	-40	-38	-26	-15	14	30	41	34	25	3	-29	-33	-40
Humidity	Dew Point	-2	2	15	27	38	50	57	54	43	32	17	1	28
	Max % RH	80	81	82	80	76	81	86	87	86	83	84	80	82
	Min % RH	75	74	70	50	44	52	53	52	54	56	71	76	60
	% Days with Rain	1	3	16	25	42	52	48	45	47	35	12	3	27
	Rain Inches	1	1	1	1	2	3	3	3	2	1	1	1	20
Sky	% Overcast Days	39	39	38	29	26	24	16	19	27	34	46	42	31
	% Clear Days	19	19	19	17	11	6	9	11	12	13	12	18	14
Wind	Prevailing Direction	S	S	S	S	S	S	S	S	S	S	S	S	S
	Speed, Knots	11	11	11	11	11	10	10	9	11	11	11	12	11
	Percent Calm	3	5	3	3	3	4	5	6	4	4	4	3	4
Days Observed	Rain	0	1	5	7	13	16	15	13	14	11	4	1	99
	Fog	13	11	9	5	4	6	4	5	7	6	8	11	89
	Haze	0	0	0	0	0	0	0	1	0	1	0	0	5
	Snow	23	19	13	6	1	0	0	0	0	5	16	22	106
	Hail	0	0	0	0	0	0	1	0	0	0	0	0	2
	Freezing Rain	3	2	2	1	0	0	0	0	0	0	3	2	13
	Blowing Sand	0	0	0	0	0	0	0	0	0	0	0	0	1

weather during more than 40 percent of the annual hours over seven months, from October through April. Eleven percent of the annual hours are below 0°F. There are more than 100 days of snow in the average year. Winnipeg straddles the same 50-degree latitude as Frankfurt, Prague, and Kiev, and its day length varies from 8 hours in December to 16 hours in June. Skies are generally overcast. Most of the normal summer conditions can be satisfied by ventilation with 100 percent outside air.

INTENTION

Design Team

IKOY was founded in 1968 by Ron Keenberg. The firm's work has generally centered on industrialized systems and the act of converting functional hardware components into dynamic works of architecture. In 1978, for example, the firm constructed its own two-story headquarters in downtown Winnipeg from prefabricated concrete and plug-in utilities in just 90 days. Perhaps as a consequence of this industrial focus, IKOY is best known for institutional, educational, and industrial work, in which cost control and ease of construction are vital. As a well-published and frequently honored architectural firm, however, IKOY's designs represent a respectable breadth of building types.

Philosophy

When people walk through a building, they should feel it as a living thing. Our buildings have excited the public because people see the reality of the building displayed through the texture and kinetics of its mechanics and their delightful forms.

RON KEENBERG

IKOY describes its architectural practice as "high-tech humanist." Its approach can also be defined through its process of design. A strong belief in industrialized system techniques has stimulated statements from IKOY on design method, systems selection, teamwork, and modes of construction:

- Architecture consists of basic systems rather than a "collection of details."

- Engineering systems are architectural systems and are therefore "part of the original design concept."

- Architects select systems. Engineers "proportion" them.

- Poor design substitutes expensive components for imagination.

- A building should outlive changes in its function.

- Manual labor construction sites have become prefabricated-component "assembly sites."

Intent

True to IKOY form, the Wallace Laboratory was intended and realized as an assemblage of industrial systems and an integrated set of dynamic working parts. Further, components systems and pieces were all required to be readily available from multiple suppliers so that no assembly would readily become obsolete. Most important, however, and what distinguishes the architectural quality of intention here, the product was to have expressionistic character and meaning through articulation of what each part does.

Development of the brief and selection of the site led to the formal intention of making the building into a gateway and providing a crucial linkup of the campus's tunnel circulation system.

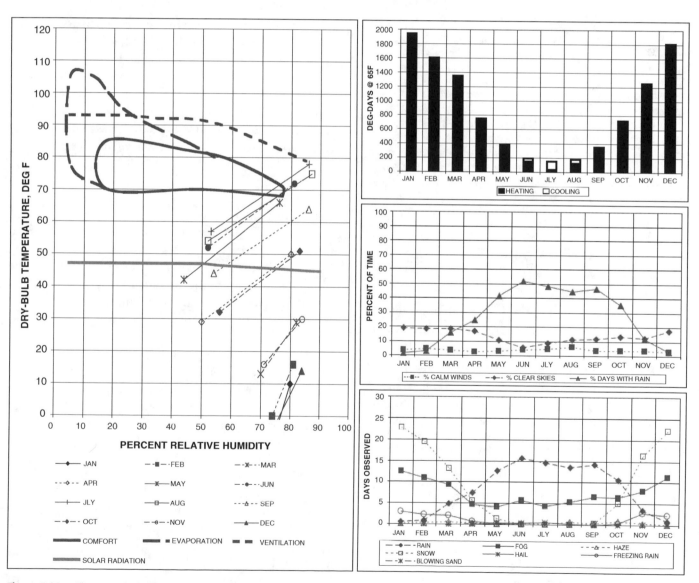

Figure 5.28 Climate analysis graphics.

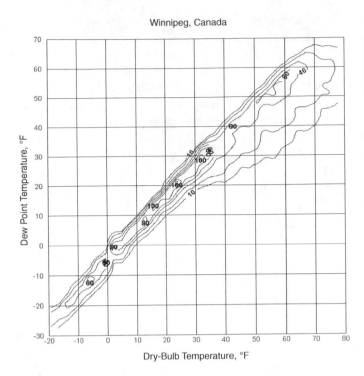

Winnipeg, Canada

Figure 5.29 Bin data distribution for Winnipeg. Concentric areas of graph indicate the number of hours per year that weather conditions normally occur in this climate. Similar to elevation readings on topographic maps, highest frequency occurrences of weather are at the center peaks of the graph. (Data sources: *Engineering Weather Data*, typical meteorological year (TMY) data from the National Climatic Data Center, and the ASHRAE Weather Data Viewer *from the American Society of Heating, Refrigerating and Air-Conditioning Engineers.*)

CRITICAL TECHNICAL ISSUES

Inherent

- Instructional laboratories have more occupants than standard research facilities and need greater amounts of space for circulation and gathering.

- Public university classroom buildings are frequently associated with a modest initial budget and are expected to have long useful lifetimes with minimal maintenance.

- Security of the elaborate laboratory equipment was given very high priority.

Contextual

- The code-required two-hour fire rating dictated concrete construction rather than steel.

- Clay soils required the foundation to be set on pilings.

- Long, cold winters made site construction and scheduling difficult.

Intentional

- Extensive research was required to find and combine suitable components available "off-the-shelf."

- Exposed systems and hardware required visual integration.

APPROPRIATE SYSTEMS

Precedent

Philosophically, the Wallace Building and much of IKOY's work are in the vein of the Bauhaus ideal. The true kit-of-parts assembly and industrial-quality components speak to that part of the Gropius legacy, even if the complementary artisan work of the Bauhaus manifesto is not in full evidence. It is certainly IKOY's ambition to meld mass-produced pieces together into an integrated and artistic whole.

Formally, and in the continuity of the firm's projects, the Wallace Laboratory is most readily compared to the studio IKOY members built for themselves in 1978. The use of prefabricated concrete structure in both projects shows how their exploration of this industrialized system was fostered and refined. Though many of their projects use concrete plank floors and color-coded technical systems, most of IKOY's other works have shown a preference for steel frame construction.

Site

There are few external landscape features of the Earth Sciences Building. Site systems per se are generally limited to a north-south lobby and entryway that bisects the building's long axis and an obligatory loading dock. The plinth that transitions the building into the landscape and matches the native stone of older campus buildings is the most overt aesthetic gesture. Even the north elevation to the Red River side is left blank and mostly windowless, relieved only by the bisecting lobby. The grass between the building and the river appears to be more a victim of the severe Winnipeg climate than a landscape opportunity.

The real site system is the building itself. It becomes both a formal entry piece to the campus and a literal pedestrian gateway. Location and orientation make the formal setting by placing the building between the parking and campus proper and by setting it alone outside the perimeter service road. Shifting the building's footprint off axis with the rest of the campus emphasizes its key role. The overall arrangement does much to mend the rift between the older campus core buildings and the surrounding ring of less graceful constructions.

Pedestrian gateway functions are served by the interior gallery. With its galleria-scale width, full-height openness, and connection to the tunnel system, passersby and occupants alike use it for purposes beyond the internal function of the building. Associating an interior mall space with site system mandates may be confusing, but the gallery is intentionally made as much a part of campus circulation patterns as it is part of the Earth Sciences Building.

Structure

This prefabricated concrete building begins with three- and four-story precast concrete columns resting on driven piles. Haunches formed in the continuous columns project to carry precast concrete floor and roof beams. The finished frame forms twenty-two 18 ft bays dividing the long axis of the building. Across the long axis, a center bay of 18 ft is used as the pedestrian street. On either side are 50 ft span bays. There are no load-bearing walls. Twelve-inch deep prestressed hollow-core concrete slabs, each about a meter wide, are placed on the beams with their exposed cores open to the central corridor. The floors have a dead load capacity of 150 lbs/ft^2, and holes up to 9 in. $\times$ 12 in. can be cut into them for utility routing in the hollow cores. At the second and third levels the floor slabs cantilever over the northern half of the center corridor to form open walkways with views down into the public areas of the ground floor.

Clay soil conditions dictated the use of driven precast concrete piles for foundations. Pilings also avoided much of the poured-in-place concrete work required for drilled pier or continuous beam foundations. Site-cast concrete was avoided wherever possible because of the difficulties of freezing temperatures and maintaining proper hydration of the pours. Scheduling concrete work around the harsh seven-month Winnipeg winters would have been extremely difficult.

Envelope

Energy efficiency goals and harsh winters combined to dictate a tight envelope configuration. Extensive passive solar heating would require large areas of glazing, which would be useful sometimes but a great liability in severe cold weather. Winnipeg's winter extremes make passive heating, without R-6 night insulation being used over glazing, impractical in any case. Consequently, insulated glass is used sparingly in occupied spaces and is distributed with a strong preference for a southern orientation. The sunless north side is practically unglazed. Large window areas are reserved exclusively for illuminating and publicly announcing the interior gallery, where occupancy is transitional and thermal control is less critical.

The remaining skin of anodized 20-gauge corrugated aluminum siding protects the insulated wall construction.

It was probably chosen both because of IKOY's predisposition to industrial materials and because of a desire for the building to blend in with some of the adjacent service buildings sited on the perimeter road.

Mechanical

The architects decided to use the 9 in. diameter floor slab cores for distribution of services wherever possible. To keep duct sizes small enough to fit, they placed small independently controlled heat pumps throughout the building in many small zones. This has the additional advantage of operating only as much capacity as is needed for spaces actually being occupied. Water-to-air heat pumps are located above the ceiling and are served by a four-pipe system delivering energy from the campus central plant. Ventilation air was dealt with separately because of the large quantity of air exhausted from the laboratory vent hoods and experiment stations. Ventilation makeup air

Figure 5.30 View of interior gallery. *(Photograph courtesy of Ron Keenberg, IKOY Architects.)*

required more heating capacity than small heat pumps could handle. Consequently, conditioned ventilation air is introduced in the long corridor through larger ductwork.

In a scheme similar to that of the PA Technology Laboratory (case study #4), the Wallace Laboratory's central axis is both a pedestrian street and a service spine. Aside from the red ductwork and its branches snaking into the concrete slab cores, there are also sprinklers and electrical systems routed along the same axis. Electrical distribution was prewired and prefinished, then installed along the laboratory side of the main beams. Circuits are distributed through the concrete slab cores. Conduit and electrical outlets are routed across workstations, lab benches, and even desktops. There are no services in the exterior walls or partitions.

Toilet rooms are handled as independent pods. Each toilet is a freestanding prefabricated room module with its own sink and accessories. They are constructed with standard metal studs and prefinished wallboard. Ideally, they can be relocated with a forklift or the building's overhead gantry crane.

Interior

All exposed concrete surfaces are sandblasted—the precast floor planks, the columns, and the beams. For visual contrast to the brute structure, exposed services, stair rails, and the like are painted bright colors. Interior partitions are all steel studs with plastic-laminate-covered wallboard. Because none of the partitions are load bearing or contain any services, they can be quickly dismantled and reassembled as needed.

Corners are taken from the long rectangular plan at the southeast and southwest ends of the building to open up the view from the pedestrian street and allow natural light. Three of the 50 ft bays are omitted from the south half of the building to the west, and two on the east. Two bays are also carved from the center of the plan in the middle of the south side for a formal entry into a lobby that occupies the north half of the same two bay widths.

The full basement level is predominantly for storage and mechanical systems. The ground floor, with its broad pedestrian street, is a mix of offices and classrooms. Second-floor use is laboratory and faculty offices, and the partial third floor is where the equipment-intensive laboratories are installed.

Vertical circulation is provided by six stairs paired down the length of the corridor. One elevator is provided at each end of the building. Five bridges cross the upper levels of the central core to double as stair landings, and all of these can be relocated with a forklift.

TECHNICAL INTEGRATION HIGHLIGHTS

Physical

- Floor-ceiling layers containing hidden services are eliminated by placing pipes, ducts, and conduits in the open cores of concrete slabs. This decreases overall floor-to-floor heights without lowering the ceilings.

Visual

- Hardware systems and color-coded services provide visual interest in the long public space.
- Exposed structure creates the planning module of interior space by visually dividing it into bays. The sandblasted concrete surfaces are durable and attractive.

Performance

- The corridor "street" serves as an 18 ft (5.5 m) wide covered walkway entry to the campus. On upper floors the corridor/gallery doubles as social and academic gathering space.
- The main corridor is also the systems axis of the building. It even features a craneway for heavy laboratory equipment and movable building elements such as bridges across the open "street."
- Hollow 9 in. cores in the prestressed concrete slabs serve as HVAC ducts, pipe raceways, and electrical conduits. The hollow cores of the slabs still leave a solid 12 in. deep concrete web to support the floor at 12 in. centers.

DISCUSSION

Strong visual impressions of laboratory spaces probably occur to many people who pass through the Wallace pedestrian street each day. From the overhead gantry crane to the candy-colored display of ducts and pipes, the components of this central space evoke a friendly workplace. For the students and scientists who work there, the central street is a core for the laboratory spaces and a communal forum.

Architectural clarity connects the cold Winnipeg climate, the prefabricated construction strategy, selection of systems, response to laboratory requirements, and the organization of spaces. The success of the design is inherent in the integration of these disparate aspects of the program into one guiding architectural concept.

Ron Keenberg generously contributed to portions of this case study.

Offices

Corporate headquarters and speculative office towers dominate our city skylines. Office space also spreads from the urban core into suburban office parks and the outer rings of regional mixed-use centers. As the industrialized world turned to service-based economies, corporate patronage played a parallel "skyscraping" role in architectural design activity.

The U.S. Energy Information Administration's 1995 study, *Commercial Buildings Energy Consumption Survey,* reveals the magnitude of office-building impact on the built environment. In number alone, office buildings in the United States rank second only to retail buildings and just ahead of warehouses. There were more than 700,000 office buildings in the United States in 1995. In terms of occupants, offices housed 35 percent of the commercial U.S. workforce, or some 27 million people. With the 10.5 billion ft^2 of floor space these buildings comprise, the average office is only about 15,000 ft2 and holds some 40 workers, at an average 387 ft^2 per occupant. Completing the statistics, 90 percent of office buildings are smaller than 25,000 ft^2 and only 3 percent exceed 100,000 ft^2. Finally, and amazingly enough when we consider the typical city skyline, only 1 percent of all U.S. office buildings (roughly 8,000 of them total) are more than ten floors in height.

Because of their dense occupancy patterns and intense use of equipment for producing work, these same offices (still taking the U.S. Energy Administration's perspective)

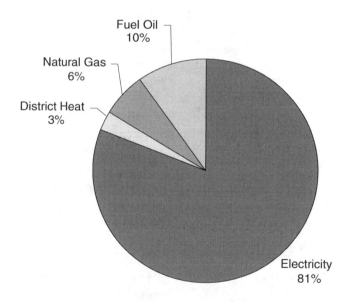

Figure 6.1 Annual site energy use in office buildings.

are the single most intensive commercial energy users. Spending well over $15 billion per year in 1995 dollars, office energy averages more than $1.50 per ft^2 per year.

The real cost of business in an office building, however, is the working staff. A $60,000 per year employee occupying a 400 ft^2 workspace costs an annual equivalent of $150 per ft^2. This amount surpasses what the floor space cost to build and is more than ten times the annual ener-

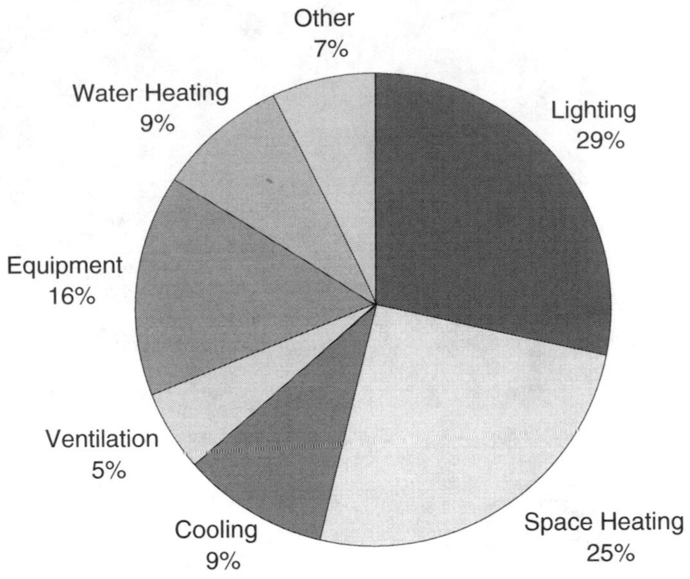

Figure 6.2 Annual cost of energy use in office buildings, $15.85 billion. (Data source: *Energy Information Administration,* 1995 Commercial Buildings Energy Consumption Survey.)

gy expense of fueling the office. Recognition of this proportion has led from the design of efficient office buildings that save energy to a more humanistic and profitable focus on productive office environments where comfort and health are the main priorities. It is easy to see that a small change in the design of a $120 per ft² construction cost of an office building could have great impact on long-term business economics, even if it has only a small effect on worker productivity, absenteeism, or workforce recruitment and retention.

Critical relationships between occupant comfort, office productivity, and bottom line economics offer significant opportunities for design. Leveraging office environment resources to enhance occupant health, comfort, and well-being can import enormous value to effective architectural services. It is the role of architects, as the stalwart champion of what is human about good buildings, to serve these needs.

A number of other stimuli of change must also be considered. Management strategies like rightsizing, outsourcing, and total quality management (TQM) change the office dynamic. Information technology (IT), along with office automation, affects how work is produced and collaborated on. Worker productivity levels are finally beginning to reflect the vast improvements anticipated from use of computers. There is growing awareness of indoor air quality (IAQ), sick buildings, and personal control of environmental conditions. Ergonomics has become an everyday office science. The list goes on, but all these issues reflect the focus on productivity — and, consequently, the trend toward designing for human comfort factors.

From the systems perspective, then, offices present a specific set of challenges, best defined as energy, comfort, and flexibility. The first two of these, judicious use of energy and occupant comfort satisfaction, completely overlap. Efficient lighting means using light to its best and most comfortable effect. Daylighting saves energy and psychologically enhances the workspace. Passive envelope systems restore contact with the outdoors. Tight thermal control provides balanced air distribution and accurate control of comfort levels. Regulated mechanical ventilation and IAQ ensure a good environment.

The third challenge, flexibility, involves attention to two areas. First, personal workstations have to offer occupants a great deal of control. Repetitive motion injuries (like carpal tunnel syndrome) illustrate that no one is sufficiently "average" to fit satisfactorily into a desk made for some idealized model worker. Adjustable-position workstations also suggest adjustable lighting, air motion, and background sound levels.

The second area to be examined for flexibility is the office building itself. Modern offices must rearrange workspaces, re-form project teams, or even sublease floor space during business downturns. An adaptable infrastructure is needed for environmental services, communications, networking, and a general "plug-in" modular approach to interior systems from telephones to partitions.

6

JOHN DEERE ADMINISTRATIVE HEADQUARTERS, 1956–1964

Moline, Illinois
EERO SAARINEN AND PARTNERS

DESCRIPTION

Eero Saarinen's headquarters for a farm equipment manufacturer is a success of modernist design and industrial technology. It is the prototypical office-in-the-garden where nature and building complement each other. As classic modern architecture, the John Deere Headquarters also offers an excellent model for the integration of technical innovation with design sensitivity.

The major building materials at Deere were new to building construction, or at least made new through design inventions. With his technology specialist John Dinkeloo and chief designer Kevin Roche, Saarinen brought weathering steel and reflective glass into the mainstream architectural palette via the Deere building. Saarinen identified, refined, and adapted these technologies—not as new materials waiting to be pioneered, but as ideal answers to a particular design proposition.

Figure 6.3 Overview of the headquarters office. *(Photograph courtesy of John Deere & Company.)*

TABLE 6.1 Fact Sheet

Project	Client	John Deere & Company, with William Hewitt as CEO
	City	Moline, Illinois
	Lat/Long/Elev	41.47N 90.45W, 650 ft (198 m)
Team	Architect	Eero Saarinen and Associates; Kevin Roche and John Dinkeloo, partners
	Structural Engineer	Ammann & Whitney
	Mechanical Engineer	Burns & McDonnell Engineering Company
	Acoustics	Bolt, Beranek & Newman, Inc.
	Lighting	Richard Kelly
	Landscape Architects	Sasaki, Walker and Associates Inc.
	Project Manager	Booz, Allen and Hamilton
	General Contractor	Huber, Hunt & Nichols
General	Time Line	Commissioned in 1956. Eero Saarinen died September 1, 1961—four days after the construction contract was let. Building was dedicated June 5, 1964.
	Floor Area	350,443 ft^2 (32,541 m^2) total. Administration building 297,132 ft^2 (27,591 m^2); Exhibit Hall, 23,000 ft^2 (2136 m^2), and Auditorium, 30,311 ft^2 (2815 m^2).
	Occupants	800 to 1000 office occupants.
	Cost	Estimated at $10 million, actual price is unpublished. About $28.54/ft^2.
	1995 Cost in US$	$49.8 million or about $142/ft^2 based on the $10 million estimate.
	Stories	Administration building, seven stories plus full basement, but entered at level four by bridge from Exhibit Hall.
	Plan	North- and south-facing rectangle about 330 ft × 96 ft 100m × 29m), floor plates of 31,600 ft^2 (2934 m^2) on 3 × 6 ft (0.9m × 1.8m) grid module.
Site	Site Description	Three farms of rolling hillside were purchased for the project, totaling about 720 acres (288 hectares), for about $600 per acre. Total cost of about $432,000 in 1956, or about $2.26 million ($3141 per acre) in 1995 dollars. Two lakes totaling 4 acres (1.6ha) were constructed immediately south of the administration building.
	Parking, Cars	718.
Structure	Foundation	Not determined.
	Vertical Members	Welded external frame of high tensile strength A-242 Cor-ten steel. Columns at 30 ft wide by 42 ft deep bays, center bay of 12 × 30 ft.
	Horizontal Spans	Welded trusses of same A-242 steel. No diagonals were required.
Envelope	Glass and Glazing	Upper five floors use laminated glass with bronze reflective interlayer. Performance is given at 47.7% solar transmission and 38% visible transmission. Lower two floors are set back from perimeter and use clear glass. Neoprene gaskets rest directly on ¼ in. thick flanges and steel plates welded to structure. All glazing is set in these gaskets.
	Cladding	Spandrels are glass exterior over metal panels. Some brick is used at lower levels and at the Exhibit/Auditorium buildings.
	Roof	Tar and gravel built-up roof on insulation on 0.5 in. metal deck.
HVAC	Equipment	1600 ton cooling plant. The larger lake is used as a spray pond to reject heat in lieu of a cooling tower. Space heating is from two gas-fired boilers, each of 25 million Btuh (747 horsepower or 7328 kW each).
	Cooling Type	Direct expansion.
	Distribution	Dual duct with 727 mixing boxes serving 516 thermostat zones. Fan capacity totals 1 million ft^3 per minute.
	Duct Type	Round flex duct to continuous base register at perimeter sill and to ceiling registers above louvered ceiling.
	Vertical Chases	Shafts.
Interior	Partitions	Movable steel partitions and glass infill.
	Finishes	Wood, carpet, and glass.
	Circulation	Center axis open corridor in 12 ft space between the 30 ft × 42 ft structural bays.
	Furniture	Custom-designed furnishings by the architect. Secretarial desks are set pedestal style on floor-mounted posts.
	Lighting	Luminous ceiling fluorescent lighting with open cell grid diffusers.

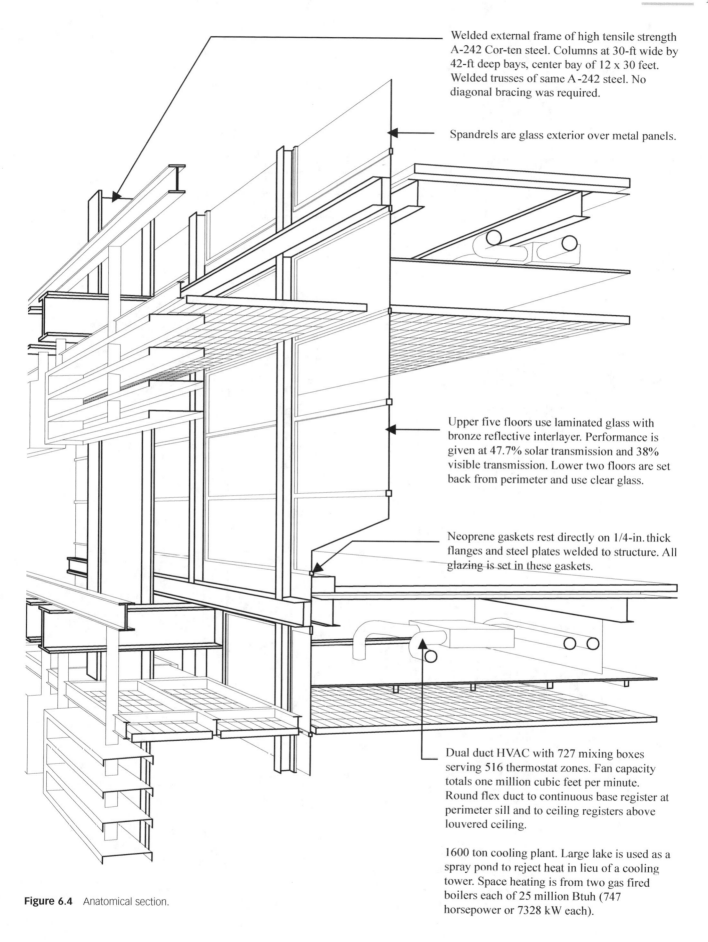

Welded external frame of high tensile strength A-242 Cor-ten steel. Columns at 30-ft wide by 42-ft deep bays, center bay of 12 x 30 feet. Welded trusses of same A-242 steel. No diagonal bracing was required.

Spandrels are glass exterior over metal panels.

Upper five floors use laminated glass with bronze reflective interlayer. Performance is given at 47.7% solar transmission and 38% visible transmission. Lower two floors are set back from perimeter and use clear glass.

Neoprene gaskets rest directly on 1/4-in. thick flanges and steel plates welded to structure. All glazing is set in these gaskets.

Dual duct HVAC with 727 mixing boxes serving 516 thermostat zones. Fan capacity totals one million cubic feet per minute. Round flex duct to continuous base register at perimeter sill and to ceiling registers above louvered ceiling.

1600 ton cooling plant. Large lake is used as a spray pond to reject heat in lieu of a cooling tower. Space heating is from two gas fired boilers each of 25 million Btuh (747 horsepower or 7328 kW each).

Figure 6.4 Anatomical section.

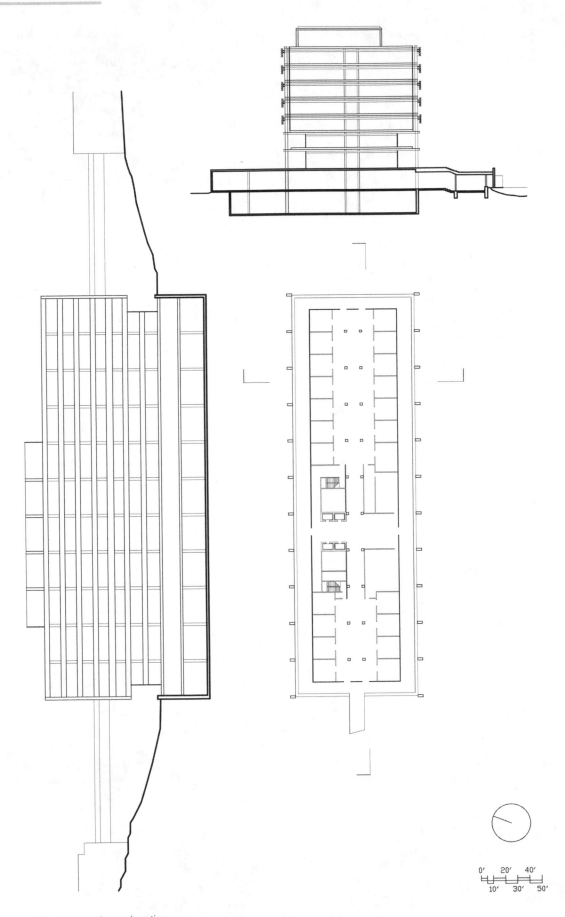

Figure 6.5 Plan and section.

PROGRAM

Client

John Deere was a Vermont blacksmith who invented the moldboard plow in 1837. The polished wrought iron of this implement's upper surface was designed to shed the Midwest prairie clay that clogged other plows. Deere moved to the Mississippi River settlement of Moline, Illinois, in 1847 to found his company. At the time, Moline (from the French *moulin* or "mill"), some 160 miles west of Chicago, was better known as a Mississippi River lumber mill. Before long however, conductors would announce the town stop by simply shouting, "John Deere."

John Deere & Company was incorporated in 1868 and today employs about 10,000 people in the community and 41,000 worldwide. It is the largest farm equipment manufacturer in the world and now also makes construction machinery and gardening implements. The company's financial arm, John Deere Credit, is among the top 25 finance companies in the United States.

In 1955, William A. Hewitt became chief executive officer of the company and served in that role until 1982. It was under his direction that John Deere achieved international standing. Deere's sales surged from less than $300 million when he became president in 1955 to more than $5 billion by the time of his retirement as chairman in 1982. Two corporate decisions were made when he assumed leadership. The first was to build a new headquarters in rural Moline. Second, and for the first time in its existence, the company decided to hire an outside architect.

In a quest to find what he described as "the best architect we could persuade to design our new headquarters," Hewitt studied architectural magazines and sought the

TABLE 6.2   Normal Climate Data for Moline, Illinois

		Jan.	Feb.	Mar.	Apr.	May	June	July	Aug.	Sept.	Oct.	Nov.	Dec.	Year
Temperature	Degree-Days Heating	1355	1093	861	444	175	22	3	8	107	369	775	1192	6413
	Degree-Days Cooling	0	0	1	13	65	209	316	261	100	18	0	0	977
	Extreme High	69	71	88	93	95	101	103	103	99	92	78	69	103
	Normal High	30	34	46	61	72	82	85	84	76	65	48	34	60
	Normal Average	21	26	37	51	61	71	75	73	65	54	39	27	50
	Normal Low	12	17	28	40	50	60	64	62	53	42	30	18	40
	Extreme Low	-27	-25	-19	7	26	39	46	40	30	16	-9	-24	-27
Humidity	Dew Point	13	18	27	37	48	59	64	63	54	42	30	19	40
	Max % RH	76	78	79	78	79	81	85	89	87	82	80	79	81
	Min % RH	66	63	57	50	49	50	54	55	52	49	59	67	56
	% Days With Rain	20	22	35	47	48	43	41	37	38	36	33	24	35
	Rain Inches	2	1	3	4	4	5	5	4	4	3	2	2	37
Sky	% Overcast Days	52	54	55	50	45	40	29	32	33	35	53	58	45
	% Clear Days	27	29	23	25	25	24	27	30	35	36	26	23	28
Wind	Prevailing Direction	WNW	WNW	WNW	WNW	S	S	S	S	S	S	WNW	WNW	WNW
	Speed, Knots	12	12	12	13	10	9	8	8	9	10	12	12	11
	Percent Calm	6	6	5	6	9	11	13	14	14	11	7	5	9
Days Observed	Rain	6	7	11	14	15	13	12	11	12	11	10	7	129
	Fog	12	12	13	11	11	9	12	15	14	13	13	13	149
	Haze	10	12	11	8	9	9	12	14	10	9	10	10	126
	Snow	14	12	8	2	0	0	0	0	0	0	6	12	54
	Hail	0	0	0	1	0	0	0	0	0	0	0	0	2
	Freezing Rain	0	1	0	0	0	0	0	0	0	0	0	1	2
	Blowing Sand	0	0	0	0	0	0	0	0	0	0	0	0	1

advice of friends. He considered Bob McNamara, whom he knew from college days at Berkeley. McNamara had recently overseen the commissioning of a new administration building for Ford Motor Company. Hewitt also consulted industrial design pioneer Henry Dreyfuss, who did considerable product design for Deere. Finally, Hewitt went touring several buildings to look at work firsthand. After he visited Eero Saarinen's recently completed General Motors Technical Center in Detroit, the two met at Saarinen's office. Acting on impressions and the strong recommendation of Dreyfuss, Hewitt decided on Saarinen "then and there."

Brief

During the year it took to select from four potential sites and acquire the land, Hewitt and Saarinen formed a

friendship while working out a basic building program. In 1957 the management firm of Booz, Allen and Hamilton made a detailed analysis of the company's needs and projected these into 1970. The resulting brief was simple enough — offices for 800 to 1000 people, cafeteria and executive dining, auditorium for 400, and a large display area for Deere products. Overall, Hewitt desired to consolidate the different offices the company had scattered around downtown Moline. Integration of departments and improvement of working conditions would mean more productivity. He also wanted a building that would attract and retain a highly qualified workforce and one that would promote the image of Deere & Company in the community and the world at large.

Beyond setting these fundamental requirements, Hewitt thought it best to send Saarinen off on his own and

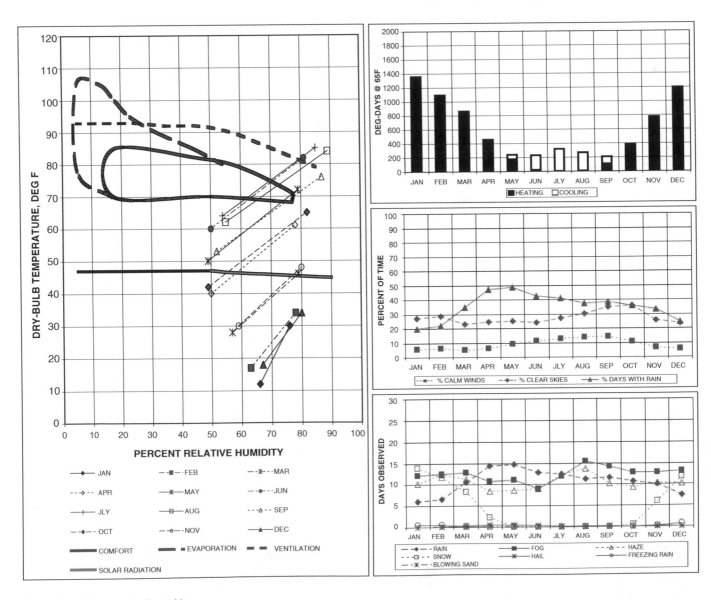

Figure 6.6 Climate analysis graphics.

Moline, Illinois

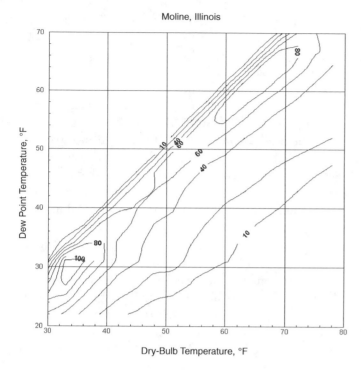

Figure 6.7 Bin data distribution for Moline, Illinois. Concentric areas of graph indicate the number of hours per year that weather conditions normally occur in this climate. Similar to elevation readings on topographic maps, highest frequency occurrences of weather are at the center peaks of the graph. (Data sources: *Engineering Weather Data, typical meteorological year (TMY) data from the National Climatic Data Center, and the* ASHRAE Weather Data Viewer *from the American Society of Heating, Refrigerating and Air-Conditioning Engineers.)*

not interfere with his architect's work. Saarinen objected and expressed a desire for interaction. Saarinen's explorations, it seems, required a driving stimulus. Without factual provocation, without clues to puzzle together, without situations to optimize, there was little real catalyst for design. It is not that Saarinen believed architecture to be limited to creative problem solving, quite the contrary. He repeatedly stated and demonstrated that his interest was in architecture as an art. The Deere Headquarters was to become one of his proofs.

Site

While scouting the four prospective sites that Deere had preselected for the project, Hewitt arranged to borrow a service truck with at 35 ft telescoping boom from the local utility company. Looking out above the treetops from the parcel that Saarinen had decided on, he may have seen the Rock River a mile to the south.

About half of the 600 acre site finally acquired was hilly and covered with mature oak trees. Saarinen thought to organize the headquarters along a high ridge that divided the site and where trees were most dense. The best sight

lines were down both sides of the 40 ft deep ravine below — running directly on a north-to-south axis and very favorable to solar protection. Site drainage would be naturally handled by the ravine as it carried storm water south to the Greenwood Slough and into the Rock River some 90 ft in elevation below the top of the ridge.

Climate

Moline, Illinois, sits on a broad peninsula between the Mississippi River to the north and the Rock River to the south. The Quad Cities area around Moline features a cool and damp climate. The regional pattern is not very different from cross-state Chicago some 160 miles to the east, except for the microclimatic influences of Lake Michigan on Chicago. Freezing temperatures normally occur in Moline from November to March, and all five of these months have more than 750 degree-days heating. In total there are 6412 annual heating degree-days to 944 cooling degree-days, a ratio of about 6.5 to 1. Measurable rain falls on more than a third of the annual days, with heaviest distribution in the spring. Freezing precipitation of some sort falls about 60 days per year. Winter winds are brisk from the WNW and summer breezes are calmer from the south. Moline is fairly comparable to Munich, Germany, except that Moline winters are somewhat shorter and more intense and Moline summers are slightly warmer than Munich's.

INTENTION

Design Team

Eero Saarinen (1910–1961) was born in Kirkkonummi, near Helsinki, Finland, 200 miles from the birthplace of Louis Kahn in Estonia nine years earlier. He was the son of celebrated Finnish architect Eliel Saarinen and Loja Gesellius, a sculptor, weaver, photographer, and architectural model maker. After growing up under his parent's tutelage, Eero studied sculpture at the Académie de la Grande Chaumière in Paris for two years and graduated from the school of architecture at Yale University in 1934. He traveled to Europe (1934–1935) and stayed an additional year in Helsinki to work with architect Jarl Eklund. Eero then returned to teach at the Cranbrook Academy of Art, where his father was serving as its architect and first president. In 1937 he met Charles and Ray Eames, who were studying at the academy, and the three became lifelong friends and compatriots. Eero worked in his father's office until Eliel's death in 1950. In 1939 Saarinen married the sculptor Lillian Swann, and they had two children, Eric and Susan. They divorced in 1953, and Saarinen was married the following year to Aline Bernstein Loucheim, an art critic. A son, Eames, named for his friends Ray and Charles, was born later that year. Tragically, Eero died of brain cancer at the age of 51 before most of his master-works, including John Deere, were even under construction. His office completed the work under the guidance of his senior partners, John Dinkeloo and Kevin Roche.

John Dinkeloo was the technologist of Saarinen's office. He was born in Holland, Michigan, in 1918. He studied architecture at the University of Michigan, after which he worked for Skidmore, Owings, and Merrill. Dinkeloo joined Saarinen's firm in 1950, becoming a part-ner five years later. He passed away in Fredericksburg, Virginia, in 1981.

Kevin Roche was Saarinen's lead design architect. Born in Dublin, Ireland, in 1922, he studied in Dublin and Illinois and then worked for Michael Scott and the United Nations Planning Office. He joined the Saarinen firm about the same time Dinkeloo did, in 1950.

Burns & McDonnell Engineering Company was founded in 1898 by two Stanford University graduates, Clinton Burns and Robert McDonnell. They based their office in Kansas City because many surrounding towns did not have municipal water or sewer systems and so were in need of civil engineers. In 1942, the Smoky Hill Army Airfield in Salina, Kansas, was the first of what would be a long line of aviation-related projects for Burns & McDonnell, and by 1953 the firm began a long association with Trans World Airlines by engineering a maintenance facility. Their airport expertise reunited them with Eero Saarinen in 1958 during master planning for Dulles International Airport (see case study #10). When Burns & McDonnell celebrated its 100th anniversary on April 1, 1998, the engineering, architectural, construction, and environmental services firm had grown from a two-man operation to an international company with more than 1300 employees.

Philosophy

Eero Saarinen is known for his meandering path through the 11 short years of his career. In each project he seemed to find new form, new technology, new expression. This led some critics to complain about his waywardness and apparent lack of direction. Other observers instead com-plimented his dedication to clients rather than to an agen-da of personal style.

Intent

Saarinen's first proposal for the Deere Company con-tained none of the naturally derived solutions or optimal selections for which he is credited in the final scheme. It consisted of an inverted concrete pyramid, hollowed in the center, the inside ringed with walkways, and the whole affair capped with a skylight. When the client committee questioned some particulars, Saarinen and his associates offered little in the way of defense or strong convictions about the scheme. Instead, the architects made polite good-byes and went back to work.

A brief three weeks later, the parties met again at Saarinen's office in Bloomfield Hills, Michigan. The sec-ond scheme was a presented in model form and, as can be seen in photos of the 1959 presentation as well as Hewitt's description, depicted a layout very close to that which was eventually built. This time the intentions were tied to strong ideas. Central in the architect's thinking was exposed steel frame construction as an iconic image for a maker of steel machines. In addition, the office interior was visually connected to the natural beauty of the site.

Spatial components of the project were separated into three individual but linked forms: formal entry through the exhibit space on top of the ridge with an adjoining auditorium, then a bridge into the ravine connecting to the mid-story of a tall, thin office block. The offices were to become the signature identity of the complex by span-ning the ravine and looking south across a lake to the parklike entry drive. The Exhibit and Auditorium blocks were nestled on top of the ridge in the tall oaks and used to separate the parking lot and public entry from the offices. Passage to the offices was gained by walking over a glass-enclosed bridge hung 50 ft above the ravine.

CRITICAL TECHNICAL ISSUES

Inherent

The client's brief for this office headquarters seems to have been structured around fairly generic workplace stan-dards. The client brought few new functional concerns or organizational relationships into the conversation. The firm's faith was in its architect, trusting Saarinen to have masterful insight into its requirements. So deep was this confidence that Saarinen was also given the task of design-ing the office furniture. Deere's operations were not then the sort of highly serviced workplace we think of now. Nor was there a long list of ergonomic and productivity crite-ria. But attracting and retaining a core of qualified per-sonnel to Moline was likely a problem. Corporate paternalism and long-term loyalty were also more charac-teristic of employers' thinking in those days of a more deeply rooted society.

An employee issue that was exaggerated by the rural locations was solved by including dining facilities. The set-ting of ravine, trees, and lakes offered a design opportuni-ty more than a challenge. The natural setting would be ideal for the best of restaurants, and employees were more likely to stay close to the office for lunch. Food service for 1000 people created functional demands for space, amenities, and systems for handling flows of groceries, waste, and services, but the benefits seemed to outweigh the resources needed.

Contextual

Given the wild natural beauty of the site and Deere's efforts to select a rural location, situating the building required sensitivity and finesse. Saarinen's decision to bridge the office block across the ravine promptly set critical design objectives for the broad façade: as an announcement of arrival, as a tractorlike image of corporate durability, and as a south façade that would require deep shading. Solar protection versus an open view to the south was a serious challenge in this regard. Proposing a lake to the sunlit side of the building did not help either. Although water absorbs about 90 percent of incident light and energy, its smooth mirror surface can create strong reflections and bright glare.

The remoteness of the site location did offer a contextual advantage—it was far enough outside the city limits to allow construction of an unprotected steel frame. Fireproofing was a problem that Roche Dinkeloo Associates would address again during Deere's expansion on the west ridge, and later in their firm's project for the New Haven, Connecticut, headquarters for the Knights of Columbus.

Intentional

Both the exposed steel frame and the visual connection of offices to the garden setting posed technical challenges. Rust and maintenance were issues for the exposed steel. After years of warning customers about rust, no one at John Deere wanted to risk the embarrassment of a high-maintenance building frame. As for open views to the site, there were questions to answer about glare and heat gain.

There was a structural challenge too. The offices were depicted as a floating mass that hovered above the lake and spanned to both sides of the ravine. An exposed structure would have to remain light to maintain this buoyancy. A heavily trussed steel support would be hard to conceal and would contradict the intended result.

APPROPRIATE SYSTEMS

The client and architect having agreed on the appropriateness of a steel building skeleton as a corporate logo suggestive of John Deere products, design development began. Saarinen was noted for exploring hundreds or even thousands of materials, details, and combinations of each

before settling on a direction. It is obvious from the failed first proposal for an inverted and introverted pyramid that the systems selections were as much reasoned out over time as they were arrived at by sudden inspiration. Thus, although the prime intention may have been declared early, further ambitions for the building were more the product of deduction and discovery than of self-guided genius.

The two most significant systems adopted for the Deere Headquarters were the exposed structure of weathering steel and the reflective glass envelope.

Precedents

The General Motors Technical Center in Warren, Michigan, was designed in halting stages but is essentially the work of Eero Saarinen. It was initially contracted by Saarinen and Swanson, that is, Eliel Saarinen working with his son and his son-in-law, from September 1945 to March 1946, when GM halted work to focus on expanding production. In December 1948 the same team resumed the project as Saarinen and Saarinen and presented a new design for GM's expanded scope, represented by a budget revised from $20 million to $60 million that eventually increased to $100 million (about $633 million in 1995 dollars). The 320 acre complex of offices, studios, shops, and laboratories eventually grew to 813 acres, and in 1951, following the elder Saarinen's death, Eero Saarinen produced a new master plan. Construction of Saarinen's 26 original buildings on the campus continued until 1956, and they have been renovated and added to many times since. Smith, Hinchman and Grylls was the project architect/engineer. Bryant and Detwiler was the general contractor.

Like John Deere, the General Motors project is an "office in the garden." Parallel features include the Technical Center, built around a 22 acre artificial lake with two fountains and several pieces of art. It was landscaped with more than 13,000 trees, 3,100 shrubs, and 56,000 ground cover plantings to surround it with a forested greenbelt. Of greater significance, the image and technology of the building complex is taken from the image and technology of the client, in this case an automobile maker.

In this part of Eero Saarinen's career, before Dinkeloo and Roche joined his firm, he was able to work closely with GM engineers to pioneer and refine several aspects of the building construction. The ceramic glazing of the end wall brickwork was perfected by spark plug engineers who used ceramics to insulate their high-performance products. The bricks were fired in a kiln custom-built by GM on the site. Windows and porcelain-enameled steel panel fittings were developed with car window gaskets. Aluminum cladding was worked out for glazing bars and column enclosures. Partition systems were made to be demountable. The GM design department helped to develop the first completely luminous ceiling, made from molded plastic pans. Aircraft technology was also employed in the form of insulated honeycomb wall panels prefinished with the porcelain-enameled steel.

With its low horizontal forms of rectangular buildings against a rectangular lake on a rectangular site, the General Motors Technical Center was decidedly of the International Style. It owes something to the influence of Mies van der Rohe, with its exposed I beams, its flexible interiors, and its conscious detailing. The campus of the Illinois Institute of Technology, designed by Mies (1939–1956) may even have been the prior precedent for Saarinen's GM Center. But Saarinen is credited with translating the International Style into an American corporate architecture and with the integration of industrial methods into architectural production.

Site

Saarinen selected a location along the ravine he deemed most pleasant and appropriate for the building he had in mind and then planned the approach carefully. A bridge across the ravine is what he had in mind for the building, with its mass suspended above two lakes. Parking would be removed from the central vista and placed above the ravine to both sides. On the east is the main entry through a separate auditorium and museum pavilion. On the west, plans were made for future expansion. From both sides the main headquarters is entered by crossing a bridge, passing through the treetops, and landing at the fifth level of the office block.

To maintain the pristine setting, an access road was routed around the perimeter of the site, hugging the ridges on both sides of the ravine. Entry from the main road splits immediately across a broad esplanade, keeping the scale of the roadways as thin as possible. The headquarters comes into view only after one clears the intervening trees and the vista opens across a large artificial lake, past a smaller lake in front of the building. Then the trees obscure the sight lines again. Finally, there is the pavilion and parking on the east.

The roadway continues to the north along its one-way loop, curving west to cross the ravine at a respectable distance from the building. A lower-level service road sneaks in from the north for deliveries and maintenance access. Exiting the site, one follows a similar path south to the main road.

The site is organized vertically by interior functions, with prime views to the south across the two lakes. Executive dining is set above the basements at the level of the small lake directly to the south of the office block. This lower mass is expressed as a plinth. Executive offices and staff dining are located in the two stories of space set above the plinth and pulled inward to create a terrace and shade the interiors. Finally, five floors of office space bridge the ravine, sheltered behind a thick eyebrow of shading devices on all four sides.

Structure

Saarinen's quest for an appropriate building material to reflect the image of John Deere & Company while gracing the natural beauty of the site began with images of farm equipment. The warm, rusted texture of plows and shears would have been unavoidable. What Saarinen discovered was a naturally weathering low-carbon or "low-alloy" steel used for railroad cars. It had been developed in response to the need for a durable unpainted surface in which to carry abrasive agricultural grains, such as wheat and corn, that would scrape away the painted surfaces during handling and ruin the purity of the grain cargo. The trade name was Corten, and it still carries that name and the ASTM A-242 alloy designation today. The chemical properties of this steel are that it forms a natural weathered surface of rust, or hydrated iron oxide, when exposed to moisture. Rather than rusting like regular mild steel, this finish crystallizes into a hard protective surface layer, thus arresting further oxidation. Alternating wet and dry conditions maintain this barrier by continually closing microcrevices in the inner layer via the alloying of copper from the underlying steel. New microcrevices form when the patina dries, but when the material is rewetted, the cycle continues and the protective surface develops a chemical equilibrium with very little surface corrosion. The finished product, after adequate wetting and drying cycles, is a permanent micro-crystalline finish similar to the mineral hematite (Fe_2O_3, also called bloodstone or iron rose) in appearance, with a red-brown color. Because of its maintenance-free weathering surface and its high strength, weathering steel has been used in the construction of more than 2300 bridges in the United States since 1970. Whereas mild steel has a tensile strength of 60,000 psi, A-242 is rated at 70,000 psi. This extra strength allows for the use of lighter sections with corresponding economies of cost.

At Deere, the weathering steel frame members are assembled stick-like, with welded connections formed as beams and columns pass and overlap each other, rather than intersect at their web and flange. Purlins sit on top of beams rather than inside their web to visually emphasize the strength of each steel section. For the same reason, end and corner connections expose the protruding section profiles rather than finishing flush. To maintain this image of vigorous steel, there are no diagonals and no bolted connections.

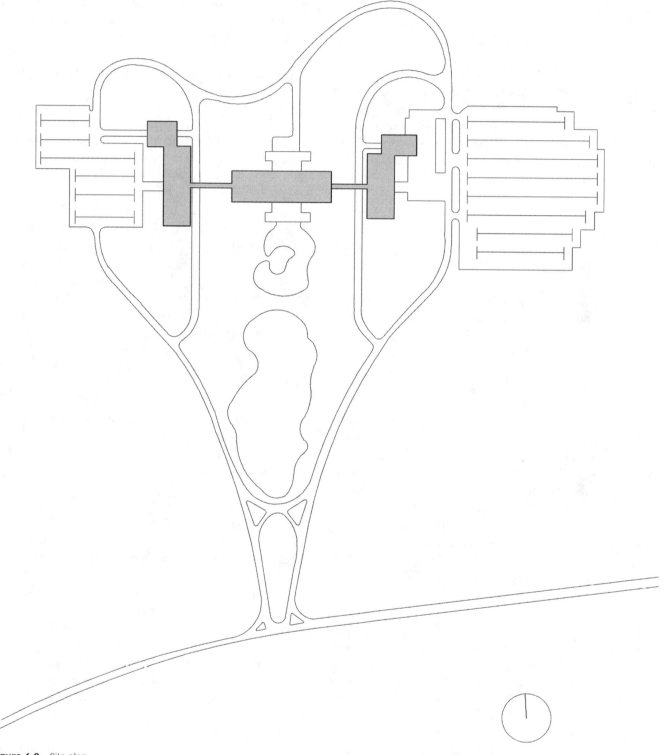

Figure 6.8   Site plan.

Main columns are 30 WF 108 along the perimeter and 10 WF 39 on both sides of the center corridor. Bay spacing is 30 ft (9.1 m) across and 42 ft (12.8 m) deep to the center corridor from both sides. The center circulation bay is 12 ft deep. The building is 11 bays wide, yielding a footprint of 330 ft × 96 ft (100 m × 29 m), or 31,600 ft^2 (2934 m^2) on a 3 ft × 6 ft (0.9 m × 1.8 m) grid. Each column is flanked by two 21 WF 82 main girders spanning north to south and extending past the column far enough to accept 10 WF 29 purlins at the outside perimeter. Six feet (1.8 m) inside the column line are two more purlins of the same shape. The outside purlin of this pair forms the base of the curtain wall, and the inside purlin forms the edge of a 2.5 in. (63 mm) concrete floor slab poured within its web on a 2.0 in. (50 mm) cellular deck. Successive 10 WF 29 purlins at 6 ft centers carry the remainder of the floor loads. All concealed steel inside the envelope is fireproofed. At the perimeter, vertical 6 B 12 steel sections rest directly on the outside 10 WF 29 purlins to frame the wall glazing. Beneath the main beams, 6 JR 4.4 purlins are mounted against the outside edge of the columns to carry the sunscreens.

Envelope

Most of what we see of this building is the signature steel frame and its articulation as a horizontal shading system. The glass envelope is held back behind the perimeter columns, making the structure brutally exoskeletal. Walls of clear glass at the lower two floors are pulled back several feet, forming a deeply shaded walkway at the plaza level and well-protected views from the adjoining dining rooms and executive offices. The five main office floors above are protected by a *brise soleil* that melds into the structural system by use of the same weathering steel and overlapping welded connections. At these upper levels the primary floor beams cantilever past the columns and support a smaller-profile secondary 6 B 12 purlin running parallel to the exterior wall. Hung from the purlin are vertical members supporting four horizontal 5.25 in. wide hat sections that form the thick eyebrow. The suspended hat section shading device and its supports extend from the floor level above, down across a glass-clad steel spandrel panel in the section of the main floor beams, and then a full third of the way down in front of the vision glass.

Above the hat section eyebrow, in the same horizontal plane as the interior ceiling grid, a second shading strategy is deployed. A 3 in. thick steel grate, with 3 in. × 3 in. cells of the same proportions as the interior suspended ceiling grid, is framed midway down from the floor beam to the bottom of the eyebrow. This 6 ft deep secondary horizontal shade helps eliminate high solar altitude sun angles and provides a sturdy walkway for window cleaning.

This assembly of thick eyebrow and horizontal grate is more than adequate, even for the long south-facing façade. It is a strong formal device that is wrapped uniformly around all four exposures of the upper floors. The suggestive value of its machine image seems to have outweighed Saarinen's respect for views, particularly from north glass where little or no solar protection is needed anyway.

To further soften the view and blunt the sun, Saarinen's group devised yet another layer of protection: reflective glass. They used 0.25 in. laminated glazing, with a bronze reflective interlayer to bond the glazings and protect the coating in the middle of the sandwich. The glass is set in neoprene gaskets that affix directly to the steel frame. There are no mullions or other dedicated glazing frame components. The vertical jamb is formed by the inside edge of the 6 B 12 vertical steel framing, and the horizontal sill and head are made by welding 0.25 in. × 11 in. steel plate closures between the jambs. The window gaskets fit directly onto the steel frame. The priority of reflective shading is curious in that it replicates the job of the external sunscreens and ignores the effects of winter weather on inside surface temperatures and comfort conditions close to the windows. Not only does protection this decrease comfort and increase thermal losses for much of the year, it also requires drier inside air in order to avoid condensation on the inside glass surface, as warm, moist interior air easily meets dew point temperatures against the cold glass surface. Hewitt later reportedly stated that insulated glass should have been selected despite its premium cost at that time.

Mechanical

Air distribution to the main offices is provided at floor level in the space between the two outer steel purlins. This cavity serves as a continuous air grille at the building perimeter. The distribution system uses 727 dual-duct mixing boxes serving 516 thermostats to maximize temperature and humidity control, with little regard for energy efficiency. Delivery to each zone is ducted in the floor-ceiling layer above the egg crate luminous ceiling. Fan capacity totals more than 1 million ft^3 per minute.

Central heavy plant equipment is located in the basement. There is a 1600 ton cooling plant. Space heating is produced by two gas-fired boilers, each of 25 million Btuh (747 horsepower or 7328 kW each). In lieu of cooling towers, the larger of the two lakes is used as a spray pond to reject heat from the chillers to the environment.

Interior

The entrance to the main office block at the fourth floor directly from the ridge level pavilion strategically places circulation in the middle of the workspaces. There are three floors above and one office level below. The interior plan and the structural scheme reflect each other with a 12 ft wide central passageway and 42 ft open spans at each side. Stairs, toilets, and elevators are located in core areas on the north side of the sixth and eighth bays, counted from the west side. Lobby and lounge spaces are located across the intervening seventh bay.

Saarinen believed that large-scale mock-ups were essential to the client's clear perception of architectural decisions and effective communication. Early in the design process a $100,000 (about $515,000 in 1995 dollars) full-scale construction of a one-bay by two-story section was executed beyond what is now the main parking lot. In the same vein, furniture and equipment were mocked-up and all fixtures were carefully selected, from door handles to drinking fountains to dining flatware, down to the paper envelopes for the sugar used in the cafeteria. Saarinen designed all the furniture as well.

Movable steel frame partitions are used in the 3 ft × 6 ft module that organizes the building. Partitions are glass infill, allowing light and view across the plan. A 3 ft × 6 ft grid of 3 in. × 3 in. grillwork provides the diffusing surface for the luminous ceiling below fluorescent strip lighting.

TECHNICAL INTEGRATION HIGHLIGHTS

Saarinen favors a strong central image for each of his designs. At Deere, the generating idea was to relate the building to the client's product. Thus, this is an exposed steel building with details befitting industrial implements. Raw steel shapes are used, and connections consist largely of overlapping pieces welded together where they pass and connect. Color is important as well; the oxidized surfaces of exposed steel are romantically reminiscent of old plows but reassuringly smooth crusted and even colored. The weathering is a patina, not a stain. The rust crystallizes into a natural reddish-brown or cinnamon color. Its hue and texture are visually not unlike the bark of surrounding trees. Stalky columns are exposed and uninterrupted, like tree trunks, for the first three levels above the lake. Eyebrow shading devices make smaller horizontal branches of the building like a man-made tree. Its bony pieces protrude and hang from the building, reinforcing the visual connection to the landscape.

Deep setbacks of the lower-level walls behind the perimeter columns also float the solid mass of upper floors high above the lake. This mass-over-void suspension prepares one for the entrance to the building at the fifth level, across a bridge from the parking area on the

adjacent hillside some 50 ft above the building podium. This sudden transition from grade level orientation below the trees to an open view above them evokes a kind of weightlessness that begins with views from the entry drive.

Physical

- Glass and structure are physically connected without the use of a glazing system.
- Site and entry are organized to limit vertical travel distance by providing entrance to the building at the midpoint of its elevation.

Visual

- The image of Deere's farm implements is replicated in the weathering steel frame.
- The visual connection of naturally weathering steel structure to surrounding trees graces the site.
- The floating mass of the upper five office floors in bright reflective glass hovers above the shadowed clear glass lower stories and the lake.
- The elimination of diagonal bracing emphasizes the vigor of steel structure.
- The reflective glass as a solid wall preserves the mass of upper floors.
- The steel spandrel panels are clad in glass to make an uninterrupted glass skin.

Performance

- Functional integration at Deere begins with the conflict between favorable views and unwanted solar heat gain. The design goes to extreme precautions by using not only overhangs, shading screens, and *brise soleil* shading methods, but a defensive glazing of reflective glass as a second layer of defense.
- The lake and its fountains double as the heat rejection point of the building, eliminating the use of cooling towers.
- The structural system becomes the external shading system.
- Exterior and interior glazing preserves light and view.
- The luminous ceiling grid is extended outward as a metal grate into the exterior steel frame.
- The extended ceiling grid is used as a metal grate shading device and maintenance walkway.
- The formal device of mass-over-void works as a shading device for the lower two floors.

DISCUSSION

The difference between Saarinen's reverence for client guidelines and Louis Kahn's disdain for most notions of building program is elemental in the way it defines the starting points of design. This difference then relates to process issues of open-ended "problem-solving" exploration versus design guided by a "personally directed" set of principles. Does the first method focus on architecture for clients and the second on architecture for architects? Perhaps this is more appropriately a question of how the approach to design is bounded. The problem-solving path is bounded by external constraints or "real-world" issues. The architect seeks to illuminate their essence. This first approach is expressionist and existential. It operates on a romantic appreciation of natural dictates and a desire to transcend the mundane. The second method, via a self-directed set of principles, is bounded by intellectual ideals. It seeks to accommodate the truths and givens within a defined set of beliefs about architecture. Given that both nature and architecture are true, the fit is only a matter of finding agreement.

In the end the two approaches are complementary, coming at the same thing from different directions. In practice, the two far ends of these different approaches are usually balanced by design processes that recognize both ways of thinking. In Saarinen and Kahn, however, we have examples of how the two processes operate differently and how they can both result in great architecture. It is not necessary to have a favorite. Saarinen's modernism may seem closer to industrialized systems architecture and to the truths of his time. Kahn's insights, on the other hand, seem elevated by reverence for light, silence, space, and the materiality he lends them. We should recognize these different concepts as genius and accept them as possible origins. Even our idols had to start their work somewhere.

Because John Deere & Company is used here as a precedent study for integration in office building projects, it follows that we could trace the lineage of its ideas into buildings that came later. The easy examples are the works of Kevin Roche and John Dinkeloo, Saarinen's partners and successors, the architects who finished his greatest designs and who carried on the traditions of his office. Roche Dinkeloo and Associates' 1969 headquarters for the Knights of Columbus repeats the exposed steel frame acting as *brise soleil*. C. F. Murphy and Associates' 1965 Richard Daley Center in Chicago and Harrison & Ambramovitz & Abbe's 1970 offices for US Steel in Pittsburgh are only two of many buildings to feature a weathering steel exterior.

7

WILLIS FABER DUMAS INSURANCE HEADQUARTERS, 1970–1975

Ipswich, Suffolk, England
NORMAN FOSTER

DESCRIPTION

This early work of Foster Associates establishes many precedents of what has come to be called "High Tech" architecture. Situated on a difficult site in the urban context of Ipswich, England, the Willis Faber Dumas Insurance Headquarters (now Willis Corroon) was designed to attract company personnel from the firm's London office. The solution features a semipublic first floor with leisure facilities and two office floors above. The building is capped by a penthouse restaurant and roof garden.

With a deep floor plan that extends to the sidewalk limits of the site, the office spaces are penetrated by an escalator circulation system that serves all four levels and doubles as a light well. The roof garden restaurant thus becomes a light monitor to introduce daylight to the central areas of the deep-plan office floors. In the overcast climate of the eastern coast of England, a suspended mullionless glass skin provides a floor-to-ceiling outside view and natural light.

The grand stairway of the escalator and the distributed exit stairs serve to organize the interior arrangement of office space. A 5 ft deep perimeter circulation path is cantilevered outside the last column bay. This scheme buffers the workstations from the less controlled glass weatherskin where harsh sun or cold glass surfaces may be uncomfortable for prolonged periods of time.

Figure 6.9 View of Willis Faber Dumas Headquarters from the roundabout.

TABLE 6.4   Fact Sheet

Project		
	Building Name	Willis Faber Dumas Insurance Headquarters
	Client	Willis Faber Dumas Insurance (now Willis Corroon)
	City	Ipswich, Suffolk, England
	Lat/Long/Elev	52.06 N 01.15 E, 95 ft (29 m)

Team		
	Architect	Norman Foster
	Structural Engineer	Anthony Hunt Associates
	Mechanical Engineer	Foster Associates
	Glazing	Pilkington
	Acoustics	Acoustics Sound Research
	Quantity Surveyors	Davis Belfield & Everest
	General Contractor	Bovis Constructor Ltd.

General		
	Time Line	Design 1970 to 1972, building opened June 2, 1975.
	Floor Area	226,041 ft^2 (21,000 m^2).
	Occupants	1350.
	Cost	£4,982,062 or U.S. $11,361,094.
	Cost, 1995 dollars	$32,184,403 or $142/ft^2.
	Stories	Three stories above grade plus a penthouse restaurant and roof garden.
	Plan	Footprint covers entire site up to sidewalk.

Site		
	Site Description	Irregular shape, 1.7 acre (7000 m^2) urban site.
	Parking, Cars	Parking garage across street from building.

Structure		
	Foundation	Slab elevated above poor soil on bored concrete piers.
	Vertical Members	Circular concrete columns on a 46 ft × 46 ft grid. Ground and first floor are 39.4 in. (1 m) diameter. Higher levels have 31.5 in. (800 mm) diameter columns.
	Horizontal Spans	Concrete waffle slab, 27.6 in. thick (700 mm); 5 ft (1.5 m) cantilever at perimeter.
	Special Features	The interior column grid is complemented by a ring of closer-spaced columns at the building perimeter that define the building shape.

Envelope		
	Glass and Glazing	There are 930 panels of 2.0 m × 2.5 m of 12 mm thick glass (6.6 ft × 8.2 ft × 0.5 in.). Interior vertical fins of 19 mm (0.74 in.) glass provide lateral wind resistance.
	Cladding	All glass, Pilkington Armor plate Antisun bronze reflective.
	Roof	Single-ply rubber roofing with glass mat and sod.
	Special Features	Glass panels are all hung from roof and connected with 6.5-in. square brass plates and stainless steel screws.

HVAC		
	Equipment	Centrifugal refrigeration chilled water and boilers.
	Cooling Type	Fan coil and forced air.
	Distribution	Supply through strip diffusers in ceiling grid. Return plenum through light fixtures.
	Duct Type	Concealed single duct.
	Vertical Chases	Toilet room modules on office floors provide stacked mechanical areas.
	Special Features	Mechanical system is exposed through glazing to sidewalk at grade level.

Interior		
	Partitions	Open plan.
	Finishes	Rubber flooring on first level. Green carpet on office levels.
	Vertical Circulation	Escalator lobby rises three levels to receive toplighting from restaurant.
	Furniture	Herman Miller.
	Lighting	Parabolic strip fluorescent downlighting in aluminum louver ceiling.
	Special Features	Ground level contains leisure activity spaces (pool, coffee bar, gym), as well as mechanical.

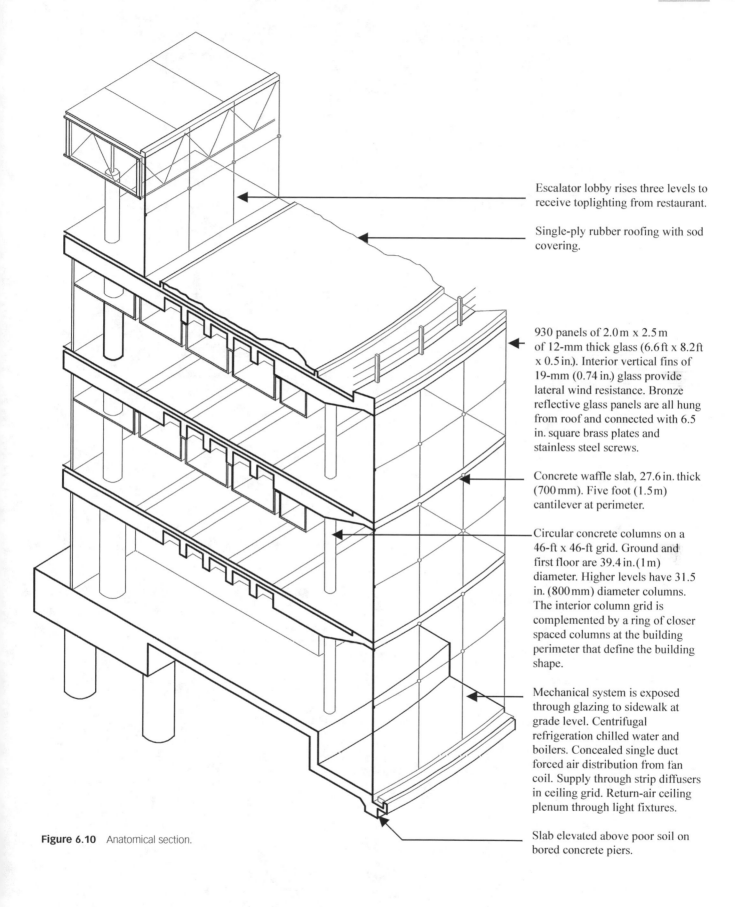

Escalator lobby rises three levels to receive toplighting from restaurant.

Single-ply rubber roofing with sod covering.

930 panels of 2.0 m x 2.5 m of 12-mm thick glass (6.6 ft x 8.2 ft x 0.5 in.). Interior vertical fins of 19-mm (0.74 in.) glass provide lateral wind resistance. Bronze reflective glass panels are all hung from roof and connected with 6.5 in. square brass plates and stainless steel screws.

Concrete waffle slab, 27.6 in. thick (700 mm). Five foot (1.5 m) cantilever at perimeter.

Circular concrete columns on a 46-ft x 46-ft grid. Ground and first floor are 39.4 in.(1m) diameter. Higher levels have 31.5 in. (800 mm) diameter columns. The interior column grid is complemented by a ring of closer spaced columns at the building perimeter that define the building shape.

Mechanical system is exposed through glazing to sidewalk at grade level. Centrifugal refrigeration chilled water and boilers. Concealed single duct forced air distribution from fan coil. Supply through strip diffusers in ceiling grid. Return-air ceiling plenum through light fixtures.

Slab elevated above poor soil on bored concrete piers.

Figure 6.10 Anatomical section.

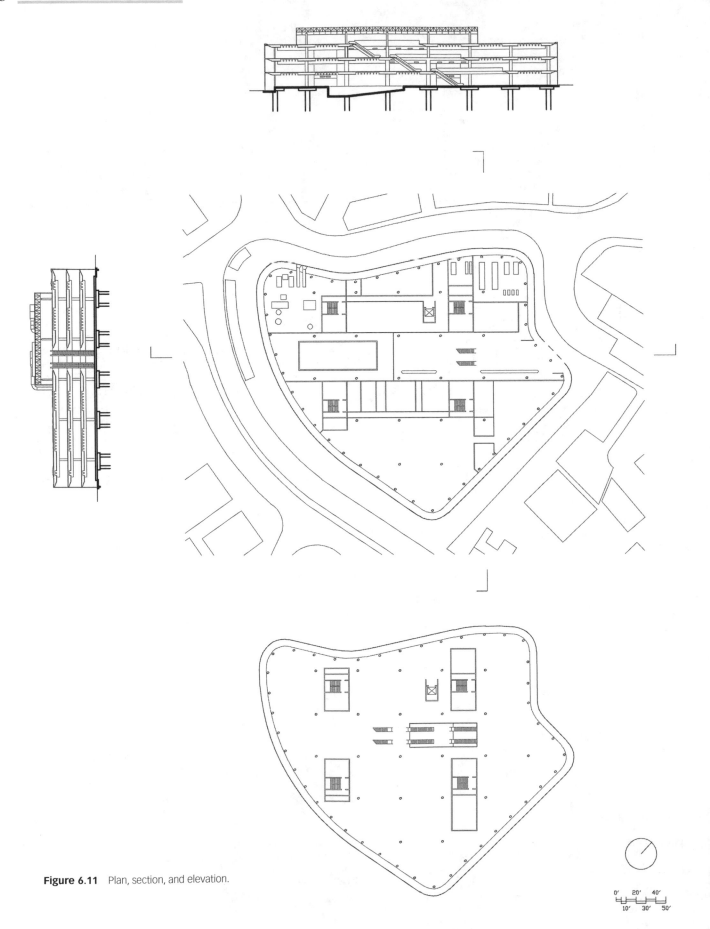

Figure 6.11 Plan, section, and elevation.

0' 20' 40'
10' 30' 50'

PROGRAM

Client

Willis Faber Dumas (now Willis Coroon) is the world's third-largest insurance firm. The company is an underwriter for Lloyd's of London and has a large interest in maritime risks. Among its insured have been the *Titanic* and the lunar exploration Moon Buggy.

In August 1971 the firm decided to reorganize its business operations and decentralize its London-based administrative departments. Ipswich was attractive for its affordable real estate, bustling port, economic vitality, and charming medieval character. But because Ipswich was a 75-minute commute by rail from London, there was some concern about persuading employees to relocate and recruiting for future needs.

Foster and Associates was selected after 12 recommended firms had been reduced to a short list that included Ahrends Burton & Koraiek, Arup Associates, and Foster Associates. The determining factor in final selection seems to have been Norman Foster's commitment to a strong personal involvement with the project. He was also known for his recent experience with open-plan offices.

Brief

The brief specified a minimum of 226,041 ft^2 (21,000 m^2) of floor space for a workforce of 1350 people using at least 1200 workstations. On the qualitative side, there were two primary criteria. First, given the need to draw and retain a workforce, the building and its work environment were seen as prospective attractions. Second, Foster responded

TABLE 6.5 Normal Climate Data for Ipswich, UK

		Jan.	Feb.	Mar.	Apr.	May	June	July	Aug.	Sept.	Oct.	Nov.	Dec.	Year
Temperature	Degree-Days Heating	764	703	667	547	368	189	94	84	179	362	580	722	5319
	Degree-Days Cooling	0	0	0	0	0	8	28	30	5	1	0	0	46
	Extreme High	59	59	63	75	79	88	91	88	82	73	64	61	91
	Normal High	44	44	48	52	59	65	69	70	65	58	50	46	56
	Normal Average	41	40	44	47	53	59	63	63	59	53	46	43	51
	Normal Low	36	36	38	41	47	52	56	56	53	48	41	39	45
	Extreme Low	12	19	27	28	30	37	45	41	39	34	27	18	12
Humidity	Dew Point	33	32	35	37	44	49	53	52	49	45	39	36	42
	Max % RH	78	77	80	80	82	83	83	81	80	81	80	79	80
	Min % RH	76	73	70	65	64	64	63	61	64	72	77	78	69
	% Days with Rain	63	46	66	60	56	56	56	50	56	63	63	66	3
	Rain Inches	2.0	1.4	1.3	1.2	1.5	1.4	1.8	1.9	1.8	2.3	2.2	1.8	20.8
Sky	% Overcast Days	49	46	42	36	31	31	27	24	29	34	40	45	36
	% Clear Days	3	9	21	8	9	3	0	3	11	4	0	14	9
Wind	Prevailing Direction	W	W	W	N	N	W	W	W	W	SW	W	W	W
	Speed, Knots	12	11	11	7	6	8	8	7	8	8	9	10	9
	Percent Calm	/	10	8	9	9	11	11	13	13	12	10	8	10
Days Observed	Rain	19	14	20	18	17	17	17	15	17	19	19	20	12
	Fog	19	18	19	19	19	18	19	21	18	21	20	21	232
	Haze	13	14	17	17	19	16	20	20	18	17	15	15	201
	Snow	5	5	3	2	0	#	0	0	0	0	1	2	18
	Hail	0	0	0	#	0	#	0	0	0	0	0	0	#
	Freezing Rain	#	#	0	0	0	0	0	0	0	0	0	#	#
	Blowing Sand	5	4	5	4	5	5	3	3	3	3	3	3	46

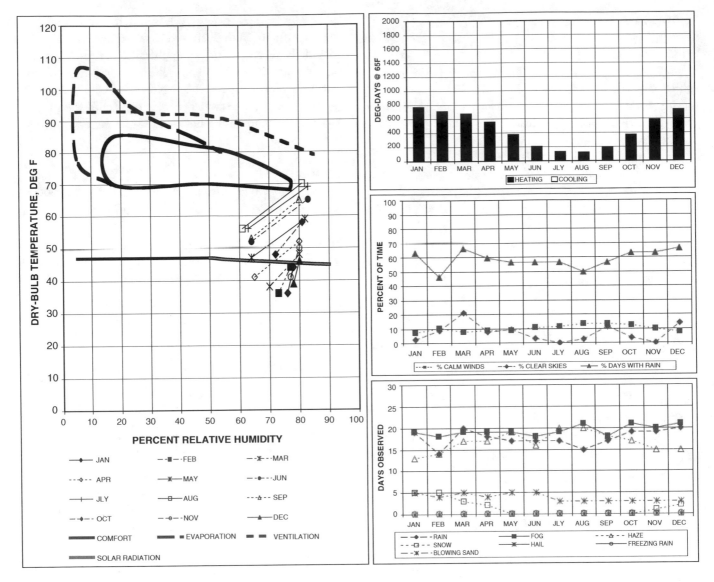

Figure 6.12 Climate analysis graphics.

Site

Ipswich is perhaps the oldest town in England. It was settled by Stone Age peoples and developed as a river port by Anglo Saxons in the seventh century. Industry, shipbuilding, and status as a port in the Napoleonic wars fostered its growth through the eighteenth century. The advent of railroad lines and a shipyard ensured growth and vitality into this century. Recently, Ipswich has been known as an engineering, commercial and insurance center.

Today Ipswich retains the flavor of a small market town. It is enlivened by its historical buildings, crowded pedestrian malls, and a soccer stadium with loud crowds

to the project scope by proposing various means of workstation flexibility and relocatable furniture for the changing office operations.

on many evenings. The historical market area has more than 600 listed buildings, including 12 medieval churches.

A 1.7 acre (7,000 m²) site for the Willis Faber Dumas (WFD) building was eventually secured between the historic markets and the river port district. Commuters would walk about 10 minutes from the train station. The irregular plot of land is anchored on one side by a traffic circle and meets curving streets on all sides.

The historic character of the setting made for a sensitive context. To preserve the low-key scale, building authorities imposed a severe height limitation, and would allow vehicle access from only one side road. There was no room for on-site parking, but space in a nearby garage was secured. The garage was later converted to more insurance office space and features a new entry tower by Michael Hopkins.

Climate

Ipswich is located on the east coast of England, 82 miles (132 km) generally east and slightly north of central London. It is also about 57 miles (92 km) east of Cambridge, 52 miles (83 km) east of Stansted Airport, and 43 miles (69 km_ south of Norwich (see case studies 24, 3, 11, and 23, respectively). A comparative look at the climate data for these neighboring locations reveals their similarity. All these locations share the same cool, cloudy, damp climate that Köppen described as Cfb (midlatitude, uniform precipitation, warm summer). This is the same macroclimate classification that covers most of central Europe. It is also found in the United States in the region around Massachusetts, in New Zealand, in New South Wales, Australia, and other scattered locations.

The mesoclimate of Ipswich, taken at the level between Köppen's macro-description of regional climates and the particular circumstances of microclimates at the site-specific scale, is moderated by its proximity to the maritime influence of the North Sea and by its geograph-

ical separation from the ocean air currents that pump moisture onto the western shores of the British Isles. Ipswich also lacks the crowded density of London and the resulting urban heat-island effects of the large city.

There is 33 percent less rainfall in Ipswich and Norwich than in London, even though all three climates have about the same number of days with rain. Both of the western coastal towns are not quite as cold as London in the winter, nor as warm in the summer.

The Woodbridge Royal Air Force weather station is located about 10 miles northeast of Norwich. According to bin data collected there, Norwich can normally be expected to experience warm temperatures, exceeding 75°F for less than 1 percent of the year, comfortable conditions for 7 percent, cool temperatures ranging from 65°F to 55°F for 30 percent, cold temperatures below 55°F but above 35°F for 57 percent of annual hours, and frigid conditions below 35°F for 6 percent of the year.

INTENTION

Design Team

The rich creative environment that begat this building centers on Norman and Wendy Foster, who had just left the company of Richard and Su Rogers and their Team 4 partnership (see case study #22 for more of the early story). The group also included Jan Kaplicky, the Prague-born architect who had settled in Britain to work with Denys Lasdun (see case study #23 for more architectural genealogy) and then Piano & Rogers before coming to Foster Associates. Kaplicky would eventually found Future Systems with David Nixon in 1979. Michael Hopkins was also on the team, having worked with Foster on the IBM buildings at Chatum before moving on to form a partnership with Patty Hopkins in 1976 and designing the Schlumberger Research Laboratory in Cambridge in 1982 (see case study #3). Foster's current partner, Ken Shuttleworth, was at Willis Faber Dumas as well.

Foster's association with the structural engineer, Anthony Hunt, also dates to Team 4 days and began with the 1966 design for the Reliance Controls Electronics Factory. Hunt founded Anthony Hunt Associates in 1962 and has strong participation in High Tech architecture, having worked with most of the major design firms in the United Kingdom. Some engineering seems to have always been done in-house at Fosters. Loren Butt and Chubby Chhabra, for example, were on the Willis Faber Dumas roll of Foster Associates to handle the mechanical engineering.

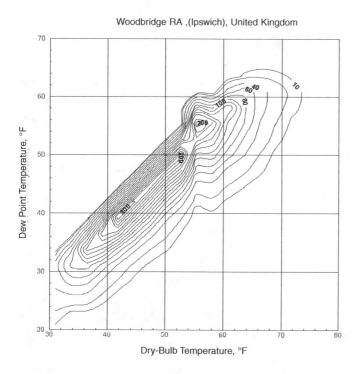

Figure 6.13 Bin data distribution for Ipswich, United Kingdom. Concentric areas of graph indicate the number of hours per year that weather conditions normally occur in this climate. Similar to elevation readings on topographic maps, highest frequency occurrences of weather are at the center peaks of the graph. (Data sources: *Engineering Weather Data, typical meteorological year (TMY) data from the National Climatic Data Center, and the* ASHRAE Weather Data Viewer *from the American Society of Heating, Refrigerating and Air-Conditioning Engineers.)*

Philosophy

Norman Foster believes that architecture has a moral obligation to push technological boundaries. The ethics of this proposition are founded, in part, on Foster's desire to improve workplace environments and the architectural accommodation of the human condition in general. He sees office buildings as places in which many people will spend most of their waking hours. Commodifying technology to the service of these individuals thus makes technology useful and connects architecture to society in a relevant way.

Intent

As in all credible works of architecture, it is Norman Foster's habit to question the client's brief, to raise doubt about its preconceptions, to probe into the hidden needs, and then to propose alternative and possibly more enlightened goals. This is the architect's inherently obligatory role, to transcend the routine of fulfilling the client's limited perspective of what is possible, what is necessary, and what the appropriate means are for connecting the two. This "interpretation of the brief" is one of Norman Foster's greatest talents toward innovative design.

Intentions at WFD were impelled by the irregular site and pressed by the large area requirements versus the low allowable-height building code. This condition was also complicated by the historical context of central Ipswich and the desire to create appealing, commodious spaces that would attract prospective office staff to commute or move from London. The resolution led to an amorphous form that fills the site to its edges. Lack of a definite shape and the absence of detail on its smooth face make a passive statement about the building, but asserts its ability to coexist with the context while satisfying its own needs internally.

CRITICAL TECHNICAL ISSUES

Inherent

- Flexible use of floor space and the uptake of office technology were stated goals of the client.
- Circulation and communication among the 1300 people in the building had to be accommodated, and large floor plan areas could lead to long walking distances between desks, to the copy machines, and between floors.
- Paper storage and records retrieval were important to the client to the extent that their dead load and storage space were programmatic issues.

Contextual

- The historical context of the site, including a 1700s Unitarian church complex on one side and the central conservation district of the old town on two other fronts, demanded a sympathetic low-rise form of response.
- Poor soil conditions and a high water table complicated construction and prohibited basements, limiting the available building space for mechanical and utility areas.
- The small site area available, along with the high water table and height restrictions, made for a cramped plan.
- Deep floor plan areas necessary to meet the area requirements resulted in many desks being far removed from the perimeter windows.

Intentional

- Providing numerous amenities to attract and retain workers further taxed the available building space needed for work areas.
- A full-height glass wall would increase the amenities of light and view, especially in the deep floor plan areas, but heat loss would have to be considered along with solar heat gain and glare.
- A roof garden was proposed to add amenity lost by the site's being covered by the building footprint, but the details of drainage and dead loads would have to be resolved.
- Daylight distribution was going to be a problem, even with full-height windows.

APPROPRIATE SYSTEMS

Precedents

The turning point for Norman Foster came with the Reliance Controls project of 1966 while he and Wendy Foster were still with Richard and Su Rogers as Team 4. The Reliance design was the beginning of their experimentation with prefabricated materials and industrial components, a direction that marks the continuum of both Rogers & Partners' and Foster Associates' practices.

Reliance Controls had asked for a 31,000 ft^2 (2,880 m^2) building that could be delivered for less than $10/ft^2 (about $48/ft^2 in 1995 dollars) and eventually expanded to three times its initial size. A very short time frame of ten months was allowed for the design and completed construction. Working with engineer Anthony Hunt, the team employed prefabrication and industrialized construction ideas they had seen at the Eames House and Studio (see case study #18) and the Smithson's Hunstanton School. An exposed steel frame was used with overhanging steel roof beams, exaggerated tubular diagonal braces, and a profiled metal roof deck and siding. Phase One was completed on time, and Phase Two followed six years later.

Site

The Willis Faber Dumas building occupies its entire site. With a limited footprint plan area, low height restrictions, and high water table, the office program swells against its physical boundaries. Parking is handled off-site. Loading docks are pushed inside the smooth skin. Mechanical systems are situated in the front window, save for cooling towers and supplemental heating, cooling, and air-conditioning (HVAC) units on the roof. The only site-related elements not contained within the building skin are storm drainage and the roof garden.

As a site system, the roof garden is more than a staff recreational amenity. It also imparts a great deal of thermal mass to the roof structure. The resulting temperature inertia provides some energy savings, even as compared with a well-insulated roof assembly. More important in this case, the thick sod restricts thermal expansion and contraction of the roof to the extent that no expansion joints are required.

Storm drainage around the building is accomplished by allowing water simply to flow down the glass skin to its base. The bottom edge of the glazing wall extends below the sidewalk level into a concealed gutter. Area drains at 62.8 ft (20 m) spacing route rainwater from the roof garden to downspouts running through four interior service cores.

Structure

Several site conditions constrained structural design to grade-level construction. First, the soil was irregularly filled over various depths of chalk and dictated a structural system based on bored pilings. Basements were precluded by a high water table and extensive underground services already in place. Finally, because the building was to occupy the entire property, excavation work would have been hampered by lack of space for earth-moving equipment. The substructure was designed around exceptionally deep 980 ft (30 m) bored pilings to bedrock.

A structural grid of 45.9 ft (14 m) column spacing was constructed of cast-in-place concrete supporting a 27.6 in. (700 mm) thick waffle slab at every floor and the roof. Columns are 39.4 in. (1 m) diameter at the ground floor and 31.5 in. (800 mm) diameter at the upper levels. Each column rests on a minimum of four 37 in. (1.0 m) pilings.

The waffle slab is based on a 3.1 ft (1.0 m) grid with 9.8 in. (250 mm) wide ribs and has extra reinforcing to serve heavy storage of paper. The entire system was designed to provide for shifts in dead loads from one area to another as office space uses change.

At the edges of this column-and-slab superstructure is a perimeter system that accommodates the irregular curved contours of the outer wall. This secondary system uses a wavy line of columns at 23.0 ft (7.0 m) spacing, each resting on two bored pilings. The floor slab changes from waffle cells inside these perimeter columns to a tapering 9.8 ft (3.0 m) cantilevered slab whose thickness at the glass exterior wall is a mere 10.5 in. (266 mm).

Envelope

Foster's first reaction to optimizing the glass façade also incorporated a response to context. By suspending a mullionless glass curtain from the top of the structure, a more or less seamless façade would be created to mirror and blend in with the surrounding buildings more than compete with them visually. This strategy also took advantage of the tensile strength of glass and reduced the skin to glass and glue with small corner clips for stability. At first this idea met resistance from suppliers and contractors, but eventually enough work was done to provide assurances and the detailed design of the glazing system was begun.

There are 930 panels of 6.6 ft × 8.2 ft × 0.5 in. (2.0 m × 2.5 m) bronze reflective glass. Each panel is 0.5 in. (12 mm) thick, and all the glass is laminated for safety, strength, and ease of drilling boltholes. Only the topmost panel is affixed to structure, held by a single bolt through the center of its top edge. This panel is stiffened by a clamping strip that is secured with four additional bolts. Five more panels are suspended below this one by means of a patch plate with one bolt in the corner of four intersecting panels. The joints are filled with clear silicone. Interior vertical fins of 0.74 in. (19 mm) glass provide lateral wind resistance by butting up against the suspended wall from inside. These fins extend 8.2 ft (2.5 m) down from each concrete slab and are fixed to it by means of a bolted angle on each side of the fin. The bottom corner of each fin extends through the inside of the patch plate connection at midheight of the story. This connection mechanically restrains glass movement horizontally between two projecting flanges of the patch fitting that embrace the glass fin. The flanges are left loose enough to allow vertical movement of the wall so as to accommodate thermal expansion and contraction.

Outside the fourth-level restaurant, grass sod was laid on a layer of soil above the roof slab to create an outdoor terrace and to replace the natural features of the site that the building footprint completely covers. A walkway or jogging track is provided at the perimeter, where it shares space with a window-cleaning gantry.

Mechanical

Basement construction was impractical because of the high water table, so heavy service equipment was located at grade level. Designers decided to display the equipment rooms directly to the sidewalk at the leading corner of the building. This not only glorifies the gas boilers and electric chillers, it also encourages good maintenance of the equipment and visually reminds workers of the resources provided for their comfort.

Four shafts run vertically through the office floors to fan rooms, through the ceiling layer, and via cable troughs formed into the floor slabs. The integrated design of a suspended ceiling and a raised floor platform allows services to be distributed from above and below.

Interior

With the exception of the mechanical and utility spaces, overall design strategies resulted in 50 percent of the plate area being dedicated to office space on two floors and the other 50 percent being used for staff amenities at the ground floor and the roof terrace. Vertical circulation is minimized by placing it in the middle of the plan and limiting the main areas of the building to three floors. A taller building would have needed the same size exit area on more floors, resulting in a higher circulation area ratio.

Finish materials become more polished as their application moves through the building. The ground floor contains a lobby, a café, an 82 ft × 26 ft (25 m × 8 m) swimming pool with locker rooms, the loading docks, and mechanical services. The lobby has a painted but exposed concrete ceiling, steel panel partitions, and rubber flooring. The two open plan office levels above are carpeted and have a mirror finish ceiling. The top-level restaurant and roof garden are connected to the lower floors by an escalator core that also serves as a daylight atrium. The glass-roofed restaurant is a lantern for the spaces below and shines into the deepest parts of the large plan area.

The office-level ceilings integrate air supply, air extract, and lighting fixtures into a continuous plane of 1.2 in. (30 mm) wide brightly polished aluminum channels. Sprinkler heads, smoke detectors, and emergency lighting are all concealed in an aluminum plate that runs along the light fixture track. Each of the two office levels

uses some 2500 light fixtures. The raised floor provides flexible connections to electrical buses and telephone and data lines.

TECHNICAL INTEGRATION HIGHLIGHTS

Physical

- The sod-covered roof replaces the natural features of the site that are covered by the footprint of the building.
- Flexible utilities are physically distributed within the floor-and-ceiling sandwich layers.

Visual

- The suspended glass exterior camouflages the mass of the office block by mirroring the surrounding low-scale buildings. The reflective quality of the glass and the location of workspace above the ground floor maintain visual privacy. At night, when lights are still on in the offices, the effect is reversed and the building turns inside out with floor-to-ceiling and ground-to-roof transparency.
- Mechanical systems are made an interesting visual element of the building; much like the brick ovens seen by passersby of streetside pizza kitchens that open to the sidewalk.

Performance

- A centralized escalator core is located under the restaurant to double as a daylight atrium. Its strategic position also minimizes the walking distance between any two points in the building. As the primary vertical circulation path, it relieves elevator usage and substitutes a social space, animated by the people who move through it.
- The ceiling layer system actively integrates lighting, fire sprinklers, conditioned air distribution, electrical connections, and acoustical absorption. The lighting fixture support also carries the sprinkler piping and the ceiling channels. The fixtures themselves have integral connections to each other, eliminating the need for wiring. Return air fittings are also incorporated into the lights to remove the heat at its source. Fiberglass matting on top of the ceiling channels isolates the return air stream and provides acoustical absorption. The raised floor serves the same flexible purposes of distributing electrical outlets and telephone and data lines.

- The earth cover for the roof terrace also insulates the roof membrane and provides enough thermal inertia with its mass to negate the stress of daily thermal expansion and contraction cycles. This eliminated the need for an expansion joint and saved the construction of a supporting line of columns that would have to extend from the roof to an extra line of foundation footings.

- Restaurant and café spaces can also be used for informal business and staff meetings.

- Interior circulation around the cantilevered perimeter floor slabs matches the reduced structural capacity of the frame there to the interior organization scheme and accommodates the cold and drafty or hot and glary conditions that sometimes exist close to the glass exterior. By pulling desks a few ft away from the glass and using the perimeter as a transitory walkway, these potential structural and environmental problems are avoided.

DISCUSSION

Kenneth Knight served on the Willis Faber Dumas client's building committee and coordinated with Foster and his team. He credits part of the headquarters' success to the architect's diligent survey of office staff and provision for their comfort. Foster's dedication to friendly workplace design created a desirable destination through strategic integration of dining, play, and exercise areas in an already crowded building plan and difficult site.

Envelope performance is poor by today's standards, and the full-height glazing was probably not the most efficient approach to daylighting or energy conservation, even with 1970s technology, but it was an early use of solar reflective glass and its electrical lighting energy was half of what was standard at the time. The main features of the skin, of course, are its structural elegance, amorphous shape, and camouflage by mirror of its historic setting.

8

BRIARCLIFF HOUSE, 1978–1983

Farnborough, Hampshire, United Kingdom
ARUP ASSOCIATES

DESCRIPTION

Briarcliff House is a four-story office building designed for Leslie & Godwin Insurance. The offices are integrated into a regional shopping mall with a busy transit station and public parking lot. The street noise is compounded by occasional air shows, for which Farnborough is famous.

Briarcliff features a U-shaped plan embracing a protected terrace. Conference rooms and a café close the open side of the building where it abuts the retail mall. This arrangement creates two separate relationships between inside and out, interpreted by different envelope systems. The outward-looking street-side enclosure is a double skin with 4 ft (1.2 m) of separation between layers. Service walkways and vertical ducts are sandwiched in the buffer space. This embracing exterior assembly provides critical noise isolation, air distribution, as well as passive thermal control for both heating and cooling. Inward-looking walls facing an acoustically protected terrace are single-leaf noninsulated glass and are protected by motorized exterior sunshades.

Servicing components dominate the design from every view. From the street side, the double layer of glazing lends a milky reflectance and translucent depth to the skin. Bright red air-conditioning ducts are visible from the exterior, their details shrouded behind the solar control glass. A projecting glass canopy bends out from the walls to cover the walkway, exposing a suspended metal frame and the meshed interstitial ductwork. Office interiors have a clear view of vertical ducts through the alternating glass and metal in-fill panels of the interior wall layer. An integrated light fixture/return air device radiates across the office ceilings between ribs of the exposed concrete structure. Air supply and cabling erupts from the raised floors. Against the terrace side of the interior, a continuous circulation path is lined with radiators for winter and automated shades for summer.

Figure 6.14 Aerial photograph of Briarcliff House from the south. *(Photograph courtesy of Arup Associates.)*

TABLE 6.5 Fact Sheet

Project	**Building Name**	Briarcliff House
	Client	The Leslie & Godwin Group
	City	Farnborough, Hampshire, United Kingdom
	Lat/Long/Elev	51.29 N 00.76 W, 207 ft (63 m)
Team	**Architect**	Arup Associates (Mike Bonner)
	Structural Engineer	Arup Associates (Terry Raggett)
	Mechancal Engineer	Arup Associates (Peter Warburton)
	General Contractor	Laing Management Contracting Ltd.
General	**Time Line**	1978–1983.
	Floor Area	101,364 ft^2 (9,417 m^2) with 88,684 ft^2 of office and 12,364 ft^2 of retail (8239 m^2 and 1178 m^2).
	Occupants	450.
	Cost	$11.3 million.
	Cost, 1995 US$	$18.0 million or $178/ft^2.
	Stories	Four, including roof terrace at second level. Underside of ceiling rib height is 7.9 ft (2.4 m), underside of trough is at 9.8 ft (3.0 m).
	Plan	U-shaped offices overlooking a central roof garden.
Site	**Site Description**	1 acre (4,047 m^2) on the southern end of a shopping center, facing a large parking area and surrounded by noisy streets.
	Parking, Cars	Covered parking for 20 cars, 649 public spaces shared with Kingsmead Mall and transit terminal.
Structure	**Foundation**	Driven pilings.
	Vertical Members	Round concrete columns at 17.7 ft (5.4 m) centers inside and 23.6 ft (7.2 m) outside the plan.
	Horizontal Spans	Curved perimeter beams on concrete columns. Inside beam is radiused at 47.2 ft (14.4 m) and outside beam at 94.5 ft (28.8 m). Radial posttensioned concrete beam ribs span 47.2 ft (14.4 m) from concrete perimeter beams. The ribs are spaced at 3.0 ft (0.9 m) along the inside beam and 5.9 ft (1.8 m) at the outside.
Envelope	**Glass and Glazing**	Street façade is double envelope of exterior 0.4 in. (10 mm) bronze glass to a 3.9 ft (1.2 m) cavity air space where supply air ducts and service walkways are placed along the interior clear single-glazing and solid panels. Solar cells automatically control horizontal blinds on the outside surface of the interior leaf.
	Skylights	One large skylight at the connection to the existing retail mall at ground level.
	Cladding	Double glass envelope with services in air space.
	Roof	Built-up flat roof and glass penthouse.
HVAC	**Equipment**	700 kW boiler and 400 kW chiller. Maximum electrical demand is about 500 kva.
	Cooling Type	Original cooling towers have been replaced with air-cooled condensers.
	Distribution	Underfloor supply air plenum and light fixture integrated return air path.
	Duct Type	Vertical exposed metal ducts visible to interior and exterior.
	Vertical Chases	Service space between two glass leaves of exterior wall.
Interior	**Partitions**	Non-load-bearing gypsum board.
	Finishes	Carpet and painted concrete.
	Vertical Circulation	Two elevators in entrance lobby serve the offices.
	Furniture	By client.
	Lighting	Ducted fluorescent troffer integrated into structural ribs.

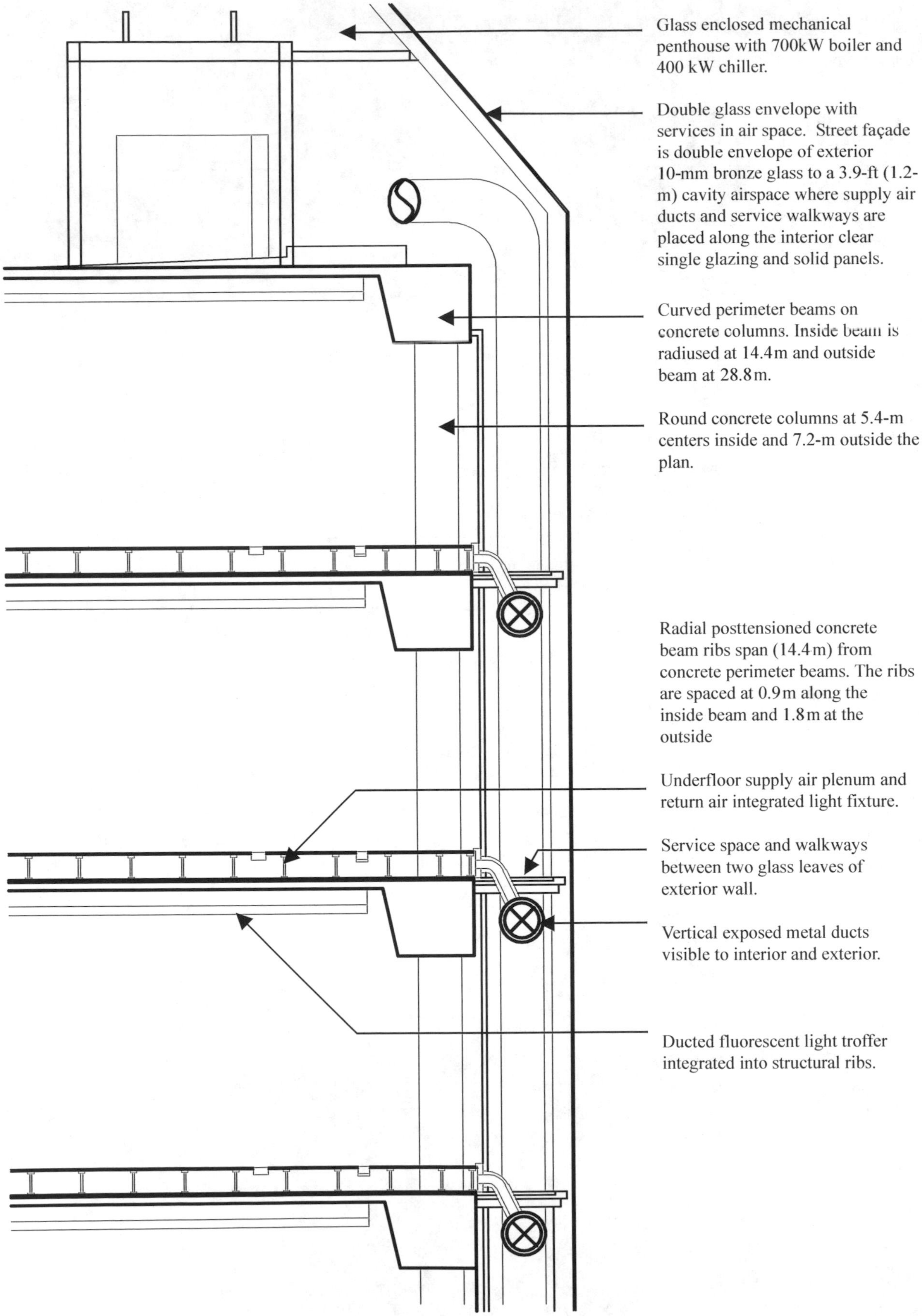

Glass enclosed mechanical penthouse with 700kW boiler and 400 kW chiller.

Double glass envelope with services in air space. Street façade is double envelope of exterior 10-mm bronze glass to a 3.9-ft (1.2-m) cavity airspace where supply air ducts and service walkways are placed along the interior clear single glazing and solid panels.

Curved perimeter beams on concrete columns. Inside beam is radiused at 14.4m and outside beam at 28.8m.

Round concrete columns at 5.4-m centers inside and 7.2-m outside the plan.

Radial posttensioned concrete beam ribs span (14.4m) from concrete perimeter beams. The ribs are spaced at 0.9m along the inside beam and 1.8m at the outside

Underfloor supply air plenum and return air integrated light fixture.

Service space and walkways between two glass leaves of exterior wall.

Vertical exposed metal ducts visible to interior and exterior.

Ducted fluorescent light troffer integrated into structural ribs.

Figure 6.15 Anatomical section.

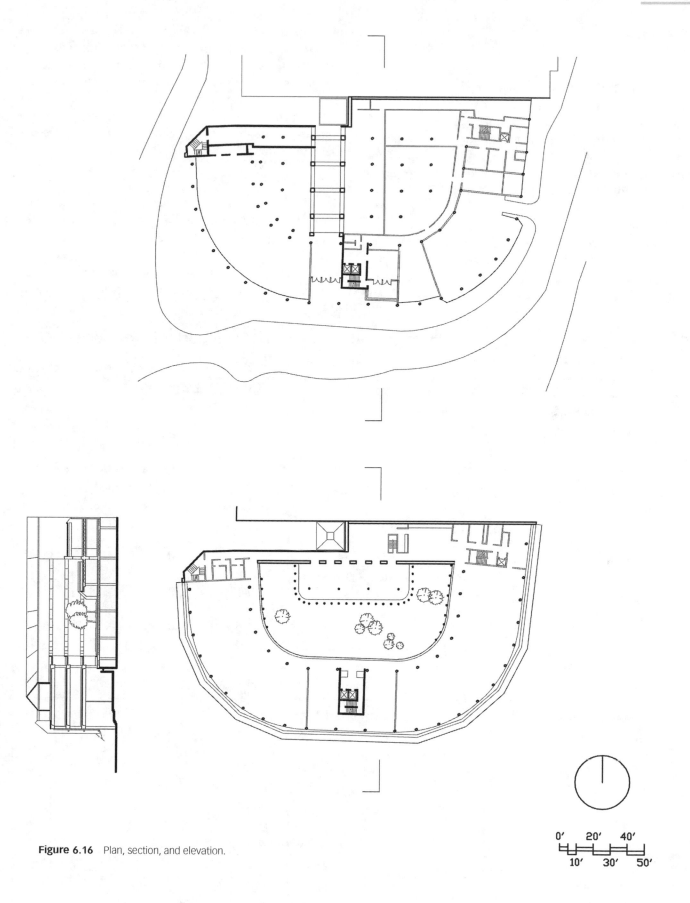

Figure 6.16 Plan, section, and elevation.

0' 20' 40'
10' 30' 50'

PROGRAM

Client

The Leslie & Godwin Group, now merged with Aon Group Ltd., was an insurance actuary engaged in portfolio risk management and reinsurance services. The company acquired the site by trading another of its properties to the city. Based on the noise environment and south orientation, the design team developed a double envelope concept and gained their clients' go-ahead. Before much progress had been made, Leslie & Godwin merged with a larger company. The new principals decided that L&G was not in the real estate business and should focus on insurance activities. The firm was advised to find a developer to assume the construction risk and then lease the building back for its own use. Long delays ensued, and more than a year passed. When an agreeable investor was finally found, the design team had to resell their innovative double envelope scheme with its underfloor plenum air supply strategy to a new company with different ideas about how to invest in the project. The investor conducted its own internal review of the project costs and options before, fortunately, accepting the design essentially unchanged.

Brief

The clients had a one-page brief for the Arup Associates team. It asked for a quiet building on their noisy site and a south-facing exposure that would warm but not cook them.

The revised brief developed for the building was more in line with speculative office space. It called for spaces no

TABLE 6.7 Climate Data for Farnborough, UK, as Compiled from Northolt and Benson RAF Stations

		Jan.	Feb.	Mar.	Apr.	May	June	July	Aug.	Sept.	Oct.	Nov.	Dec.	Year
Temperature	Degree-Days Heating	728	690	643	517	365	221	132	140	250	421	589	608	5443
	Degree-Days Cooling	0	0	0	0	9	29	58	48	11	1	0	0	44
	Extreme High	61	63	67	73	84	90	89	89	86	81	65	59	90
	Normal High	45	45	51	55	62	68	72	72	66	58	51	46	58
	Normal Average	41	41	45	48	54	60	64	64	59	52	46	43	51
	Normal Low	36	36	38	41	47	52	56	55	51	45	40	38	45
	Extreme Low	10	12	10	21	30	36	43	39	34	24	19	1	1
Humidity	Dew Point	36	35	37	39	44	50	54	53	51	46	41	38	44
	Max % RH	88	88	87	87	86	85	86	89	91	91	90	89	88
	Min % RH	77	72	65	58	58	57	56	56	62	70	76	80	65
	% Days with Rain	20	15	20	18	19	19	18	17	17	19	19	19	18
	Rain Inches	4	3	3	2	3	3	3	3	3	4	4	4	36
Sky	% Overcast Days	37	37	33	25	23	21	18	16	20	26	30	36	26
	% Clear Days	6	6	6	6	6	4	4	8	6	6	6	5	6
Wind	Prevailing Direction	WSW	ENE	WSW	NNE	NNE	WSW	W	SW	WSW	WSW	SW	WSW	WSW
	Speed, Knots	10	10	10	10	10	8	8	8	9	9	9	9	9
	Percent Calm	2	2	2	2	2	2	2	2	2	2	2	2	2
Days Observed	Rain	21	18	21	18	19	19	18	17	17	19	20	19	226
	Fog	9	7	7	7	8	8	6	9	12	13	12	12	110
	Haze	13	15	16	15	16	15	13	12	14	15	16	15	175
	Snow	4	5	2	1	#	0	0	0	0	0	#	1	13
	Hail	0	0	#	#	0	#	0	0	0	0	0	0	#
	Freezing Rain	#	#	0	0	0	0	0	0	0	0	0	0	#
	Blowing Sand	0	#	#	0	0	0	0	0	#	0	0	0	#

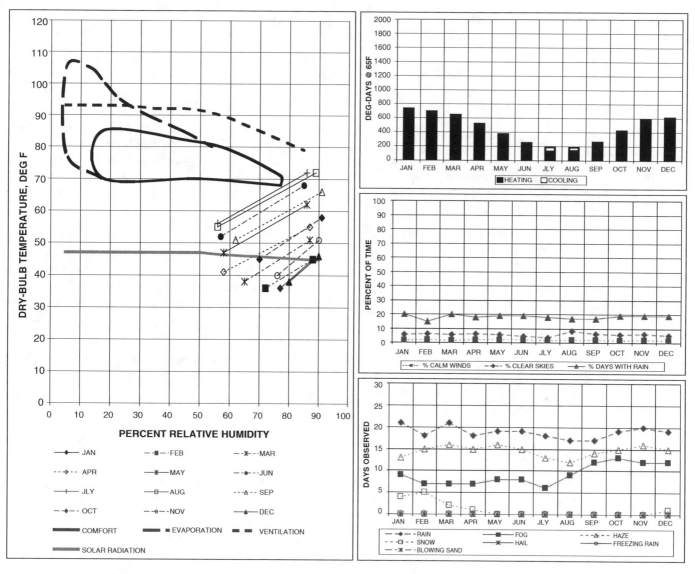

Figure 6.17 Climate analysis graphics.

more than 59 ft (18 m) deep that could be subdivided into leaseable areas of 5400 to 8600 ft² (600 to 800 m²). Exterior zones would be capable of enclosure for private offices. The restaurant was to include separate coffee bar and lounge areas. For greatest leasing potential, retail space at the ground level was to be maximized and covered parking for 20 cars was to be provided.

Site

Farnborough evolved from the township as it was established in the church records of 1599. Some 25,000 acres of shrubby wilderness between Farnborough and nearby Aldershot, known as the heaths of Rushmoor, were laid out as a permanent military camp in 1853. By 1974 the two towns had basically grown together and much of the military site had been redeveloped. Their adjoining communities constitute Rushmoor Borough.

In 1908, the HM Ballon Factory (later called the Royal Aircraft Establishment) was developed in Farnborough, and the site has been associated with aircraft ever since. Several aviation research agencies set up shop there in the 1990s. Along the way, in 1948, Farnborough Airfield began hosting an annual air show. This industrial activity brings a great deal of prosperity to Rushmoor, but also a disturbing amount of noise.

During redevelopment, the Farnborough Town Center complex was formed into three adjoining retail markets. Kingsmead and Princes Mead are shopping malls, and Queensmead is a pedestrian district. Briarcliff House is located on a 1 acre plot at the south end of the Town Center. It envelops the entry to Kingsmead Mall and meets the south terminus of the Queensmead mall. Just to the west of the complex is a series of long pedestrian malls; the south and east sides of the site are bordered by busy roads.

London (Gatwick), United Kingdom

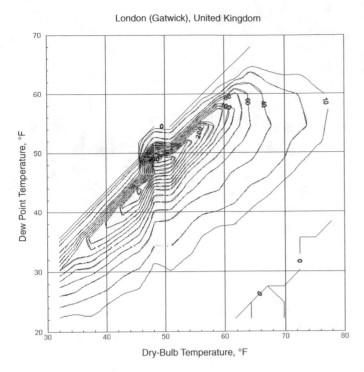

Figure 5.18 Bin data distribution for Benson RAF Station. Concentric areas of graph indicate the number of hours per year that weather conditions normally occur in this climate. Similar to elevation readings on topographic maps, highest frequency occurrences of weather are at the center peaks of the graph. *(Data sources: Engineering Weather Data, typical meteorological year (TMY) data from the National Climatic Data Center, and the ASHRAE Weather Data Viewer from the American Society of Heating and Refrigerating and Air-Conditioning Engineers.)*

Climate

Normal climate data for Farnborough is taken from two airfields 30 miles north of town, the Northold (51.5N 0.3W) and Benson (51.62N 1.08W) Royal Air Force (RAF) stations. Heathrow airport (51.48N 0.45W) is somewhat closer to Farnborough, but the smaller stations were chosen to reflect the lower density of the smaller town and avoid the heat island effect associated with the large developed area of the Heathrow station. The Heathrow data shows slightly warmer conditions than that of the two smaller stations.

As is common in southeastern England, this is a cool and gray climate. There are normally 5443 degree-days heating and 44 negligible degree-days cooling. Rain is likely on two-thirds of the days of any month, and 26 percent of all days are overcast. Clear days account for 5.9 percent of the year, with little or no seasonal deviation. The normal high in July is 72°F with a low of 56°F, and January days range from 45 to 36°F. Summer design conditions are 73F dry bulb with a 62°F wet bulb temperature and 8.9 mph winds from the west. Winter design levels are 30°F with 5.1 mph winds from the NNE.

INTENTION

Design Team

Ove Arup & Partners is best known to the architecture community as a building engineering firm that has worked with a wide array of architects and high quality buildings around the world. Arup Associates is a separate business included in Arup's Special Practices Board along with Arup Fire Control, Arup Acoustics, Arup Project Management, and several other organizations. Along with the Building Europe Board and the Special Practices Board, other Arup businesses operate under the Infrastructure, Industrial Engineering, Corporate Services and East Asia Boards. The focus of the firm continues to center on innovative and efficient buildings.

Arup Associates originated in 1963 as a partnership between Ove Arup & Partners founder, Sir Ove Arup, and architect Sir Philip Dowson. The Arup Associates arm continues as a multidisciplinary office that provides architectural, surveying, and engineering services. The firm's overall success is based on Ove Arup's founding belief in "total architecture," in which design fulfills social and public needs. In practical terms, Arup Associates allows for involvement in architectural rather than solely engineering pursuits. Because each Arup business, and even each individual workgroup, acts as an individual entity, this arrangement protects the architects who engage Arup from concerns about hiring their own competition.

The Arup Associates team for Leslie & Godwin consisted of architect Mike Bonner, mechanical engineer Peter Warburton, structural engineer Terry Raggett, and Brian Carter.

Philosophy

The underlying spirit of what is now a global organization begins with Sir Ove Arup (b. 1895, knighted in 1971, d. 1988). He founded the firm in 1946 with offices in London and Dublin. The firm now has a worldwide staff of more than 6500. Arup & Partners has worked with a great many architects of note, so it is no coincidence that the company's work contributed to many of the case study buildings in this text.

Arup Associates, an architectural concern, works as a separate entity from Arup & Partners and generally does not work with other architects. The firm operates on the premise of "total architecture" and forms multidisciplinary teams for each project. All team disciplines are involved in formulating design priorities, trade-offs, and decisions. This teamwork approach is carried through from project inception to completion.

Intent

Motivations for the design team were essentially rational ones. Energy, efficiency, flexibility, and servicing dominated the thinking. These formative goals were to inspire the architectural solution. The scheme the team proposed featured a ventilated double-skin glass wall with services between the two layers.

CRITICAL TECHNICAL ISSUES

Inherent

Daylighting is always useful in the daytime occupancy of this building type. If internal loads were low, then solar gain would also be useful most of the year in this cool, gray climate. Client needs in this program were straightforward but complicated by the site context. Interior requirements were dominated by criteria of flexibility. With computer networks in place and the prospect of subleasing parts of the building designed in, space allocations, workstations, and all the attendant servicing would have to be responsive to change.

Contextual

Farnborough is renowned for its air shows, and these cause periodic noise problems. The Royal Aircraft Establishment is less than a mile from Briarcliff House, and normal flight paths carry low-flying aircraft across the site daily. Another persistent source of noise at the site is automobile traffic. The A325 Farnborough Road to the M3 motorway is a major thoroughfare to the east of the building. A main artery, Meudon Avenue, runs across the south end of the site. Large park-and-ride asphalt lots cover the ground between the building and Meudon. A major bus stop is located immediately in front of the building, where waiting passengers stand under Briarcliff's glass canopy.

The office functions of Briarcliff are physically connected to a series of shopping malls that make up part of the city center. A feature of the Briarcliff program was to connect the parking and bus areas to the enclosed mall with an independent entry. The physical connection between the two structures was also problematic during construction; when piles foundations were being driven, bottles rattled precariously on the store shelves next door.

Intentional

The design team's approach to the problems of noise and sun dictated an introverted plan and a buffer to the noisy aspects of the east and south orientations. South sun was desired though, so these aspects had to be reconciled. Contextually, the new building was envisioned as a key link between the parking, transit centers, pedestrian routes, and the adjoining town center office and retail spaces. Spatially, the design called for a building that would "contribute an element of order and visual interest to the undisciplined and rather drab character of the neighborhood."

APPROPRIATE SYSTEMS

Precedent

There are too many similarities between this project and the Willis Faber Dumas (WFD) headquarters to ignore (see case study #7). Suspended and mullionless glass façades are the most obvious parallel to Foster's design. The grass sod terrace at Briarcliff and its greenhouse pavilion café are also interestingly similar to those at WFD. No explicit reference or statement by the design team has ever connected the two buildings, but the progression of technologies from one office headquarters to the other is clear enough to provide linkage. One identifiable but tenuous tie between the two projects is the prior association of their mechanical engineers—Arup's Peter Warburton and Foster's Loren Butts previously worked together for the U.K. engineering firm Haden Young.

Site

The 1 acre site is configured as an introverted arrangement whereby the building wraps around and protects an interior terrace. Connections from the building's ground floor to its immediate exterior surroundings are made via a generous glass-canopied walkway with separate entrances to the retail mall and the insurance offices. The south edge of the building and its covered walkway provide shelter for bus passengers and access to outlying public parking lots. Along the east side of the building is a service dock and a gated entrance to covered parking for 20 cars off Farnborough Road. To the west are a service access and then a pedestrian mall connecting to the retail shops of Queensmead.

The building footprint takes up its entire site but gives back some important elements. The first of these is the continuous glass canopy around the south and east sides, which keeps off the weather without darkening the wide walkway. Another public feature is the commercial space and mall entrance next to the transit stop. The designers also provided a generous skylight at the northwest corner of the first floor roof where the extension of the retail area connects to the existing mall.

Internally, the building remakes its own site, with the garden terrace captured inside the plan at the second level. The ground level is a solid mass dedicated to retail, park-

Figure 6.19   The garden terrace.

ing, service cores, and a computer center as well as a double-height lobby entry. The three levels of office space above look out to the captured terrace and across to the restaurant and coffee bar.

Structure

Construction is cast-in-place posttensioned concrete. The supporting soil is acidic sandy loam (pH about 3.5) with a meter of peaty clay topsoil. The water table is 5.9 ft (1.5 m) below grade, so the building rests on driven pilings. Arup Acoustics was brought in to monitor the ground vibrations for fear of damage to the connecting retail shops. A supermarket kept its wine and spirits bottles against a common wall, which had to be monitored visually during piling operations. Houses less than 328 ft (100 m) away were also surveyed, but the only damage revealed was restricted to an aquarium in one of the houses. It seems the resident observed that vibrations during construction caused wave motions in the aquarium and made his fish seasick.

The U-shape form of the plan generated a radial organization to the main structure. It is entirely of poured-in-place concrete. Round columns at the exterior wall carry a perimeter beam supporting one end of the posttensioned floor beam ribs. A second column line 10 ft (3.0 m) inside the interior wall carries another beam. The floor beams cantilever over the inside beam and leave the

captured terrace view unobstructed at the perimeter. The space between the inside column line and the solid glass wall to the terrace is used for circulation.

The rib beams were designed to complement the underfloor air supply plenum by incorporating the return air path. Ridges at the center of each beam are left for a fluorescent light strip, which feeds the return air duct in the floor plenum above. This required careful design for the placement of reinforcement cable in the beams and resulted in a slightly deeper profile.

Envelope

A double skin assembly wraps the exposed perimeter of the building. Its exposure takes in the east side to Farnborough Road, the broad south exposure toward the parking areas, and the west orientation facing a pedestrian mall. The interior layer of the double envelope consists of alternating clear single glazing and solid metal panels. The exterior rain skin is 0.4 in. (10 mm) reflective bronze glass in panels 11.9 ft high by 5.9 ft wide (3.6 m × 1.8 m). Each of the rain skin glass panels is suspended from its aluminum substructure by six 0.25 in. (6 mm) stainless steel bolts through gasketed connections countersunk in the glass. Joints in the glass panels are silicone sealed, giving the exterior a smooth face. Behind that is a 3.9 ft (1.2 m) cavity airspace where supply air ducts and grated metal service walkways are located within a thin tubular steel frame. The outside bronze glass skin continues upward past the fourth floor to enclose a penthouse containing all the heavy mechanical equipment. The same exterior skin turns outward at the base of the building to form a canopy over the entire length of the street side. A gutter is tucked into the corner transition from vertical wall to projecting canopy so that rainwater is diverted from the sidewalk.

On the courtyard side of the offices is clear single-pane glass. Toward both northern corners of the terrace the office windows are protected by automatically controlled horizontal blinds on the outside surface. These blinds are activated by solar cells. The cladding of the restaurant and coffee bar is also single-pane clear glass.

The base of the south side double envelope is left open where the canopy glass turns outward. Winter air is drawn up the air cavity and preheated to provide tempered make-up air for ventilation. During warmer months the rising air is exhausted by stack effect on the north leeward side of the penthouse, taking with it absorbed solar heat gain. In all seasons the air cavity serves as a thermal buffer to the interior and circumvents uncomfortable glass surface temperatures to the interior office space.

A few vented-skin buildings were built prior to Briarcliff: Cannon Design Group's office for the Hooker Chemical Company, 1981, GEW Colonge by Kraemer and Sieverts, 1982, and British Sugar Corporation by Arup Associates, 1975.

Mechanical

All heavy HVAC equipment is located in the glass-covered penthouse that runs the length of the building. There are four sets of fans serving equal portions of the offices. Return air is brought up through the ducted light fixtures and into a duct in the floor cavity of the interior circulation corridor above. Outdoor air is taken from the solar-heated south side air cavity and either mixed with return air when the space is underheated or exhausted from grilles on the north side of the penthouse. The three-story air cavity produces a stack effect, acting as a chimney to enhance the movement of air and heat in both seasons. Summer ventilation air is taken directly through the mechanical plant room walls. Air balance is maintained throughout the year by exhausting an appropriate portion of the return air. A computerized monitoring system switches to 100 percent ventilation air or evaporative cooling whenever mechanical cooling can be averted. Supplemental heat is provided by perimeter radiators that are controlled by thermostatic valves.

Cooling and outside air requirements are provided by air handling units in the penthouse. These recirculate a mixture of return air and outside air, conditioning it and then supplying it back to the offices via vertical ducts in the air cavity south wall. Interior raised floor plenums are pressurized with supply air without the use of horizontal ducts or terminal units. Floor-mounted twist pattern dif-

Figure 6.20 Construction at Briarcliff. *(Photograph courtesy of Arup Associates.)*

fusers can be located wherever needed and closed when not in use.

Heat transfer simulations were developed to account for the large thermal storage mass provided by the exposed concrete floor ribs. This thermal inertia was predicted to smooth temperature fluxuations during a daily cycle by absorbing peak heat gains from the offices during the day and slowly radiating it back during unoccupied night hours. The resulting design prescribed a supply air temperature of 65°F (18.5°C) with up to six air changes. The anticipated peak return air temperature was 82°F (28.0°C).

Energy monitoring at Briarcliff validated the design strategy. The sophisticated combination of vent skin envelope, solar chimney, internal mass, and underfloor supply air plenum proved to be comfortable, flexible, and efficient.

Interior

The environment at Briarcliff integrates several aspects of what would become the prototypical highly serviced workplace. Flexibility is provided by a raised floor of pedestals at 2.0 ft (0.6 m) on center, supporting particleboard panels finished with carpeting. Below this are organized routes of cabling for electrical, data, and telephone systems. The raised floor plenum also provides supply air to any spot in the building without the need for ducts. Despite fears of drafty air from low-level diffusers causing discomfort, the system drew no complaints, per-

haps because supplying from the floor allows warmer supply air temperatures and lower flow volumes to be used.

The air-handling light fixtures in the ceiling ribs are fitted with T8 warm white fluorescent lamps with an average lighting power density of 3.67 W/ft^2 (39.5 W/m^2) to provide 60 fc (600 lux). Custom-made fixtures run down the center of the circulation path. These are indirect fluorescent sources with curved housings painted white to match the ceiling. Lighting in the double-height reception entry is provided by 250 W tungsten halogen downlights and wall washers.

Organizationally, the three floors of office space above the ground level are identical. A central elevator and stair shaft at the main entry is complemented by fire stairs at both ends of the plan. Circulation around the open office plan happens at the courtyard side of the plan along a continuous open corridor cantilevered outside the column line.

TECHNICAL INTEGRATION HIGHLIGHTS

Physical

- The floor plenum incorporates flexible space for cabling.
- The rain screen glass skin encloses the mechanical penthouse and duct chase.
- The rain screen also becomes a walkway canopy.

Figure 6.21 The mechanical penthouse.

TABLE 6.8   Energy End-Use Estimates at Briarcliff House Offices

Energy in Millions of Btu's per Year						
	Electric	Gas	Total	Total/ft²	Total/occ	Percent
Heating	646	2101	2747	0.0383	7.55	46%
Cooling	455		455	0.0051	1.01	8%
Hot water		200	200	0.0023	0.44	3%
Small power	467		467	0.0053	1.04	8%
Lights	1307		1307	0.0200	3.94	22%
Elevators	102		102	0.0012	0.23	2%
Cooking	171		171	0.0019	0.38	3%
Computing	512		512	0.0058	1.14	9%
Energy used	3661	2301	5962	0.0672	13.25	100%

(Data derived from Gordon Nelson, "Energy Revisit: Briarcliff House," *Architects' Journal*, February 12, 1986; Gordon Nelson, "The Glass of '84," *Architects' Journal*, September 5, 1984.)

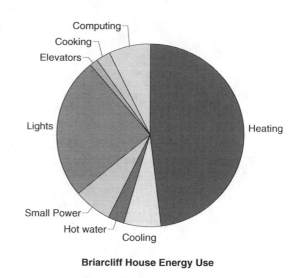

Briarcliff House Energy Use

Figure 6.22   Energy use graphic.

Visual

- The exposed structure is finished and painted white.
- Services are exposed to view through the double-envelope glazing and directly from the walkway.
- A view is provided to the captured courtyard garden and maintained by the circulation path.

Performance

- The double envelope provides solar and acoustical buffering. It also helps with radiant temperature control of inside glass surface.
- The double envelope provides passive thermal and acoustic benefits with its vented skin strategy.
- The double envelope houses and shelters the HVAC distribution system.
- Structural ceiling ribs provide thermal mass and become part of the light fixture diffusers.
- The raised floor plenum makes for flexible servicing of the interior and ease in reorganizing workstations.

DISCUSSION

Double envelope and vented skin technologies like those developed for the Briarcliff House have opened new possibilities for configurations of served and servant spaces. Where Louis Kahn developed a rational aesthetic of separation, the Arup team advanced an active layering that visually and functionally emphasizes the roles of envelope and services in providing shelter. Architectural possibilities for incorporating ductwork, other service elements, or even complete systems within the vented layer are increasingly popular avenues for refinement and integration of their thermal, luminous, and acoustical benefits. Locating service systems within the double skin is also superior to exposing it in the interior space or on the exterior of buildings because it isolates the associated noise, upkeep, and replacement while still protecting their components from harsh weather and dirt. Finally, like the exposed mechanical room fronting the sidewalk at Willis Faber Dumas, these windows through the layered technical systems of buildings can add to the visual reading of buildings as dynamic shelters.

Briarcliff House was double skinned for several reasons, but control of noise produced by a bus route and airplane traffic was the deciding rationale. In crowded urban situations the extra layer of separation may be the best practical solution for some sites. Ultimately, however, the most significant benefit of double envelope construction is the opportunity to fulfill the "barriers, filters, and switches" mandate of envelope performance. Bimodal operation of vented skins in response to summer versus winter, sun versus shade, breeze versus still air, and day versus night may be the least exploited of these opportunities to date.

Peter Warburton and Terry Raggett generously contributed to portions of this case study.

9

LOCKHEED BUILDING 157, LOCKHEED MISSILES AND SPACE COMPANY, 1979–1983

Sunnyvale, California
LEO A. DALY ARCHITECTS

DESCRIPTION

Large rectangular footprint plan areas such as that of Lockheed Building 157 offer efficient and economical construction schemes. This economy occurs because the resulting minimal external surface areas can contain rather large interior volumes—less skin to build, more space to use. The same characteristics pose problems, however, if daylight is expected to reach deep into the interior. Daylighting design dictates long, thin shapes, with lots of perimeter floor area close to windows and minimal buried interior space. So although deep plan areas offer construction cost savings, they can also require extensive amounts of electrical lighting energy and extra air-conditioning capacity to handle the waste heat from artificial

illumination. Leo A. Daly architects and engineers earned the commission for this large single-building office project by contending that they would resolve the conflict between "structurally stocky" and "environmentally slender." They proposed to provide a building that used half the energy of what would normally be expected. The resulting design exceeded expectations.

The roof of these engineering offices is considerably larger than two football fields. Yet no one inside sits more than 40 ft (12.2 m) from a source of natural light, and the systems of the building are integrally configured to maximize daylighting efficiency. The relatively small construction cost premium for this achievement, some 4 percent of the total cost, provided annual energy savings of nearly $500,000 and a four-year simple payback on the investment.

The real "bottom line" is an even better story. It is about intelligent and reasoned design for humane workplaces. In this case, an engineering work group of 2700 people collectively moved from their old quarters into Building 157. Comparing that one-time cost with the ongoing annual salary and benefits of an average employee indicates the relatively small cost of erecting an office building versus the never-ending expense of maintaining an efficient workforce. Small increases in workplace productivity can easily offset the price of a more humane and comfortable environment. This is an equation that Leo A. Daly solved very neatly. At Lockheed, while moving a known workforce, absenteeism reportedly dropped 15 percent and productivity increased another 15 percent. So although the daylighting system purportedly paid off in four years of energy savings, the entire Lockheed building, and everything under its 2.3 football fields' worth of roof, likely paid for itself completely in even less time.

Figure 6.23 Overview of Building 157 from the northeast. *(Photograph by the author, permission courtesy of Lockheed Martin.)*

TABLE 6.9 Fact Sheet

Project		
Building Name	Lockheed Building 157	
Client	Lockheed Missiles and Space Company, Inc.	
Location	Third Avenue, Sunnyvale, California	
Lat/Long/Elev	37.41 N 122.03 E, 12 ft (3.7 m)	

Team	
Architects	Leo A. Daly
Mechanical Engineer	Leo A. Daly
Daylighting	Lawrence Berkeley Laboratories
Lighting	Michael D. Shanus
Fire Protection	Richard M. Patton
Construction	Hensel Phelps
Interior Landscaping	Interior Landscape Design
Acoustics	Richard Hamme

General	
Time Line	1979–1983.
Floor Area	585,000 ft^2 (54,300 m^2).
Occupants	2700 engineers and support staff.
Cost	$50 million.
Cost in 1995 dollars	$76.5 million or $127.41/ft^2.
Stories	Five stories totaling 90 ft height (27.9 m)
Plan	560 ft × 250 ft (73.2 m × 170.7 m)

Site	
Site Description	Large campus adjacent to Moffet Air Field.
Parking, Cars	Abundant surface parking in surrounding campus.

Structure	
Foundation	Not published.
Vertical Members	Steel frame.
Horizontal Spans	Steel frame.

Envelope	
Glass and Glazing	15 ft (4.6 m) high north and south glazing with tinted glass below light shelf and clear glass above.
Skylights	Diffusing glass (south sloping) and clear glass (north vertical glazing) above central atrium.
Cladding	Glass on north and south.
Roof	Built-up roof with skylight monitors and elevator penthouse.

HVAC	
Equipment	Central plant system located elsewhere on campus.
Cooling Type	Chilled water from central plant.
Distribution	Variable air volume.
Duct Type	Above ceiling.
Vertical Chases	At east and west walls.

Interior	
Partitions	Open office systems.
Finishes	Cool green carpet.
Vertical Circulation	Central core escalators.
Furniture	Predominantly workstations.
Lighting	Daylighting and photocell-dimming cool white fluorescent ambient lighting. Ambient fluorescents are ceiling suspended and also integrated into perimeter light shelves. Supplemental direct/indirect task lighting from lensed warm white fluorescent fixtures integrated into workstations.

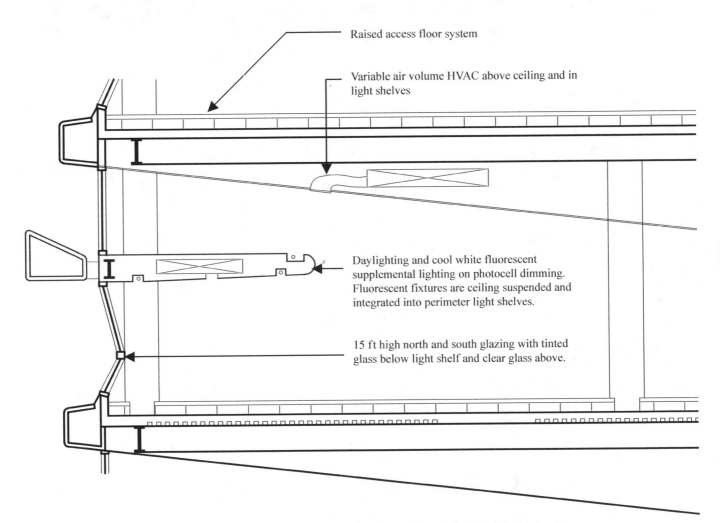

Five story building totaling 90-ft in height (27.9-m)
560 ft x 250 ft (73.2 m x 170.7m) in plan

Raised access floor system

Variable air volume HVAC above ceiling and in
light shelves

Daylighting and cool white fluorescent
supplemental lighting on photocell dimming.
Fluorescent fixtures are ceiling suspended and
integrated into perimeter light shelves.

15 ft high north and south glazing with tinted
glass below light shelf and clear glass above.

Supplemental direct/indirect task lighting from
lensed warm white fluorescent fixtures integrated
into workstation.

Figure 6.24 Anatomical section.

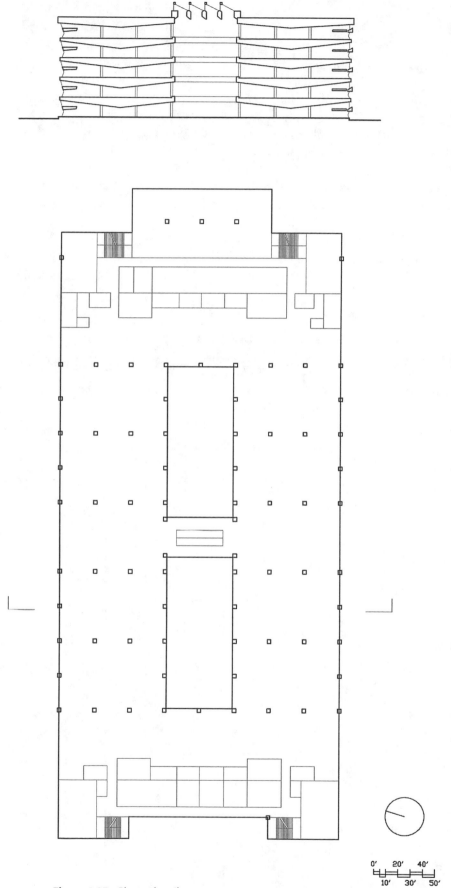

Figure 6.25 Plan and section.

PROGRAM

Client

Lockheed Missiles and Space Company (now part of Lockheed Martin) supplies satellites for civil, commercial, and military use. It is part of an aerospace and aviation industry leader with more than 180,000 employees world-wide and commerce approaching $30 billion per year.

Brief

In 1979 Lockheed developed an in-house design for a new five-story office building. One of its existing engineering work groups would be moved into this facility. Before the project was initiated, however, Sacramento imposed a moratorium on new buildings. The San Francisco office of Leo A. Daly used the delay to make a proposal for a com-

plete redesign of the proposed facility based on energy cost reduction. Accepting the offer, Lockheed encouraged research and exploration. The architect assembled a research team and began looking closely at a daylighting solution. Lockheed, meanwhile, retained the original parameters of the building. It would be five stories tall with 100,000 ft² (9,290 m²) floor plates and 18 ft (5.5 m) floor-to-floor heights.

Site

Moffett Field Naval Air Station provides the 1000-acre setting for Lockheed, its campus of offices, and the neighboring aviation/aerospace research industry. Founded in 1933, Moffett Field was originally created to house dirigible airships. It is the site of 211 ft high Hanger One and the first Goodyear blimp, the *Macon*. The 785 ft *Macon*, 10 ft

TABLE 6.10   Normal Climate Data for Sunnyvale, California

		Jan.	Feb.	Mar.	Apr.	May	June	July	Aug.	Sept.	Oct.	Nov.	Dec.	Year
Temperature	Degree-Days Heating	468	338	323	227	146	60	27	23	32	103	277	456	2488
	Degree-Days Cooling	0	0	1	8	23	56	70	72	76	33	2	0	346
	Extreme High	76	82	83	95	103	104	105	101	105	100	87	76	105
	Normal High	58	61	63	67	70	74	75	75	76	72	65	58	68
	Normal Average	50	53	55	58	61	65	66	67	66	63	56	50	59
	Normal Low	42	44	46	48	51	55	57	58	57	53	47	42	50
	Extreme Low	21	26	30	32	38	43	45	47	41	33	29	23	21
Humidity	Dew Point	56	56	44	42	38	40	33	34	33	48	46	54	56
	Max % RH	82	81	79	76	73	73	77	79	79	79	81	82	79
	Min % RH	61	59	56	52	53	54	58	58	55	54	59	63	57
	% Days with Rain	39	41	39	26	16	7	3	5	8	19	33	39	23
	Rain Inches	3	2	2	1	0	0	0	0	0	1	2	2	13
Sky	% Overcast Days	32	32	28	22	17	14	15	16	15	18	24	30	22
	% Clear Days	20	18	19	24	27	35	44	39	42	36	23	21	29
Wind	Prevailing Direction	SE	NNW	NNW	NNW	NNW	NNW	NNW	NNW	NNW	NNW	NNW	NNW	NNW
	Speed, Knots	8	7	8	9	10	10	11	11	9	8	6	6	9
	Percent Calm	29	26	20	18	16	15	inc	inc	inc	inc	inc	inc	Inc
Days Observed	Rain	12	13	12	8	5	2	1	1	3	6	10	12	83
	Fog	13	11	5	4	3	3	6	7	8	10	12	15	95
	Haze	16	13	9	9	10	11	17	18	18	17	16	17	171
	Snow	0	0	0	0	0	0	0	0	0	0	0	0	0
	Hail	0	0	0	0	0	0	0	0	0	0	0	0	0
	Freezing Rain	0	0	0	0	0	0	0	0	0	0	0	0	0
	Blowing Sand	0	0	0	0	0	0	0	0	0	0	0	0	0

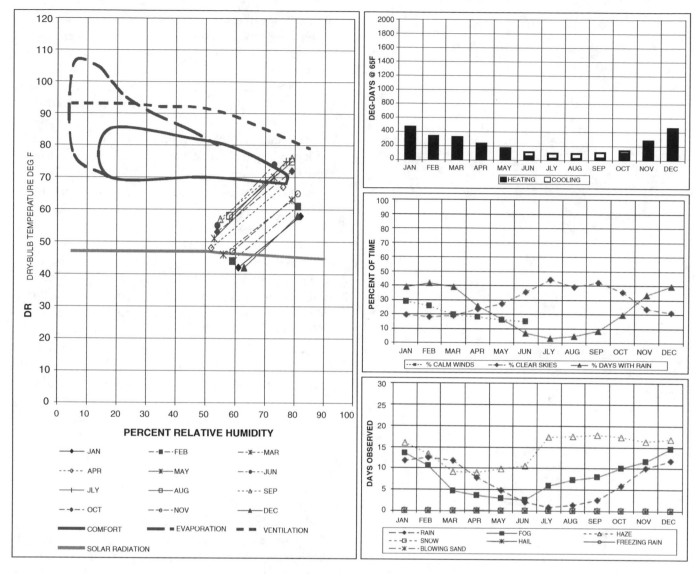

Figure 6.26 Climate analysis graphics.

longer than the *Graf Zeppelin*, was built for $2.5 million ($29.4 million 1995 equivalent) and berthed at Moffett after her maiden voyage from Akron, Ohio.

Moffett became a haven for aviation research with the establishment of a $10 million laboratory in 1939. Partly due to the abundance of electrical power available locally, and partly due to the proximity of Stanford University brainpower, the air station became the first site of the National Advisory Committee for Aeronautics (NACA) in 1940 with the establishment of Ames Research Center. It is the site of what was once the nation's largest wind tunnel, a feature still clearly visible in aerial photos. NACA later became NASA, which still maintains a 430 acre (172.0 hectare) campus across Moffett's two landing strips from the Lockheed campus.

After several years of deliberation and military budget cuts, Moffett Naval Air Station was decommissioned in December 1992. It is now in the hands of NASA, and discussions for redevelopment of the airfield and military facilities are being undertaken in the community. Along with NASA and Lockheed, Hiller Aircraft and the TRW subsidiary ESL anchor the remaining aviation interests on the site.

Climate

Sunnyvale is in the middle of Silicone Valley about 40 miles south of San Francisco. Geographically, it lies in the Santa Clara Valley about 25 miles to the east of the Pacific Ocean, whose tempering breezes moderate the local climate. The Santa Cruz mountains follow the western edge

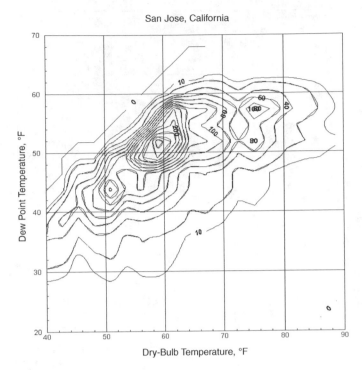

San Jose, California

Figure 6.27 Bin data distribution for Sunnyvale, California. Concentric areas of graph indicate the number of hours per year that weather conditions normally occur in this climate. Similar to elevation readings on topographic maps, highest frequency occurrences of weather are at the center peaks of the graph. (Data sources: *Engineering Weather Data, typical meteorological year (TMY) data from the National Climatic Data Center, and the ASHRAE Weather Data Viewer from the American Society of Heating, Refrigerating and Air-Conditioning Engineers.*)

of the San Francisco peninsula up the coast, and the Sunol and Valpe ridges of the Diablo range to the east complete the bowl of mountains around the valley.

Moffett Field borders the southern end of the San Francisco Bay. It is separated from the marshes of the bay by a two-mile belt of commercial salt evaporation ponds. Microclimatic differences make inland Sunnyvale considerably warmer than the peninsula of San Francisco. Degree-days at the Lockheed site are 2439 heating and 498 cooling, as compared with San Francisco's 3341 heating and 241 cooling. Sunnyvale data from Moffett Field is available for normal weather records and San Jose, 11 miles west into the desert, is adequate for bin data.

The climate of Sunnyvale is generally pleasant and Mediterranean, with 28 percent of all hours being comfortable (65°F to 75°F) and another 53 percent cool (50°F to 65°F). The rest of the hours are 13 percent cold, 5 percent warm, and 1 percent hot (over 90°F). Sea breezes through the valley keep summer temperatures mild and within a narrow margin between the daily high and low. Low clouds bring cool, moist air in summer mornings and evenings. In September ocean breezes become less pro-

nounced and may be overcome by very hot air off the western deserts, occasionally bringing temperatures in excess of 100°F. Summers are also quite dry with almost negligible rainfall. September is the warmest month, with a normal high of 76°F and a low of 57°F. January typically varies from 58°F to 42°F, and freezing temperatures are rare.

About 80 percent of the annual 13.5 in. of rain falls in the cooler months. Precipitation amount and rain days are fairly uniform November through March. Fog is prevalent November through February. Clear weather dominates about 30 percent of all days, with July through September being the clearest. Daylighting design must respond to these sky conditions because they define the resources and qualities that the final solution must deal with. Sunnyvale seems appropriately named in this regard. The other daylight resource factor to be considered is the variation of natural light through a typical day and across the seasons. At this latitude, 37.4°N, earth:sun geometry has a significant effect on both seasonal day length and the angles at which direct sunlight will impact a building. June 21 days last 14.5 hours, with the sun rising and setting 120 degrees from south. At noon the sun is 76 degrees above the horizon. A window facing 15 degrees west of south, like the Lockheed site, will receive high incidence angles of direct sun from 9:30 A.M. to 5:40 P.M. This summer sunlight will not penetrate far into a south-facing window, but it is very intense. December 21 days are a different matter: daylight lasts 9.5 hours, with sunrise and sunset 60 degrees from south and a noon sun only 29 degrees above the horizon. The same window would receive full sun at very low angles from 8:30 A.M. to 5:50 P.M. This winter sunlight is less intense but often becomes a visible source of blinding glare.

INTENTION

Design Team

Leo A. Daly is an architecture and engineering firm in its third generation of leadership under the Daly family banner. Founded in 1915 by Leo A. Daly Sr., the firm later grew under the direction of his son Leo A. Daly Jr. After the war years of the 1940s, the firm's work was founded on government projects. The 1950s and 1960s brought a specialization in high-technology defense projects. The 1970s focus was on health, education, and research buildings. In 1981, Leo A. Daly Jr. passed away and Leo A. Daly III began his service as chairman and president. Today, Leo A. Daly is the largest privately held architecture firm in the United States, with about 230 architects and a total staff of 730 in 15 offices.

Philosophy

Leo A. Daly Jr. instituted a practice of organizing projects around a multidisciplinary team approach that the firm carries on to this day, bringing architects, planners, engineers, and interior designers together as collaborators. They strive to bring an understanding of the project's inherent characteristics to the initial client meeting.

Intent

Lee Windheim, project architect of Building 157 and a principal of Leo A. Daly, predicted that passive daylighting could cut annual energy bills to 50 percent of what Lockheed's in-house generic design would use. This contention generated the most formative design directions. Windheim also pointed out the General Services Administration study: construction of Building 157 would account only for 2 percent of Lockheed's 30-year expenditure. Energy and maintenance would be 6 percent, and employee salaries would make up the other 92 percent. Keeping the staff comfortable and productive, as well as healthy, was the best investment Lockheed could make.

CRITICAL TECHNICAL ISSUES

Inherent

Daylight availability is normally not the critical issue of daylighting design. Even on a cloudy day there are 500 footcandles (fc) of illumination available on a horizontal surface, far more than needed on most task surfaces. The real problem is usually distribution—getting some of those 500 fc deep into a space and dealing with the overabundance of brightness close to windows. In Building 157 this problem was exaggerated by the extreme depth of the plan, 240 ft (73.2 m).

Contextual

Lockheed, now Lockheed Martin since the 1995 merger of aerospace giants, is commonly engaged in secret defense industry contracts for the federal government. We will never know the full implication of the security requirements that entails; suffice it to say that security is vital and well maintained on the entire campus. This constraint implies an introverted building design, whereas daylighting suggests a more open and extroverted approach.

Intentional

Because of the classified nature of work that goes on in this building and the scarcity of publications on its design, there is no information available concerning critical issues that arose from the architects' intentions.

APPROPRIATE SYSTEMS

Precedent

Frank Lloyd Wright's Larkin Building of 1904 is a good link between what Richard Saxon (*The Atrium Comes of Age*, 1993) calls the prehistory of atrium daylighting and its rediscovery during the energy crisis of the 1970s. The Larkin Building has sometimes been mentioned as a technical precedent of Building 157. Both buildings are five stories tall and include corner stairwells, open galleries, and pursue the general objectives of daylighting and quality workspace.

Site

Building 157 is set on a southeast street corner at the east end of the Lockheed campus. Its orthogonal orientation along the street is an advantageous 15 degrees west of south, easy to shade but open to the brightest part of the sky. The general area, being an industrial campus, is mostly paved, and there is little thought given to vegetation or landscape. A sea of parking and smaller structures surrounds the building on three sides. The overwhelming size of the building belies its function as a workplace of secrets and a factory of engineering know-how. There is even something sinister about the cool gray color it was painted in 2000. The surrounding complex of buildings on the Lockheed campus is not much different. The scale of the building does seem to match the scale of the science and machines produced there.

Structure

This is a straightforward steel frame building with eight 30 ft (9.1 m) column bays running north to south. East-to-west columns are spaced at 60 ft (18.3 m) within the plan but return to 30 ft (91. m) spacing at the building perimeter and around the atrium. Diagonal bracing across the 60 ft (18.3 m) ends of the atrium provide the only relief in the general scheme of the building. The atrium skylights, however, are dramatically framed by their supporting beams.

Envelope

The daylighting design was developed with project consultant Michael Shanus. The strategy adopted a target daylight level of 30 to 35 fc (323 to 377 lux) for general ambient illumination. Supplemental fluorescent lighting was planned to balance the daylight, continually dimming down in work areas where natural light was bright and dimming up where daylight levels fell below the target. Task lighting fixtures at each workstation would provide additional footcandles as fill light on desk surfaces. This task/ambient scheme would ensure full harvesting of day-

Figure 6.28 Skylights on the Lockheed roof.

light by making electrical lighting strictly a supplement. Equally important was lighting quality. Excess brightness ratios between the task areas and background could produce discomfort or disability glare and foil the illumination design. Any design option that allowed direct sun, for example, would be disregarded. Overlighting was also to be avoided because it introduces more heat, regardless of whether the source is electric or natural.

Daylight levels in different versions of the building design were tested over a three-month period with scale models at 1/8 in. and 3/8 in. These models were built with materials of accurate reflection and light transmittance properties. Controlled tests were performed in San Francisco at Lawrence Berkeley Laboratory's hemispherical sky simulator for clear and overcast sky conditions. More tests were performed on the site, under varying sky conditions, with a tilting heliodyn sun-table to simulate the seasons. Office widths of 80 to 100 ft (24.4 m to 30.5 m) were tested with atriums of 40 to 120 ft (12.2 m to 36.6 m) width. Models were made to represent 120 ft long sections of the building. Various materials and configurations were tried in combinations: light shelves, louvers, fins, different glazing materials, and several skylight configurations. Following refinement of the model design, numerical simulation of the annual contribution of daylight indicated that more than 70 percent of the electrical energy required to meet the target 30 to 35 fc could be saved with the use of constant dimming controls. Final model testing was performed at the Owens-Corning

Fiberglass Technical Center in Granville, Ohio. A 30 × 45 ft (9.1 × 13.7 m) full-scale section of a typical south wall office was used to study not just illumination, but also HVAC air patterns, wire management, acoustics, workstation design, and material finishes.

The final design retains an efficient five-story rectangular form but punctures it with a 60 × 300 ft (18.3 × 91.4 m) central atrium covered by sawtoothed glass skylights. South-facing skylight apertures are sloped 45 degrees and use light-diffusing glass, north-facing elements are vertical and made with clear glass. Serving as a light well, the "litetrium," as the designers call it, divides the offices into two thin bars, each lit from both sides.

The east and west sides of the building are unglazed because daylight on these orientations varies greatly with time and season. Windows on those elevations would also be difficult to shield from glare and excessive solar heat gain. Continuous glazing on the more amenable north and south faces is divided into a view window and a daylight aperture by a horizontal light shelf. The shelf extends 12 ft (3.7 m) deep into the interior, with a 7.5 ft (2.3 m) high window below and a 6.0 ft (1.8 m) clear glass daylight aperture above. The south side has an additional 4.0 ft (1.2 m) exterior extension of the light shelf that is tilted up at 30 degrees to reflect direct sunlight onto the horizontal part of the shelf. Lower windows for view on the south use reflective solar cool glass with 17 percent total transmission and a shading coefficient of 44 percent to reduce heat gain and sky glare. On the shadier north side, however, a

41 percent daylight transmission solar-gray-tinted glass with a shading coefficient of 69 percent is used in the vision panel, and the light shelf does not provide external shading.

Mechanical

Building 157 and about 50 other Lockheed buildings on the campus receive chilled water from a central plant. Air-handling units transfer cooling to each office zone. About 80 percent of the year, however, the outside air is cooler and drier than the return air from the office floors. Whenever possible, the HVAC system runs on 100 percent outside air and exhausts slightly less room air from the return ducts so that the building stays positively pressured relative to the outdoors. Note that the abundance of outside air also promotes good indoor air quality and occupant health.

A low-pressure variable air volume (VAV) system distributes air from above the ceiling and through the light shelves. Return air is taken from above the light shelves where most solar absorption occurs, so a great deal of heat is removed before it becomes a room load. For the same reason, air is also exhausted directly from the top of the litetrium skylights, where warm air stratifies. As the climate data indicates, outside air in Sunnyvale is frequently cooler and drier than this return air stream is, so return air is frequently exhausted and replaced with outdoor air.

With energy savings as a design priority and HVAC loads tempered by the mild climate, the focus of performance naturally turns to lighting. The 1980 California Energy Code dictated a budget of 40,000 Btu/ft²/yr (454 million joules/m²/yr) for new commercial buildings in this region. Because the proposed construction systems for the building did not comply with prescriptive sections of the code dealing with insulation levels and glass area ratios, the building had to qualify on the basis of calculated performance. The design firm's predictions put Lockheed 157 at 50 percent of the allowable, just meeting the designer's initial goal. Energy use at the building is not monitored, owing to the unmetered consumption of chilled water from the campus central plant, but daylighting performance was successful in a postoccupancy evaluation by Lawrence Berkeley Laboratories (Benton and Fountain, 1990).

All told, an extra $2 million, or 4 percent of the total cost, was invested in the final version in excess of what would have been spent on Lockheed's generic plans. The improvements save $500,000 per year, mostly in lighting energy. So a 25 percent return on the investment was certainly satisfactory. Furthermore, the relocation of a known work group population from an old building to a new one

provided a good comparison case for studying productivity improvements. Independent reports claim that absenteeism at Building 157 dropped 15 percent after the move and that productivity on the first new job contracted by the group rose another 15 percent. A 1983 first cost of $83/ft² indicates that each personal workspace accounts for about $18,000 worth of the building's initial construction. Leveraged against the 40-year costs of the building, 92 percent of which is typically represented by employee salaries, the actual savings are staggering.

These findings were supported by several industry studies performed at about the same time the building was completed. The General Services Administration study mentioned by Windheim was just one such investigation. Other studies showed that white collar knowledge workers were subject to the same productivity influences of many blue collar trade "outputs." The quality of the interior environment appears to make a 5 to 15 percent difference in productivity.

Interior

Luminous zoning organizes the interior in much the same way that solar zoning arranges the envelope response. Ground floor functions include a large cafeteria off the south side of the atrium, deliveries, reception, and some general office space. The north entry side glazing at street level is translucent glass block for privacy and security. Above, all four upper floors are dedicated to workstations. The atrium lightwell bisects the depth of the plan so that the north and south office floors are effectively each 90 ft deep and 420 ft long (27.4 m × 128.0 m). Each 90 ft (27.5 m) wide workspace is then divided lengthwise by a circulation aisle, leaving every workstation within 40 ft (12.2 m) of a daylighting source. To each side of the atrium is a 60 ft × 30 ft (18.3 m × 9.1 m) open office space backing up to the core areas. Ceilings slope from 15 ft (4.6 m) high at the exterior and atrium perimeters to 10 ft high at the center of the main floors 45 ft (13.7 m) in. Model studies showed that at 40 ft (12.2 m) from the windows, a sloping ceiling would produce a 41 percent improvement in footcandle levels as compared with a flat ceiling.

Seven zones of indirect fluorescent lighting were installed at a lighting power density of 0.92 W/ft². These consisted of suspended fixtures with cool white lamps and were run in lines parallel to the windows. An eighth zone was installed under the inner portion of the light shelf. Each of these eight sets of lights is dimmed in response to a photocell measuring available daylight in the zone. Adjustable lighting fixtures are built into each workstation to provide supplemental task light on desktops. The ambi-

Figure 6.29 The interior atrium at Lockheed.

Figure 6.30 Lightshelf along the south wall.

ent light coming off the ceiling from the combined fluorescents and daylight is just enough to keep contrast ratios between task lighting and background illumination comfortable.

The interior space arrangement is based on luminous and solar zoning. Mechanical rooms, toilets, and storage areas are all pushed to the unfavorable east and west walls. Open fire stairs are located at both corners of the east and west end walls. Conference rooms and computing centers, which do not require task lighting levels, are also moved to the side wings to allow the maximum utilization of daylight in the workstation-filled open office floors. The only interrupting element in this scheme is a central stair tower in the atrium that acts as a bridge across the 60 ft span. Otherwise, a walk around the atrium perimeter would be as much as 360 ft (109.7 m) long.

Because 70 percent of Lockheed's staff was being moved around each year, workstation areas at Building 157 were planned with flexibility in mind. First, the floor is raised 10 in. (255 mm), allowing for unlimited wire management. Then the modular workstations can be literally unplugged, set on wheels, rolled down the central aisle, and reconfigured elsewhere in about an hour and a half. Russell Robinson, the manager of facility interior development, set the cost of moving an employee in Building 157 at $60, one-tenth of the cost at Lockheed's other offices.

TECHNICAL INTEGRATION HIGHLIGHTS

Physical

- Lightshelves on both sides of the building incorporate ductwork and electrical lighting systems.
- A raised floor system allows for cable management and plug in. workstation flexibility.

Visual

- Indirect lighting of the ceiling mitigates the perception of fluctuating daylight levels by blending electric and natural sources. Both use the ceiling to distribute light.
- The litetrium breaks down the scale of the 100,000 ft^2 (9286 m^2) floor plates by dividing them into four areas and allowing a central public space at the ground floor.

Performance

- HVAC return air removes solar heat at the daylight apertures before it becomes a large cooling load in the building.
- The envelope design maximizes thermal and luminous performance.
- Interior zoning incorporates solar and luminous design strategies.

DISCUSSION

Integration is successful only if it achieves architectural benefits. To say that Lockheed's office building is only an economic success overlooks the root of its real accomplishments—people work better in Building 157 because it is a better place to work. The building should be recognized for its humane environment and comfortable conditions as well as its pro forma economics and return on investment.

Technically, the building has needed some fine-tuning from time to time. During a 1989 postoccupancy evaluation by Lawrence Berkeley Laboratory's Chris Benton and Marc Fountain, the calibration and placement of the photosensors was corrected. It also seems that the litetrium was perhaps more successful than desired—the east and north ledges of the upper workstation floors have been lined with metal shades and canvas parasols for some time.

7

Airport Terminals

Airport terminal buildings are principally intended to provide passage for large and concentrated numbers of pedestrians and luggage between two modes of transportation. For this reason, airport terminals are typically described as having a "landside" and an "airside." Between the two modes is where the prominent public experience of airport architecture occurs—in the terminal building. The case studies in this chapter will illustrate the central role of the terminal in airport design.

Inherent problems of pedestrian circulation in terminal buildings are prime generators of architectural response. Complex networks of separate arrival and departure paths become compounded by ticketing, food and retail services, baggage handling, immigration procedures, and security. At one end of the circulation path the designer has to cope with connections to private car, taxi, bus, shuttle, and rail transit terminals. At the other circulation end there is the problem of passengers waiting for and boarding large, hulking aircraft spread across great distances by the spacing of their immense wingspans.

The terminal building is surrounded, of course, by a vast and complex array of infrastructure. Airports are urban-scale planning projects that respond to two large-scale issues: aircraft operations and regional ecology. Operational activities are largely pragmatic and dictated by the needs of servicing and operating aircraft as they land, taxi, park, fuel, board, load, taxi out, and take off. Although these issues require strategic planning for huge

plots of land, they are not essentially within the architect's domain. Ecological issues, on the other hand, must be addressed by many large-scale land-planning tasks from an architectural perspective.

The large parcels of land required for aircraft services and safe operating conditions create both design opportunities and long-term management problems. Immense land requirements begin with the runways—current standards are 12,000 ft (3,658 m) long, 150 ft (46 m) wide, with a spacing of 4,300 ft (1311 m) to allow simultaneous use. Airside operational areas for taxiing of aircraft, service hangers, and cargo operations stretch the airport farther into the landscape. Landside needs for passenger approach and parking add still more area. Around all these designated-use areas, there is a buffer zone for noise attenuation added to the airport perimeter and restricted land use for miles around the airport proper. Finally, all airports have to plan for continuing expansion.

Ecology

The size and complexity of land use in airports creates nothing less than a regional ecology. Airports are universally associated with at least three prime environmental concerns: ground traffic, aircraft noise, and storm water. The vast no man's-land beyond the runway areas generally provides the resources for addressing all three of these problems. Parking can be handled in outlying lots, from which passengers are shuttled directly to their terminals. Alternately, and with increasing preference, mass transit terminals can be integrated into the terminal building itself. Storm water from the massive roof and paving areas can be channeled into surrounding ponds and wetlands, providing floodwater retention, sediment and chemical remediation, and natural habitat.

In addition, storm drainage and runoff from extensive runway and parking areas pose flooding problems and water quality issues not only to the airport but also to its neighbors. This is another problem that grows along with the success of most any airport. Typically, storm water is captured in retaining ponds. A more environmentally responsible practice is to use larger and shallower ponds to better allow filtration of solid material and dissolved sediments back into the land instead of being transported to other ecosystems by runoff. Most acceptable is the provision of planted wetland ecologies to purify storm water and provide natural habitat. As the environmental impact is minimized, however, the land area required for ponds and wetlands increases.

Complexity comes with size. Wetland habitats, for example, attract bird populations that are inherently incompatible with aircraft. Most airports have full-time biologists on staff who use everything from propane cannons to plastic snakes in order to reduce the risk of "bird strikes" and potential mechanical disaster with operating aircraft. Scare tactics seldom fool the birds for very long, however, and more systemic solutions are often needed. Dogs have been valiantly rescued from abandoned pet shelters and retrained to chase away nesting birds, for example. But design offers the best and most elegant answer. The new Hong Kong airport of Chek Lap Kok (Norman Foster, 1998) spent $50 million on landscape improvements, including plantings of 2,287 bauhinia trees and 25,800 bauhinia seedlings. The bauhinia, or Hong Kong orchid tree, whose five-petaled flower is the emblem of Hong Kong, was selected for more than symbolic importance: This tree family also has the important property of being unattractive to bird populations.

Addressing another large-scale issue, the new Denver International Airport (DIA) offers a well-documented case history in airport planning in general and noise problems in particular. The first facility to be constructed as a totally new airport in the United States in more than 20 years, DIA was built to replace the aging Denver Stapleton Airport. Stapleton suffered from overcrowded flight traffic, narrow runways, frequent weather delays, and urban noise control problems. So in place of Stapleton, seven miles from downtown Denver, DIA was placed 35 miles (56 km) away. The new $5 billion airport (C. W. Fentress

J. H. Bradburn & Associates, 1995) covers 53 square miles (137 square kilometers), or an area twice the size of Manhattan, and can be expanded from its original five runways to eleven. Its terminal buildings enclose a quarter-mile of ticket counters, 48 food service establishments, and some 60 stores and shops. The 1.5 million ft^2 (139,284 m^2) main concourse is covered by a Teflon-coated fabric roof and connects to three outlying airside concourses via underground rail trolleys and an automated baggage system. The entire operation was designed to turn planes around in 30 minutes at each of the 94 total gates. Outside, four deicing pads can each handle up to five aircraft at a time, and the alcohol-based chemicals are captured for recycling after spraying down the planes.

Despite the advantages of starting new rather than expanding an existing facility, DIA suffers many typical airport problems. The automated baggage system was to use photocells and radio tracking to take luggage from the terminal directly to the aircraft on 17 miles of track. When televised tests showed luggage flying off conveyer belts in every direction, the system was declared a $200 million bust and required a $51 million alternative. Later, despite the rationale of moving the new airport an hour's drive from downtown to avoid noise problems, DIA was fined $4 million for violating its own noise standards over surrounding neighborhoods.

Airport noise problems are certainly the most apparent complication of airport operation. With length of service and success, airports become bigger and noisier. As time passes, surrounding communities sprawl into its economically attractive activities. Houses, schools, and churches get closer, as airports get bigger and louder. Eventually, conflicts arise. The issue often comes to fore when an airport is forced to consider expansion and a neighborhood reacts defensively. Several sorts of efforts have been made to deal with these problems, all with limited success. Many airports have spent hundreds of millions of dollars adding sound insulation to outlying houses and buildings as noise remediation, at a cost of about $25,000 per building. A great many studies and computer models have been developed to predict airport noise footprints and levels of disturbance in surrounding communities. DIA is, in fact, among the first airports to deploy active sound measurement systems in outlying areas to monitor ongoing noise levels. The generally accepted standard in the United States has been a maximum average day and night noise level of 65 decibels, as established by the Federal Aviation Administration (FAA). There are at least three scientific studies that look specifically at sleep disturbance levels caused by air traffic. The greatest hope for progress in this "must grow" irresistible force versus "not in my back yard" immovable objection seems to lie in the development of quieter aircraft. The transition from Stage II noise-classified planes to Stage III was supposed to be completed in 1999 and to supply substantial relief, but some airports had already reported substantial compliance with Stage III before 1998. Until silent flight is perfected, the battle is likely to persist. Architects and urban planners will continue to cope with problems like those that closed Denver's Stapleton and still shadow DIA for the foreseeable future.

Flexibility

Once the designer comes to grips with all the functional and architectural characteristics of airports, there is still the issue of adaptability. Changes in airport use are constantly dictated by advances in technology. New airplanes, for example, grow ever bigger and consequently need larger gates (and runways)spaced farther and farther apart.

Flexibility issues are also driven by the need to accommodate more and more travelers. According to the Airport Council International, the 50 largest airports in the world experienced a mean 1999 growth of 5.1 percent in number of passengers served, averaging more than 32 million passengers per year each, or some 1.6 billion travelers total. At that rate of growth, airports must somehow double their passenger-handling capabilities every 14 years

Other needs for flexibility are evidenced by progress in baggage handling, people movers, ticketless traveling, Internet reservations, E-commerce, and "just-in-time" product management. Safety issues are also prominent: Hijacking, terrorist bombings, and aircraft failures are too frequent news items. Finally, consider the plight of flight traffic control in light of the fact that a sizable majority of the world's aircraft fleet is in the air at any given time.

TABLE 7.1   Annual Passenger Growth at the World's Busiest Airports (1999)

Rank	Airport	1999 Passengers	Growth
1	Atlanta Hartsfield(ATL)	78,092,940	6.30%
2	Chicago O'Hare(ORD)	72,609,191	0.10%
3	Los Angeles (LAX)	64,279,571	5.00%
4	London Heathrow (LHR)	62,263,365	2.60%
5	Dallas/Ft. Worth (DFW)	60,000,127	−0.50%
6	Tokyo Haneda (HND)	54,338,212	6.00%
7	Frankfurt (FRA)	45,838,864	7.30%
8	Paris Charles De Gaulle (CDG)	43,597,194	12.90%
9	San Francisco (SFO)	40,387,538	0.70%
10	Denver (DIA)	38,034,017	3.30%
11	Amsterdam Schiphol (AMS)	36,772,015	6.80%
12	Minneapolis/St. Paul (MSP)	34,721,879	14.40%

Conclusion

Modern airports are increasingly distinct institutions in world culture. Popular and affordable air travel has permeated industrial society. Consider, for example, the stimulus that affordable business air travel provided in the infant years of franchise hotel chains and to the continuing alliance of pleasure travel and hotel accommodation. Consider as well the increasingly isolated, "island-unto-itself" governance of airports that divorces them from the surrounding urban fabric. Airports have their own security forces, fire departments, traffic and parking systems, mass transit stations, restaurants and shopping centers— all operating more directly under the auspices of the airport authority than of local government. These not-so-small island cities operate as increasingly independent communities.

10

WASHINGTON DULLES INTERNATIONAL AIRPORT, 1958–1964

Chantilly, Virginia
EERO SAARINEN AND ASSOCIATES

DESCRIPTION

Techno-society and techno-design converge in this modernist terminal building for the first passenger jet airport. True to Eero Saarinen's prototype form seeking, the unique building requirements evoked several opportunities for inventing new architectural form by way of advanced technology.

Saarinen's response to pedestrian pathways and the inherent car-to-plane changeover was both radically practical and idealistically modern—so radical and ideal that the building was designed for a fleet of detachable appendages, mobile lounges replacing conventional terminal waiting areas. The Chrysler-built lounges married waiting room with docking jetway with cocktail bar. A few of them would carry an entire flight of passengers directly from the ticket counter to their waiting jet out on the "service station" tarmac.

The building served for more than convenient flying, of course. It was also to be a monumental and international gateway to the nation's capital 26 miles to the northeast. Saarinen's structural inventiveness is manifested in this aspect of the project as a 600 ft (182.9 m) long catenary roof. It is slung hammock-style across 170 ft (51.8 m) between two rows of inclined pylons. Eliminating the need for walkway fingers sprawling out to airplanes simplified the terminal, allowing it to remain an uncluttered and gracefully thin form. The final result is a revolutionary airport design inspired by the issues it confronts and enriched by the technology it employs.

Figure 7.1   Overview of the terminal building at Dulles. *(3-D rendering by Travis Hughs.)*

TABLE 7.2   Fact Sheet

Project	**Building Name**	Dulles International Airport
	Client	United States Federal Government
	City	Chantilly, Virginia
	Lat/Long/Elev	38.95 N 77.45 W, 322 ft (98 m)
Team	**Architect**	Eero Saarinen
	Structural Engineers	Ammann & Whitney, chief structural designer Boyd Anderson
	Mechanical Engineers	Whitney, Burns and McDonnell
	Landscape	Dan Kiley
	Airport Consultant	Charles Landrum
General	**Time Line**	Commisioned Saarinen in 1958. Dedicated November 17, 1962, by President John F. Kennedy and former president Dwight D. Eisenhower.
	Floor Area	362,422 ft^2 (33,653 m^2).
	Occupants	50,000 passengers served the first year.
	Cost	$108.3 million total, $16.0 million for terminal building.
	Cost in 1995 US$	$583.8 million total, $80.8 million for terminal building, or $223/ft^2.
	Stories	Two.
	Plan	600 ft × 150 ft zz9182.9 m × 45.7 m) in 15 structural bays of 150 ft × 40 ft (45.7 m × 12.2 m).
Site	**Site Description**	Fifteen square mile site located 26 miles (41.6 km) west of Washington D.C. 10,000 acres (4000 hectares) in Loudoun and Fairfax Counties in Chantilly, Virginia; 4,880 acres (1952 hectares) used for aircraft operations. Dulles is approximately 30 minutes from downtown Washington, D.C. The site is a large flat plain. Access from Washington, D.C., is via a toll road.
	Parking, Cars	Campus lots.
Structure	**Foundation**	Not published.
	Vertical Members	Cantilevered columns using up to 16 tons (14.5 metric tons) of reinforcing steel each.
	Horizontal Spans	Precast concrete slabs laid on 1 in. (25 mm) diameter steel cables at 10 ft (3.1 m) centers, grouted together to form a homogeneous catenary draped membrane.
Envelope	**Glass and Glazing**	Inclined walls of 0.25 in. (6 mm) clear plate glass in aluminum-clad steel framing.
	Skylights	None.
	Cladding	Glass.
	Roof	Single-ply neoprene membrane.
HVAC	**Equipment**	Remote central plant.
	Cooling Type	Fan rooms in lower level.
	Distribution	Located in floor-ceiling layer beneath concourse floor.
	Duct Type	Concealed.
	Vertical Chases	None.
Interior	**Partitions**	Low-level kiosk-style areas in the concourse pavilion.
	Finishes	Plaster ceiling, concrete floor, glass walls.
	Vertical Circulation	Interior stairs.
	Furniture	Eames.
	Lighting	Direct downlighting in kiosks and indirect lighting off concourse ceiling reflected from kiosks' uplights.

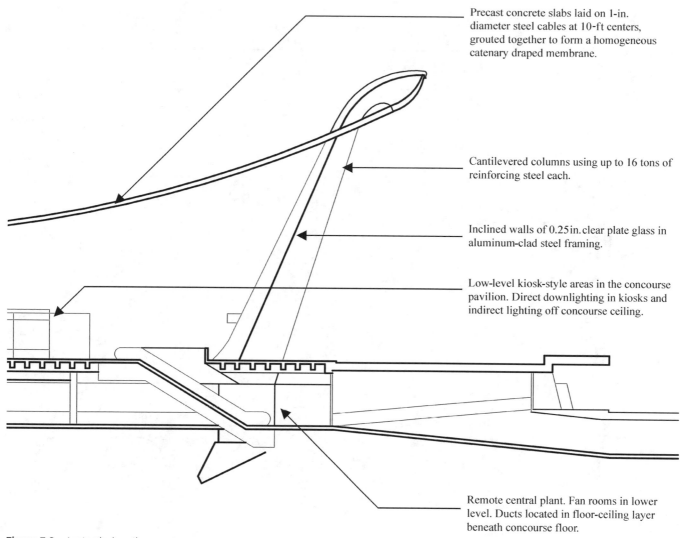

Precast concrete slabs laid on 1-in. diameter steel cables at 10-ft centers, grouted together to form a homogeneous catenary draped membrane.

Cantilevered columns using up to 16 tons of reinforcing steel each.

Inclined walls of 0.25 in. clear plate glass in aluminum-clad steel framing.

Low-level kiosk-style areas in the concourse pavilion. Direct downlighting in kiosks and indirect lighting off concourse ceiling.

Remote central plant. Fan rooms in lower level. Ducts located in floor-ceiling layer beneath concourse floor.

Figure 7.2   Anatomical section.

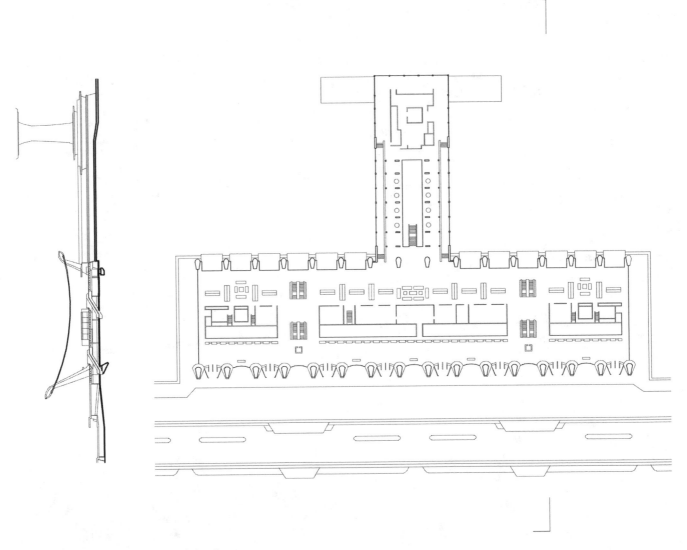

Figure 7.3 Plan, section, and elevation.

PROGRAM

Client

The approaching introduction of jet airliners and a series of midair collisions spurred passage of the Federal Aviation Act of 1958. A new office, the Federal Aviation Agency, was given rule-making authority to prevent aviation hazards and responsibility for developing and maintaining a system of civil and military air traffic control. The scope of the Federal Aviation Act owed much to the leadership of Elwood "Pete" Quesada, an Air Force general who had served as President Eisenhower's principal advisor on civil aeronautics. After becoming the first administrator of the agency he had helped to create, Quesada mounted a vigorous campaign for improved airline safety.

Brief

Also in 1958, the U.S. government contracted architects and engineers Eero Saarinen & Associates, Amman & Whitney, Burns & McDonald, and local Washington architect Ellery Husted, with planning consultant Brunham Kelly, to develop the master plan for Dulles International Airport. A set of regulations was drafted and submitted for approval of federal authorities. It would establish a unique organization to administer the plan and to coordinate with local governments in controlling the development of the region surrounding the new airport. Although the proposed site was quite remote from Washington, D. C., or any other urban complex, it was to generate immediate growth of housing and commercial facilities. The Developmental Advisory Board was appointed to ensure

TABLE 7.3 Normal Climate Data for Dulles Airport, Washington, D.C.

		Jan.	Feb.	Mar.	Apr.	May	June	July	Aug.	Sept.	Oct.	Nov.	Dec.	Year
Temperature	Degree-Days Heating	1039	869	668	360	132	18	1	4	60	317	582	902	4927
	Degree-Days Cooling	0	0	3	11	65	210	351	302	131	15	2	0	1097
	Extreme High	75	79	89	92	97	100	104	104	99	90	84	78	104
	Normal High	41	44	55	66	75	83	87	86	79	68	57	45	65
	Normal Average	31	34	44	53	63	71	76	75	67	55	46	36	54
	Normal Low	22	23	32	41	50	59	65	63	55	42	34	26	43
	Extreme Low	-18	-14	-1	17	28	36	41	38	30	15	9	-4	-18
Humidity	Dew Point	21	22	30	39	52	61	65	64	58	45	35	26	43
	Max % RH	77	77	78	77	82	84	86	89	89	88	82	78	82
	Min % RH	57	52	49	46	53	54	54	55	55	52	54	57	53
	% Days with Rain	31	32	44	50	52	46	46	42	39	35	41	37	41
	Rain Inches	3	3	3	3	4	4	4	4	4	3	3	3	40
Sky	% Overcast Days	52	50	52	43	45	40	39	39	40	39	47	55	45
	% Clear Days	23	23	22	22	19	17	17	19	23	30	24	22	22
Wind	Prevailing Direction	NW	NW	NW	NW	S	S	S	S	S	S	NW	NW	NW
	Speed, Knots	11	11	11	11	7	6	6	6	6	6	10	11	9
	Percent Calm	10	10	8	9	10	12	13	16	16	17	12	12	12
Days Observed	Rain	9	10	13	15	16	14	14	13	12	11	12	11	150
	Fog	13	11	12	11	14	16	19	20	19	14	12	12	174
	Haze	4	4	5	4	8	14	19	18	12	7	5	4	105
	Snow	8	8	4	1	0	0	0	0	0	0	2	6	30
	Hail	0	0	0	0	0	0	0	0	0	0	0	0	1
	Freezing Rain	1	1	0	0	0	0	0	0	0	0	0	0	2
	Blowing Sand	0	0	0	0	0	0	0	0	0	0	0	0	0

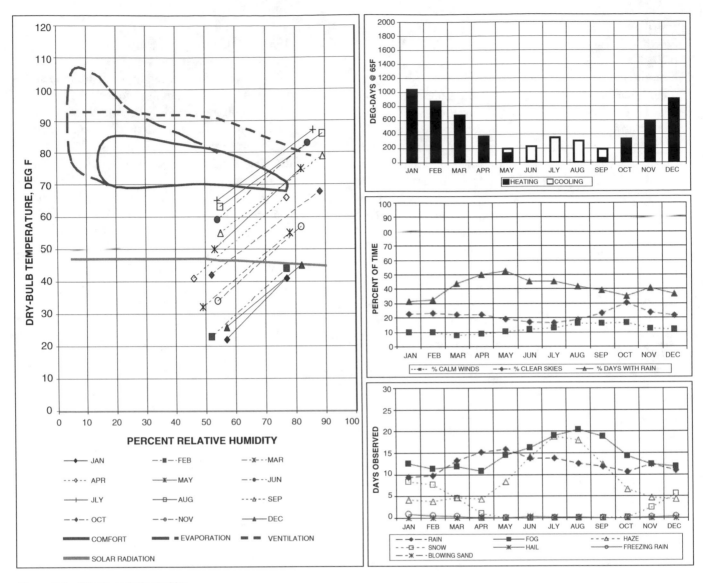

Figure 7.4   Climate analysis graphics.

compliance with federal regulations. The board met regularly to review the physical development of the airport and the state of airport community relations, reporting its conclusions and recommendations to the FAA.

Site

Ten thousand acres of Virginia prairie were selected for the airport and approved by President Eisenhower. The site was deemed remote enough to keep air traffic out of the District of Columbia airspace and near enough to be conveniently accessible. A 14-mile-long (22.4 km) air corridor was established for air traffic, and 4,880 acres (1952 hectares) were set aside for aircraft operations. A dedicated toll road was built to provide a conduit directly to the terminal from the fringes of the capital.

Master planning for the project established 2000 ft boundaries along the runways and 8000 ft borders at both ends of the airstrips (610 × 2438 m). Along the entire perimeter of the site a 1000 ft (304 m) band of trees was planted as a noise barrier and visual separation from the surrounding landscape. Vehicles reach the site from the toll road on the east side of the property. Approach to the terminal building is from the north and passes another of Saarinen's lakes (see case study #6) before reaching the main parking area.

Climate

A generally westerly atmospheric flow maintains a continental climate at Dulles Airport, with four distinct seasons. There is a degree-day ratio of 4.5 heating degree-days to each cooling degree-day (4927 heating to 1097 cooling). Normal bin data indicates that 9 percent of the year is hot (above 85°F), 11 percent warm (above 75°F), 19 percent comfortable, 16 percent cool (55°F to

65°F), 32 percent cold (35°F to 55°F), and 17 percent of annual hours are below 35°F. The frost-free growing season averages 169 days.

There are, on average, 30 days with snowfall per year, with a total of 24 in. Rainfall is evenly distributed at 3 to 4 in. precipitation per month and a total of 40 in. per year, with measurable rain occurring on about 150 days annually.

Dulles fits Köppen's classification of Cfa climates: midlatitude, uniform precipitation, hot summer. Barcelona, Spain, and Tokyo, Japan, are also Cfa category climates, typically lying on an eastern seaboard between the tropics at about 40 degrees latitude.

INTENTION

Design Team

Biographical information and the association of Eero Saarinen with Charles and Ray Eames are presented in the study of the John Deere Administrative Headquarters (see case study #6). The engineering firms of Ammann &

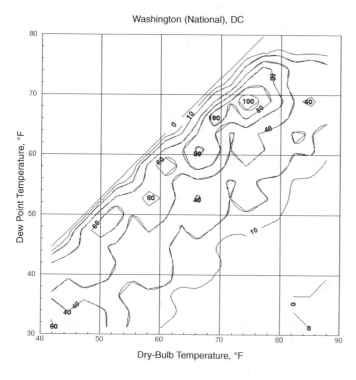

Washington (National), DC

Figure 7.5 Bin data distribution for Dulles Airport. Concentric areas of graph indicate the number of hours per year that weather conditions normally occur in this climate. Similar to elevation readings on topographic maps, highest frequency occurrences of weather are at the center peaks of the graph. (Data sources: *Engineering Weather Data, typical meteorological year (TMY) data from the National Climatic Data Center, and the ASHRAE Weather Data Viewer from the American Society of Heating, Refrigerating and Air-Conditioning Engineers.*)

Whitney (structural) and Whitney, Burns & McDonnell (mechanical) also continued their work with Saarinen's team after the Deere project. Whitney, Burns & McDonnell (now Burns & McDonnell) had been working with airport construction for some time.

Philosophy

Washington Dulles Airport reflects Saarinen's concern for functionally inspired architecture and a solution unique to its constraints and context. The complexity of Dulles is introduced through the sophistication of airport issues in general and the advent of jet travel in particular. This concern was not a dictate of the client or the original brief; it was introduced by Saarinen and his team out of the belief that architecture should embrace this functionalist philosophy.

Intent

Considering the building as a formal object and a monumental gateway, Saarinen thought of a form that would rise above the Virginia prairie, "something between earth and sky." A hovering roof with an upswept shape that suggested flight came to mind. He might have thought of Le Corbusier's chapel at Ronchamp, where the mass of the roof is dematerialized by a thin strip of glass as it joins the perimeter walls.

As a technical challenge, Saarinen determined that jetways from the terminal waiting lounges for boarding the aircraft would be eliminated and replaced with mobile lounges. This decision was supported by the bus systems he saw servicing airports in Europe. But Saarinen went beyond the simple notion of replacing jet-ways with another passenger inconvenience of boarding buses and unloading at the aircraft. He saw this substitution as a negative step. For the approach to be successful, it would be necessary to transform the mobile lounges into luxurious spaces. He decided to eliminate the lobby entirely and make the transit from ticket counter to the jet liner door directly. The mobile lounge would be the waiting lobby.

CRITICAL TECHNICAL ISSUES

Inherent

Washington Dulles International Airport was necessitated by the advent of commercial jet aircraft. After World War II, aircraft manufacturers had to find new markets for their military-industrial capabilities. With certain knowledge that they needed different products for these new markets, interest in innovation led to developments in jet engines. Britain's Sir Geoffrey de Havilland (1882–1965) was the first to see the commercial advantages of pressurized-cabin jet aircraft that could comfortably fly above the weather. He started British Overseas Air Carriers (BOCA) in 1949 to capitalize on the Comet jet plane developed from wartime technology. On May 3, 1952, scheduled BOAC passenger service from London to Johannesburg began. The Jet Age was born.

The safety of jet aircraft and their operational practicality were thoroughly demonstrated during the Korean War. One advantage was that jets used cheap kerosene fuel rather than the high-octane gasoline required by piston engine propeller airliners. By 1957, Boeing had converted its enormously successful military refueling jet, the KC-135, for commercial service as the Boeing 707 passenger plane. It replaced the propeller-driven Boeing 377. Simultaneously, McDonald Douglas began production of the DC-8 to replace the prop engine DC-7. It was at about this time that Washington, D.C., decided it needed a new airport.

Saarinen recognized that the new jet engine planes were bigger and would thus have to be more widely spaced around a conventional terminal building at greater distances than smaller propeller driven aircraft. The Boeing 707 was 34 ft longer (10.4 m) than the 377. The DC-8 had a wingspan 25 ft wider (7.6 m) than the DC-7. Just as important, both jets seated about twice as many passengers as their predecessors. It seemed to the design team that the airport terminal was in serious danger of being overwhelmed by crowds of people and the distances they would have to walk.

The team, with Charles Landrum as airport project consultant, did extensive research at terminals around the world to consider walking distances and times. They studied nearby Washington National, Willow Run in Detroit, Chicago's O'Hare Field, Dallas' Love Field, and Lambert Field in St. Louis. Charles Eames condensed much of their findings in about 40 illustrations and a five minute film presentation.

Contextual

With the federal government as client and owner of the project, Washington International Airport became a part of the capital complex. Visitors' first and last impressions of their Washington visit would be made in the terminal building. Thus, the building would assume importance as a reference symbol of the government and technology of the United States.

Intentional

Saarinen's intention of collapsing the path from airside to landside into a narrow pavilion made the development of mobile lounges highly critical. These chariots would have to serve as comfortable waiting rooms and cater to the tastes of elite patrons. Flying was not a middle-class institution in the United States until after deregulation of the airlines in the late 1970s.

Two other issues were generated by the general nature of the design intention. The first was structural and related to the desired image of "something between earth and sky" that would span the concourse as an uninterrupted space. Second, all of the service functions would have to be cleared from the concourse, swept into the lower level and the floor-ceiling layer between the two floors.

APPROPRIATE SYSTEMS

Precedent

Technical precedents for a jet airport were, of course, nonexistent in 1958, but the systems of baggage and passenger accommodation in airports were already being explored for commercial travel in propeller aircraft. The European model of taking buses from the terminal to the waiting aircraft on the taxiways must have appealed to Saarinen as the most viable means of minimizing passenger inconvenience. Today many large European airports like Paris's Charles de Gaulle still use these remote boarding procedures. Some of them use shuttles more similar to Saarinen's mobile lounges than to conventional shuttles.

The team developed a roof form that suggested a suspended structure. Saarinen worried that the roof might look heavy from inside, but his project for the Ingalls Hockey Rink at Yale University provided him with a satisfactory model for the airport terminal.

Site

The terminal structure itself is divided into three levels on the landside. Entry from parking is the lowest. A ramp at baggage level for passenger pickup meets the base of the building to make the second level. Rampways from these first two levels meet at the lower level of the terminal. The third level is the open-plan pavilion of the ticketing lobby and concourse. A passenger drop-off ramp hugs the building under the overhanging pylons.

The enclosed volume of the lower baggage claim level is expressed as a massive base that berms into the earth on both narrow sides. The three levels of the complex are set back successively from the parking area. This molds the supporting lower-level functions of the building into the site and minimizes their presence. It also elevates the compact concourse pavilion with its soaring roof as a discrete object that forms the image of the entire terminal as "something between earth and sky."

On the airside of the terminal, the pavilion is separated into two wings by a two-level structure that forms

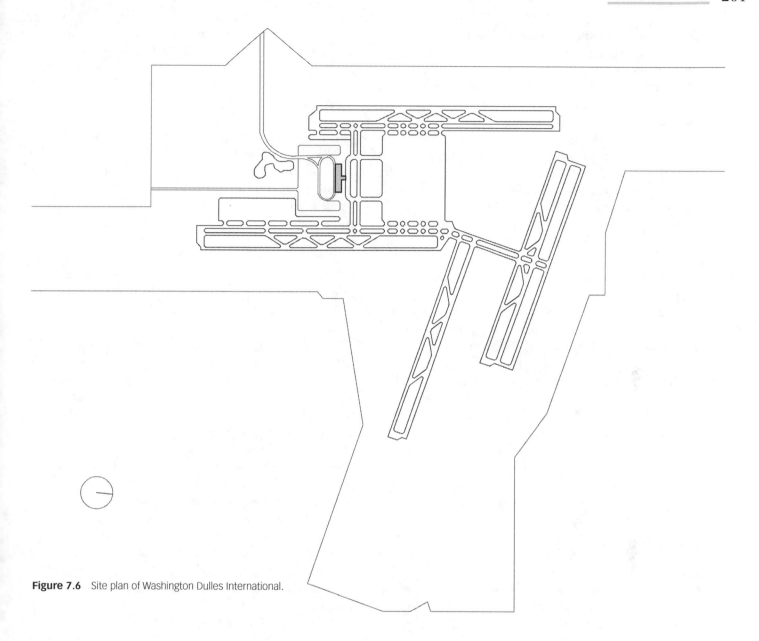

Figure 7.6 Site plan of Washington Dulles International.

courtyards for the mobile lounge docking gates. Its lower level is occupied by airline offices and terminal management. The upper level is given to passenger lounges and a restaurant. At the southern end of this extension is the 14-story air traffic control tower. The southern extent of this structure was planned as the base of future boarding platforms for more mobile lounges, ironically introducing the "fingers" that the design intention sought to avoid.

Landscape design was given to Dan Kiley, whose work would grow to include collaborations with I. M. Pei, Kevin Roche, and others. A lake at the entryway of the airport and the 1000 ft (304.8 m) deep perimeter of trees surrounding the property are his most evident contributions. For safety reasons, potential bird habitats are kept clear of the runways and most of the area around the terminal is mowed grass.

Structure

The ground floor of the terminal is concrete slab on grade. The next level of main floor beams supporting the concourse is reinforced concrete and spans generous distances between supporting columns. These concourse floor beams are widely spaced to clear the baggage handling machinery and passenger facilities. The principal floor beams, therefore, are positioned in line with the main vertical rib frames and then supplemented by intermediate columns at midpoint of the span.

The curved concrete roof is made by suspending pairs of 1 in. (25 mm) cables at 10 ft (3.0 m) centers across the plan and allowing them to hang in a natural catenary curve. The floor of the terminal is 150 ft (45.7 m) wide, but the outwardly inclined pylons with their connecting edge beam form overhangs of more than 20 ft (6.1 m) on each side. Together, the total span is close to 200 ft (61 m). The cables are supported on both sides of the long span by stiff concrete edge beams. The poured-in-place edge beams are carried, in turn, on inclined concrete pylons at 40 ft (12.2 m) centers. Once the cables were in place, a roof deck was laid by setting 5.9 ft (1.8 m) wide × 7.5 in. (190 mm) deep precast double-T concrete panels between the cables. The double-T shape and the use of lightweight concrete for the roof panels kept dead loads across the long span to a minimum. Exposed reinforcing bars projecting from the end of the panels were simply laid over the suspension cables. Then the roof was temporarily loaded with sandbags to form the design curvature and to pretension the cables. Next, concrete beams at 10.0 ft (3.1 m) on center were poured between each row of roof panels along the line of the suspension cables. These form inverted arch beams that resist the dead load of the roof as well as wind uplift forces. Pretensioning the suspension cables with the sandbags stiffened these beams significantly.

Roof edge beams along both long sides of the terminal were poured to support the three pairs of suspension cables between pylons. These thin beams are inclined in the plane of the cables to resist the dead loads of the roof and the resultant vertical component of tension forces in the cables. Because these beams form the roof overhang outside the line of the pylons, their weight counterbalances the horizontal force of the cables and resists inward rotational forces on the pylons.

The structural action of the concrete pylons is to resist tension forces from the roof suspension cables, which explains their inclined profile. They are spaced at 40 ft (12.2 m) centers across both long sides of the building, and each contains about 20 tons (18.1 metric tonnes) of reinforcing steel. During their construction, workmen had to vibrate the concrete pours from inside the reinforcement cages. On the landside, pylons are 65.3 ft (19.9 m) tall. On the airside, they reach 42.6 ft (13.0 m). The pylon colonnades on both sides rest on supporting fins at the lower level that extend their total height by another 19.2 ft (5.8 m). Openings through the overhanging roof allow the pylons to pass uninterrupted up to the curved roof parapet.

Storm water is removed from the roof by one large central drainpipe. This drain can handle 12,500 gallons of water per minute (788 liters per second), carrying it through the terminal to a lake north of the parking area.

Envelope
The 0.25 in. (6.3 mm) clear plate glass skin of the terminal is framed in an aluminum-clad steel curtain wall that slopes outward with the inclined pylons. The taller land-side wall has a ceiling height of 48.7 ft (14.9 m), and the airside wall reaches 42.7 ft (13.0 m). A suspended plaster ceiling covers the underside of the concrete roof deck, concealing the structure. Rigid insulation, 1.5 in. (38 mm) thick was installed against the double-T deck panels.

The glass wall presented two problems. First, its slope would tend to make the system sag outward. This was handled by bowing the horizontal mullions so that the frame would always be in compression under its own weight. The frames are nonetheless still made of 5.5 in. × 4.5 in. (140 mm × 114 mm) steel T's in both horizontal and vertical members to resist wind loads. Second, a system of entry had to be devised for moving through the inclined wall. This was achieved by the design of low pavilions that project through the wall at every second bay across the north entry side of the concourse. Similar construction is used for the interior ticketing kiosks and the south-side mobile lounge docks.

To accentuate the perspective and curvature of the bowed curtain wall, Saarinen modulated the size of the glass panels very carefully. Size increases with height (8.3, 11.2, 12.7, and 14.0 ft successively), and panels are wider in the center than at the pylons. The long orientations of the glass walls to favorable north and south elevations are shaded by generous overhangs. More shading is also effected by the inclined angle of the wall, which increases the sun's angle of incidence and therefore increases the amount of solar energy reflected from the glass. East and west walls are unprotected, however. Treatment of these vertical sidewalls is limited to a splayed pattern of vertical mullions that harmonize geometrically with the inclined pylons framing them on both sides. Trussed mullions are used on the east and west curtain walls for added wind bracing.

Saarinen specified a number of cement mixes for the terminal building, all made from the same limestone deposit for uniformity of color. He then varied the aggregate finishes to differentiate the three levels of the complex. Parking level surfaces are rough exposed aggregate; the columns are crandalled (bush-hammered with a mallet of pointed steel bars) for a rusticated texture. Finally, the terminal floor is polished smooth.

Mechanical
Mechanical rooms are located on the lower level, and the floor-ceiling layer beneath the main concourse is used to distribute mechanical and electrical services. Return air ducts are the only obvious element. These are integrated into the sill of the exterior glazing along with electrical outlets.

Lighting is provided at occupant level by task fixtures incorporated into door canopies and the ticketing, concession, and other kiosks in the concourse. Ambient light and definition of the enclosing roof is achieved by uplighting the high plaster ceiling from the top of the kiosks. A pattern of façade downlights is incorporated into the roof overhang along the bow of the exterior glazing.

Interior

Plan dimensions were established by the 40 ft (12.2 m) width needed to service two mobile lounges and the 150 ft (45.7 m) depth needed to accommodate ticketing and baggage functions from landside to airside. In theory, this system was extensible to allow for the addition of more gates as needed.

To maintain the pavilion flavor of the interior, kiosks are used to enclose functional areas in the concourse. After entering the concourse through low canopies, matching kiosk-style construction is used inside. At the center of the space is a row of ticketing lobbies; backing up to these and facing the departure lounge is a row of snack bars, shops, and toilets. The kiosk-type construction is repeated a fourth time at the mobile lounge docking gates. Overall, it is a 150 ft (45.7 m) walk from the front door to the mobile lounge. The open interior space is dominated by the monumental colonnades on both sides, making the interior and exterior "one thing" as Saarinen intended. The only interruption to the volume of the concourse is the drainpipe from the center of the roof down through the space. This unavoidable element resembles a sculptural funnel pressed against the plaster ceiling and running down through the concourse floor.

Mobile lounges dock against the airside of the building, on the south. These can be thought of as detachable rooms of the terminal where passengers assemble to be taken to their flights. It took two of the 60 ft (18.3 m) long carriages, at 72 seats each plus standing room for 19, to fill a Boeing 707. Initial construction provided for 24 lounge gates. Bulky undercarriages raised the vehicle's floor level several feet off the ground. Accordion lifting mechanisms raised and lowerd the cabins to boarding-height level at the terminals and to aircraft emplaning height on the taxiways. Chrysler Motors developed the lounges for the project at a cost of about $100,000 each (about $510,000 each in 1995 dollars).

Arriving air passengers depart the mobile lounges and go directly downstairs to baggage claim and customs. From there, one ramp leads up to the midlevel pickup drive and a second ramp leads down to the parking area. The lower level, which forms the plinth of the building, also contains mechanical rooms, car rental agencies, and a restaurant, with the southern third of the floor given over to baggage sorting and an interior roadway for baggage trolleys.

From either level of the concourse, connection to the control tower is made across a projecting wing to the south that bisects the main terminal building. At the lower level of this wing are airline and airport management offices; at the upper level are lounges and restaurants with a view of the mobile lounge gates and the airfield beyond. Observation decks on the control tower offer more views. The southern extent of this projecting wing is planned for future expansion as another wing of boarding gates for mobile lounges. Its initial use was for boarding of helicopters and small planes unsuited to mobile lounge docking.

TECHNICAL INTEGRATION HIGHLIGHTS

Physical

- Services are contained in the floor-ceiling layer between the lower level and the concourse level without interrupting the pavilion.

Visual

- The dynamics of the structure are expressively dramatized by the suspended roof and inclined pylons.
- The structural system is the dominant element of the envelope and interior.
- The pathway from landside to airside is clarified and minimized.

Performance

- Circulation and holding areas of the interior are replaced by the amenity of the mobile lounge.
- Inclined pylons create overhanging roofs above passenger drop-off and lounge boarding areas.
- Aircraft are not required to taxi and maneuver up to the terminal, saving the expense of time and fuel. Instead, jets park on a taxiway fueling station, resembling a giant truck stop for airplanes, and the lounges come out to them.

DISCUSSION

Saarinen thought that Washington Dulles Airport was the best thing he had done. The link between this statement of quality and the prototypical development of a new kind of airport for a new kind of aircraft is a great lesson in technical integration. It illustrates how the fit between function, formalism, technology, and architectural ambition generates the design process.

11

STANSTED INTERNATIONAL AIRPORT, 1981–1991

Stansted, United Kingdom
SIR NORMAN FOSTER ASSOCIATES

DESCRIPTION

Sir Norman Foster Associates design for London's third major airport revisits some of Eero Saarinen's ambitions for Dulles International in Washington, D.C.—namely, to simplify the travel experience and to whisk travelers

directly to their flights (see case study #10). At both Dulles and Stansted, passengers cross the terminal on one level while baggage and support functions are handled below. Stansted also uses a railed transport system to move passengers from the terminal that is conceptually similar to the rolling passenger lounges of Dulles. This transport strategy enables both airports to separate the terminal building from the aircraft boarding area and simplify passenger transition from land to air and back again. At Stansted, however, shuttles leave departure lounges from the terminal and carry passengers to satellite mini-terminals out on the runway. These small satellites arc easily accessed by aircraft through conventional gates and jetways and are geared to higher-volume passenger flows than the Dulles mobile lounges could ever accommodate.

Simplicity at Stansted is achieved by repetition of modular "trees" that integrate structure, daylighting, artificial light, mechanical services, terminal and flight information, and even fire safety requirements. Where Saarinen used the sophisticated cable hammock roof to span the entire Dulles terminal, Foster maintains the effect of a single room while breaking the span down into 118 ft (36 m) grids. Instead of the monumental concrete roof of Dulles, Stansted is covered with a lightweight series of skylit domes supported by transparent structure.

Figure 7.7 View of the landside passenger level. Note the 59 ft wide structural trees located at alternate bays. *(Photograph courtesy of Ove Arup & Partners.)*

TABLE 7.4 Fact Sheet

Project	**Building Name**	Stansted International Airport Terminal Building
	Client	British Airport Authority
	City	Stansted, Essex, England
	Lat/Long/Elev	51.88 N 0.23 E, 348 ft (106 m)
Team	**Architect**	Sir Norman Foster Associates
	Structural Engineer	Ove Arup & Partners
	Mechanical Engineer	BAAC with Beard Dove and Currie & Brown
	Acoustics	ISVR Consultancy (airport noise), Institute of Sound and Vibration Research (ISVR) at the University of Southampton, in the United Kingdom
	Lighting	Claude & Danielle Engle
	Wind Tunnel	University of Bristol
	Landscape Architects	Adrian Lisney & Partners
	Ecology	Penny Anderson Associates
	Quantity Surveying	Bernard Dove, Cyril Needleman, Corduroy
	Construction Management	Laing Management handled 150 major work contracts and 150 minor ones. There were more than 20,000 pages of drawings.
General	**Time Line**	Predesign: January 1981 to December 1984. Construction: June 1986 to March 15, 1991.
	Floor Area	922,463 ft^2 (85,700 m^2) including departure gates. Terminal is 780,380 ft^2 (72,463 m^2).
	Occupants	About 3600 in the concourse.
	Cost	US $196,743,600 or £108,000,000 UK. About $213/ft^2. About 50% of the total cost was for information technology, movement systems, and environmental controls.
	Cost in 1995 US$	$220,071,140 or about $239/ft^2.
	Stories	One passenger story plus full undercroft services level.
	Plan	Compact rectangular, 650 ft deep × 532 ft wide footprint (198 m × 162 m).
Site	**Site Description**	Former military airfield and surrounding farmland totaling 2400 acres (960 hectares). Ten percent of the site was reserved for landscape restoration.
	Parking, Cars	2500 short-term adjacent to terminal and 6500 long-term located along M11 roadway.
Structure	**Foundation**	Concrete piers with reinforced concrete slab on grade over compacted gravel fill.
	Vertical Members	Steel trees of 13 in. (330 mm) and 7.2 in. (183 mm) diameter tubes in 9.8 ft × 9.8 ft (3 × 3 m) base on an 118.1 ft × 118.1 ft (36 × 36 m) grid support the roof structure. A total of 2850 tons (2588 metric tons) of structural steel were used in the building. Undercroft level supports concourse floor with concrete columns.
	Horizontal Spans	Concourse is separated from undercroft by poured-in-place waffle slab supported on 26 ft (8.0 m) high concrete columns.
Envelope	**Glass and Glazing**	Envelope of concourse is glazed with double-pane low-emmisivity units measuring 11.8 ft × 6.6 ft (3.6 m × 1.8 m). The glass sits in a thermally broken aluminum frame.
	Skylights	4 triangular skylights of 34.8 ft^2 totaling 139.2 ft^2 (13 m^2) in each roof dome (4% glazed).
	Cladding	Envelope of undercroft is clad with 11.8 ft × 3.1 ft × 4 in. insulated panels with aluminum skin and plastic frame.
	Roof	59 ft × 59 ft (18 m × 18 m) prefabricated aluminum domes with skylights.
	Special Features	Stainless steel roof drain system siphons down rainwater through external downspouts.
HVAC	**Equipment**	Two 5.2 megawatt capacity gas boilers and heat recovery from chillers.
	Cooling Type	Two 711 ton reciprocating chillers with dual compressors and heat recovery. Two cooling towers are located away from the terminal.
	Distribution	24 constant volume air handlers for concourse, and 33 smaller variable air volume boxes serve the freestanding cabins.
	Duct Type	Four rectangular ducts form walls at each structural tree service pod.
	Vertical Chases	Most services provided through information pods integrated in structural trees. Core of waffle slab provides penetration for services to retail and office cabins.
	Special Features	Air-to-air heat exchangers reclaim energy from ventilation exhaust air.
Interior	**Partitions**	Cabins are clad in graphite-reinforced plastic panels.
	Finishes	Granite floor in concourse. White polyester power coat paint throughout.
	Vertical Circulation	Two escalators and four elevators from rail station plus two pedestrian ramps. Total of 7 passenger and 10 service elevators.
	Furniture	Wire-framed modular seating system with upholstered cushions.
	Lighting	400 W metal halide lamps at about 0.7 W/ft^2 (7.5 W/m^2) are fixed on top of each information pod, illuminating the ceiling domes and indirectly lighting the terminal. As many as 24 lamps are used on each of the pods.

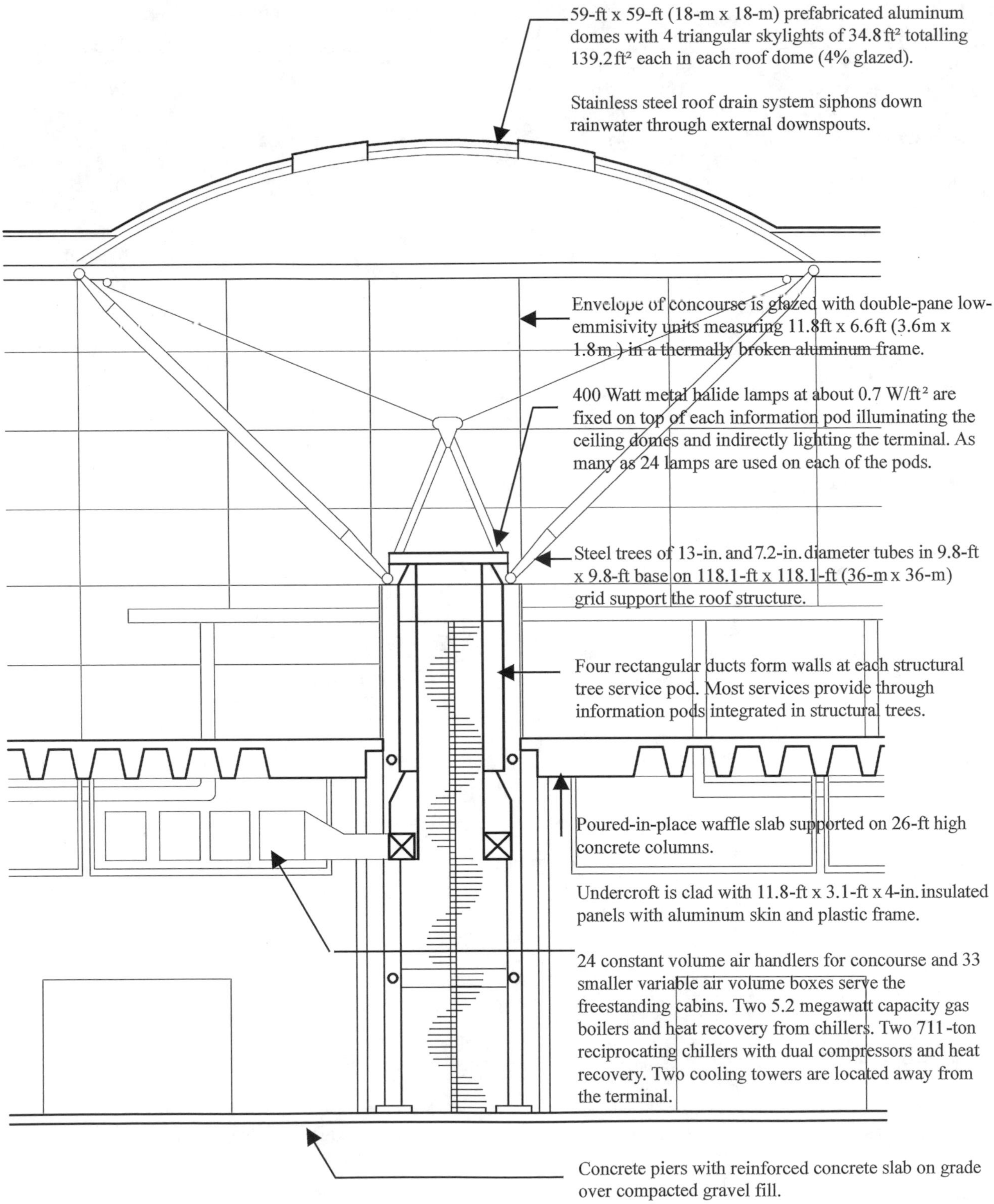

59-ft x 59-ft (18-m x 18-m) prefabricated aluminum domes with 4 triangular skylights of 34.8 ft² totalling 139.2 ft² each in each roof dome (4% glazed).

Stainless steel roof drain system siphons down rainwater through external downspouts.

Envelope of concourse is glazed with double-pane low-emmisivity units measuring 11.8 ft x 6.6 ft (3.6 m x 1.8 m) in a thermally broken aluminum frame.

400 Watt metal halide lamps at about 0.7 W/ft² are fixed on top of each information pod illuminating the ceiling domes and indirectly lighting the terminal. As many as 24 lamps are used on each of the pods.

Steel trees of 13-in. and 7.2-in. diameter tubes in 9.8-ft x 9.8-ft base on 118.1-ft x 118.1-ft (36-m x 36-m) grid support the roof structure.

Four rectangular ducts form walls at each structural tree service pod. Most services provide through information pods integrated in structural trees.

Poured-in-place waffle slab supported on 26-ft high concrete columns.

Undercroft is clad with 11.8-ft x 3.1-ft x 4-in. insulated panels with aluminum skin and plastic frame.

24 constant volume air handlers for concourse and 33 smaller variable air volume boxes serve the freestanding cabins. Two 5.2 megawatt capacity gas boilers and heat recovery from chillers. Two 711-ton reciprocating chillers with dual compressors and heat recovery. Two cooling towers are located away from the terminal.

Concrete piers with reinforced concrete slab on grade over compacted gravel fill.

Figure 7.8 Anatomical section.

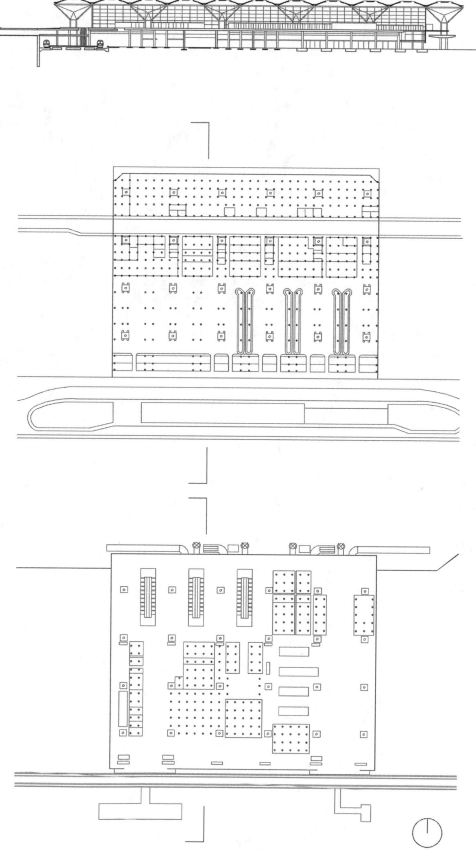

Figure 7.9 Plan and section.

0'   50'   100'

PROGRAM

Client

As early as 1961, government agencies had identified an abandoned military runway at Stansted as the only logical site for a third London airport. Other locations remained on the list of possibilities until a 1978 White Paper avowed the immediate need for increased regional flight capacity. In 1979 a plan to expand Stansted from 150,000 passengers per year to 15 million was announced. Controversy over potential environmental impacts led to a public hearing that lasted two years before a compromise plan was announced for phased expansion to 8 million passengers per year.

The client, the British Airport Authority (BAA), owns seven airports in the United Kingdom and manages all or parts of nine others. These include terminals in the United States, Australia, and Italy. The BAA Lynton subsidiary is a leading developer of airport locations for office, warehouse, and hotel developments around the world.

BAA saw Stansted as an eventual necessity early on. It began preparing studies for a new terminal building in 1981. The intent was to have a fast-track plan ready to implement as soon as parliamentary approval was granted. Air traffic was reaching critical levels at London's Heathrow and Gatwick airports, and any delay in updating Stansted could mean trouble for London air traffic.

Brief

Passenger services at Stansted were differentiated from those at London's Gatwick and Heathrow airports by slotting it with a collection of budget flights to continental Europe and including some domestic flights. This strategy was seen by BAA as a method of integrating the total resources of the three London airfields. It also limited the traffic at Stansted by restricting it to the sort of flights that

TABLE 7.5 Normal Climate Data for Stansted Airport

		Jan.	Feb.	Mar.	Apr.	May	June	July	Aug.	Sept.	Oct.	Nov.	Dec.	Year
Temperature	Degree-Days Heating	814	738	709	575	397	225	122	119	231	433	635	746	5726
	Degree-Days Cooling	0	0	0	0	1	10	26	24	2	0	0	0	60
	Extreme High	57	63	69	72	82	91	91	93	84	79	63	61	93
	Normal High	43	43	48	53	60	65	70	70	64	57	49	45	56
	Normal Average	39	39	42	46	52	58	62	62	57	51	44	41	49
	Normal Low	34	33	36	38	44	50	54	53	50	45	39	36	43
	Extreme Low	12	10	22	25	30	36	41	41	34	28	21	7	7
Humidity	Dew Point	35	34	36	38	44	50	53	53	50	46	40	38	43
	Max % RH	90	90	91	90	90	90	90	92	92	93	91	91	91
	Min % RH	82	77	70	61	62	62	59	57	62	73	80	84	69
	% Days with Rain	50	40	36	43	36	36	36	40	36	43	46	46	41
	Rain Inches	2	1	1	2	2	2	2	2	2	2	2	2	22
Sky	% Overcast Days	37	34	33	24	21	19	16	16	19	25	29	33	26
	% Clear Days	6	7	6	7	6	4	6	7	6	6	7	5	6
Wind	Prevailing Direction	SW	E	W	N	N	N	W	SW	SW	SW	SW	SW	SW
	Speed, Knots	9	10	11	9	9	8	8	8	8	9	9	9	9
	Percent Calm	3	3	3	3	3	3	3	4	3	5	3	2	3
Days Observed	Rain	15	12	11	13	11	11	11	12	11	13	14	14	148
	Fog	16	14	14	12	14	14	11	15	14	17	16	17	174
	Haze	16	17	18	18	18	18	16	19	17	18	17	17	209
	Snow	8	6	5	3	#	#	0	0	0	#	2	4	28
	Hail	#	0	#	#	#	#	0	0	0	#	#	0	1
	Freezing Rain	#	1	0	0	0	0	0	0	0	0	0	0	1
	Blowing Sand	0	0	#	#	#	#	#	0	#	#	#	#	1

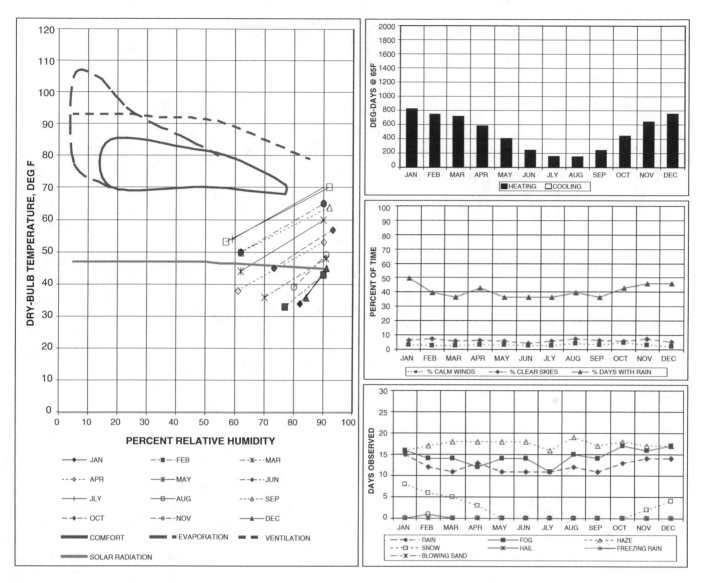

Figure 7.10 Climate analysis graphics.

typically do not involve passengers transferring from one flight to another. By 1981 the large terminals at London's Gatwick and Heathrow airports were already booked to capacity. Total traffic in southeast England airports was approaching 80 million passengers per annum (MPPA), and shortfalls were already being forecast for the early 1990s. Stansted was initially intended to handle about 2 MPPA and grow to 8 million. In a review, the government's Civil Aviation Authority (CAA) stated, "There is no alternative." Somehow, the CAA continued, London airports would have to cope with more than 120 MPPA by 2005, of which Stansted's share would be about 33 MPPA.

The brief called for phased terminal construction so that growth could be accommodated with minimal disruption to ongoing service. Both airside and landside traffic to the remote location had to be considered along with

the expansion of the terminal and sensitivity to the rural setting. BAA chairman Sir Norman Payne made it clear that commercial considerations would outweigh architectural ones, but at the same time sought an architect with both the vision and the resources to maximize the result. BAA prepared six alternative schemes and asked Foster to review them for building merit and to work out the relative costs of each. When Foster came back with his own alternative scheme number seven, he was able to convince BAA's planners of its superior merit. In January 1981, Foster Associates was given a limited appointment and in September 1984 received a full commission.

Site

Located about 37 miles northeast of downtown London, Stansted is the most remote of the three airports serving

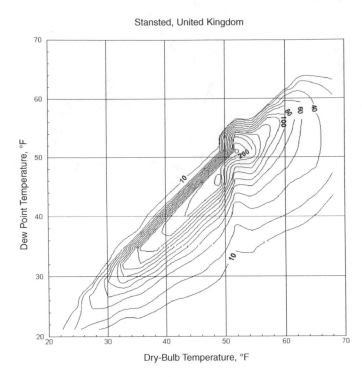

Stansted, United Kingdom

Figure 7.11 Bin data distribution for Stansted Airport, United Kingdom. Concentric areas of graph indicate the number of hours per year that weather conditions normally occur in this climate. Similar to elevation readings on topographic maps, highest frequency occurrences of weather are at the center peaks of the graph. (Data sources: *Engineering Weather Data, typical meteorological year (TMY) data from the National Climatic Data Center, and the* ASHRAE *Weather Data Viewer from the American Society of Heating, Refrigerating and Air-Conditioning Engineers.)*

the city. Transit time from central London is about 40 minutes by rail and an hour by car. It occupies 2400 acres (960 hectares) of level terrain and is neighbor to the rural parishes of Stansted Mountfichet, Bishops Stortford, and Takeley. The surrounding landscape is dotted with farms, archeological sites, parish churches, and vernacular timber barn structures.

Construction at Stansted dates to August 1942 when the airfield began as an alternate bad weather site for World War II allied warplanes. In the 1950s the single runway was extended to a imposing 10,000 ft to accommodate B47 bombers during the Cold War. At about the same time, a small terminal at Stansted began handling long-distance charter flights. The 1960s found the airport developing into a major freight center. In 1961 the fateful position paper was published by BAA, promoting the rural location as the site of London's next major airport.

Climate

As mentioned earlier, Stansted is only 37 miles from the heart of London and not many more miles removed from the Gatwick airport weather station (see case study #24 for

London data). There are, however, some differences between patterns at the two locations.

INTENTION

Design Team

Foster Associates engaged the familiar services of Ove Arup & Partners as consultants at Stansted. The two firms were already collaborating on the Renault Distribution Center at Swindon. Adrian Lisney & Partners were the landscape architects, and Laing Management was the general contractor. Airport noise acoustics consultant was ISVR Consultancy Institute of Sound and Vibration Research at the University of Southampton in the United Kingdom. Wind tunnel testing was performed at the University of Bristol.

A series of public hearings on Foster's proposal opened on September 29, 1981, and were held for 258 days over a two-year period. It was December 1984 before the project was approved and June 1985 before the government gave the final go-ahead. The team used the two-year delay during the public hearings to develop and compare several design scenarios. When final approval was granted, they moved immediately into detailed design work.

Philosophy

Sir Norman Foster was born in 1935 in Manchester, United Kingdom. He entered the Manchester University School of Architecture at age 21 and later studied at Yale. After working with Team 4, he founded Foster Associates in 1967. Foster was knighted by the queen in 1990 and renamed his practice Sir Norman Foster and Partners. His wife, Sabiha, is a director of the London firm, which now numbers more than 200 architects and 500 employees with offices in Europe and Asia.

Foster flies his own small jet on shorter business trips. His love of flying is certainly one of the inspirations for the ideas incorporated into the Stansted terminal building. Other constants of Foster's work also surface here: emphasis on the social dimension of design, a preoccupation with natural light, high quality of components and details, and a relationship between ecology, energy, technology, and their links with poetic meaning (see case studies #7, 23, and 25).

Chronologically, among the works of Sir Norman Foster, Stansted can be listed after designs for Hong Kong and Shanghai Bank (1979–1984) (see case study #25) and Renault Distribution Center (1980–1982) were being executed, parallel with Century Tower (1987–1991), and before Carre d'Art (1984–1993) and Stockley Office Park (1987–1989). His reputation for bringing in large buildings on time and within budget was clearly established and matched the priorities of BAA. The 1978 Sainsbury Center for Visual Arts (see case study #23) must have sparked BAA's vision of what sort of terminal building Foster would deliver.

Intent

Foster's ideas for this airport embody a notion of romantic and functional simplicity evoked through convenient and direct visual links from ground transit to air. To make flying an uplifting experience, he reasoned that architecture should celebrate the events of arriving and departing. Consequently, rather than emphasize the experience of the terminal building, Foster aimed at subjugating all its complexities and distractions to the dominant clarity of hopping off a train and onto an airplane.

The rural context also shaped his design intent. Given the flat countryside and rural setting, the scale was to be kept low and unobtrusive.

CRITICAL TECHNICAL ISSUES

Inherent

Of all the typical issues that new airports commonly deal with, expansion was probably the most elemental at Stansted. From the very beginning this facility was intended to relieve the overburdened terminals at London's Gatwick and Heathrow airports. Growth had to be planned for.

Contextual

The distance of Stansted from the center of London added two important design considerations. First, the terminal would have to include a rail transit station with direct service from the city. This was essential to maintaining reasonable commuting times to Stansted and making it competitive with London's Heathrow and Gatwick airports. Second, the relatively remote rural location led authorities to appoint Stansted as the designated landing field for hijacked flights. Antiterrorist measures heightened the need to incorporate security measures into the terminal scheme by controlling access and flow between the terminal areas. Ultimately, all of these restrictions conflicted with Foster's intention of providing passengers with an easy stroll to the airplane.

Within the Stansted Mountfichet village community (1991 population of 5361 living in 2037 households) there were other issues to address. Quiet rural neighborhoods and noisy international airports are naturally not a good mix. Local authorities and the general populace of the sleepy Essex communities around Stansted had opposed

the project on environmental grounds for years. It did not help that Stansted was also a large freight carrier and therefore featured frequent night flights with noisier cargo planes. Of course, as the airport grows and traffic increases, noise becomes an ever-increasing problem. In suburban Denver this noise problem led to environmental nuisance lawsuits and the eventual relocation of the airport.

Other challenges were presented directly by the client. Working for BAA, Foster Associates was dealing with an experienced group of experts who had detailed requirements. Here was a rare opportunity for BAA to plan a new airport from the ground up rather than expand an existing facility piecemeal. After enduring several years of waiting for the project to find a home and then two more years of public hearings, BAA was anxious to get Stansted completed. The client also expected everything to be optimized, efficient, and reconsidered from first principles. Moreover, after experiencing some "sticker shock" associated with expansion at Gatwick's North Terminal, BAA was in no mood for cost overruns. Time and budget were established with very strict limitations. The project time frame was compressed, and thus construction started before design was complete. Further, the construction would have to be sequenced so that a dry enclosure would provide shelter for uninterrupted work to completion, regardless of the weather.

Intentional

Airports are inherently complex programs, and Foster's intention of dramatizing travel required clarity and simplicity. The model of Saarinen's airport at Dulles was close to Foster's vision of the pioneering days of commercial flight when passengers walked from their cars to their planes. But modern requirements and the escalating number of air travelers conspired against those romantic notions. The complexities of baggage handling, ticketing, security, high occupancy flows, concessions, retail shops, and the expansive dimensions of wide-body aircraft would have to be dealt with. Keeping the terminal simple and maintaining clarity in how passengers would move directly through it required a new prototype.

Mixed into the formal and experiential intentions was a response to the rural context. In agreement with the BAA, the terminal building would have a profile no higher than a mature tree: 49.2 ft (15 m). Given the resistance of local authorities who opposed the environmental threats of Stansted and the pressures imposed by its growth, Foster and the BAA would have to work diligently at creating neighborly relationships. An 800,000 ft^2 (74,285 m^2) terminal building with a 2 mile long runway and 8 million passengers per year was not going to blend easily into the village setting.

APPROPRIATE SYSTEMS

Precedents

The romantic precedents for Stansted come from Foster's affection for small airports. Spencer de Grey, the director of Foster Associates in charge of the project, also likens the terminal to the vast skylit interiors of nineteenth-century iron and glass railway stations.

In regard to function, the design team looked at Dulles airport as the old prototype for direct passage through a terminal. Upon analysis, the economy of a mobile lounge solution was attractive enough, but its carrying capacity was too small for modern passenger movement and wide-body aircraft. The new prototype at Stansted would have to maintain the simplicity of Dulles, but substitute something else for the mobile lounge. A comparison of the two building sections shows the similarities of flow through the two-level terminal buildings. Both maintain simplicity by minimizing the distance passengers walk across the main concourse, and both banish all the mechanical and baggage functions to the understory.

As a continuum of Foster's architecture, Stansted shares elements of its scheme with his earlier sheds for the 1977 Sainsbury Art Center and the 1982 Renault Distribution Center. There is also some mention of the steel masted Fleetguard factory by his former partner, Richard Rogers. The Renault building in particular reveals features that were important in the development of Stansted, especially its steel mast structure and square roof grids.

Site

During the ten-year debate and two-year public hearing over where London's third airport should go, ecological impacts on its setting became a focus issue. In 1980 a consulting ecologist firm, Penny Anderson Associates, was commissioned to survey the proposed development area at Stansted. Included in the firm's study was a 100 acre (40 hectare) tract of ancient woodlands next to the development area, which had been officially designated as a Site of Special Scientific Interest by the Nature Conservancy Council. The airport site and the rest of the adjacent Essex County lowlands were mostly farms. Among them was an eroded network of woodlands, some small areas of grassy fields, a few ponds and streams, and some surviving hedgerow. Much of the natural woodlands environment had already been lost to postwar agricultural development.

Working with the planners and landscape architects, the ecologists helped to identify the areas of highest value to be preserved and worked with transplanting some of the hedges and grasses. This work had to be completed before construction was scheduled to start in the spring of

1986. A 2 acre (0.8 hectare) area was identified, and the ecologists set out to move the best of the transplanted vegetation and soils there. Some of this farmland area had been contaminated with enhanced nitrate and phosphate levels from fertilizer residue. After the topsoil was cleared away and replaced, the reserved plot was restored to a native wildlife setting. Other areas of the airport site were seeded with native grasses or plants, and a wetlands was developed on one end of the runway so as to attract dragonflies and frogs rather than birds. Maintenance programs such as mowing were established to match the growing cycle of the landscape. As the ecologists began working more directly with the landscape architects, Adrian Lisney & Partners, the restored wildlife area was used as a model for the landscape redevelopment of the entire site. Plantings were made according to the characteristics of the ancient woods and grasslands that are indigenous to Stansted. Eventually, 10 percent of the total land area was devoted to landscape and more than 250,000 trees and shrubs were planted.

Development of the terminal area and other structures on the site began with transportation links on both the landside and airside access. Passenger arrival is situated along the south edge of the terminal, where a drop-off and covered entry court are situated in front of the concourse level beneath an open bay of structural trees and covering roof canopy. Below that, in the undercroft level, is a 21,600 ft^2 (2,006 m^2) British Rail station. The south wall of the rail station doubles as a retaining wall for a large earth berm above the short-term parking lots. This wall is penetrated by a walkway leading from the surface parking to elevators and ramps up to the concourse. Passengers depart to aircraft boarding gates from the other side of the terminal via a tracked transit system to airside satellite terminals. The automated double-track transit system carries up to 100 passengers along 8900 ft (2713 m) of track and operates continuously in a four-stop loop. Four of the outlying terminals were planned, but only one was built in the first phase. An additional domestic flight terminal is so close to the terminal that it is connected by an enclosed walkway, and passengers walk to the jetways in the usual fashion.

To keep the volume of the terminal below the 49 ft (15 m) height barrier, Foster selected a rolling area of the site and burrowed the building into it. More than 1.3 million yd^3 (1 million m^3) of soil were excavated and used as fill around the building. The rail station and the undercroft floors are about 10 ft (3 m) below grade and are 29 ft (9 m) high. A service road runs through the undercroft from east to west and divides the south mechanical services zone from a larger north baggage handling zone. Above, the concourse level extends south from the terminal floor to cover

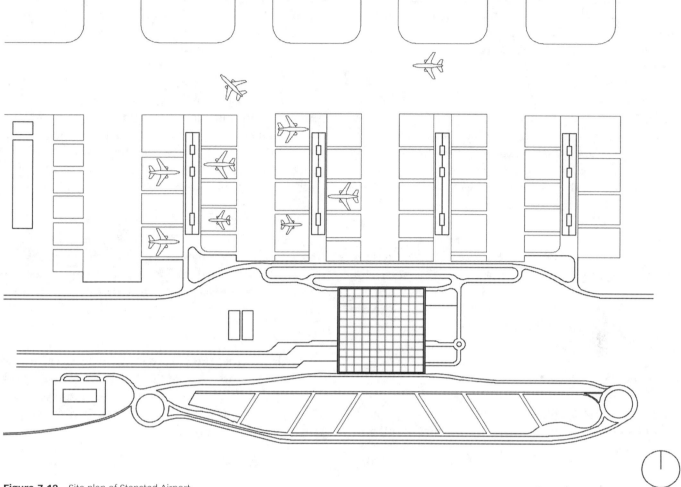

Figure 7.12   Site plan of Stansted Airport.

the rail station and provide a forecourt entry under the extended roof. The forecourt deck is penetrated with thick glass skylights set flush into the concrete slab between the trunks of the structural trees. The skylights are centered over the British Rail station platform. On the north side of the terminal, the concourse floor is interrupted by the terminal rail transit system. A bay of structural trees and their canopy provide cover for the passenger boarding platforms. The east and west sides of the terminal are left blank so that the building section can be extruded in both directions to meet expansion requirements.

Structure

Overall, the undercroft is 26.3 ft (8 m) high and the passenger concourse level reaches another 39.4 ft (12 m). In plan the terminal is based on repetition of a 59 × 59 ft (18 m) grid of 11 × 11, or 121 equal bays. Thirty-six structural trees sit at the centers of alternate grid squares, 118 ft (36 m) on center and 59 ft (18 m) high from undercroft floor to roofline. Horizontal bay spacing between the trees was

determined by the minimum bay size of the baggage handling system. Each tree rises as an 11.5 ft × 11.5 ft (3.5 m) trunk of four 18 in. (457 mm) diameter steel tubes from the building's foundation to 13.1 ft (4 m) above the concourse floor. To this point, the frames are similar to the clustered column towers Foster used at the Hong Kong and Shanghai Bank (see case study #25). Above that point, the frame branches outward to pin connected tubular steel booms. The outrigger booms of 7.2 in. (183 mm) steel tube reach another 26 ft high and out to the corners of the 59 × 59 ft (18 m) bay to support the 12 in. (323 mm) diameter roof grid frame. Prefabricated roof canopies fill the span above the trees as well as the open bays between them.

Within the branching outriggers are two pyramidal frames for bracing. The first rests on top of the four vertical trunk members and converges 13.1 ft (4 m) above it, halfway to the roof. The second pyramid is inverted and consists of 1.6 in. (40 mm) steel tension bars prestressed from the top of the first pyramid out to the four corners of the roof frame.

The shallow dome roof shells, or "bubbles," are each prefabricated at grade level from a square frame, steel lattice supports, and a deck of simply curved aluminum panels. Once assembled, they are lifted by a crane to rest on the structural trees and connected by a gutter system. The decks are covered with 6 in. (150 mm) mineral wool insulation and sealed with PVC single-ply roofing. The canopies provide rigid bracing to the 59 × 59 ft (18 m) roof frame. Dimensional tolerances in the whole system are so close that no expansion joints are required. Expansion and contraction, as well as wind loads, are taken up by flexure in the steel frame. There is a scissors-like connection at the eave line between the roof structure and glazing wall that allows 7.9 in. (20 cm) of movement. The fascia is actually closed with a plastic membrane at the eave.

The concourse floor is a 12 to 24 in. (305 to 610 mm) thick waffle slab of precast and cast-in-place concrete. It is supported by concrete columns on a 20 ft (6.1 m) grid on the southern side, where the 29 ft (8.8 m) high undercroft area is used primarily for the mechanical and electrical plant. The northern half is supported on a 39.4 ft (12 m) square grid to allow minimum clearance for the baggage handling system.

Construction sequence was planned for uninterrupted speed. The strategy was to close in the envelope quickly and allow work to continue out of the weather. So the structural trees were erected first, followed by the roof canopies. Structural components were factory prefabricated, and all joints ultrasonically tested before delivery and assembly at the site. The tree trunk bases of 55.8 × 11.5 × 11.5 ft (17 × 3.5 × 3.5 m) came first. Their size was the largest that could be transported by truck. The towering bases were erected from the truck to their four foundation pads and bolted into place. Pin connections carry the connecting branches, and a custom casting ties tubular members to the tension bars. The final connection and pretensioning is via a "Jesus nut" that holds everything in place at the top of the upright pyramid frame where the four tension rods connect.

After the steel structure was in place, the roof canopies were assembled on the ground and lifted into the tree frame. Construction then proceeded with rain protection in place. Final excavation, drainage, and the at-grade slab for the undercroft were next. The concourse slab and the mezzanines followed.

Envelope

The sheltering roof was planned to provide cover for construction work even before the on-grade and waffle slab floors were poured. The final solution resembles a field of 121 bubbles, each weighing 11 tons (10 metric tons) and crowning out 9.8 ft (3 m) above structure at the 49 ft (15

Figure 7.13　The finished structural and service modular tree.

m) height limit above the concourse floor. Rainwater from the 421,000 ft² (39,092 m²) roof is collected without interior drains that would interrupt the concourse space. Instead, drainage is accomplished by horizontal stainless steel pipes laid in gutters between the canopy modules. These are drained by siphon action to 16 exterior downspouts. Wind uplift across the roof is countered by an air foil section along the eaves. This foil was developed during predesign in wind tunnel tests at Bristol University.

Each of the 121 roof canopy sections incorporates four triangular skylights around a rotated solid aluminum square at its center. The 139 ft² (13 m²) area of glazing cositute 4 percent of the total roof area. Daylight levels, based on a design daylight factor of 3 percent, provides 17 footcandles on a clear winter day. Energy savings via reductions in lighting power are expected to amount to $500,000 per year. Beneath each skylight is a perforated metal reflector with a white finish. This reflector diffuses daylight and reduces glare; it also acts as a reflector for artificial uplighting from the service pods below.

Several materials were considered for the ceiling side of the roof canopies. Metal panels would be durable but acoustically reflective, creating a noisy interior. Fibrous surfaces would be quieter but hard to clean and less light reflective. Tensioned fabric panels were too expensive. The final solution meets all requirements: Perforated steel trays with fibrous mineral fiber backing provide both light reflection and sound absorption.

Glass encloses all four sides of the terminal at concourse level. The insulated tempered glazing units are argon filled and low-emissivity coated. An exterior (8 mm) pane, an air cavity, and a 0.25 in. (6 mm) inside pane make up each unit. Set in an aluminum frame, the window wall provides an effective R-3.5 insulation level. Each glass panel measures 11.8 ft (5.6 m) across by 6.6 ft (1.85 m) high, dimensions that open the view and limit heat losses through metal framing members. The solar orientation of the building is actually skewed so that the entry façade faces southeast. The reason is probably that the runway was long ago designed to face into the predominant southwest winds and the terminal building is aligned to look out onto the runway. On the unprotected northeast and southwest elevations, where there are no projecting structural trees or roof canopies, double pane laminated glass with a reflective inner layer reduces solar gain by more than 60 percent. The glazed walls are supported by a frame of 3.4 × 2.3 in. (86 × 58 mm) steel mullions. This frame is stiffened by a vertical truss of 3.2 in. (80 mm) steel tube running up the inside of the wall.

The undercroft is wrapped with 11.8 ft wide × 3.3 ft (3.6 m × 1.0 m) high insulated aluminum panels with an R-value of 20.0 and a polyester powder coat finish. Set in with them are double-glazed acrylic vision panels of the same size. Aluminum louvered panels are used where air intakes are required. Any of these panels can be removed and relocated within the vertical supports of 8 in. × 8 in. (203 mm) steel channel mullions that span the 26.3 ft (8.0 m) high undercroft. In order to allow service access for large equipment, there are no horizontal supports.

Mechanical

The services concept was another factor determined largely by the desire for an uncluttered roof that allowed for expansion and daylight. The major mechanical and electrical equipment would be housed below the concourse floor and feed through the structural trees.

Distribution of services was coordinated by reserving layers of space below the undercroft floor. Each layer is for services running in a specific direction. The lowest layer is 4.6 ft (1.4 m) deep and is dedicated to primary ducts and pipe work running north to south. This includes exhaust air ducts from kitchens, toilets, and smoke exhaust fans. Below that is a 2.3 ft (0.7 m) deep layer for east-to-west services. Air handlers, chillers, boilers, and electrical works fill the lower 13.8 ft (4.2 m) to the floor. Computer simulation was used to identify "interference" points where services were likely to clash.

Air is delivered through service pods integrated into the structural trees. Two sides of each of the 24 interior trees contain rectangular supply ducts that discharge air at the top of the pod through four adjustable drum diffusers. Return air is extracted through a register in the center of the pod's roof and down through ducts similar to those used for supply air. Service access for each pod is reached by metal spiral stairs from the undercroft mezzanine.

Fire detection, sprinklers, and smoke exhaust are provided in the open-sided kiosks. Smoke extraction ducts draw air down to the undercroft and then exhaust it through chimneys on the east and west walls. The closed wall cabins handle smoke exhaust with the mechanical air conditioning system. In event of a fire the air handler goes to 100 percent outside air and 100 percent exhaust. A fire research computer program, "Jasmine," was used to simulate fire spread and occupant exit patterns in the main concourse area. It predicted that 20 to 23 ft (6 m to 7 m) of air above floor level would still be breathable ten minutes after fire was detected and that evacuation could be safely accomplished in less than five minutes. A color animation of the smoke and egress calculations assured officials that no other measures were required in the main concourse.

Figure 7.14 Interior of the concourse.

Interior

The concourse is arranged with all passenger movement on one level. Arrivals are on the east side and departures on the west. Overlaying this arrangement with landside functions to the south and airside on the north of the terminal creates a grid of four squares that can be extended laterally as the terminal grows. To board aircraft, passengers pass through the departures lounge and ride small rail transit cars to satellite terminals. This rail system was favored because it not only kept the terminal uncluttered, it also achieved the separation of arrival from departure areas so vital to security. BAA had already had a favorable experience with the same system at Gatwick airport.

To keep the concourse clear and open, Foster limited the height of all structures within the terminal to 11.5 ft (3.5 m). This maintained the desired sense of orientation that comes with seeing all the way through the building from landside to airside. You can see trees outside from the baggage claim and airplanes from the front door. The route is straight and clear both ways.

The lighting design by Claude Engle is intended to raise the apparent height of the ceiling by making it the brightest object in view. Each of the service pods has four luminaries mounted behind the diffusers. These fixtures hold four to six 400 W metal halide lamps, the number depending on their position in the concourse. Wide flood angle distribution and the long throw of light onto the high ceiling ensure uniform reflected brightness. The reflector panel below the skylights obscures the black sur-

faces at night. Step switching allows the lamps to be dimmed in response to available daylight, and battery powered backup provides emergency lighting from the same fixtures. Task illumination is provided at service desks with modular fluorescent lamps, and halogen fixtures are used in concession areas.

Finishes and furnishings in the terminal are meant to be background. Sufficient drama is created by the structural system, the floating roof, and the see-through enclosure; further sophistication was deemed as conflicting and potentially confusing. The white painted ceiling and structural trees along with tame interior color schemes diffuse interior light levels and balance the brightness of the view outside. This design scheme also allows the eye to be appropriately drawn to the bright information signage designed by the Pentagram group (see NMB, case study #27, for more on Pentagram).

The structural trees are the basis of interior organization in the terminal. The 13 ft (4.0 m) vertical bases below their pyramid branches are wrapped on all four sides with service elements. Along with directional signs and flight information monitors, the pods contain maps, clocks, alarms, public address (PA) speakers, security cameras, staff telephones, and fire hoses.

Foster designed the various freestanding functions in the terminal as demountable "cabins." They are kept below the 11.5 ft (3.5 m) height limit and constructed of steel frames with plastic composite panel cladding. The cabins cover about 25 percent of the concourse floor area.

Mezzanines are prohibited not only because they would restrict view, but also because they would be up in a smoke-affected zone in the event of fire.

INTEGRATION HIGHLIGHTS

Physical

- The modular character of the structural trees facilitates expansion.
- Extensive computer modeling was used to coordinate the routing of services through two independent layers below the concourse floor.

Visual

- Placing services in the undercroft simplified the terminal environment and lowered the building scale.
- The transparent structure allows views from the front door arrival point to waiting airplanes on the departures side, enhancing the expectancy of travel.
- White painted surfaces and neutral finishes keep the terminal bright and clean but leave the emphasis on arrival and departure.

Performance

- Integrated service pods provide multiple functions.
- The placement of mechanical equipment in the undercroft frees the roof for daylighting.
- The lightweight roof structure allows long spans and uninterrupted floor space.
- The high ceiling also acts as a smoke reservoir, so the main concourse can remain one large space.
- The splayed branches extending from the tree columns reduce the roof span to 59 ft from the 118 ft (36 m) free width required by the baggage system in the undercroft.
- The project was 15 percent under budget.

DISCUSSION

In January 2000 construction work began on Phase II of the airport, along with planning for an anticipated final capacity of 15 MPPA. The successes of the initial design are being repeated with more of Foster's tree service columns.

12

UNITED AIRLINES TERMINAL AT O'HARE AIRPORT, 1984–1988

Chicago, Illinois
MURPHY JAHN ARCHITECTS

DESCRIPTION

O'Hare Airport's United Airlines Terminal is among world's the busiest and fastest growing passenger service terminals. United's flights represent about 80 percent of the O'Hare Airport business, with American Airlines making up most of the rest. With 54 aircraft boarding gates, 11,000 employees, and 40,000 passengers on 800 flights per day, United's concourses are logistically challenging and very fast moving. At 1.3 million ft^2 (121 million m^2), United's terminal is also 30 percent larger and three times more crowded than the 47-story Hong Kong and Shanghai Bank.

United's new terminal represented about one-third of a $1.6 billion expansion program undertaken at O'Hare beginning in 1984. Helmut Jahn's solution for the facility relies on a combination of opposites that unites the lacey steel frame of an industrial-era train station with some modern magic of advanced daylighting and electrical illumination technology. The building is conceptually a romantic nineteenth-century structural frame with a subservient high-tech infill. To the traveler, it is a very large expanse of two linear buildings linked by an 800 ft (244 m) light sculpture under which passengers drift between concourses on moving walkways.

Figure 7.15   Image of United O'Hare Terminal. *(Photograph courtesy of Bruce Haglund.)*

TABLE 7.6 Fact Sheet

Project		
	Building Name	United Airlines Terminal at O'Hare
	Client	United Airlines and the Chicago Airport Authority
	City	Chicago, Illinois
	Lat/Long/Elev	41.97N 87.90W, 673 ft (205 m)

Team		
	Architect	Helmut Jahn, Murphy/Jahn Architects
	Engineer	A. Epstein & Sons
	Structural	Lev Zetlin Associates
	Lighting	Sylvan R. Shemitz Associates, Inc.
	MEP	Cosentini Associates

General		
	Time Line	Begun in 1984, opened December 1988.
	Floor Area	1.3 million ft^2
	Occupants	11,000 employees and, initially, 40,000 passengers per day on 400 arriving and 400 departing flights. Planning allows for growth up to 80 million passengers per year.
	Cost	$446.0 million or $334/ft^2.
	Cost in 1995 US$	$582.2 million or $448/ft^2.
	Stories	One, plus mezzanine and tunnel.
	Plan	Extended wings from central ticketing lobby plus remote terminal.

Site		
	Site Description	Existing airport to the west of Chicago.
	Parking, Cars	Central garage.

Structure		
	Foundation	Not published.
	Vertical Members	Steel frame exposed to interior.
	Horizontal Spans	Steel frame exposed to interior.

Envelope		
	Glass and Glazing	Clear, reflective, and ceramic fritted glazings.
	Skylights	Extensive and various glazings
	Cladding	Glass and insulated aluminum panels.
	Roof	Glass.

HVAC		
	Equipment	Remote central plant.
	Cooling Type	8000 tons or about 160 ft^2 per ton.
	Distribution	70 variable volume air handlers.
	Duct Type	Concealed.
	Vertical Chases	None.

Interior		
	Partitions	Largely open plan.
	Finishes	Terrazzo floors.
	Vertical Circulation	Escalators to tunnel.
	Furniture	Not determined.
	Lighting	Wall-mounted metal-halide in concourse.

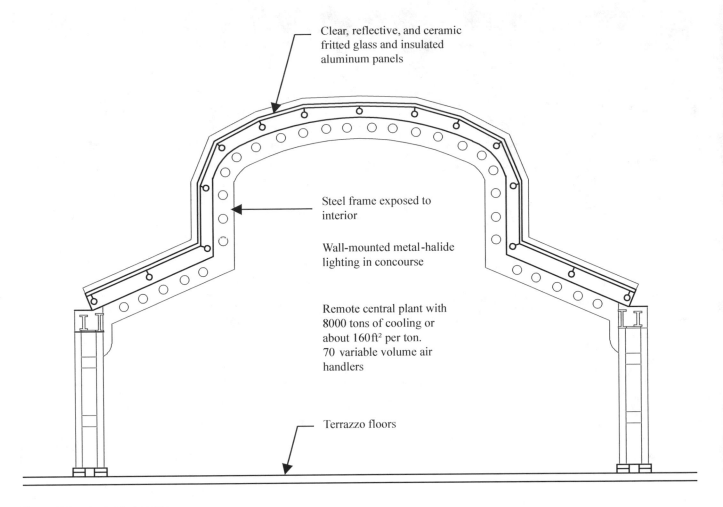

Clear, reflective, and ceramic
fritted glass and insulated
aluminum panels

Steel frame exposed to
interior

Wall-mounted metal-halide
lighting in concourse

Remote central plant with
8000 tons of cooling or
about 160ft² per ton.
70 variable volume air
handlers

Terrazzo floors

Figure 7.16 Anatomical section.

PROGRAM

Client

O'Hare, Chicago's second airport, was originally a World
War II airstrip named Orchard Field. The military gave the
land to the city, and Chicago annexed a narrow connecting strip of territory leading from the site to the north side
of its existing boundaries, making Orchard part of the city.
The official designation is still ORD, but the name was
changed in 1949 to honor fighter pilot Lt. Comdr. Edward
H. O'Hare after he was posthumously awarded the
Congressional Medal of Honor. O'Hare was a godson of
mobster Al Capone, but the award was given before the
time of Capone's conviction for tax evasion. In these days,
most people still traveled by train or ship and the world's
big airport was still south-side Chicago Municipal, likewise renamed in 1949 for the World War II Battle of
Midway.

The first commercial passenger terminal at O'Hare
Airport was commissioned in 1956 by Mayor Richard J.
Daley with the architects Naess & Murphy, and the airport
was expanded to 7200 acres (2880 hectares). Commercial
jetliners entered service during the design phase in 1959,
prompting sweeping changes in physical requirements for
the runways, the buildings and the service infrastructure.
The Miesian structure that was eventually built on the site
was flexible enough to meet the facility's needs into the
late 1970s. But, as happened at many airports, new security requirements, bigger aircraft, and rapidly increasing
passenger demands made the terminal obsolete. In the
meantime, Naess & Murphy became C. F. Murphy, and
later, Murphy Jahn.

In 1962 all Midway operations were transferred to jet-
ready O'Hare. United Airlines built its $500 million termi-
nal at O'Hare in 1987 as part of a $1.5 billion expansion.
American Airlines remodeled Terminal 3 in 1990, and

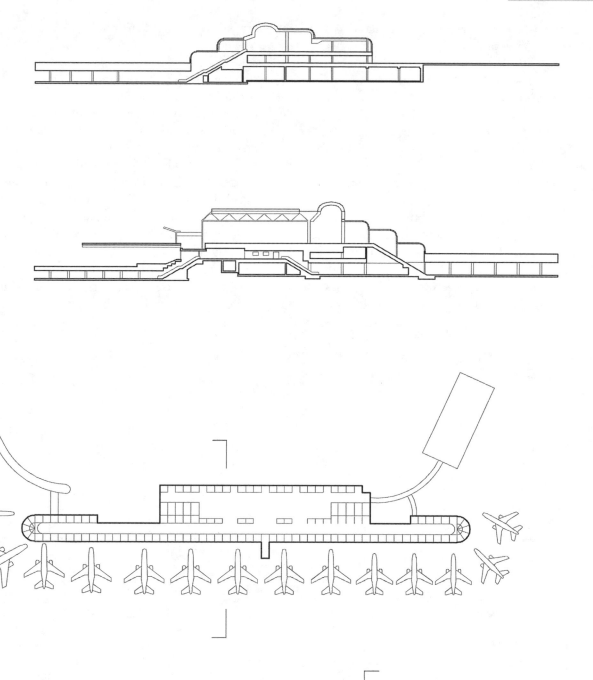

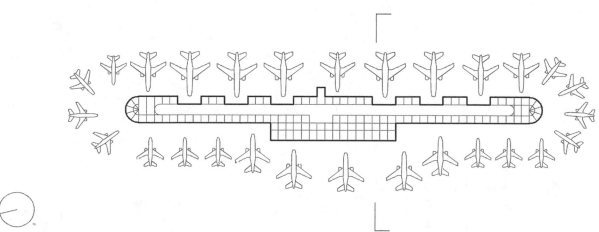

Figure 7.17   Plan and section.

Terminal 5, the new international terminal, was added in 1993 for $618 million.

Meanwhile, the number of passengers per annum (PPA) who flew through O'Hare in 1949—1 million—zoomed to 10 million in 1959 after the first terminal was completed. It served 30 million PPA in 1968, and 38 million ten years after that. O'Hare's business reached 50 million PPA before the two new concourses of United Airlines terminal were opened in 1988. The 72 million PPA that O'Hare served in 2000 may even reach 100 million in the next ten years.

The U.S. government passed the Airline Deregulation Act of 1978 primarily because it believed that passengers were paying $2 billion more per year than they would in a free market. Further, as a regulated industry, the airlines had no incentive to compete through lower fares and no ability to use innovative pricing schemes. Airlines no

longer needed market protection, and large carriers had no significant advantage over smaller ones. It was reasoned that deregulation would lower prices, increase competitive efficiency, and popularize air travel. United Airlines was slow to adjust to the new market, and its share of the industry decreased. By 1984, Number 2 American Airlines was catching up and the budget-niche airlines were cutting into its flanks.

United Airlines also suffered internal stress. The problems started in 1969 when the Civil Aeronautics Board decided against its bid for international routes. This not only cost United profitable business, it made its purchase of jumbo Boeing 747s look foolishly premature. From a $45 million profit in 1969, the company went to a $46 million loss in 1970.

In the next 18 years the company went through a series of six CEOs. It purchased Westin Hotel in 1970 and

TABLE 7.7   Normal Climate Data for Chicago

		Jan.	Feb.	Mar.	Apr.	May	June	July	Aug.	Sept.	Oct.	Nov.	Dec.	Year
Temperature	Degree-Days Heating	1345	1094	868	497	228	48	7	12	111	389	751	1165	6511
	Degree-Days Cooling	0	0	1	10	53	160	270	236	97	13	0	0	839
	Extreme High	65	71	88	91	93	104	104	101	99	91	78	71	104
	Normal High	29	34	45	58	70	80	84	82	75	63	48	35	59
	Normal Average	22	26	37	49	59	69	74	72	65	53	40	27	49
	Normal Low	13	18	28	39	48	57	63	62	54	42	31	20	40
	Extreme Low	-27	-17	-8	7	24	36	40	41	28	17	1	-25	-27
Humidity	Dew Point	14	18	27	36	46	56	62	61	54	42	31	21	39
	Max % RH	77	78	79	77	77	78	82	85	85	82	81	80	80
	Min % RH	66	63	59	53	51	52	54	55	55	53	62	68	58
	% Days with Rain	36	30	40	43	36	33	33	30	30	30	36	36	34
	Rain Inches	2	1	3	4	3	4	4	4	4	3	3	2	35
Sky	% Overcast Days	58	57	55	53	45	37	29	32	37	42	57	61	47
	% Clear Days	23	21	19	20	22	22	24	24	25	28	19	20	22
Wind	Prevailing Direction	W	W	W	NNE	NNE	SSW	SW	SSW	S	S	SSW	WNW	SSW
	Speed, Knots	10	9	10	11	10	9	8	8	8	9	11	10	9
	Percent Calm	2	2	2	2	4	5	6	6	5	3	2	2	3
Days Observed	Rain	11	9	12	13	11	10	10	9	9	9	11	11	125
	Fog	12	11	12	10	10	8	9	12	11	11	12	13	131
	Haze	11	12	13	11	12	13	15	17	14	11	11	11	150
	Snow	16	15	11	4	0	0	0	0	0	1	7	15	69
	Hail	0	0	0	0	0	0	0	0	0	0	0	0	2
	Freezing Rain	1	1	0	0	0	0	0	0	0	0	0	0	2
	Blowing Sand	0	0	0	0	0	0	0	0	0	0	0	0	0

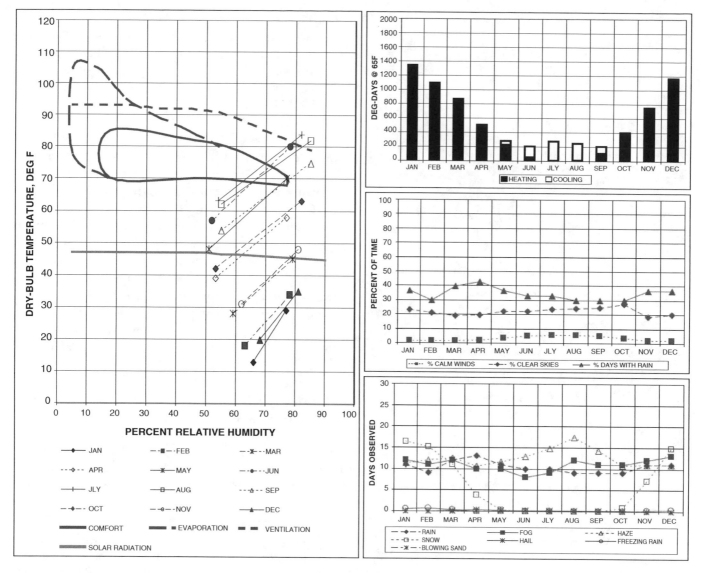

Figure 7.18 Climate analysis graphics.

named its president to run United. Seeking to become a travel conglomerate, it also bought the car rental firm Hertz Corporation in 1985. It acquired Australian and Asian air routes from Pan American in 1986 and bought Hilton International from Transworld in 1987. Finally, a shareholder revolt forced a change of direction. The hotel and car rental businesses were sold off, and United went back to focusing on its airline. The new strategy led to interest in the new home terminal.

The City of Chicago was suffering as well. Noise nuisance lawsuits were brought against the city repeatedly in the early 1980s by municipalities and school districts neighboring O'Hare airport. Finally, in 1982, the courts banned construction of new runways at O'Hare until 1995 and ordered the city to implement a set of noise control measures. This led Chicago, which owns the airport and

leases its facilities to the airlines, to promote the use of quieter engines and to begin the expensive task of soundproofing public buildings and even private residences in the approach and take-off paths. Despite these problems, air traffic at O'Hare was growing rapidly and was a vital part of the city's economy. To satisfy both the noise problem and the traffic growth, the airport would have to use newer, bigger, quieter aircraft. This led to the 1984 redevelopment plan and eventually to Terminal 1 for United Airlines.

Brief

General space requirements for United's terminal were to include facilities for ticketing, baggage handling, and airline operations supporting two concourse areas with 54 new boarding gates. With waiting areas and concessions,

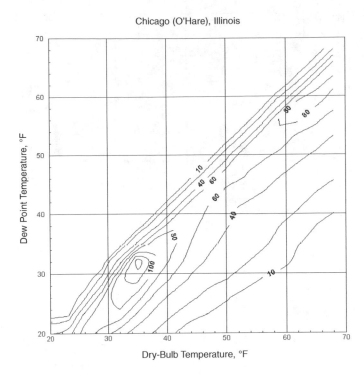

Chicago (O'Hare), Illinois

Figure 7.19 Bin data distribution for Chicago, Illinois. Concentric areas of graph indicate the number of hours per year that weather conditions normally occur in this climate. Similar to elevation readings on topographic maps, highest frequency occurrences of weather are at the center peaks of the graph. *(Data sources: Engineering Weather Data, typical meteorological year (TMY) data from the National Climatic Data Center, and the ASHRAE Weather Data Viewer from the American Society of Heating, Refrigerating and Air-Conditioning Engineers.)*

this came to about 1.3 million ft² (121 million m²). Because of ongoing operations, the project was phased into two parts. The second phase would replace existing gates after Phase One was occupied and the old terminal facilities demolished. Phase One would include 958,000 ft² (88,956 m²) and Phase Two would comprise 342,000 ft² (31,757 m²).

Site

O'Hare is 15 miles west of Lake Michigan and about 20 miles from the central business district. Geographically, the terminal is on a flat plain about 670 ft above sea level and about 100 ft above Lake Michigan. The most significant site considerations were the remote location of the airport from the central business district and the growth of noise-sensitive neighborhoods adjacent to the airport. Access from downtown and other outlying areas was addressed by the construction of a rapid transit line to the airport with a station beneath the parking garage. Helmut Jahn was also the architect for that project during earlier parts of the airport expansion.

Climate

Chicago, nicknamed the Windy City for its lakeshore breezes and the torrents of wind between buildings, has a predominantly cool climate. Köppen's classification (see Chapter 4 for a discussion of Köppen's work) for Chicago borders Dfa and Dfb, meaning cool with warm-to-hot summers and uniform precipitation.

Normal data reflects the cool climate, with 6511 heating degree-days and 839 cooling degree-days, a nearly 8:1 ratio. Chicago's inland location is associated with continentality that exaggerates the extremes of each season; winters are long and severe with short spring and fall periods. Summers are warm and humid. The lake tempers frontal movements by warming air masses in the winter and cooling them in the summer as they move across the water. The most extreme winter temperatures come from west of the city in northern air masses that sometimes miss the Great Lakes entirely. The heaviest snowfall occurs right along the lakeshore, driven by fronts that do cross the water and pick up additional moisture. Inland snowfall is generally lighter.

Chicago is underheated 52 percent of hours during a normal year. It is also comfortable about 24 percent of the time and overheated the remaining 24 percent of annual hours. There are, however, 2362 hours per year (26 percent) of freezing cold temperatures, as compared with only 167 hours (2 percent) of sultry weather above 85°F. Normal temperatures in January range from 13°F to 29°F and in July from 63°F to 84°F.

Rain, fog, and haze frequently obscure sky conditions; only 22 percent of all days have clear skies. Hours of day length vary seasonally between 9.0 hours of low sun in December and 15.8 hours of bright skies in June. Rainfall occurs on 30 to 40 percent of the days of any month, with about an equal chance of fog.

The United Terminal is a daylight-saturated environment with a great deal of internal heat gain. Its sensitivity to the climate needs to be balanced between desirable daylight illumination and the unwanted solar heat gain that comes with it. This is a trade-off between replacing electric light with cooler daylight to reduce cooling loads on one side, and fending off unwanted solar heat gain on the other. Usually, the United Terminal is overheated internally by people, lights, and equipment. This internal heat gain makes it likely that the facility will have a low balance point temperature and need cooling much of the year, even during moderately cold weather. There is not much potential from winter solar heat gain in Chicago's climate of cloudy skies and short winter days. For the warmer half of the year, however, at comfortable temperatures or above, the building is continuously overheated by internal sources and heat gains from the environment.

The potential for ventilation cooling with 100 percent outdoor air could offset the terminal's cooling loads from internal and solar heat gain when outside temperatures are below 55°F. Ventilation cooling is useful only when humidity levels are low, however, and the summer months in Chicago are on the humid side. If a 55°F outdoor wet-bulb temperature is used as the upper threshold of heat and humidity beyond which ventilation cooling is not practical, then 83 percent of the hours in Chicago between June 1 and October 1 are eliminated from consideration.

INTENTION

Design Team

Helmut Jahn studied architecture at the Technicsche Hochschule in Munich and finished graduate studies at the Illinois Institute of Technology in Chicago in 1967. He then worked at C. F. Murphy, where he became director of design in 1973. In 1981 he was made president of the company, and its name was changed to Murphy Jahn.

An oversight team, O'Hare Associates, was given responsibility for strategic planning and management of the entire $1.6 billion O'Hare redevelopment. This team was a joint venture of the Chicago firms Murphy Jahn, Envirodyne Engineers, Inc., and Schal Associates.

Structural engineering for the United Terminal was provided by Lev Zetlin Associates. The Chicago-based architecture and engineering firm A. Epstein & Sons provided the mechanical, electrical, and structural service engineering services. Sylvan R. Shemitz Associates Inc. of West Haven, Connecticut, performed the lighting design.

Philosophy

"Romantic Modernism" is one of the principles Helmut Jahn uses to describe the work of Murphy Jahn. He cites the stagnation of the Modern movement following the death of its masters, particularly Mies van der Rohe, as a disconnection from site, place, humanism, and history. He recognizes that Modernism fell short in its mission to harness technology and industrialization. In his own work, Jahn seeks to continue the Modernist ideals and reclaim the role of architecture as creative assertion, simultaneously avoiding the position of technical-translator-to-appropriate-form.

Intent

In addition to his Miesian education and Chicago heritage, Helmut Jahn has an attraction to the Art Deco movements of the 1920s and 1930s. His North Western Terminal (Chicago, 1987) and Bank of the Southwest (project for Houston, 1982) are good examples of his interest. He sees Deco as a much overlooked contribution to architectural history that is skipped over in the connections from Sullivan to Mies. For Jahn, Art Deco portrays a sentimental affection and public spirit of architecture. This clearly softens the High-Tech style he developed from his pragmatic and Miesian beginnings.

At O'Hare, Jahn mixes the romance of the exposed and articulated steel frame with some High Tech envelope pieces and meticulous lighting design. The intended effect is romantic, even if the technical means are necessarily more frugal, pristine, and modern. Jahn also wanted to invoke the excitement of flying in simpler times when passengers boarded in the hangar. It is interesting to compare Jahn's interpretation of this simplicity to Norman Foster's airport at Stansted (see case study #11).

CRITICAL TECHNICAL ISSUES

Inherent

Parking wide-body jets at many of the 54 new gates dictated greater distances between gateways and therefore longer concourses. The new aircraft technology emphasized the problems of long walking distances and overbearing linearity between boarding gates, just as Eero Saarinen had encountered at Washington's Dulles International (see case study #10). Another generation of jets had renewed the issues.

Contextual

Crowded working conditions and difficult construction sequences plagued the project. The construction staging area, including offices and parking for 2000 cars, had to be located two miles from the site at the northwest corner of the airport. Moreover, the existing United gate areas would not be demolished until the new ones were in operation, so construction equipment and moving aircraft would sometimes be competing for space. Excavation for the terminal buildings and connecting tunnel, for example, required the removal of 500,000 yd³ (382,000 m³) of earth with as many as 65 trucks driving across active taxiways.

Intentional

Given the intentions of exposed steel structure and daylight saturation of the terminal through large areas of glazing, the design was faced with two critical problems. First, exposed steel structure in this occupancy did not meet the fire codes. This issue was solved by negotiation with city officials and the provision of sprinkler systems. Second, and more significant to the design solution, the balance between daylighting and solar heat gain would have to be

Figure 7.20 Musée D'Orsay.

resolved if the terminal was going to be both naturally lit and affordably cooled.

Seasonal variation in day length and available light seem to suggest either that the envelope should have shading controls that distinguish between winter and summer sun angles or that the glazing be specified with low solar and luminous transmission values. The architectural intention probably led to the abandonment of external shading, though the Musée D'Orsay in Paris (Figure 7.20) would have made a suitable precedent. The Paris museum was converted from a train station designed by Beaux-Arts architect Victor Laloux and built on the Seine embankment for the Paris Universal Exposition of 1900. Remodeled in 1978 by ACI Architects with interiors by Gae Aulenti, the 183,000 ft^2 (17,000 m^2) exhibition space features a 450 ft (137 m) long nave beneath a 103 ft (31 m) barrel vault of glass and iron. The vault is glazed at both the upper and lower chords of its truss work, and sun-

tracking louvers were installed that allow the museum to control the introduction of solar light and heat. This is the path not taken by Helmut Jahn. [insert Fig. 7.20]

Instead, United was to be given a thin and static smooth skin, more in keeping with inspirations from the Crystal Palace. Envelope performance can still be responsive to different seasons in this scheme because the geometry of low winter sun will address the terminal differently than the high summer sun. Certainly, the huge expanse of enclosure required for the terminal building makes this less complicated solution quite attractive. The designers may have reasoned that careful distribution of glass in correspondence to solar geometries would resolve the problems of solar heat versus natural light, perhaps not with the same daily and seasonal flexibility as the converted Paris train station, but with less expense and complication.

APPROPRIATE SYSTEMS

Precedent

The formal and historical precedent for the United Terminal has already been discussed in terms of its romantic inspiration derived from Victorian industrial structures. There is also a similarity to the 1851 Crystal Palace, especially at the terraced aircraft gates where the arching glass vaults march along like the modular bays of Paxton's glass pavilion.

Site

The terminal is arrayed as two malls of passenger gates: Concourse B, a 1725 ft (526 m) long bar, and Concourse C, a parallel 1622 ft (494 m) island sitting 860 ft (262 m) to the west. There is just enough space between them for two Boeing 757s to roll past one another. This arrangement maximizes the available docking space on the airside. It also leaves the landside of the main concourse open for 1200 ft (366 m) of street access to the ticketing lobby. A tunnel beneath the taxiway connects the concourses with escalators and moving walkways. Beside the tunnel is the underground baggage handling hall, one of the first to use bar code readers for sorting luggage. [insert Fig. 7.21]

Helmut Jahn designed a 105,000 ft^2 (9,750 m^2) rapid transit station beneath the airport parking garage. Commissioned in March of 1979 and completed in the spring of 1984, the station is walled with undulating glass block on both sides, much like the new tunnel connecting the two United Airlines concourse areas. A railed people-mover system connects the central parking garage, the transit station, and all the O'Hare terminals. Originally, this people mover was going to run along the front wall of the United ticketing lobby and car access would have been from the level below. In the final scheme, the people mover is attached to the international terminal across the street and connected by a pedestrian bridge to the United side.

Structure

The desire for large spans and clear views dictated a steel frame structure. In order to change Chicago building codes, a committee was formed and fire consultants were hired. Local officials were eventually convinced that a supervised sprinkler system would make the exposed steel structure safe.

A folded-truss ticketing lobby precedes the dominant steel skeleton of the concourse and holding rooms. The 14 ft (4.3 m) deep folded-trusses are set in pairs at 37 degrees from horizontal at a 25 ft (7.6 m) clear height. They are made of welded 6.6 in. (168 mm) diameter steel tube and span 120 ft (36.6 m) from the landside entry to the concourse area. Twenty-seven bays of these trusses form a column-free space 810 ft (246.9 m) long. Columns on the airside are set outside the envelope and also support a cantilevering upswept canopy.

Concourses B and C use a more expressive skeleton of 24 in. (610 mm) deep vaulted steel arches accentuated by 12 in. (305 mm) diameter perforations. The visual effect, true to Jahn's intention, is reminiscent of nineteenth-century train depots or the inside of a dirigible airship. The 1725 ft (526 m) long vault over Concourse B spans 40 ft (12.2 m) and reaches a height of 45 ft (13.7 m). In Concourse C, where planes dock on both sides, the span is 50 ft (15.2 m). The structural bays repeat along the long axis every 30 ft (9.1 m). Passenger lounges flanking the concourses are 30 ft deep. Supporting columns are made of 8.6 in. (218 mm) steel tubes in clusters of one to five, depending on the load carried. The clusters are formed by 12 in. (305 mm) deep steel batten plates drilled to the diameter of the pipe columns. The batten plates are also lightened with 9 in. (229 mm) diameter drilled holes to unify the aesthetic. Welded 1 in. (25 mm) steel plate fins between the batten flanges add to the turn-of-the-century classical look of column capitals.

Structural elements arrived at the site prepainted and were lifted into place with padded slings. The careful erection process was complicated whenever poor weather restricted visibility to the point where cranes near the runways had to be shut down.

Envelope

Exterior skin elements of the terminal are insulated aluminum panels and insulated glass in clear, tinted, and

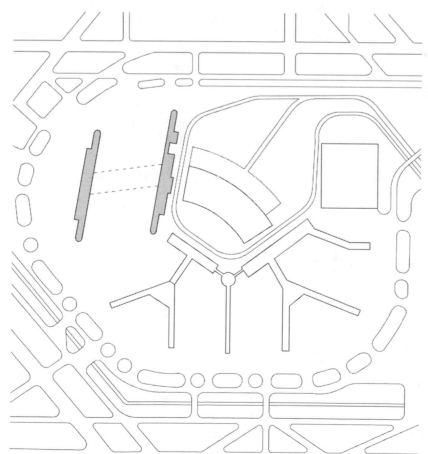

Figure 7.21 Site plan of United O'Hare Terminal.

Figure 7.22 Interior daylighting. *(Photograph courtesy of Bruce Haglund.)*

ceramic fritted materials. Each 30 ft (9.1 m) wide concourse bay and passenger lounge area is divided into five differently glazed vaults in a pattern of 2.5, 10.0, 2.5, 10.0, and 2.5 ft (0.76 m and 3.0 m) widths. At the center is a 5 ft (1.5 m) strip of clear glass spanning east to west. The two 10 ft bays are aluminum panels on the east and white ceramic fritted glass with a 50 percent daylight transmission oriented west. The outer 2.5 ft on each side of the bay is always filled with aluminum panels.

Mechanical

The airport's central plant delivers chilled water and steam as source energy. Heating and cooling are provided in the terminal by more than 70 VAV air handlers delivering in excess of 8000 tons of capacity. There is about 1 ton of peak air-conditioning for each 160 ft^2 of floor space. Primary duct distribution runs parallel to the long axis of the concourse in a triangular structural bay above the ticketing lobby.

Lighting

Lighting design for the terminal integrates a daylight top-lighting scheme with indirect artificial lighting. In the ticketing lobby this begins with continuous 5 ft (1.5 m) wide strip skylights at the top of each folded truss vault on 30 ft (9.1 m) centers. Beneath the skylights is a matte white light diffuser reminiscent of Louis Kahn's solution for the Kimball Art Museum. A vertical baffle breaks up solar penetration, and a perforated gull-wing diffuser introduces it into the space. The aperture size and spacing and the baffle/diffuser design were tested with scale modeling techniques in order to refine the solution.

The lobby's skylight diffuser system also integrates artificial lighting hardware. At the outer tip of each gull-wing is a linear light source alternating fluorescent and low-wattage metal-halide lamps. These two sources have about the same color rendering, but the metal-halides were needed to reach the desired footcandle (fc) illumination level. An additional baffle is suspended beside the linear fixtures to screen excess brightness from both the skylight and the artificial light strip.

In the concourse areas, sunlight is allowed directly into the space. The white ceramic frit pattern on the coated glass area diffuses light to the underside of the opaque aluminum panels and prevents high contrast ratios at the ceiling level. The structure and ceiling are painted white to increase brightness levels in the space and maximize diffusion. By night, opaque panels on the east side of the long axis are lit from below and across the corridor with fixtures using four 400 W metal-halide lamps. Reflections from the white-finished panels are caught by the ceramic fritting on the west side glass panels. This reflection gives the glass its own brightness and prevents it from becoming a black mirror surface at night. Each typical bay uses two of the fixtures with four lamps each to provide something less than the Chicago-required 25 fc of illumination, but the lighting designer was able to argue that the 25 fc level was based on direct downlighting. The indirect uplighting scheme used at O'Hare would satisfactorily provide a higher quality of light by directly illuminating the room enclosure rather than relying on light reflected off the floor. It would also save energy—in a typical 1200 ft^2 (111.4 m^2) bay the two fixtures of four lamps at 400 W equates to less than 2.7W/ft^2 and are operated only at night.

The passenger lounge holding areas are lit with a system similar to that used in the ticketing lobby. The 5 ft (1.5 m) strip of clear glass that bisects each 30 ft (9.1 m) bay of the concourse continues across the roof of the passenger lounges. The rest of the ceilings are opaque panels, but the west-facing walls and curved eaves are glazed. Between the skylight and the service desk below is a white painted and

Figure 7.23 Lumetric light sculpture by Michael Hayden. *(Photograph courtesy of Bruce Haglund.)*

perforated metal gull-wing diffuser. Fluorescent uplights and directional metal-halide fixtures light the ceiling and indirectly illuminate the space to 25 fc. Task lighting on the service desk comes from an indirect fluorescent fixture suspended below the centerline of the reflector. Additional ambient room light is provided by two strips of indirect fluorescent fixtures under inverted V-shaped ceiling coves running parallel to the skylight.

The connecting tunnel between the terminals is also the inside of a light sculpture. Four moving walkways carry passengers through an installation by artist Michael Hayden. His computer-generated "lumetric" sculpture pulsates over its 800 ft (243.8 m) length in rhythm with music by composer William Kraft. The $1 million commission, titled *Sky's the Limit,* consists of 23,600 ft² (2191.4 m²) of mirror reflecting more than 1 mile of neon tubes.

Jahn repeats a sidelighting scheme from the rapid transit station in the pedestrian tunnel. In both instances, glass block sidewalls are illuminated to relieve the impression of being underground. In the case of the transit station there is an empty space between the excavation and the sidewalls that allows the glass block to be backlit with high-pressure sodium lamps. In the terminal walkway tunnel the walls are flush to structure, so they are washed from the interior side with concealed fluorescent fixtures.

Interior

Both landside levels have 810 ft (247 m) of curb frontage. Check-in happens at 56 "flow-through" ticketing counters, where luggage disappears beneath the floor and passengers walk directly through security gates to the concourse. Walking time between the two farthest points in the ter-

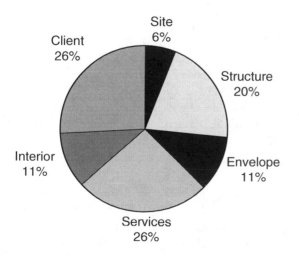

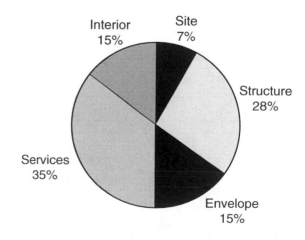

Figure 7.24 Cost data by system with and without UAL client systems cost.

TABLE 7.8   Cost Data for United O'Hare

Category	Item	$1,000s	% of total
Client	UAL systems	76,960	17.26%
	Security system	2,200	0.49%
	Apron paving	35,960	8.06%
Envelope	Ornamental and storefront	8,300	1.86%
	Waterproofing	4,320	0.97%
	Elastic sheet roofing	1,930	0.43%
	Pavilion roofing	1,070	0.24%
	Hollow metal	1,080	0.24%
	Rolling doors	510	0.11%
	Curtain wall	31,680	7.10%
	Window washing equipment	160	0.04%
Interior	Finish hardware	630	0.14%
	Drywall and ceilings	7,080	1.59%
	Ceramic tile	500	0.11%
	Resilient flooring	60	0.01%
	Terrazzo	3,220	0.72%
	Painting	2,720	0.61%
	Toilet partitions	130	0.03%
	Casework for club and offices	32,510	7.29%
	Special signage	1,840	0.41%
	Toilet accessories	90	0.02%
Site	Demolition	686	0.15%
	Excavation	9,500	2.13%
	Slurry wall	4,730	1.06%
	Exterior landscaping	860	0.19%
	Roadways	490	0.11%
	Garage tunnels	790	0.18%
	Site utilities	7,590	1.70%
Services	Loading dock equipment	40	0.01%
	Temporary terminal links	2,780	0.62%
	Elevators and dumbwaiters	2,610	0.59%
	Escalators	2,130	0.48%
	Moving walkways	3,230	0.72%
	Plumbing	8,390	1.88%
	Ventilation	15,540	3.48%
	HVAC	31,200	7.00%
	Electrical	48,650	10.91%
	Special lighting	1,730	0.39%
	Cathodic protection	1,070	0.24%
Structure	Caissons	2,430	0.54%
	Concrete	28,830	6.46%
	Masonry	7,070	1.59%
	Structural steel	30,790	6.90%
	Canopy	1,170	0.26%
	Miscellaneous iron	12,260	2.75%
	Rough carpentry	2,070	0.46%
	Spray-on fireproofing	1,180	0.26%
	Fire protection	5,450	1.22%

		$1000's	% Total
Subtotals	**Site**	24,646	5.53%
	Structure	91,250	20.46%
	Envelope	49,050	11.00%
	Services	117,370	26.32%
	Interior	48,780	10.94%
	Client	115,120	25.81%

minal, the north end of Concourse B through the tunnel to the north end of Concourse C, is estimated at 16 minutes without walking along the moving walkways. The north and south ends of both concourses terminate under half-dome canopies. The floors are terrazzo squares in a black-and-white diagonal checkerboard pattern.

The passenger lobby loading halls are built with the potential for adding a mezzanine level. This contingency allows for faster boarding of airplanes when aircraft of the future reach double-deck size.

TECHNICAL INTEGRATION HIGHLIGHTS

Physical

- Burying the baggage hall beneath the taxiway relieves the ticket lobby area of obstructions and promotes clear walking paths.

Visual

- Detailing of the steel structure achieves a classical quality relating to the design intentions.

Performance

- Ticketing lobby skylight diffusers are also the artificial lighting supports, ensuring that light comes from the same set of room distribution controls both day and night.
- Ceramic fritted glass in the concourse areas diffuses light by day and becomes a bright ceiling surface by night.
- Indirect artificial lighting complements the daylight strategy and maintains the daytime brightness of room surfaces.

DISCUSSION

There are 15 acres of glass in the United Terminal, and most of it faces west or horizontal. Despite the cool, temperate, and overcast character of the Chicago climate, the rationalization of this strategy is doubtful. Given warm, humid summers; high rates of internal heat gain; and long bitter winter nights; the aperture areas of the building seem less than thermally optimal.

The terminal's saving grace is the high quality of natural and electrical lighting and their mutual integration with the envelope system. With its alternating patterns of clear and ceramic fritted glass interspersed between opaque aluminum-clad panels, the envelope is always the glowing source of illumination.

13

KANSAI INTERNATIONAL AIRPORT, OSAKA BAY, 1987–1994

Honshu, Japan
RENZO PIANO WORKSHOP

DESCRIPTION

Kansai Airport was built to resolve a series of difficult compromises between economic needs and environmental requirements. A large part of this $15 billion project went to civil engineering challenges, beginning with the creation of an artificial island for the project. The problem, and the justification for Kansai's expensive existence, grew from the conflicting needs for a 24-hour airport to serve the region and the lack of available space where aircraft would not create a noise disturbance. Crowded cities and rugged terrain prohibited such a facility on any existing mainland site. In 1968 officials decided to build Japan's first around-the-clock airport on an artificial island in the waters of Osaka Bay.

Focus on the $2 billion main terminal building (MTB) begins with Renzo Piano. The MTB was to resemble a great, gleaming bird come to rest — its stainless steel body arching over a four-story "canyon" atrium, check-in counters, arrival/departure halls, 27 restaurants, 46 shops, and myriad other conveniences, its wings spread over glass-walled concourses and two extended gate wings, each stretching 2231 ft (680 m) along the runway.

Figure 7.25 View of Kansai International Airport. *(Photograph courtesy of Renzo Piano Building Workshop.)*

TABLE 7.9   Fact Sheet

Project	Building Name Client City Lat/Long/Elev	Kansai International Airport Kansai International Airport Company, Limited Izumisano City (serving Osaka and Kyoto), Osaka Prefecture, Japan 34.4N 135.3E, 14.8 ft (4.5 m)
Team	Architect Engineer Other Team Members Acoustics Façades Cost Control Cost Control Landscaping Construction Steel Contractors	Renzo Piano Building Workshop Ove Arup & Partners Aeroports de Paris, Japan Airport Consultants, Inc., and Nikken Sekke Peutz R. J. Van Santen David Langdon & Everest Futaba Quantity Surveying Co. Ltd. Koung Nyunt Obayashi Corp., Shimizu Corp., Fleur Daniel, Toda Corp., Okumura Corp., Konoike Construction Co., Ltd., Nishimatsu Construction Co., Ltd., Hazama Corp., Sato Kogyo Co., Ltd., with Fudo Construction Co., Ltd. joint venture, Takenaka Corp., Kajima Corp., Obayashi Corp., Overseas Bechtel, Fujita Corp., The Zenitaka Corp., Asanuma Corp., Matsumura-gumi Corp., Tokyo Construction Co., Ltd., with Tobishima Corp. joint venture. Watson Steel /Nippon Kawaski
General	Time Line Floor Area Occupants Cost in 1995 US$ Stories Plan	January 1987 (seawall begun); May 1989 (passenger terminal begun) to September 4, 1994 (opening). 3.1 million ft² (291,270 m²) main terminal building (MTB), including the 1 mile (1.7 km) long Passenger Gate Wings. 10,000 passengers per day capacity. Annually, 160,000 takeoffs/landings, almost 31 million passengers, and 1.4 million tons of air cargo. $15 billion, including construction of island and bridgeways, $2 billion for passenger terminal building, or about 1.5 trillion yen. Four (passenger terminal building), reaching 119.9 ft (36.54 m) high. MTB is approximately 900.9 ft × 492.1 ft (274.6 m × 150.0 m), totaling 604,456 ft² (56,156 m²) footprint and 2.1 million ft² (192,462 m²) of floor space. With the gate wings included, this reaches 1.2 million ft² (113,879 m²) footprint and 3.1 million ft² (291,270 m²) of floor.
Site	Site Description Parking, Cars	2.5 mile long × 0.76 mile wide (4.37 × 1.25 km) artificial island in Osaka Bay, 1277 acres (455 ha) located 3 miles (5 km) from mainland. 6500 in garages.
Structure	Foundation Vertical Members Horizontal Spans	Basement slab with jacks under each column to compensate for differential settlement. Vertical and inclined tubular steel columns with pin connections to trusses. 271.7 ft (82.8 m) clear-span arched warren trusses in MTB with two 10.5 in. (267.4 mm) top chords and one 16 in. (406.4 mm) bottom chord at 47.2 ft (14.4 m) centers spacing.
Envelope	Glass and Glazing Skylights Cladding Roof	Clear and heat absorbing glass in 0.5 in. (12 mm) units. Gable walls are 0.5 in. (14 mm) laminated heat-absorbing glass. All glazing is single leaf, not insulated. Band of glass skylights extends over entry canyon. Small extent of 2.4 in. (60 mm) extruded cement panel. 90,000 identical stainless steel panels, 5.9 ft × 2.0 ft and 0.04 in. thick (1.8 m × 0.6 m × 1 mm) with nonreflective finish.
HVAC	Equipment Cooling Type Distribution Duct Type Vertical Chases	Central plant located at west end of island serves about 50 airport buildings. Steam and chilled water from central plant. Local air-handling units with fan coils. Macro and micro systems. Macro air jets in each of 19 bays deliver air at 1400 ft/min (7 m/sec). Macro and micro systems. Macro air jets deliver air across open Teflon duct deflector. Return air shaft in canyon, exposed ducts for macro air jets.
Interior	Partitions Finishes Vertical Circulation Lighting	4.2 miles (7 km) of glass fences for separation of arrival and departure paths. Compartmentalized retail cabins with individual fire safety systems. Rock wool acoustical board ceilings, metal wall panels, artificial stone and rubber tile floors. Color-coded fixtures throughout. 87 elevators and 76 escalators. Service trees provide direct downlighting and indirect uplighting throughout the MTB.

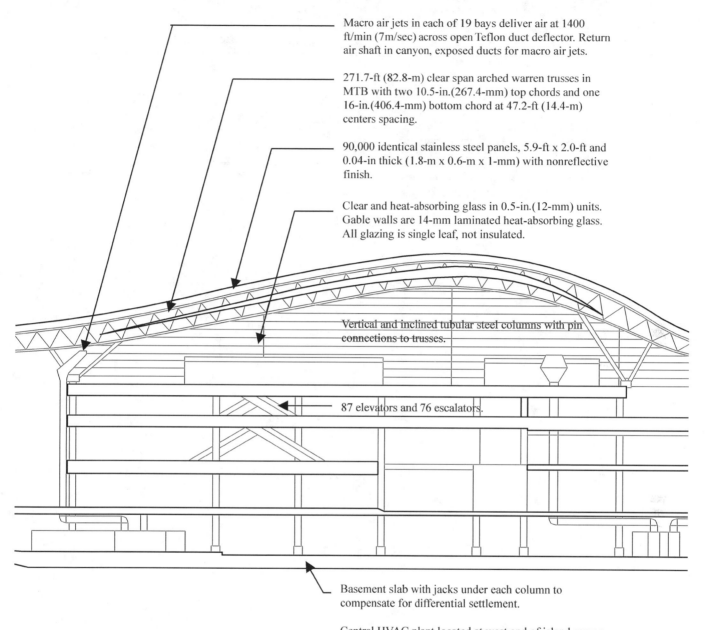

Macro air jets in each of 19 bays deliver air at 1400 ft/min (7m/sec) across open Teflon duct deflector. Return air shaft in canyon, exposed ducts for macro air jets.

271.7-ft (82.8-m) clear span arched warren trusses in MTB with two 10.5-in.(267.4-mm) top chords and one 16-in.(406.4-mm) bottom chord at 47.2-ft (14.4-m) centers spacing.

90,000 identical stainless steel panels, 5.9-ft x 2.0-ft and 0.04-in thick (1.8-m x 0.6-m x 1-mm) with nonreflective finish.

Clear and heat-absorbing glass in 0.5-in.(12-mm) units. Gable walls are 14-mm laminated heat-absorbing glass. All glazing is single leaf, not insulated.

Vertical and inclined tubular steel columns with pin connections to trusses.

87 elevators and 76 escalators.

Basement slab with jacks under each column to compensate for differential settlement.

Central HVAC plant located at west end of island serves about 50 airport buildings. Steam and chilled water from central plant. Local air handling units with fan coils.

Figure 7.26 Anatomical section.

PROGRAM

As early as 1968, Osaka International Airport was reaching its passenger and flight capacity. There was no room for expansion. The surrounding Kansai region of 22 million people, consisting of Osaka and sister cities Kobi and Kyoto, constitute the second largest urban and industrial complex in Japan. An airport capable of supporting a robust economy was required. Osaka also wanted to keep pace with competition from other airports that were coming on line with new terminal plans at Hong Kong, Seoul, Shanghai, Macao, and Kuala Lumpur. Asia-Pacific air passenger traffic increased more than 10 percent in each of the years between 1985 and 1995. By 2005 it is expected to double again, reaching 50 to 65 million passengers per year. Wishing to capitalize, the Japanese Ministry of Transportation put a plan into motion.

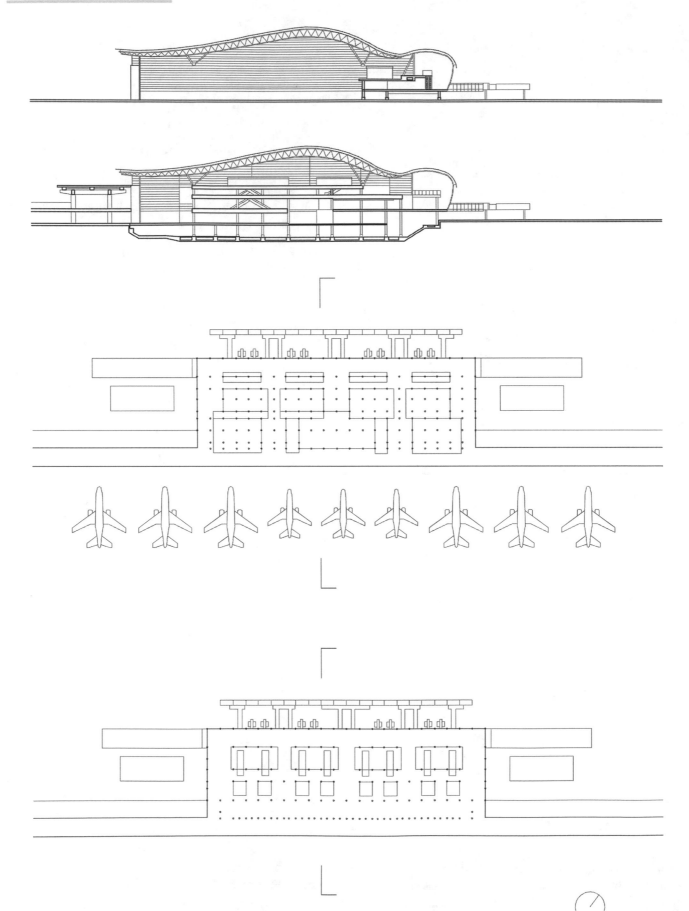

Figure 7.27 Plan and section.

Client

Kansai International Airport Company, Ltd. (KIAC) was established in 1984 with investment capital from the national and regional governments as well as the private sector. Its purpose was the construction and operation of Kansai International Airport, KIA. A separate entity, the Kansai International Airport Promotion Council, was also created with representatives of local government, private enterprise, and academia. The Promotion Council's task was to guide KIAC policy in parallel with the wishes of the local community and of airport patrons.

Land reclamation work to form the 1278 acre (511 ha) island 3 miles (5 km) into Osaka Bay began in 1987 and was to continue into early 1992. Eighty automated barges worked 24 hours per day to carry 233 million yd^3 (178 million m^3) of earth and sand from an entire Osaka mountain to build a 108 ft (33 m) thick layer of earth in 60 ft (18 m) of sea. A total of 26,000 6.2 ft (2 m) diameter pilings and 7 miles (11.2 km) of concrete embankments were placed to support the earthworks. The connecting 2.3 mile (3,750 m) Sky Gate Bridge from Izumisano on the south shore of the bay was begun in mid-1987 and not completed until early 1994. This is a double-deck truss bridge with a six-lane 98 ft (30 m) wide roadway 141 ft (43 m) above the water and a double-track rail on the lower level. In addition, the bridge carries all the utility services to the island: electricity, water, gas, and telephone.

Construction of the Passenger Terminal Building was to begin in mid-1991 and be complete by mid-1994. The semipublic KIAC held an international competition for the design of the main terminal building in 1988. Because of the short construction time table, a closed competition of 15 invited architectural firms was opened. Design requirements were based on consultations with Aéroports de Paris vice president, Paul Andreu.

Competition requirements called for a single building to centralize all functions of the terminal. Unlike the conventional land-based high-capacity airports of the world, Kansai would not be a distributed scheme where additional terminals could be added to accommodate growth at a later date. To conserve space further, the brief called for a layering of five single-purpose floors with direct-path circulation and "linear boarding" from landside to airside:

- Basement level for infrastructure and baggage handling. This 26.3 ft (8 m) deep space was designed by the firm Nikken Sekkei and was not in the design architect's scope of services.
- Level One is for international arrivals.
- Level Two serves domestic arrivals and departures.
- Level Three contains shops and restaurants.
- Level Four is international departures. This is the main departure hall.

Renzo Piano Building Workshop was awarded the contract in joint venture with Aéroports de Paris, Japan Airport Consultants, Inc., and architectural/engineering firm Nikken Sekkei. KIAC also awarded separate design contracts for a terminal train station, more than a dozen other buildings, 75 acres (30 ha) of cargo terminals, and the Aeroplaza hotel and shopping mall. To meet construction deadlines, KIAC split the MTB in half and hired two contracting firms to complete separate ends of the building.

On September 4, 1994, the Kansai International Airport became Japan's first full-scale round-the-clock operation. KIA has links to 39 cities in 21 countries over-

TABLE 7.10   Competition Participants for Kansai International Airport

Ellerbe Becket / Parsons / Shimizu, a Joint Body
Taller de Arquitectura Ricardo Bofill
Design System Kiyoshi Seike /JD Architekten-BDA
Foster Associates /Ohbayashi Corporation
Kazuhiro Ishii, Architect & Associates
Kiyonori Kikutake, Architect & Associates
Jean Nouvel et Associés
Helmuth, Obata & Kassabaum / Kajima Corporation
I. M. Pei and Partners / Kumagai Gumi Co., Ltd.
Cesar Pelli & Associates Inc. / Takenaka Corporation
Renzo Piano Building Workshop / Ove Arup & Partners
Sato Kogyo
Bernard Tschumi Architects

TABLE 7.11   Competition Jury Members

Yoshio Takeuchi	President of Kansai International Airport Company
Toru Akiyama	Deputy Chair of the Aviation Council
Soichi Nishimura	Vice Governor of Osaka Prefecture
Arata Isozaki	Architect
Kiyoshi Kawasaki	Architect
Kisho Kurokawa	Architect
Helmut Jahn	Architect
Richard Rogers	Architect

seas, and maintains the capacity to handle 160,000 take-offs/landings, almost 31 million passengers and 1.4 million tons of air cargo each year.

Brief

The design competition brief described a well-established set of criteria for the proposed Kansai International Airport. These rules were based on predesign studies by Aéroports de Paris done in consultation with the Japan Ministry of Transportation. Civil engineering and airport planning issues dictated several factors. To minimize the size of the island, it was designed around a single runway extending from one end to the other. The breadth of the island was covered by the runway, aircraft taxi areas, and a bordering complex of buildings. The main terminal building was placed close to the center of the island, and boarding gates were arrayed down a mile-long wing to allow for 42 docking gates. To keep the main terminal building (MTB) small, arrivals and departures for domestic and international flights were sandwiched into a four-story building scheme with direct circulation from landside to airside.

Initially, the airport was to serve 334 international flights a week, connecting to 21 countries. In addition to the airport facilities, there were requirements for a 576-room hotel, an international post office, a power plant, an energy center providing air-conditioning, a wastewater treatment center, and a waste disposal plant. Kansai Airport would be a self-contained city.

Site

The artificial island is 1.1 miles (1.7 km) long and covers 1277.5 acres (511 hectares). It rests 3 miles (5 km) offshore from Izumisano, 30 miles southeast of Osaka, in 60 ft (18 m) of water in the shallow Osaka Bay. It took robot-controlled

barges three years of 24-hour-per-day hauling to move 178 million yd³ (136 million m³) of earth and stone to complete the job. The earthwork is supported on more than 1000 piers sunk in 65 ft (20 m) of water and 65 ft of mud, then driven into 130 ft (40 m) of rock. To compensate for general and differential settlement of the island, the terminal building is constructed with hydraulic pier jacks supporting each structural column and equipped with monitoring instrumentation to measure any foundation movement.

The remote location of the site necessitated new infrastructure for transportation to the airport. The 2.2 mile long (3.5 km) Skygate Bridge from Izumisano was constructed with six automobile lanes on the upper deck and two train rails on the lower deck. Boat service is also available on Boeing 979 jet-foil passenger ferries running 30 minutes to and from Kobe at a speedy 50 mph (80 km/h).

Climate

Japan is roughly the size of the British Isles, but its climate is driven by the presence of the large Asian continent. Monsoonal circulation describes the seasonal reversal of flow caused by the large land areas that are warmer than oceans at the same latitude in summer and colder in the winter. (The word "monsoon" comes from the Arabic word *mawsim,* which means "season.") Japan's seasonal variation is driven by this Asian monsoon and the moderating effect of surrounding waters. The mountainous inland terrain accounts for substantial variation in local conditions, and tropical storms are frequent summer and fall. September brings the greatest threat of destructive typhoons (tropical cyclones).

The winter monsoons begin in November, ushering in cold dry polar winds from the north. These pick up moisture across the Sea of Japan, bringing rain and snow to the

Figure 7.28 Aerial view of the airport island. *(Photograph courtesy of Renzo Piano Building Workshop.)*

TABLE 7.12   Normal Climate Data for Osaka, Japan

		Jan.	Feb.	Mar.	Apr.	May	June	July	Aug.	Sept.	Oct.	Nov.	Dec.	Year
Temperature	Degree-Days Heating	717	635	541	215	47	1	0	0	1	61	285	570	3065
	Degree-Days Cooling	0	0	0	7	68	232	456	530	309	66	3	0	1667
	Extreme High	63	66	70	80	88	93	98	101	94	85	77	66	101
	Normal High	46	47	53	64	71	77	84	87	80	70	60	51	66
	Normal Average	42	42	48	58	66	73	80	82	75	65	56	47	61
	Normal Low	37	37	42	52	60	68	75	77	70	60	50	42	56
	Extreme Low	25	19	25	34	46	54	63	66	54	43	34	27	19
Humidity	Dew Point	28	29	34	44	53	63	71	71	65	53	44	34	49
	Max % RH	67	69	70	71	75	81	84	82	82	75	73	69	74
	Min % RH	52	53	52	53	56	64	67	62	63	58	56	54	58
	% Days with Rain	33	40	53	50	43	53	43	40	50	43	36	36	43
	Rain Inches	2	2	4	5	6	9	6	4	7	4	3	1	52
Sky	% Overcast Days	17	24	31	33	32	40	27	17	29	24	19	15	25
	% Clear Days	12	11	14	18	14	6	4	5	5	12	15	17	11
Wind	Prevailing Direction	WNW	W	N	ENE	N	W	W	ENE	N	N	N	W	N
	Speed, Knots	9	10	7	9	6	7	6	11	7	7	6	10	8
	Percent Calm	3	2	2	1	1	2	1	1	2	2	2	3	2
Days Observed	Rain	10	12	16	15	13	16	13	12	15	13	11	11	157
	Fog	2	2	3	3	4	6	9	5	3	3	5	5	50
	Haze	3	3	5	5	8	7	5	5	3	5	6	6	61
	Snow	4	5	2	0	0	0	0	0	0	0	0	1	12
	Hail	#	0	0	0	0	0	0	0	0	0	0	0	#
	Freezing Rain	0	0	0	0	0	0	0	0	0	0	0	0	0
	Blowing Sand	#	#	1	2	1	0	0	0	#	0	0	#	4

windward slopes of the northern islands. On the southern islands, winter is the dry season and precipitation comes from storms riding the leading edge of polar air masses. Spring weather across the islands is pleasant, drier even than summer and fall. The cloudy summer monsoon brings heavy rain to the southern islands from tropical storms and typhoons off the South China Sea or the Western Pacific. Maritime summers are hot and humid, driving city dwellers to the cool mountain retreats. The Japanese rainy season, *tsuyu,* usually slows by mid-July. The weather cools rapidly in October, and by November the storms subside and the winter monsoon season repeats. The southern islands, Shikoku and Kyushu, have a mild, almost subtropical climate similar to that of the southeast coast of the United States.

The climate in Kobe, Nara, and nearby historic Kyoto is similar to that of Osaka, on which the following Kansai

climate analysis is based. This is a humid cool temperate climate with 3065 heating and 1667 cooling degree-days, a ratio of about 2:1 indicating the dominance of cool weather. The bay area generally separates the cooler climates to the north from the subtropical southern islands. Constant maritime humidity keeps the daily temperatures within narrow ranges between high and low.

As the fingerprint graph of bin data indicates with its four different peaks, there are pronounced seasons in Kansai. Winters last from November to April, with freezing temperatures expected to occur most days of February through December. Summers are quite humid and brutal during July and August. There are more than 60 hours per year with temperatures over 93°F and 1150 hours over 80°F. Summer design conditions are 90°F dry bulb with a 77°F wet bulb temperature. Winter design conditions are a corresponding 32/29°F.

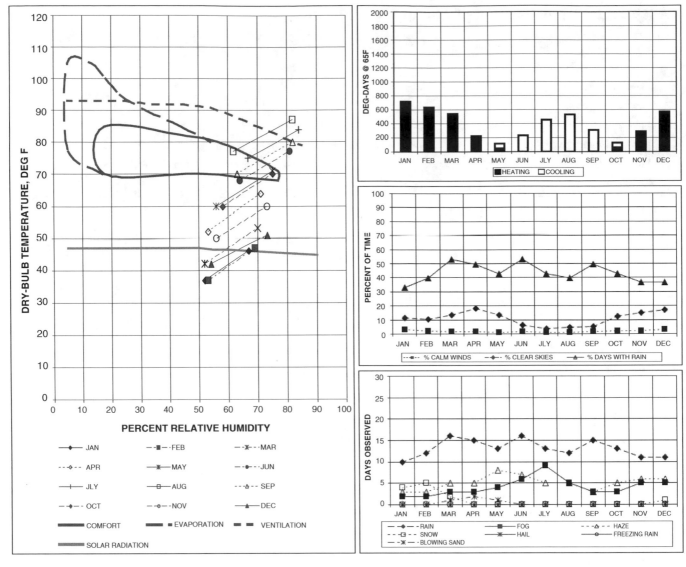

Figure 7.29 Climate analysis graphics.

INTENTION

Design Team

The competition and design project team of the Renzo Piano Workshop was complemented by the engineering work of Ove Arup & Partners, with Peter Rice and Tom Barker as the principals. The rest of the consortium consisted of Aéroports de Paris, represented by architect and vice president Paul Andreu, and Japan Airport Consultants, led by Takeshi Kido and Yoshiaki Niina. Noriaki Okabe, head of Piano's Paris office, was the project leader for the Renzo Piano Workshop. Each of these firms and the many other organizations that participated in the conception and birth of Kansai dedicated large pools of staff expertise and resources to the project. In proportion to everything else about KAI, this is an enormous amount of expertise for the architect to employ and coordinate.

Philosophy

The guiding spirit of the project was, of course, Renzo Piano himself. Piano was born in Genoa, Italy, and attended Milan Polytechnic University. He worked with Louis Kahn from 1965 to 1970, where he met Jean Prouve. In 1971, Piano began his collaboration with Richard Rogers on the Centre Pompidou (see case study #22). In 1981 he opened the Renzo Piano Building Workshop, which now has offices in Genoa and Paris.

Intent

The design team's response to the competition brief's outline of the terminal and its gate wings was graphically sug-

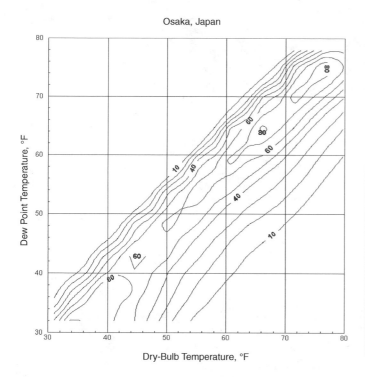

Osaka, Japan

Figure 7.30 Bin data distribution for Osaka, Japan. Concentric areas of graph indicate the number of hours per year that weather conditions normally occur in this climate. Similar to elevation readings on topographic maps, highest frequency occurrences of weather are at the center peaks of the graph. (Data sources: *Engineering Weather Data, typical meteorological year (TMY) data from the National Climatic Data Center,* and the ASHRAE *Weather Data Viewer from the American Society of Heating, Refrigerating and Air-Conditioning Engineers.)*

gestive. It reminded them of a glider plane with the MTB as its fuselage and the gates as its wings. The soft form of its roof also suggests organic images, such as birds.

CRITICAL TECHNICAL ISSUES

Inherent

- Kansai would have to become a gateway to Japan for the project to become economically viable.
- The organization and unity of a mile-long building would have to maintain clarity and order for passengers.

Contextual

- Because of the remote location and the anticipated settlement of supporting earthworks, the building would have to be as lightweight and efficient as possible.
- Construction on an artificial island required a reliable all-weather transportation system for materials and as many as 10,000 workers.

- Amenable passenger transportation from the airport to the mainland and back would have to interface with the terminal.
- Japan has a strict set of seismic design regulations that dictates specific levels of severity and allowable building failure.

Intentional

- With more than 35 million ft³ (1 million m³) of volume, the design intention of maintaining one open continuous space in the MTB was at odds with fire code requirements for fire separation. The Building Standard Law of Japan (BSJL) stipulates a 529,717 ft³ (15,000 m³) limit.
- Maintaining clear sight lines from the air traffic control tower to the airport apron and gateways imposed height restrictions at the same time that fire safety design called for higher ceilings to serve as smoke reservoirs.

APPROPRIATE SYSTEMS

Precedent

Two man made islands had already been constructed in Osaka Bay, Port Island Terminal and Rokko Island Terminal at Kobe. Neither of these land reclamation projects was in waters as deep as those where Kansai was to be located, however, nor were they as far from shore.

Architecturally, there were few other modern, urban, centralized terminal airports to draw from at the time of the Kansai competition. Certainly, there were none on tiny, crowded artificial islands. Kennedy Airport in New York, for example, carries fewer passengers annually than Kansai, but uses four times as much land area. Chicago's United O'Hare Terminal (see case study #12) and Denver International were both new, but quite suburban. The prototypical Dulles terminal is formally similar to Kansai in some ways, and a good example of direct linear boarding, but the early days of the small jet were long gone. Kansai had to be invented.

Site

Features of the site were organized and dictated by the design competition guidelines. There was little room for exception, and all of the highly considered design entries conformed to the same basic layout finalized by Piano and his team. The civil engineering of the site was central to the project, and all of its features were optimized from the start for the single purpose of creating an offshore airport.

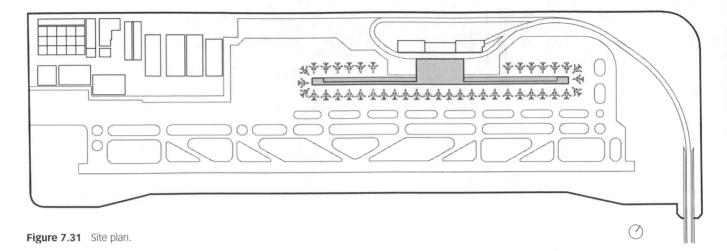

Figure 7.31   Site plan.

Figure 7.32   The Eiffel Tower. The tower is 10,100 tons total weight and 324m high (with flagpole). It takes 50 tons of paint to refurbish the structure every five years.

The southeast half of the island is given over to taxiways and a single aircraft runway. The northwest corner is apportioned to maintenance, central energy plant, and air cargo operations. On the northeast corner is a domestic cargo facility with a small water port. Passenger terminal operations were given the central northern portion of the island and pushed against the aircraft apron. Transportation to the island by train, bus, or car arrives from the Sky Gate Bridge at the southeast corner of the site and curves along the northeast end of the island, past the domestic cargo port to the northwest edge of the island, between the passenger terminal building and the water. Parking and transit terminals are located between the main terminal building (MTB) and a hotel/retail complex on the water's edge.

Structure

To appreciate the enormous scale of the Kansai MTB, consider the following proposal:

- Start by removing the top 50 percent of the Eiffel Tower, exactly 492 ft (150 m) of it.
- Break the four corners apart and lay these frames horizontal.
- Bend them into 14 different radii across their lengths.
- Repeat the first three steps 5.5 more times.
- Cut each of the completed 22 frames into nine 70 ft long segments.
- Prepaint the 198 frame segments and ship all 13,860 ft of them to Japan.
- You are now ready to frame the main Kansai MTB roof trusses, but the 1 mile long gate wing with its 244 structural ribs will have to wait.

How fitting that Eiffel of France, the same company responsible for the original monument in Paris, would become one of the steel subcontractors for KAI.

TABLE 7.13 Parameters of Truss Shape in the MTB from Landside to Airside

Cantilever over the airside entrance

Water accumulation and drainage around skylights

13 ft (4 m) fire safety height requirement above Level 4 concourse for smoke accumulation

Vertical rise to center of space for structural efficiency

Form of 270 ft (82.4 m) span to promote airflow in main concourse

Need to ensure visibility of jets from air control tower located on landside of terminal

Water accumulation and drainage on airside of roof

Ceiling height at third floor of wings, especially at their ends where structure tapers down

Curvature over gateway lounges to gain advantage of shell structural form

Volume requirements at wing ends

Cantilever shading over gate wing glazing

Need to limit cantilever of second floor over first

The volume of the main terminal building is formed under 18 of those Eiffel-Tower-proportioned arched trusses 492 ft (150 m) in length. Each truss is an inverted triangle with a 16 in. (406 mm) lower cord and two 10.5 in. (267 mm) top cords. The cords and their 5.5 in. (140 mm) diagonal bracing maintain constant external diam but vary in wall thickness according to varying loads. This reinforces their visual continuity while minimizing structural weight. Wall thicknesses in the top and bottom cords vary from 0.4 in. to 1.2 in. (10 to 30 mm). The thickest members are at the end supports across the 269 ft (82 m) span where loads are transferred downward. Diagonal members have wall thicknesses between 0.25 in. and 0.5 in. (6 to 12 mm). All trusses were prefabricated in seven to nine sections and welded together on-site.

Design of the truss profile was determined primarily by interior aerodynamics via the use of the underside of the ceiling as an open air duct that moves air across the MTB. That aspect is discussed in a following section on the building's mechanical systems. Other important factors, aside from structural strength, were related to sight lines from the air control tower to the tarmac, fire safety, water drainage, and so forth.

Double trusses were used at the end walls to simplify glazing from floor to deck without structural interference. The double strength also provides required lateral stability to the roof frame. Gable end glass walls run between the inner and outer trusses and bear entirely on the floor. Lateral support is provided by a row of double bow trusses with a vertical center member where the window wall is infilled. To keep the gable ends clear and distinct from the roof structure, the largest component of the bow truss is restricted to a profile of 1.4 in. (35 mm).

Envelope

The MTB roof is a double-layered system with an upper sunscreen surface of stainless steel tiles and an inside rain screen of insulated metal deck. The air space between the two layers is allowed to vent naturally and reduce the cooling load on the building. There are 82,400 identical outer roof panels on the MTB. Each is 0.04 in. (1 mm) thick and measures 5.9 ft × 2.0 ft (1.8 m × 0.6 m), a size that can be carried by one person but is large enough to be read as an individual element at a distance. The panel is composed of industrial-grade stainless steel with corrosion resistance similar to that of titanium. Their expensive quality limited the thickness to 0.04 in. (1.0 mm), about the thickness of a fingernail. To keep blinding glare from the view of jet pilots and control tower personnel, a textured finish was etched onto the panels to make them dull and light diffusing. This texture gave the panels a directional pattern that had to be followed during installation.

Figure 7.33 View of truss at gable.

Each panel is slopped across its narrow dimension on the roof and connects across its long edge to the next panel via folds in its shape that incorporate a gutter on one long side and a seamed connection where two panels meet lengthwise. Open joints are allowed at the narrow ends of each row of panels, where rainwater is diverted to the lower layer. The pitch of each panel, the integral gutter, and the open joint combine to visually accentuate each individual panel as a separate plane of the roof.

Beneath the stainless steel outer panels is a layer of double-bent steel deck. This rain screen surface is finished in fluoropolymer paint. It consists of two layers of profiled steel with a layer of insulation sandwiched between them. Clips are bolted to this deck to support the folded edges of the stainless steel cladding panels and provide a concealed edge for the connecting screws. For drainage, gutters are flashed into the lower deck surface at strategic intervals and connected to downpipes.

All vertical surfaces in the terminal are glazed. At the wing gates a 0.47 in. (12 mm) heat absorbing insulated glazing is used in panels of 11.8 ft × 2.0 ft (3.6 m × 0.6 m) for all 183,000 ft² (17,000 m²) of the southeast-facing wall. Glazing is installed in a horizontal pattern for ease of fit and glazing of joints at the curved wall structure. The panel size also matches the width of two stainless steel panels in the roof overhang.

Mechanical

The entire airport is supported by a central Energy Center supplying thermal energy to about 50 buildings on the island. Electrical service comes to the airport over the bridge from the mainland. Backup electricity is supplied by two 20 megawatt generators driven by engines capable of burning either natural gas or fuel oil.

Within the terminal building, issues of lightweight construction suggested to the designers that all systems should be removed from the ceiling. This would decrease the dead load supported by the roof, thus the weight of structure necessary to complete the span. It was therefore decided that all air distribution and lighting systems would be floor mounted. To prevent disorderly proliferation of small, distributed systems, the necessary components were divided into macro and micro systems. Large air jets would wash the entire upper concourse, and light fixtures mounted above eye level would indirectly light the ceiling. At a smaller scale, local lighting, information terminals, and signage would be positioned on service trees. Local cooling would be delivered from small air towers at floor level.

The use of an open duct to condition the fourth level concourse required aerodynamic design of the ceiling profile. If an enclosed duct had been used, several small air register openings with little air resistance would have to be included along its length for air to be released into the large volume. The use of an open duct assumes that these distribution openings are continuous. Making it work meant determining the precise path of air across the space from air jets located high on one side of the space. Once the correct profile was determined, the ceiling truss design could be curved to the correct geometry. Resolving the aforementioned param of shape for the roof from both sides resulted in a profile with 12 radii for the outside surface and 11 different inside surface radii.

Nineteen air duct risers, one per bay in the MTB, terminate in nozzles designed to generate the required flow of air across the space at a discharge rate of 1400 ft/min (7 m/sec). To reduce airflow friction and provide good reflection of uplights, a Teflon-coated canvas membrane is stretched between the trusses to guide, rather than force, air across the concourse. The canvas is hung on an aluminum frame suspended at ceiling level.

Micro systems for lighting are based on the service trees of a standard 12.5 ft (3.8 m) height and 23.6 ft (7.2 m) spacing. Metal halide fixtures in 250 W, 400 W, and 1000 W sizes are used alongside emergency lighting, public address speakers, security cameras, and information screens. Cooling and ventilation are provided at the micro level by exposed airpost columns that are clad in aluminum and fitted with eyeball diffusers. In some areas lighting and ventilation elements are wall mounted.

Interior

From three-level vehicle access on the northern airside of the terminal, or from the second-level attached train terminal, passengers enter the MTB through "the canyon." This vast four-story space encompasses the width of the building at 410 × 88 × 82 ft (125 × 27 × 25 m), and its volume continues on the ground level through the international arrivals concourse. Circulation is visually expressed in this space, and its straight-through linear boarding organization simplifies movement. Transfer from domestic arrivals to international departures, for example, is simply a matter of going straight up two floors rather than to a different concourse wing or even a different terminal, as in most airports.

Above the canyon, a band of glass skylights complements the natural landscaping within. More than 100 native trees and bamboos were planted along the center of the space. Outdoor gardens beyond the gable endwalls of the MTB were planted to match with 60 more trees each, extending the connection of inside to out. The canyon is also the only public space in the terminal where color, a terr-cotta, is used on the wall surfaces. The bridges, return air shafts, and other elements are painted ash green. All of the air delivery devices are sky blue.

A color scheme was developed for the project to unify the vast interior. Most surfaces are a shade of gray; 13 different shades were used to establish a hierarchy. Wall, ceiling, and floor, for example, are middle gray. The structure is almost white, for visual emphasis; glass is dark gray; information terminals are deep gray. Other elements use a traditional Japanese color palette: light is yellow, air is blue, movement is red, and circulation is green. These accents are used for corresponding components; thus, light fixtures are always yellow, ducts are always blue, elevators are red, and so forth.

To minimize travel time for international passengers, an automated guideway transit system called the "Wing Shuttle" carries passengers from the MTB concourse to their boarding gates in the wings. Two tracks run on the landside roof of the second floor of each long gate wing. There are two cars on each track and three stops along each wing. Departing passengers clear various control points and then walk out from the third floor of each wing area in the MTB to catch a shuttle to their gate stops. Arriving passengers do the opposite.

Fire safety design for the open spaces in the MTB was satisfied by means of a fire engineering approach. Arup engineer Margaret Lowe, a world known authority in the field, demonstrated to the Kansai study group and code officials that the vast volume of the terminal provided a sufficiently large smoke reservoir at the ceiling level to ensure safe evacuation. In addition, the steel structure was protected by GRC, a cementitious fiberglass-reinforced coating that was formed around members and finished in soft shapes that gave them a cigarlike profile. Further protection was afforded by the application of intumescent paint to all exposed steel. When exposed to high temperatures, a 1 mm layer of intumescent paint foams up to provide 1 cm or more of temperature-protective insulation around the steel. This extends the amount of time steel will maintain its structural integrity before reaching its elastic limit and collapsing. In most countries steel is assumed to fail at about 1000°F (550°C), but in Japan a more restrictive 650°F (350°C) rating is used. With all this fire protection in place, basic suppression systems were added by distributing 1091 fire sprinklers throughout the building. In the retail areas individual spaces were compartmentalized for fire control in the usual way. Each has its own mechanical smoke exhaust and fire sprinkler system.

Fire suppression is also provided by a series of water cannons with highly sensitive photoelectric heat scanning detectors. These cannons are capable of automatically calculating the amount of water and air necessary to extinguish a fire, determining angle and distance to the target, aiming at the blaze and dousing it at a distance of up to 272 ft (83 m). Smokers beware.

Figure 7.34 Gate wing interior. *(Photograph courtesy of Renzo Piano Building Workshop.)*

TECHNICAL INTEGRATION HIGHLIGHTS

Physical

- The double roof allowed for installation of the stainless steel top layer after construction was dried in.
- Bow trusses on gable walls permitted glazing of vertical members running between double roof trusses.
- The geometry of the building form was fitted to required sight lines for air control.

Visual

- The continuation of the roof truss bottom cord across the landside canopy and airside gate wing ribs reinforces the unity of the interior.
- Shingled stainless steel roof panels are a reference to the dominant roof forms of traditional Japanese architecture. They are also self maintaining and have a very long life expectancy.

- Interior use of color reinforces the direct linear boarding scheme.
- Glass fence partitions and stair rails expose the organization of space.

Performance

- Structure, interior, and mechanical systems are integrated to create open ducts.
- Open ducts eliminate ceiling ducts, reduce required structure, and provide indirect ambient lighting.
- The double roof is vented to reduce solar impact on the cooling load.
- High ceiling heights provide a smoke reservoir in the event of fire and allow the single-volume MTB space.

Figure 7.35   Kansai International Airport. Photograph taken from 118 nautical miles altitude on April 10, 1994, at 05:22 Greenwich Mean Time. The camera position is near vertical. The sun is at 48 degrees altitude and 58 degrees west of south. *(Photograph courtesy of NASA.)*

DISCUSSION

An important subplot of Kansai airport design might be titled "The Algorithm of Form." Most of the primary design features are closely linked to numerically determined criteria for the critical functions of the airport. The general configuration and orientation of the terminal building, for instance, was established by air traffic and taxiway requirements for large jets. Computer maps of computational fluid dynamics shaped the profile of the open duct ceiling. The organizational strategy for interior spaces was determined by the competition brief. Ceiling heights were set by smoke reservoir calculations. From the very beginning, the placement, shape, orientation, and size of the island and were determined by the geometry of flight patterns; everything else followed suit.

Despite this jumble of preconditions and scientific determinism, and regardless of whether they were assigned by the competition or adopted by the design scheme, the solutions offered by the competition entries show a remarkable range of innovative freedom. A few entries were disregarded for failing to accommodate all the requirements of the brief, but none of the more highly considered designs were any less innovative, despite their conformity to the guidelines.

A second point of discussion is the unusual internality of Kansai. Even relative to other airports, the visual impact of the MTB in and on its setting is slight. To begin with, the outdoor climate is marginally relevant to the traveler speeding by train to the terminal and protected in the terminal until boarding an aircraft. The entire sequence occurs in controlled environments—the airplane seat is little different from the car in which where the trip began. Except for a few glimpses of the terminal

building airside through the girders of the approach bridge, and maybe a peek from an aircraft window as it lands and taxis, the building is never experienced as an object. Once cars and trains enter the terminal garages, or as passengers arrive at the landing jetway, the exterior of the terminal could be anything, anywhere. Even those who stay at the island's airport hotel may never see more than the interior of the terminal. The setting, the form, the context, and the climatic influences are rendered irrelevant by the remote setting of the airport and the internally protected transitions in transportation modes of arrival and departure. A traveler's only concern for the weather might be in regard to snarled traffic on the way to the airport and bumpy flying conditions during storms. The envelope system and its climatic interventions, the mechanical system and its humming work, are all silent to the Kansai passenger.

A final note on the integrity of the structure: On September 29, 1994, after a spell of exceedingly hot weather, Typhoon Orchid swept across Kansai with torrential rain and winds in excess of 130 mph. Two ships were grounded by the storm off Kobe, and there were three related deaths. Sixteen months later, at 8:46 GMT on January 17, 1995, an earthquake measuring 7.2 on the Richter scale occurred in Osaka bay. Its epicenter was about an equal 30 km from both the city of Kobe to the north and Kansai Airport to the south. About 60 percent of the midrise buildings in Kobe were structurally damaged, and 20 percent of them were destroyed completely. More than 4000 lives were tragically lost in the city. Kansai Airport sustained only minor damage from both of these events, without loss of life.

Pavilions

orld's Fairs, Grand Expositions, Olympic Games, and trade pavilions are acknowledged as proving grounds for experimental architecture. Their centerpiece buildings are meant to impress with technical flair and to act as ambassador of the host or home county's progressive industry. Basically, pavilions are a chance to show off. For this reason, their design is obligated to be daringly experimental in the use of advanced materials and techniques.

Experimental Factors

Pavilions are often experimental because of their commercial mission and because they are usually temporary structures. At the end of the fair, exposition, or celebrated event, most pavilions are either converted to public use or dismantled. In either case, their primary intention has already been served and any future use is secondary. As an example of the experimental nature of these structures, consider engineer Lev Zetlin's design of a ferrocement thin shell for the New York Exposition of 1964. Built to provide experience in thin shell construction, it was loaded to destruction after the fair to validate the theoretical statics. The pavilion proved to take twice as long to build and held twice the load anticipated. The experience is documented in a three-volume report published by the Building Research Advisory Board after the fair.

Another reason for the experimental aspect of pavilions is the short and absolute time line of expositions—construction time is short, speed is vital, and opening day cannot be postponed when the whole world is arriving. From the Crystal Palace forward, this led to an extensive use of industrialized and prefabricated building design strategies. Paxton's Palace set the pace: constructed in 17 weeks from standardized parts, dismantled after the exposition, and reerected in Sydenham in 1855.

After 1900 the shift from large exposition halls that contained the exhibits, to individual pavilions for each participating country, was complete. This move transferred the burden of design and construction to individual participants. Consequently, construction components and sometimes entire buildings were designed and prefabricated in one country and assembled in another. Aside from the problems of dimensional tolerance, field assembly, and construction sequence, design-from-afar also introduced the element of transportation. Prefabricated pieces would have to be designed around their mode of transport and the maximum sizes of assemblies that could be handled.

Evolution

Given the three parameters of technical image, temporary use, and rapid construction, architects and engineers for pavilions are forced to continually innovate. There is no learning curve or reliable precedent for the next design, because each new one must be more spectacularly innovative and technically advanced than anything before it. A pavilion looks more to the utopian future than to the reliable past.

First, the expositions stimulated the designing of experimental pavilions. Then the most successful pavilions stimulated architectural history. Their huge spans and vast interiors took center stage. The pavilions immediately usurped the exhibits, and architecture became the main attraction and defining feature of expositions. The combination of innovative design and public appeal was an irresistible influence on the practice of architecture.

The history of influential exposition architecture began with Joseph Paxton's Crystal Palace at London's Great Exhibition of 1851. It continued through the early industrial years with Dutert's Gallerie des Machines, and the Eiffel Tower (both of Paris, 1889). After the turn of the century, a mid-to-early Modernist period centered on Mies van der Rohe's German Pavilion (Barcelona, 1929). It would be reasonable to consider Eero Saarinen's Gateway Arch for St. Louis in this second period as well. Even though the Arch was not built until 1961–1966, Saarinen won the design competition in 1947 and the Arch, after all, was intended to produce the same economic revitalization that motivated other trade fairs of its day. Further notable contributions include Peter Behrens's German Railway Pavilion (Brussels, 1910), Le Corbusier's Pavilion de l'Esprit Nouveau (Paris, 1925), the General Motors Building by Albert Kahn (Chicago, 1933), and Alvar Aalto's Finish Pavilion (Paris, 1937). The second period of pavilion architecture closed with the New York World's Fair of 1939–1940. The opening day celebrations were published on the same day the *New York Times* reported on Hitler's ultimatum to Poland. There would not be another major fair until 1958.

A third and equally long period runs from the postwar years to the new millennium. These 50 years saw many transitions in the nature of pavilions, and so the postwar era is not easy to typify. It has, however, generated a continuum of important buildings. The Montreal Expo of 1967 provides a dramatic sample by itself: Frei Otto's tension cable German Pavilion, Buckminster Fuller's geodesic dome American Pavilion, and Moshe Safdi's modular Habitat Housing.

Expositions grow from tremendous economic and political stimulus. The obvious mission of expressing technical and cultural prowess through the architecture of these events is to promote and market someone's home industry. But an equal impetus is the economic windfall to be gained by the host city in preparing for the event. This sometimes involves a complete overhaul of a city. Planning, financing, and logistical preparations begin years in advance. Organized lobbying and competition to become the designated host city start years before that.

Figure 8.1 The Grand Palais, Paris, built for the 1900 Universal Exposition. This is also where the 681 entries for the Centre Pompidou design competition were exhibited in July 1977, including the winning proposal by Rogers+Piano.

Cities know that they will benefit most from hosting international events not through temporary boosts in tourism or employment, but through permanent infrastructure improvements. Airports, roadways, and other transportation improvements have to be made to accommodate the mass migration of attendees. St. Louis built its first water system for the 1904 fair. At least three cities built their metro lines in anticipation of expositions: Chicago in 1893, Paris in 1900, and Montreal in 1967. Seattle built a downtown monorail in 1962. Then there are the hotel and housing projects. Architecturally, these infrastructure projects often receive the same ambassadorial status as the centerpiece pavilions, as well as some of their experimental flair. Santiago Calatrava's bridge to the fairgrounds of Expo 92 in Seville is a noteworthy example.

Development

Engineers in the mold of Paxton and Eiffel dominated the first era of exposition pavilions. The multiple challenges of long-span structures and rapid construction were beyond the general scope and education of Victorian architects. The historic evolution of exposition pavilions took the design profession by surprise. The town festivals and market day fairs that carried from medieval times to that industrial era had the right commercial basis; they even had the correct take on sideshow amusements. Tradition did not, however, prepare architects for expositions on a global scale.

The positivist ideals of the early fairs communicated an unbounded enthusiasm for technology and the future it promised. This was not only a commercial force, it was also a political motivation. Expositions were frequently targeted at popular unrest and aimed to deflect criticism away from the established order of society. This conservative role was played repeatedly. Before the Great Exhibition of 1851, for example, democratic reforms had been rejected three times in British parliament; there were protests in the streets, arrests, and shootings. British authorities thought fearfully about the French Revolution and the Reign of Terror. American fairs were organized against similar backdrops of social turmoil during cycles of industrial depression from 1870 to the First World War. After wars and during depressions, governments and industry have repeatedly mounted expositions to assure and distract the ordinary citizen.

The second age of pavilions extended from the Paris Exposition Universelle 1900 to the New York World's Fair of 1939. Industry began to turn away from the public venue of world's fairs to concentrate instead on specialized trade shows. The public in turn was less curious about the

Figure 8.2 Moshe Safdi's Habitat Housing for the 1967 Montreal Expo.

constant revelations of industry and remained content with other amusements. World's Fairs were left to focus on popular entertainment for their primary purpose and profits. Spectacles were expected, and amusement zones were emphasized.

By this time architects had reclaimed the upper hand from engineers. Pavilions of the 1893 Columbian Exposition in Chicago and the 1900 Exposition in Paris were plastered to simulate marble and decoratively painted inside; their engineered structures were covered over. In Paris, additions to the Gallerie des Machines included a domed salon heavily embellished with ornament. Adding blasphemy to sacrilege, plans were also proposed to enclose the naked skeleton of the Eiffel Tower or to gild its frame with a decorative finish. Fortunately, the tower was still the personal property of Gustav Eiffel. Similarly, San Francisco's Fair of 1915 is still recognized for the Palace of Fine Arts, but what we see today is a 1967 reconstruction in permanent materials. The original building was done in painted plaster over timber frames. The wartime economy, of course, had something to do with the construction methods, but the considerable opportunity to redevelop 76 blocks of San Francisco only nine years after the earthquake and Great Fire of 1906 eluded the fair's developers (see case study #24 for Lloyd's of London's presence in this story). It is ironic, perhaps, that much of the 1915 Fair was built over rubble fill from the 1906 disaster.

Figure 8.3 Buckminster Fuller's American Pavilion for the 1967 Montreal Expo. Photograph taken in June 1999. The acrylic cladding over the dome burned after a welding accident on May 20, 1976.

Relationships between the architecture of pavilions and the activities of world's fair expositions are rather muddled in this middle period, as were the distinctions between pavilion architecture and engineering. So the second phase of pavilion development is best described as one of theoretical change. By the late 1920s the advent of International Style modernism began to clash with the Beaux-Arts school of Art Nouveau and then Art Deco. Le Corbusier's plan for the 1925 Fair, featuring his Ville Contemporaine, went so far as to advocate the leveling of much of Paris. Mies's precious Barcelona Pavilion was as foreign to the 1929 exposition as Centre Pompidou was to the Paris of 1975; it had to be resurrected and rebuilt later, in 1959. Modernism became a theme only at the Paris 1937 Exhibition *La Vie Moderne*, where Alvar and Aino Aalto's Finnish Pavilion won first prize. The Aalto Modernist pavilion was largely prefabricated in Finland. At the 1939 New York Exposition, Aalto struck again with the Finnish Exhibit.

By the postwar third period of expositions, fascination with technology for its own sake has lost its attractive gloss. Fair themes from the 1958 Brussels Exposition Universelle et Internationale forward highlighted ideals of peace and harmony and increasingly included environmental issues. The Spokane Expo 1974, Celebrating a Fresh New Environment, was the first to claim a straightforward ecological focus, but disenchantment with technology as a utopian dream actually began just as World War II ended, with the nightmares of Hiroshima and Nagasaki.

The 1958 Brussels theme, Building the World at a Human Scale, misrepresented its own motto with a series of modern but decidedly monumental pavilions. The most architecturally successful exposition to follow was undoubtedly the aforementioned Montreal Expo 67, Man and His World. The Montreal fair succeeded where Brussels did not, taking human scale as the starting point, even for its logo of stick figure couples forming a circle of unity. Buckminster Fuller finally was given a stage there for his presentation on peace through technology and constructed the world's largest geodesic dome. Frei Otto and Rolf Gutbrod's German Pavilion set the standard for cable-supported tension structures (see case study #14). Equally lacey space frames, including Fuller's dome and the Dutch Pavilion by Eijkelenboom and Middelhoek, were a common theme. The heavy monuments of Brussels were forgotten

True high tech, in its least inhibited form, followed quickly. The $10 billion that poured into Osaka for Expo 70 for the first Asian universal exhibition found chief architect Kenzo Tange and fellow Metabolist architects Kurakowa and Kiyonori well prepared. Tange's megastructure proposal for a giant pavilion to cover the entire fairgrounds under one roof was reduced to a still enormous 354 ft × 1000 ft (107.9 m × 304.8 m) space frame pierced by Taro Okamoto's 230 ft (70.1 m) sculpture *Tower of the Sun* (see case study #25 for the Metabolist influence on the Hong Kong and Shanghai Bank).

Conclusion

The inherently experimental qualities of pavilion architecture did much to promote the tenets of Modern architecture. Prefabrication, factory subassembly, industrial standardization, machine precision tolerances, field assembly work, and all the related technologies were brought to bear. By the time of Expo 67 in Montreal these methods were commonplace and practical, but constant pressures to ephemeralize the technologies and press on to new ones kept design on the cutting edge. Like the exhibits they contained, pavilions continued to attract interest by demonstration of amazing new technologies.

Pavilions, as the following case studies will show, are also recipes for systems integration. Physical integration governs their component size, weight, and assembly detailing. Visual integration is inherent in their programmatic requirement to impress and articulate industrial know-how. Finally, performance integration is vital to the substance of their presentation and the intellectual content of their architecture.

TABLE 8.1 Some of the Major World's Fairs

Year	City	Title	Acres	Countries Represented	Visitors (millions)	Months Open	Theme
1851	London	Great Exhibition	26	28	6.0	4.8	The Industry of All Nations
1855	Paris	Exposition Universelle	165		6.8	6.7	
1862	London	International Exhibition	25		6.2	5.7	
1867	Paris	Exposition Universelle	165	32	11.0	7.2	
1873	Vienna	Weltausstellung Wein	42		7.2	6.2	
1876	Philadelphia	Centennial Exposition	285		10.1	5.3	
1878	Paris	Exposition Universelle	192		16.0	6.5	
1879/80	Sydney	International Exhibition	15	37	1.1	7.0	
1880/81	Melbourne	International Exhibition	63		1.3	7.0	
1883	Amsterdam	Internationale Koloniale	62	28	1.4	6.0	International Colonial Exposition
1885	Antwerp	Exposition Universelle	22	35	3.5	6.0	
1888	Barcelona	Exposición Universal	111		1.2	6.0	
1888	Brussels	Grand Concours	220			6.0	Science and Industry
1888/89	Melbourne	Centennial Exhibition	22		2.0	6.0	
1889	Paris	Exposition Universelle	237		32.2	5.7	The 2nd Olympic Games
1893	Chicago	Columbian Exhibition	686	50	27.5	6.1	World's Columbian Exposition
1894	Antwerp	Exposition Internationale	149		3.0	6.0	
1897	Brussels	Exposition Internationale			6.0		
1900	Paris	Exposition Universelle	267		50.8		
1902	Turin	Arte Decorativa Moderna		13		7.5	
1904	St. Louis	Louisiana Purchase Exposition	1272		19.6	6.1	1904 Olympic Games
1905	Liege	Exposition Universelle	173		6.1		
1906	Milan	Exposizione Internazionale	250		5.5	6.0	
1910	Brussels	Exposition Universelle	217	26	13	7.0	
1911	Turin	Exposizione Internazionale	247		4.0	4.5	
1913	Ghent	Exposition Universelle	309		11.0	7.5	
1915	San Francisco	Panama-Pacific Exposition	635	24	18.9	9.6	Panama Canal
1925	Paris	Arts Décoratif et Industriels	57	18	5.9	6.0	Art Deco
1926	Philadelphia	Sesquicentennial Exposition	275		6.4	6.0	
1929	Barcelona	Exposición Internacional	292			6.0	Industry, Spanish Art, and Sports
1930	Antwerp	Exposition International	171	21	5.2	6.0	Centennial of Independence
1933/34	Chicago	Century of Progress	426		48.8	12.0	Industry, Past and Future
1935	Brussels	Exposition Universelle	371	24	20.0	6.0	
1937	Paris	Exposition Internationale	250	44	34.0	6.0	Art and Practice of Modern Life
1939/40	New York	New York World's Fair	1216	33	44.9	12.0	Building the World of Tomorrow
1958	Brussels	Exposition Universelle	494	44	41.4	6.0	Building the World on a Human Scale
1962	Seattle	21st Century Exhibition	74		9.6	6.0	Century 21: Life in the Space Age
1964/65	New York	New York World's Fair	646	24	51.6	12.0	A Millennium of Progress
1967	Montreal	Universal Exhibition	1000	60	50.3	6.0	Man and His World
1968	San Antonio	Hemisphere	92			6.0	
1970	Osaka	Japan World Exhibition	865	38	64.2	6.0	Progress and Harmony for Mankind
1974	Spokane	Expo '74	100	18	5.2	6.0	Celebrating a Fresh, New Environment
1982	Knoxville	International Energy Exposition	70	21	11.1	6.0	Energy Turns the World
1986	Vancouver	173	54	22.0	4.5		
1992	Seville	Universal Exposition	415	108	40.0	5.0	The Era of Discoveries
1998	Lisbon	Expo '98	18	146	15.0	4.0	The Ocean—A Heritage for the Future
2000	Hanover	Expo 2000	400	170	17.2	4.0	Man, Nature, Technology

14

OLYMPIC STADIUM, 1966–1972

Munich, Germany
BEHNISCH & PARTNERS WITH FREI OTTO

DESCRIPTION

This stadium complex for the 1972 Summer Olympics in Munich, Germany, exemplifies the integration of site and structure. Undulating roofs and equally dramatically sculpted earthscapes unify the setting. Visitors and competitors alike are provided with a sophisticated series of experiences both inside the event halls and out among its park setting.

As a pavilion, Olympiapark sets several keynotes. The tension structure and translucent skin were revolutionary and remain visually and technically impressive today. Architects Behnisch & Partners make a strong favorable statement about the host country and its capabilities. Built on an abandoned airfield covered with piles of rubble from the war, the project reclaimed a significant site in urban Munich. And after serving brief duty for the Olympics, the entire complex has been put to permanent use as a sports stadium and well-visited park.

Figure 8.4   Overview of Olympic Stadium. (Photograph courtesy of Architekten Behnisch & Partners.)

TABLE 8.2 Fact Sheet

Project	**Building Name**	Olympic Stadium
	Client	City of Munich
	City	Munich, Bavaria, Germany
	Lat/Long/Elev	48.17 N 11.56 E, 1744 ft (162 m)
Team	**Architect**	Behnisch & Partners, Stuttgart
	Engineer	Frei Otto; Leonhardt + Andrä
	Landscape	Günther Grzimek
	Graphics	Otl Aicher
General	**Time Line**	Competition awarded October 13, 1966. Construction: 1968 to 1972.
	Floor Area	Size of acrylic roof: 915,000 ft² (85,100 m²)
	Occupants	Capacity: 69,216 seated, 11,800 standing, 100 wheelchair spaces.
	Cost	$26,059,375 excluding land. Roof over the Stadium, Sports Arena, and Swimming Arena, including suspended ceilings, $43,750,000. Landscaping entire site, including artificial lake, $28,696,875.
	Costs in 1995 US$	Stadium only, $95,1 million. Tension roofs, $159.7 million. Landscape, $104.7 million.
	Stories	One, plus utilities under seating and connecting underground service roads.
	Plan	Earthscaped and irregular.
Site	**Site Description**	Spiridon-Louis-Ring Road, Munich, Germany. Abandoned 1930s airstrip located 3 miles north of central city. There are 700 acres (280 hectares) in the entire Olympic complex.
	Parking, Cars	8000.
Structure	**Foundation**	Concrete pilings providing gravity load reactions to tension structure.
	Vertical Members	Tapering tubular steel masts up to 230 ft (70 m) high, 9 ft (2.7 m) diameter and 3 in. (76 mm) wall thickness.
	Horizontal Spans	Cable tension structure of saddle-type nets.
Envelope	**Glass and Glazing**	Reflective bronze-tint acrylic panels averaging 32 ft² (3 m²) by 1 in. (25 mm) thick.
	Cladding	Sports Hall and Swimming Hall are enclosed under cable roof by glass walls.
HVAC	**Equipment**	Physical plant located off-site.
	Cooling Type	Fan coil.
	Distribution	Hydronic.
	Duct Type	Concealed.
	Vertical Chases	None.
Interior	**Partitions**	None.
	Finishes	None.
	Vertical Circulation	Stairs.
	Furniture	Fiberglass seats.
	Lighting	Stadium.

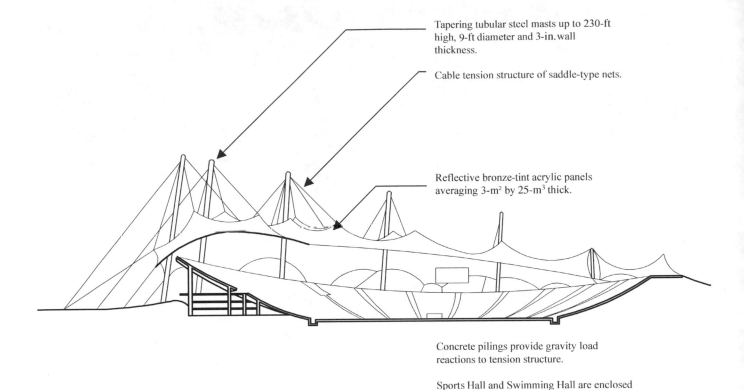

Tapering tubular steel masts up to 230-ft high, 9-ft diameter and 3-in. wall thickness.

Cable tension structure of saddle-type nets.

Reflective bronze-tint acrylic panels averaging 3-m² by 25-m³ thick.

Concrete pilings provide gravity load reactions to tension structure.

Sports Hall and Swimming Hall are enclosed under cable roof by glass walls.

Physical plant located off-site.

Figure 8.5 Anatomical section.

PROGRAM

Client

The Olympic Stadium was a project for the West German government and the 20th Olympic Games. Willi Daume was the West German National Olympic Committee president. Architects Günter Behnisch & Partners, following the program established by Daume, proposed a dramatic reversal of what Germany had shown the world when Hitler's Nazis ruled at the 1936 Olympics. The design featured almost 1 million ft² (92,865 m²) of undulating canopy on a 3 million ft² (68.9 acre or 27.5 hectare) site of green hills and a placid lake. Behnisch's scheme was championed by Egon Eiermann, chairman of the competition jury. Eiermann believed that the design was an expression of the political and intellectual reorientation of Germany in the 1960s. It helped matters that Frei Otto had completed the acclaimed German Pavilion at Expo 67 in Montreal with architect Rolf Gutbrod. Though the Montreal cable structure was much smaller, it proved the feasibility of the concept. Behnisch's proposal would construct the largest self-supporting roof in the world at that time.

Brief

Functional requirements of the competition called for a stadium of 80,000 seats, a smaller enclosed sports hall, and a swimming hall. Other facilities for the competitions included a warm-up arena and an enclosed workout facility. In addition, an Olympic Village complex was to provide 3000 living units and support functions. These facilities were to be of permanent quality and convertible to public use and parkland after the three-week Olympic games. Thematically, the competition used the motto "Olympics in the Green."

Site

When the International Olympic Committee awarded the 1972 Olympic Games to Munich in 1966, the city had no large sports arenas. Previous planning, however, had already selected the best site for the new facility, an empty tract of land known as the Oberwiesenfeld just three miles north of central Munich.

The 700 acre setting was the site of a 1930s airfield. A former drill ground of the Bavarian Royal Army, it was also the site of Munich's first civil airport. Abandoned

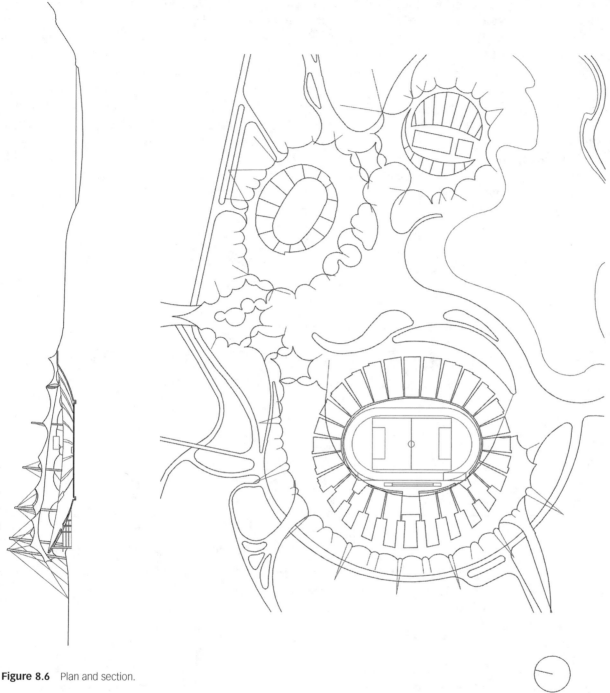

Figure 8.6 Plan and section.

before the war, it had been used as a dump yard for the rubble of ruined buildings afterward. The site is divided twice by slices from east to west. First, a major roadway bisects the land fairly neatly in two. The northern half was used for the Olympic Village and later converted to housing and dormitories. The southern half contains the stadium complex and is divided by a second geographic slice, the Nymphenburg Canal. The other key physical features of the site were a 4,200 ft long and 200 ft high (1300 m × 60 m) hill of building debris and a 984 ft (300 m) tall broadcast tower.

Climate

Munich lies at about 1,744 ft (162 m) altitude on the upper Bavarian plains. To the south, the Danube River drains the Black Forest highlands from the Swiss and French borders to Munich. The Isar River makes an 8 mi (14 km) path through the city. Overall, Munich has a continental climate with mild summers and cold winters. The city is 30 mi (50 km) north of the Alps and 86 mi (140 km) north of Garmisch, site of the 1936 Winter Olympics and Germany's highest mountain, the Zugspitze (9,730 ft or 2,966 m).

The proximity of the Alps has a strong influence on Munich's climate. Prevailing winds from the SE and SW loose their moisture as they cross the mountains, bringing warm breezes, known as Föhn, to Munich with spectacular clear weather and panoramic views of the mountains. When Föhn conditions dominate, unseasonably warm temperatures can occur in any season. Fortunately, this happens most commonly in autumn and winter and is quite rare in summer.

An opposite climate condition, Alpenstau (or Stau), is more common in spring and summer. This condition comes with NE and NW frontal movements that get trapped against the mountains and can lead to extensive rain or heavy snow, accompanied by unseasonably cold temperatures.

The outdoor setting of the Olympic stadium and the summer schedule of the competitions were well suited to the Munich weather. The average daily temperature in July ranges from a morning low of 54°F to an afternoon high of 72°F. An average of five days with some rainfall are expected in each of the summer months. Summer days are quite long at this latitude, with 15 hours from sunrise to sunset and more than 250 hours per month of sun. Winter, in contrast, has days about 8 hours long with about 50 hours of sun per month.

Despite the temperate weather, the design of a cable net roof for this application had to address two critical factors: wind and snow. Freezing rain, snow, or hail falls an average of 75 days per year in Munich, and wind gushes can exceed 40 knots during stormy weather. Heavy snow and ice accumulations on the unheated roof could impose dangerous structural loads.

TABLE 8.3   Normal Climate Data for Munich, Germany

		Jan.	Feb.	Mar.	Apr.	May	June	July	Aug.	Sept.	Oct.	Nov.	Dec.	Year
Temperature	Degree-Days Heating	1073	937	780	612	347	188	92	100	236	532	810	1006	6701
	Degree-Days Cooling	0	0	0	0	1	16	51	50	9	0	0	0	130
	Extreme High	63	70	74	80	86	93	97	95	86	79	66	69	97
	Normal High	36	38	48	53	63	68	72	73	66	55	44	38	55
	Normal Average	30	32	40	45	54	59	64	63	57	48	38	33	47
	Normal Low	24	25	32	36	44	50	54	54	48	40	32	27	39
	Extreme Low	-16	-9	4	21	27	36	39	39	32	21	6	-6	-16
Humidity	Dew Point	26	26	32	35	44	50	53	53	49	42	33	28	39
	Max % RH	88	90	87	86	84	85	84	89	91	92	90	89	88
	Min % RH	80	74	62	57	55	58	55	55	61	71	80	81	66
	% Days with Rain	47	37	51	63	68	73	64	62	55	57	54	49	56
	Rain Inches	2	2	2	3	4	5	5	4	3	2	2	2	37
Sky	% Overcast Days	38	33	29	28	22	22	17	16	19	28	35	37	27
	% Clear Days	10	15	11	11	10	6	12	16	14	12	9	8	11
Wind	Prevailing Direction	WSW	WSW	WSW	WSW	E	WSW	WSW	WSW	WSW	WSW	WSW	WSW	WSW
	Speed, Knots	14	12	12	10	7	9	9	8	9	10	12	13	10
	Percent Calm	5	5	3	2	3	3	4	5	5	5	5	4	4
Days Observed	Rain	14	11	15	19	21	22	19	19	17	17	16	15	205
	Fog	17	19	15	12	11	12	10	15	17	20	18	16	182
	Haze	2	7	7	4	3	2	2	4	5	4	2	1	44
	Snow	15	14	10	8	1	0	0	0	0	1	9	13	69
	Hail	0	0	0	0	0	0	0	0	0	0	0	0	1
	Freezing Rain	2	1	0	0	0	0	0	0	0	0	1	1	5
	Blowing Sand	0	0	0	0	0	0	0	0	0	0	0	0	0

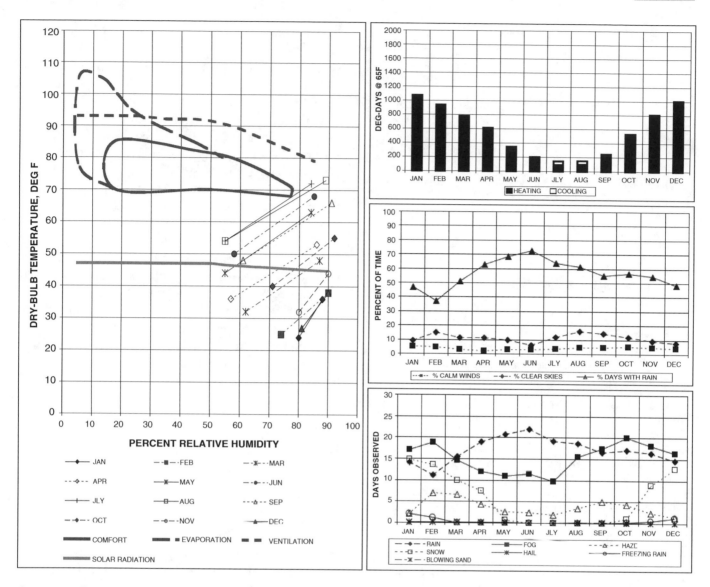

Figure 8.7 Climate analysis graphics.

INTENTION

Design Team

Dr. Günter Behnisch was born in Dresden, Germany, in 1922. He studied architecture at the Technical University of Stuttgart before working in the office of Rolf Gutbrod. He struck out on his own in 1952, and in 1967 he formed Günter Behnisch & Partners. In 1984 he completed a doctorate at the University of Stuttgart and serves on its faculty. Behnisch is a modernist who believes that innovative building techniques inspire architectural possibilities.

Dr. Frei Otto was born in Siegmar, Germany, in 1925. Both of his parents were sculptors and activists in labor unions. He developed an interest in gliders and model

building at an early age. After his schooling, from 1931 to 1943, he served as a pilot in World War II but spent most of the war designing structures for the French as a prisoner of war. From 1948 to 1950 he studied architecture at the Technical University of Berlin. After graduation he studied for two months in the United States at the University of Virginia before working in the New York office of Fred Severud. In Severud's office Otto participated in the design of the State Fair Arena in Raleigh, North Carolina, which had the largest cable net roof ever constructed at that time. This experience led to the publication of his doctoral thesis, *Das Haengende Dach* (The Suspended Roof) in 1953. In 1952 he founded a studio in Zehlendorf, and in 1957 founded the Developmental Center for

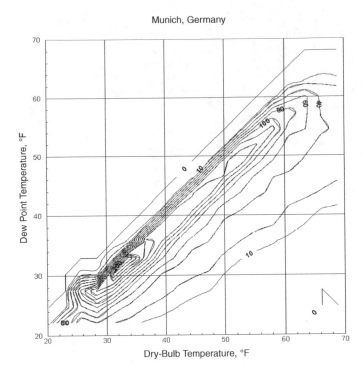

Munich, Germany

Figure 8.8 Bin data distributions for Munich, Germany. Concentric areas of graph indicate the number of hours per year that weather conditions normally occur in this climate. Similar to elevation readings on topographic maps, highest frequency occurrences of weather are at the center peaks of the graph. (Data sources: *Engineering Weather Data, typical meteorological year (TMY) data from the National Climatic Data Center, and the* ASHRAE Weather Data Viewer *from the American Society of Heating, Refrigerating and Air-Conditioning Engineers.*)

Lightweight Construction in Berlin. Hampered by the absence of a durable fabric membrane material, Otto focused on theoretical development and education. He developed his talents for developing lightweight tensile structures and pioneered scale model and computer based simulation techniques for their design. In 1964 he transferred his activities to the Institute for Lightweight Structures in Stuttgart. Frei Otto works largely in collaboration with other architects, serving as a specialist on lightweight construction.

Philosophy

Otto exhibits both rational constructionist design logic and a romantic affinity to organic forms. Since 1972 he has studied the mimicry of biological structures, a pursuit that parallels the interests of Buckminster Fuller and, more particularly, of D'Arcy Wentworth Thompson (*On Growth and Form,* 1917), the British biologist (1860–1948) who wrote about self-organizing form before the concept of self-organization was ever developed.

INTENTIONS

Behnisch & Partners submitted the design proposal and were awarded the competition before Frei Otto was involved with the project. After the firm encountered several difficulties in resolving the structural scheme for the vast roof however, Frei Otto and Leonhardt & Andrä were added to the team. The general intention was to provide a low, undulating roof form that merged with the site topography and to construct a sports complex that would become a series of park pavilions after the Olympics.

Two concepts shaped the general intentions. The first was Behnisch & Partners' maturity from an early practice involved primarily with prefabricated industrialized construction of academic buildings to a richer and more contextually responsive architecture. The evolving second concept is what Behnisch refers to as "situation architecture," which he defines as bringing together the constellations of forces that make up the design problem and expressing them as visible objects. As the culmination of these ideas, the Olympic Park became, in Behnisch's words, "a metaphor for an open, modern society."

CRITICAL TECHNICAL ISSUES

Inherent

A stadium of Olympic importance must respond with corresponding attention to the primary functions it hosts. Orientation to sun and wind have to ensure equitable outdoor conditions for all competitors. The stadium itself must accommodate hundreds of thousands of spectators, most of them visitors to the city. Traffic, parking, circulation, site lines to the playing field, exterior event lighting, and safety concerns such as ease of egress in an emergency—all these and many similar programmatic factors are underscored by the international scope of the Olympic events that occur here.

The 20th Olympic Games of 1972 were to be conducted from August 26 to September 11, hosting 7123 athletes from 121 countries. They would participate in 23 different sports featured in 195 events. There were 600 medals to be awarded.

Special circumstances also influenced design thinking. Two questions dominated the work at Munich. The first issue that arose was speed of construction—deadlines were absolute and the time line for developing 32 million ft^2 (735 acres or 294 hectares) of site (including the Olympic Village) was short. Speed of construction and the risk of delays would have to be considered. Second, what would happen to the complex after the Olympics? Given the costs associated with such a grand occasion and the extensive facilities that would remain, their future use had to be designed for. A temporary structure would be insufficient, and a monumental one would be a perpetual burden.

A third consideration emerged later with the requirements of broadcast color television. The first live coverage of the Olympics, as well as the first satellite relay color broadcast, was transmitted worldwide from the Tokyo Olympics in October 1964. By then, color television had become the standard and had achieved considerable market penetration. Television revenue, in only its third Olympic showing, provided US$17.62 million (US$64.31 million in 1995 dollars, but still a small amount as compared with the US$894 million already contracted for the 2008 Summer Olympics). Television would have its say. As a media event, the Games would also be host to 4587 journalists from around the world.

Contextual

Like most events of global proportions, the 1972 Olympics presented Munich with an opportunity to overhaul its infrastructure. Not only would the existing site be reclaimed, it had to be reconnected to the city. Freeway and subway systems were extended, and new bus routes were established.

Aside from urban reintegration, the design team also had to consider the impact of broadcast television requirements for lighting, shadow reduction, and acoustics. Finally, the huge roof would produce mass amounts of rainwater runoff that had to be retained on-site. Other than the requirement of very conservative foundations for the innovative structure, there was no mention of special considerations in the building code.

Intentional

To realize his metaphor for an open and modern society and to express all the essentials of forces acting on the problem, Behnisch decided on a soft, sculptural treatment for both the enclosure and the reclaimed topography of the site. This was a direct resistance to monumental forms. It led him to burrow the stadiums into the site and then to mold the roof forms into extensions of the new earthworks.

Cable net structures posed a number of direct challenges. First, accumulated snow loads can lead to leaks or structural failure. This had been dealt with in Montreal, at Otto's German Pavilion of 1976, by placing large fans under the canopy to melt snow off the top. Second, although fiberglass and Teflon-coated fabrics came into use shortly after, there was no good solution at that time for a permanent canopy material. Canvas was a decidedly

temporary material. Finally, there were acoustical problems. Tensioned fabric is reflective of sound energy and can cause noise defects. The doubly curved contours of tensile structures are particularly susceptible to focusing sound.

APPROPRIATE SYSTEMS

Precedent

Frei Otto's first major project, the German Pavilion at Montreal Expo 67 (with Rolf Gutbrods and Leonhardt & Andrä), served as the technical precedent for the Munich Olympics. At Montreal, the 86,000 ft^2 (7,986 m^2) structure was much more modest than its Munich successor, but it served to establish the feasibility of what would, at Munich, become the largest cable-supported roof of its time.

The mast-supported net at Montreal was made of single strands of 0.47 in. (12 mm) cable clamped into a 20 in. (508 mm) grid mesh. It was prefabricated in Germany in 45 ft (13.7 m) wide strips. Binding steel ropes of 3, 5, and 6.5 in. (76, 127, and 165 mm) were used to tie the structure together and hold it down. For a canopy, Otto used a vinyl-coated canvas suspended 20 in. below the cable net.

Site

Behnisch exploited the site conditions by sculpting the sporting arenas into the ground and mounding around them. An existing canal was widened into a lake feature and bordered by an open air amphitheater. Arenas were located between the six-lane roadway and the new lake. Their footprints are expressed as the rounded shapes of stadium seating. The sculpted curvature is accented by the fluid form of the lake and winding pedestrian pathways everywhere. The low, hovering roof nets repeat these curves in section. Except for the masts, guy wires, and suspension cables, the site is devoid of straight lines.

Across the lake from the arenas, the rubble of 66 World War II bombings was piled up and covered over. The resulting hill provides a viewpoint across the complex and to the flat topography of central Munich. It also serves as a historic landmark and preserves something of the heritage of the site. Its visual appeal has made it a popular gathering place. At the base of the mountain, against the lake, is a small amphitheater.

The low, curving masses and mounded landscape allowed Behnisch to avoid monumental masses. It is difficult to see the buildings without thinking of them as integral with the site. To mold the form of the roof construction into the site and to transform the abandoned dumping ground into a park, 3.3 million yd^3 (2.5 million m^3) of earth were moved and 222,000 yd^3 (170,000 m^3) of concrete were placed.

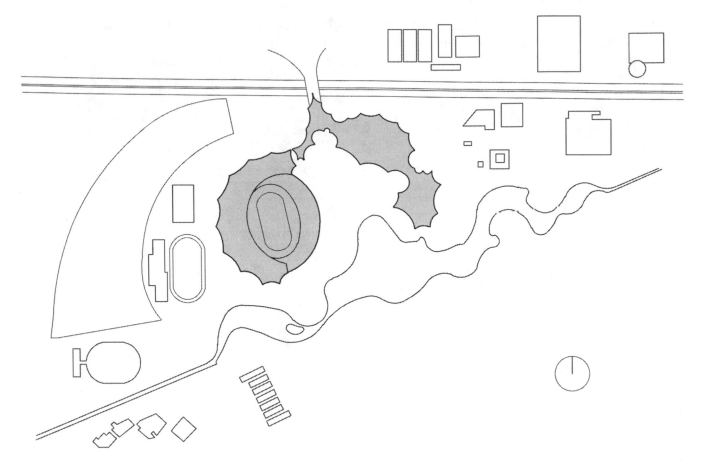

Figure 8.9   Site plan of the Olympic Park.

The 113,189 ft² (34,500 m²) main stadium was placed toward the center of the site, just west of the 8,000 car parking area. It connects to outlying practice stadiums and locker rooms via underground tunnels that lead directly to the playing field. To the north is the 71,358 ft² (21,750 m²) sports arena, and to the east is the 39,042 ft² (11,900 m²) swimming hall. There are 19,685 ft² (6,000 m²) of connecting roof sections that unify the structures into one continuous canopy, but the sports arena and the swimming hall have enclosing sidewalls as well as the roof.

Structure

The roof grid over the main stadium is formed by nine saddle-shaped nets of 1.0 in. (25 mm) steel cables spaced in a 30 in. (762 mm) square grid. The saddles span up to 213 ft (65 m) and reach a maximum height of 190 ft (58 m). The nets are supported over the seating areas by eight tapering masts behind the stadium, ranging from 165 to 262 ft (50.0 to 70.0 m) high. Smaller bow-shaped nets connect the larger membranes and wrap around the supporting masts. Each of the nine tensile roof modules over the main stadium is lifted by two 4.7 in. (120 mm) cables from the mast tops and propped up by two smaller understaying masts called "air supports."

The cable nets are doubly curved. There are no two points where a straight line could be drawn on their surface. The resulting double-curved saddle shape prevents the canopies from easily fluttering in the wind.

Where the nine canopies join in a continuous edge along the west edge of the playing field, a 1443 ft (440 m) long floating eave forms a sweeping crescent-shaped catenary arch of ten cables, each 4.7 in. (120 mm) in diameter. Each of these ten cables consists in turn of seven wires with 55 strands each. An additional 3.2 in. (81 mm) periphery cable is sheathed into the leading edge of the roof net. Guy connections from the masts to supporting concrete piers are 4.7 in. cable. The total length of steel cable in the complex exceeds 255 mi (408 km). The masts themselves are up to 11.5 ft (3.5 m) in diameter and have walls as thick as 3 in. (75 mm). The 262 ft (80 m) high Swimming Hall mast has an inspection hatch at the peak, where workers can climb through the hollow masts and check the integrity of the cable connection.

Tension loads in the cable net are as much as 5000 tons. The foundation design was originally intended to consist of prestressed anchors. Local code officials, however, insisted on more conservative gravity piers to provide stability by their sheer weight. In some cases these are as much as 60 ft deep and 20 ft wide (18.3 × 6.1 m), about the size of a small house. These huge foundations were required to resist the tremendous tensile stresses in the cable network and the live loads imposed by winds across and under the open structures. Compressive footings were needed under the mast supports, and earth anchors were called for where restraining cables kept the masts in place by tension.

Intersection points of the cable pairs were clamped at the factory with aluminum joints at exactly 750 mm (2.5 ft) centers under controlled levels of prestress. This ensured accurate and rapid field construction. The close cable spacing even saved the need for scaffolding. Passing cable pairs were joined at the aluminum clamps with one bolt, resulting in a rotating joint. The cable nets were completely assembled on the ground and then hoisted into position. Thereafter the geometry and stresses in the cables were adjusted until the final form was attained.

Development of the roof structure was worked out by Otto with Leonhardt & Andrä. The computational work was usually done manually. Otto started, however, with physical models. Beginning with 1:125-scale constructions, Otto measured the mechanical forces in individual wires of the net with gauges he had developed at the Institute for Lightweight Structures and used for the Montreal temporary pavilion. Several fixed cameras were used to record the loaded and unloaded shape of the model for comparative measurements. These experiments were followed by the development of larger models and more detailed investigations, with hand calculations for verification. Eventually, Otto brought in Professors Linkwitz and Argyris, who had developed computer programs to calculate the exact geometry of the cable nets just in time to prove them on the Munich roof. Finally, workshop drawings were produced at a scale of 1:10. This required 41,000 ft² (3,800 m²) of drawings for the entire roof.

Stadium seating and the supporting structure make up the rest of the construction. These are poured-in-place concrete slab and walls with precast beams forming the stairs and terraced seating levels.

Envelope

Originally, the designers intended to hang a canvas fabric below the cable net, just as Otto had done in Montreal. As television companies and their technical production teams became involved, however, the issue of excessive contrast for broadcast photography suggested modification. In the end, bronze-tinted acrylic plastic panels were used. These were installed in 2.9 m × 2.9 m (9.5 ft²) panels above the cable wires. Connections between the panels had to allow for thermal expansion and structural movement of up to 1.0 m (39.4 in.) deflection under heavy

Figure 8.10 Acrylic panel canopy. *(Photograph courtesy of Architekten Behnisch & Partners.)*

wind loads. Finally, a neoprene gasket membrane was used and attached to the edges of each acrylic panel with continuous clamping strips. Although unsightly and not as pure as a true translucent canopy, the opaque connections were too small to create contrast glare against the transparent plastic panels and too fine to cast shadows onto the playing field.

Acrylic panels were attached to the supporting net at the intersection points of the cables. A neoprene pedestal was attached to the fixing bolt in each cable clamp. Drilled holes in the acrylic panels were bolted to the top of the pedestal and sealed. Because of the irregular geometry of the net, panels sometimes overlapped the cable grid at varying angles, but overall the two grids matched fairly well.

Mechanical

Buried under stadium seating in the enclosed sports hall and the swimming pavilion are 49 air-handling units. These are served with hot and cold water from a central plant located on the other half of the site, north of the freeway. In addition, a 19 km (62,000 ft) network of hot water piping was buried 25 cm (9.8 in.) below the grass

Figure 8.11 Overview of Olympic Park.

surface of the stadium playing field so that it would be usable year round.

Lighting and loudspeaker hardware are mounted in clusters suspended below the cable net. Freestanding poles and fixtures were largely eliminated.

Interior

Although there are few interior considerations for the stadiums, there were several items that had to be incorporated into the design. Refreshment stands, information kiosks, and other matching appointments were all designed as site furniture, using elements sympathetic with the architecture.

TECHNICAL INTEGRATION HIGHLIGHTS

Physical

- Circulation up and down the stadium seating is shortened by berming the grandstands into the topography and entering the bleachers at half level
- Cut and fill from the canal, where it was expanded to create the lake, was used on site to create the grass covered mountain over the piles of rubble.

Visual

- The form of the cable roof embraces the topography and greenery of the site.

- Structural mass and mechanical hardware are bermed into the ground.

Performance

- Otto's dominant roof is the structural, solar, aerodynamic, hydrologic, luminous, and acoustic form of the complex.
- The lightweight cable structure was quickly and accurately assembled.
- Bronze tinting of the glazing helped reduce heat gain and glare without casting shadows as a canvas canopy would have.
- Open-walled pavilions are naturally ventilated and resistant to storm winds.
- Rainwater is channeled by the shapes of the roof and directed toward the lake.

DISCUSSION

From wasteland to parkland, from canal to lake, and from rubble to pavilion, the transformation of Oberwiesenfeld into an Olympic complex was rapid, thorough, and convincing. The single gesture of an undulating roof married into the undulating relief of the sculpted site produces a harmonious and delightful setting for the festivities. Its ongoing operation has also been a complete success.

15

INSTITUT DU MONDE ARABE, 1981–1989

Paris, France
JEAN NOUVEL

DESCRIPTION

Between two cultures, two landscapes, and two urban fabrics, Jean Nouvel interposes a building of dialectics. A rectangular shape meets a curved one; there is a side reflecting Arab culture and another for Paris; a screened elevation and a shuttered one; a transparent tower and a colonnaded underground.

The Arab World Institute, or Institut du Monde Arabe, is a pavilion of culture. It plays the ambassadorial role of representing Arab culture in Paris, addressing not only French citizens and tourists, but also a large number of ethnic Arab citizens from the former French colonies in Algeria and sub-Saharan Africa, who began settling in France after 1960. In 1998 there were 4 million Muslims living in France, and Islam was second in membership only to the Catholic church.

Figure 8.12 South elevation of IMA with its screen wall of light-sensitive diaphragms.

TABLE 8.4   Fact Sheet

Project	**Building Name**	Institut du Monde Arabe (IMA), the Arab World Institute
	Client	Institut du Monde Arabe
	City	Paris, France
	Lat/Long/Elev	48.85 N 02.36 E, 315 ft (96 m)
Team	**Architect**	Jean Nouvel-Architecture Studio
	Engineer	Louis Gruittet
	Acoustics	M. Armagnac
	Mechanical	Setec
	Lighting	Light Design
	Signs/Graphics	Pierre Martin Jacot
	Diaphragms	Epsi
General	**Time Line**	Competition awarded November 1981; design: 1985–86; construction: 1987–89.
	Floor Area	As built, the center contains about 286,965 ft^2 (26,660 m^2).
	Cost	Originally budgeted at FF 50.3 million or about US$ 10.1 million ($32/ft^2). The final cost was reported at FF 389.5 million or US$77.9 million ($270/ft^2).
	1995 US$ Cost	$100.4 million or $350/ft^2.
	Stories	Ten levels reaching 105 ft (31.9 m).
	Plan	Rectangular plan compressed against a curving street and split by a narrow passage to a central courtyard.
Site	**Site Description**	Central Paris, on the left back of the Seine, with a view of Notre Dame de Paris, just down the river. IMA borders historical Paris and is adjacent to the modern urban fabric to the southeast, beginning with the university building at Jussieu.
	Parking, Cars	150 below grade.
Structure	**Foundation**	Concrete with below-grade basements.
	Vertical Members	Steel and concrete.
	Horizontal Spans	Steel.
Envelope	**Glass and Glazing**	Insulated glass with silk-screened silhouette on northeast. Insulated glass with active sunscreen diaphragms to southwest. Insulated glass with translucent marble panel screen at courtyard.
	Skylights	Extensive glass skylights.
	Cladding	Mostly glass.
	Roof	Roof terrace at restaurant level.
HVAC	**Equipment**	Not published.
	Cooling Type	Not published.
	Distribution	Ducted through ceiling layers.
	Duct Type	Not published.
	Vertical Chases	Service core at east end of towers.
Interior	**Partitions**	Translucent glass.
	Finishes	Bitumen floor in auditorium, exposed steel structure, glass.
	Vertical Circulation	Glass-cage elevators and open stairs.
	Furniture	Custom-built display cases in steel and tempered glass.
	Lighting	Recessed.

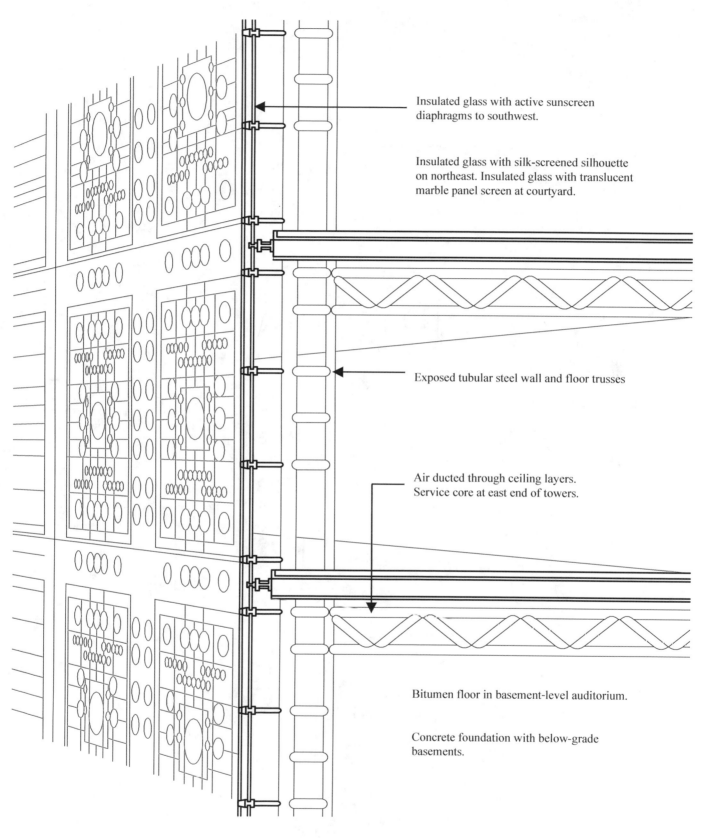

Insulated glass with active sunscreen diaphragms to southwest.

Insulated glass with silk-screened silhouette on northeast. Insulated glass with translucent marble panel screen at courtyard.

Exposed tubular steel wall and floor trusses

Air ducted through ceiling layers. Service core at east end of towers.

Bitumen floor in basement-level auditorium.

Concrete foundation with below-grade basements.

Figure 8.13 Anatomical section.

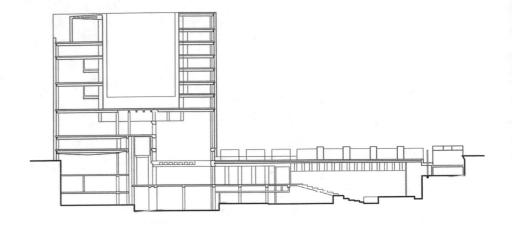

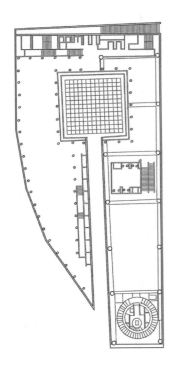

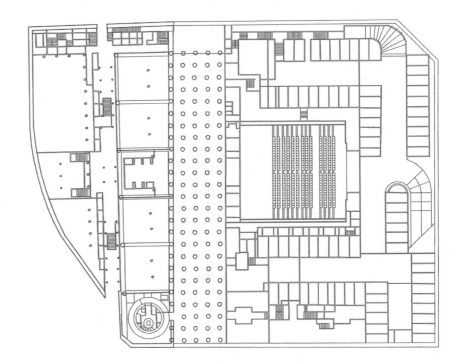

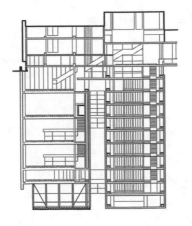

Figure 8.14 Plan and section.

PROGRAM

Client

The Institut du Monde Arabe is a collaborative cultural mission of France and several Arab countries. Its mission is to promote commerce and cultural relationships between the parties and to represent Arab culture to the French populace. The center hosts more than one million visitors per year and features a museum, a library for browsing and cultural research, an events auditorium, and a restaurant. France paid half of the project costs from then-President François Mitterand's socially enthusiastic *Grands Travaux* coffers. Several participating Arab nations paid the other half.

Mitterand began his FF15 billion (about US$3.0 billion) program of modern monuments intending to reclaim a central role for France in art, politics, and the world economy at the end of the twentieth century. In addition to the IMA, works included the Grande Arche de la Défense, Parc de la Villette, the Pyramid in the Grand Carré of the renovated Louvre, the Opéra de la Bastille, and the Bibliothèque de France. This series of costly building projects gained widespread endorsement, even though the individual buildings were not always met with popular approval.

TABLE 8.5 Approximate Space Allocation in the IMA Multiuse Cultural Center

Space Inventory	Areas		Percent of Total Areas		
Description	ft²	m²	Occupied	Interior	Planned
Museum	47,361	4,400	43%	25%	17%
Library	20,451	1,900	19%	11%	7%
Auditorium	8,181	760	7%	4%	3%
Offices	23,142	2,150	21%	12%	8%
Conference	4,628	430	4%	2%	2%
Audiovisual	1,722	160			
Restaurant	6,458	600	6%	3%	2%
Terraces	62,215	5,780			22%
Parking	36,059	3,350			13%
Plant and Circulation	78,469	7,290		42%	27%
Occupied	110,222	10,240			
Interior	188,691	17,530			
Planned	286,965	26,660			

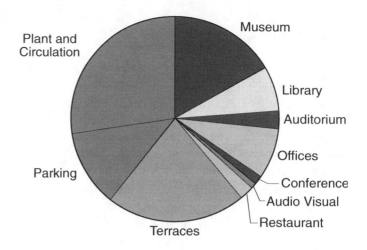

Figure 8.15 Space allocation graphic.

Brief

The competition brief was simple: Following the mission of the foundation, the architects were charged with developing a program to "encourage a knowledge and understanding in France of the Arab world—its language, civilization, and development." The public space was to include 54,000 ft² (5,000 m²) of museum display, a 100,000-volume library, an auditorium, a café, and a reception area. Additional areas for the foundation would provide offices, meeting rooms, and support facilities. An initial budget of FF 50.3 million (about US$ 10.1 million) was set for a program area of 318,600 ft² (29,600 m²).

Site

The central Paris location provided for the IMA is on the left bank of the Seine with a direct view of Notre Dame Cathedral and Île Saint-Louis to the immediate west. It is within walking distance of its French culture center equivalent, Centre Pompidou (see case study #22). The building site lies between the river at the Pont de Sully (bridge) and the university buildings to the southeast. It is, in fact, tucked into the northwest corner of the Université de Jussieu. To the west is Faubourg St. Germain and the Latin Quarter cafes where modern literature and art were incubated in the 1920s. To the east and south are the university and a part of Paris more reflective of the 1960s.

The meandering Seine flows from east to west at this point along the left bank (facing downstream). The water is about 30 ft (9.1 m) below the street, bordered by stone-cobbled quays and busy with *bateaux-mouches* tourist boats. The Pont de Sully crosses the river just in front of the site. Quay St. Bernard meets St. Germain at the head of the bridge and continues between the river and the IMA across the northern edge of the site.

Climate

Central Paris is defined by a circle six miles in radius from the square in front of Notre Dame Cathedral on the Île de la Cité where the city was first settled. It occupies a mere 34 mi² (88 km²) if its two major parks are omitted. The city rests in a level shallow bowl, carved by the Seine over time, and is surrounded by seven hills, the highest of which is Butte de Montmartre, at 423 ft (129 m) above sea level. The outlying ring of hills is still respected as the limits of Paris proper. In recent years, however, the population of the city has dispersed to the suburbs. In 1999 only 2 million of greater Paris's 19 million remained in the central area. Until 1950 the central ring density was about 70,000 people per square mile (27,000 per km²); in recent years it has hovered between 60,000 and 70,000. Paris remains, nonetheless, one of the most densely populated urban centers in the world, at twice the density of Tokyo and three times that of New York or London.

Usually the flat Parisian plain benefits from ocean winds and a wet climate that sweeps and cleanses the atmosphere and disperses pollution. During calm or dry weather, however, the City of Lights and Number 1 tourist attraction in the world can reach pollution concentrations of more than 20 times the normal levels. This is most pronounced when warm weather accelerates the formation of secondary pollutants with heat and ultraviolet energy. The *rentrée* of travelers from the ritual Parisian July vacation is a critical occasion. With more commuters and a decrease in the popularity of mass transit (ridership declined 10 percent from 1995 to 1997), smog is increasingly becoming a factor in the Paris climate.

TABLE 8.6 Normal Climate Data for Paris

		Jan.	Feb.	Mar.	Apr.	May	June	July	Aug.	Sept.	Oct.	Nov.	Dec.	Year
Temperature	Degree-Days Heating	819	714	615	464	260	128	47	43	144	378	617	752	5028
	Degree-Days Cooling	0	0	0	0	10	41	93	93	23	2	0	0	253
	Extreme High	59	68	75	79	87	95	95	99	90	85	79	63	99
	Normal High	43	45	51	57	64	70	75	75	69	59	49	45	59
	Normal Average	39	40	45	50	57	62	67	67	61	53	44	41	52
	Normal Low	34	34	38	42	49	54	58	57	52	46	39	36	45
	Extreme Low	1	10	21	26	32	39	41	43	41	28	21	14	1
Humidity	Dew Point	34	33	37	39	47	52	55	54	52	47	40	36	44
	Max % RH	89	87	87	86	86	86	85	87	91	92	91	89	88
	Min % RH	79	71	65	58	57	58	54	51	59	69	76	81	65
	% Days with Rain	60	46	56	53	53	46	43	40	46	56	53	60	51
	Rain Inches	2	2	2	2	3	2	2	2	2	2	2	2	26
Sky	% Overcast Days	39	32	27	19	19	16	11	9	14	23	29	36	23
	% Clear Days	8	14	12	13	10	8	13	14	14	10	11	8	11
Wind	Prevailing Direction	SW	E	W	NE	NE	W	W	W	W	W	SW	SW	W
	Speed, Knots	12	6	10	9	9	9	9	8	9	9	11	11	9
	Percent Calm	2	3	2	2	2	2	2	2	3	3	2	2	1
Days Observed	Rain	18	14	17	16	16	14	13	12	14	17	16	18	185
	Fog	13	14	10	8	7	6	5	7	10	13	14	13	120
	Haze	0	0	0	#	#	#	#	0	#	0	#	#	1
	Snow	4	4	2	1	#	0	0	0	0	0	1	2	14
	Hail	#	0	#	#	#	#	#	0	0	#	#	#	1
	Freezing Rain	1	1	#	0	0	0	0	0	0	0	#	1	3
	Blowing Sand	0	#	0	0	0	0	0	0	#	#	0	0	#

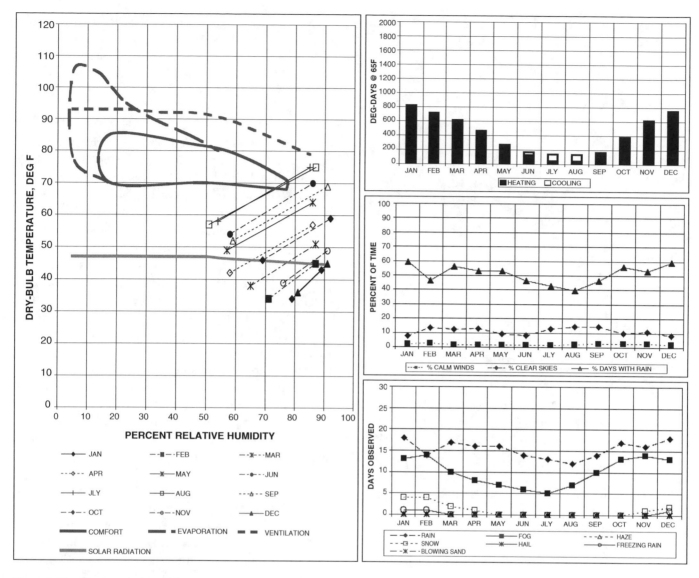

Figure 8.16 Climate analysis graphics.

INTENTION

Design Team

Paris lies at the junction of marine and continental climate regions. So despite the 107 miles (172 kilometers) distance up the Seine to its discharge into the English Channel, Paris enjoys mild, almost maritime weather. This location also makes the weather changeable and moody.

The climate of Paris (48.85N, 02.36E) is remarkably similar to that of coastal Seattle (47.50N, 122.29W). Temperatures range from January's normal high of 43°F and low of 39°F to a July range of 75°F to 58°F. Rainfall is fairly consistent, with about an even chance of rain on any day of the year. Rainfall amounts are comparatively uniform at about 2.0 in. (50 mm) per month. Sky conditions are usually mostly cloudy to overcast. The heavy gray skies of Paris have their own moody name, *la grisaille*.

Born in Fumel, France, Jean Nouvel graduated from the Ecole des Beaux-Arts in 1972, where he studied under Claude Parent and Victor Virilio. He credits them for the basis of his education and for persuading him to forgo Postmodernism and the Modernist orthodoxy of 1970s Paris. He was part of the 1968 student uprising over the quality of modern French life that led to general strikes and ushered in new political ideals. He participated in March 1976, a movement whose participants marched in the streets of Paris and wrote manifestos on architectural issues. Later, Nouvel aligned himself with the radical

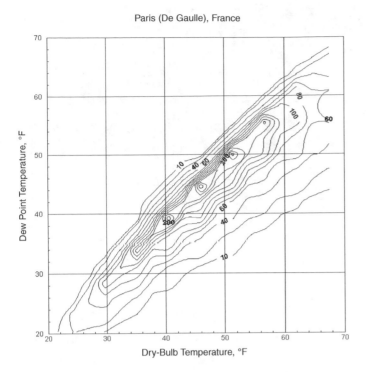

Figure 8.17 Bin data distribution for Paris. Concentric areas of graph indicate the number of hours per year that weather conditions normally occur in this climate. Similar to elevation readings on topographic maps, highest frequency occurrences of weather are at the center peaks of the graph. *(Data sources: Engineering Weather Data, typical meteorological year (TMY) data from the National Climatic Data Center, and the* ASHRAE Weather Data Viewer *from the American Society of Heating, Refrigerating and Air-Conditioning Engineers.)*

group *Syndicat de l'Architecture.* After brief partnerships, Nouvel won the IMA design competition with Lezènes, Soria, and Architecture Studio. That collaboration dissolved, and he assumed the IMA project as Architectures Jean Nouvel.

Philosophy

Jean Nouvel would like to dematerialize architecture, to, as Steven Peterson (writing on Mies for *Inland Architect*) describes it, "eliminate the object as form that obscured the transcendental reality, revealing an infinite universal space, itself unformed, conceived as the void." This idea has a kinship with Buckminster Fuller's goal of technical ephemeralization, but is based on emotional goals more than Fuller's rational pursuits. Nouvel wants technology to do more than express its own function in a Modernist way; he wants it to be directly and emotionally evocative. He wants technology to disappear and leave nothing behind except its magic to silently intervene between inside and out. This is not a pop fiction dream—Nouvel understands the advances in miniaturization and materials that can give the mechanical underpinnings of a building a smaller and smaller face. He can play on the paradoxes of simplicity and complexity. Nor is this belief in transcendent technology a resistance to function—Nouvel believes that buildings have to be real and that architects have to build for today.

Within his idea of a minimalist, transparent, gravity-defying, dematerialized architecture, Nouvel also refers to a tangible fragility and frozen moment-in-time quality that he seeks to evoke. He is fond of photographic and cinemagraphic allusions to the experience of buildings, not just in their temporal quality, but also in their production

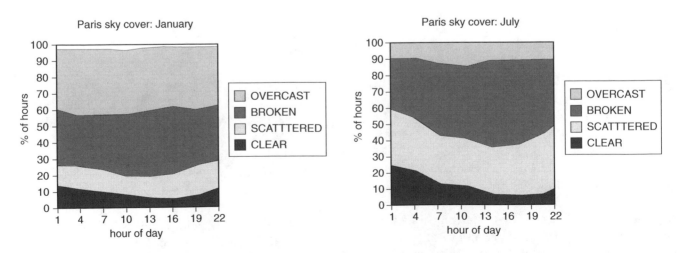

Figure 8.18 Clear, scattered, mostly cloudy, and overcast skies in Paris for January and July.

methods. Here perhaps his personal notions of light also come into play. For Nouvel, light invigorates space with the sense of moment; he compares this to the way Chartres Cathedral is illuminated by a passing sunbeam across its rose window.

Nouvel's urban statements are more grounded in context, and it is possible to regard his work, especially IMA, as urban planning. This aspect is covered in the following discussion of site systems at IMA.

Intent

From a dematerialist philosophy and a cultural program, the design found overlapping territory in the traditional Arab transformation of space through complex geometry. Nouvel intended to make a transparent building and leave its minimalist frame open to reveal only the symbolic and evocative pieces. Among the objects remaining, he injects light, reflection, and mirrored transparency. The objects will float.

CRITICAL TECHNICAL ISSUES

Inherent

Mixed-use buildings are simultaneously challenges of the individual needs of different spaces, their appropriate separation, and the shared functions of the building. The library and the museum pose security constraints, the library has its dead load of book stacks, the café needs services and view. But the noise of the café has to be segregated from the quiet library. The auditorium needs wide egress, but the reception area needs narrow control.

Contextual

As a cultural center, the pavilion would have to represent Arab society sensitively and appropriately. This has traditionally entailed the use of central courtyards, sunscreens, and water features in residences and a central tower in town plans. The aesthetic of vernacular Arab architecture is partly based on an abstraction of matter and space through complex patterns like those that westerners are accustomed to seeing in oriental carpets. By Islamic principle, these patterns avoid images of humans and animals and rely on intricate geometry for composition.

Problems of site context made for external constraints. How would IMA engage so many of the different conditions around it? A river, a street, a university, a cathedral, and a historic skyline all influence the setting.

Intentional

With "technology at the service of emotion," how would Nouvel decide what was Arab and how to portray it, what vocabulary to use, what to evoke? Technically, how would "fragile transparency" be reconciled with museum security? How would solar impacts affect the building environment and its cooling loads? Could art be kept safe from ultraviolet radiation?

APPROPRIATE SYSTEMS

Precedent

Part of the visual vocabulary Nouvel selected for the project is drawn from Arab and Mediterranean traditions. The *moucharabieh* solar screens are only the most obvious of these elements. The Arab influence is combined with the context of central Paris to produce a set of historical precedents for the IMA.

Within the lineage of the architect's work, the IMA represents Nouvel's grand debut. His later work, like the Cartier Headquarters (Paris, 1991) and the Hotel Les Thermes (Dax, France, 1992), demonstrates the continuation of his ideas, but it is equally important to note a building Nouvel wished to distance his work from: Centre Pompidou. For him, the Modernist expression of technology "for its own sake" is passé. While committing to the highest possible level of technology, Nouvel wants to fulfill a different mission than the one played out by High Tech expressionism. Rather than ascribing to functionalist honesty, he pursues technologies that have minimalist form. Rather than articulating "served and servant," Nouvel tends to a more abstract "served and ghostly servant." Technology permeates his buildings, but its image is ephemeralized, vaporous, and misty. He is more interested in the emotional effect of technology working in the space than the shapes of its machines.

Site

Originally, the IMA was intended to cover the entire 1.8 acre (80,000 ft^2 or 7,500 m^2) site. The final design compressed many of the spaces and placed the less manageable ones underground, beneath the plaza. This decision left Nouvel free to choose as to which elements to arrange in the transparent tower and which to bury. It also meant that a large part of the program would have to fit in a small part of the site. Legal and competition requirements limiting the design scheme to the height of surrounding six-story structures implied further constraints on space. The resulting building has a footprint of about 24,000 ft^2 (2,230 m^2), covering only 30 percent of the site.

The complex is divided into two glass structures connected by a brick core mass on the east and separated by an open atrium above the fifth-level courtyard. This courtyard, like its vernacular Arab precedent, filters light

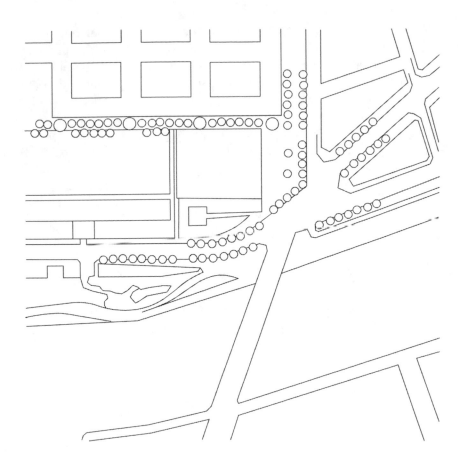

Figure 8.19 Site plan of the Arab World Institute.

softly down to an inner patio. Originally at its center was a fountain of pure mercury. An entry axis to the court ramps down to the northwest to complete the division of the two building wings. The sight line of this entry is aimed directly at Notre Dame Cathedral. Spectacular views from the rooftop café and its terrace are aligned along this same axis to the cathedral and across the river. Centre Pompidou (see case study #22) is visible in the near distance, with Basilique du Sacré Cœur on the hills beyond.

To the southwest of the complex Nouvel reserved a 190 ft × 190 ft (58 m × 58 m) public plaza. This open space politely disassociates the IMA from the university buildings and gives it a separate public approach. The plaza also aligns with a long open expanse of lawn between two rows of classroom blocks to the east. An entry pavilion is set on the west side of the plaza to direct visitors to the south entrance doors under the bright screen wall.

Structure

The primary organizing geometry of the building is a square measuring 9.5 ft (2.9 m) on a side. This is the grid of the large plaza and of the southwest facing screen wall. It is also the module of the structural grid—four incre-

ments equal the 38.1 ft (11.6 m) column bay width across the south block, and the same 9.5 ft is the basic floor-to-floor height.

Three-dimensional steel tube trusses, about 12.0 in. (400 mm) wide, span from column to column of a steel frame and are also used as columns themselves in different places. Outside the west wall of the library tower, which is the most visible side of the building to passing traffic, the truss is exposed and the glass wall is pulled in. Parts of the frame are fire protected and then wrapped in an aluminum skin. Wherever possible, the steel and its bolted connections are left exposed.

In the north tower, the structural grid is broken down to slender columns at 9.5 ft (2.9 m) on center. Floors are flat concrete slabs carried on various steel sections. With suspended ceilings, they form a typical combined thickness of 9.8 in. (248 mm).

Envelope

The Arab Institute's defining architectural feature is its 204.7 × 85.3 ft (62.4 × 26.0 m) southwest façade hung above the recessed ground floor. Between the walls' inside and outside layers of glass are 27,000 electromagnetic irises continually dilating or contracting in response to interior light levels. There are 240 diaphragm assemblies of these irises in 6.9 ft (2.1 m) square panels made of two layers: an outer aluminum plate cut into geometric grilles and an interior layer of several irises. Each diaphragm is a composed pattern of several different irises of varying size. A separate 15.8 in. (40 cm) band of irises wraps around each of the large panels, creating a border geometry. Overall, one large panel and two of the margin widths complete the 9.5 ft (2.9 m) module size of the building. Each iris is controlled by two solenoids. The full open-to-closed range of dilation gives the wall an effective aperture with an opening of between 30 percent and 10 percent.

To the exterior of the diaphragm assemblies is a 20 mm sheet of insulating glass. Behind them is a single pane of 6 mm glass that swings open for maintenance and cleaning. Aluminum glazing frames are heavily expressed across the façade to create visual complexity and multiply the effect of the shutters.

The giant solar screen formed by the diaphragms is a visual reference to traditional Arab sunshades, or *moucharabieh*. These screens are familiar sights in North Africa and the Middle East where they typically provide privacy and view from second-story windows that project onto the street. They came to France from colonial presence in Africa. In traditional construction their latticework grille is formed of wood bobbins turned on a lathe and put together in intricate geometries. Jean Nouvel's interpretation of the screen uses high-tech metal shutters suggesting the mechanical aperture of a camera.

The north and northeast Quay St. Bernard face of the complex addresses the Paris skyline. It is pressed into the curve of the river right up to the street. If the southwest side is given to Arab forms, then the northeast is definitely Paris. To mark this duality with certainty, glass across the river side was silk-screened with a panorama of the old city skyline, leaving a ghostly but identifiable image visible from inside and out, as if it were a shadow or a reflection cast onto the IMA. The 9.5 ft (2.9 m) module of the south tower is also repeated here, but in three vertical and horizontal divisions of 96.6 cm. The wall is covered in one layer of insulated glass and protected by an external *brise soleil* of horizontal slats. This shading device is held in place by stainless steel cables stretched in front of the wall and separated by metal collars between the slats. It is proportioned like a half-drawn Venetian blind. At the top of the building the slats are close together but then are evenly distributed across the wall. Extending above the glass, the slats form a low wall across the roof terrace.

The interior side of the north glass is veiled by a thin mesh fabric shade to diffuse and soften daylight. The multiple shading devices across this exposure address problems of solar geometry—solar orientation of much of the riverside elevation is closer to northeast than true north so

summer mornings can receive direct sun up to about 10 A.M. Even at the west end of the wing where the glass wall faces almost directly north, there is morning and afternoon summer sun to deal with.

Walls surrounding the central courtyard are glazed and then covered with thin translucent slabs of marble. These are held in place with a delicate metal frame and decorative attachment clips at each corner of the 10.25 in. × 10.25 in. (260 mm × 260 mm) marble squares. The whole assembly is held 27.5 in. (700 mm) outside the exterior wall by frames cantilevered from the floor structure. The space at each floor level between the outside glass wall and the marble panels is filled with a steel grate walkway.

The east side of the complex is shielded from the university buildings by a windowless service core containing fire stairs, elevators, and toilet rooms. A stairway runs from the roof terrace down the outside of this east wall and lands at the entry plaza on the south side of the building. Originally, Nouvel intended the stair also to be a waterfall, part of a water garden and moat covering the

Figure 8.20 Some of the 2.9 m light-sensitive diaphragms made of several electromechanical irises between two layers of glass.

plaza, but those features were postponed because of budget restraints.

Mechanical

Services are routed through ceiling cavities beneath the floor slabs. Air diffusers are distributed in the ceiling plane among recessed light fixtures. Heavy plant equipment is located in a lower basement level.

Interior

The plan is organized horizontally by using the north tower for museum purposes, giving display areas the priority of diffuse and even daylight. Spaces on this museum side of the complex are double height, 19 ft (5.8 m). South tower spaces, on the other hand, begin with the spiraling library stacks in the southwest corner. This spiral form is expressed as an independent structure within a glass and steel cage. It winds up the building, with bookshelves arranged on both sides of its ramp and various views to the outside. At the top floor, the minaret-like tower becomes a lounge area with spectacular views over a wide panorama. In addition to the multilevel library are reading, study, and conference areas. The east side and the upper floors of the south tower are filled with offices and meeting rooms. South tower floor-to-ceiling height is low, at 8.7 ft (2.6 m), but alternate floors on this side have lightwells opening to the area below. Core functions and fire stairs are grouped in a narrow bay to the east that adjoins both of the towers.

Entry from the south plaza is gained through the center of five open bays in the south block. This bay is dedicated to vertical circulation through all ten levels. The rest of the ground floor on the south side is a reception hall. Its floor is pulled away from the outside wall, creating a lightwell to the lower-level exhibit spaces. A connecting passageway from the center bay leads through to an entrance lobby on the north street side. This north lobby also bridges above exhibit spaces below, starting the alternating floor level pattern of single-height spaces on the south and double-height spaces on the north.

The central courtyard between the towers acts as an armature for museum circulation. Mezzanine walkways from the south block divide the double-height display volumes in the north block in half and connect the museum exhibits vertically with open stairs. Display areas that back up to the courtyard atrium are daylit through a suspended curtain of thin translucent marble panels hung a few feet outside the glass wall. A passageway bridges across the VIP entry path from the north to the south tower at the fifth level, allowing a continuous spiraling circulation from the sixth-level museum entry down to the exhibit space below street level. To view the exhibits, patrons walk along interior paths that circle the central courtyard and its marble veiled walls.

Nothing in the interior is allowed to interfere with transparency. Stairs are open treads with open rails. Structure is steel, slender, and exposed. Elevators are glass enclosures. Even the private office suites on the upper floors have partitions and doors made of translucent glass. Wherever possible, elements are transformed into objects of light.

The sum effect of staggered floors, open lightwells, and bridged entries fulfils Nouvel's intention of dematerializing the building. The lifting force is light, and this is

Figure 8.21 Interior view of circulation core.

allowed to come through the thin mesh filters of the envelope and infiltrate everywhere. Even where the light source is far from an interior position, there are plenty of bright surfaces to reflect and refract the flow of light through the space. With light so all-pervading and places to stand so fractured, the effect is certainly what Nouvel was after.

Vertical organization of the interior starts with the occupied level below the south plaza. This begins with a double-height hypostyle hall, 25 rows of five columns spaced 9.5 ft (2.9 m) on center both ways to make a corridor more than 246 ft (75 m) long and 38.1 ft (11.6 m) wide across the lower level plan. An auditorium with 350 seats is centered along the south side of the hall, surrounded by a corridor of support spaces and then the underground parking. The north side of the hall abuts the lower level of the south tower where current and temporary exhibitions are displayed. These lower galleries are daylit by lightwells and through voided floor space of the ground level above. The narrow width of plan between the two towers and below the central courtyard is used for a stairway connecting the lower galleries to the street-level entry.

The progression of library and museum spaces dominates the midlevels of the building. Upper levels are given over to the institute's offices and, at the top floor, a double-height council meeting room adjacent to the lounge above the library tower. The restaurant is also at this level, wrapped around the north side of the center court's marble walls. Outside the restaurant is the large roof terrace café with views of central Paris.

Fire safety egress is ensured by exit stairs at both corners of the service core as well as within the center shaft of the library tower. Auditorium exit paths meet these stairs at the hypostyle hall. From the roof there is an open stair running down the eastern flank of the complex and emptying on the southern plaza.

TECHNICAL INTEGRATION HIGHLIGHTS

Physical

- Breaking the complex into two towers maximized the exterior skin and the potential to introduce light.
- Pushing the auditorium and parking, as well as some of the display areas, under the south plaza allowed the two towers to remain open and transparent.

Visual

- The architectural intention of dematerialization is achieved through careful selection and deployment of envelope, structure, and interior systems.
- Arab cultural references are incorporated abstractly, as opposed to represented or referenced literally.
- Moving the envelope about a foot outside the line of structure captures the building skeleton and allows the interior to play off it.
- The transparent skin of the building gives it a bimodal day/night quality like that of the Willis Faber Dumas building (see case study #7). With lights on inside at night, the building puts on a performance for the street.
- The library tower, intended as a landmark (especially at night) occupying the corner of St. Germain and Quay St. Bernard, has also proven to make a good billboard. Many of the published photographs of this elevation show it draped with large banners.

Performance

Although the giant *moucharabieh* on the plaza side of the building has never functioned as planned, it can still be operated seasonally. The screens were never intended to move noticeably or create sudden dramatic changes in light. At best, they could have brought light transmission down gradually from 30 percent opening to 10 percent. Perhaps it is best to regard their performance as a sort of tunable *brise soleil*.

DISCUSSION

For many architects, especially those espousing High Tech Style, the profits of technical systems are achieved through the visual expression of structural and mechanical functions as an inherent part of building. At the Arab Institute, on the other hand, Jean Nouvel wants technology to be omnipresent, but only as an evocative magic. For this reason the orderly existence of structural systems, even though they are largely exposed, is diffused in many-layered ghostly reflections between polished glass surfaces. Their existence is highly amplified and the purity of their technical shapes is evident, but they are far from legible in the traditionally High Tech way. Mechanical services are completely hidden for the same reasons. They would only distract from the effect.

16

LINZ DESIGN CENTER, 1988–1989

Linz, Austria
THOMAS HERZOG

DESCRIPTION

In 1420, the Italian Renaissance architect, goldsmith, and craftsman Filippo Brunelleschi found it necessary to invent the building technology and equipment of construction necessary to win a competition. His design and construction of the 138.5 ft (42.2 m) diameter dome and its spire over the existing base of the Florence Cathedral was prototypically Renaissance. Peter Murray, in *The Architecture of the Italian Renaissance,* says that Brunelleschi was the first to "begin to comprehend the structural system of classical architecture and to adapt its principles to modern needs."

Shifting from cathedrals to pavilions, the prototype of large exhibition pavilions was established by the Crystal Palace. Constant reference to its influence is unavoidable. Creative reinterpretation of Paxton's 1851 masterpiece is an inherent goal in the architecture of many pavilions since. The objective of "adapting principles to modern needs" has inspired a number of Brunelleschi-scale innovations in pavilion design, but none quite so dramatic perhaps as Thomas Herzog's development of the Linz Design Center.

The crowning glory of the Linz pavilion was not a dome, but a freespan 670.3 ft × 249.3 ft (204.3 m × 76.0 m) glass-skinned barrel vault. Like Brunelleschi, Herzog and his team were required to include a detailed structural engineering study with their competition submission. This was an unusual requirement in modern times, one that might have stymied more speculative projects like the Sydney Opera House. The real innovation at Linz, however, was the glass skin across the vault. Herzog recognized that the Crystal Palace scheme failed to satisfy the thermal insulation, glare control, and solar shading requirements of modern buildings. At the same time, he intended to capture the airy lightness of a daylight-saturated space. To resolve his interpretation, Herzog would oversee the deployment of radically new glazing technologies and the means of their manufacture.

Figure 8.22 CAD rendering of the Design Center. *(3-D rendering by Travis Hughs.)*

		TABLE 8.7 Fact Sheet
Project	Building Name	Linz Design Center
	Client	Landeshauptstadt Linz (Linz City Council)
	Location	Linz, Austria
	Lat/Long/Elev	48.23 N 14.18 E, 1027 ft (313 m)
Team	Architect	Thomas Herzog
	Structural Engineer	Fritz Sailer + Kurt Stepan
	Mechanical Engineer	Mathias Bloos
	Daylighting	Lichtplanungsbüro, Christian Bartenbach
	Acoustics	Muller BBM
General	Time Line	Fall 1988 (competition). Design phase: February 1989 to July 1989. Construction: July 1991 to October 1993. Opening: January 1994.
	Occupants	Not determined.
	Cost	US$643.7 million.
	1995 Cost US$	$790.8 millon.
	Stories	6.9 million ft^3. (197,000 m^3). One story plus mezzanine and basement.
	Plan	333,680 ft^2 gross floor area, 670.3 ft × 269.0 ft footprint (31,000 m^2, 204.3 m × 82.0 m).
Site	Site Description	8.45 acre site (34,182 m^2).
	Parking, Cars	360 underground, 241 surface.
Structure	Foundation	Flat pad and strip foundation on compacted gravel.
	Vertical Members	Reinforced concrete walls.
	Horizontal Spans	Precast concrete Tee floor above basement with two prestressed steel cables between each box girder to resist the outward thrust of the arched roof. The roof span consists of 34 steel arched girders at 23.6 ft (7.2 m) centers spanning 243 ft (74 m) with a radius of 194.2 ft (59.2 m) and a maximum height of 49.2 ft (15 m).
Envelope	Glass and Glazing	See skylights.
	Skylights	148,541 ft^2 (13,800 m^2) of double glazed roof in 3,456 panels measuring 2.6/3.0 ft × 8.9 ft (80/90 × 270-cm) with a 0.63 in. (16 mm) grid of aluminized plastic micro mirrors sandwiched between the two layers of glass. The grid is oriented in the glazing to allow small shafts of indirect light from the north sky and provide an overall daylight transmission of 33%.
	Cladding	Metal curtain wall and ceramic tile.
	Roof	See skylights.
HVAC	Equipment	Not determined.
	Cooling Type	Ventilation rates: north zone: 107,726 ft^2/hr (183,000 m^2/hr), south zone: 90,066 ft^2/hr (153,000 m^2/hr).
	Distribution	Not determined.
	Duct Type	Round metal ducts.
	Vertical Chases	Minimal.
Interior	Partitions	Not determined.
	Finishes	Various.
	Vertical Circulation	Two elevators.
	Furniture	Not determined.
	Lighting	3550 fixtures plus 282 stage lights.

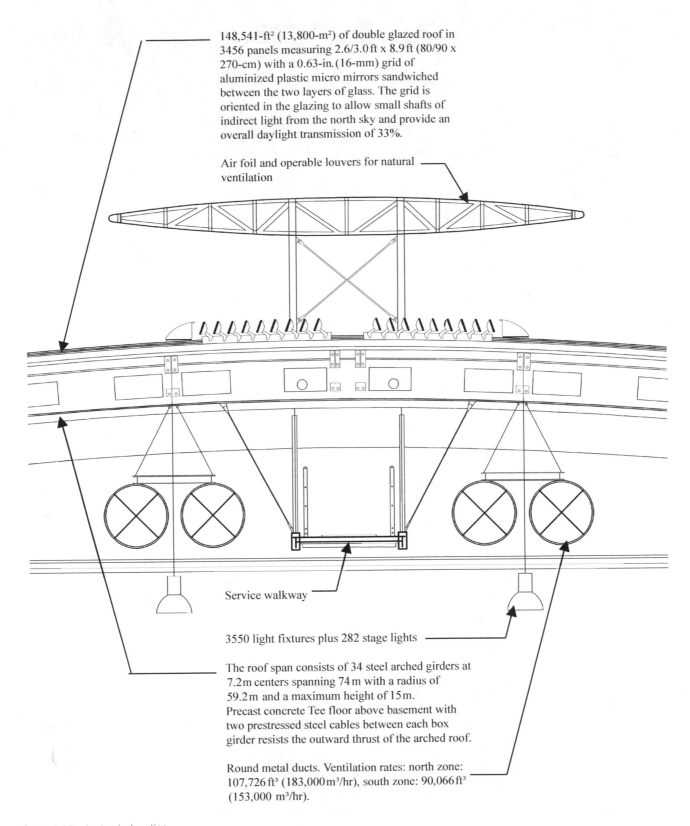

148,541-ft² (13,800-m²) of double glazed roof in 3456 panels measuring 2.6/3.0 ft x 8.9 ft (80/90 x 270-cm) with a 0.63-in. (16-mm) grid of aluminized plastic micro mirrors sandwiched between the two layers of glass. The grid is oriented in the glazing to allow small shafts of indirect light from the north sky and provide an overall daylight transmission of 33%.

Air foil and operable louvers for natural ventilation

Service walkway

3550 light fixtures plus 282 stage lights

The roof span consists of 34 steel arched girders at 7.2 m centers spanning 74 m with a radius of 59.2 m and a maximum height of 15 m. Precast concrete Tee floor above basement with two prestressed steel cables between each box girder resists the outward thrust of the arched roof.

Round metal ducts. Ventilation rates: north zone: 107,726 ft³ (183,000 m³/hr), south zone: 90,066 ft³ (153,000 m³/hr).

Figure 8.23 Anatomical section.

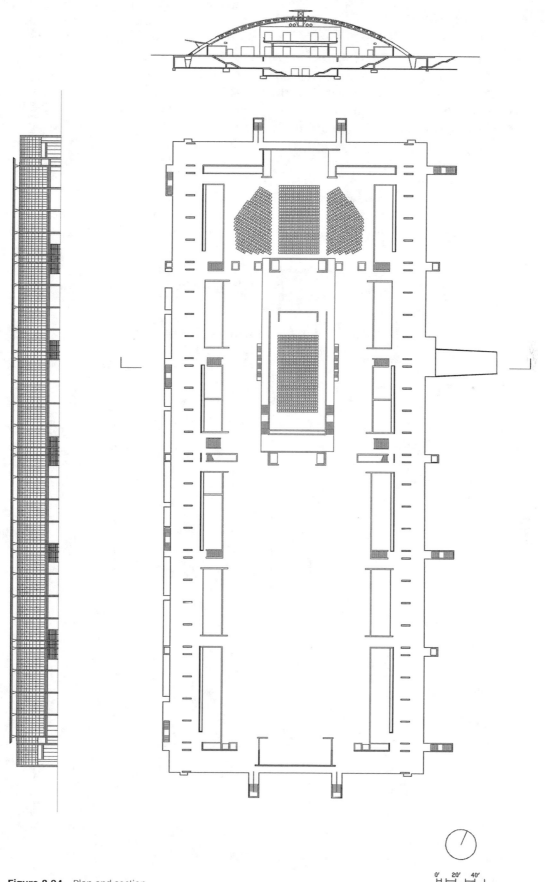

Figure 8.24 Plan and section.

0' 20' 40'
10' 30' 50'

PROGRAM

Client

As Mayor of Linz in January of 1988, Dr. Franz Dobusch announced his intention to build a commercial exhibit and trade center. Its purpose was the stimulation of a modern urban core for the city and the related commercial activity it would bring. In autumn of that year, a competition was announced for the project.

Brief

Aside from the stipulation that entries would include a detailed structural analysis, the project was given an urban planning perspective. The exposition hall would knit together an extensive area around the site and give it focus and definition. It would include a companion four-star hotel on the same site. The Austrian Broadcasting Authority (ORF) facility on the west side was to be given specific attention.

The city also desired to integrate works of visual art into the pavilion. After the commission for the building was awarded to the Herzog team, a second round of competition was held and five artists were selected by the jury to work with the architects until the building was completed. Pepi Meier, Waltraut Cooper, Ferdinand Götz, Nickolaus Lang, and Rainer Wittenborn all contributed permanent installations.

Site

Linz (population 210,000) is the state capital of Upper Austria, one of the nine Austrian provinces. The city is located on the banks of the Danube River about 100 miles (60 km) east of Salzburg and 100 miles (60 km) west of Vienna. Linz is an important center for industry and com-

TABLE 8.8 Normal Climate Data for Linz, Austria

		Jan.	Feb.	Mar.	Apr.	May	June	July	Aug.	Sept.	Oct.	Nov.	Dec.	Year
Temperature	Degree-Days Heating	1101	916	751	527	260	137	68	72	205	505	823	1016	6396
	Degree-Days Cooling	0	0	0	0	7	36	72	68	11	0	0	0	184
	Extreme High	55	61	75	77	86	90	99	94	86	77	63	57	99
	Normal High	34	38	48	56	66	70	74	74	67	56	42	36	74
	Normal Average	29	32	41	47	57	62	65	65	59	49	38	32	48
	Normal Low	25	26	33	39	47	53	56	55	50	41	33	28	25
	Extreme Low	-18	-9	-8	27	28	36	45	41	34	23	7	-2	-18
Humidity	Dew Point	26	27	32	36	45	51	54	54	50	42	33	29	40
	Max % RH	91	91	90	88	86	87	88	91	94	94	92	91	90
	Min % RH	84	71	57	53	49	52	51	50	55	65	80	85	63
	% Days with Rain	40	33	53	60	60	66	63	60	50	50	53	46	52
	Rain Inches	2	2	2	3	3	4	5	4	3	2	2	2	34
Sky	% Overcast Days	45	39	30	28	20	23	19	17	23	28	43	47	30
	% Clear Days	7	15	14	12	10	7	11	16	16	15	8	7	11
Wind	Prevailing Direction	W	W	W	W	W	W	W	W	W	W	W	W	W
	Speed, Knots	10	8	8	8	7	7	7	7	7	7	8	9	8
	Percent Calm	10	9	8	6	7	7	9	11	12	11	10	9	9
Days Observed	Rain	12	10	16	18	18	20	19	18	15	15	16	14	191
	Fog	23	20	19	14	14	14	16	19	22	24	23	24	32
	Haze	6	10	12	8	6	6	6	11	12	12	6	3	98
	Snow	15	11	7	4	#	0	0	0	0	1	7	12	57
	Hail	#	#	#	#	0	#	#	0	#	0	#	0	1
	Freezing Rain	2	1	#	0	0	0	0	0	0	0	1	2	6
	Blowing Sand	#	0	0	#	0	#	0	0	#	#	#	0	#

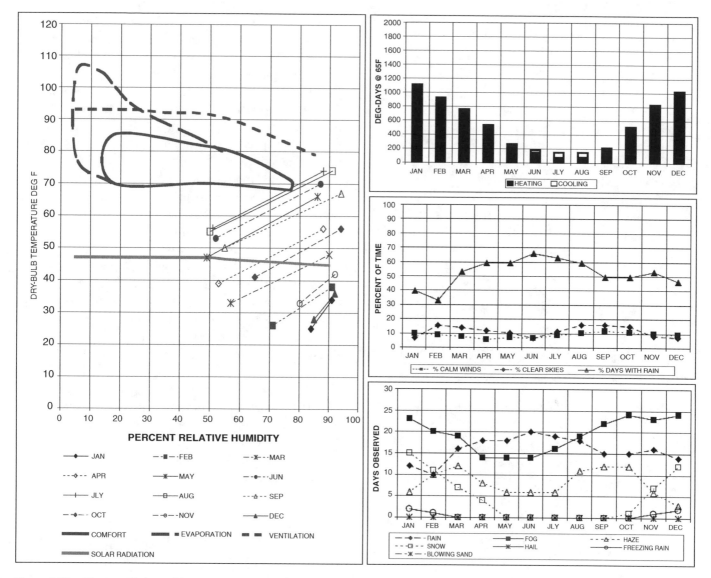

Figure 8.25 Climate analysis graphics.

merce. Although Austria is landlocked, it sails a merchant marine fleet of 32 vessels on the Danube. Linz and Vienna share the nation's port facilities. Linz is also home to three universities with a combined enrollment of more than 17,000 students. Beethoven, Napoleon, and Johannes Kepler all spent time here. The town square dates to 1230. Munich, Germany, is 150 miles to the west and the Czech border is 35 miles away to the north.

In 1990, after the Design Center was complete, Linz adopted a policy to implement low-energy construction and conservation in their public housing stock. More than 12,000 homes were needed in the area. By 1996 this project evolved into the Solar City project, and 630 pilot residences were constructed south of Linz in the district of Pichling. Notably, three of the design partners in the project are the offices of Norman Foster, Richard Rogers, and Thomas Herzog.

The Design Center building site is located on the southern end of central Linz, on the fringe of an industrial area. Major thoroughfare streets run along all three sides of the site, Franckstrasse to the west, Liebigstrasse to the east, and Goethestrasse to the north. Heavy rail yards and the industrial docklands are to the south and west of the site.

Climate

Austria is divided into different climate zones by the extension of the Alps through its central region. South of the mountains is the sub-mediterranean or *Illyrisches* climate with characteristically more sunshine than the rest of Austria. East of the mountains is the *Pannonisches* climate, which has a higher degree of continentality because of the

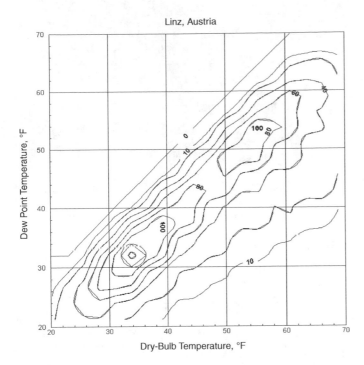

Linz, Austria

Figure 8.26 Bin data distribution for Linz, Austria. Concentric areas of graph indicate the number of hours per year that weather conditions normally occur in this climate. Similar to elevation readings on topographic maps, highest frequency occurrences of weather are at the center peaks of the graph. (Data sources: *Engineering Weather Data, typical meteorological year (TMY) data from the National Climatic Data Center, and the ASHRAE Weather Data Viewer from the American Society of Heating, Refrigerating and Air-Conditioning Engineers.*)

sheltering effect of the Alps. The Alpine region itself is covered by grassland pastures on the south and deep forests to the north. Cold air currents often roll down the mountains into the Alpine valleys.

Linz lies in the fourth climate zone, Upper Austrian. Because of geographic similarities the climate of Linz is quite like that of Munich and is classified as typically Central European. Salzburg and Vienna are in the same general classification. This region is strongly influenced by wind currents and frontal movements from the Atlantic. Both Linz and Munich lie just beyond the northern extent of the Alps but the eastward distance of Linz from Munich has a moderate continental effect, producing more extreme temperatures and reduced rainfall in Linz.

Snow falls in Linz an average of 54 days per year from November to April, and about 20 percent of all annual hours are below freezing. The January temperature range averages 34°F high and 25°F low. Summers are pleasant, with July normal highs of 74°F and lows of 55°F. Rain in excess of 1 mm (trace precipitation) falls on half the days of any month, with more abundant precipitation amounts in the summer. There are 6396 degree-days heating and only 184 annual degree-days cooling. Design data for Linz are 79°F dry bulb and 63°F wet bulb for summer and 12°F/9°F for winter. Both summer and winter winds are from the east at design conditions, but winds prevail annually from the southeast.

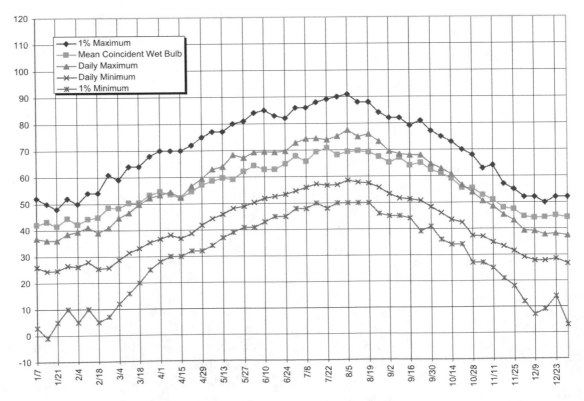

Figure 8.27 Temperatures in Linz.

Sunshine for the daylit Design Center is diffused somewhat by cloudy skies. Linz is 30 percent overcast annually. On average there are 191 days with rain, 232 days with fog, and 98 days with haze, all about evenly distributed through the year. The critical summer months, when solar heat gain is undesirable, have the bluest skies, at about 15 percent clear, 70 percent scattered, and 15 percent overcast conditions.

INTENTION

Design Team

Thomas Herzog completed a diploma of architecture at the Technical University of Munich in 1965 and received his Doctorate in architecture from the University of Rome in 1972. Dr. Herzog became the chair of Design and Building Technology at the Technical University of Darmstadt in 1986 and chair of Design and Building Construction at the Technical University of Munich in 1993. Along the way, he has worked for the European Commission, the policy initiative arm of the European Union, and championed solar architecture at several other European organizations.

Herzog's work has been a continuing series of partnerships and collaborations. He approaches each project as a prototype design for state-of-the-art technology, and this research and development requires teamwork. Since 1981 he has worked "hand in hand" with the Freiburg Institute of Energy Research, he says, because "no architect can ever master all the forces at work on solar buildings" (Herzog, 1994). He believes in the necessity and synergistic effect of multidisciplinary teams.

For the Linz Design Center, Herzog worked closely with Hanns Jörg Schrade and a team of six assistants. Daylighting for the project involved the participation of Christian Bartenbach, whose office in Innsbruck includes a staff of 60 and provides lighting expertise internationally. Energy simulation was performed at the Fraunhofer Institute for Solar Energy Systems in Freiburg, Germany. Wind tunnel experiments were directed by Dr. Rudolf Frimberger at the Technical University of Munich. Internal airflow modeling was performed by Design Flow Solutions in Cardiff, United Kingdom.

Philosophy

The research and development background of Herzog's academic pursuits find Modernist expression in his professional practice. He constantly seeks to experiment and apply the best and most advanced technologies to the service of his buildings. For him, Modernist architecture is still involved in a transition from the 1970s attitude in which energy efficiency was sacrificed to achieve visual statements of material minimalism. Herzog sees the emerging role of Modern architecture as just the opposite —using new materials and configurations to exploit a building's functional relationship with the environment. This evolution is evident in his own career as well. After following in the footsteps of Frei Otto and publishing his doctoral dissertation, *Pneumatic Constructions,* Herzog abandoned the lightweight minimalist envelope solution in favor of far more proactive and environmentally sophisticated techniques.

Intent

As a continuously toplit building, the Linz Design Center is a direct technical descendent of the Crystal Palace. Adapting the wonder of a clear span and fully glazed pavilion to the needs and capabilities of modern science was clearly the founding architectural intention. In keeping with Herzog's philosophy, this would involve a great deal of research and development and the participation of several experts.

CRITICAL TECHNICAL ISSUES

Inherent

- Exhibition halls and conference centers serve multiple functions. Trade shows, technical conferences, home/car/boat shows, religious conventions, local celebrations, banquets, concerts, lectures and so forth—all had to be accommodated at the Design Center.

- Flexibility to serve small and large functions, and even multiple events simultaneously, had to be planned for.

- Exhibition halls need services distributed beneath the floor so that electricity, water, phone, and other utilities can be brought to each display booth.

- Auditoriums need acoustical planning and protection from noise in adjacent areas.

- Food services must be provided for large crowds, and catering for small dinner functions.

Contextual

- The Design Center was conceived as a stimulus to the urban fabric and an organizing element of its neighborhood. With scattered housing and commercial buildings to the south and the urban fabric of central Linz to the north, there was considerable mending to be done.

- Energy efficiency and industrial-quality construction were cultural expectations.

Intentional

- The height of the exhibition hall would be kept to a minimum to reduce the volume of space that needed to be conditioned.
- Thermally insulated glass with infrared-reflective coatings would be used to minimize heat gain while maximizing light.
- An "active spatial environment" would be achieved through daylight saturation without the presence of uncomfortable glare. This dictated that skylight would be admitted but direct-beam sunlight would be shielded from the interior.

APPROPRIATE SYSTEMS

Precedent

The historical paradigm of the Crystal Palace left Herzog with a search for a modern archetype. His use of the barrel vault resolved a fundamental question: the need for wide-span exhibit spaces versus the desire for a restricted, economical interior volume. This basic form served as the structural model for the development of the program. Brunelleschi's dome was an arch rotated to make a three-dimensional form. Herzog's vault would be an arch extruded to form a long hall. In *Archetypes in Architecture*, Thomas Thiis-Evensen (1987) discusses the modeling and articulation of the arch. He then chooses E. L. Boullée's skylit Bibliothèque Nationale project of 1792 to illustrate the barrel vault, saying, "A space is created in which the details intensify the main tendency of the vault." This seems like a fitting description for Herzog's articulation of the form. The other general reference to the vaulted glass cover was the popular glass-roofed galleria. A nearby historical reference would be Otto Wagner's Post Office Bank (1912), also a competition winner, in neighboring Vienna. Wagner's glazed vault is suspended from cables above a room with a glass floor that transmits light into the lower stories.

Site

Herzog placed the exposition hall on the eastern half of the site and used the minor hotel structure as a wall to the busy Franckstrasse side. This left the entire north half of the site open to the central cityscape, including the northwest corner as a paved public terrace at the street intersection, complete with flagpoles and a splashing fountain. A restaurant was located between the two buildings for shared use and to promote the open terrace between them as an exhibition court. This arrangement maximized the available length of the hall and exposed both of the narrow ends to streets where large trucks could dock easily. A surface parking lot and basement parking entrance are located at the northeast quadrant of the site.

Structure

The two-story basement substructure measures 670 ft × 269 ft (204 m × 82 m). Its reinforced concrete walls and footings are the principal load-bearing elements. The perimeter of the basement is a double-loaded parking loop, and interior zones are used for meeting rooms. A lower level connects to a tunnel leading to the pavilion's companion hotel. The floors above the basement are on a 23.6 ft × 27.6 ft (7.2 × 8.4 m) grid with precast concrete double-T beams spanning the long dimension across cast-in-place beams. A 5.9 in. (150 mm) finishing floor slab is poured over the double-Ts. Within this finishing slab are two steel cables that connect arch footing pads on opposite sides of the building. Prestressing these cables to 1000 to 1200 kN resists the tremendous horizontal thrust of the main roof arches. Three lateral expansion joints separate the building into structural areas of less than 269 ft × 203 ft (82 m × 62 m).

The dominant structural element of this pavilion is the 248.0 ft (75.6 m) span of 34 flat-arched (large radius) girders at 23.6 ft (7.2 m) centers. These box beam constructions were built up from cut steel and welded into form. At either end of the arches was a footing abutment held in place by the floor slab and tied back by the steel cables. Arches were bolted to each footing with 16 ribbed steel anchor rods 1.6 in. (40 mm) in diameter and 47.2 in. (1.2 m) long.

Each arch had a fixed cross section of 35.4 in. × 14.6 in. (900 × 370 mm). They were fabricated in four segments with a constant radius of 194.2 ft (59.2 m) and bolted together at the site. In place, the arches reached a crest height of 42.7 ft (13 m). Secondary span purlins were fabricated in similar welded construction and spaced at 8.9 ft (2.7 m) centers across the arches longitudinally to the building. The end 25 percent of each of the purlins was splayed apart at its centerline giving the effect of an arched bottom chord and a flat top chord. This reduced the required size and weight of the purlins by enhancing their spanning action.

A portal crane was used to erect the steel frame and then employed for the rest of the assembly work as well. The crane spanned across the building from towers on both sides to a height of 75.5 ft (23 m). The towers ran up and down the building on rails. Arch segments for the roof were bolted together in a standing position at one end of the hall and then carried the length of the building by the crane to be bolted to the footings. This assembly strategy was a response to the small site and short construction

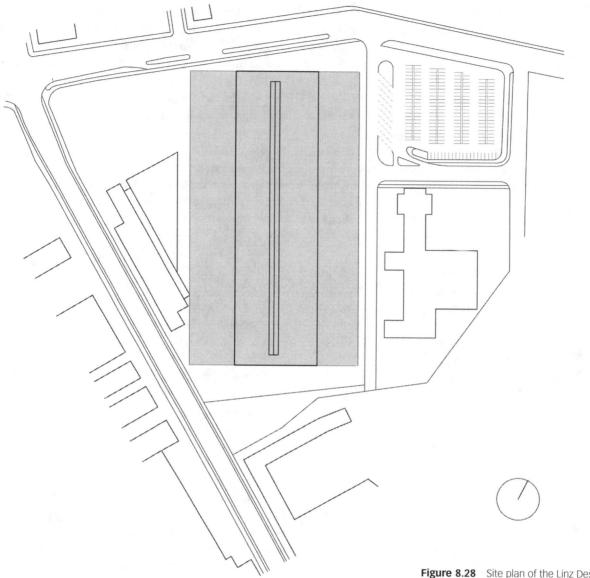

Figure 8.28 Site plan of the Linz Design Center.

schedule. Arches, purlins, and bracing, all 1600 tons of them, were erected in five months.

Envelope

Herzog worked with Austrian daylighting scientist Christian Bartenbach on the development of a glazing system for the Design Center. Bartenbach also worked on the Lloyd's of London Headquarters (1984) with Richard Rogers and the Hong Kong and Shanghai Bank (1985) with Norman Foster (see case studies #24 and #25), as well as many other daylighting projects across Europe.

What the team developed was a system of sealed double-glazing around an inner grid of plastic baffles. The baffles are coated with a fine layer of pure aluminum, creating a "retro reflecting" screen between inside and out. For this idea to be effective, each of the twenty 8.9 ft × 2.6

to 2.9 ft (2.7 m by 0.80 to 0.90 m) glazing panels in the cross section of the roof had to be considered separately. Not only was each panel oriented differently along the roof slope, their solar exposure changed with the seasonally changing path of the sun.

Simulations indicated that the grid pattern would vary from roof panel to roof panel and that the grid would be turned at different angles for each glazing. These parameters led to the design of a 0.63 in. (16 mm) grid of double-curved light channels through which all direct light is obscured. In profile the grid looks like a series of small periscopes. Heat-absorbing glass was used above the aluminized plastic grids, and laminated safety glass was used below them. The units were produced by optimizing each of the required grid profiles for its specific place on the roof. Tests at the Institute for Solar Energy Systems in

Freiburg, Germany, rated the assembly with an overall solar transmission of 42 percent and a visible light transmission of 33 percent.

Visually, the grid screen produces two effects. When the viewer is standing in the hall looking south, reflections of the floor are pixilated on the tiny reflective surfaces of the roof. Looking north, however, gives a view of the sky through the fine network of the roof grids.

The second major envelope feature was a continuous vent along the ridge of the roof that opened under an airfoil wing. Carefully contrived as a passive ventilation strategy, this system was tested in wind tunnels at the Technical University in Munich with 1:250 scale models that included a 1312 ft (400 m) diameter of the Design Center surroundings. The building's orientation worked into this configuration as well. Because the prevailing winds in Linz are from the west all year, the long axis of the building would produce a large wind shadow of negative pressure on the east side of the roof. The airfoil cover protected the operable louvers from rain and enhanced the ventilation by directing air across its curved profile.

Wind tunnel tests suggested a natural ventilation strategy utilizing outside air intakes at the floor level and exhaust at the roof ridge. Inlets were placed across the floor, and additional louvers were placed in the roof eaves for complete washing of the space with air movement and to provide flexible use of the floor space that might cover the floor louvers. Supplemental fan-powered ventilation on the order of 212,000 cfm (360,000 m³/hr) takes hot air from the top of the hall. In colder months this extracted air is fed through a heat exchanger to preheat outside air before it is used to ventilate the building.

Mechanical

Electrical power for the building is drawn from the city utility grid at 10 kW through five 630 kva transformers. There are six power centers in the building for electrical distribution. Two automatic emergency generators come on line in the event of a power failure and can be used to reduce peak electrical demand from the utility grid. There is also a 200 kva uninterruptible power supply. To provide electrical service to the exhibit floor, a bus bar system was laid in the basement corridor ceiling and connected to floor gutters in the hall. Fiber optics connect the Design Center to the Austrian Broadcasting network headquarters across the street.

Thermally, the hall was divided into several zones to tailor operation to occupied spaces only and minimize the amount of energy being used at any one time. Calculations indicated that the maximum cooling load in the building was 42.5 Btu/ft² (134 W/m²). Solar heat gain and temperature difference through the glazed roof accounted for 60 percent of this, 26.0 Btu/ft² (82 W/m²). The total connected cooling load for the building was 1,530 kW which, assuming an EER of 12.0 Btu/W, equates to the same number of tons in cooling capacity, 1530 tons. The cooling load contribution of the roof has to be discounted against the reduction in total cooling load provided by daylighting. An opaque roof with the same level of light provided by artificial sources would have resulted in a need for much greater cooling capacity.

Four distribution ducts for fan-powered ventilation and return air to the mechanical plants are placed under the center of the roof. Supply air ducts are run along the lower edge of the roof above the perimeter cabins that occupy the low ceiling curve of the roof vault.

Interior

The Design Center is organized on the main floor by two congress halls (650 and 1200 seats) with shared foyer making up the north half of the plan. A large exhibit hall occupies the other portion. By locating the larger hall on the north end wall, circulation is allowed to flow around the interior 650 seat hall to and from the exhibit floor. This facilitates the use of the three facilities together or separately in any combination.

The smaller auditorium is actually depressed into the basement level. Its long, thin plan necessitated raked, theater-style seating. The space above this auditorium is recovered as a mezzanine that overlooks the foyer area and its perimeter café. Elevators serve all levels of the building from two lift shafts where the foyer meets the exhibit hall in the center of the floor plan. The remaining functions on the ground floor are, like the café, swept to the perimeter and housed in low cabins. This includes meeting rooms, offices, toilets, and entry vestibules.

The exhibit hall allows for displays of up to 39.4 ft (12 m) in height. Above that is a service zone accessed by a central catwalk running down the long axis of the entire building. Suspended light fixtures are hung to the level of the catwalk floor. For acoustical purposes, a set of extendible cloth sails is fixed across the exhibit hall under the arches and at the luminaire plane. These translucent sails add sound absorption to the hall and lower reverberant sound levels without blocking natural light.

The basement level contains a perimeter loop driveway of double-loaded parking. A central foyer with elevators and stairs feeds into the main foyer at the ground level. A central mechanical equipment core occupies the broad part of the basement's central axis and is flanked by corridors with small offices, meeting rooms, and support spaces to both sides.

TECHNICAL INTEGRATION HIGHLIGHTS

Physical

- The basement provides infrastructure for servicing exhibit hall floor utilities.
- The ground floor finish slab also contains tensioned steel cables to resist roof thrust.
- The low ceiling cabins are meshed into lower areas of the roof vault at the building's perimeter.

Visual

- Ductwork for heating/cooling and ventilation systems is exposed and ordered.
- Envelope and interior are meshed by the daylighting system.
- The exposed structure orders all other systems, including the site.

Performance

- Roof glazing incorporates daylight distribution and solar shading.

- Acoustical sails can be used to diffuse and soften daylight on bright days.
- The natural ventilation scheme is meshed with the aerodynamics of the envelope.
- Natural ventilation works with mechanical ventilation on warmer days when fan power is needed.

DISCUSSION

The Linz Design Center illustrates the integration of structural form with daylighting saturation from the envelope, joined by an interior function responding to the same form-seeking logic. This performance integration concept is central to the architecture. Visually, this is reinforced by the articulation of the sweeping glass enclosure, mechanical ducts, and the structural vault with its webbed purlins.

Research aspects of the project and intense collaboration with building scientists were necessary to achieve these integrations. Solar geometry, natural ventilation, airflow modeling, heat transfer, and structure were all pushed far beyond the scope of standard practice. It took an integrated work of architecture to pull them all together.

17

BRITISH PAVILION, 1988–1992

Seville, Spain
NICHOLAS GRIMSHAW AND PARTNERS

DESCRIPTION

The theme for Expo 92 in Seville was "The Age of Discovery," a remembrance of the 500th anniversary of Christopher Columbus' voyage to the Americas and a time in history when Seville was the center of trade for the Spanish foothold in the New World.

To mark British participation in the event, Nicholas Grimshaw and Partners created a modern Crystal Palace. Reinterpreting indigenous building response to the hot dry summers of Seville, the UK Pavilion combines High Tech vocabulary with solar technology to produce a showpiece of British know-how.

Figure 8.29 Overview of the pavilion. *(Photograph courtesy of Ove Arup & Partners.)*

TABLE 8.9 Fact Sheet

Project		
Building Name	British Pavilion, Expo 92	
Client	U.K. Department of Trade and Industry	
City	Seville, Andalucia, Spain	
Lat/Long/Elev	37.4 N 6.0 W, 30 ft (9 m)	

Team		
Architect	Nicholas Grimshaw and Partners	
Engineer	Ove Arup & Partners (structure and mechanical)	
Quantity Surveyors	Davis Langdon & Everest	
Exhibition Design	RSCG Conran Design Ltd.	
Water Wall	William Pye Partnership	
Contracting	Trafalgar House Construction Management Ltd.	

General		
Time Line	Competition invitations: December 1988. Construction September 1990 to April 1992, with substantial completion December 1991 to allow for commissioning and exhibit installations.	
Floor Area	63,480 ft² (5,897.5 m²) in a 22,320 ft² (2,073.6 m²) footprint.	
Occupants	Up to 20,000 visitors per day.	
Cost	$ 35.4 million (£20.0 million), or $557/ft². About 70% of the budget is in the building shell and core, with the other 30% for interior fittings. This does not include the cost of the exhibits.	
1995 cost in $US	$ 39.6 million, or about $623/ft²	
Stories	Four levels in a single volume reaching to 59 ft (18 m) at the top of the glass wall and 81.4 ft (24.8 m) to the roof.	

Site		
Site Description	95 pavilions on an island in the Guadalquivir River, with a 1.5 acre (6,200 m²) site for the U.K. Pavilion.	
Parking, Cars	Shared parking for fairgrounds located to west of building.	

Structure		
Foundation	Concrete piers and slab on grade.	
Vertical Members	Ten 71.2 ft (21.7 m) tall wall frames provided ten column points on east and west wall.	
Horizontal Spans	Ten 105 ft (32 m) inverted bow roof trusses	

Envelope		
Glass and Glazing	Walls are 8.2 ft × 5.9 ft (2.5 m × 1.8 m), east wall is clear at the first 16.4 ft (5 m) and fritted glass at the top 42.7 ft (13 m).	
Skylights	None.	
Cladding	Glass to east, fabric sails on north and south, and water wall to west.	
Roof	PVC membrane over insulation on metal deck. Photovoltaic array on fabric shades.	

HVAC		
Equipment	Two chillers located in ground floor service area beneath the concourse.	
Cooling Type	Direct expansion with river water heat rejection rather than cooling towers.	
Distribution	Raised floor plenums under exhibit, office, and auditorium floors.	
Duct Type	Elliptical metal ducts.	
Vertical Chases	None.	

Interior		
Partitions	Enclosed auditorium pods.	
Finishes	Glass handrails and exposed structure.	
Vertical Circulation	Inclined moving walkway travelators and two elevators.	
Furniture	Exhibit design for display.	
Lighting	Metal halide floods, recessed downlighting, concealed strip lights in walkways and handrails.	

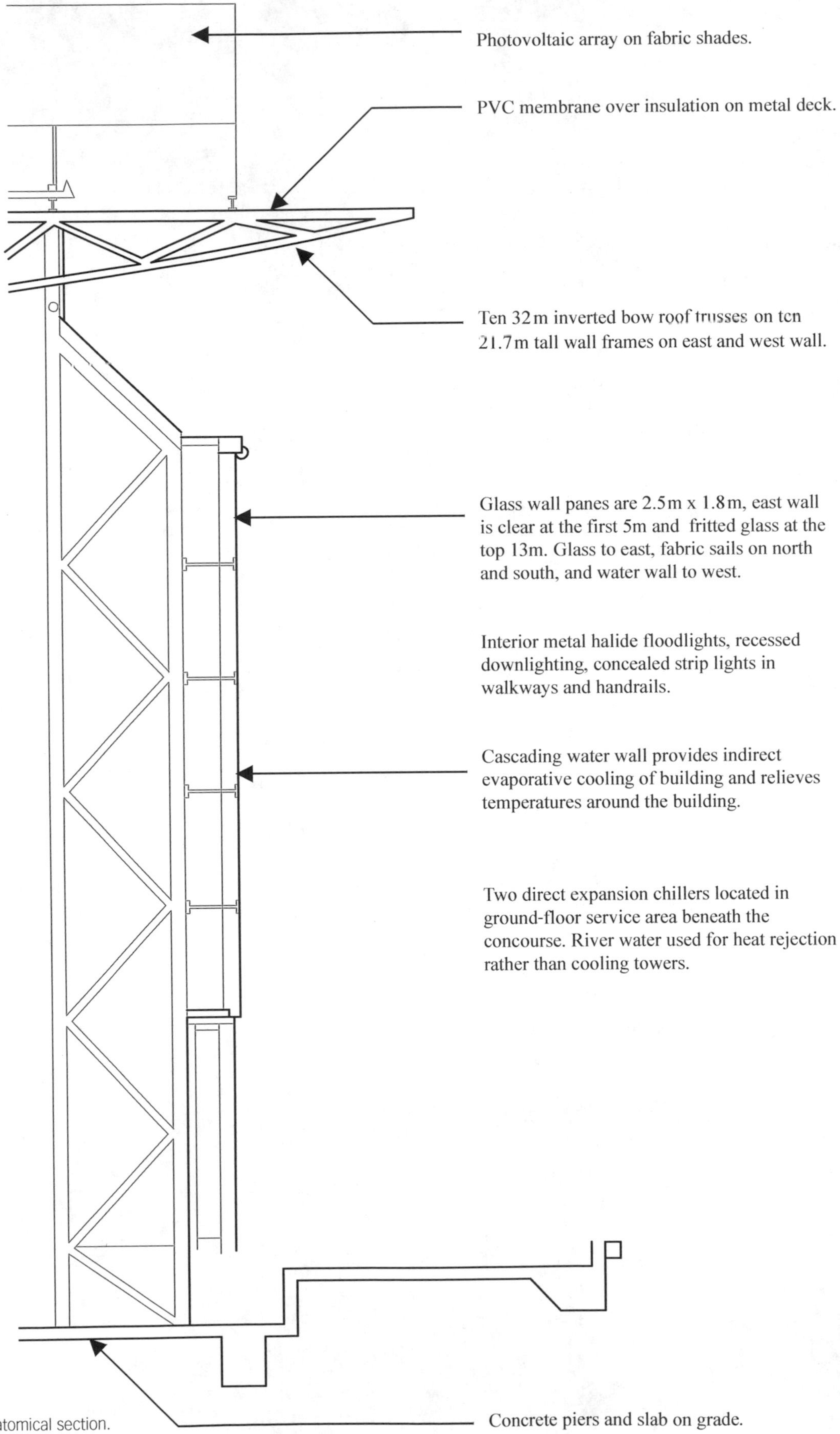

Photovoltaic array on fabric shades.

PVC membrane over insulation on metal deck.

Ten 32 m inverted bow roof trusses on ten 21.7 m tall wall frames on east and west wall.

Glass wall panes are 2.5 m x 1.8 m, east wall is clear at the first 5 m and fritted glass at the top 13 m. Glass to east, fabric sails on north and south, and water wall to west.

Interior metal halide floodlights, recessed downlighting, concealed strip lights in walkways and handrails.

Cascading water wall provides indirect evaporative cooling of building and relieves temperatures around the building.

Two direct expansion chillers located in ground-floor service area beneath the concourse. River water used for heat rejection rather than cooling towers.

Concrete piers and slab on grade.

Figure 8.30 Anatomical section.

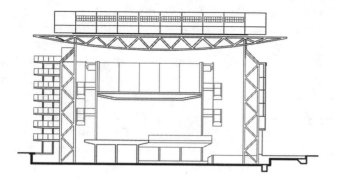

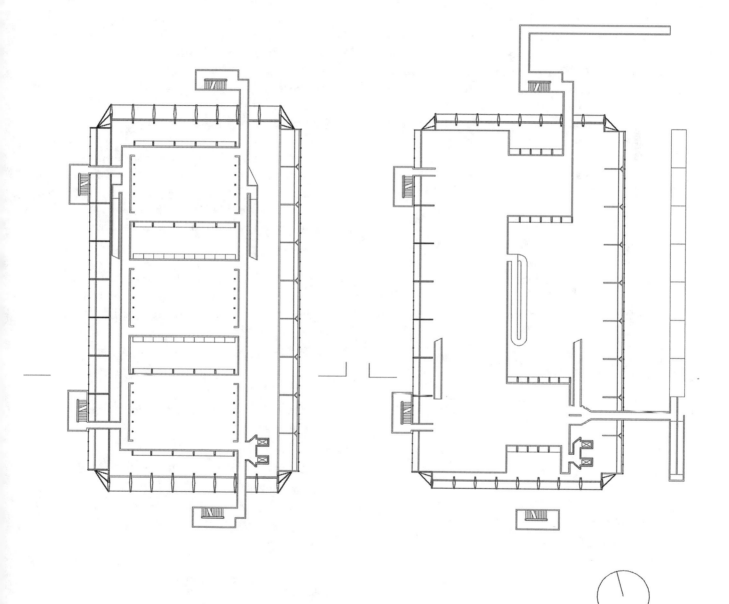

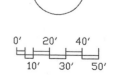

Figure 8.31 Plan and section.

0' 20' 40'
10' 30' 50'

PROGRAM

Client

The British government's Department of Trade and Industry (DTI) states its mission thus: "To increase competitiveness and scientific excellence in order to generate higher levels of sustainable growth and productivity in a modern economy." DTI promotes commerce at home and abroad through regulatory policy and direct support of British interests.

In keeping with its mission, DTI had several goals in mind for participation in Expo 92. Most of these were ambassadorial, such as promoting the image of British enterprise and technical excellence. The agency could rationalize the expense of such a grand gesture only by the stimulus it would provide for the U.K. economy. Along these same lines, the building design had to promote a high level of private commercial participation and financial contribution to the pavilion. A survey performed to poll Spanish perceptions of British culture revealed an image of stogy conservatism. DTI had something much different in mind and set out to build a progressive and forward-looking icon that would represent an advanced industrial nation.

Brief

Operationally, the client's brief established three categories of design objectives. Programmatically, the pavilion would serve national interests with a strong image easily identified with the United Kingdom. Functional goals were described by their themes without distinct area requirements:

- Unobstructed floor space for exhibition design
- Concession areas for fine dining
- Retail areas
- Circulation for 20,000 visitors per day for the six month duration of the Expo, from April through October 1992
- Access for disabled persons
- Staff offices
- Separate VIP entry, reception, and dining facilities
- A third category of requirements proposed that the pavilion be dismantled after the Expo and reassembled on a site to be determined later

Site

Expo 92 was sited on reclaimed land along the Guadalquivir River, a name bequeathed by the Arabic rulers of the eighth century as Wadi al-Kabir, meaning "Great River." The island site, La Cartuja, is on the north side of Seville about 50 miles (80 km) from the Mediterranean coast. It is reportedly the spot from which Christopher Columbus sailed to the New World. From Roman times to the Middle Ages and Moorish occupation, the river was navigable from the Atlantic Ocean inland past Seville and as far as Córdoba. The Muslim city of Granada fell just ten months before Columbus sailed, ending nearly eight centuries of Muslim rule in Iberia. In recent history silt accumulation has made the river impassable to commercial navigation upstream north of Seville.

Seville is the administrative capital and largest city in the autonomous state of Andalucía. Central Seville had a 1985 population of about 800,000, with some 1.5 million residents in the 5400 mi^2 (14,000 km^2) region. Andalucía had a 1990 population of 7,100,060. Expo 92 was held there partly in hopes of invigorating its chronically underdeveloped economy. Agriculture is the primary industry, but Andalusían farm laborers are among the poorest in Europe and many had migrated to the industrial centers of Madrid and Catalonia, seeking new employment. Seville, embellished by Moorish architecture and once celebrated as a center of culture, art, and science, saw tourism and the related service industry as a new means of vitality. Expo 92 was envisioned as a way of promoting its attractions. Perhaps now, 500 years after Seville set forth to discover the New World, the world would rediscover Seville.

Expo 92 Time Line

- May 1976 — King Juan Carlos of Spain announces the intention to host Expo 92, vowing to promote the qualities of Spain and the Latin-American nations.
- March 1982 — Seville applies to the Bureau International des Expositions (BIE), requesting to host a world exposition commemorating the fifth centennial of Columbus's first voyage.
- June 1982 — The Isle de la Cartuja is announced as the exposition site.
- June 1983 — The Internal Bureau of Exhibitions in Paris approves the general provisions of the fair.
- November 1984 — Manuel Olivencia Ruiz is appointed commissioner general of the exposition.
- April 1985 — The Spanish government launches the organizational structure of the exposition. Sociedad Estatal para la Exposicion Universal Seville 92 SA is founded. The exposition budget is placed at 183.7 million pesetas.
- February 15, 1986 — The Spanish Council of Ministers approves the general plan for the exposition.

Architect Ricardo Bofill was an early candidate for commissioner general of the Expo, but Manuel Olivencia was eventually chosen. Infrastructure projects to support the event were put in motion, including five new bridges to Isle de la Cartuja. Notably, one of two bridges designed by Santiago Calatrava was erected: the 656 ft (200 m) span, El Alamillo, with its 466 ft (142 m) mast at the northern end of the island. Seville's San Pablo Airport was completely renovated for the fair by Rafeael Moneo (1987–1991), and a new city ring road constructed to keep things moving. A high-speed railway was built to connect Seville with Madrid, joining the new Santa Justa Station rail terminal, by Seville architects Cruz and Ortiz, with their mentor Moneo's Atocha Station in Madrid. These and other works—some public infrastructure and some for tourism industries—would benefit Seville and Andalucía long after Expo 92 was converted to other uses.

Cartuja Island was a 538 acre (215 hectare) strip of desolate and unused territory harboring the old Carthusain monastery of La Caruja de las Cuevas. It lay just across the river from Old Quarter Seville. The monastery, where Christopher Columbus stayed before his journey and was buried briefly, was conserved on the southern end of the island. The northern two-thirds of the site were gridded for 70 major pavilions. To the east side of the pavilion blocks, an entertainment zone was erected around a 40 acre (16 ha) artificial Lake of Spain. Parking was placed along the western waterfront of the island. Canals were dug to separate the lake from the pavilion zone. For site circulation and elevated viewing of the fair there was a monorail system circling the site, and a 6.6 mi (11 km) cable car system ran above the central fairground avenue and into the old town. Barqueta Bridge spans into the entertainment zone, and Calatrava's Cartuja Bridge crosses at the Monastery.

Climate

Seville is hot and dry. It has, in fact, arguably the hottest climate in Europe. Daytime temperatures can reach 115°F (46°C), with lows of 40°F (5°C) the same night. The average daily temperature range between daily high and daily low in July is 29°F (16°C). Dryness promotes these large daily swings. Low relative humidity levels allow both massive solar heat gains during the blue-sky day and correspondingly high radiant flux back to the clear night sky. The large daily temperature range negates the usefulness of degree-days—there are statistically only 980 degree-days cooling and 1780 degree-days heating annually, because degree-day calculations are based on average daily temperature and tend to cancel out warm days with cool nights. Hourly bin data more accurately shows that there are 1363 hours per typical year when temperatures exceed 80°F. In comparison, Albuquerque, New Mexico, experiences only 1063 such hours. Seville's hot temperatures account for 15.6 percent of all annual weather. The same analysis limited to daytime hours of 6:00 to 18:00 is more telling: 25 percent of all daylight hours are over 80°F, 11 percent over 90°F, and 2 percent over 100°F annually. Further isolating the climate to a typical July day, the same analysis reveals that 100 percent of all daylight hours are over 80°F, 68 percent over 90°F, and 20 percent over 100°F. Coincidently, Expo 92 was held during Seville's dry weather period, when

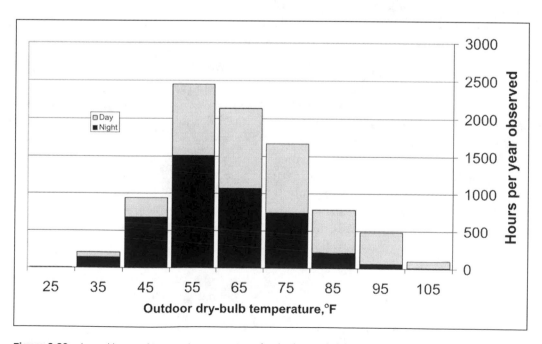

Figure 8.32 Annual hours of temperature occurrence for daytime and night hours in Seville.

TABLE 8.10   Normal Climate Data for Seville, Spain

		Jan.	Feb.	Mar.	Apr.	May	June	July	Aug.	Sept.	Oct.	Nov.	Dec.	Year
Temperature	Degree-Days Heating	417	308	221	143	41	2	0	0	0	30	188	358	1712
	Degree-Days Cooling	0	0	4	17	98	292	497	505	370	115	8	0	1915
	Extreme High	75	79	88	93	102	111	111	113	111	97	88	75	113
	Normal High	61	63	69	71	79	87	95	95	90	78	69	62	77
	Normal Average	52	54	58	61	67	75	81	81	77	67	59	53	66
	Normal Low	42	44	46	50	55	62	66	67	64	56	49	44	54
	Extreme Low	25	27	32	34	43	46	57	55	48	39	30	23	23
Humidity	Dew Point	43	44	45	48	51	56	59	59	58	53	49	45	51
	Max % RH	87	87	84	86	85	83	77	77	80	83	87	87	84
	Min % RH	59	57	47	48	42	37	31	32	35	46	56	61	46
	% Days with Rain	30	30	23	36	23	13	3	7	10	26	26	36	22
	Rain Inches	3	2	4	2	2	0	0	0	1	3	3	3	23
Sky	% Overcast Days	15	17	10	14	8	5	1	2	3	9	13	17	10
	% Clear Days	37	31	37	24	29	42	67	67	50	36	36	35	41
Wind	Prevailing Direction	NE	NE	NE	SW	SW	SW	SW	SW	SW	NE	NE	NE	SW
	Speed, Knots	7	7	7	9	9	9	9	9	8	7	7	7	8
	Percent Calm	35	30	29	26	23	23	24	26	30	32	32	30	28
Days Observed	Rain	9	9	7	11	7	4	1	2	3	8	8	11	80
	Fog	12	10	9	9	10	9	6	6	8	7	8	11	105
	Haze	8	9	9	9	11	13	12	11	11	7	7	9	116
	Snow	0	0	0	0	0	0	0	0	0	0	0	0	0
	Hail	0	0	#	0	#	0	0	0	0	0	#	#	#
	Freezing Rain	0	0	0	0	0	0	0	0	0	0	0	0	0
	Blowing Sand	6	5	4	4	4	6	4	4	4	3	3	3	50

all of these hot hours occur: April to October. At least it was cool as soon as the sun went down; 30 percent of all July hours from 18:00 to 6:00 are below 70°F.

Passive and indigenous building response to this climate emphasizes the usual hot-arid solutions: high envelope and internal mass construction with small well-shaded openings and lots of moisture for evaporative cooling. At the Expo, misting towers were distributed around the fairgrounds to provide atomized jets of cooling humidity in the open air

INTENTION

Design Team

Nicholas Grimshaw and Partners, NGP, is a London firm founded in 1967; today this office is about the same size as Richard Rogers & Partners. Though slightly younger than Rogers and Norman Foster, Grimshaw is usually associated with the same High Tech movement and pursuit of technical rigor. A remarkable aspect of his office is youth; the average age of the staff and directors, including Grimshaw, is presently about 32. Four members of his 1988 office who have remained are currently directors: David Harriss, Chris Nash, Andrew Whalley, and Neven Sidor.

The 1992 British Pavilion marks NGP's return to Modernism, a coup that was followed by the equally remarkable 1993 Waterloo International Terminal in London. Since that time NGP has continually expanded the scope of its work in every way—project volume, building type and size, design context, and geographical location around the world. It is also one of the few firms to operate a semi-independent product design firm with whom it collaborates on most NGP building projects.

Philosophy

> Our work is concerned with producing buildings and products which are noticeably more joyful, interesting and understandable than the norm through intelligent process.

Chris Nash, NGP Director

Nicholas Grimshaw studied architecture at the Edinburg College of Art and at the Architectural Association. As a young graduate he fell under the influence of the avant-garde Archigram, its technophilia, and its countercultural mission to destroy Modernism as a stylistic pursuit and restore its sociotechnic ideals. Archigram is still remembered for a series of underground-style publications and surreal futuristic proposals for rebuilding the world—Instant City, Plug-In City, even Walking City—but none of its members' designs were ever built. Grimshaw felt an affinity for Archigram's ideas, but he wanted to build and his passion for building well led to the founding of his own practice.

Crafted detail and technical rigor are keynotes of NGP architecture. The firm also subscribes to another of the Archigram visions—the merging of information systems and buildings. In 1988 it converted to design-by-computer in a single reorganization of the office, without trying to phase it in gradually. Working with its product division, the firm uses the computer media as a design tool that closes the gap between design and making, as well as between the extravagance of custom components and the precision of industrial fabrication.

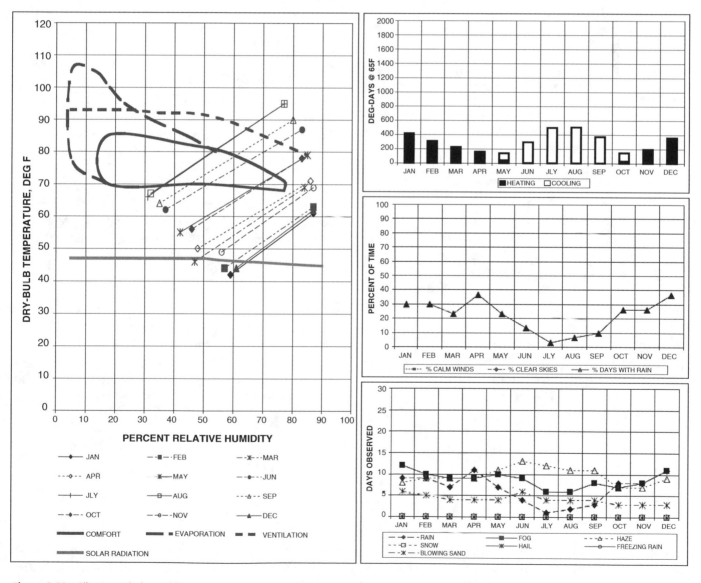

Figure 8.33 Climate analysis graphics.

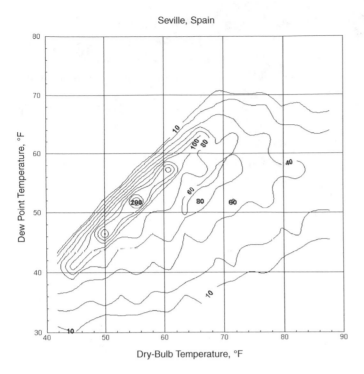

Figure 8.34 Bin data distribution for Seville. Concentric areas of graph indicate the number of hours per year that weather conditions normally occur in this climate. Similar to elevation readings on topographic maps, highest frequency occurrences of weather are at the center peaks of the graph. (Data sources: *Engineering Weather Data, typical meteorological year (TMY) data from the National Climatic Data Center, and the* ASHRAE *Weather Data Viewer from the American Society of Heating, Refrigerating and Air-Conditioning Engineers.)*

Intent

On one hand, Grimshaw and his team brought a devotion to technically expressed systems to the project as a means of evoking Britain's industrial and scientific prowess. On the other hand, the design would have to deal with the uncompromisingly hot-arid climate in elegant style. Oppositions between these two ideals, the use of High Tech kit of parts versus climate-responsive building techniques, stimulated the directions this pavilion would take. Rather than taking the typical Modernist universal machine approach, Grimshaw and his team would fine-tune the universally adaptable kit of industrial parts to serve the particular environmental criteria of a specific place.

CRITICAL TECHNICAL ISSUES

Inherent

World's fairs are always challenging from the perspective of time, construction, and economics. Anticipating these constraints, DTI committed to Expo 92 early and was reward-ed with the choice of a prime building site from the many parcels still available. An early start was something of a disadvantage later, however, because the British construction team was always the first to encounter minor coordination problems with site regulations or Seville building officials. Other participants came to rely on the DTI's experiences to smooth the way for their own projects.

Everyone attending Expo 92 would have high expectations of the pavilions they came to see. The final building product would have to be impressive enough to communicate its British message. Architectural innovation and expression had key roles in achieving this objective and would play to the theme, "The Age of Discovery."

Climate would also play a role. Seville is mostly hot and sunny April through October, with 100°F temperatures possible any day and certain on many. With crowds of up to 20,000 visitors to the pavilion per day, satisfying the need for an indoor oasis would attract attention and appreciation.

Contextual

It was decided early on to prefabricate the building in the United Kingdom and ship it to Seville for on-site assembly. This was seen as the most reliable way to control quality and meet the construction schedule. Transportation strategies dictated that nothing shipped to the site could exceed 82 ft (25 m) in length or weigh more than 8.4 tons (7.5 tonnes).

Spanish building codes were also something of an issue. First, the earthquake resistance standards for the Seville area were relatively strict. Second, the problems of language and building conventions would have to be overcome.

Intentional

The brief's requirement for technical wizardry fit well with the architects' philosophy of elevating finely refined technical solutions to the status of pure architecture.

The minimalist aesthetic of glass and steel building vocabulary was challenged by a climate that was best tempered with deep shade, thick massive construction, and open surfaces of water.

APPROPRIATE SYSTEMS

Grimshaw's general solution to the program placed the building under a shading array of photovoltaic collectors and surrounded it with pools of water. The envelope employs different passive cooling strategies on each surface and houses a single grand volume where most activities are placed on an elevated concourse. Partial floors are suspended above the concourse for exhibit space and reached by inclined moving walkways rather than stairs. Service and office functions are buried below the concourse. Heat is allowed to stratify and exhaust at roof level, so the pavilion environment is buffered but not mechanically controlled. Air-conditioned cooling is reserved primarily for auditorium spaces contained in upper-level pods. The structural frame is expressed to the exterior as part of an extended envelope system that mediates between inside and out. On the interior the frame becomes an armature for the circulation system and platform floors that lead to the auditoriums.

Precedent

The progression from Paxton's Crystal Palace, to Dutert's Gallery of Machines, and on through the history of pavilion architecture remains an inspiration, especially to Modernist architects who favor the industrial systems mode of construction and its premises in design. Nicholas Grimshaw, for one, is not shy about direct references to the Crystal Palace.

Site

A 1.5 acre (6200 m^2) building plot was selected, fronting on the fair's principal International Avenue and adjacent to the west gate entry from the parking areas. Its long sides face west-northwest (WNW) to a row of service buildings and ESE to International Avenue. Views east from the pavilion entry façade look down European Avenue to the lake, where the Spanish Pavilion was sited on the water's edge.

Direct solar radiation would have greatest impact on the roof, the south and west sides of the building (SSW and WNW). The entry side to the ESE would only receive a few hours of direct sun per day. On July 21, for example, the long entry elevation is illuminated by sunlight at a 25-degree profile angle at 7:00 A.M. and receives some direct sun until 11:00 A.M. when the profile angle is 70 degrees. This exposure happens during cooler hours of the day, however, and some potential shading of low sun may be provided by surrounding pavilions. The July sun actually rises and sets 25 degrees north of the east-west horizon points at this latitude. Because the building is shifted clockwise in plan about 15 degrees east from true north, the east wall is spared some sun and the west wall exposure is exaggerated. The sun faces squarely on the entry wall at 9:00 A.M. solar time, when the July sun is already 60 degrees above the horizon. Meanwhile, the back wall west orientation is sunlit during the hot July afternoon from 1:00 P.M. to 7:00 P.M. without much shading from surrounding structures. Profile angles are quite low on the west side after 4:00 P.M., and the incidence angle to the window approaches normal right at 5:30 P.M.

Structure

This site is about 30 ft (9 m) above the Guadalquivir's normal flow and was previously used as farmland. Soils consist of soft alluvial silts deposited by the river and a lower level of dense gravel down to 60 ft (18 m). A grid of driven piles was placed to support the column loads of the building, followed by pile caps and a concrete slab that was poured slightly below existing grade. A basement level was constructed for services and office space.

Superstructure work began with framework for the interior, essentially an autonomous support system for suspended partial floor levels and moving walkways leading up to the enclosed auditorium pods. Four pairs of column feet supported each of three structural trees rising from the basement to the base of the auditoriums. The 65.6 ft (20 m) distance between columns was spanned by thick wall pipe Warren trusses that supported floors of poured concrete over profiled deck. The Warren trusses tapered toward both ends of the span and were supported at both ends between the paired columns. Cross bracing from north to south at the center bay of the interior frame provided lateral stability.

This interior frame penetrated the exterior superstructure and envelope systems to join outside open fire stairs on the north, south, and west elevations. For lateral support the interior frame was shifted off center to the west wall. This spacing provided more open area on the east entry side and simplified bracing of the two frames together above the pods at the west wall. Moving walkway "travelators" crisscrossed the platforms on the east and west edges of the interior frame. These were hung from the interior frame by attachment to the pod column feet and supported on prismatic pipe trusses. Each of these had two top chords and two more chords paired at the narrow base. The profile of the walkway trusses was formed by passing the chords through steel cross plates.

After the interior structure was in place, work started on the exterior frame. The exterior superstructure consisted of 12.9 in. (327 mm) tubular steel wall frames 4.9 ft (1.5 m) deep and 71.2 ft (21.7 m) tall. Five of these were placed along the east wall and five along the west. Each of these frameworks formed two vertical trusses, making a support grid of 10 columns across each long side of the building at 23.6 ft (7.2 m) centers. They were shipped full height and erected in one day. Next, ten 105 ft (32 m) inverted bow trusses for the roof were shipped in two parts and connected during erection at their midspan with pin joints. These roof trusses overhang the wall columns and are connected to them by more pin joints. Lateral stability of the frame was achieved by cross bracing the center bay along both sides and the roof. This one stiff bay was

Figure 8.35   Construction. *(Photograph courtesy of Ove Arup & Partners.)*

attached to all the other bays by slender horizontal tubes and roof purlins.

North and south walls are framed by mast-shaped trusses with pin connections at their base and a roller bearing connection at the roof that prevented the transfer of vertical loads. Each truss has three vertical members. A curved 12.8 in. (324 mm) diameter pipe forms the center and main structural element. Tapered spreaders project spinelike from the center pipe to hold off the other two vertical members, which are stainless steel rigging rods. These inside and outside riggings hold the truss in tension against wind loads.

Envelope

The six-month duration of Expo 92 extending through the dry summer season meant that the British Pavilion's envelope would have a single purpose, cooling. This logic motivated the dramatic use of different strategies on each of the exterior envelope surfaces as well as in their carry-over expression into the site and interior systems. Because of the extension of its parts into other systems, even the

articulated frame of the structure appears to be an active participant in this environmental servicing.

The east wall is a waterfall that cascades from roof eave level down across an entry canopy. The entry is itself elevated up a sloping ramp and suspended as a bridge across a lake fronting the entry and the east side of the building. The entry canopy diverts the cascading waterfall from the covered doorway but surrounds approaching visitors with streams of water from nozzles at its side edges. The wall actually consists of 0.5 in. (12.5 mm) gray-tinted glass panels hung from rectangular steel sections at the top of the wall. The upper 41.0 ft (12.5 m) of glass is patterned to enhance the translucent effect of the waterfall. At the 16.4 ft (5 m) level, a thin gutter converts the waterfall film to thin streams that splash into the lake at the base of the wall. The glass below the gutter is clear and untinted to give an inviting view into the interior and is recessed a few inches away from the waterfall.

A high mass wall was instantly created to the long west-facing orientation by an interlocking stack of 24 water-filled metal freight containers that were piled to a height of 49.2 ft (15 m). Each container was 23.6 ft long × 3.3 ft wide × 8.2 ft deep (7.2- × 1.0 m × 2.5 m), lined with a waterproof membrane, internally insulated on the interior wall side, and painted white to reflect unwanted solar heat gain. This wall acted as a giant thermal flywheel, warming by day and cooling by night but effectively remaining at about average daily air temperature. The containers held 18,300 ft³ (518 m³) of water, constituting a thermal mass of some 1.2 million Btu/°F. At the average daily July dry-bulb temperature, this wall would remain at about 81°F all day, the same temperature as human skin. According to the engineers at Arup & Partners, the inside surface stayed constant at 86°F (30°C) while the exposed face experienced a 77°F (25°C) temperature swing between day and night extremes. As a bonus, seven of these tanks were used as part of the potable water supply system.

Closure of both the east and west walls is made outside the truss column structure. At the top of the wall, however, eaves between the ten roof trusses had polycarbonate ventilation louvers set back to the plane of the inside structural member. Insulated glass-reinforced plastic (GRP) glazing panels on the top diagonal chord of the wall truss connected the eave to the wall.

The narrow 105.0 ft wide × 82.0 ft high (32 m × 25 m) north and south walls are translucent fabric screens. Panels 13.2 ft (4 m) wide of a PVC-coated polyester sail fabric were stretched over the structural center steel pipe member of the masts outside both end walls. There is no glass. On the south side, an additional layer of pennants was attached to the frames to block sunlight, but these were not needed on the shady north elevation. A 0.75 in. (20 mm) glass panel closes both of these walls at their base.

On the roof, a PVC membrane over rigid insulation on a steel deck provided the weather closure. Above that, an array of photovoltaic solar panels was installed over south-facing fabric sunshades stretched across an S-shaped metal frame. The shades were held above the roof to allow cooling breezes to wash the roof surface. There is no storm drain system on the roof. The infrequent summer rains were to be allowed to evaporate in place, providing some extra cooling relief to the interior. It happened that 1992 was an unusual summer, with some heavy rainfall and unusually low temperatures during the Expo. Even in these extreme conditions, runoff from the roof was usually contained and any discharge over the eaves quickly evaporated on the envelope.

Electricity from the photovoltaics was used to pump water across the east wall via 26 submersible pumps. Four larger pumps driven by on-line power were used for backup and nighttime duty.

Mechanical

Night flush cooling was incorporated into the mechanical design with four air-handling units (AHUs) totaling 46,615 ft³/min (22 m³/sec) drawing air through the eaves and ducting it below the pods across the pavilion about 30 ft (9 m) above the concourse. By day, air was allowed to stratify in the space and be exhausted through the east or west eave louvers. Sensors monitored wind direction and opened the leeward side louvers accordingly. This tended to keep cooler air at the lower concourse levels circulating upward after it had been cooled evaporatively by the water features.

Offices and restaurants at the lower ground level had separate AHUs distributing mechanically cooled air through pressurized floor plenums. The auditorium pods and the VIP suite had individual units that drew air from the upper levels, cooled and delivered it to occupants, then returned it to the pavilion space still cooler than before its use. Limiting the mechanically cooled areas to spaces with high occupancy density helped keep the total building energy use an estimated 33 percent lower than a fully conditioned version of the pavilion would have consumed. In addition, water was conserved by the elimination of cooling towers and evaporative condensers. Instead, a community-sized system took river water from upstream and distributed it to each Expo pavilion for heat rejection before discharging it back into the Guadalquivir downstream.

Daylighting through the translucent east waterwall and the sail-fabric north and south walls provided most of the required illumination by day. There was, in fact, some conflict with the desirable low level of background light in the exhibits where accent lighting and computer screens were muted by the abundant natural light. At night, however, several artificial lighting systems produced a more controlled and dramatic effect. Floodlighting with 150 W cold white metal halide fixtures was used to highlight the wall trusses. Underwater 300 W spotlights washed the lower 16.4 ft (5 m) of the waterwall. Downlights in the floor decks held ambient illumination to about 4 fc (40 lux). Spotlights at the top and bottom of the end walls made the sails glow. The fabric roof shades were uplit with floodlights. At the pedestrian scale, travelators were lit with fluorescent strip lights in the side skirting and handrails.

Interior

An entry ramp elevated 8.2 ft (2.5 m) above the site runs through the east waterwall as a bridge at the northeast corner of the pavilion. This brings visitors over a 210.0 ft × 52.5 ft (64 m × 16 m) pond that runs across the entire east side of the building and extends about 26 ft (8 m) away from the east wall as well as 26 ft (8 m) inside the building. The bridge finally lands at the 14,746 ft² (1370 m²) concourse level 8.2 ft (2.5 m) above the pond and 13.8 ft (4.2 m) above an open courtyard and café that are depressed 5.6 ft (1.7 m) below grade on the 26,370 ft² (2450 m²) floor slab. Offices and service areas are buried beneath the concourse itself. Two elevators are located against the north wall, but most circulation through the pavilion is by long moving walkways slowly inclined from platform to platform across the open volume above the concourse. The +8.2 ft concourse level contains the sponsors' exhibits, a shop, and the information desk. The main exit ramp leaves through the south wall from the other end of the concourse.

At the next level, +24.6 ft (7.5 m), platform floors are used for an additional 6,243 ft² (580 m²) of exhibit space. Connecting walkways between the platforms at every level extend to the exterior fire stairs. Above is the 11,840 ft² (1100 m²) pod level, at 41.0 ft (12.5 m), with the two enclosed auditoriums and a central deck between them. The highest level, +57.4 ft (17.5 m), contains the 3,875 ft² (360 m²) VIP suite.

INTEGRATION HIGHLIGHTS

Physical

- Prefabrication ensured accurate field fit of all components and allowed a small construction crew to erect the building rapidly.

Visual

- High Tech expressiveness was used to convey the DTI-mandated image of an innovative business culture.
- Spitting the pod columns into pairs reduced their visual bulk.

Performance

- Climatic challenges posed by the Seville heat were transformed into architectural features: the waterwall, pools and fountains, shading sails, and photovoltaic panel roof shades are relevant examples.
- Prefabrication of a kit of parts for the building facilitated its reuse after the Expo. Following disassembly, the solar panels, submersible pumps, and water storage containers could be recycled into infrastructure systems for sites in developing countries. Alternately, the building could be reassembled at a site to be determined. Ideally, though, the building would remain in Seville and be converted, altered, or expanded for a different use.
- The waterfall on the east wall was evaporatively cooled to about 75°F (24°C), leaving it cooler than body temperature and providing a source of radiant relief to occupants.
- The pin-connected structural system provided ductility of frame to meet seismic codes. It also allowed for rapid on-site assembly by small crews.

DISCUSSION

In the end, Seville was a popular success. More than 42 million people passed through its gates to see the 95 major pavilions and the expositions representing 110 participating organizations and nations. Thirty percent of the exposition buildings on Cartuja, or about 1.3 million ft² (125,000 m²) were to remain standing after the event closed. The American Pavilion, for example, is now part of the local university.

9

Residential Architecture

The century of the great works of engineering and architecture, the century of airports and the consolidation of the railway stations, has woven its architecture around the concern with the domestic space, with decent and just housing, with spaces for harmonious coexistence.

Anatxu Zabalbeascoa, Houses of the Century *(1998)*

The middle of the twentieth century witnessed a rush in postwar housing construction and a simultaneous population boom. These events roughly coincided with Frank Lloyd Wright's turn from his Prairie House designs to the Usonian mode of the "Solar Hemicycle" Jacobs House in Madison, Wisconsin. Usonian motifs are still evident in residential design today. Smaller houses with open rooms, kitchens flowing into the living space, expansive views to the garden, and alignment of the house with its climatic and site influences are all Usonian innovations that continue to typify residential design challenges.

The later part of the century brought escalating energy costs, the evolution of high-performance envelope materials, and affordable air-conditioning systems. All of these had subsequent technical influences on residential design and single-family home communities. Moreover, as a reflection of construction economics, the growing trend has been to build houses of lighter-weight materials and on smaller lots. In an increasingly mechanized environ-

ment of pool pumps, air conditioners, and busy streets, the savings in material costs of lightweight construction are offset by noise control problems.

Cultural shifts have also come into play. Two-income families, single-parent households, infant daycare and a generation or two of latchkey children, suburban lifestyles and long commutes, mall hopping and electronic entertainment all combine to disrupt the traditional roles of home life. These intrusions are symptomized in the United States by the distribution of spending on home cooking versus restaurant food. According to the U.S. Department of Agriculture Economic Research Service (1995), 81 percent of the average food dollar and 18 percent of disposable income was spent in the home kitchen of 1950. By 1995 only 61 percent of the average food dollar and less than 7 percent of disposable income were spent in the same way. Dining out, on the other hand, has doubled, from 18 percent to 36 percent of the average family food dollar, during the same period despite the fact

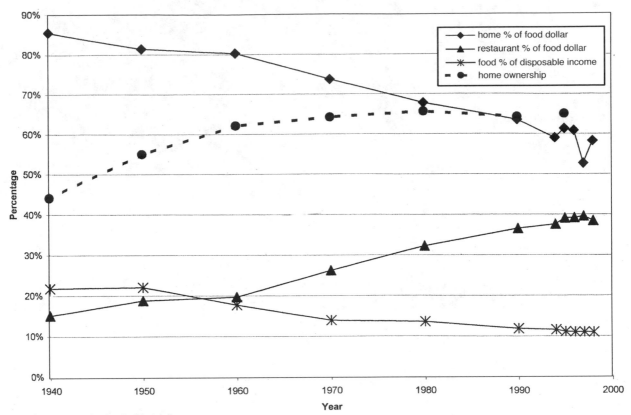

Figure 9.1 The family food dollar.

that total food costs have fallen by one-half from 22 percent to 11 percent of disposable income. Thus, as expressed in 1995 dollars, disposable income increased by a factor of 7 while spending on home food rose by a factor of 2.5. Restaurant spending increased 9-fold, whereas total food spending went up by a factor of only 3.5. Meanwhile, the percentage of home ownership in the United States rose from 44 percent to 65 percent (U.S. Census and American Housing Surveys, 1995). Home ownership is increasingly important to us, but the way houses are used has changed dramatically over the last 45 years.

Externalities aside, residences have generic characteristics that qualify them as unique design challenges and distinguish them from other building types. Because of their low internal heat loads, small footprint size, and large exposed surface area relative to contained volume of space (ft²/ft³), single-family dwellings are more sensitive to climatic influences than any other building type and thus are the best candidates for careful site design and passive energy approaches. Single-family homes also have their own inherent needs for flexibility — families grow, children mature, and parents age. The users of a house change even if the original owner/occupant remains. Homes are also most frequently subject to modification, by everything from rearranging the furniture to remodeling to large additions.

In considering them as case studies, residences are elusive subjects. A whole series of introverted characteristics usually obscure insight into the complete story. Not only are residential programs, sites, functions, and technologies less complicated and critical than those of larger buildings, but some of their design issues often remain discreetly undisclosed in consideration of the client's privacy. Further, because homes are more individual and intimate in character than public buildings, it is more difficult to distinguish where the client's brief ends and the architect's intention begins. In this respect, residential design is quite different from larger projects, in which the architecture is usually meant to extrovertly promote the client's public image. On the positive side, as Anatxu Zabalbeascoa (1998) points out, the last century has seen a great deal of architectural design devoted to private residences and their significant influence cannot be overlooked.

The four residential case studies included here are scaled down somewhat to reflect the level of information available about them and the less complicated nature of their building solutions. Inherent issues, site specifics, mechanical systems, and other items routinely discussed in the other case study chapters are not as vital here, and they are covered only as the available background information allows.

18

THE EAMES HOUSE AND STUDIO, 1945–1949

Pacific Palisades, California
CHARLES AND RAY EAMES

DESCRIPTION

Set in the period of Modernist styles for postwar living, the Eames House marks the beginning of industrial design in residential architecture. There are earlier examples of houses employing similar aspects of thinking and materials, but this design is widely regarded as the true starting point, most likely because it was the first such project to earn widespread appreciation for blending incredibly rich domestic-scaled space with industrial construction systems.

The prefabricated steel structure for the house and studio was erected in one and a half days with some 90 man-hours of labor. The welded-to-structure steel window frames were in-filled with various solid and glazed panels to suit conditions of separation and communication of inside and out. The result is a Modernist precedent that blends rational simplicity with compositional sophistication.

Figure 9.2 View of the Eames House and Studio from the east. *(Photograph courtesy of the Eames Office © 2002 Eames Office [www.eamesoffice.com].)*

TABLE 9.1 Fact Sheet

Project	**Building Name**	Eames House and Studio
	Client	Charles and Ray Eames
	City	Pacific Palisades (Santa Monica and Los Angeles area), California
	Lat/Long/Elev	34.03N 118.53W, 150 ft (46 m)
Team	**Architect**	Charles and Ray Eames
	Engineer	Edgardo Conti and McIntosh & McIntosh
	Other Team Members	Eero Saarinen collaborated on the initial idea
General	**Time Line**	1945–1949.
	Floor Area	3000 ft^2 (279 m^2), house 1650 ft^2 (153 m^2), studio 1050 ft^2 (97.5 m^2), courtyard 600 ft^2 (55.7 m^2).
	Occupants	Two.
	Cost	Not available.
	Stories	Alternating double-height spaces and two-story spaces joined by a courtyard.
	Plan	Bays are 7.3 ft (2.2 m) wide and 20 ft (6.1 m) deep. House is 7 bays or 51.1 ft × 20 ft (15.6 m × 6.1 m) footprint. Studio is five bays or 36.5 ft × 20 ft (11.1 m × 6.1 m). Courtyard is four bays, 30 ft × 20 ft (9.1 m × 6.1 m). Overall footprint is roughly 124 ft × 20 ft (37.8 m × 6.1 m).
Site	**Site Description**	3 acres (1.2 ha) on south-facing bluff 150 ft (46 m) above the Pacific Ocean.
	Parking, Cars	Open parking.
Structure	**Foundation**	Slab on grade.
	Vertical Members	4 in. (102 mm) steel H columns.
	Horizontal Spans	12 in. (305 mm) open-web steel joists.
Envelope	**Glass and Glazing**	Tempered clear glass, wired glass, and translucent fiberglass in steel frame window units.
	Skylights	None.
	Cladding	Plywood, asbestos, and stucco-finished wood lathe set in steel window frames.
	Roof	Flat roof on insulated metal deck.
HVAC	**Equipment**	None.
	Cooling Type	None.
	Distribution	Gas heating in both house and studio.
	Duct Type	Enclosed.
	Vertical Chases	Minimal.
Interior	**Partitions**	Frame.
	Finishes	Various.
	Vertical Circulation	Spiral stair.
	Furniture	Eames.
	Lighting	Various.

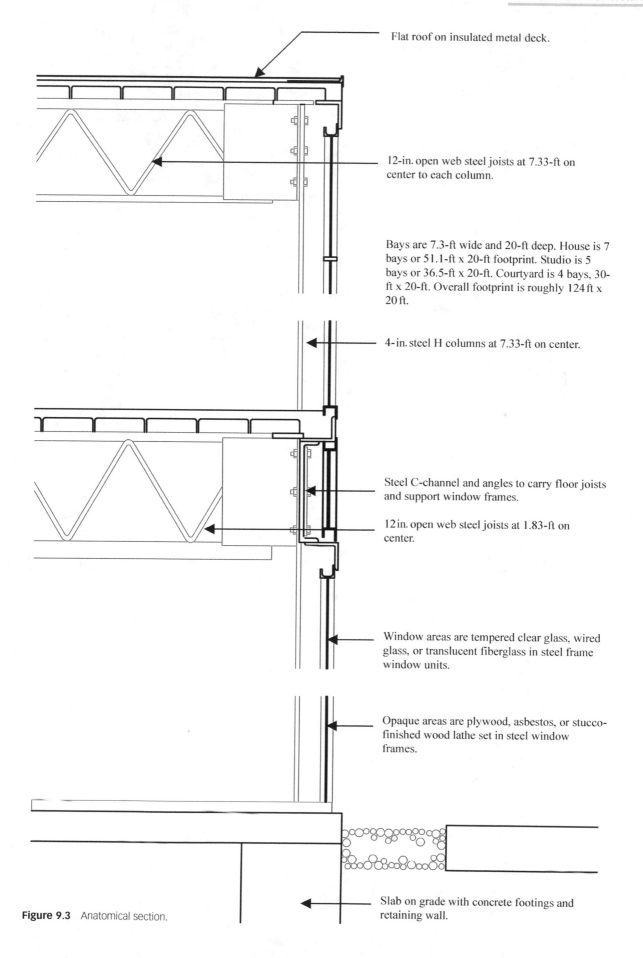

Flat roof on insulated metal deck.

12-in. open web steel joists at 7.33-ft on center to each column.

Bays are 7.3-ft wide and 20-ft deep. House is 7 bays or 51.1-ft x 20-ft footprint. Studio is 5 bays or 36.5-ft x 20-ft. Courtyard is 4 bays, 30-ft x 20-ft. Overall footprint is roughly 124 ft x 20 ft.

4-in. steel H columns at 7.33-ft on center.

Steel C-channel and angles to carry floor joists and support window frames.

12 in. open web steel joists at 1.83-ft on center.

Window areas are tempered clear glass, wired glass, or translucent fiberglass in steel frame window units.

Opaque areas are plywood, asbestos, or stucco-finished wood lathe set in steel window frames.

Slab on grade with concrete footings and retaining wall.

Figure 9.3 Anatomical section.

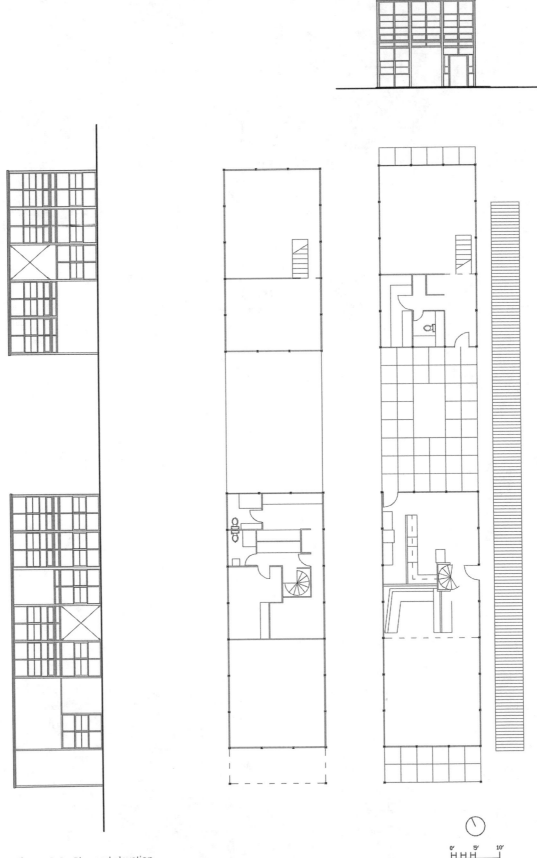

Figure 9.4 Plan and elevation.

PROGRAM

Client

The Eames couple met at the Cranbrook Academy of Arts in 1940, where Eliel Saarinen was serving as president of the Academy and head of the architecture department and Charles Eames headed the Department of Industrial Design. Ray (born Beatrice Alexandra Kaiser) assisted in the preparation of models and drawings for a competition entry developed by Charles with Eero Saarinen. In 1941, Charles and his first wife, Catherine Dewey Woermann, were divorced. Charles and Ray married that same year and moved to Los Angeles. They apparently met publisher John Entenza immediately, as he seems to have helped them settle into a Strathmore Avenue apartment designed by Richard Neutra.

The Eameses went on to create their own personal 37-year epoch of design excellence. The Library of Congress has collected more than 130,000 documents from their office. The 300 boxes they fill require 120 linear feet of shelf space. In the abundance of all this work there is an equal breadth of scope. Trained as artist and architect, the Eameses' legacy encompasses a diverse mix of accomplishments. Included is the furniture that is still made under license around the world, most notably perhaps the Eames Chair of molded plywood and leather. They made more than 100 films, including the ubiquitous 1968 *Powers of Ten,* still obligatory viewing for architecture students everywhere. They also designed showrooms, games, toys, storage units, exhibits, and the media to produce them all. Along the way, they defined a mode of design thinking that incorporated a way of living. The essence of the Eameses as designers is understood best through this interaction. All of it, for them, was a constant and giddy celebration. Work was always play—and play was to be taken very seriously.

Brief

The Eames House project began as a demonstration program of invited house designs by a number of Modernist architects. The idea was to establish new prototype designs and popularize their features. As usual for the popular Eames couple, their involvement came about through working relationships with a friend. In this case that friend was John Entenza, publisher of the Los Angeles–based journal, *Arts and Architecture.* Entenza decided to focus on the postwar housing shortage by sponsoring a series of Case Study Houses in his journal. He recognized, no doubt, that the 50 million potential American home buyers of the day had already piqued the interest of architects. What he intended was to provide a means by which the general population could profit from the best possible

design expertise. Working from the start with Ray and Charles Eames, some principle criteria for the Case Study Houses were set:

- Industrialization and Modernist ideals were to be brought to service of the home environment.
- Design solutions should define an ideal and artful way of living, "the good life," in the postwar economic boom.
- The building solutions should be "capable of duplication," if not as complete designs, then as design and construction methods.
- The solutions should offer practical assistance to the average American home buyer.

The second criterion, emphasizing "artful living," set the Case Study Houses program apart from any narrow Modernist goals based on simple fixation with the machine aesthetic. It would do the housing public no good to repeat earlier architectural styles that were based on more limited technology. Those earlier styles were restricted to imitating industrial qualities solely for their potent imagery. The difference the case study program was reaching for was driven by two critical factors. First, the housing shortage created a real need for innovative technical solutions. New methods and materials would have to be applied if architects were to serve this need. Second, the design proposed an important subplot: Technology would be brought to bear not so much on the problem of housing construction as on the notion of what Karsten Harries termed the "vision of an ideal way of living."

Site

The Eames House was located on prime ocean view acres secured by John Entenza for the Case Study Houses program. The Eames House (published as Case Study House 8) and the Entenza House (Case Study House 9), were to share a 3 acre plot on a south-facing bluff above the Pacific Coast Highway and the ocean.

The site is about two miles from the amusement park on the Santa Monica Pier and adjoins the "Rolls Royce Avenue" neighborhoods on the beach. It is located between West Sunset Boulevard to the north and the ocean front Pacific Coast Highway to the south and is part of the Santa Monica bedroom community of Pacific Palisades. In this community are some of the most famous and expensive seaside resort and residential properties in the country. Property value in Santa Monica reached its peak around 1920, in the heyday of residents like William Randolph Hearst, Douglas Fairbanks, Mae West, and Cary Grant. At that time beach property could sell for $20,000 per lineal

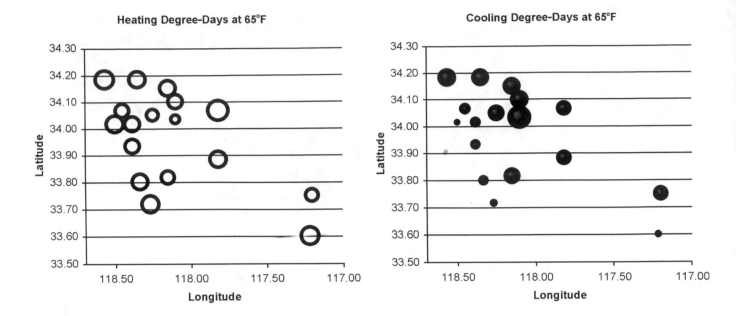

Figure 9.5 Los Angles area microclimates. The width of the circles corresponds to the number of degree-days at each location.

foot of frontage (equivalent to $150,000 in 1995 dollars). Malibu beach, just to the west, was the exclusive property of the Rindge family until 1938; all 27 miles of its coastline was kept chained off and patrolled by guards on horseback.

Despite ongoing interest in the Pacific Palisades site where the Eames House was eventually built, cowboy comedian Will Rogers would not sell the property from his personal 187 acre ranch. John Entenza had to wait until after his death in 1935 to purchase it from the estate.

Natural grade on the site rises steeply to the west, where the property is bounded by an internal circulation road. A thick stand of eucalyptus trees clings to the western edge of the site. The eucalyptus, or gum tree, is extremely hardy, sun loving, and evergreen. It is naturally desirable for both winter wind breaks and summer shade. Many species easily grow to 150 ft. The black peppermint eucalyptus can reach an astounding 475 ft high. Mature trees of flowering species generally bloom from April to November. Because these trees are important to the final Eames design and a major site feature, they merit some description.

There are more than 500 eucalyptus species, most extremely fast growing, especially the aromatic *Eucalyptus globulus*. About 100 species are well adapted to California today, the most popular being what is commonly called blue gum. All are native of Tasmania and Australia, where they were discovered in 1642. The eucalyptus was first brought to California in 1849 by Australian settlers during the California gold rush. At that time, the supply route from Australia was shorter than the route from the eastern United States, because there was no transcontinental rail-

road and no Panama Canal. Ships from the East Coast had to sail all the way around South America to reach the West Coast. Because the desirable land in California was so dry and barren in those frontier days, eucalyptus seeds were widely imported for sale and cultivation. Their initial popularity as a windbreak, fuel source, and medicinal oil suffers today because of the temperamental quality of curing its wood, the natural toxins from its roots and leaves that kill native plants, and the extreme combustibility of its dense litter and oil-rich wood in wildfires.

Climate

Pacific Palisades is gifted with the most moderate of maritime weather. The Santa Monica Pier weather station is about two miles from the Eames House and provides enough data to be a good indicator of climate factors. Generally, conditions in the region are moderated by the proximity of the ocean, which acts as a huge thermal buffer, and by the surrounding mountain ranges that shelter the Los Angeles basin from the outlying deserts. The summer and winter design conditions for Santa Monica are identical to those of Los Angeles, but this is a misleading coincidence. Comparing Santa Monica data to that of three surrounding stations shows how extremely sensitive Los Angeles area microclimates are to proximity of the ocean and elevation above sea level. This sensitivity results in large variations in temperature, rainfall, humidity, fog, and sunshine over distances of less than a mile. Closer to the ocean, daily temperature ranges are narrower and rainfall is diminished. So although the Los Angeles International Airport is located only 15 miles away, its climate data has to be interpreted carefully. Mugu Naval Air Station is 44 miles west of Pacific Palisades. But Mugu climate data better represents the Eames House location than Los Angeles International in some respects, probably because its instrumentation is closer to the water. Note the similarity of degree-days cooling, for instance. Interestingly, of all the relevant local weather stations, Santa Monica has the most moderate cooling season, a fact that explains the weekend traffic jams of vechicles leaving Los Angeles dating all the way back to 1920.

What can be said conclusively about the Pacific Palisades/Santa Monica climate is that it is quite comfortable, if frequently on the cool side. Temperatures range between 50°F and 75°F for 80 percent of annual hours. The average daily high in August is 72°F, with a morning low of 63°F. The average daily low in January is 50°F, with an afternoon high of 64°F. No freezes have occurred in the

period since 1948, before the Eames House was erected. At a 65°F base temperature, there are only 1647 degree-days heating, and these are distributed smoothly across the winter months. A good number of them occur during summer nights. As for the warm season, there are a negligible 300 degree-days cooling at the same 65°F base temperature.

Weather events at the site are mild mannered as well. There are normally less than 12 in.es of rain per year and fewer than 90 days per year with precipitation. Most of the rain occurs in the winter months, and summers are quite arid. Mornings and evenings year-round are frequently covered with low clouds that promote cool, humid conditions. Fog makes up for some of the dryness, especially close to the coast where the Eames House sits in the eucalyptus grove. The airport reports 194 days per year when some fog can be expected. Mugu Naval Air Station experi-

TABLE 9.2 Normal Climate Data for Santa Monica and Los Angeles

		Jan.	Feb.	Mar.	Apr.	May	June	July	Aug.	Sept.	Oct.	Nov.	Dec.	Year
Temperature	Degree-Days Heating	277	215	220	146	84	22	2	1	3	27	122	244	1355
	Degree-Days Cooling	5	6	6	13	17	52	134	167	143	80	24	5	656
	Extreme High	88	92	95	102	97	104	97	98	110	106	101	94	110
	Normal High	65	66	65	68	69	72	75	76	76	74	71	66	70
	Normal Average	56	58	58	61	63	66	69	70	70	67	62	57	63
	Normal Low	47	49	50	53	56	59	63	64	63	59	52	48	55
	Extreme Low	27	34	37	43	45	48	52	51	47	43	38	32	27
Humidity	Dew Point	42	44	46	49	53	56	60	61	59	54	46	42	51
	Max % RH	70	72	76	76	77	80	80	82	81	76	69	68	76
	Min % RH	61	62	64	64	66	67	67	68	67	66	61	61	64
	% Days with Rain	26	26	26	19	17	13	6	6	12	14	17	21	24
	Rain Inches	3	2	2	1	0	0	T	0	0	0	1	2	12
Sky	% Overcast Days	29	32	29	27	26	20	3	3	9	20	20	26	20
	% Clear Days	33	33	32	35	31	34	36	38	39	36	39	37	35
Wind	Prevailing Direction	WSW	WSW	WSW	WSW	WSW	WSW	WSW	WSW	WSW	WSW	WSW	WSW	WSW
	Speed, Knots	8	8	9	9	9	9	8	8	8	8	8	7	8
	Percent Calm	7	7	6	5	5	6	6	7	8	8	8	8	7
Days Observed	Rain	8	8	8	6	5	4	2	2	4	4	5	6	89
	Fog	11	11	8	7	6	6	7	8	10	11	11	11	194
	Haze	19	18	17	18	19	22	25	25	24	23	20	19	7
	Snow	0	0	0	0	0	0	0	0	0	0	0	0	20
	Hail	0	0	0	0	0	0	0	0	0	0	0	0	0
	Freezing Rain	0	0	0	0	0	0	0	0	0	0	0	0	0
	Blowing Sand	0	0	0	0	0	0	0	0	0	0	0	0	0

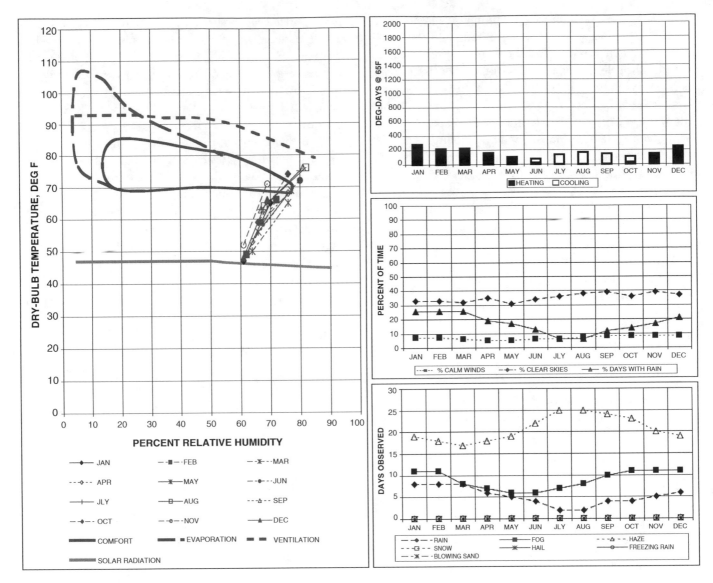

Figure 9.6   Climate analysis graphics.

ences a very similar 187 days with fog. The Santa Monica station does not keep this level of detailed data, but can logically be expected to experience similar conditions. Although the fog is heaviest in winter, there is sufficient morning fog in the warmer months to provide some relief, especially to vegetation.

Thunderstorms occur only one or two days per month, mostly during November through April. Wind is generally from the west, bringing mild temperatures to the coast. At night, as the deserts behind the mountain ranges cool, winds reverse and move toward the ocean. The hot, dry Santa Ana winds from the inland deserts seldom reach the coast.

As the Eames House is thermally a surface-load-dominated environment, an analysis of passive heating potential will help demonstrate the importance of climatic influ-

ences. There was not much available in terms of sophisticated solar design tools in 1945, but Walter Gropius's 1937 personal house in Lincoln, Massachusetts, had already established the wisdom and practicality of passive techniques. Frank Lloyd Wright's "Solar Hemicycle" Jacobs House in Madison, Wisconsin, was designed in the 1940s and built in 1948, the same period as that of the Eames House.

The Load Collector Ratio (LCR) method (Balcomb et al., 1980) is commonly used to size and predict the performance of passive heating systems. It is largely based on the ratio of the building heat loss coefficient in Btu per degree-day to the area of south-facing glass. Basing performance on Los Angeles climate data with 1579 degree-days heating, a simple direct-gain system with an LCR of 90 results in a solar heating contribution of 50 percent.

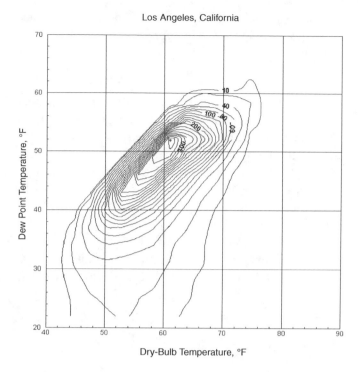

Los Angeles, California

Figure 9.7   Bin data distribution for the Los Angeles area. Concentric areas of graph indicate the number of hours per year that weather conditions normally occur in this climate. Similar to elevation readings on topographic maps, highest frequency occurrences of weather are at the center peaks of the graph.. (Data sources: *Engineering Weather Data, typical meteorological year (TMY) data from the National Climatic Data Center, and the* ASHRAE Weather Data Viewer *from the American Society of Heating, Refrigerating and Air-Conditioning Engineers.)*

This roughly means that each 90 Btu of energy loss per degree-day heating would be countered by 1 ft² of unshaded south-facing glass, and that the result would be a 50 percent reduction in heating load. This assumes that the appropriate amount of sunlit thermal mass is provided in the occupied space. Note that higher performance savings require lower LCR heat loss ratios and imply higher levels of insulation. An 80 percent savings would require an LCR of 31 and a 30 percent solar savings fraction (SSF) could be achieved with an LCR of 187. In Sacramento, California, for comparison, with 2843 degree-days heating, the 50 percent savings LCR would be 27 and the 30 percent SSF would work for an LCR of 124. The 80 percent SSF is not achievable in Sacramento with direct gain unless night insulation is deployed over the south glazing.

INTENTION

Design Team
Ray and Charles Eames worked with Eero Saarinen on the first scheme for their house and studio while collaborating

on the design of the adjoining Entenza house. The friendship and working relationship between them would continue until Saarinen's death in 1961. Engineering assistance was provided by Edgardo Conti. McIntosh & McIntosh provided engineering consultation for the redesign.

Philosophy
Ray Eames (1912–1988) was born in Sacramento, California. She studied art with the German painter Hans Hoffman in Massachusetts from 1933 to 1939. Hoffman introduced her to Cubism and, in particular, to works of Mondrian, Kandinski, Arp, and Miró. In 1936 she became a founding member of American Abstract Artists. In 1937 she exhibited her paintings at the first American Abstract Artists show in New York.

By 1940 she was auditing classes at the Cranbrook Academy of Arts. She met Charles Eames there while working on models and drawings for entries that Eames and Eero Saarinen were preparing for the Organic Design in Home Furnishings competition at the Museum of Modern Art in New York. In June 1941, six months before Pearl Harbor, Charles and Ray married and moved to California.

Charles Eames (1907–1978) was born in St. Louis, Missouri. He studied architecture there at Washington University from 1925 to 1928. Allegedly, he left the university because of a controversy in which he argued for the ideals of Frank Lloyd Wright. The next ten years were spent in two architectural partnerships and an eight-month spell of travel, painting, and work in Mexico. In 1938 he received a fellowship at the Cranbrook Academy of Art, where he later became the head of the Department of Industrial Design.

Together, Ray and Charles Eames were frequently described as "ridiculously happy." Every moment was an event and every event was a celebration. And celebrations were taken very seriously. Their zest for life left nothing to the mundane; everything was an opportunity to design something special: toys, games, furniture, movies, exhibits, houses, or just an elaborate setting on the dinner table. Gifts were made on every occasion, elaborately wrapped in precious papers and ribbons. Even their clothes were carefully selected with Hollywood flair, part stylish apparel and part movie costume. The couple dedicated their work to things that interested them and looked for common interests in their clients. This interest transformed labor into work and work into play—and into more opportunities to celebrate life. They always sought to instill joy and pleasure into whatever they produced. True to form, the couple moved to their new home and studio on Christmas Eve of 1949.

The Eameses were also pioneer technophiles. A great deal of their work is devoted to demonstrations and instructional media on the potentials of new technology. In the postwar transformation to an information society they were producing movies, books, and exhibitions that promoted the benefits of scientific progress. IBM, Boeing, Polaroid, and Westinghouse were among the many clients who worked with the Eames studio to popularize the progressive aspects of their products.

Intent

Aside from the Case Study parameters of technical accommodation and service to lifestyle, the primary intent was to popularize well-designed mass-production housing. Ideally, industrial building systems would be made to provide a neutral background for the warm decoration of personal lifestyles and technology would produce a flexible environment for everyday activities. These challenges fit neatly with the Eameses attitudes about combining work with play and art with science as well as with their special abilities to find wonder in mundane objects.

This approach, parallel to the ideas of Buckminster Fuller's ephemeralization, included the idea that more and more could be accomplished with fewer and fewer resources through elegant design thinking and technical progress. It also mirrored the Bauhaus ideal of wedding art and craft with science and industry to produce democratically accessible, affordable architecture. Finally, it echoed Karsten Harries' (see Chapter 4) description of architects' recurrent desire "to reflect an ideal way of living."

CRITICAL TECHNICAL ISSUES

The inherent, contextual, and intentional issues of the Eames House and Studio are combined in a single section for this case study. The interwoven nature of the program, intention, and, particularly, the site context muddles the exact classification of critical design and technical issues.

Residential design in community settings is always confronted by issues of view, privacy, and respect for adjoining properties. The Eames House would have to share the bluff-top meadow overlooking the Pacific with Entenza's own Case Study house, and this seems to have influenced the redesign of the Eames House as well as its repositioning along the west property line. Its being nestled into the earth at the edge of the property makes for a very different and more introverted house than the first "Bridge House" scheme that was proposed. Where the first scheme would have been open and elevated to capture ocean vistas, winter sun, and summer breezes, the final

scheme was cloistered in shade and privately huddled behind captured views of its courtyards. With the maturity of the eucalyptus trees and landscape plantings over the years, this introverted position has been gradually solidified.

The kit-of-parts approach to detailing and craftsmanship was the most critical aspect of the building construction, and its finished quality was essential to the architectural intent of providing a high-quality, well-designed, mass-manufactured housing prototype. What systems would be used, and how would they be visually integrated into the image of this new ideal way of living? How reliably could industrial components be substituted for on-site craftsmanship? How would brute technology be given a human face that fulfilled the common expectations about a house that could become a graceful family home?

APPROPRIATE SYSTEMS

Precedent

The technical development of industrial-component residential construction begins with Richard Neutra's 1929 Lovell House in the Santa Barbara section of Los Angeles. The Eames House is a progression from this precedent in its intentional use of off-the-shelf building materials from commercial and industrial systems. Neutra employed industrial materials exclusively, including a steel frame of the same basic members later repeated in the Eames House. Moreover, it was Neutra who made earlier statements about the need for modern architecture to serve the needs of humankind. He also held a strong position on the relation of indoor to outdoor spaces as defining the human condition in nature. The Lovell House is often recognized as a milestone in the Los Angeles architecture scene and as a founding part of the region's avant-garde design mystique.

If the Lovell House is the technical precedent of the Eames House, then a scheme of Mies van der Rohe is the more direct formal and stylistic one. The Eames House and Studio went through two complete design schemes. The first unbuilt version, the Bridge House, was allegedly based on a 1937 design for a glass house by Mies van der Rohe. Mies's design was unrealized as well, and it is not clear how any of the team would have been knowledgeable about its details. Opinion holds that Charles Eames was somehow aware of it through professional channels.

As published in *Arts & Architecture* of December 1945 as Case Study #8, the specifics of the first scheme offered a number of features that might have made it quite satisfactory. The house was a simple rectangular volume, elongated from east to west with glass-covered truss walls making up the south and north façades. Sketches show the diagonal bracing through full-height glass. The west end wall sat on high ground at the edge of the property. The volume spanned the meadow below and was cantilevered across two slender supporting columns. A stair spiraled up from a covered parking area into the single-story living space. The studio space was separate and set among the eucalyptus against the west property line, making an L-shaped compound.

In the Mies precedent, or what became Eames's scheme #1, there would have been a wide view of the ocean directly to the south. This also would have afforded efficient natural ventilation in the mild climate and made for easy passive solar heat gain in the long, cool seasons. Despite these advantages, there were some significant drawbacks. First, placing the house in the middle of the site was judged to be too strong a mark on the landscape. A more gentle honoring of the hilltop meadow demanded subtler massing. This problem was emphasized by the fact that view and open space were shared with the adjoining Entenza residence, Case Study House #9, and a central position for the Eames house monopolized the entire bluff. Nonetheless, the design was published and steel was ordered.

In November 1947, however, Charles Eames traveled to New York to see an exhibit of Mies van der Rohe's work at the Museum of Modern Art. This exhibit, incidentally, included the first public display of Mies's glass house inspiration for the truss wall Bridge House scheme. Something in the exhibit persuaded Eames to redesign the house, even though he would have to rework the kit of parts already on order. In doing so he was able to expand the enclosed area from the 2500 ft² of the first scheme to a final 3,000 ft² of house and studio.

Site

The final scheme situated the house and studio some 350 ft away from the Pacific Coast Highway and 120 ft above it. Across the three acre site from the Eames House, to the east, is the one-story Entenza House, Case Study House #9. Another two adjoining acres were reserved for other Case Study Houses, including one by Richard Neutra.

Redesigning the house involved pulling it out of the center of the meadow and leaning it close into the west property line. This aligned the axis of the house with that of the studio. A 30 ft wide and 20 ft deep courtyard was captured between the two 17 ft high structures. The entire compound made a slender footprint of 20 ft by 124 ft.

Placing the building at the edge of site left an expanse of meadow open to view from the interior. Rather than bisecting the site, this placement left it whole. Views toward the ocean were still accessible from the fully glazed

south elevation at a two-story living space and from the bedroom balcony above. This location also stationed the house in deep shade amidst the grove of eucalyptus trees. It did, however, transgress on the privacy of separation between the Eames House and the Entenza House.

The second site redesign problem was more pragmatic, but the steep grade from the meadow up to the trees at the edge of the site required an expensive 200 ft long concrete retaining wall. An additional $5,000 ($32,000 in 1995 dollars) was needed for the retaining wall, sacrificing any savings that were gained in redesign by the more efficient use of the steel frame. The cut behind the wall made a level area where the house could be situated just above the meadow. Soil removed from the cut did help resolve the privacy separation issue. It was used to make a berm between the two residences. Shrubs and trees were planted on top of the earth berm and liberally spread between the two houses to provide visual screening. To the west of the retaining wall the site is left wild for separation from the street. A path above the wall provides space for the everyday paraphernalia of ladders and garden tools.

Structure

The final design is constructed from a prefabricated kit of parts made to order for the project. A steel frame on 7.3 ft centers is bolted together to make the 20 ft wide shell, and steel angles are welded to it to receive steel window frames, also welded in place.

Vertical support is provided by 4 in. × 4 in. steel × 10 lb H-section columns, with the hollow areas concealed in the walls and the inside flanges factory drilled for bolting. Eighteen columns on 5 in. × 5 in. × 0.5 in. welded base plates form the long walls of the house, and 12 more line the long axis of the studio, all at 7.3 ft on center spacing. The southernmost column bay of the house is hollowed out to enclose a patio that is walled on the west and covered with an overhang. Columns are 17 ft high on the main east elevation, but to the west they rest on a continuous 8 ft high retaining wall. All columns are set into concrete and secured by 0.625 in. × 10 in. anchor bolts set in the foundation. Each of the four narrow end walls facing north or south are divided by two additional 4 in. × 4 in. columns, but these are basically window frames and do not carry floor or roof loads. Diagonal X-bracing is set between columns in a few of the opaque sections of the exterior wall, and one of these is expressed on the main east elevation.

Horizontal structure starts with a band of 12 in. steel channels with welded end tabs that are bolted to the columns at the second floor level. These channels support 14 in. prefabricated steel bar joists at 1.83 ft on center where there is a second floor, but no channels are used across the double-height spaces. Floor joists are fitted with 10.5 in. × 4.5 in. × 0.25 in. steel plate connections and secured to the channel with 0.5 in. bolts. The top and bottom of the 12 in. channel receives a welded 4 in. × 3 in. steel angle, which forms the second floor edge and makes a continuous frame for the envelope infill. The vertical face of these angles is welded flush to the outer flanges of the columns. The second floor is formed of 2x6 tongue-and-groove wood planks on a metal deck. For the roof, prefabricated 12 in. steel bar joists at 7.3 ft on center span east to west from each column and support a metal deck, 0.43 in. insulation board, and a built-up tar and gravel roof. Because the roof joists span directly from the columns, no edge beam is needed, but a 3 in. × 3 in. × 0.17 in. steel angle is welded to the top of the columns to receive the envelope infill. Roof joists were fabricated with 0.38 in. steel plate connectors and then fastened to the column flanges with 0.5 in. bolts, in the same manner in which the second floor joists are bolted to the horizontal 12 in. channel.

Envelope

The exterior skin of the design is a composition of rectangles provided by steel window frames welded directly to the steel superstructure in a plane formed by the outer flange of the columns and the horizontal steel angles. Even the 12 in. edge beam is covered by a steel window frame.

By using variously subdivided window mullions, the design achieves a playful pattern of sizes and shapes across its façades. Within the frames are fitted both clear and opaque materials, and these are intentionally varied from panel to panel. Clear and wired glass is used, as well as translucent fiberglass panels. Opaque infill pieces are insulated wood panels, asbestos board, or stucco over wood. Painted color is used on the opaque panels to heighten the compositional effect. The elevations are derived from Ray Eames's abstract cubism, Mondrian-like with large and small rectangles of bright color moving in front of the transparent and translucent frames.

The colors and transparencies also have a functional character. They modulate between the inside and outside conditions and vary according to the need for light, air, privacy, and view. Exterior color is used to designate the interior activity. There is also the suggestion that the panels can be replaced or rearranged to suit the occupant's fancy and changing needs.

The passive performance of the skin seems to have been decided in favor of cooling season priorities. With the long axis shifted to a north-south orientation, the only south sun orientation left was the double-height wall at the end of the living space. Even so, this wall is protected by a 7.5 ft deep overhang and an equal-sized west shading fin above the retaining wall. There is little emphasis on view here, let alone beneficial solar heat gain. The surrounding shade of evergreen eucalyptus trees satisfies the cooling priority.

Mechanical

Mechanical heating and cooling requirements are minimal in this climate. The summer design weather conditions for sizing equipment are 78°F dry bulb and 64°F wet bulb, which is almost no requirement at all. There are about 835 degree-days cooling in the Los Angeles area where that data is taken, but only 446 annual cooling degree-days in Santa Monica, so even the mild 78/64 overstates what actually occurs at the site. Consequently, there are no cooling systems in the home or studio. Winters are also mild, but design conditions of 43°F and the 1819 annual degree-days heating on the Santa Monica beach front (considerably more than the 1419 recorded in Los Angles) dictate the need for some space heating. The studio and the residence each have a gas-fired furnace and duct system for winter comfort. These systems are readily contained within the kitchen and utility areas of the divided-height spaces and in the cavity of the second floor above the finished ceiling of the lower floor. Wood-burning fireplaces are also provided in both the residence and the studio, and these have a much greater impact on the design than do the furnaces.

Interior

Indoor-outdoor relationships are established by treating the house as seven cubes. These cubes alternate between open-height spaces and divided-height spaces. The central courtyard is an open-height space flanked on the north by a two-story studio cube divided into service spaces below and a storage mezzanine above. South of the courtyard is the divided-height cube of the house, kitchen and dining below with bedrooms above. Then there are the two outer open cubes, the double-height studio to the north end and the double-height living room on the south. Two additional outdoor rooms are captured by the retaining wall at either end of the compound, parking to the north and a patio to the south.

Interior plans are mostly open, with the ground floor of the residence being kitchen, dining, and living space and the studio consisting largely of a double-height room and an open mezzanine. Private spaces are provided by a loft bedroom, a small guest room, two baths and lots of closet space upstairs in the house and by a small bath/utility area downstairs in the studio.

Interior walls are framed into the structure by means of a 10.5 in. × 4.5 in. × 0.25 in. steel plate support bolted to the columns. Finishes are mostly gypsum board or plaster, but the roof joists and metal deck are left exposed to the interior.

TECHNICAL INTEGRATION HIGHLIGHTS

Physical

Structure and envelope systems are physically meshed, and to a certain point, indistinguishable. The steel structural frame has welded elements that are more for connection to the enclosing skin than they are for support, and the steel window frames are just smaller-scale supports for the actual envelope panels. This scheme greatly simplifies construction, just as the prefabricated subsystems of columns, channels, joists, and metal deck facilitate on-site assembly.

The building foundation is also physically merged with the site. This provides a level of privacy and defends the perimeter boundary while opening vistas across the meadow. The house is unapproachable from the steep west side slope below the street.

Visual

The overall image of the Eames House and Studio is one of abstract composition with black painted structural frames supporting interchangeable envelope panels of various glass or painted surfaces. This expression is perhaps meant to be a playful arrangement, but one that harmonizes the exterior pieces and conveys something about what happens behind them. Their modular patterns suggest the possibility of personalized arrangement.

Structure also interacts with the site elements to create other visual benefits of integration. Three walled outdoor rooms are formed by the long retaining wall—at the central courtyard and at the north and south ends of the house and studio. As the wall turns back into the site on its north and south ends, it embraces a semicovered patio area outside the living room and parking for two cars at the end of the drive outside the studio. The wood paneling on the west wall of the double-height living room is extended into the patio area to visually reinforce the status of the patio as an outdoor room.

Performance

Three thousand feet is a generous space for two people, though there must have been lots of visitors and staff in the Eames Studio plus many friends to entertain in their home. Still, space utilization does not seem to have been a challenging mandate. Nor was there much to worry about in the way of climate forces that might have pushed the design response and the integration of systems and their performance. The environment is friendly and benign to the point of benevolence. This helps with luminous performance as well, because sun and shade are not sufficiently critical to prohibit large unobstructed areas of glass for view and daylight. Perhaps this is an example of enve-

lope and site integration between the open view and the evergreen eucalyptus shade. Certainly, it helps that the house looks east rather than west.

The real need for performance integration is suggested by the idea of affordable mass production graced with good design. This called for inventive design by elegant simplicity rather than sumptuous complexity, and the Eames House meets that challenge fairly well in the selection and deployment of all its systems. The prefabricated structural system and welded envelope frames minimized expensive site labor. The decidedly low-performance envelope works well enough in the mild climate. Except for the expensive retaining wall, the site systems are mostly left to nature. Performance integrations are less spectacular in this early example of industrialized systems because there are fewer performance requirements to deal with, but the Eames House nonetheless establishes that economical mass production is suited to high-quality architectural results.

DISCUSSION

This is the perfect house for a perfect client, on a perfect site, in the perfect climate. Although the Eames House reflects many ideals of architectural design and is justifiably celebrated as the marriage of industrial design with architecture, perhaps it was just too perfect to be reproducible, and in an important sense this perfection fell short of the intent to provide the best possible vocabulary of design features to the general population.

In the end, direct and immediate applications of lessons from the Eames House and the other Case Study Houses were as inaccessible to the general postwar population and conventional construction as were the elitist mansions of Rolls Royce Avenue. What started as design propositions for the masses through mass production ended with the same magazine-cover gloss as most design-by-architects, for-other-architects, idealized showpieces. The hard issues of climate, affordable detailing, lot planning, and middle-class suburban living are mostly lost in the formal exuberance and technical inventiveness of architectural expression. It did not help that returning soldiers and their families probably felt little affinity for the California-styled good life. These were the days long before popular television programs were filmed on the beaches of Malibu.

As compared with the lessons of Wright's Usonian houses, there are very few traces of the Case Study Houses to be found in typical residential construction today. The "Case Study House #8" tag certainly suggests a prototype design, but it seems that some combination of common practicality on the consumer industry side clashed with unrestrained idealism from the architects' camp. Or perhaps the Case Study program was just too visionary for easy consumption, too advanced for its day.

Although the Eames House and the Case Study program had less than the desired impact on the home building industry, they certainly made significant impressions on the minds of architects. The list of participating designers, by itself, added critical legitimacy to the movement that Entenza and his cohorts inaugurated. When the last of the Case Study Houses (27 of the 34 designs were built) was being constructed in 1966, Entenza sold the magazine that had featured them. By then the program had influenced a Modernist movement and established an industrial systems motif that was taken up by a generation of architects.

Allison and Peter Smithson are England's, and perhaps all of Europe's, closest counterparts to Charles and Ray Eames. They were close friends with the Eameses and avid innovators of industrialized systems architecture in their own work. The Smithsons have made several mentions of their own intellectual debt to the landmark Eames House and the many endeavors of the prolific Eames office.

A number or impacts of the Eames House are clear:

- For perhaps the first time, domestic warmth and industrial construction systems were proven to be compatible. Allison and Peter Smithson described this house as the artful arrangement of everyday items so that they become "honorable objects."

- Modernist architecture had proved that it could provide neutral backgrounds for individual lifestyles without the articles of everyday living invading and destroying purist design intent. The Eames House makes this statement through the idea of architect as "host" and the building as "shock absorber."

- Rearrangement of personal spaces and belongings could be enhanced by interchangeable building components. Envelope panels could be unplugged and reused. Their color could be changed to signal the kind of activity that happened inside the skin.

- Establishing the merits of "functional décor" encouraged many Modernist architects to wander away from Spartan modernism into explorations of richly dimensioned space.

19

MAGNEY HOUSE, 1983-1985

Bingie Bingie Point, New South Wales, Australia
GLENN MURCUTT

DESCRIPTION

The roof floats like a seagull claiming the open expanse of the site, but its form is more deliberately that of a dry creek bed waiting for monsoon rains. There is also an intentional reference to the enclosure of soft tent forms. Then, of course, it is a sharp-brimmed hat shading the clerestory windows. Perhaps it is also a visual cue to the swell of ocean waves heard crashing nearby. Or, one last formal conjecture, the roof is an aerodynamic foil, capturing and venting air with its upturned wings.

To Glenn Murcutt, the roof is all these things, but mostly to him it is just a roof. Its form only reflects multiple understandings of the landscape it inhabits, a form contorted by the obvious clues as well as the invisible ones.

In an existential sense, the roof simply articulates what is already there. It is part of the land, in harmony with it despite the assertive distinction of its being an industrial artifact commanding the open seaside. Murcutt calls this assertion "confronting the site," a term defining his ecological perspective as disciplined and functional. He opposes sentimental attempts to blend buildings into the environment by imitating its forms or colors.

Under the roof is a long pavilion programmatically divided by a veranda into two quasi-independent retreats. On the east and ocean side is the parents' suite, complete with its own kitchen. To the west side are rooms for the grown children and guests, along with communal kitchen, dining, and general use areas.

The pavilion is divided phenomenologically across its other axis from north to south. The north wall (the sunlit side in the "down-under" Southern Hemisphere) is a series of filters, barriers, and switches controlling sun, wind, light, and view. It makes a thin but controlled edge between inside and out. Lined along the north wall are the open bays of activity spaces. There is a fireplace in the parents' suite, a woodstove in the common gathering space. Behind the rooms is a continuous corridor with seven doors of separation along the long axis and an open view out both ends of the house. Next, the south interior zone contains a narrow service core with all the kitchen, bathing, toilet, and utility spaces. The final layer of the south wall is made of service components absorbed into cabinetry and plumbing fixtures. This extra thick south layer ensures protection from the cold winter winds of August.

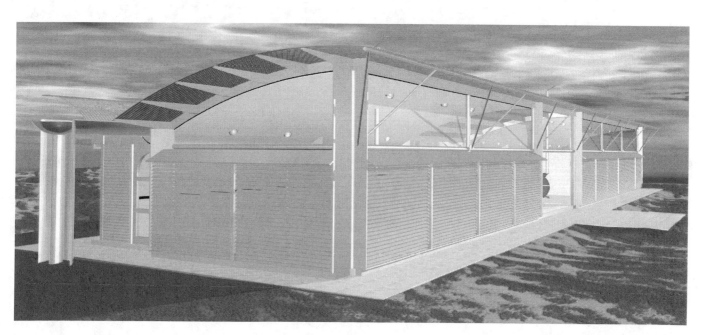

Figure 9.8 Overview of the house from the northeast. *(3-D rendering by Travis Hughs.)*

TABLE 9.3   Fact Sheet

Project	**Building Name**	Magney House
	Client	Magney Family
	Location	Bingie Bingie Point, Moruya, New South Wales, Australia
	Lat/Long/Elev	36.02 S 150.17 E, close to sea level
	Design	Glen Murcutt
General	**Time Line**	1983–1985.
	Floor Area	1919 ft² (178.3 m²) plus 222 ft² (20.8 m²) terrace.
	Occupants	Three bedrooms.
	Cost	Not determined.
	Stories	One.
	Plan	Long, single story, one-room-deep pavilion with six bays each 18.4 ft (5.6 m) across and 19.4 ft (5.9 m) deep.
Site	**Site Description**	Rural and treeless open seaside between rocky point and inland waters. The 82.5 acre (33 hectare) site is covered with tall native grasses and a line of exposed granite boulders. Topography slopes up to south and southeast. Bingie Bingie Point is 17 km southeast of Moruya, 12 km south of Congo, and 200 km south of Sydney.
	Parking, Cars	Two, with canvas canopy for cover.
Structure	**Foundation**	Insulated slab on grade.
	Vertical Members	Hot dip galvanized steel tube frame of 4.5 in. (114 mm) pipe columns. Solid exterior walls are corrugated steel over insulation over brick with plaster interior finish.
	Horizontal Spans	Steel purlins support roof spans over interior spaces.
Envelope	**Glass and Glazing**	Tempered or laminated glass with insect screen. Glazed gable ends above 7.2 ft (2.2 m) walls. Operable aluminum louver shading below 7.2 ft wall line on north façade.
	Skylights	None.
	Cladding	Corrugated zinc-galvanized steel over fibrous insulation blanket.
	Roof	Corrugated zinc-galvanized steel with aluminum gutter section and insulated, vented air cavity. Roof drains into large rainwater cisterns.
HVAC	**Equipment**	Fireplace.
	Cooling Type	None.
	Distribution	None.
	Duct Type	None.
	Vertical Chases	None.
Interior	**Partitions**	Glazed transoms above 7.2 ft (2.2 m) interior walls. Continuous corridor down long axis.
	Finishes	Ceramic floor in 12.5 in. (318 mm) gray tiles, plaster walls, gypsum board ceilings.
	Vertical Circulation	None.
	Furniture	Ikea.

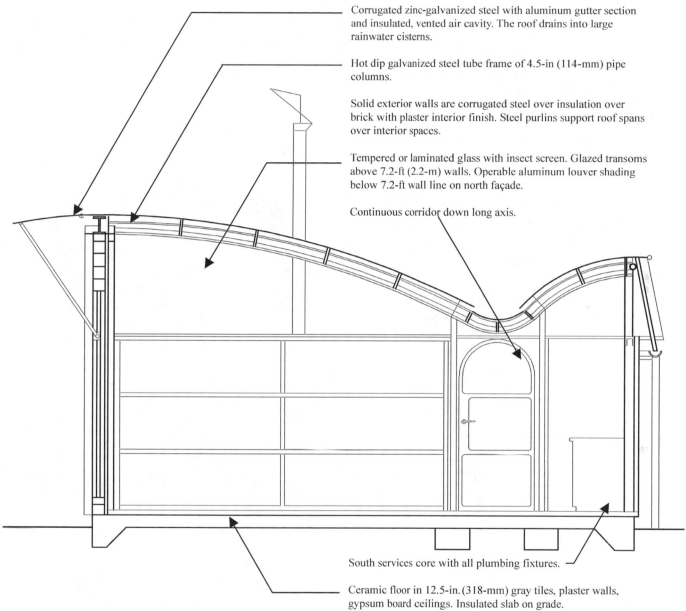

Corrugated zinc-galvanized steel with aluminum gutter section and insulated, vented air cavity. The roof drains into large rainwater cisterns.

Hot dip galvanized steel tube frame of 4.5-in (114-mm) pipe columns.

Solid exterior walls are corrugated steel over insulation over brick with plaster interior finish. Steel purlins support roof spans over interior spaces.

Tempered or laminated glass with insect screen. Glazed transoms above 7.2-ft (2.2-m) walls. Operable aluminum louver shading below 7.2-ft wall line on north façade.

Continuous corridor down long axis.

South services core with all plumbing fixtures.

Ceramic floor in 12.5-in. (318-mm) gray tiles, plaster walls, gypsum board ceilings. Insulated slab on grade.

Figure 9.9 Anatomical section.

Another system of layers organizes the scheme from bottom to top. An insulated concrete slab foundation sets a plinth for the house and is covered in the same gray ceramic tiles inside and out, dissolving the separation. The plinth visually anchors the house to the windswept site. Exterior walls form a strong horizontal band of enclosure, defined by a terminating line at door-head height. Interior base walls are constructed of plaster on brick, stopping at the same 7.2 ft height. Above the wall band are a mullionless clerestory and glazed gables providing low continuous views of the sky. The clerestory is complemented inside by laminated glass transoms that close the plastered base interior walls to the ceiling while maintaining light and view. And then, resting above the ribbon of glass, there is the floating, flying, shading, splashing, sloshing, and breathing roof.

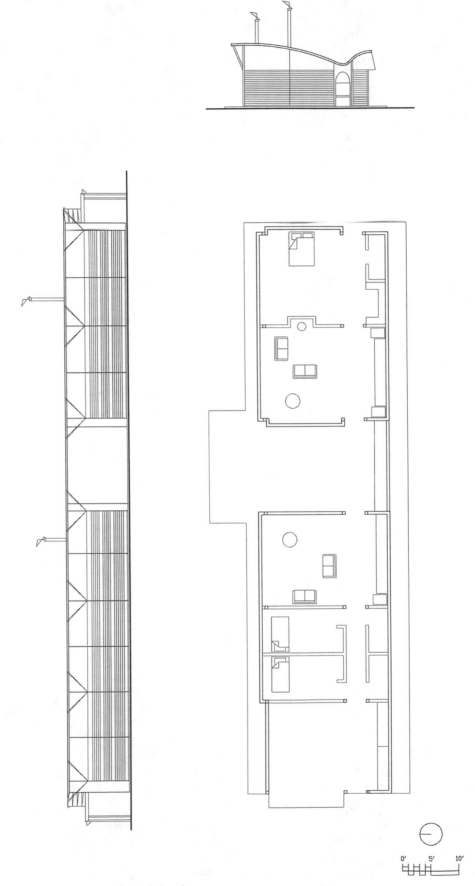

Figure 9.10 Plan and elevation.

PROGRAM

Client and Brief

The Magney family camped on this site many times before acquiring it in the mid 1970s. Their idea for a vacation house on the 82.5 acres was to maintain the memories of experiencing its natural beauty, temperament, and climatic events. They envisioned something perhaps reminiscent of a tent, for this would be a place to live in nature. As for city life, the Magneys would later commission Murcutt to redesign their Sydney house as well.

Site

The rural houses of Glenn Murcutt's architecture are sophisticated responses to his sense of place. The sophistication does not result in cluttered complexity because Murcutt imposes clear and poetically minimalist interpretations on their forms. To appreciate these qualities, it would be necessary to experience something of the place and come to know it directly. All that can be offered here is a short description of the characteristics of the place where the Magney House is set.

Bingie Bingie Point and the inland town of Moruya lie within southeast Australia's Eurobodalla Coast of New South Wales. The region encompasses the present-day towns of Batemans Bay, Moruya, and Narooma. Eurobodalla is a primary vacation area for the Australian capital Region of Canberra and is situated on the South Coast of New South Wales, 273 km south of Sydney and 150 km east of Canberra. The shire is 101 km long and 40 km wide, with a total area of 1,313 mi^2 (3,402 km^2). The 1981 population of 16,497 had almost doubled by the 1996 census.

The Eurobodalla, or "Many Waters," region was originally the home of South Coast nomadic Aborigines tribes, the Bugelli-Manji and the Yuin. The 60,000-year history of Aboriginal life and knowledge is an important insight to the land of Australia, and Glenn Murcutt spent years studying their culture to inform his sense of place. Aboriginal sites including stone quarries are found at Bingie Bingie Point. Folklore is perpetuated by Aboriginal names still used in the region, or by names given by Captain Cook.

The shire of Eurobodalla stretches along 100 km of undeveloped coast and pristine forest. The woods are dominated by eucalyptus species: spotted gum, Sydney blue gum, and Sydney peppermint, among others. Magnificent old-growth forests cover 150,000 acres (60,000 hectares) of the Eurobodalla, more than 16 percent of the South Coast Forest. Its wetlands are host to migratory waterfowl, whose habitats are now protected here and by joint treaties with Japan and China. More than 400 species of native mammals, birds, reptiles, and amphibians live in this natural paradise—more than a fifth of all Australia's native species.

Gold was discovered in Moruya in 1851, and by 1861 the entire Eurobodalla had gold fever. By the end of the 1890s gold was mined out, and thousands of hopeful immigrants dispersed or settled down to become dairy farmers, fishermen, or to work in local industries. In early 1924, the British engineering firm Dorman Long and Company won the contract to erect the Sydney Harbour Bridge, and the firm decided to take granite for bridge pylons from a quarry on the Moruya River. A plant for preparing the stone, a light-gauge railway, and a stone crusher benefited Moruya's economy.

Today tourism is big business in Eurobodalla. It generates many more economic benefits by preservation than the lumber industry does by harvesting—about 100 times more. Ecotourism provides a rational case for preserving the natural ecology of the region as opposed to exploiting its resources, an example for the world to follow.

Twelve km west of Moruya, Bingie Bingie Point is named for a narrow jetty of rock protruding 750 m from the open beach into the Pacific. From the point's promontory the town of Tuross Head is visible to the south, and Mullimburra Point to the north. The Magney property is immediately adjacent to the point and is surrounded by beaches on three sides while facing a lake to the north.

Climate

The climate of Bingie Bingie, based on data from Moruya Heads Pilot Station just up the coast, is as mild as that of Los Angeles or Santa Monica, but, of course, their seasons are reversed. Moruya also receives considerably more rainfall than the Los Angeles basin, 38 in. (965 mm) versus 12 in. (304 mm), and the region does not have a typically dry season like the arid Los Angeles summers. The similarity and mildness of temperatures in these cities is a result of their maritime locations. Moreover, although they are in separate hemispheres, they are about the same distance from the equator, so their latitudes have comparable effects on the climates, especially on factors of solar availability. In the case of Australia's New South Wales coast, the East Australian current brings warm water from the Coral Sea into the cooler Tasman Sea and keeps the climate relatively warm. Sydney, 200 km up the coast, is considerably warmer than Moruya year-round.

The low inland mountains of the Great Dividing Range mark the western extent of the Eurobodalla. They have a profound effect on regional rainfall. Southwesterly winds must pass over the mountains before reaching the coast and often lose their moisture on the western slopes.

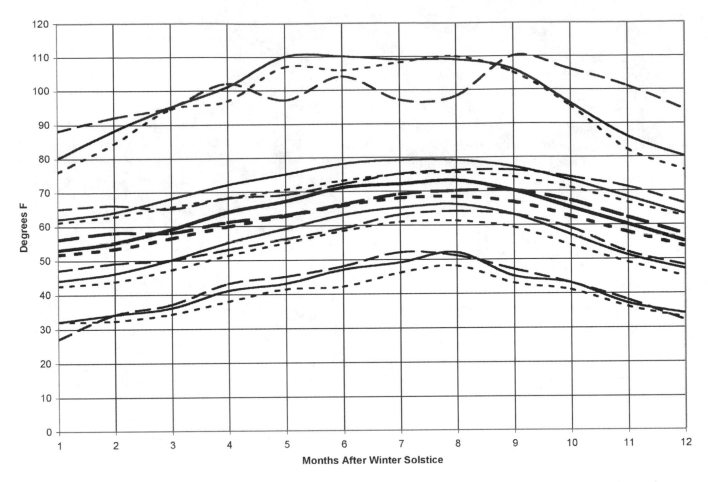

Figure 9.11 Extreme high and low temperatures as well as normal monthly high, low, and average temperatures for Moruya (short dashes), Sydney (long dashes), and Los Angeles (solid line).

Tropical depressions and the "westerlies" frontal systems of moist air masses bring more reliable winter rains. Large variations in day-to-day weather are common because of fluctuations in maritime depressions.

Flooding occurs from time to time, especially in La Niña or El Niño years. The worst floods were in 1973–74, but the springs of 1992 and 1993 were also inundated. Summer rain can be quite intense. The highest recorded daily rainfall is 10.2 in. (259.4 mm) and the highest monthly recording is 22.6 in. (575.8 mm). There are about 20 thunderstorms per year on average. Drought strikes unpredictably as well. Nine grave periods of drought have occurred in southeast Australia since 1888, including a severe drought in 1972–73, ironically, just before the floods.

The 3:1 degree-day ratio favors heating considerations at Bingie Bingie Point. Winter days are relatively clear; note the fortunate correlation between the curves for degree-days heating and percentage of days with clear skies. The normal daily low in July is 52°F with an afternoon high of 68°F. The summer pattern is not much different, with January highs averaging 75°F and normal daily lows of 61°F. It never freezes at Bingie Bingie Point. Rainfall is generally uniform through the year, with a slight decrease in winter months. There is measurable precipitation on about 30 percent of all days. Foggy days are rare.

INTENTION

Design Team

Glen Murcutt is fiercely independent. He works without partners, assistants, or secretaries. He does this in order to maintain complete control over his work and to avoid what he considers the mediocrity of design by committee. His work is predominantly rural for the same reason — Murcutt believes that the urban context and the codes that protect it are based on mediocrity and hopelessly destined to perpetuate it.

Glenn Murcutt grew up in the Morobe district of New Guinea, where he developed a preference for simple, primitive architecture. His father introduced him to the architecture of Ludwig Mies van der Rohe and the philosophies of Henry David Thoreau, both of which influenced his architectural style.

In an initial exploratory phase Murcutt established a mastery of the Miesian style. His second phase was more regional in nature. Using a mixture of pragmatism and lyricism, Murcutt creates simple houses that resemble open verandas. He is chiefly admired among his contemporaries for creating an identifiably Australian idiom in domestic architecture.

Philosophy and Approach

Glenn Murcutt was born in 1936. His father, Sydney Arthur (Sam) Murcutt, had left home at the age of 11 to make his own life as a naturalist, philosopher, musician, and home builder. Discussion of his mother is reverent but less specific. Glenn's grandfather, a mathematician and musician, managed to pass down his patriarchal discipline quite successfully. Glenn himself was raised on a steady diet of Henry David Thoreau's philosophy and never-ending stacks of architecture journals featuring his father's favorite—Modernist simplicity.

From 1956 to 1961, Glenn Murcutt studied architecture at the University of New South Wales and worked for a number of architects. After traveling for two years, he worked in the office of Ancher, Mortlock, Murray, and Wooley from 1964 to 1970. He then established his own firm in Sydney.

Sydney Ancher (1904–1980) was a pioneer of the Modern movement in Australia. His houses were described by Robin Boyd as being "in the best Australian tradition of horizontally bleached colors and decorative shadows…a line of development, unaffected, uncomplicated and an undeviating search for simplicity." Ancher's houses and buildings were designed to adapt to the conditions of their Australian bushland sites. He made extensive use of open planning, pergolas, and wide terraces,

TABLE 9.4 Normal Climate Data for Moruya, Australia

		Jan.	Feb.	Mar.	Apr.	May	June	July	Aug.	Sept.	Oct.	Nov.	Dec.	Year
Temperature	Degree-Days Heating	9.1	5.9	22.3	81.8	219.8	338.6	402.1	353.4	242.5	146.5	78.1	27.4	1912.5
	Degree-Days Cooling	157.8	149.2	104.8	27.9	2.6	0.1	0	0.3	6.5	27.8	61.8	120.9	666.8
	Extreme High	108.14	109.94	105.08	95.18	82.04	75.92	75.92	84.2	94.46	96.8	106.88	105.8	109.9
	Normal High	74.8	75.4	73.9	70.9	66.4	62.2	61.0	62.8	65.5	68.2	70.5	73.0	68.7
	Normal Average	67.8	68.3	66.6	62.4	57.7	53.5	51.7	53.2	56.3	59.7	62.7	65.7	60.5
	Normal Low	60.8	61.2	59.2	54.0	48.9	44.8	42.4	43.7	47.1	51.3	54.9	58.3	52.3
	Extreme Low	46.0	48.0	43.0	41.0	36.0	32.7	32.0	32.2	34.2	37.8	41.4	42.1	32.0
Humidity	Dew Point	60.71	61.61	59.54	54.05	50	45.23	42.53	43.52	47.3	50.9	54.14	59	52.4
	Max % RH	79	82	80	75	77	76	74	71	71	71	75	76	75.6
	Min % RH	71	72	71	66	65	63	59	59	62	66	69	71	66.0
	% Days with Rain	35.7	32.4	34.4	28.8	26.5	25.8	22.8	23.5	28.4	33.4	35.1	35.4	30.0
	Rain Inches	3.8	3.6	4.4	3.5	3.4	3.5	2.2	2.1	2.4	3.1	3.0	3.0	38.0
Sky	% Overcast Days	39	36	34	26	29	27	19	22	24	33	34	39	30.0
	% Clear Days	31	31	35	42	42	41	49	50	42	35	30	27	38
Wind	Prevailing Direction	S	S	S	W	WNW	W	W	W	W	W	W	S	W
	Speed, Knots	9	10	8	9	10	11	12	12	12	13	14	10	11.0
	Percent Calm	26.2	28	35.8	33.7	28.5	20.3	18.4	20.5	22.6	26.3	24.4	24.5	25.7
Days Observed	Rain	10.8	9.8	10.4	8.7	8.0	7.8	6.9	7.1	8.6	10.1	10.6	10.7	109.5
	Fog	4	4	5	4	3	2	2	2	3	4	5	3	41.0
	Haze	21	17	19	14	10	5	6	10	13	15	18	19	167.0
	Snow	0	0	0	0	0	0	0	0	0	0	0	0	0.0
	Hail	#	#	#	#	#	0	0	#	0	#	#	#	1.0
	Freezing Rain	0	0	0	0	0	0	0	0	0	0	0	0	0.0
	Blowing Sand	#	#	#	#	#	#	#	#	#	#	#	#	1.0

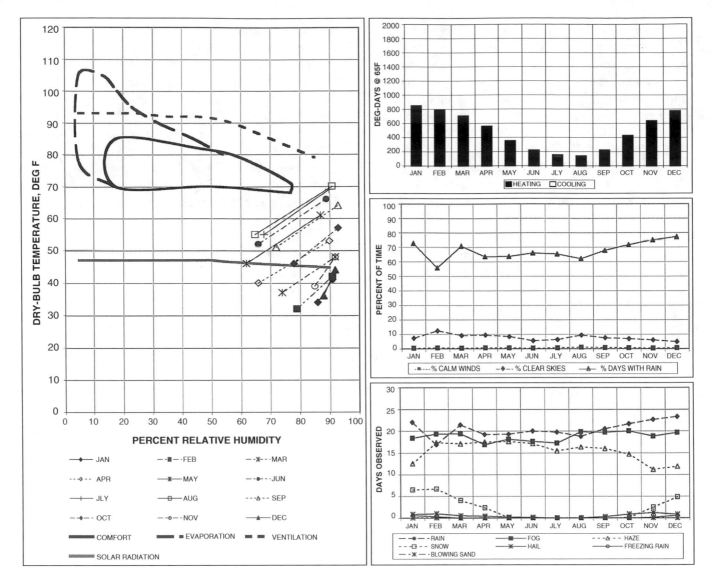

Figure 9.12 Climate analysis graphics.

opening the interior of his white painted houses to the landscape.

Murcutt still acknowledges the influences of Thoreau and can quote him at length. The Modernist beliefs have also stayed with him, with a central place for the work of Mies van der Rohe and the Farnsworth House. The *Arts and Architecture* series of Case Study Houses played a role in his early education as well. He mentions the Eames House in particular.

Influences aside, Glenn Murcutt is completely original. His work has earned him the highest esteem for his poetic fusion of vernacular regionalism with indigenous Aboriginal sensitivity and Modernist rationalism. Glenn Murcutt was awarded the 2002 Pritzker Prize for architecture and the Magney House was featured in the award presentation.

CRITICAL TECHNICAL ISSUES

Because this was to be a house for weekends and vacations, the design had to compensate for the house's remote location. Security is a prime issue because the house would be unprotected by proximity to neighbors and would be frequently unoccupied. Although Moruya (1996 population 2600) is only 12 km away, the location is also a logistical concern for construction work and building materials.

With southern California and the south of France, Australia is one of the world's most dangerous environments in regard to wildfires. Coincidentally, major burns occurred near the Eurobodalla at about the same time the Bingie Bingie Point property was bought and again at about the time that design work began. At the time of this

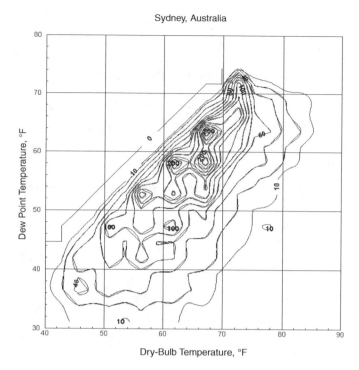

Sydney, Australia

Figure 9.13 Bin data distribution for Moruya. Concentric areas of graph indicate the number of hours per year that weather conditions normally occur in this climate. Similar to elevation readings on topographic maps, highest frequency occurrences of weather are at the center peaks of the graph. (Data sources: *Engineering Weather Data, typical meteorological year (TMY) data from the National Climatic Data Center*, and the ASHRAE Weather Data Viewer *from the American Society of Heating, Refrigerating and Air-Conditioning Engineers.*)

writing in December 2001, more than 100 wildfires with a total perimeter of 360 km were burning around Sydney and into New South Wales and were being contained by some 15,000 firefighters. Lighting starts most wildfires, but human carelessness and vandalism are also problematic. With no available public source of water for fire fighting, the house would have to be constructed of fire-resistant materials and able to collect its own water in case surrounding brush fires broke out.

Passive design would also be incorporated into the design for practical, economic, and logistical reasons. More significant, passive interaction with the climate would fulfill the intention of making the house an integral part of the site. Fostering the balance of connection and protection between indoors and out naturally leads to purposeful interventions that define and configure the architecture. The inspiration of camping on the picturesque coastal site made this a romantic and poetic opportunity as well, especially given the mild winters with daily lows around 45°F and temperate summer days normally below 75°F.

APPROPRIATE SYSTEMS

Precedent

The root simplicity of the Magney House may be traced to Murcutt's early studies of Mies's abstract pavilion for the 1951 Farnsworth House, but the model for its actual design comes from the progression of Murcutt's original work in Australian regionalism. His pavilions are more akin to verandah-style living than to pristine ideals of International Style design.

Site

The house is situated about 700 m from Meringo Beach and 350 m from a lake. It rests on the only area of level grade in the center of the site. About 1500 m to the west is an inland bay. Elevations rise south and east of the house. Vegetation is sparse, consisting of coastal grasses and scrub brush. A curious row of granite outcroppings makes a directional line to the house from the north.

Perhaps in keeping with the Aboriginal tradition, there is no strong sign of an entry or even an approach to the house. A driveway marks the territory of the site, cornering around to the north and east before landing from the south. The house is aloof and individual, fitting its surroundings through Murcutt's gesture of "confronting the site."

Structure

A galvanized steel pipe frame on a concrete slab foundation makes up the open skeleton of the house. Six bays each 18.4 ft (560 cm) across and 19.4 ft (590 cm) deep, define the 110.4 ft by 19.4 ft (590 cm) footprint. Columns are 4.5 in. (114 mm) in diameter with corners and connection details formed by welded angles and channels. Stiffness and bracing of the frame are provided by partial height brick walls that run north to south across the interior walls of the house and along the south exterior. The brick terminates at door head height to leave an opening for continuous transom windows.

The roof frame is formed by metal purlins laid east to west. Overhangs are supported at the drip line by a 2.4 in. (60 mm) galvanized pipe purlin carried by two 1.7 in. (42 mm) pipe struts flared out from each column at the base of the transom.

Envelope

The low valley formed by the spread wings of the roof acts as a dry creek bed that collects rain to be stored in underground cisterns. It covers the 1.0 m wide circulation spine of the house matching the flow of people to the hydrological form of the roof. From there the south wing of the roof arches up over another 1.0 m bay, the utility core of the house. The broad north expanse of the roof covers the living spaces and the terrace and overhangs the sunlit north wall. Sheathing is corrugated galvanized steel that overhangs the north glass far enough to protect the transom from summer sun. Two layers of insulation form a ventilated air cavity in the roof, with 3.0 in. (75 mm insulation against the roof and 2.0 in. (50 mm) against the ceiling.

Transoms line the perimeter of the house, affording continuous views of the sky even when the windows are covered for privacy. Most of this infill layer between a line at 7.2 ft (2.2 m) high and the underside of the undulating roof is cut from laminated glass, but on the south the glazing is kicked out away from exterior wall to leave a 7.0 in. (178 mm) space. This gap is fitted with insect screen and hinged vent flaps to provide cross ventilation in the absence of operable south windows.

Brick wall construction is clad in horizontal-pattern galvanized steel screwed to 1.5 in. (37 mm) battens with 3 in. (75 mm) insulation compressed in the cavity. Murcutt observes that the horizontal corrugations pick up different colors of the site, as the lower bands catch the red-gray grasses and the upper bands reflect the sky. Two large doors clad in the same galvanized steel close the west end of the house.

Large sliding doors with three horizontal sash divisions and sliding insect screens fill the rest of the walls below the transom. These are protected on the exterior by natural anodized aluminum blinds that can be lowered and adjusted to suit the need. Blinds are stored in the raised position inside a channel welded to the pipe frame.

Mechanical

There are no mechanical systems for interior comfort except for two fireplaces. Low winter sun likely provides comfort on all but the most blustery winter days at Bingie Bingie Point. Gray ceramic tile on concrete slab floors and plaster-covered brick partition walls act as thermal storage to stabilize indoor temperatures for nighttime and cloudy weather.

Interior

The rooms of the house are extroverted and lightly enclosed. The continuation of ceramic tile floors out onto the veranda and the perimeter slab areas reinforces the indoor-outdoor intention. Interior finishes are kept white to welcome the outdoor brightness and reduce contrast ratios. Cabinetry, appliances, fixtures, and other potential interruptions are closeted into the south wall zone.

TECHNICAL INTEGRATION HIGHLIGHTS

Physical

- The south 1.0 m zone aggregates and simplifies all the services.
- The pipe frame structure allows lightweight construction with generous glass infill.

Visual

- The razor-thin edge of corrugated steel maintains the lightness of the roof.
- Openness to the site is achieved by the pavilion plan.

Performance

- The roof provides shade but allows sun, sheds rain but collects water, and directs breezes but deters winds.
- Solar, aerodynamic, and hydrological functions of the envelope are integrated with view, privacy, and the divisible plan of the house.
- The circulation spine is also the standing workspace of the interior, freeing the living space of both requirements.

DISCUSSION

The Eames House illustrated how industrial systems and materials could be transformed into a neutral background for family living, how Modernist design could provide for warmth and complexity without imposing pure and rigid spaces. The Magney House demonstrates further that these materials can provide vernacular warmth and relate poetically to site. Murcutt also shows how systems integration works in simple buildings and that the benefits provided are similar to those of larger-scale buildings.

20

EXPERIMENTAL HOUSE AT ALMERE, 1982–1984

The Netherlands
BENTHEM & CROUWEL ARCHITECTS

DESCRIPTION

This radical design was a winning entry in a competition for demountable housing. Most designs for High-Tech residential projects seek to identify technologies that are transferable from commercial building systems. This house takes the reverse approach. It is actually a residential laboratory for working out a construction scheme the architects were developing for a commercial project. Its location in the new town of Almere makes it part of an even larger experiment, because Almere itself is a laboratory of urban development in a country where high population density and sparse land area place constant demands on resources.

Working with store-bought pieces, the architects erected the house themselves in only three days. One of them, Jan Benthem, lived in it with his family during the five-year design award period.

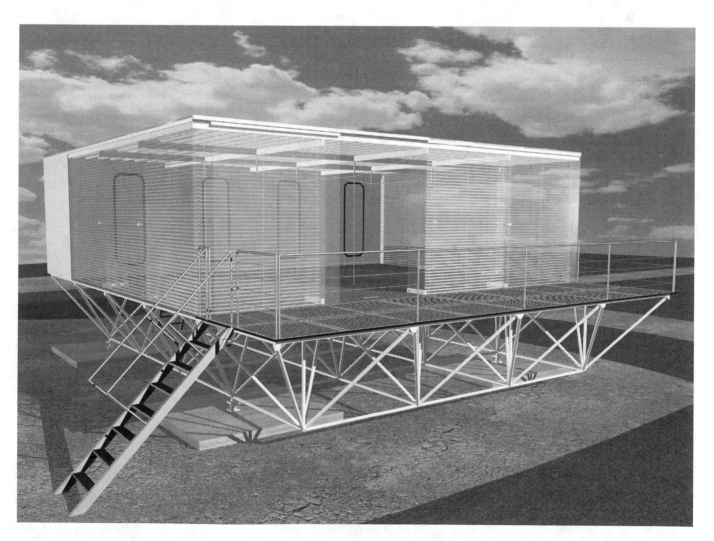

Figure 9.14 View of the house from the southwest. (*3-D rendering by Travis Hughs.*)

TABLE 9.5 Fact Sheet

Project	**Building Name**	Experimental House at Almere
	Client	Almere—Competition for Temporary Architecture
	City	Almere, The Netherlands (20 mi (32 km) east of Amsterdam)
	Lat/Long/Elev	52.38 N 5.22 E, −7 ft (−2 m)
	Design	Benthem & Crouwel Architects
General	**Time Line**	1982–1984.
	Floor Area	689 ft^2 (64 m^2) on a 26.3 ft × 26.3 ft plan using a 6.6 ft grid (8 m × 8 m overall on a 2 m grid). A cantilevered 6.6 ft × 26.3 ft (2 m × 8 m) deck extends across one glazed side, forming the main entry.
	Occupants	Single family.
	Cost	Not published.
	Stories	One.
	Plan	Two bedrooms, the kitchen and bath form a 6.6 ft (2m) bay on one end of the house. The main 19.6 ft × 26.3 ft (8 m × 6 m) living area extends to the other end and meets a 6.6 ft × 26.3 ft (2 m × 8 m) deck.
Site	**Site Description**	Competition provided a 4850 ft^2 (450 m^2) temporary site for movable structure of minimal environmental impact. A storage container sits adjacent to the small house.
	Parking, Cars	None.
Structure	**Foundation**	Four prefabricated concrete pads supporting a steel space frame of 6.6 ft (2 m) bays. The space frame uses thin tube members flattened at the ends, bolted together on 0.2 in. (5 mm) octagonal welded steel connectors.
	Vertical Members	Roof is supported on three sides by frameless glass walls and supporting glass fins.
	Horizontal Spans	Roof span rests on inverted truss of steel angles and tension cables. Roof grid is vertically tied back to floor by two interior cables to resist uplift.
Envelope	**Glass and Glazing**	8.2 ft high × 6.6 ft wide (2.5 m × 2.0 m) tempered 0.5 in. (12 mm) glazing with interior aluminum blinds. One panel forms a suspended sliding door to the front deck.
	Skylights	None.
	Cladding	1.6 in. plywood composite panel with insulating polyurethane foam core.
	Roof	Loose-laid EPDM membrane on 2.0 in. (50 mm) extruded polystyrene insulation over profiled steel metal deck.
HVAC	**Equipment**	A fan coil heat exchanger in the house is fed by a district water heating system.
	Cooling Type	Forced-air ventilation using 100% outside air drawn from below the house.
	Distribution	Forced-air perimeter supply ducts and floor registers.
	Duct Type	Exposed round duct hung below floor.
	Vertical Chases	Return air and heat exchanger form a vertical chase at the kitchen/bathroom core.
Interior	**Partitions**	1.6 in. (40 mm) plywood composite panel with insulating polyurethane foam core (same as exterior).
	Finishes	Non-slip rubber tile floor, glass envelope, exposed steel deck. White interior and green plywood exterior painted surfaces.
	Vertical Circulation	Open metal stairs to deck and rear exit.
	Furniture	Integral closet and sleeping bunks.
	Lighting	Clamp-mounted fixtures with long spiral-wound power cords in living room.

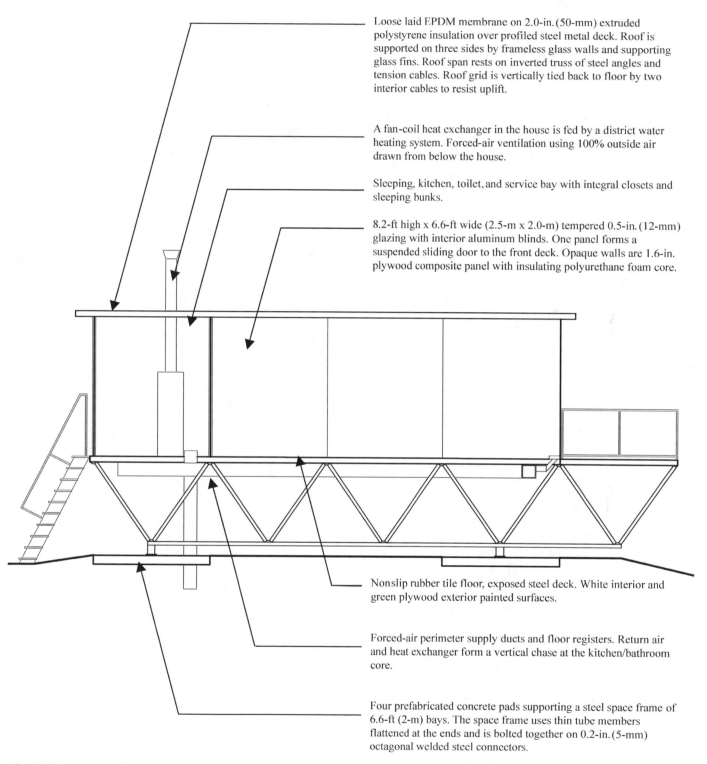

Loose laid EPDM membrane on 2.0-in. (50-mm) extruded polystyrene insulation over profiled steel metal deck. Roof is supported on three sides by frameless glass walls and supporting glass fins. Roof span rests on inverted truss of steel angles and tension cables. Roof grid is vertically tied back to floor by two interior cables to resist uplift.

A fan-coil heat exchanger in the house is fed by a district water heating system. Forced-air ventilation using 100% outside air drawn from below the house.

Sleeping, kitchen, toilet, and service bay with integral closets and sleeping bunks.

8.2-ft high x 6.6-ft wide (2.5-m x 2.0-m) tempered 0.5-in. (12-mm) glazing with interior aluminum blinds. One panel forms a suspended sliding door to the front deck. Opaque walls are 1.6-in. plywood composite panel with insulating polyurethane foam core.

Nonslip rubber tile floor, exposed steel deck. White interior and green plywood exterior painted surfaces.

Forced-air perimeter supply ducts and floor registers. Return air and heat exchanger form a vertical chase at the kitchen/bathroom core.

Four prefabricated concrete pads supporting a steel space frame of 6.6-ft (2-m) bays. The space frame uses thin tube members flattened at the ends and is bolted together on 0.2-in. (5-mm) octagonal welded steel connectors.

Figure 9.15 Anatomical section.

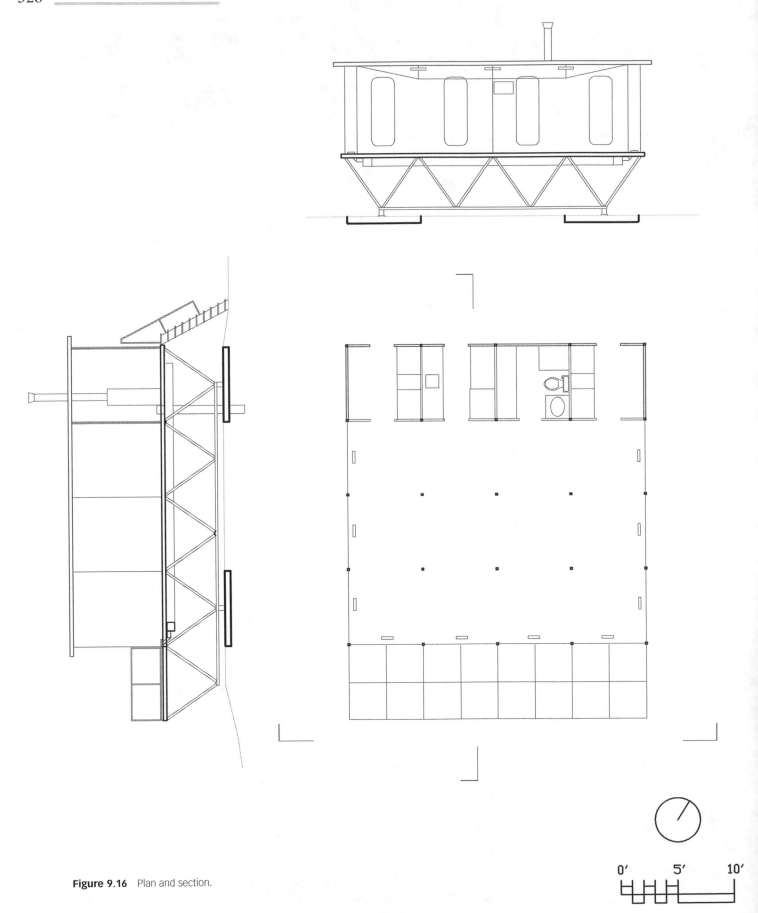

Figure 9.16 Plan and section.

0'   5'   10'

PROGRAM

Client

The competition served as the client for this project. The goal was to design and build the winning solutions as an exhibition in two adjoining neighborhoods: The Reality and The Fantasy.

Brief

The competition emphasized a concern about the impact of permanent architecture. It asked whether society would not be better served by having a portion of its buildings designed as deployable temporary structures to be erected, disassembled, warehoused as components, then erected again. This was postulated as a more intelligent response to changing needs and land use patterns than heavy investment in monumental buildings that constantly become obsolete and burdensome. Accordingly, the guidelines stipulated that entries must be removable in five years and leave no scars on the site. To ensure the ease of construction and commissioning, the rules required that the houses could be readily assembled by the user.

Site

Almere is a new town and a working experiment in urban design. Its development was undertaken by Dutch authorities in 1977 in an effort to relieve overcrowding and the housing deficits that have plagued Holland since World War II. Located just east of Amsterdam, it was planned as a bedroom community of five residential neighborhoods. Recreational green space and waterways connect the five housing nodes and finger into them at every possibility.

TABLE 9.6   Normal Climate Data for Amsterdam

		Jan.	Feb.	Mar.	Apr.	May	June	July	Aug.	Sept.	Oct.	Nov.	Dec.	Year
Temperature	Degree-Days Heating	840	778	695	548	342	197	117	106	215	421	628	768	5663
	Degree-Days Cooling	0	0	0	0	6	19	32	28	3	0	0	0	83
	Extreme High	57	61	70	80	84	90	90	93	83	77	64	59	93
	Normal High	41	42	48	53	61	66	69	70	64	57	48	44	55
	Normal Average	38	37	43	47	54	59	62	62	58	51	44	40	50
	Normal Low	34	32	37	40	46	52	55	55	51	46	39	36	44
	Extreme Low	3	6	18	25	30	37	39	32	36	30	20	7	3
Humidity	Dew Point	35	33	38	40	46	52	56	56	53	47	41	37	44
	Max % RH	91	91	92	90	87	89	90	91	93	93	92	92	91
	Min % RH	86	79	74	66	62	66	68	65	72	78	85	88	74
	% Days with Rain	73	56	71	64	64	66	65	62	68	72	75	77	67
	Rain Inches	3	2	4	2	2	2	3	2	3	4	3	3	32
Sky	% Overcast Days	42	36	35	25	21	23	19	15	21	27	35	41	28
	% Clear Days	7	12	9	10	8	6	6	9	8	7	6	5	8
Wind	Prevailing Direction	S	E	WSW	N	N	W	W	W	SSW	S	SSW	SSW	W
	Speed, Knots	11	11	15	10	9	9	10	10	10	9	13	12	11
	Percent Calm	0	1	1	1	1	1	1	1	1	1	1	1	1
Days Observed	Rain	22	17	21	19	19	20	20	19	21	22	23	23	245
	Fog	18	19	19	17	18	18	17	20	20	20	19	20	225
	Haze	13	17	17	17	18	17	15	16	16	15	11	12	185
	Snow	6	7	4	2	0	0	0	0	0	0	3	5	27
	Hail	1	1	1	0	0	0	0	0	0	1	1	1	7
	Freezing Rain	1	0	0	0	0	0	0	0	0	0	0	1	2
	Blowing Sand	0	0	0	0	0	0	0	0	0	0	0	0	1

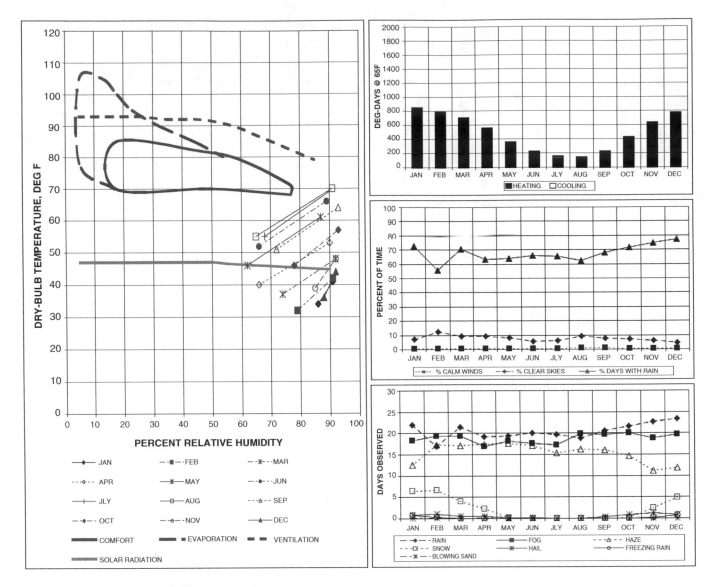

Figure 9.17 Climate analysis graphics.

Traffic around each of the centers is limited to a system of ring roads. Internal circulation is reserved for public transit and bicycles.

Almere Stadt is the neighborhood designated as town center of Almere. The development was planned by architects J. van Stigt, A. Mastenbroek, and D. Apon.

Climate

Almere is a bedroom community of Amsterdam, for which detailed climate data is plentiful. The data resembles that of a large group of other midlatitude, low-elevation European weather stations with 5000 to 6000 degree-days heating and minimal degree-days cooling. In Amsterdam's case the numbers are 5663 and 83, respectively. Amsterdam and most of central Europe lie in

Köppen's Cfb climate zone: midlatitude, uniform precipitation, warm summer. The maritime moderating effects of the North Sea are reduced by Amsterdam's high latitude and are less potent than in southern California or southeast Australia where the warm Pacific dominates. Nonetheless, conditions here are relatively mild, considering the 52°N latitude.

The normal low in February is 32.0°F, and the normal high in August is 70.0°F. More extreme weather can produce temperatures as low as 3°F and as high as 90°F. Normal daily averages in the coldest month and the warmest month vary only from 37°F to 62°F, and the daily temperature range is also a narrow 10°F to 15°F; both factors indicate a constant high relative humidity. Rain falls on about 66 percent of days in Amsterdam; there is no dry season, and light snows are common from November to March. Fog and hazy conditions occur on more than half of the days of any normal month. Winds in Amsterdam are fairly brisk and seldom calm, as one would expect, seeing all those still-working ancient windmills and the new generation of wind turbine machines.

Passive solar heating and daylighting are the natural strategies most appropriate to the comfort conditions of Amsterdam, but the climate resources are less than ideal for their application. Winter solstice days are 7.5 hours long, but the sun never rises more than 15 degrees above the horizon. This means that solar energy goes through the atmosphere at such a low angle and in such a long path that it is mostly absorbed or scattered before it reaches the ground. Low sun angles prevail from November to February during periods when the earth's declination angles are greatest. This makes substantial passive heating difficult and daylighting a potent source of direct glare. In summer this geometry is reversed, and day length reaches 16.5 very pleasant hours at the June equinox.

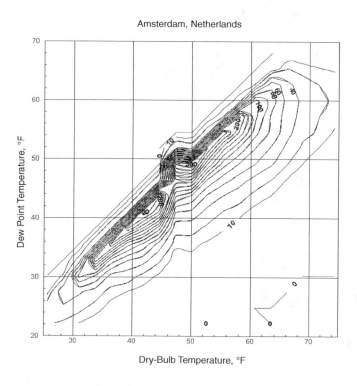

Amsterdam, Netherlands

Figure 9.18 Bin data distribution for Amsterdam. Concentric areas of graph indicate the number of hours per year that weather conditions normally occur in this climate. Similar to elevation readings on topographic maps, highest frequency occurrences of weather are at the center peaks of the graph. (Data sources: *Engineering Weather Data, typical meteorological year (TMY) data from the National Climatic Data Center, and the ASHRAE Weather Data Viewer from the American Society of Heating, Refrigerating and Air-Conditioning Engineers.*)

INTENTION

Design Team

Jan Benthem and Mels Crouwel graduated from Delft University together in 1978. In January 1979 they formed Benthem & Crouwel Architecten. Their work includes the Customs Office (1980–1987), Airport Buildings (1982–1988), and an extension to Shiphol Airport (45 minutes from Almere).

Intent

This design was put together hurriedly when the architects realized they could use its construction as an experiment. They were devising an integrated building system for a customs house project and believed that the hands-on experience would help them refine its details. When they were awarded one of the prizes that allowed them to use the site for five years, they decided to make it a working laboratory. After the architects assembled the building with their own hands in three days, Jan Benthem and his family of four moved in.

CRITICAL TECHNICAL ISSUES

Inherent

There are about 15.9 million people living in Holland, a nation roughly the size of southern England or slightly smaller than twice the size of New Jersey. The population density is a staggering 1191 people per square mile, or 16 times that of the United States, at 73 per square mile. The 0.57 percent Dutch population growth rate is not expected to decline. As in most countries of the world, life expectancy there is continuously increasing. Holland is especially prosperous and anticipates serious growth demands.

Despite the dense population, more than 60 percent of Holland is open space or agricultural land. With only 0.008 percent of the world's land area, it is still the third largest exporter of food after the United States and France. The Dutch economy depends heavily on this agricultural sector, which accounts for 3.5 percent of the gross domestic product. Consequently, there is considerable control and restriction on new building development.

Population density and scarce natural resources critically stress the Netherlands environment. Housing is scarce near sources of employment, and traffic is increasingly snarled. Pollution sources are denser than in other countries, and there is less room for waste. Water and soil quality are endangered by industrial waste and by runoff from intensive agriculture. There are also important external factors. Three major rivers flow into Holland toward the sea—the Rhine, the Maas, and the Schelde. They bring pollutants from central Europe beyond the control of Dutch management. Then, of course, there is the threat of rising oceans resulting from global warming. It is important to remember that 50 percent of Holland is already below sea level, and 33 percent of its land is reclaimed from the sea.

The point of this synopsis of Dutch ecology is to stress the critical technical issue of resource management and its impact on architecture. Holland has been dealing effectively with the decoupling of economic growth from environmental destruction for many years. The Dutch now enjoy the highest standard of living in the European Union while simultaneously decreasing pollution levels. They have managed for today what the rest of the world will soon face with population growth and resource depletion. The Dutch spirit of collaboration and proactive planning is an exemplary model that deserves close attention. Perhaps if the rest of us lived below sea level or experienced some other environmental mandate so directly and personally, then our collective priorities about architecture would take a similar turn.

Contextual

The dictates of the competition objectives led to the design of a lightweight building with demountable connections so that it could be easily assembled and dismantled by its occupants. It also had to be inexpensive to construct and provide efficient use of space and energy in order to be practical. Finally, it had to be benign, having a small environmental footprint and leaving no scars on the earth when it was gone.

Intentional

When Modernist minimalism succeeds in both technical and human terms, it does so by satisfying its most lofty claims. Among these stated goals are the expression of function as the essence of design and an unornamented vocabulary that legibly defines its working parts. One more particular idea was dealt with explicitly here, that of avoiding the complexities and capturing the possibilities of modern Dutch life.

The architects were also intent on developing and refining a high-tech building system for a series of custom houses they were designing for the government. The experimental house gave them a chance to prototype the systems under consideration and actually try them hands-on.

APPROPRIATE SYSTEMS

Precedent

Two buildings come to mind in considering this the experimental house. Buckminster Fuller's Dymaxion Dwelling

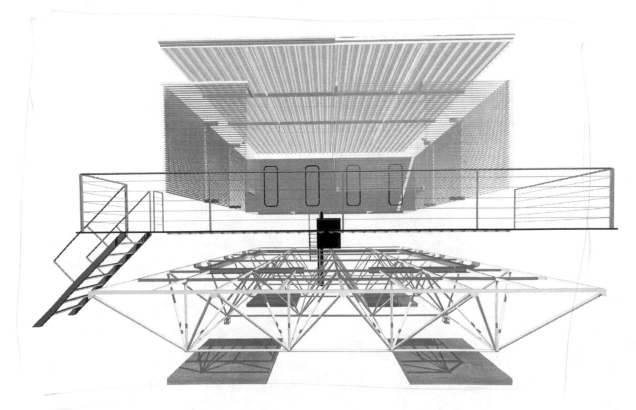

Figure 9.19 Exploded diagram of the Experimental House. *(3-D rendering by Travis Hughs.)*

Unit is the first, perhaps because it also is a house and has similar intentions. It was named for three of Fuller's favorite ideas—DYnamic, MAXimum, and tensION—and constructed with aircraft technology and materials. Dymaxion is really a series of three projects, all designed to be hung from a central mast by cables. The 4D house of 1927 was 50 ft in diameter and elevated above grade. Fuller's fully deployable Dymaxion Dwelling Unit was prototyped for the U.S. Army in 1940 and resembled a 20 ft diameter grain silo. In 1946, the Dymaxion Deployment Unit was built as a demonstration house from three tons of parts that could fit in a 300 ft³ cylinder and be delivered by helicopter anywhere.

The other project is Renzo Piano's 1983 traveling exhibit pavilion for IBM, which also was also a deployable building, but Benthem & Crouwel's house at Almere actually preceded the IBM project by about a year.

Site

Site systems are minimal because the house is a temporary five-year installation. The whole concept of the temporary house makes for an interesting challenge—"short-cycle architecture" that is durable enough to comfortably enjoy but transient enough to remove without a trace of its tenure on the site. The solution had to be both easily constructed and demountable to the last nut and bolt.

With nothing permanent to remain, two site provisions were made for the house. The first was an electrical connection pole with no real presence. The second was a steel shipping container serving as the industrial High-Tech equivalent of utility shed and storage room. The container securely relieves the small house of storage burdens. It also seems like a favorable parallel to the increasingly popular practice in the United States of renting self-storage mini-warehouse space. Probably, though, it is just an exigency that evolved when the Benthem family of four actually moved into the tiny house.

Structure

The house sits to the north side of the site and faces an open view southward to a 40 ft (12 m) wide waterway. Because no piers could be used, which would leave scars of the building five years later, another system of support had to be devised. The architects chose prefabricated concrete industrial floor slabs as supporting pads. Four of them support the house on a 19.7 ft (6.0 m) grid.

Adjustable jacks centered on each of the pads support an off-the-shelf space frame system. The frame is configured in a 6.6 ft (2.0 m) grid of steel tube struts at 45-degree angles and bolted end connections where the tubes are flattened. This lifts the house 6.6 ft off the ground, plus the height of the jacks and the exposed concrete pads. A

deck extends 2 m past the house, making a 9.4 ft (3 m) cantilever from two of the supporting pads.

The floor structure and membrane are prestressed panels used for refrigerated truck bodies. They consist of two layers of plywood sandwiched above and below 1.2 in. (30 mm) of polyurethane insulation and secured to steel Z-sections at the perimeter. The same panels are used for the enclosed bays of the house on the far side from the deck. The wall panels are structural and are screwed into steel Z-sections at the floor and ceiling lines.

The remaining vertical structure is provided by mullionless 8.2 ft high × 6.6 ft wide (2.5 m × 2.0 m) tempered 0.5 in. (12 mm) glass panels with 0.6 in. (18 mm) thick supporting fins at the glass joints. The fins are bolted to steel angles, and the angles are screwed into the roof and floor decks. A profiled steel roof deck is laid in the perimeter steel Z-section, which in turn rests directly on a steel channel laid over the head of the wall of glass panels. The glass is made structural by bearing carefully on the large, thick panels and then bracing them with fins to prevent lateral deflection.

The roof is supported by three tensioned stainless steel cables spanning from the deck side wall to the enclosed bays and two more cables spanning the other direction. This makes a 2 m grid of cables under the metal roof deck, matching the joints of glass and supporting fins. It both holds the roof up and holds it down. Pairs of steel angles run under the exposed metal deck on the same grid. Adjustable struts lift the middle of the roof from the six intersection points of the cables, pressing down against the cables and up against the steel angles. The cable, struts, and angles form a shallow and whispery two-way tension truss, preventing deflection in the roof and perhaps introducing positive camber to ensure rainwater drainage. In addition, the center two strut points are tied back to the floor in the middle of the room by vertical steel cables to counter wind uplift forces. These two tie-back cables pull directly down from the adjustable struts and are secured to the floor at points where there is direct support from the space frame undercarriage.

Envelope

The sheltering skin of the building is formed by the insulated plywood panels for the floor and walls of the enclosed bay. Unshaded glass makes up the rest of the walls, forming the enclosure of the large living room. One sliding panel of the glass separating the living room from the steel grated deck creates the entry. Doors, formed from the insulated stress skin panels, are provided from each of three rooms in the enclosed bay.

Roof construction is formed by simply laying rigid 2.0 in. (50 mm) insulation board on top of the metal roof deck and covering it with a loose-laid EPDM membrane. At the edge of the roof the membrane is held down by a small steel angle bolted through the perimeter steel Z-section.

Mechanical
The house is provided with a central fan-coil unit and underfloor duct distribution. Heat is from a neighborhood-shared district heating plant somewhere in the community and is piped in as steam to each residence. Fresh air ventilation provides cooling in warmer periods. Thin-slot air registers are located in the floor at the outside wall, centered on each of the ten glass wall panels.

Interior
Like the building's envelope, much of the interior is covered in the discussion of other systems. The ceiling is exposed metal deck, painted white. The walls are either glass or plywood, painted bright lime green on the exterior but white on the interior. Polished aluminum blinds are provided for sun control and privacy in the living room. The floor is covered with non-slip black rubber tiles.

Four rooms, more properly called compartments because of their size and configuration, make up the north side enclosed bays of the house. Each is 6.6 ft × 6.6 ft (2.0 m × 2.0 m) in plan. Bedrooms with built-in bunks are in the two outside corners. The kitchen and a bath / laundry / mechanical room complete the plan. Except for the bathroom, each compartment has its own exterior door, so there are two exits from each occupied space. Only the kitchen door is equipped with a stair, so the other two doors qualify as emergency exits. All four of these compartments are windowless.

TECHNICAL INTEGRATION HIGHLIGHTS

Physical
The light weight of the building components has a synergistic effect in reducing the physical size and structural requirements of its other systems, except for heating and cooling. The light roof needs little support and enables the glass walls to act structurally, thin wall and floor construction in turn allow for a thin-membered space frame, and

the whole featherweight package can rest on four concrete pads. A lightweight prefabricated kit of parts was, of course, dictated by the design parameters as interpreted by the architects. The reduction of the kit to standardized bolt-together construction took a great deal of design ingenuity and coordination.

Visual
The Modernist minimalism of the project means that all of the systems are exposed and that each of them has visual qualities. Detailing on the project is sparse, but what is exposed is well ordered and visually interesting. The cable-truss roof support system is especially High-Tech in its use of connecting hardware at the strut points. The six point connectors in the center of this cable network resemble the space frame undercarriage of the floor, but at a finer and more machined level of detail. The overall impression of the house is of something almost insubstantial, but its radically innovative look and High-Tech appeal are strong. Consistent use of materials and details that are functionally expressive is both honestly presented and visually appealing.

Performance
The glass wall does a great deal of the work in this design, fulfilling mandates of both the envelope and structural systems as well as addressing interior concerns for light, air, and egress. Similarly, the wall panels provide structure, insulation, and two finished surfaces. These features eliminate the need for a vertical structural frame, with the minor exception of wood battens at the corners of walls, roof, and floor.

DISCUSSION

Aside from rooms that are tight by most standards, the Almere-Stad experiment is rather convincing. Holland's history of environmental conservation and housing issues makes an excellent proving ground for the idea that good architecture can be simple, affordable, technical, efficient, and even transient.

21

TWO-FAMILY HOUSE, 1986–1989

Pullach, Germany
HERZOG + PARTNERS

DESCRIPTION

Despite its High-Tech look of glass on laminated wood frame with steel tie cross bracing, this house has its beginnings in the traditional Alpine timber frame barn. Like its vernacular precedent, the Pullach house starts with an elegantly small substructure and cantilevers outward, like Eames House, at each successive upper level. The roof becomes a huge overhanging form in comparison to the thin proportions of its base. A relatively small and well-protected structure rests beneath the sheltering eaves.

The vernacular barn uses this outwardly cascading form defensively to keep its wood frame and rough board cladding dry and covered. Structurally, the scheme provides an economy of support and cantilevered spans. Thomas Herzog acknowledges this as a formally appropriate beginning point and then opens up a series of complex interactions with the climate via technical components and Modernist ambitions. Glass is used wherever possible, then solar collector panels are strategically integrated as insulated wall wherever privacy dictates an opaque barrier. There is an exposed industrial wood structure, a galvanized metal screen for climbing summer vines on the south, and a corrugated metal roof that turns to glass beyond the exterior wall line to become a broad and transparent rain canopy.

Figure 9.20   Overview of the Two-Family House. *(3-D rendering by Travis Hughs.)*

Figure 9.21   Vernacular farm building from 1650, Düdingen, Switzerland, near Fribourg. This grain-storage structure was restored by its proprietor, Leo Jungo, in 1999.

TABLE 9.7 Fact Sheet

Project	**Building Name**	Two-Family House
	Client	Private
	City	Pullach, Germany
	Lat/Long/Elev	48.13 N 11.70 E, 1736 ft (529 m)
Team	**Architect**	Thomas Herzog, Michael Volz, Michael Streib
	Engineer	Structure: Jullus Natterer
	Energy	Fraunhofer Institute for Energy Systems, Freiburg
General	**Time Line**	1986–1989.
	Floor Area	2475 ft^2 (230 m^2) including basement of 642 ft^2 (59.6 m^2).
	Occupants	Two families.
	Cost	Not available.
	Stories	Two plus partial basement.
	Plan	Pavilion-style long rectangle, one room deep with perimeter circulation.
Site	**Site Description**	Open meadow to south with trees to north.
	Parking, Cars	Two-car covered parking.
Structure	**Foundation**	Basement with pier and beam.
	Vertical Members	Laminated timber columns in 5.9 in. × 5.9 in. (150 × 150 mm) and 2.0 in. × 5.9 in. (60 × 150 mm) sizes.
	Horizontal Spans	Laminated wood beams at 11.8 ft (360 cm) centers across the long east-to-west axis.
Envelope	**Glass and Glazing**	Double glazing with laminated inner lites.
	Skylights	Sloped glazing at second-story exterior wall on north and south.
	Cladding	6.0 in. (150 mm) insulation clad on both faces with cementitious chipboard.
	Roof	Corrugated metal roof with laminated glass overhanging eaves.
HVAC	**Equipment**	Radiant heating from boiler in basement.
	Cooling Type	None.
	Distribution	Radiant heat with heat recovery ventilation.
	Duct Type	Exposed round metal duct at second story.
	Vertical Chases	Central core of 11.8 in. (300 mm) reserved for services.
Interior	**Partitions**	Wood frame.
	Finishes	Exposed wood frame, glass, and gypsum board.
	Vertical Circulation	Stairs.
	Lighting	Daylighting and task lamps.

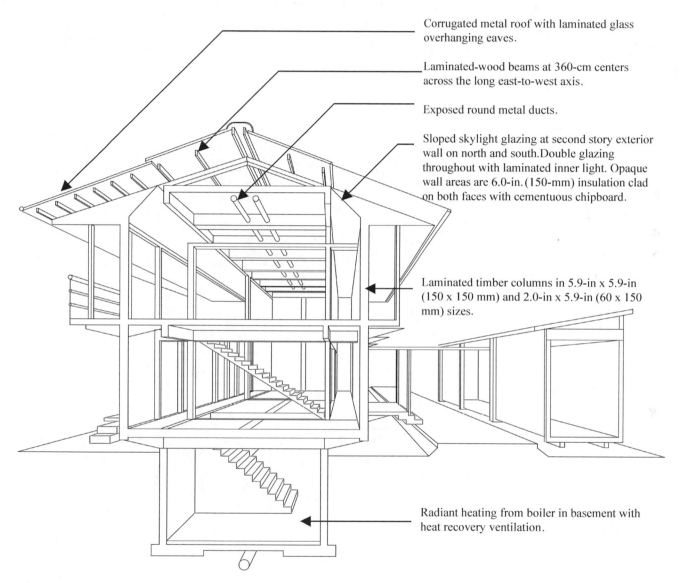

Corrugated metal roof with laminated glass overhanging eaves.

Laminated-wood beams at 360-cm centers across the long east-to-west axis.

Exposed round metal ducts.

Sloped skylight glazing at second story exterior wall on north and south. Double glazing throughout with laminated inner light. Opaque wall areas are 6.0-in. (150-mm) insulation clad on both faces with cementuous chipboard.

Laminated timber columns in 5.9-in x 5.9-in (150 x 150 mm) and 2.0-in x 5.9-in (60 x 150 mm) sizes.

Radiant heating from boiler in basement with heat recovery ventilation.

Figure 9.22 Anatomical section.

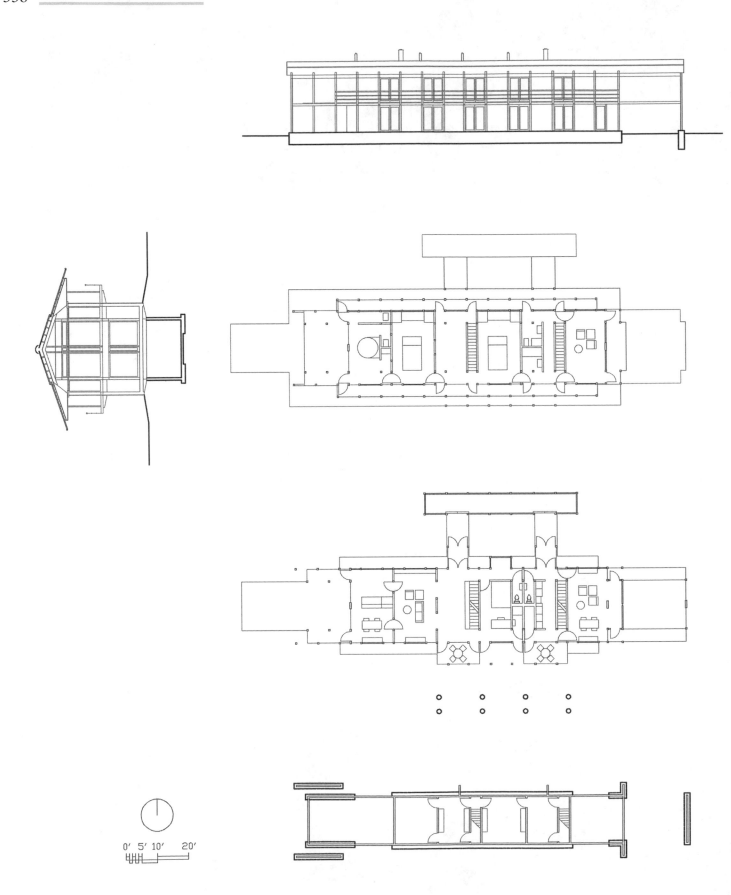

Figure 9.23 Plan, section, and elevation.

0' 5' 10'   20'

PROGRAM

Client and Brief

The client for this project requested a two-family house in wood frame. Emphasis on energy efficiency and moderate construction cost were also given as criteria. No other information has been made public.

Site

The site occupies a long east-to-west strip of land bordered on the north by large evergreen trees. The rest of the site is open.

Climate

Pullach is a southside suburb of Munich and is well described by the larger city's climate data. The general region, Southern Bavaria, lies in the south catchment of the Danube River. Pullach specifically is 40 miles north of the Austrian border, a great barrier formed by the north face of the Alps mountain range. The climate is characterized by cool, temperate weather and a degree of inland continentality. Conditions are generally mild but quite variable from season to season and year to year. The average daily high in August is 73°F, and the average daily low in January is 30°F. Cold weather often coincides with long periods of low, gray, overcast skies; there are only 55 hours of sun in the month of December and 28 in all of January.

A degree-day ratio of 6701 heating to 130 cooling generalizes the temperate, cool conditions of Munich. The climate resembles that of Chicago, Illinois. Measurable rainfall occurs on more than half of the annual days as does fog. There is no dry season, and April through August are the wettest months in both frequency and total precipitation. From November to April there are normally 69

TABLE 9.8 Normal Climate Data for Pullach

		Jan.	Feb.	Mar.	Apr.	May	June	July	Aug.	Sept.	Oct.	Nov.	Dec.	Year
Temperature	Degree-Days Heating	1073	937	780	612	347	188	92	100	236	532	810	1006	6701
	Degree-Days Cooling	0	0	0	0	1	16	51	50	9	0	0	0	130
	Extreme High	63	70	74	80	86	93	97	95	86	79	66	69	97
	Normal High	36	38	48	53	63	68	72	73	66	55	44	38	55
	Normal Average	30	32	40	45	54	59	64	63	57	48	38	33	47
	Normal Low	24	25	32	36	44	50	54	54	48	40	32	27	39
	Extreme Low	−16	−9	4	21	27	36	39	39	32	21	6	−6	−16
Humidity	Dew Point	26	26	32	35	44	50	53	53	49	42	33	28	39
	Max % RH	88	90	87	86	84	85	84	89	91	92	90	89	88
	Min % RH	80	74	62	57	55	58	55	55	61	71	80	81	66
	% Days with Rain	47	37	51	63	68	73	64	62	55	57	54	49	56
	Rain Inches	2	2	2	3	4	5	5	4	3	2	2	2	37
Sky	% Overcast Days	38	33	29	28	22	22	17	16	19	28	35	37	27
	% Clear Days	10	15	11	11	10	6	12	16	14	12	9	8	11
Wind	Prevailing Direction	WSW	WSW	WSW	WSW	E	WSW	WSW	WSW	WSW	WSW	WSW	WSW	WSW
	Speed, Knots	14	12	12	10	7	9	9	8	9	10	12	13	10
	Percent Calm	5	5	3	2	3	3	4	5	5	5	5	4	4
Days Observed	Rain	14	11	15	19	21	22	19	19	17	17	16	15	205
	Fog	17	19	15	12	11	12	10	15	17	20	18	16	182
	Haze	2	7	7	4	3	2	2	4	5	4	2	1	44
	Snow	15	14	10	8	1	0	0	0	0	1	9	13	69
	Hail	0	0	0	0	0	0	0	0	0	0	0	0	1
	Freezing Rain	2	1	0	0	0	0	0	0	0	0	1	1	5
	Blowing Sand	0	0	0	0	0	0	0	0	0	0	0	0	0

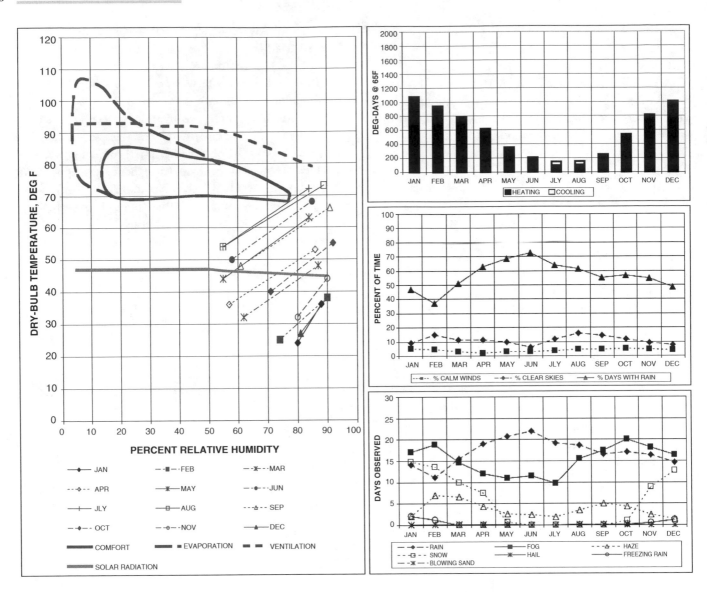

Figure 9.24 Climate analysis graphics.

days of snowfall, corresponding with the months when normal daily low temperatures are below freezing. Clear weather occurs on about 11 percent of annual days with no clear relationship to temperature. Winds are generally from the WSW and calm only 4 percent of the time. Summer breezes are particularly generous.

INTENTION

Design Team

Thomas Herzog practices architecture from a strong academic and research base. After completing a diploma of architecture at the Technical University of Munich in 1965, he received his doctorate in architecture from the University of Rome in 1972. Dr. Herzog became the chair for Design and Building Technology at the Technical University of Darmstadt in 1986 and chair for Design and Building Construction at the Technical University of Munich in 1993. Along the way, he has worked for the European Commission, the policy initiative arm of the European Union, and championed solar architecture at several other European organizations. His more recent work includes the Wikahn Furniture Factory (1992), Linz Design Center (1993), Expo Hall 26 at the Hanover Trade Fair (1996), and a collaboration with Sir Norman Foster for a solar village at Regensburg, Germany (1998) for the European Commission.

Herzog's work has been a continuing series of partnerships and collaborations. He approaches each project

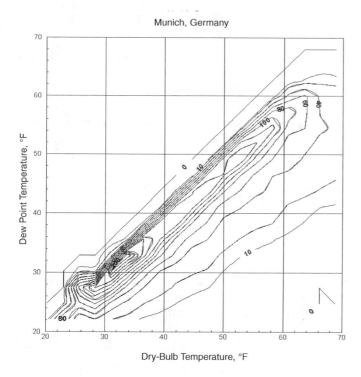

Munich, Germany

Figure 9.25 Bin data distribution for Munich. Concentric areas of graph indicate the number of hours per year that weather conditions normally occur in this climate. Similar to elevation readings on topographic maps, highest frequency occurrences of weather are at the center peaks of the graph. (Data sources: *Engineering Weather Data, typical meteorological year (TMY) data from the National Climatic Data Center,* and the ASHRAE Weather Data Viewer *from the American Society of Heating, Refrigerating and Air-Conditioning Engineers.*)

as a prototype design for state-of-the-art technology, and this research and development requires teamwork. Since 1981 he has worked hand in hand with the Freiburg Institute of Energy Research, because he says, "no architect can ever master all the forces at work on solar buildings." He believes in the necessity and synergistic effect of multi-disciplinary teams. His partner for the Pullach House was Michael Volz, with assistance from Michael Streib. Structural engineering was provided by Jullus Natterer. Herzog, Volz, and Natterer have also cowritten a book on timber structures.

Philosophy

The emphasis on research and development in Herzog's academic pursuits find Modernist expression in his professional practice. He constantly experiments and seeks to apply the best and most advanced technologies to the service of his buildings. For him, Modernist architecture is still involved in the transition from the 1970s attitude whereby energy efficiency was sacrificed to achieve visual statements of material minimalism. Herzog sees the emerging

role of Modern architecture as just the opposite—using new materials and configurations to exploit a building's functional relationship with the environment. This evolution is evident in his own career as well. After following in the footsteps of Frei Otto and publishing his much translated doctoral dissertation *Pneumatic Constructions,* Herzog has essentially abandoned lightweight minimalist envelope solutions in favor of far more proactive and environmentally sophisticated techniques.

Intent

Specific statements about design intentions for this project have not been identified, and the architect has been careful to protect his client's privacy. From the philosophical statements and lineage of Herzog's practice and research, however, a few ideas can be identified in the finished building. Primarily, this building was to utilize cutting-edge technology, with provisions for uptake of new technologies as they emerged into practical application.

CRITICAL TECHNICAL ISSUES

Inherent

Programmatic challenges for this project seem to have been centered on how to provide glazed solar access and airy ventilated spaces without sacrificing interior privacy. The predominantly glass skin was one antagonizing factor. The need to provide two separate homes within the same see-through building scheme was another.

Contextual

Most of Herzog's residential-scale work has been met with resistance, and often rejection, by conservative-minded building authorities, a problem he shares with Glenn Murcutt. His response is philosophical: He declares no desire to impress with originality and feels no obligation to conform, further saying that our love for new technology has to be made compatible with our love for our old towns and historic cities. Herzog has, along the way, learned to warn his clients about the bureaucratic challenges of designing solar-oriented prototype buildings in tradition-oriented communities.

Intentional

Basing the design scheme on the traditional timber frame barn, Herzog adapted a climatically appropriate form and one that was also suitable for the wood framing suggested by the client. This set the challenge of finding suitable transformations of a romantic form into a high-performance building of modern construction.

APPROPRIATE SYSTEMS

Precedent

Alpine barn structures like the Swiss example pictured in Figure 9.21 are well adapted to the cold climate of southern Germany and to construction with indigenous wood timber. Some forms of this building are called *spicher,* and some are named *stöekli;* in either case they were once traditionally transformed into cottages for retiring parents when the oldest son took over the farm.

The cantilevering masses of the barn start with a minimal basement, usually excavated into a sloping hillside for direct access to the lowest level and dug deep enough to avoid frost heave. Above this foundation increasingly larger rooms are built, taking advantage of overhanging projections to increase joist spans and floor area where the seeds for next year's crop are dried and stored. The structural projection also shelters storage for materials and tools outdoors under the overhanging eaves. Surrounding walkways at the upper levels flank the central rooms, providing insulating buffer zones, and these are used for storage of hay, onions, or other goods less susceptible to frost. A steep and broad roof overhangs the building on all four sides, resisting the accumulation of snow and shedding moisture away from the foundation.

All in all, the farm building is an appealing traditional form and a practical means of constructing a climate-appropriate house with minimum materials and resources. Herzog adapted it as both an appropriate historical and functional precedent.

Site

The open site is bordered on both sides by tree-lined fences. This allowed Herzog to press the house against the north property line for protection from the most bitter northerly winter winds and leave it exposed to low angles of winter sun from the south.

The form of the house, a thin pavilion, is worked into the site by indoor/outdoor buffers on all four sides. To the north and south are overhanging balconies and shaded decks. On the east side is a carport whose roof is a terrace accessed from the second floor. Finally, on the west, there is a conservatory greenhouse opening to a tree-covered deck at grade level.

Structure

The rich density of conifers and temperate hardwood trees in Bavaria suggest the appropriateness of a wood structure, but heavy timber framing is no longer competitive with engineered wood framing. Adherence to sustainable construction practice would also dictate the use of more reasonable resources. Herzog's adaptation of the traditional barn building uses laminated wood structure as both an economical and practical material for translation into industrialized construction. The building is essentially a heavy wood frame for glass infill with a great sheltering roof.

The narrow basement in this case is an 11.8 ft × 47.2 ft (3.6 m × 14.4 m) excavation under the center of the house with grade beams extending out to both ends. A 3.9 in. × 15.8 in. (100 mm × 400 mm) beam spans across the basement, cantilevering 2.9 ft (900 mm) past the basement wall on both sides. This structural platform places the first floor level a couple feet above grade and allows for the basement to be daylit and ventilated through panels set between the beams.

Vertical support starts with 5.9 in. × 5.9 in. (150 mm) laminated wood columns set along the basement wall on 11.8 ft centers, which establishes the interior planning grid of seven 11.8 ft × 11.8 ft (3.6 m × 3.6 m) bays. External columns of 2.4 in. × 5.9 in. laminated wood are set on the edge of the floor platform and divide each bay into modules of 2.9 ft, 5.8 ft, and 2.9 ft (900 × 1800 × 900 mm) sequentially. The main floors beams taper to 7.1 in. at their ends and are bound by a 2.4 in. × 7.1 in. (60 mm × 180 mm) edge beam, also of laminated wood.

Beams for the second floor and roof levels do not cantilever past the basement walls but terminate at the interior columns instead. The perimeter area of the second floor and the projecting north and south balconies are balanced on a built up support that spans out 2.9 ft (900 mm) both sides of the external column at the second floor level. The external column continues past this support and is capped by a triangular support member at 5.8 ft (1.8 m) spacing that resembles an inverted and wood clad truss. One leg of this support spans up to the second floor ceiling, another cantilevers horizontally 6 ft out to the eave of the roof, and the sloping top chord supports the roof itself. Beyond the interior columns the roof is glazed in anticipation of replacing them with photovoltaic cells when they are economically viable. The closure from internal column to external column is likewise in-filled with a sloping glass skylight. Purlins of laminated wood run across the inverted trusses to support the glass area of the roof and a more conventional rafter system supports the central opaque roof that covers the 11.8 ft (3.6 m) interior bays. In contrast to the narrow foundation at the 11.8 ft × 47.2 ft (3.6 m × 14.4 m) basement, the outline of the roof measures 31.9 ft × 91.5 ft (9.7 m × 27.9 m).

Transverse bracing is provided by several solid partition walls across the internal columns that divide the house into minor pavilions facing east and west. At the west end of the structure is a two-story-high bay that serves as a conservatory, and its north and south walls are secured with tubular steel X-bracing to aid in longitudinal stiffness. The east end of the house terminates in a covered carport, with its roof serving as a large terrace accessed from the second floor balcony. To the north there is a 41.3 ft × 5.9 ft (12.6 m × 1.8 m) storage building with connecting canopies to both dwellings.

Envelope

External cladding of the house is typical of passive heating schemes, with extensive glass to the south and opaque insulated construction to the north. Herzog uses 5.9 in. (150 mm) insulation blankets in all the opaque walls with cement-bound chipboard on both sides. The primary vertical glazing is insulated clear glass, and the skylights are insulated with a laminated inner light. The glazed portion of the roof is tempered single pane.

An experimental solar collector was built into four of the 5.8 ft (1.8 m) bays of the south wall. These resemble unvented Trombe wall construction, except that they are filled with translucent insulation fibers inspired by the light-transmitting hairs of the well-insulated polar bear. Glass is used as the panel's outside covering, and a 4.0 in. (100 mm) thick precast concrete slab with a black painted surface is placed behind the insulation to absorb sunlight and store heat. The collectors total only 194 ft² (18 m²) but succeed in providing 10 percent of the annual heating requirement.

In the summer, shade from the high sun is provided at the ground floor by the overhanging balconies, and sunlight at the upper floor is screened by the roof purlins below the glass canopy. Two-story-high trellises are planted in front of three bays of the south wall. The plants grow from wood decks outside the middle bays to the bottom of the eave line. For air, a great number of exterior doors on the house accommodate the separate occupancies, and these can also be used for natural ventilation in warmer weather. No less than 27 doors open to decks and balconies, and the end wall of the conservatory has an additional pair of sliding doors. The attic space above the center bay width is ventilated at both ends by louvers sheltered beneath the projecting roof gable. A continuous roof ridge vent provides ample exhaust for hot air from the attic.

Mechanical

Backup mechanical heating is a necessity in the 6701 annual degree-day heating climate of Munich. The winter dry-bulb design temperature is a frigid 10°F (−12.5°C), and the summer design conditions are a mild 78°F dry-bulb and a 63°F wet-bulb temperature (25.5/17.4°C). Supplemental heat is provided by a conventional boiler in the basement and distributed by radiators. In addition, there is a wood-burning stove in each dwelling.

While the house is closed tight in winter, indoor air quality is maintained by an air-to-air heat exchanger that reclaims warmth from exhausted indoor air and passes it to incoming outside makeup air. These simple devices pass the two air streams by each other with lots of high-conduction surface area separating them. Usually some 90 percent of the heat can be reclaimed from kitchen, toilet room, and other exhaust air streams. Ideally, slightly more outdoor air is brought in than indoor air is exhausted to keep the house positively pressurized relative to the outdoors and thereby reduce infiltration of cold air.

Interior

The one-room-deep pavilion plan of the Pullach House is not unlike that of Glenn Murcutt's Magney House. Even the quasi-division into two independent living units expresses a similarity of scheme. These affinities are largely due to the shared goals of blending interior rooms with the outdoors, both for environmental reasons — sun and ventilation — and for communion of interior space with its natural setting. Herzog's scheme is quite different, though, in its sectional qualities and in the arrangement of circulation at the perimeter of occupied space rather than through a central axis as in the Magney House. The two-story construction of the larger Pullach House obviously makes for a different kind of section as well.

The seven bays of the interior are planned in three major sections, from east to west, as two bays for a small one-bedroom dwelling with an internal stair, two bays for a double-height gallery with an open stair and two guest rooms, and two bays for a grander one-bedroom dwelling opening onto the gallery on one side and terminating in the extra third bay of the double-height conservatory on the other. From south to north the plan is layered into a 2.9 ft (884 mm) wide sunlit circulation path, the 11.8 ft (3.6 m) wide center bays, and another 2.9 ft (884 mm) boundary to the north, where the insulated walls are supplemented by an assortment of storage compartments, closets, and other built-in buffers.

TECHNICAL INTEGRATION HIGHLIGHTS

Physical

- Most of the system-to-system interfaces in this project are put together to achieve performance levels of integration, but it seems that the structure is physically meshed with other systems as a consequence. Daylight and air flow to the basement between beams; the interior planning module is based on the structural bay; solar heating and shade elements wrap into the structural frame; and even the basic circulation paths follow along the structural cantilevers.

Visual

- Structural framing is exposed throughout the house with good effect. Reducing the envelope to skeleton and infill emphasizes the timber qualities of the laminated wood frame. The prevalence of glass also accentuates the wood. It is a plus that all the timber is engineered from plentiful small-dimension lumber.
- The pavilion plan opens communication from interior rooms to the open site, and the shading strategies manage to protect against glare and overheating.

Performance

- Trombe wall indirect-gain solar collectors with their integral concrete thermal mass make up the opaque wall elements of the south façade.
- Solid north-to-south interior walls give the structure diaphragm strength and partition the separate occupancies.
- Overhanging glass eaves keep the wood structure protected while allowing solar penetration to the interior. The glass canopy can eventually be replaced with photovoltaic panels.
- The cantilevered structure provides overhanging shelter while minimizing loads and member sizes.
- The exterior storage building promotes openness of the house by removing potentially interrupting interior storage closets and other elements. It also acts as a freestanding buffer against winter winds.
- The one-room depth of the pavilion plan allows shorter spans and facilitates natural cross ventilation.

- The interior storage provides extra thermal insulation to the opaque areas of the envelope.
- The interior planning strategy allows for flexible use of floor space, especially the shared middle bays that seem to belong to either of the two dwellings.

DISCUSSION

Other than the 10 percent solar contribution of annual heating requirements by the solar collectors integrated into the south wall, no performance figures are given for this project. It is safe to assume, however, that the additional glazing area provides a much larger portion of the heating by direct gain. Even on a completely overcast winter day, some 40 percent of the solar energy available on a clear day can still be usefully collected. Guidelines for passive heating in Chicago, Illinois, for example, suggest that a 35 percent south glass-to-floor-area ratio would provide 23 percent of the annual heating requirement. The long pavilion plan of the Pullach House has more like 0.5 ft^2 of glass for each square foot of floor, a 50 percent ratio.

The solar inventiveness of this house is a major physical feature, but success in integration is largely strategic rather than physical. Most of the performance benefits are attained more by design logic than by system-to-system interfaces. Consequently, a rather simple plan reveals a very sophisticated combination of thoughts about interior planning, structural spans, solar penetration, summer shading, circulation, privacy, and view, as well as the aesthetics of timber framing with the transparency of glass infill.

10

High Tech Architecture

Approaching the various aspects of integration from the perspective of High Tech architecture entails a look at design beyond the building use "types" as discussed in the case studies of the five previous chapters. Although High Tech design is often associated with a particular range of open-plan building types, it is clearly not restricted to any particular applications. It is also true, as rated in the declarations of its champions, that High Tech is not simply understood or pursued in practice as a "style." The best description left for this architectural venue, and one particularly appropriate to integration issues, is probably the label of "method."

High Tech is easily identified by its imagery—revealed structure, exposed ducts and building services, industrial kit-of-parts appeal, machine precision aesthetics, and open-span spaces. These expressionistic qualities vary from the pyrotechnic spectacular to the factory spartan. The Medical Faculty at Aachen (Webber, Brand and Partners, 1984) and the Cummins Engine Company (Ahrends, Burton and Koralek, 1983) perhaps illustrate the two extremes. Either way, technical expressionism is a clear visual marker of High Tech ideals—admire the results or not, they are nonetheless provocative. In fact, the buildings produced by leading High Tech architects are undeniably the most published, discussed, and generally visible buildings today.

In the time line of architectural history, High Tech emerges as a logical extension of thought along the lineage of Paxton's Crystal Palace, through Corbusian Brutalism and Bauhaus industrial craft, to Louis Khan's articulation of served and servant spaces. These turning points, as discussed in Chapter Two, were advanced by the accelerated pace of scientific progress, technological commodification, and the economics of modern construction. Along the way, however, High Tech incorporated many new ideas and original interpretations.

From its heritage, then, High Tech embodies ideals of functional rationalism, expressionistic honesty of materials, a dislike for applied finishes, scale through detail, articulation of joint, legibility of systems, and an overriding glorification of technology. The inheritance is less certain in some areas—many High Tech buildings are made of custom-designed pieces rather than off-the-shelf kits and are easily among the most expensive buildings in the world to construct. But these shortcomings can also be seen as part of the struggle to emerge from standard building practice and a limited array of ingredients of acceptable quality for machine-made buildings. Sufficient numbers of High Tech kit buildings have been produced affordably, proving that it is certainly possible to do so.

In good keeping with its techno-logic legacy, High Tech has played a major role in developing the systems approach to architectural design. This is as true of compositional or formalist aspects as it is of the functional or rationalist ones. The integration of these two aspects is precisely why High Tech is discussed in a separate set of case studies. Not only have its methods provided a new way of visually reading buildings and appreciating them as legible constructions of articulated parts, it has also extended our palette of building components and expanded the vocabulary of architectural thought. These new realms take us into an anatomical exploration of buildings. They introduce building dynamics of flexibility and component obsolescence. They also allow for accommodation of yet-to-be-invented systems to replace the current ones.

High Tech modes of exposing hardware and refining the details of connections made much of this new exploration necessary. As long as elements such as ducts and diagonal bracing were covered over by smooth finish materials or buried in basements and floor-ceiling layers, architects were primarily concerned with their physical requirements for space. As they became glamorized elements of occupied rooms and public street elevations, greater care was given to how they worked, what they did, how they were deployed, and what potential for architectural realization lay in their essential characteristics.

New preoccupations with the now architecturally legitimized hardware also fostered new attitudes about what buildings are supposed to do and how they are evaluated. The whole notion of air-conditioning, for example, finally became important to architecture. No longer just a machine that "had to be given its place," in Louis Khan's phrase, air-conditioning hardware became a design opportunity. In order to deploy it advantageously and to work in concert with mechanical engineering team members, architects exercised greater concern for the impacts of air-conditioning on the design, cost, appearance, performance, and life cycle of buildings. In consequence, the servicing and serviceability of buildings has rapidly become as ennobled as their constructability and structure have always been.

22

CENTRE GEORGES POMPIDOU, 1972–1975

Paris, France
PIANO+ROGERS

DESCRIPTION

Centre Pompidou is a museum and cultural center in central Paris situated on a five acre plaza between the Louvre and Notre Dame. This location, known as Plateau Beaubourg, gave the complex its original name, "Centre Beaubourg." In relation to modern buildings, it is just east of I. M. Pei's Pyramid at the Louvre and northwest of Jean Nouvel's Arab World Institute. The Pompidou's strategic location had previously languished as a parking lot for the nearby food markets of Les Halles.

Originally, Centre Pompidou was to be a "live center of information" with dynamic video displays of cultural events on the plaza side and traffic information on the street side. This concept was gradually squashed by political, budget, and time constraints. Instead, the building portrays its own datum—spreading vertical circulation components across the length of a pedestrian plaza on the west side and its mechanical workings across the long east street side elevation. This public display of components is framed by an external structure. The pedestrian escalators to the west and the mechanical fittings to the east are both contained within 25 ft (7.6 m) deep zones of exposed steel skeleton and diagonal bracing. To ensure legibility of the technical vocabulary and its visual articulation, external systems are color coded by function. To do honor to the original intent, huge banners are frequently hung from the structural frame, announcing current events at the center.

The external display of structure and services is actually generated by programmatic requirements for flexibility of the interior spaces. These machine infrastructures were moved outside the glass skin to leave unobstructed and adaptable interior volumes. The exterior zone of the structural frame is there to provide tension forces outside the main volume's external columns, pulling the cantilevered horizontal members downward to reduce the bending forces on the floor span. This complementary structural strategy eliminates the need for supporting columns across the unencumbered interior span of 157 ft (53.3 m). The mechanical and air-conditioning services are then placed in the exoskeletal frame, leaving the interior open and adaptable.

Figure 10.1 Overview of Centre Pompidou. *(Photograph courtesy of Renzo Piano Building Workshop.)*

TABLE 10.1 Fact Sheet

Project	**Building Name**	Centre Georges Pompidou
	Client	French Ministry of Culture and Ministry of Education
	City	Paris, France
	Lat/Long/Elev	48.85N 2.36E, 550 ft (168 m)
Team	**Architect**	Piano+Rogers
	Engineer	Ove Arup & Partners
	Other Team Members	Gianni Franchini
General	**Time Line**	1972–1975.
	Floor Area	692,117 ft^2 (64,300 m^2) of occupied space and 1,076,388 ft^2 (99,950 m^2) of total planned area.
	Occupants	10,000 visitors per day.
	Cost	FF 345 million or 1973 US$ 75.9 million.
	Cost in 1995 US$	$260.8 million or $377/ft^2.
	Stories	Six stories of 23 ft (7 m) height.
	Plan	557 ft × 157.5 ft (170 m × 48 m).
Site	**Site Description**	Originally a parking lot for the food markets at Les Halles, 4.9 acres (20,000 m^2) between Rue du Renard and Rue St. Martin, "Plateau Beaubourg." Rue St. Martin was closed to create a piazza on the vertical circulation side west of the building.
	Parking, Cars	700 cars below grade
Structure	**Foundation**	Main columns carrying vertical loads of 4,000 tons and moment loads of 18,000 tons are supported on wall piles 29.5 ft long by 3.3 ft wide by 45.9 ft deep (9 m × 1 m × 14 m).
	Vertical Members	26 centrifugally cast steel tube compressive columns of 33.5 in. (850 mm) outside diameter (each carrying 3000 tons), 26 solid steel round bar tension ties of 8 in. (200 mm) diameter located 19.7 ft (6 m) outside the compressive columns
	Horizontal Spans	147 ft (44.8 m) main truss girders. Gerberette beams of monolithic cast steel, each weighing 9.6 tons, cantilevered inward approximately 6.6 ft (2 m) and supporting main truss girder.
Envelope	**Glass and Glazing**	Various clear, single, double, and fire-resistant glazings.
	Skylights	None.
	Cladding	Insulated metal panel.
	Roof	Not determined.
HVAC	**Equipment**	47,000 cfm of air supply (80,000 m^3/hr), high-velocity dual-duct variable air volume distribution located in structural frame on east elevation.
	Cooling Type	Centrifugal refrigeration, double bundle condensers.
	Distribution	High-velocity variable air volume, dual duct.
	Duct Type	Color coding of ducts.
	Vertical Chases	External distribution on west façade.
Interior	**Partitions**	Movable dry construction.
	Finishes	Various, as there are several different uses of the building.
	Vertical Circulation	Escalators and four elevators located on west façade, eight fire escapes on each floor, with four on east and four on west elevation.
	Lighting	Modular lighting tracks at 4.5 to 7.5 W/ft^2 (50 to 80 W/m^2).

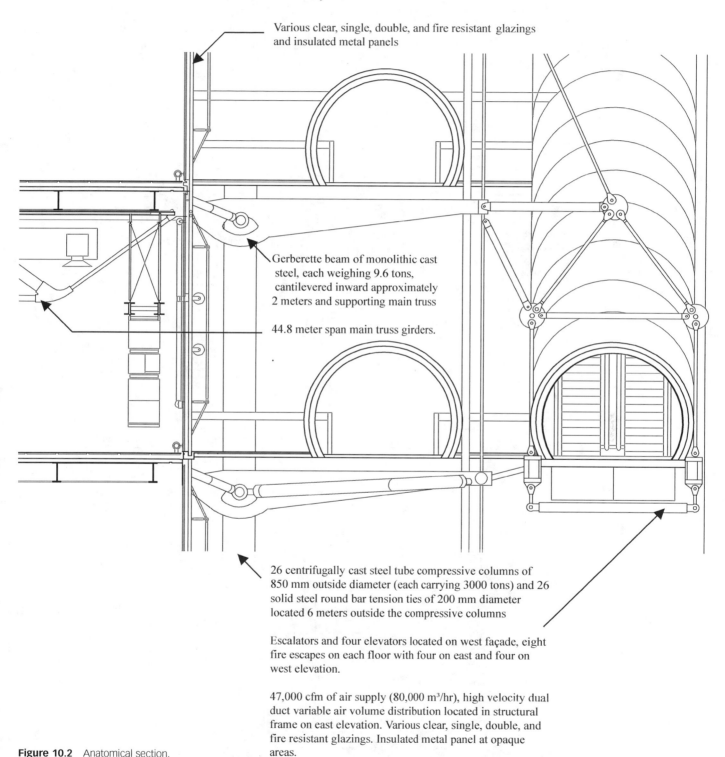

Six stories of 23-ft (7-m) height and 557-ft x 157.5-ft (170-m x 48-m) in plan.

Main columns carrying vertical load of 4,000 tons and moment loads of 18,000 ton meters are supported on wall piles 29.5-ft long by 3.3-ft wide by 45.9-ft deep (9-m x 1-m x 14-m).

Various clear, single, double, and fire resistant glazings and insulated metal panels

Gerberette beam of monolithic cast steel, each weighing 9.6 tons, cantilevered inward approximately 2 meters and supporting main truss

44.8 meter span main truss girders.

26 centrifugally cast steel tube compressive columns of 850 mm outside diameter (each carrying 3000 tons) and 26 solid steel round bar tension ties of 200 mm diameter located 6 meters outside the compressive columns

Escalators and four elevators located on west façade, eight fire escapes on each floor with four on east and four on west elevation.

47,000 cfm of air supply (80,000 m³/hr), high velocity dual duct variable air volume distribution located in structural frame on east elevation. Various clear, single, double, and fire resistant glazings. Insulated metal panel at opaque areas.

Figure 10.2   Anatomical section.

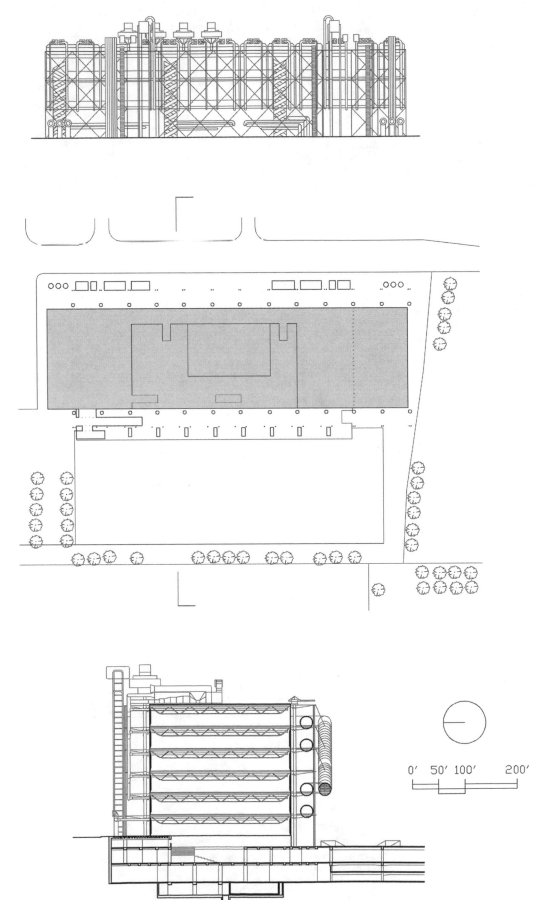

Figure 10.3 Plan, section, and elevation.

PROGRAM

Client

In 1971, French president Georges Pompidou announced an architectural competition for the center. The jury included Philip Johnson, Oscar Niemeyer, and its chairman, Jean Prouve, among others. The design was awarded to the newly formed partnership Piano+Rogers on July 18 of the same year. Ove Arup & Partners was brought on as the engineering consultant. Arup's Peter Rice, whose first major project was the Sydney Opera House, was an integral member of the team. The state client was represented by senior representatives from the ministries of culture, education, and finance.

Brief

The competition brief called for an "architectural and urban complex which will mark our century" and be visited by some 10,000 people per day. It included spaces for a museum of modern art, a reference library of one million volumes, an industrial design center, an acoustical and music research facility called IRCAM, multipurpose performance halls, plus a restaurant and parking. The budget was set at FF 280 million or about 1971 US $50,778,000 (the equivalent of 1995 US $190,894,736). Completion was scheduled for December 1975. Although the IRCAM acoustical research center was dropped from the first phase of construction, the final cost still totaled some FF 345 million (in 1973 equivalents) or about 1973 US $75,900,000 (the equivalent of 1995 US $ 260,824,742). IRCAM, with its 400-seat variable acoustics auditorium, was completed separately beneath the southern end of the plaza in 1977.

Centre Beaubourg was seen as a focal French cultural center. It would house the existing Centre Nationale d'Art Contemporain (CNAC) and a poorly provided for National Museum of Modern Art. In addition to its museum collections, the cultural center would house the Public Information Library and an industrial design center. The industrial design agency, Union Centrale des Arts Décoratifs, was responsible for the 1925 Paris World's Fair, Arts Décoratifs et Industriels. Above all, the program called for a novel and modern solution to house novel and modern culture. The brief contains several references to reexamination of the past and speculation about the future. The character suggested is that of a landmark statement about contemporary twentieth-century culture and its "service for the diffusion of knowledge." Centre Pompidou was a predecessor of later president François Mitterand's mammoth Great Works projects that were to reclaim French mastery of culture and art by the end of the millennium (see case study #15).

Site

A critical aspect of the Plateau Beaubourg location, apart from its proximity to other sites of historical and modern architecture, is its relationship to the neighboring market of Les Halles. From Roman times until its 1969 redevelopment, Les Halles had been the largest of the Parisian markets. Plateau Beaubourg had been used merely as a parking lot for the market since the 1930s. Having outgrown the space available in the heart of Paris, the market and its food stalls were moved to the southern suburbs of the city. A large retail mall and transit center were developed in their place. Of equal historical note, the surrounding Les Marais quarter had been rescued from the swamps during the reign of Henry IV (1589–1610) and had been home to French aristocracy in the seventeenth century. But the neighborhood of pre-Revolutionary medieval streets and stone buildings was in steep decline, and several projects were sited to revitalize it. Centre Pompidou was at the focus. Les Marais is now a heavily populated residential district.

Climate

Paris (48.85 N latitude, 2.36 E longitude) is part of the large "temperate, mid-latitude, no dry season, warm summer" region of northern Europe. This is the world's largest zone of what Köppen classified as cfb climates. It stretches from central Spain and northern Greece to eastern Bulgaria and the central coast of Norway. Of all the climates discussed in this text, however, that of Paris most closely resembles the patterns of Seattle, Washington, at about the same latitude (47.50 N, 122.29 W). Nearby London and Amsterdam are also close matches to Paris, but both have somewhat cooler climates.

Rain falls in Paris on 50 percent of all days and is fairly constant from month to month, both in frequency and

TABLE 10.2   Outline of Space Inventory

	ft²	m²
Public Reception and Retail	57,049	5,300
Museum and Library	402,569	37,400
Auditoriums and Temporary Exhibits	78,576	7,300
Administration, Storage, and Workspace	153,923	14,300
Open Space	75,347	7,000
Total Built Space	692,117	64,300
Total Program Space	767,464	71,300
Parking for 700 Cars (located below plaza)		
Site Area	215,277	20,000

TABLE 10.3   Normal Climate Data for Paris

		Jan.	Feb.	Mar.	Apr.	May	June	July	Aug.	Sept.	Oct.	Nov.	Dec.	Year
Temperature	Degree-Days Heating	819	714	615	464	260	128	47	43	144	378	617	752	5028
	Degree-Days Cooling	0	0	0	0	10	41	93	93	23	2	0	0	253
	Extreme High	59	68	75	79	87	95	95	99	90	85	79	63	99
	Normal High	43	45	51	57	64	70	75	75	69	59	49	45	59
	Normal Average	39	40	45	50	57	62	67	67	61	53	44	41	52
	Normal Low	34	34	38	42	49	54	58	57	52	46	39	36	45
	Extreme Low	1	10	21	26	32	39	41	43	41	28	21	14	1
Humidity	Dew Point	34	33	37	39	47	52	55	54	52	47	40	36	44
	Max % RH	89	87	87	86	86	86	85	87	91	92	91	89	88
	Min % RH	79	71	65	58	57	58	54	51	59	69	76	81	65
	% Days with Rain	60	46	56	53	53	46	43	40	46	56	53	60	51
	Rain Inches	2	2	2	2	3	2	2	2	2	2	2	2	26
Sky	% Overcast Days	39	32	27	19	19	16	11	9	14	23	29	36	23
	% Clear Days	8	14	12	13	10	8	13	14	14	10	11	8	11
Wind	Prevailing Direction	SW	E	W	NE	NE	W	W	W	W	W	SW	SW	W
	Speed, Knots	12	6	10	9	9	9	9	8	9	9	11	11	9
	Percent Calm	2	3	2	2	2	2	2	2	3	3	2	2	2
Days Observed	Rain	18	14	17	16	16	14	13	12	14	17	16	18	185
	Fog	13	14	10	8	7	6	5	7	10	13	14	13	120
	Haze	0	0	0	#	#	#	#	0	#	0	#	#	1
	Snow	4	4	2	1	#	0	0	0	0	0	1	2	14
	Hail	#	0	#	#	#	#	#	0	0	#	#	#	1
	Freezing Rain	1	1	#	0	0	0	0	0	0	0	#	1	3
	Blowing Sand	0	#	0	0	0	0	0	0	#	#	0	0	#

precipitation amounts. The total annual rainfall of only 26 in. indicates light showers more than torrential downpours. Nonetheless, a scant 11 percent of Paris days have clear skies. The generally gray skies are complemented by cool temperatures—less than 5 percent of annual hours are above 75°F. Temperature ranges from daily low to daily high are kept narrow by constant humidity and cloud cover. Overall, Paris is 59 percent cold, 25 percent cool, 14 percent comfortable, 14 percent warm, and 0 percent hot.

Art collections and libraries in this climate have to plan for humidity control. Even in winter there is some need to cool air to below its dew point by mechanical air-conditioning, so as to drive off the excess moisture before reheating it to serve occupant temperature comfort. With the large number of visitors expected, ventilation by provision of outdoor air means a constant introduction of additional humidity loads. [tab. 10.3; Figs 10.4–5]

INTENTION

Design Team and Their Philosophy

Piano+Rogers was formed expressly to enter the Pompidou competition. The team consisted of the remnants of Team 4, which had formerly included Norman Foster. Renzo Piano had previously joined forces with Rogers to collaborate on other projects. As a group of young architects, they were quite inexperienced for a project of this scale. The evolution of this group is a story in its own right.

Richard Rogers (b. July 23, 1933, in Florence) returned to his family's native England with his parents in 1938 to escape the early rumblings of war in Mussolini's Italy. After an adventurous and frequently turbulent youth during the war years and an early education troubled by mild but undiagnosed dyslexia, he entered the army in November 1951. He was immediately stationed back in

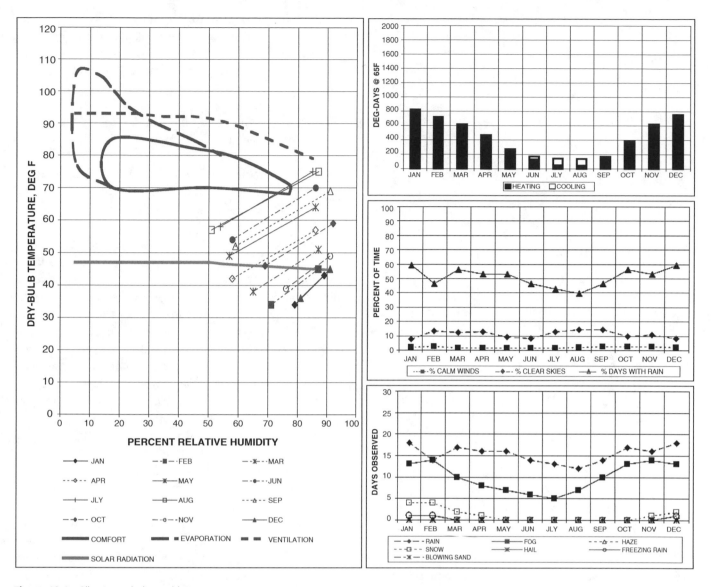

Figure 10.4 Climate analysis graphics.

Italy, where he met up with his cousin, Ernesto Rogers, also dyslexic and an architect. Ernesto became the editor of *Domus* in 1945 and, in 1954, of *Casabella*. It was in Ernesto's studio with partners Ludovico Belgiojoso and Enrico Peressuti that Richard Rogers first decided to become an architect and, on the advice of his cousin, targeted an education at London University's Architectural Association (the AA). In the autumn of 1953, done with military service and avowed against discipline and authority in general, he returned to England.

The early 1950s was the era of several Modernist transitions. Alison and Peter Smithson were teaching at AA. Giedion had published *Mechanization Takes Command* in 1948, and its message was taken to heart. By 1952, Le Corbusier's Unité d'Habitation was nearing completion in Marseilles. Reyner Banham (1966) called it all, collectively, the New Brutalism.

Rogers entered the Epsom College of Art for two terms to take foundation courses in preparation for the AA. Here he met fellow students Georgie Cheeseman and Brian Taylor, and another series of adventures began. Georgie, coincidentally the daughter of a wealthy Lloyd's of London underwriter, became his first true love and his total obsession. Her father forbade her to travel with Rogers on summer outings, and so he struck out on his own. An excursion to Milan in the summer of 1957 led to Rogers's meeting and romance with Su Brumwell. In the time that followed, Rogers's parents, Dada and Nino, as well as Su's parents, Marcus and Rene, seemed to bond around the young couple.

Despite his intellectual interest in architecture and his efforts to work in professional practices, Rogers seems to have suffered a lack of drawing skills that threatened his academic progress. Peter Smithson apparently saw

Paris (De Gaulle), France

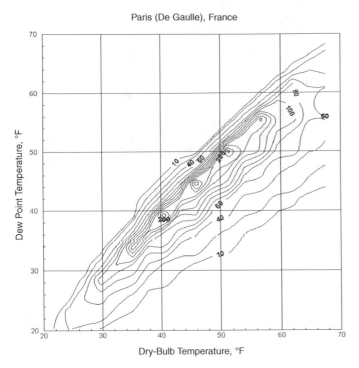

Figure 10.5 Bin data distribution for Paris. Concentric areas of graph indicate the number of hours per year that weather conditions normally occur in this climate. Similar to elevation readings on topographic maps, highest frequency occurrences of weather are at the center peaks of the graph. (Data sources: *Engineering Weather Data, typical meteorological year (TMY) data from the National Climatic Data Center,* and the ASHRAE *Weather Data Viewer from the American Society of Heating, Refrigerating and Air-Conditioning Engineers.)*

Rogers's real potential and fostered his academic growth. Meanwhile, Su Brumwell was studying sociology nearby at the London School of Economics (LSE). Rogers eventually won the fifth year prize at AA for a school design project set in Wales and constructed of local materials. On August 27, 1960, Richard and Su were married. They flew to the south of France for their honeymoon and stayed with Georgie Cheeseman before traveling on.

After Su's last year at LSE, both she and Richard were accepted at Yale. Rogers had to decline an offer to study under Louis Kahn at the University of Pennsylvania to do so, but he preferred to study at Yale with his wife. She took up urban planning and he was awarded a Fulbright scholarship in architecture. Paul Rudolph, then dean at Yale, had an authoritarian character that did not sit well with Richard Rogers. Vincent Scully's history lessons had more appeal to Rogers's intellect.

Norman Foster was attending Yale at the same time. He and Rogers worked on several projects in school together, including a science laboratory inspired by Louis Kahn's design for the Richards Medical Research Building.

Philip Johnson, a juror for the young team's project, is said to have flattened its towers with his bare fists. The trio of Su, Richard, and Norman were also exposed to the Yale teachings of James Stirling and met Craig Ellwood of Case Study House fame and the avant-garde California design scene. The three traveled to Chicago, visiting the works of Frank Lloyd Wright and Mies van der Rohe. Sometime in 1962 they visited the Eames House together. After graduating, Rogers and Su remained in California to do drafting and model making for the firm of SOM. Along the way they visited works of Rudolf Schindler, including the 1953 Lovell Beach House on which Rogers had written an essay for Vincent Scully.

By 1963, Su and Richard Rogers had returned to England to pursue their own prospects, designing a house for her parents, the Brumwells. They contacted Georgie and Wendy Cheeseman, who were now qualified architects, and set up an office in a corner of Wendy's apartment. When Norman Foster joined them later, the Team 4 group was complete. Rogers was 30 years old, Foster was 28. After settling into the relationship of four architects in partnership, the group balance was disturbed by Georgie's withdrawal. Eventually, in 1964, Norman Foster and Wendy Cheeseman were married. In 1967, Rogers and Foster decided to close Team 4 after the success of the Reliance Controls Factory failed to bring in new work. Wendy and Norman Foster established their own independent office that same year.

Another important collaborator was structural engineer Anthony Hunt. He had been associated with Wendy Cheeseman on some domestic projects, and she introduced him into the group. Together, Team 4 and Anthony Hunt finally completed the project for the Brumwell home and a few other small domestic designs. The Michael Jaffe house in Radlett, Hertfordshire was later used as a film set for *A Clockwork Orange.*

Other more successful projects followed, most notably the bold steel frame Reliance Controls Factory, a job that James Stirling had them short-listed for. Anthony Hunt again provided the engineering and stretched the materials to their economical and functional limits. In spite of awards and recognition, Reliance brought no new work, and the cooperative forces of Team 4, especially between the powerful personalities of Rogers and Foster, began to disintegrate. In June 1967, Rogers and Su left the firm's projects to Norman Foster and Wendy Cheeseman. John Young, chief assistant, stayed with the Fosters to finish his term at the Architecture Association, but Rogers later worked a deal for Young to complete his education in his office, where he has remained to this day.

Eventually, the work of the Rogers caught the attention of Renzo Piano, who was practicing in Genoa.

Following some correspondence, Piano came to London and began working with Richard and Su. In 1969, Marco Goldschmied joined the firm at the urging of John Young, and by 1970, Piano was an official team member.

Su and Richard had their third child, Ab, in July 1968. Meanwhile, Rogers had started a romance with Ruth Elias, a New Yorker whom he had met through an introduction from Georgie Cheeseman. By mid-1970, Richard Rogers organized a lecture tour in the United States to spend three months with Ruth and meet her family.

After returning to London to find the firm plodding along without him, Rogers eventually met an engineer from Ove Arup & Partners by the name of Ted Happold (see case study #3 for more on Happold and his work with Michael Hopkins and Frei Otto). Arup & Partners had recently finished the Sydney Opera House, and despite that project's political difficulties and cost overruns, the firm was determined to do another international project. In early 1971, Happold contacted Piano+Rogers to enter a competition in Paris. Rogers was against it, but Piano and Su outvoted him. Gianfranco Franchini was persuaded by Piano to move to London from Genoa and join the effort.

At about 10:30 on a Friday morning in the middle of July, John Young appeared at the office to find Richard and Su Rogers dancing gleefully. They had won the Centre Pompidou competition.

Intent

The team's architectural intention was defined in its competition statement as "A Live Center of Information." This focus was played out in the design by three media. First, there were the library and museum collections. For these interior functions to remain dynamic, a large degree of flexibility would be required. Originally, the team's competition entry proposed a series of movable floors, uninterrupted by partitions. Although the moving floors were eventually abandoned, the 157 ft (48 m) clear span across the narrow dimension of the plan was maintained. An interactive component of the interior information systems would include newsrooms, galleries, libraries, cinemas, and documentary services.

Second, the open plaza area was seen as a vital extension of the interior functions. Life would be instilled here by temporary exhibits and outdoor events, promoting continuity between the interior and pedestrian life. To broaden the plaza, a crossroad to the west would be closed and incorporated as pedestrian space. Not coincidentally, the plaza also provides an open place to see the building from.

Finally, the long façades of the building were to become three-dimensional surfaces layered with interest. With the building pushed up against Rue Renard on the east, the building was transformed into two information surfaces. The street side would display traffic-related data, and the plaza side would present entertainment and information to pedestrians. Developmental design sketches from late 1972, after most major elements of the building had been decided, show how images might be projected onto the building from neighboring structures across the plaza. Other images show how digital displays, of the "multivision" blinking screens variety, might have been employed.

The building was also to be a protagonist for Modernist architecture. It would be a flexible container of changing functions rather than a monumental form housing fixed installations. The Pompidou would be a dynamic servicing machine. To make this proclamation while still embracing the functional intention of providing live information, a number of bold moves were required. First, the building would be turned inside out, thus liberating the interior spaces from the permanent accommodation of circulation and servicing. This move also implied a strategy of expressively revealed technical systems. Second, the building would estrange itself from the historic character of its urban context in every way imaginable: scale, height, form, and expression. Reintegration with the cityscape would rely on attractive differences rather than soft-edged harmony.

CRITICAL TECHNICAL ISSUES

Inherent

Art museums and cultural libraries are first dominated by concerns for their collections, and second, by accommodation of visitors as they roam through the facilities. Security, environmental control with an emphasis on humidity levels, artificial and natural lighting, circulation, and storage are all vital. Live load allowance for exhibit spaces was set at 102 lbs/ft² (500 kg/m²)

As a national culture center, Beaubourg would also have significant popular importance and serve as a nerve center for the country's artistic interests. Gestures of great magnitude were required to recognize and serve the high status of the building's prominent position.

Finally, Centre Pompidou is a museum of modern art. Classical works are collected at the expansive Musée de Louvre, which is only a short walk from Centre Pompidou to the west, past Les Halles.

Contextual

The French ministries wanted the project to be completed by November 1975, largely because Georges Pompidou wanted the building completed before the end of his presidential term. Consequently, the site was excavated in

March 1972, two years before the design was completed. Construction continued during design development at the rate of about $3 million (£1.5 million or FF 20 million) per month. Speed, accuracy, and decisiveness were paramount throughout the project's evolution. Further, the original brief for the building essentially relegated the architect's work to design of the façades and structure. Piano+Rogers had to negotiate to gain control of interiors and furniture. Debates about the plaza and other parts of the project were ongoing.

Placing the center within its environs was also a challenge. It was assumed that most people would come by car, so 700 spaces were allocated for parking. Connection to the existing metro line was also important and would help merge the center into the everyday experience of local neighborhoods. Furthermore, there was a matter of scale. Huge floor area requirements, extensive ceiling heights, and the desire for a large plaza around the building combined to increase the overall height and mass of the building beyond the legal limits of the building code. The building mass also threatened to outgrow the stature of the existing five- and six-story urban fabric.

Intentional

The architects' "Live Center of Information" interpretation of the program fell into a period of uncertainty following the 1968 student political uprisings in Paris. Part of the motivation for the cultural center may have been stirred by those events, just as some of the world's fair expositions were motivated by domestic appeasement. Consequently, there was a lack of will on the part of the client to empower the potent media aspects of the architect's intention. Who would control what information was displayed? How would the messages be formatted? These questions gave Pompidou's ministries pause for concern.

Turning the building inside out, as it were, exposed the technical systems and released the interior loft floors for flexible use. Although serving the main architectural intentions quite well, this decision also posed problems. What would it take to span 157 ft (48 m), and how would the structure be fireproofed? How would view and daylighting work? How would the exterior be finished, and how would it be cleaned?

The megastructure scale of the building added a new dimension. More than 60 percent of the 14,560 tons (13,000 tonnes) of structural steel was of rolled, cast, or forged steel exceeding 6.3 in. (160 mm) thickness, and this was quite unusual for building construction. The steel casting industry in particular was unfamiliar with architectural requirements. No one on the team had experience with a building structure of this scale, and all of their previous experience had to be viewed with some caution.

APPROPRIATE SYSTEMS

Precedent

Peter Rice visited Kenzo Tange's cast steel Metabolist megastructure in Osaka, Japan, in 1971. It was the featured Expo 1970 space frame Festival Plaza pavilion designed by Kenzo Tange and Professor Tsuboi (see introduction to Chapter 8). The Metabolist's work would also have an influence on Norman Foster's Hong Kong and Shanghai Bank (see case study #25). In addition, Expo 70 was big on information technology, interactive displays, and huge data screens.

A merging of information and architectural technologies was originally rooted in the central tenets of Archigram, a group of young graduates who published techno-utopian manifestos from about 1961 to 1974. Their work took the form of futuristic drawings and terse declarations that read like telegrams, hence "Archi-gram." Led by Peter Cook, David Greene, Michael Webb, Ron Heron, Warren Chalk, and Dennis Crompton, they proclaimed an agenda in which, in the words of David Greene (Wolfe, 1999), "nomadism is the dominant social force; where time, exchange and metamorphosis replace stasis; where consumption, lifestyle and transience becomes the programme; and where the public realm is an electronic surface enclosing the globe." If this sounds prophetic of the Internet as we know it entering a new century, it was certainly portentous and pregnant with possibility when Piano + Rogers wrote the competition statement for Centre Pompidou.

Site

Below-grade substructure work was expedited by detailed programming work under preparation for two years before the competition was awarded. The architects' winning design pushed the building footprint against the eastern boundary of the site, but everything from Rue du Renard to the western edge of adjoining buildings, and from the St. Merri church to the south to the northern edge of the property, was hollowed out to the depth of four or five floors, reaching down 196 ft (60 m). The underground work led to the development of a large cover at surface level that formed an interconnected set of exterior spaces. The largest of these is the sunken main plaza in front of the building that covers the main garage area. This plaza leads gradually down to the building entryway one level below the surrounding streets. The slow slope of this plaza is usable as an amphitheater but not so steep as to prohibit outdoor exhibits. Two 7 m video screens were originally planned to be arrayed on the wall frame above. Large air ducts rise on the tree-lined western site boundary from the parking garage to visually claim the plaza for

Figure 10.6 Public plaza of Centre Pompidou.

the Pompidou center. Other parts of the plaza flow south to St. Merri across a large fountain pool in front of the IRCAM, further west along a broad pedestrian axis and park leading to Les Halle and north to encompass the end of the site where Brancusi's studio was permanently relocated. Most of the buildings that front these exterior spaces have been converted to commercial uses opening onto the plaza, effectively binding the Pompidou back into its fabric.

Structure

Below-grade construction was started by boring along the perimeter and inserting steel sections. The bottom portions of these holes were filled with concrete to anchor them structurally, and the upper parts were filled with weak grout that could be easily replaced with shoring between the steel sections as excavation progressed. Bearing foundations for the building's main columns were set on reinforced and posttensioned concrete wall footings 29.5 ft long by 3.3 ft wide by 45.9 ft deep (9 m × 1 m × 14 m). Each footing was reckoned to carry a vertical load of 4,000 tons and moment loads of 18,000 ton m.

There are six floors of 23 ft (7 m) floor-to-floor height above grade spanning 157.5 ft (48 m) with 9.3 ft (2.8 m) deep lattice trusses. In plan the superstructure of the building consists of three zones forming a footprint of 196.9–ft × 550.2 ft (60 m × 167.7 m) in 13 bays of 42.3 ft (12.9 m), about 26,412.8 ft² (2,452.6 m²) overall. The middle zone contains the 157.5 ft (48 m) clear span across the building interior between the main columns. The outside two zones make up structural wall frames to support and cantilever the main span lattice girders. These outer frames visually resemble oversized scaffolding. The inside wall frame support consists of 34 in. (850 mm) diameter steel tube columns, which were delivered to the site in two sections and welded together after erection of the lower elements. Each column has a tapering wall thickness from 3.4 in. (86 mm) at its base to 1.6 in. (41 mm) at the upper level.

Outer tension rod members of 7.9 in. (200 mm) solid steel in the wall frame act to reduce the bending moments on the center of the span by producing a 19.7 ft (6 m) cantilever outside the main columns. This cantilever force acts through horizontal 9.6 ton cast steel gerberette beams that are threaded around the main columns. Compression forces in the top chord of the long-span lattice trusses are thus transferred through the main columns without acting on them laterally or torsionally. Instead, the compressive shortening forces in the trusses move through the gerberettes and are transferred in tension down the outer frame wall rods to the foundation. Consequently, rotational forces on the columns are greatly reduced and they are required to act only in pure compression. Each of the 28 total assemblies of compressive column-to-gerberette-to-tension bars rest on one of the 29.5 ft × 3.3 ft × 45.9 ft (9 m × 1 m × 14 m) deep concrete wall footings.

The frame is stiffened laterally by cross bracing in the vertical plane across the long façades attached to the ends of the gerberette beams. Stiffening in the other vertical plane is added by diagonal braces between the lattice girders on both gable walls. Horizontal stiffening is provided by bracing rods between the gerberette ends and the columns at alternate floor levels. Alternate bays of the lattice beams are braced horizontally for torsional stiffness. The floors are constructed of rolled steel sections spanning the 42.3 ft (12.9 m) between bays and act compositely with a 4 in. (11 cm) concrete deck.

Figure 10.7 South end wall.

The lattice trusses are the largest elements of the building. They are literally of bridge construction proportions. Each truss weighs 88.5 tons (79.0 tonnes) and measures 9.3 ft deep (2.82 m) by 157.5 ft (48 m) long. They were formed by two 16 in. (41.9 mm) diameter top chords and two 8.9 in. (225 mm) bottom chords, the double chords being used to reduce the depth of the structure and improve lateral stability. The original contract for the trusses called for them to be brought to Paris by barge and transported from the Seine by trailer. In fact, they were brought by rail to Port de la Chappelle and then trailered to the site at night. Rue du Renard had to be reinforced prior to the start of delivery. The trusses arrived at the rate of three per week and were lifted into place with a single 500-ton-capacity crane that could handle the weight of the trusses out to a 111 ft (34 m) radius. Bays were erected at the rate of one every ten days. Following erection of the trusses, prefabricated floor sections measuring 34.6 ft × 21.0 ft (10.5 m × 6.4 m) were bolted directly to the trusses and concrete decks were poured one bay behind steel erection. The entire structure was erected in eight months.

Fire-resistance requirements dictated a two-hour rating for the steel, meaning that temperatures in the structural members would not exceed 840°F (450°C) after two hours of exposure to a standard fire. This was handled in the columns by filling them with circulating water so that their maximum temperature in any fire would be controlled to below 340°F (170°C). Truss members were wrapped with mineral wool or ceramic fibers and clad in stainless steel. Floor beams were sprayed with a vermiculite and cement compound. These passive measures were supplemented by an active fire sprinkler system mounted outside within the wall frames.

Envelope

The north, west, and south façades are fully glazed to overlook the plaza and provide views from, of, and into the building interior as well as the glazed escalator tubes. From the restaurant terrace on the south end there is a good view toward Notre Dame Cathedral; the Eiffel rises far off to the west across the plaza with traces of La Defense behind; and to the north is a view toward Montmartre and the Basilica of Sacré Coeur. These three elevations are provided with roll-down fire curtains. Because of the service elements outside the east façade, however, that side was unexpectedly required to use solid panels for adequate fire resistance.

Walls on all the elevations are held back 5.3 ft (1.6 m) from the columns and gable trusses to distance the structure from potential fires. In addition, glass wall frames are fitted with metal roll-down shutters, which are activated by fire to protect the external structure from heat coming from an inside fire. The shutters can also be operated manually for solar control.

Mechanical

Heavy equipment, boilers and chillers of the building's central plant, is located in the basement of the building along with thermal storage water tanks, main electrical distribution gear, and water treatment equipment. These services are distributed vertically within the east wall frame to equipment on the lower levels and finally to the roof level air-conditioning plants and four prominent rooftop cooling towers. Some horizontal distribution occurs across the east façade. This wall frame zone also contains freight elevators opening to the basement service areas and access gantries for servicing. Color coding of the service elements provides legibility and visual interest.

Within each floor level, there are exposed below-ceiling services for air delivery, ductwork, and lighting, as well as above-floor delivery of wiring and small pipes within an 11 in. (280 mm) raised floor resting on the concrete deck. Each bay of interior floor space is an independent thermal

Figure 10.8 East service wall from Rue du Renard.

Figure 10.9 Ceiling level services in the museum.

zone that receives air from the rooftop air handlers and delivers it accordingly.

The central plant has a total cooling capacity of 3500 tons (10 megawatts) and three boilers totaling 6800 kW. There are 26 high-velocity variable volume air handlers on the roof, each feeding conditioned air down to and back from one of the 13 bay widths of each floor. To lower the scale of the rooftop equipment, each air handler is broken down into its component parts: filters, air washers, fans, coils and air vents. Air-handling equipment and the cooling towers cover the east half of the roof. Trumpeted air vents are clearly visible from the east side terraces and the outdoor plaza.

Interior

Public access to the museum areas is not from the escalator tubes, as the building exterior seems to suggest, but from doors located centrally at the lower edge of the plaza. A double height interior forum connects the street level with the plaza level in a single volume. This room contains the general reception area, retail facilities, and temporary exhibits on the plaza level. The street-level mezzanine of the forum holds an exhibit area with a café to the south of the double height entry reception, plus a large theater to the north. The plaza-level reception area also looks down into a performance-level basement where a theater and meeting rooms are situated. From ticketing booths on the plaza level an interior escalator takes visitors to the street level on the northwest corner of the building. Here a small lobby connects to elevators and the exterior escalator. At this point in the journey, visitors can already look down 46 ft (14 m) onto the plaza. Four elevators are located at this corner. An emergency exit is located at the bottom end of the two-way escalator tube, and this is left open after museum hours for direct public access to the restaurant and its terrace at the top floor, five levels (115 ft or 35 m) above the street. The 13.1 ft (4 m) diameter escalator tube is suspended outside the 26.3 ft (8 m) wall frame. In reality, the escalator accesses only the mezzanine, level four, and level six. Horizontal circulation platforms occur inside the frame—most of them restricted to staff access and emergency exits.

Levels two and three contain the library. These are reached not from the exterior tube, but from a separate set of interior escalators off the street-level mezzanine. This arrangement is necessary so that the typical measures of control over the book stacks can be exercised. Entry to the museum collections from the escalator is at level four, and an interior stair connects to the rest of the collection on level five. Level five also has a sculpture terrace on the west side, dominated by a shallow reflecting pool, a similar terrace across the south end, and a dry sculpture terrace on the northwest corner outside the emergency exits. Finally, level six is cut away above the three sculpture courts of level five, opening them to the sky. The restaurant and its outside terrace overlook the fifth-level south sculpture garden. Galleries and a small bookstore have a view over the other two terraces. The horizontal walkway in the wall frame of level six is glazed from the southern end to the elevators shafts, affording spectacular views of the low-rise central Paris and outlying grand monuments.

Fire stairs are located at the four corners of the building, and the two on the west generally connect with the horizontal walkways within the wall frame. Four additional fire stairs are placed five bays in from each corner. The top floor is treated like a mezzanine of the fifth level, and the connecting terrace across the south façade connects the two sides of the building for fire egress.

There are no permanent partitions on any of the floors, but a relocatable, bolted-together two-hour firewall divides each typical level into two zones of less than the allowable 106,000 ft^3 (3000 m^3) compartment size. The trusses were all designed to carry a bolt-on system of demountable mezzanines within the 23 ft (7 m) story height, but because of client disinterest, few of them were ever deployed.

TECHNICAL INTEGRATION HIGHLIGHTS

Physical

- Structural, movement, and servicing zones share physical space in the external wall frames.

- Underground parking and utility areas helped create a large urban plaza.

Visual

- Structural and service systems are the dominant visual features.
- Site, terrace, and circulation systems maximize views of the city.

Performance

- Flexibility is attained by the structural scheme and the inside-out servicing of the building.
- Isolating the escalator tube from the floor plates provides for security and alternate accessibility to the restaurant.

DISCUSSION

Turning the building inside out was the most successfully realized architectural intention. The wall frames, with their captured servicing and movement systems, are unavoidably read as the corpus of the building. Static monumentalism is out; dynamic servicing and flexible floor space is in. The envelope hardly exists as a statement of the architecture, except in its transparency. Extensive and strict fire safety requirements mitigated many of the architectural ambitions related to these concepts, such as the transparency of the east wall and the fireproofing of structural members, but the intention is realized nonetheless. The inside-out aspects of the building truly failed only when it came to cleaning and maintenance of the painted finishes. It is interesting in this regard to note the differences between Pompidou and Richard Rogers's next major project, Lloyd's of London.

The plaza is another successfully realized architectural intention in terms of its integration with the west façade and the pedestrian neighborhood. This is a significant accomplishment of the project and an important part of how its incongruent features meld into the urban fabric surrounding it. Without the plaza, the building might not work at all.

Failure of nerve by the client effectively prevented the main architectural intention from being seriously attempted. The live center of information may be realized as part of the cultural center's activities, but the idea of the building as a flashing, shining, continuous information medium was abandoned. Perhaps this idea will resurface at a world's fair sometime soon.

23

SAINSBURY CENTRE FOR VISUAL ARTS, 1976–1977

Norwich, East Anglia, England
NORMAN FOSTER & PARTNERS

DESCRIPTION

The Sainsbury Centre probably represents the first prominent use of insulated cladding panels for a public institution. Its efficient shape and the adoption of industrial-quality building materials, not unlike those of the Boeing 737, have earned it the description of resembling something between a dirigible airship and a dirigible hangar. Wrapped into the building's structural frame are the mechanical, utility, and service spaces along with a highly tuned daylighting system. Inside, the single-volume space brings together an art collection, a school of fine art, and an assortment of public spaces.

Figure 10.10 The Sainsbury Art Centre.

TABLE 10.4   Fact Sheet

Project		
	Building Name	Sainsbury Centre for Visual Arts
	Client	Sir Robert and Lady Sainsbury and the University of East Anglia
	City	Norwich, East Anglia England
	Lat/Long/Elev	52.62 N 01.24 E, 95 ft (29 m)

Team		
	Architect	Norman Foster and Partners
	Engineer	Anthony Hunt Associates
	Cladding	Tony Pritchard
	Drainage	John Taylor
	Landscape Architect	Lanning Roper
	Acoustics	Sound Research
	Lighting	Claude Engle
	Exhibit Lighting	George Sexton
	Quantity Surveyors	Hanscomb Partnership

General		
	Time Line	1976–1977, with addition in 1987.
	Floor Area	66,585 ft^2 (20,295 m^2) and 8000 ft^2 (2438 m^2) addition.
	Site Description	Level end of rolling campus in an open grassy field toward a lake.
	Parking, Cars	Campus parking.
	Occupants	Not determined.
	Cost	$4 million or $60/ft^2.
	1995 $US Cost	$10.5 million or $152/ft^2.

Structure		
	Stories	One, plus mezzanines. Total height is 32.8 ft (10.3 m) with a clear inside height of 24.0 ft (7.3 m).
	Plan	Rectangular 114.83 ft × 431.1 ft (35 m × 131.4 m) for a 49,503 ft^2 (15,089 m^2) footprint. Subtracting the occupied 6.9 ft (2.1 m) perimeter structural zone leaves an interior clear room of 401.6 ft × 95.1 ft (122.4 m × 29.0 m), equaling 38,192.2 ft^2 (3,549.6 m^2). About 70% of the footprint is in the continuous central space.
	Foundation	Continuous 9.8 ft (3.0 m) concrete strip footings with integral floor slab.
	Vertical Members	37 prismatic truss assemblies on 11.8 ft (3.6 m) centers made of welded steel tubes form supports measuring 5.9 ft (1.8 m) across the plan and 8.2 ft (2.5 m) deep.
	Horizontal Spans	Trusses similar to the vertical members are bolted to the truss columns, forming a portal frame.

Envelope		
	Glass and Glazing	The 98.4 ft wide × 24.0 ft high (30 m × 7.3 m) end wall glazing is 0.6 in. × 24.0 ft × 7.9 ft (15 mm × 7.5 m × 2.4 m) laminated glass supported by 1.0 in. thick × 10 in. deep (25 mm × 254 mm) glass fins.
	Skylights	Interchangeable cladding panels in curved and flat fiberglass-reinforced plastic. Panel modules are 7.9 ft × 3.9 ft (2.4 m × 1.2 m).
	Cladding	Interchangeable insulated cladding panels in curved and flat superplastic aluminum 0.06 in. (1.5 mm) facing. Rigid foam is 3.9 in. (100 mm) thick. Overall heat transfer coefficient is 0.08 Btu/ft^2 °F (0.47 W/m^2 °C).
	Roof	Wall and roof are of identical construction. All panels fit in a continuous neoprene gasket grid incorporating an integral rain gutter in the profile. The gasket lattice was molded together on site from large prefabricated sections and has a total weight of more than 14.8 tons (13.2 tonnes or 12,000 kg).

HVAC		
	Equipment	Forced air from 40 fan/coil units housed in truss wall thickness.
	Cooling Type	Heat from campus central plant. No cooling is provided.
	Distribution	High side-wall diffusers with long throw design. Usually mounted in sets of four per fan/coil unit.
	Duct Type	None. Fans discharge directly into space.
	Vertical Chases	None. Mechanical systems are housed in wall thickness.

Interior		
	Partitions	Perforated aluminum shutter systems are fixed to inside of vertical structural frame and backed with acoustically absorbing blanket.
	Ceilings	A deeper aluminum shutter system is used on the ceiling than on the walls, and openings are left for downlighting fixtures.
	Vertical Circulation	Entry is via a long bridge from the hillside campus buildings on a 45 degree axis into the upper level of the building. A spiral stair descends to the ground floor. Two fully glazed hydraulic elevators are provided for movement from basement storage to art galleries and mezzanines.
	Furniture	Freestanding display panels, cases, and screens designed by the architect.
	Lighting	High bay metal halide.

Rectangular plan of 114.83-ft x 431.1-ft (35-m x 131.4-m) for a 49,503-ft² footprint. Subtracting the occupied 6.9-ft (2.1-m) perimeter structural zone leaves an interior clear room of 401.6-ft x 95.1-ft (122.4-m x 29.0-m) equaling 38,192.2-ft² (3,549.6-m²). About 70% of the footprint is in the continuous central space. Total height is 32.8-ft (10.3-m) with a clear inside height of 24.0-ft (7.3-m).

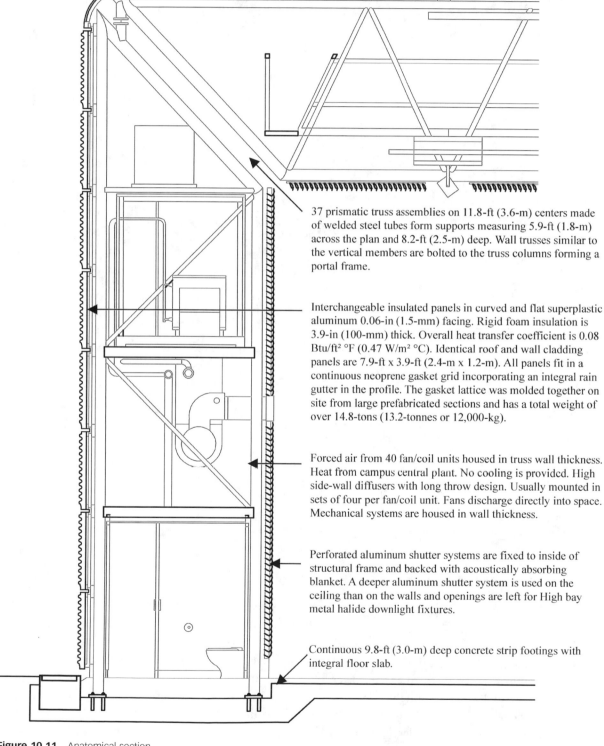

37 prismatic truss assemblies on 11.8-ft (3.6-m) centers made of welded steel tubes form supports measuring 5.9-ft (1.8-m) across the plan and 8.2-ft (2.5-m) deep. Wall trusses similar to the vertical members are bolted to the truss columns forming a portal frame.

Interchangeable insulated panels in curved and flat superplastic aluminum 0.06-in (1.5-mm) facing. Rigid foam insulation is 3.9-in (100-mm) thick. Overall heat transfer coefficient is 0.08 Btu/ft² °F (0.47 W/m² °C). Identical roof and wall cladding panels are 7.9-ft x 3.9-ft (2.4-m x 1.2-m). All panels fit in a continuous neoprene gasket grid incorporating an integral rain gutter in the profile. The gasket lattice was molded together on site from large prefabricated sections and has a total weight of over 14.8-tons (13.2-tonnes or 12,000-kg).

Forced air from 40 fan/coil units housed in truss wall thickness. Heat from campus central plant. No cooling is provided. High side-wall diffusers with long throw design. Usually mounted in sets of four per fan/coil unit. Fans discharge directly into space. Mechanical systems are housed in wall thickness.

Perforated aluminum shutter systems are fixed to inside of structural frame and backed with acoustically absorbing blanket. A deeper aluminum shutter system is used on the ceiling than on the walls and openings are left for High bay metal halide downlight fixtures.

Continuous 9.8-ft (3.0-m) deep concrete strip footings with integral floor slab.

Figure 10.11   Anatomical section.

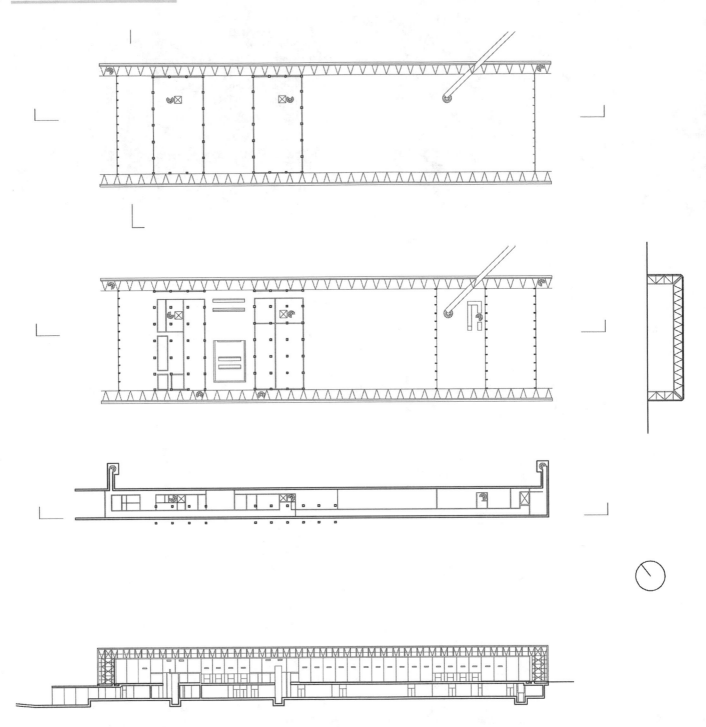

Figure 10.12 Plan and section.

PROGRAM

Client

Sir Robert and Lady Sainsbury described their interest in art as the "passionate acquisition" of works that appealed to them intuitively and sensually. They thought that the Centre for Visual Arts was the best way to convey their own appreciation and to promote the academic understanding of others. Norman Foster was commissioned to create a place where art could be experienced sensually in the course of daily life. Sainsbury was chosen because it was a new school whose scope and format could accommodate new ways of thinking about art education.

The Sainsbury's art collection at that time consisted of about 500 works of drawing, painting, and sculpture from the late-nineteeth and twentieth-century periods of European art and a second group of antiques from Africa, Oceania, the Orient. and the pre-Columbian period. Most of the objects are quite small, anthropomorphic, and constitute a selection based more on individual taste than rarity or cohesive inclusion.

The University of East Anglia's (UEA) School of European Art Studies was founded in 1964 with a focus on European art and architecture. Acquisition of the Sainsbury collection greatly expanded the program's scope and ambition. It was later renamed as the School of World Art and Museology.

Brief

The client's initial brief was quite short. The Sainsburys wished for the art to be experienced in a casual fashion by everyone in the East Anglia program. The art collection would be shared between academic studies and public display in a "living room" environment. There would be a restaurant, a display area, and a library. In consultation with UEA, the program was extended to include a school of fine art, a faculty club, and a public restaurant. A site was selected for the project where a grassy field could be incorporated into the public aspect of the center along a 40-acre lake, or broad, that would be included in the project.

Site

The University of East Anglia is located on the western edge of Norwich (population 300,000) in the east coast county of Norfolk, United Kingdom. The Yare River runs west of the campus, closest to the Sainsbury Centre site, flowing through the broadland lakes of East Anglia to the coast at Yarmouth.

The master plan for UEA was created by Sir Denys Lasdun in 1962 and developed through 1968. Lasdun is a Modernist in the mode of Le Corbusier's Brutalism. The

TABLE 10.5 Climate Data for Norwich, UK (compiled from several sources for nearby stations)

		Jan.	Feb.	Mar.	Apr.	May	June	July	Aug.	Sept.	Oct.	Nov.	Dec.	Year
Temperature	Degree-Days Heating	764	703	667	547	368	189	94	84	179	362	580	722	5319
	Degree-Days Cooling	0	0	0	0	0	8	28	30	5	1	0	0	46
	Extreme High	59	59	63	75	79	88	91	88	82	73	64	61	91
	Normal High	44	44	48	52	59	65	69	70	65	58	50	46	56
	Normal Average	41	40	44	47	53	59	63	63	59	53	46	43	51
	Normal Low	36	36	38	41	47	52	56	56	53	48	41	39	45
	Extreme Low	12	19	27	28	30	37	45	41	39	34	27	18	12
Humidity	Dew Point	33	32	35	37	44	49	53	52	49	45	39	36	42
	Max % RH	78	77	80	80	82	83	83	81	80	81	80	79	80
	Min % RH	76	73	70	65	64	64	63	61	64	72	77	78	69
	% Days with Rain	63	46	66	60	56	56	56	50	56	63	63	66	58
	Rain Inches	2	1	2	2	1	2	2	2	2	2	3	2	22
Sky	% Overcast Days	42	38	37	29	13	23	20	18	22	29	32	38	29
	% Clear Days	6	8	7	7	7	5	6	9	7	7	7	6	7
Wind	Prevailing Direction	W	W	W	N	N	W	W	W	W	SW	W	W	W
	Speed, Knots	12	11	11	7	6	8	8	7	8	8	9	10	9
	Percent Calm	7	10	8	9	9	11	12	13	13	13	10	7	10
Days Observed	Rain	19	14	20	18	17	17	17	15	17	19	19	20	212
	Fog	19	18	19	19	19	18	19	21	18	21	20	21	232
	Haze	13	14	17	17	19	16	20	20	18	17	15	15	201
	Snow	5	5	3	2	0	#	0	0	0	0	1	2	18
	Hail	0	0	0	#	0	#	0	0	0	0	0	0	#
	Freezing Rain	#	#	0	0	0	0	0	0	0	0	0	#	#
	Blowing Sand	5	4	5	4	5	5	3	3	3	3	3	3	46

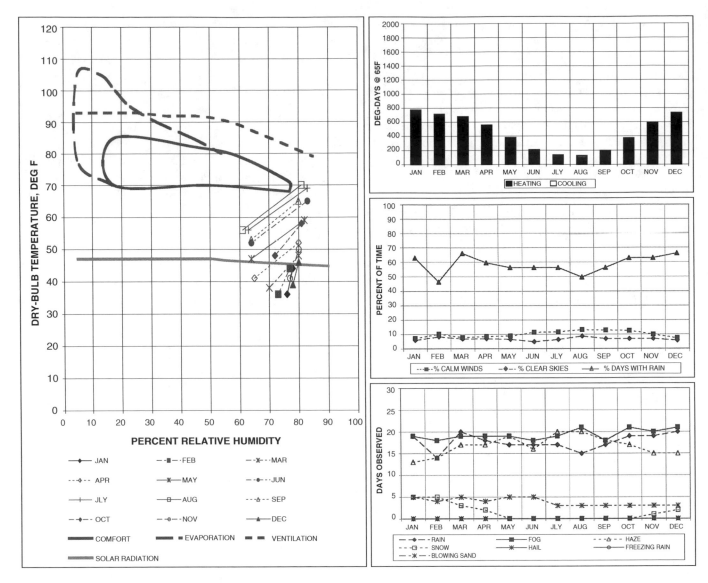

Figure 10.13 Climate analysis graphics.

platformed concrete architecture of the campus reflects Lasdun's views of buildings as strata of interlocking levels. He refers to the campus in this regard as a single entity: "University Town." His row of "ziggurat" student residences, elevated walkways, and terraces lead directly into the Sainsbury Centre.

Climate

The Eastern Counties climate region of England includes Norwich and Ipswich on the coast and stretches inland to Cambridge, Northampton, and Milton Keynes. This area is separated to some degree from the moderating Gulf Stream maritime influences on the eastern half of the British Isles. Its winter climate in particular is subject to influence by cold air masses from the continent. Warmer

air across the English Channel frequently provides enough energy and moisture to produce winter rain and snow in the British Eastern Counties.

Overall, Norwich is drier than most of England because of its west coast separation from the moisture-bearing Gulf Stream. Annually, there are 22 in. (550 mm) of precipitation in Norwich versus 24 in. (600 mm) in London, 32 in. (800 mm) in Brighton, and 40 in. (1000 mm) in easterly Cardiff and Plymouth. Parts of the west coast Cambrian Mountains, in comparison, receive more than 78 in. (2000 mm) per year.

Temperatures in Norwich seldom exceed 75°F, normally for fewer than 174 hours per year. Readings over 85°F are very rare, and the extreme high on record is 91°F. Using the summer design conditions at Hemsby (20 miles

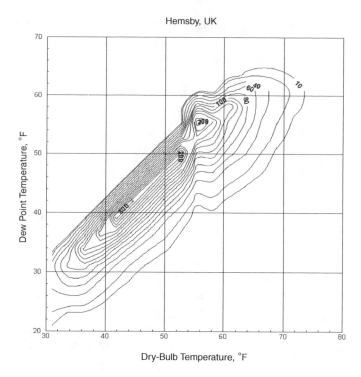

Hemsby, UK

Figure 10.14 Bin data distribution for Norwich. Concentric areas of graph indicate the number of hours per year that weather conditions normally occur in this climate. Similar to elevation readings on topographic maps, highest frequency occurrences of weather are at the center peaks of the graph. (Data sources: *Engineering Weather Data, typical meteorological year (TMY) data from the National Climatic Data Center, and the* ASHRAE Weather Data Viewer *from the American Society of Heating, Refrigerating and Air-Conditioning Engineers.)*

east of Norwich at 52.7N 1.7E, 46 ft) as a guide, the 69°F dry-bulb / 62°F wet-bulb condition is exceeded only 2 percent of the time, and 71 / 63 is exceeded only 1 percent of the time. The corresponding relative humidity for those conditions is a rather dry 60 to 63 percent. Weather is comfortable 7 percent of the time, cool 62 percent and below 45°F about 28 percent of the time. There are 5319 annual degree-days heating and fewer than 50 degree-days cooling.

INTENTION

Design Team

Overlapping Norman Foster's 1970–1975 work for the Willis Faber Dumas Insurance Headquarters (see case study #7), the office began a series of projects that opened the potential for translating industrial building systems into wider applications. The flexible IBM offices in Cosham (1971) and the Factory Systems Studies (1972) publication initiated this sequence. Projects for Olsen Ltd., VW/Audi (1972), the Retail/Leisure Research Studies

(1973), and the Modern Art Glass facility in Thamesmead (1973) all foreshadow Sainsbury in different ways. Both IBM and the Retail/Leisure Studies portend the "clustering of uses usually found in different buildings" concept that is employed at Sainsbury.

Philosophy

Beginning in 1971, Foster established a working relationship with Richard Buckminster Fuller. This relationship lasted until Fuller's death in 1983, only ten days after he personally delivered the address at Norman Foster's award of the RIBA Gold Medal. Among their collaborations was the unbuilt 1978 design of a domed theme pavilion for Knoxville, Tennessee's 1982 International Energy Expo, which was a refinement of Fuller's dome at Montreal Expo 67 (see Chapter 8).

Foster admired Bucky Fuller's ideals of ephemeralization. They fit well with his own social and ethical motives for architecture. When Fuller saw the Sainsbury Centre, for example, he asked Norman Foster for an evaluation based on the building's total weight of construction.

Intent

As Foster developed the brief, he soon arrived at a solution that put the gallery, art school, seniors' common, and restaurant functions all under one roof. This was more efficient than creating a cluster of smaller buildings and satisfied the Sainsburys' desire for the collection to be available for casual viewing. By grouping everything together, the design would allow more opportunity for leisurely interaction. Foster also decided that a mechanically cooled building would suggest an institutional character that was unfriendly to a casual setting, so the building would rely on natural cooling strategies.

CRITICAL TECHNICAL ISSUES

Inherent

The display and lighting of art are the prime aspects of an art gallery. But these goals presuppose the security and protection of the collection. With art valued at more than £5 million, or about US$ 10 million in 1977, this is a serious concern. Making the collection available to the general public means securing it from theft and vandalism, from aging caused by humidity or ultraviolet degradation, and from accidental damage due to vagaries such as roof leaks.

The actual display and viewing enjoyment of art in the gallery required the design of lighting, display, storage, delivery, packaging, security systems, and inconspicuous visual monitoring of visitors. Provisions for gallery visitors, like the café, the information desk, and so forth, are a secondary overlay to the requirements of the art.

Contextual

Lasdun's master plan for the campus and its execution in raw massive concrete forms were formalistically adverse to Foster's philosophy of lightweight ephemeralization. Options to site the Sainsbury closer to the campus entryway or in various other locations were all rejected because of interference with planned growth or similar objections. The situation chosen seemed the most appropriate to Foster and was reasoned out with Lasdun.

Intentional

Putting all the program spaces under one roof introduces problems of separation between the functions: security, acoustics, privacy, scheduling, and so forth. This makes circulation and separation within a single volume multi-use space quite difficult. It also raises issues about flexible space versus differentiated space. Foster's choice of a large open plan, adaptable to any number of purposes, had to prove satisfactorily better than a compartmented series of differentiated spaces optimized for specific uses.

A low-energy solution that would forsake mechanical cooling would also be a challenge, even in Norwich's cool climate. High humidity and high temperature levels accelerate the material degradation of art objects and also play a role in photodegradation via ultraviolet light. Lighting for museum viewing and art study, on the other hand, must provide task-level illumination on the order of 50 footcandles (540 lux) with excellent color rendering. Natural cooling with outdoor air ventilation would have to be able to offset not only the envelope heat gains from temperature and solar impacts, but also the internal heat gain from people, lights, and equipment.

APPROPRIATE SYSTEMS

Precedent

Members of the design team explored functional precedents on extensive visits, accompanied by the Sainsburys, to several museums:

- The Louisiana Museum, Copenhagen, by Jørgen Bo and Vilhelm Wohlert, 1956–1958—A modern Danish art collection based in a villa on the coast and expanded with several pavilions and connecting glass corridors. The facility was expanded in 1966 and again in 1971. It houses modern art by international artists such as Arp, Francis Bacon, Calder, Dubuffet, Max Ernst, Sam Francis, Giacometti, Kiefer, Henry

Moore, Picasso, Rauschenberg, and Warhol. This museum was appreciated for its response to its natural surroundings. Created by private art collector, Knud W. Jensen, it is in a beautiful setting overlooking the Sound, a few kilometers south of Elsinore and Kronborg, Denmark.

- Alvar Aalto's Nordjyllands Museum, Aalborg, 1958, 1968–1972—Designed by Elissa and Alvar Aalto with Jean-Jacques Baruël, built between 1968 and 1972. This is a 19,685 ft^2 (6000 m^2) toplit museum on a site similar to Sainsbury's, adjoining a large wooded area and set on a ziggurat-terraced landscape. It has a mobile partition wall system for flexibility.
- Berlin New National Gallery, Mies van der Rohe, 1962–1968—Mies's glass box pavilion, 166 ft (50.6 m) square in plan with a 213 ft (65.0 m) dimension overhanging roof. The 27,000 ft^2 (2507 m^2) upper level is one great room walled in glass and spanned by the world's first rigid plate roof constructed over 6 ft deep web girders at 12 ft on center. Large-scale sculptures occupy the outside terraces. The lower-level gallery has one glass wall looking out to a sculpture court.

These precedents established several influences on the design:

- Daylighting strategy with tunable toplighting
- Flexibility for growth and adaptive use
- Useable storage space
- Security with a minimum number of docents
- Service of infrastructure and lighting without disruption to exhibits
- Sociable atmosphere
- Coordination of furniture and display elements with building design

Site

The building is sited at the southeast end of the campus. For a public space, it is in a remote corner location, far from parking or other public amenities of the university. It makes for a very long procession from the bus stop to the Sainsbury Centre. The saving grace is the luscious open field and neighboring trees and, of course, the new lake. Its placement gives the impression that the site was reserved for this building long ago. Sitting to one side, the Sainsbury respects an open vista in the center of the campus that captures the new broad. Nestled against the tree line, the building mass terminates the long axis of the science classrooms on one side and claims its private garden

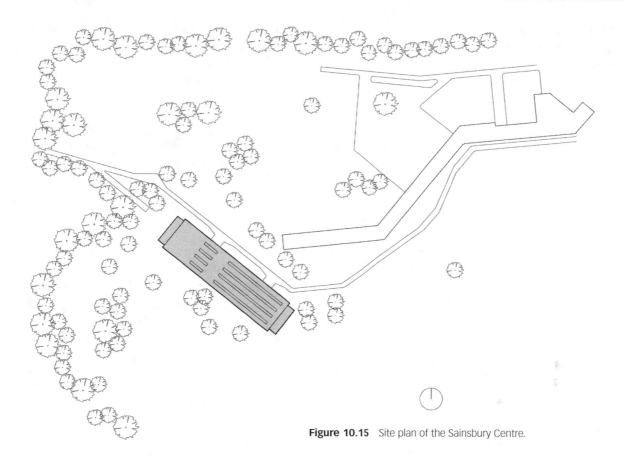

Figure 10.15 Site plan of the Sainsbury Centre.

on the other. Entering the building from the campus terraces above, a level bridge conducts visitors above the street and into the midlevel at a 45 degree angle to the plan. A spiral stair winds down to the reception area. The bridge is narrow and low-key; the entryway and reception area are scaled to be friendly, and the café is right there to provide a domestic greeting. Walk-up entry at street level is through a door below the bridge. The art school has its own doors farther up the same campus side elevation.

With so much roof glazing, the building's solar exposure is horizontal and wall orientation is less important. Foster pushed the footprint back against the open end of the campus, preserving and capturing all available green space to the southeast. This also affords the best view from the special exhibits area toward the broad, rather than back at the residences had the long axis of the Sainsbury faced south. If there is an environmental angle to the orientation, it must be aerodynamic. The prevailing summer breezes in Norwich hail from the west to southwest and stream directly onto the long axis of the building.

Service access to the basement storage and workshop comes from the other side of the campus. A drive veers off toward the building and burrows down unseen below the sculpture terrace outside the restaurant. All loading and unloading of artwork happens securely and unnoticed in the basement.

Structure

There are 37 sets of triangular steel tube trusses spanning the 113 ft (34.4 m) width of the building. They provide a clear inside height of 24.6 ft (7.5 m) and rest on lattice columns. Both truss and column have their flat base supporting the envelope and their pointed ends facing the interior. Both members measure 8.2 ft (2.5 m) deep by 5.9 ft (1.8 m) across. Substantial camber is introduced to the roof span by use of lower chord members that are shorter than the upper cords. A two-pin connection of the trusses is made with bolted connections where the outside vertical tubes meet the top two horizontal tubes. At the end walls all three points of the trusses are bolted together to protect the full-height glass from lateral motion.

Prefabricated columns were delivered to the site in one piece, and the trusses arrived in two sections. Trusses are pin-connected at their top two points to the columns except at the end condition. Glass walls at both ends of the building require those two bays to have pin connections at all three truss-to-column points. This provides the stiffness of a rigid frame that is needed to prevent distortion of the glazing mullions.

The concrete foundation consists of a 9.8 ft (3 m) deep continuous perimeter beam. There is also a narrow but full-length basement connected by an underground service drive to the street north of the building.

Envelope

The void of the tubular structural system frames a double-layer envelope for the long walls and roof of the building. The exterior side is clad with an interchangeable system of panels 6.9 ft wide × 3.9 ft high (2.4 m × 1.2 m). Solid aluminum, fiberglass-glazed, and aluminum louvered options are mounted in a continuous neoprene gasket and secured with six bolts each. Although all of the panels are interchangeable, the general scheme is laid out with four long rows of mostly continuous skylights down the long axis of the roof. The curved eaves are transparent where they match the skylight pattern. Transparent fiberglass panels are also used on sections of the south wall to display the mechanical units and announce the ground-level doorways.

Interior claddings consist of perforated aluminum louvers. The ceiling panels are automatically adjusted to regulate daylight. The wall panels are backed with a fibrous acoustical blanket for noise and reverberation control. Both walls and ceilings are painted white.

Between the exterior and interior layers, within the structural thickness of the frame, is a continuous service zone. The wall contains offices, toilets, and storage at the ground and mezzanine levels, with mechanical systems and more storage interspersed above. The 9.8 ft (3 m) thick ceiling zone is webbed with a walkway used for adjusting illumination.

Daylight is diffused by photosensor-controlled louvers under the horizontal skylights, through the structural frame, and, finally, through the adjustable ceiling louvers. The two sets of louvers are set at right angles to each other, with the skylight controls running across the plan and the ceiling louvers reinforcing the line of the long room. This crisscrossing lattice creates a fine mesh and thus prevents direct glare much more effectively than parallel louvers would have. Ambient supplemental light is supplied by high-voltage track light fixtures, and display lighting by low-voltage fittings. The lower ceiling louvers are spaced in long rows, and artificial sources are mounted in the open gaps between them. All of the display lighting is provided from this level. Although it is less energy-efficient to light the art from 15 ft above than at the display, this ceiling-mounted strategy keeps much of the heat of light up high in the space where it can be exhausted before affecting room temperatures.

Glass walls measuring 98.4 ft × 24.6 ft (30 m × 7.5 m) fill both ends of the long building. The glazing rests in steel channels anchored to the floor slab. The glass lites measure a full 8.0 ft × 24.6 ft (7.5 m × 2.4 m) and are joined by structural silicone sealant. Full-height reinforcing glass fins, like those at the Willis Faber Dumas Headquarters (see case study #7), are set perpendicular to each joint on the interior for wind bracing.

Insulation in the aluminum-clad envelope panels is rated at R–12 or u = 0.08 Btu/ft^2 °F (0.47 W/m^2 °C). The panels are also light reflective to keep sunlit surface temperatures, and therefore heat gain, more managable.

Roof drains, downspouts, and leader lines have all been eliminated by the neoprene gasket system behind the envelope panels. Its profile incorporates a small gutter, and the entire assembly makes a distributed drainage system. At the base of the building is a continuous rain gutter to carry away the water shed from the building skin.

Mechanical

The technically inventive contribution of the Sainsbury Centre comes in the form of a reinvented wall as a layering interpretation of both served and servant spaces and interior to exterior environments. Instead of using a thin-leaf wall with finished surfaces on either side and pipes and wires in the middle, Foster fills the 6.9 ft (2.1 m) thick

Figure 10.16 Ventilation system. Fan/coil (midlevel) and ventilation system (upper) meshed in the structural frame above the art school doorway. Note the four levels of space below the curved eave.

structural frame with occupied and mechanical servant spaces. Fan/coil units, darkrooms, offices, storage, toilets—everything not contributing to the public use of the daylit gallery is swept away to the interstitial wall. This emancipates the grand central space for open circulation, daylighting, and shared volume. The entire structural frame is engaged in this scheme. Ground-level spaces serve private occupancy needs and storage. Two intermediate wall levels are primarily mechanical. The ceiling-roof space is the moderator of light, both natural and artificial.

With the envelope strategy geared to minimizing cooling loads, HVAC systems are limited to heating and ventilation. Heat is distributed to the building from a campus central plant in the form of high-temperature water. Ventilation is supplied directly through grilled panels of the envelope, and air is discharged into occupied spaces via long-throw sidewall diffusers. In all, there are 40 fan/coil units housed in the upper three levels of the south wall. Ducts do not penetrate beyond the service wall. Additional exhaust ventilation is provided for kitchens, toilets, darkrooms, and basement areas.

Interior

From end to end, the central interior space is divided into seven areas surrounded by the thick service core wall. Each of these can be described as bays of the structural grid, of 11.8 ft (3.6 m), between truss centers. At the southeast gable is a four-bay special exhibits area, followed by a four-bay entryway and service desk adjoining the café. Next is the eleven-bay collections gallery, followed by a four-bay mezzanine with reserved study space fronting the gallery and art school offices facing the opposite direction on the lower level, and more exhibit/study space above. Beyond are the four-bay art school and another four-bay mezzanine with more offices facing into the art school area, a kitchen facing away, and the faculty club above. Finally, there is the restaurant dining area on the northwest end. A one-bay-deep covered terrace is recessed under each end of the long roof. Roughly one-third of the floor space (15 of 45 total bay widths) is dedicated to exhibits.

Every public area except the restaurant and the mezzanines are skylit by four double rows of translucent roof panels and a continuous translucent eave of one curved and one flat wall panel. There are 32 panels across the roof, so it is effectively 25 percent glazed above these areas. Counting the wall and eave panels, the enclosure is 46 panels across sill to roof to sill and 12 panels are glazed in the daylight critical rooms. In addition, where the south elevation is fitted with doorways at the art school and main entry, the wall is covered in translucent panels up to the curved eave. All of these panels are subject to being rearranged, but this is the original scheme.

TECHNICAL INTEGRATION HIGHLIGHTS

Physical

- Mechanical spaces are meshed within the structural frame, liberating the open plan.
- Mezzanines divide the space functionally without imposing on openness.
- Natural surroundings provide a public setting for outdoor sculpture.

Visual

- Mechanical systems are exposed on the south elevation.
- The structural frame is exposed at both sculpture terraces.

Performance

- The envelope, roof structure, and interior louvers work together to daylight the space.
- Interchangeable envelope panels enhance the flexibility of use.
- Ceiling-level catwalks negate the need for scaffolding and ladders in the gallery.
- Interstitial wall spaces and removable exterior wall panels eliminate the need to work on mechanical or electrical equipment from the interior.
- Sidewall discharge of heating and ventilation air across both sides of the open space eliminates the need for ducts.
- High ceilings combine good daylighting with the ability to display large works of art. They also promote stratification of warm air to be exhausted and replaced with outdoor air.
- A neoprene gasket lattice behind the panel system incorporates small rain gutters.

DISCUSSION

When Fuller asked Foster to produce calculations on the total weight of the Sainsbury wing, the results proved that the basement accounted for 80 percent of its weight and 30 percent or so of its budget. More significant, the building reportedly weighs less per square foot than a Boeing 737. For High Tech buildings, weight, cost, and benefit ratios are interesting metrics. Lightweight, inexpensive, and interchangeable materials, in this case, are providing much of the benefit with a lower share of resources. More with less.

24
LLOYD'S OF LONDON, 1979–1984

London, England
RICHARD ROGERS PARTNERSHIP

DESCRIPTION

Richard Rogers and Partners' design for the 1984 Lloyd's of London Insurance building is a response to the client's need for flexible space to accommodate its growing needs over the next 50 years. From a systems integration perspective, it is among the most spectacular realizations of Louis Kahn's "served and servant spaces" scheme.

Lloyd's modernity is set against the medieval streets of old London in a stylistic juxtaposition reminiscent of the Pompidou Centre in central Paris. Its image has also been likened to the North Sea oil platforms as an emulation of technical clarity, as an homage to Lloyd's wealthy oil company clients, or both. Indeed, the six service towers encircling the glass office block and its 13-story central atrium space were conceived first as a system of solutions rather than as a building design. The High Tech touches are thus inherent in the approach. But the machine platform aesthetic is less of a stylistic manipulation than a refined and well-integrated response to a cramped site coupled with demanding space requirements.

Figure 10.17 General view of Lloyd's of London.

TABLE 10.6 Fact Sheet

Project	**Building Name**	Lloyd's of London
	Client	Lloyd's of London Insurance
	City	London, England
	Lat/Long/Elev	51.51 N 0.08 W, 203 ft (62 m)
Team	**Architect**	Richard Rogers Partnership
	Engineer	Ove Arup Associates
	Right of Light	Anstey Horne & Co
	Quantity Surveyors	Monk Dunstone Mahon & Sears
	Acoustics	Sandy Brown Associates
	Catering	GWP Associates
	Audio	Visual Theatre Developments Limited
	Lighting	Friederich Wagner of Lichttechnishe Planung
	Bovis Construction	Brian Pettifer, Director; John Smith, Project Director
General	**Time Line**	1978–1984.
	Floor Area	561,874 ft^2 gross, 403,645 ft^2 net.
	Occupants	5000 underwriters, 8000 total, or up to 70 per 1000 ft^2 in the market area and an average density of about 20 occupants per 1000 ft^2.
	Cost	£75 million, or $135 million. $240/ft^2, $15.3 million on foundation alone.
	Cost in 1995 $US	$197.9 million or $352 per gross ft^2.
	Stories	12 above grade, 3 below grade, 276 ft (84 m) to top of atrium, steps from 12 stories at north to 6 at south, typical floor-to-ceiling height is 10 ft (3 m).
	Plan	224 ft × 153.5 ft (68.4 m × 46.8 m); atrium is 36 ft × 108.3 ft (11 × 33 m) and 240 ft (84 m) high.
Site	**Site Description**	Adjacent to the food stalls of Leadenhall Market, among the crowded and twisted streets of "The Square Mile," in the older City of London (now called just "The City").
	Parking, Cars	None.
Structure	**Foundation**	300 pilings, 30 in. (762 mm) diameter, driven to 85 ft (25.9 m) depth, within lines of previous basement and adjacent to other tall buildings.
	Vertical Members	Precast and poured-in-place concrete columns on 35.3 ft × 59 ft (10.8 m × 18.0 m) grid.
	Horizontal Spans	Open two way concrete with 11.8 in. (300 mm) wide and 21.6 in. (550 mm) deep beams around 23.6 in. × 23.6 in. (600 mm × 600 mm) void. Stub columns on structural grid create raised floor.
Envelope	**Glass and Glazing**	Triple-glazed wall with stippled exterior panel, operable center sash, 1.6 in. (40 mm) return air cavity between exterior and interior glazing units.
	Skylights	275 ft (84 m) high atrium, opening into offices below the eighth floor.
	Cladding	Glass and stainless steel with exposed concrete frame, 2.2 acres (8903 m^2) of glass; thermally broken aluminum-frame curtain wall system. Return air cavity in curtain wall.
	Roof	Glass-vaulted atrium.
HVAC	**Equipment**	Basement-located central plant with fan rooms atop service towers.
	Cooling Type	Two 425 ton chillers, one 340 ton chiller (1190 total tons), perimeter zones with supplemental heat pumps.
	Distribution	Fan rooms on four satellites, forced air external ducts, induction fan units.
	Duct Type	External stainless steel with internal insulation over rigid fiberglass.
	Vertical Chases	External service towers
Interior	**Partitions**	Mostly open plan.
	Finishes	Exposed concrete grid ceiling with custom light fixtures.
	Vertical Circulation	12 elevators at exterior satellites, escalator system in atrium to first four levels.
	Furniture	Custom demountable workstations.
	Lighting	Custom light fixtures fill the 10,000 ceiling voids in concrete grid of structure. User-controlled task lighting at workstations.

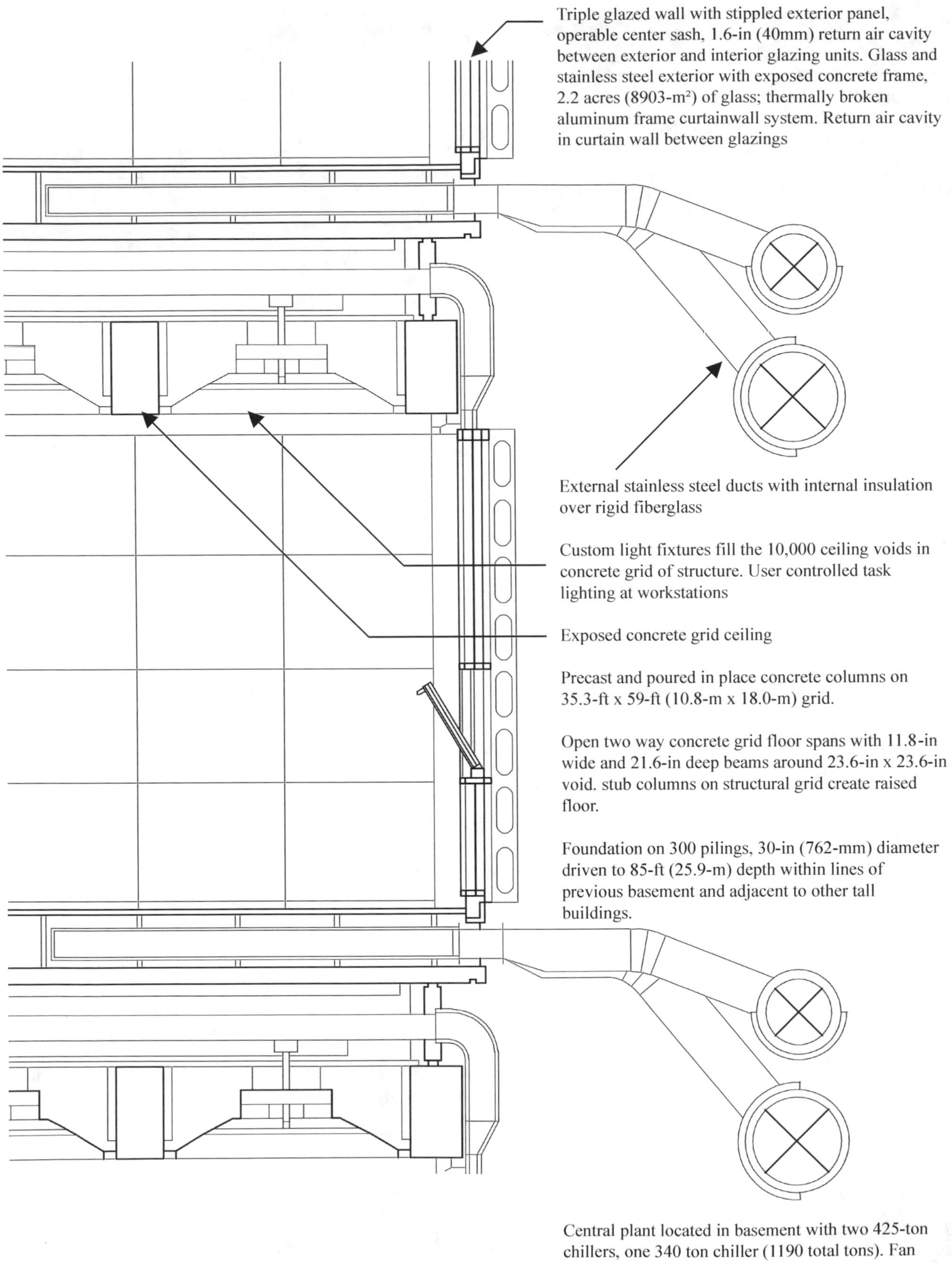

Triple glazed wall with stippled exterior panel, operable center sash, 1.6-in (40mm) return air cavity between exterior and interior glazing units. Glass and stainless steel exterior with exposed concrete frame, 2.2 acres (8903-m²) of glass; thermally broken aluminum frame curtainwall system. Return air cavity in curtain wall between glazings

External stainless steel ducts with internal insulation over rigid fiberglass

Custom light fixtures fill the 10,000 ceiling voids in concrete grid of structure. User controlled task lighting at workstations

Exposed concrete grid ceiling

Precast and poured in place concrete columns on 35.3-ft x 59-ft (10.8-m x 18.0-m) grid.

Open two way concrete grid floor spans with 11.8-in wide and 21.6-in deep beams around 23.6-in x 23.6-in void. stub columns on structural grid create raised floor.

Foundation on 300 pilings, 30-in (762-mm) diameter driven to 85-ft (25.9-m) depth within lines of previous basement and adjacent to other tall buildings.

Central plant located in basement with two 425-ton chillers, one 340 ton chiller (1190 total tons). Fan rooms placed atop service towers.

Figure 10.18 Anatomical section.

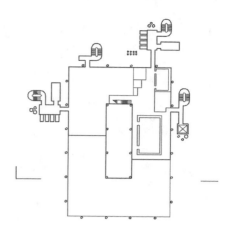

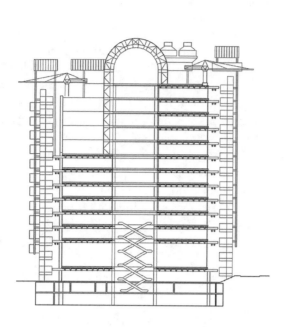

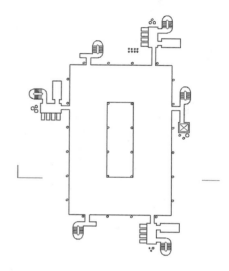

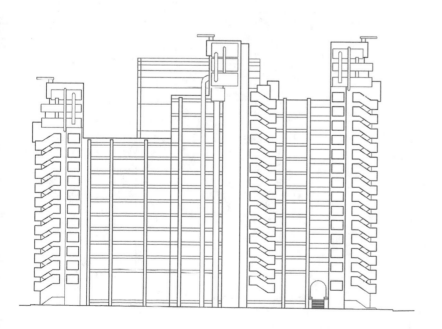

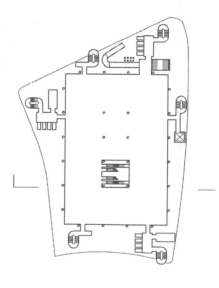

Figure 10.19 Plan and section.

PROGRAM

Client

Lloyd's of London is an institution named for the dockside coffee house where it originated in the seventeenth century. Edward Lloyd's Coffee House at 16 Lombard Street, just above London Bridge, was the working center and gathering place of marine underwriters. Even today, Lloyd's is more an insurance marketplace than a company —its underwriters all compete and participate in risks just as at its inception. The activity inside Lloyd's resembles that of the trading floor of a stock market rather than the business of a typical office. The 384 insurance syndicates that made up Lloyd's of London in 1984 represented some 28,000 "names" or underwriters whose personal investments backed the risks assumed by each syndicate.

Brief

As Lloyd's grew over the centuries, it continued to operate its market from a single large room where communication between brokers, and thus information about risks and opportunities, was maximized. By 1979, however, the firm had outgrown "The Room" three times in the previous 50 years. The need for a different approach to the Lloyd's working environment was critical enough to open a design competition for a new building. The first solid mandate would be for a new facility to serve the organization continuously for the next 50 years. A total of 40 firms were invited to participate, and six were eventually asked to submit design proposals.

Rogers and Partners' winning proposal addressed the client brief by describing not a building, but a set of strategies for incorporating Lloyd's needs into a built solution.

TABLE 10.7 Normal Climate Data for London

		Jan.	Feb.	Mar.	Apr.	May	June	July	Aug.	Sept.	Oct.	Nov.	Dec.	Year
Temperature	Degree-Days Heating	792	717	700	565	389	211	108	124	241	431	623	724	5570
	Degree-Days Cooling	0	0	0	0	1	10	26	19	2	0	0	0	62
	Extreme High	55	63	68	73	83	91	93	95	82	77	63	59	95
	Normal High	44	45	49	54	61	66	71	71	65	58	50	46	57
	Normal Average	39	39	43	46	52	58	62	62	57	51	44	42	50
	Normal Low	34	34	36	38	44	50	53	52	48	44	38	36	42
	Extreme Low	9	7	19	23	26	34	39	36	34	24	18	12	7
Humidity	Dew Point	36	35	37	38	44	50	54	54	51	47	41	38	44
	Max % RH	90	90	91	90	90	90	91	94	94	93	92	90	91
	Min % RH	80	74	68	60	59	61	59	59	64	72	78	82	68
	% Days with Rain	76	56	73	63	63	60	56	56	60	69	69	76	64
	Rain Inches	3	2	2	2	2	2	2	2	3	3	3	3	30
Sky	% Overcast Days	37	35	32	24	22	19	17	15	19	25	29	34	26
	% Clear Days	6	8	7	7	6	5	6	8	7	6	8	5	7
Wind	Prevailing Direction	SW	SW	SW	NE	SW	SW	SW	SW	SW	SW	SW	SW	SW
	Speed, Knots	10	10	11	10	9	8	8	8	9	8	10	10	9
	Percent Calm	6	7	7	7	8	7	7	10	10	9	9	6	8
Days Observed	Rain	23	17	22	19	19	18	17	17	18	21	21	23	235
	Fog	14	13	16	14	18	19	17	22	20	21	17	16	207
	Haze	13	14	15	15	13	14	13	13	13	12	13	14	162
	Snow	6	6	4	2	#	0	0	0	0	#	1	4	23
	Hail	#	#	#	#	#	#	#	0	0	#	0	#	2
	Freezing Rain	#	1	0	0	0	0	0	0	0	0	0	#	1
	Blowing Sand	0	0	0	0	0	0	0	0	0	0	0	0	0

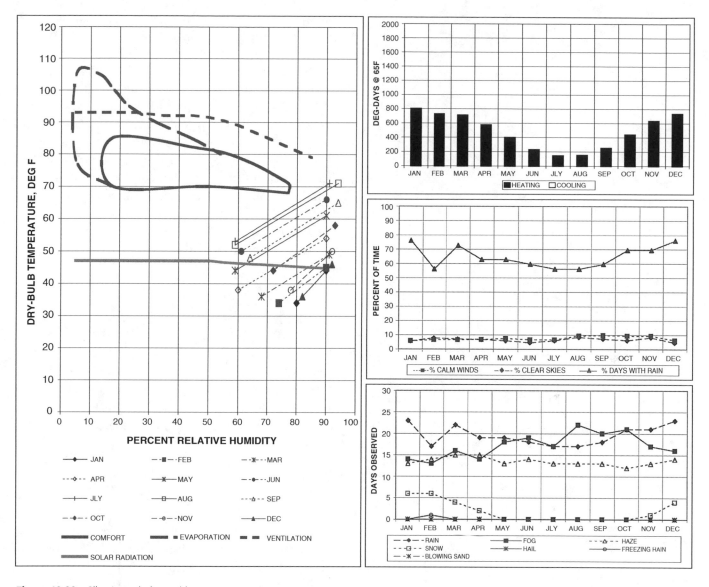

Figure 10.20 Climate analysis graphics.

The program required an expandable market room that would grow from 70,000 ft² to perhaps 200,000 ft² (6500 m² to 18,580 m²) in the early twenty-first century. Lloyd's expected this building to serve its expansion, or even potential contraction, for the next 50 years. Investment in a facility with such a long project life implied the eventual replacement of obsolescent components and office technologies along the way. Flexibility of spaces and the ability to change their functions without disruption were vital.

Site

Lloyd's sits among the twisted streets of the old City of London, now called just "The City" or "The Square Mile." These were the ancient quarters of Londinium settled by Romans in A.D. 43, easily predating the other London of Westminster, founded in 1061. Walking out from the wide pedestrian galleries and steaming food stalls of Leadenhall Market, one encounters Lloyd's of London.

The challenge of placing the Lloyd's building into this medieval street pattern lay in maximizing the use of an irregular site plan to ensure the greatest-size Room with the best possible communication between its levels. Further, the occupancy density would be as much as ten times that of conventional office space, so circulation, exits, toilets, and other support spaces had to be distributed on the site accordingly. Then there was the prospect of constructing the new building in close proximity to surrounding foundations and within the height limitations imposed by the "right to light" of neighbors to the south and west.

The site already belonged to Lloyd's when the decision to build was made. This was the location of its 1928 offices, adjoining the 1958 Lloyd's building across Lime Street to the east.

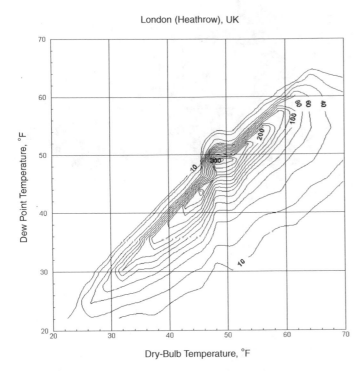

London (Heathrow), UK

Figure 10.21   Bin data distribution for London. Concentric areas of graph indicate the number of hours per year that weather conditions normally occur in this climate. Similar to elevation readings on topographic maps, highest frequency occurrences of weather are at the center peaks of the graph. (Data sources: *Engineering Weather Data, typical meteorological year (TMY) data from the National Climatic Data Center, and the ASHRAE Weather Data Viewer from the American Society of Heating, Refrigerating and Air-Conditioning Engineers.*)

Climate

The climate of London is comparable to that of Boston. Köppen's climate classification places London in the Cfb zone labeled "Mid-Latitude, Uniform Precipitation, Warm Summer," describing an area across Europe from northern Greece to central Norway. The weather specific to London is characterized as cool temperate, windy, rainy, and overcast, but it is also subject to sudden and dramatic mood shifts when the wind changes. Londoners just call it "fickle." Temperatures are generally moderated by the maritime influence, but extreme variability produced by sudden frontal movements is an important factor. The high latitude is another influence of variation, producing an exaggerated difference of season—a mid-June day is as much as 16.6 sunny hours long, whereas a bleak December day is only 7.4 hours long from sunrise to sunset. With 5319 heating degree-days F and only 46 cooling degree-days F, London weather is experienced as being decidedly on the chilly side. Some 50 percent of London hours are below 56°F. About 27 percent of the annual hours are normally cool (between 65°F and 55°F), and 65 percent of them cold

(below 55°F). Considering daylight hours alone, these percentages are 5 percent warm, 16 percent comfort, 29 percent cool and 50 percent cold.

An internally load dominated building, however, has a lower equilibrium "balance point" temperature than the 68°F to 75°F of human comfort balance. Lloyd's, with its intense occupant density and office equipment requirements, is almost always overheated from within. So even in this cool climate, designers had to recognize the special thermal metabolism of this building and plan for a predominant cooling need. This, in turn, placed priority on daylighting to reduce internal loads. It also suggested separate thermal zoning of perimeter areas, where the internal surfaces of cold walls and windows had to be addressed.

INTENTION

Design Team

Richard Rogers formed the Richard Rogers Partnership (RRP) in 1977 following the completion of the Centre Pompidou with Renzo Piano. The original RRP partners were, and remain at this printing, John Young, Marco Goldschmeid, and Mike Davis.

Philosophy

Rogers's dedication to the principles of open plan, flexibility, functionalism, and technical imagery is widely recognized. Although these practices have strongly associated RRP's work with High Tech pursuits, the firm prefers to focus on the ideals of optimistic Modernism, eschewing stylistic labels and fascination with machines. They also point to broader goals of social and ecological promotion, as well as the particular feeling of creating "people places." Rogers himself has acknowledged the obligation of design to go beyond client program in the service of the civic realm and to give a "public performance."

Intent

RRP won the Lloyd's design competition by submitting a strategy for addressing the firms needs rather than with a polished building proposal representing formal and spatial qualities. This tact demonstrated to Lloyd's that its architect understood the problems to be confronted better than the firm's members did themselves. The building was conceived as a set of relationships between ordering systems and their functional mandates. It follows that the organizing architectural intention was to develop and express these systems along with their functional and physical connections.

Figure 10.22 Lloyd's from the Leadenhall Market.

CRITICAL TECHNICAL ISSUES

Inherent

The need for constant communication in a continuous market room and the ability to expand it to three times its initial size dominated the Lloyd's brief. There was also the difficulty of dealing with internal circulation loads, especially at peak times like the daily lunch exodus from the building. Productivity issues dictated a high level of occupant comfort. Finally, the solution had to be flexible enough to change function from office to market and back again without disrupting ongoing activities.

As the design emerged, the magnitude of internal heat gain from people, lights, and equipment soared above the conventional 3 or 4 W/ft^2 all the way past 13 W/ft^2 in the market room and over 12 W/ft^2 in the office areas. In part, this was due to the manner in which Lloyd's operates the trading floor. Moreover, it became evident in the late stages of design that computer technology would have to be incorporated into the workstation environment. This led to a doubling of the electrical power needed and to an attendant increase in mechanical cooling capacity.

Contextual

Fitting the required building area into the irregularly shaped site was further complicated by the close proximity of adjoining building foundations. Right to Light laws that protected existing buildings from the shadows of new construction carved into the vertical deployment of the building volume. Old London's urban context created a difficult backdrop for Rogers's expressionistic ideals.

Intentional

Among the many challenges shaped by the design propositions, the visual legibility of building parts seemed most critical. Exposing structural and mechanical components required careful consideration and craft in their fabrication and connection, greatly exceeding that necessary when these parts are simply covered up by layers of finish materials. The constraints of one system would affect the attributes of others in unexpected ways. Ultimately, systems such as glazing and interior light fixtures were developed exclusively for the Lloyd's building. Other systems had to be mocked-up at full scale and tested off-site. Weatherizing and cleaning externally exposed pieces had to be considered in practical as well as aesthetic terms (compare Lloyd's with Pompidou in this regard). At the macro-scale, London's cool climate threatened to invade any open-skinned expression of unbroken interior space.

The atrium in particular threatened to be an environmental problem. Fear of cold drafts flowing down the glass surfaces and spilling across the floor of the market room led to an engineering investigation. Members of Ove Arup's office performed one of the first architectural uses of computational fluid mapping to test the situation. They concluded, somewhat ironically, that warm air rising from the intense level of activity and use of equipment in The Room would more than offset the effect of heat loss against the glass.

APPROPRIATE SYSTEMS

Precedent

The service towers that surround Lloyd's are undeniable references to Louis Kahn's "served and servant" articulation of function. As in Khan's Richards Medical Research Building in Philadelphia and the Salk Institute in San Diego, the towers organize and facilitate the functional design scheme. The formal precedent of George Street's Law Courts is likewise reflected in the skeletal expression of the service towers. As a continuum of Rogers's own work, the exterior expression of services and uninterrupted expanse of interior space are clear carryovers from his work with Renzo Piano on the Centre Pompidou.

Site

With cramped perimeter boundaries and Right to Light-restricted height setbacks, there was no where to go but down. The approach to Lloyd's and its boundaries are so limiting that delivery trucks have to be taken by 10 ton and 24 ton elevators to the lower of two basement levels for unloading. Cooling towers were placed on the roof because there were no other outside areas available. There is no on-site parking.

A clever separation of public and private circulation is achieved by raising the business entry a half-level above the street and opening a pedestrian mall around the level below the street. The public spaces on the lower level connect to Leadenhall Market and to a street-level passage called "The Green."

Envelope

Enclosure of the gallery floors uses 2.2 acres (8903 m²) of a double-pane outer glazing and a single pane inner panel. The insulated unit outer glazing is 0.25 in. (6 mm) rolled glass outside plus a 0.5 in. (12 mm) air space and a 0.25 in. sheet inside. The inside layer of glass is a 0.25 in. (6 mm) pane of rolled glass. Glazing is set in a thermally broken aluminum frame and braced with perforated aluminum fins on the exterior. The 1.6 in. (40 mm) void between the two glazings is used as a return air path to warm the interior glass surface during cold days and aid thermal comfort close to the exterior wall. The outer insulated glass unit was developed by RRP as a translucent daylight lens with rolled facets or "dimples" that refract light and scatter it at different angles.

Infill panels on the gallery block, located at the raised floor level and penetrated by air ducts, are of epoxy-coated and linen-textured stainless steel. The prefabricated toilet modules, the satellite tower cladding, and the elevators are surfaced with the same material. The epoxy coating was developed for steel bridges and is expected to be maintenance free for more than ten years.

Structure

The 224 ft × 153.5 ft (68.4 m × 46.8 m) gallery is framed by poured-in-place concrete columns on a 35 ft by 59 ft (10.8 m by 18 m) grid. Eight interior columns form three center bays of 35 ft by 35 ft (10.7 m), above which a glazed steel frame atrium rises to the full 13-story height. Glass-sided escalators, reminiscent of Norman Foster's Willis Faber Dumas building, run up and down two levels from the double-height market room. The all-important Room market level is a double-height version of the typical 9.8 ft (3.0 m) floor-to-ceiling office floor. Three gallery levels above The Room extend the market area vertically and

Figure 10.23   One of the six service towers.

keep communication and walking distances compact.

Horizontal construction in the gallery is made of a two-way grid of 21.6 in. deep by 11.8 in. wide (550 mm × 300 mm) beams at 5.9 ft (1.8 m) on center both ways. The floor grid is supported by posttensioned U-beams spanning between the columns and ending in precast yokes resting on precast brackets at the column support. A return air plenum and service void is created by 17.3 in. (440 mm) high stub columns that rest on the grid intersections and support a 3.9 in. (100 mm) concrete deck above. Custom-designed light fixtures fill the 10,000 ceiling voids, 59.1 in. (1.5 m) on each side, and are suspended inside the grid beams below.

The atrium vault and exterior glazing are of exposed structural steel frame. The atrium glass is set in an external space frame tubular steel barrel vault. The barrel vault springs from a custom-cast steel bracket bearing on top of the concrete columns. Satellite towers were constructed from about 1800 precast concrete frame pieces.

Mechanical

The served-and-servant configuration pulls virtually all mechanical elements out of occupied space. Toilet rooms, elevators, electrical and plumbing risers, even firemen's lifts, are located in the towers. The toilet rooms were prefabricated as complete modules in Bristol and delivered ready to plug in.

The mechanical plant is in the lower basement level, and the cooling towers are on the roof. Distribution of air to the market room is accomplished from the basement level up through floor registers. Air for the remaining gal-

Some 1600 local fan terminals in the raised floor distribute air to the market areas. They mix 50 percent room air with 50 percent primary (supply) air and deliver it to as many as four workstations. There are also 900 perimeter water-to-air heat pumps using chilled water return lines from the fan rooms atop the service towers as a heat source in the early part of cold days.

Interior

The expressionist notion of articulating the systems externally is echoed on the interior. Exposed structure forms the ceiling grid, whose cells are completed by the sophisticated lighting fixtures. Most partitions are eliminated, leaving the exterior glass wall as a translucent boundary. The floor consists of finish surfaces over the 23.6 in. × 23.6 in. (600 mm by 600 mm) raised floor panels.

The only principal interior element consists of a custom-designed modular workstation. It is readily demountable and easily connects to distributed services beneath the floor panels. Each workstation provides individual controls for task lighting and air distribution.

TECHNICAL INTEGRATION HIGHLIGHTS

Physical

- Terraced floors above the sixth gallery level promote maximum use of the site and conform to Right of Light requirements.
- Deployment of service towers around the rectangular gallery fill the odd corners of the irregularly shaped site and maximize its utilization.
- Uninterrupted interior space is provided by pulling services to exterior service towers.
- Separate ceiling return air and raised floor supply air plenums eliminate interior ductwork.
- Light fixtures combine return air and fire sprinkler hardware.

Visual

- The expression of technical elements lends scale and clarity to the elevations.
- Service towers break up the regular surfaces of the rectangular glass-box gallery.
- A visual dynamic plays between the static box and the apparatus-covered towers.
- Craft in fabrication of exposed structure and mechanical elements creates a machine aesthetic.

Figure 10.24 External ductwork.

leries comes from three-story fan rooms located on top of four satellite towers. Vertical air distribution runs down the towers on the exterior of the elevator lobby windows. Horizontal supply and return air ducts of up to 24 in. (610 mm) diameter finger across the façade at every level at the base of each floor. Supply feeds into the floor plenum. Return draws air up through the light fixtures, across the stud column service void, through an exterior fishtail-shaped extract duct, down the window cavity and into the duct. All exterior ductwork is clad in stainless steel.

Inside, the gallery ceiling-to-floor service layer is divided into three physically separated zones totaling about 45 in. (1.1 m) in thickness. First is the concrete ceiling grid continuously in-filled with a combination return air, fire sprinkler, and light fixture. Above that is the void between the stub columns provided for horizontal distribution of services and as a return air plenum. Finally, above the concrete deck, an 11.8 in. (300 mm) raised floor is left as a service way and provides a supply air plenum.

Performance

- Tight security is provided by elevating the guarded business entry at a half-floor (8.2 ft or 2.5 m) above the street and leaving an exposed public walkway around the retail and restaurant floor a half-level below. This also creates a strong pedestrian connection to the Leadenhall Market.

- The air distribution plenums couple the heat capacity of the structure with the thermal needs of the space, provide a large thermal buffer for the cooling system, and reduce supply air temperature requirements.

- Return air cavities in the exterior glazing alleviate cold glass walls.

- Fire water storage tanks double as thermal storage reservoirs for the heating system.

- Service distributions under the raised floor are accessible for reallocation of market spaces or workstations.

- Service equipment is accessible for repair or replacement upon obsolescence.

- Return air light fixtures remove 60 percent of the convective heat from the lamps before it ever enters the room as a cooling load.

DISCUSSION

Lloyd's makes a decidedly Gothic impression. Richard Rogers's reference to Street's Law Courts in the Strand as a formal precedent seems well served by the six technical service towers, or "turrets" as Rogers has called them, that spire around glass walls and gleaming fishtail ducts. The building even responds to Rogers's desire that different views provide surprises "rather like a Gothic cathedral."

Lloyd's' visual expressionism conveys the mechano-rationalist interworkings of its architectural systems very explicitly—and this is probably the most obviously integrated building anywhere. It suggests technical integration like a red race car suggests tire-burning velocity. Service towers beyond anything Kahn could have possibly foreseen, exposed structure, exposed ducts—all the visual integrations are marshaled together around their shared mandates. Is this unified visual result the best measure of integration, or are performance factors the deeper and more critical outcome? The window wall is a return air duct after all; the light fixture is an acoustical ceiling; desks become personal air diffusers; every part of the building does two or three things. Or perhaps it is less a matter of features than of benefits: flexible space, technology uptake, folded space, personal comfort, site utilization, energy efficiency, and so on.

25

HONG KONG AND SHANGHAI BANK, 1979–1986

Hong Kong
NORMAN FOSTER & ASSOCIATES

DESCRIPTION

The Hong Kong and Shanghai Bank (HKSB) is a vertical banking city of eight villages suspended below double-height lobby spaces. The lowest of the lobbies is an open pedestrian mall at grade level that maintains an urban parkway leading from ferry landings to cultural centers. Inside the building a small number of express elevators run between the double-height lobby floors, with escalators providing quick and open circulation within each vertical village.

Custom prefabrication typifies the HKSB technical systems. The large scale of this project allowed for every component to be custom designed and fabricated. Construction on the small site proceeded as components were delivered and plugged directly in place. Modular mechanical rooms, permanent service cranes, exoskeletal structure, and sophisticated floor-ceiling service layers carry the High Tech banner of industrial precision, expressionism, and flexible servicing.

Figure 10.25 Overview of Hong Kong and Shanghai Bank. *(Photograph by Meredith L. Clausen ©1996, as selected from the Cities & Buildings Database at the University of Washington. Visit the digital image collection at http://content.lib.washington.edu/cities.)*

TABLE 10.8 Fact Sheet

Project	Building Name	Hong Kong and Shanghai Bank
	Client	The Hong Kong and Shanghai Banking Corporation (HSBC)
	City	Hong Kong
	Lat/Long/Elev	22.30°N 114.20°E, height about 33m/108 ft above sea level

Team	Architect	Norman Foster & Associates
	Structural	Ove Arup & Partners
	Services	J Roger Preston & Partners
	Quantity Surveyors	Levett & Bailey in association with Northcroft, Neighbor & Nicholson
	Project Coordinator	R. J. Mead & Company
	Management Contractor	John Lok / Wimpey joint venture
	Value Analysis	Quickborner Team
	Sunscoop	Lighting Sciences of Arizona

General	Time Line	Competition: June to October 1979; design concept May 1980; construction November 1981 to November 1985. Erection of steel superstructure actually began January 3, 1983, and practical completion was handed to the client 2 years and 11 months later.
	Floor Area	43 floor levels above a pedestrian plaza, four basement levels; gross 1,067,476 ft² (99, 171 m²); usable 757,757 ft² (70,398 m²).
	Occupants	Staff of 5000 with about 7000 customer visits per day.
	Cost	5227 million Hongkong dollars, or about US$670 million in 1985. Some 65% of the budget was committed to steel structure, cladding, elevators, and escalators by January 1982.
	Cost in 1995 US$	$949.2 million, about $890/ft².
	Stories	43 above a pedestrian plaza, reaching to 586 ft (178.8 m); 4 basement levels to 61.7 ft (18.8 m) below grade.
	Plan	Plaza is 37,826 ft² (3512 m²). Largest floor is 34,607 ft² (3215 m²). Footprint is about 177 ft × 230 ft (54 m × 70 m) overall.

Site	Site Description	Central Hong Kong along Des Voeus Road Central, looking about 16 degrees east of north over the seafront. The plot is about 223 ft (68 m) north to south and 246 ft (75 m) east to west, with a small slice taken off the southeast corner on the Queen's Road side.
	Parking, Cars	Small number of parking spaces in basement.

Structure	Foundation	Caissons to depth of 111.5 ft (34 m) below grade.
	Vertical Members	8 groups of aluminum-clad steel tube masts aligned in two rows of four.
	Horizontal Spans	External trusses at double-height levels, from which floors below are suspended on tension hangers.
	Special Features	29,736 tons (27,000 tonnes) of structural steel and 1,236,013 ft³ (35,000 m³) of concrete.

Envelope	Glass and Glazing	344,444 ft² (32,000 m²) of insulated silver reflective glass.
	Skylights	None.
	Cladding	Structure is clad in 1 million ft² (93,000 m²) of aluminum.
	Roof	Not determined.
	Special Features	Exterior sunscoop at Level 12: 480 mirrors, total weight 35.2 tons (32 tonnes).

HVAC	Equipment	3555 tons (12,5000 kW) of cooling capacity.
	Cooling Type	Direct expansion with seawater heat rejection via tunnel to bay.
	Distribution	Chilled water from basement to 139 service modules.
	Duct Type	Subfloor.
	Vertical Chases	Core functions at east and west walls.

Interior	Partitions	Movable.
	Finishes	Various.
	Vertical Circulation	23 express passenger elevators to double-height floors and 5 freight elevators, 62 escalators.
	Furniture	Various.
	Lighting	Indirect fluorescent.
	Electrical	11,880,000 ft (3,600 km or 2027 miles) of electrical and communication cabling
	Special Features	Interior sunscoop reflector at top of 170 ft high atrium (above plaza)

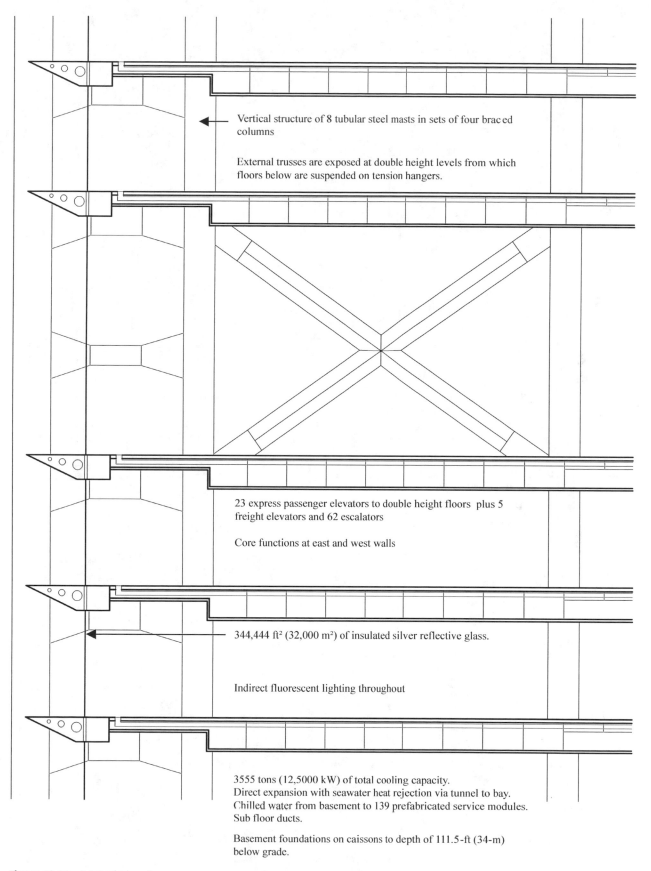

Vertical structure of 8 tubular steel masts in sets of four braced columns

External trusses are exposed at double height levels from which floors below are suspended on tension hangers.

23 express passenger elevators to double height floors plus 5 freight elevators and 62 escalators

Core functions at east and west walls

344,444 ft² (32,000 m²) of insulated silver reflective glass.

Indirect fluorescent lighting throughout

3555 tons (12,5000 kW) of total cooling capacity.
Direct expansion with seawater heat rejection via tunnel to bay.
Chilled water from basement to 139 prefabricated service modules.
Sub floor ducts.

Basement foundations on caissons to depth of 111.5-ft (34-m) below grade.

Figure 10.26 Anatomical section.

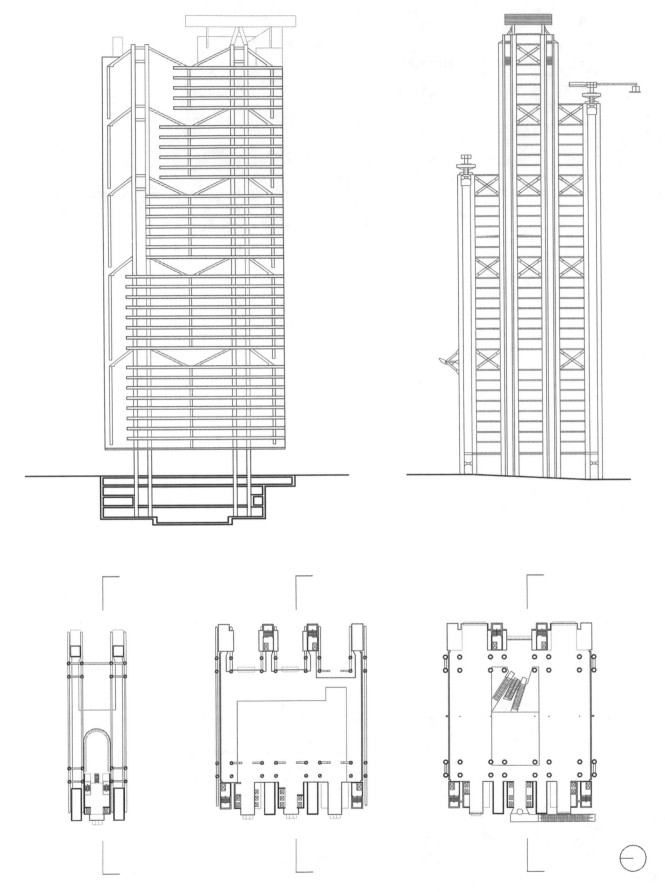

Figure 10.27 Plan, section, and elevation.

PROGRAM

Client

The Hong Kong Bank was one of the first British banks to open an overseas operation in the Far East. It was founded by local merchants in 1865 to finance their trade with China, Japan, and the Philippines. By 1900 it had branches in London, New York, San Francisco, Shanghai, Bangkok, Singapore, and dozens of other major commercial centers. In 1886 its first headquarters was constructed on the present site in Hong Kong by the architectural firm of Palmer & Turner. The same firm completed the bank's Shanghai branch office in 1923, a building that now houses the Shanghai municipal government and headquarters of the local Communist Party.

During the depression of the 1930s, the bank purchased Hong Kong's city hall next to its own building and set out to build a grand banking center. Completed in 1935, the new building covered an acre of ground and included several innovative materials, all of them imported. The only local material was a native granite cladding. Made of high-tensile Chromador steel, fully air-conditioned, glazed with plate glass capable of withstanding 130 mph typhoon winds, and completed in less than two years, the new building attracted worldwide attention. A pair of guardian lions at the main entrance would soon become a symbol of the bank's success. Today they stand at the front of the new headquarters; their paws polished smooth by generations of passersby hoping that prosperity will rub off.

By 1978 the bank had outgrown its facilities and spread its offices across central Hong Kong. Office space was in high demand, and further growth of the bank suggested that by 1985 another 50,000 ft^2 would be needed just to keep pace. Consolidation was in order.

At this time in its history, Hong Kong was a city-state of about 5.5 million people living in its most dense areas at the incredibly crowded conditions of about 74,000 people per square mile (28,500 per square kilometer). Migration from Mainland China had strained the province's resources since the end of World War II, when the Hong Kong population numbered only 600,000. Nonetheless, Hong Kong had become the fourth largest financial center in the world, after New York, London, and Tokyo. The central business district lies on Hong Kong Island, overlooking one of the world's largest deep-water container ports. From the island's summit on Victoria Peak (1,810 ft or 552 m), the wealthy elite of Hong Kong look down on a vertical city of towers that began popping up only in the 1960s.

Brief

The 1970s were prosperous in Hong Kong, reflecting the general affluence and optimism of global economics. The bank's existing site at 1 Queen's Road Central was one of the most expensive pieces of real estate in the world, and the small building that stood there neither served the bank's needs nor took advantage of the location. The bank thus began in January 1979 to set up a feasibility study and choose an architect to redevelop its facilities. Following an internal selection process, on June 14, 1979, the following firms were invited to participate in a three-month exercise, after which one firm would be chosen:

- Palmer & Turner—the bank's own homegrown architects
- Skidmore, Owings & Merrill—corporate architects extraordinaire
- Hugh Stubbins—recently completed Citicorp Center in New York
- Harry Seidler—renowned Australian
- Gollins, Melvin & Ward—designers of Commercial Union high-rise in London
- Minoru Yamasaki—Seattle-based architect of the World Trade Center in New York
- Norman Foster—44-year-old British architect known for his innovative solutions, but who had never built anything over four stories tall

The contestants were provided with little information about the bank's needs and only one day of briefing on the whole project. From their previous months of investigation, the bank set out only the broadest criteria. First, the bank would continue operations on the site throughout the redevelopment process. This meant that it wished for one of two basic schemes to be employed. Either the north tower of the existing bank would be permanently retained and married to a new south tower erected beside it, or the entire site would be redeveloped in stages while the bank's staff worked in the existing south tower temporarily.

Other general guidelines included minimally designated space allocations. A basement level would be provided for vaults and safety deposit boxes, public space for exhibitions and general use, loading and unloading of gold, normal office storage and equipment, and for HVAC and electrical plant rooms. The superstructure of the building would contain a multilevel banking hall around a central atrium, executive offices, specialist banking departments, international banking, a recreation area with swimming pool (later omitted), a restaurant and kitchen, gardens and terraces, and a helipad and a viewing gallery at the top.

TABLE 10.9   Normal Climate Data for Hong Kong

		Jan.	Feb.	Mar.	Apr.	May	June	July	Aug.	Sept.	Oct.	Nov.	Dec.	Year
Temperature	Degree-Days Heating	104	95	44	3	0	0	0	0	0	0	8	64	319
	Degree-Days Cooling	25	36	109	251	450	550	620	618	555	438	217	71	3949
	Extreme High	79	79	86	91	91	99	97	99	99	91	88	82	99
	Normal High	67	67	71	77	83	86	89	89	87	83	76	70	78
	Normal Average	63	63	67	73	79	83	85	85	83	79	72	65	74
	Normal Low	58	59	63	69	75	79	81	81	79	75	67	60	70
	Extreme Low	43	41	41	54	63	72	70	73	68	57	36	37	36
Humidity	Dew Point	51	54	60	66	72	75	76	76	73	66	58	51	65
	Max % RH	71	78	81	83	83	82	80	81	78	73	69	68	77
	Min % RH	62	70	73	75	76	76	73	74	71	66	61	59	70
	% Days with Rain	13	17	23	26	43	60	56	50	40	20	7	10	30
	Rain Inches	1	2	3	6	11	16	14	15	12	5	2	1	86
Sky	% Overcast Days	58	73	76	78	74	75	65	66	63	56	53	49	65
	% Clear Days	45	30	26	29	38	40	56	52	49	54	55	54	44
Wind	Prevailing Direction	E	E	E	E	E	E	WSW	E	E	E	E	E	E
	Speed, Knots	10	11	11	11	10	11	7	10	10	10	9	9	10
	Percent Calm	2	2	1	3	32	3	3	4	4	2	2	1	2
Days Observed	Rain	4	5	7	8	13	18	17	15	12	6	2	3	110
	Fog	5	9	13	13	4	1	#	1	#	#	#	4	50
	Haze	0	0	0	0	0	0	0	0	0	0	0	0	0
	Snow	0	0	0	0	0	0	0	0	0	0	0	0	0
	Hail	0	0	0	0	0	0	0	0	0	0	0	0	0
	Freezing Rain	0	0	0	0	0	0	0	0	0	0	0	0	0
	Blowing Sand	0	0	0	0	0	0	0	0	0	0	0	0	0

In more general terms, the bank stressed a need for maximum flexibility for operational changes and technology uptake. Its requirements, and the realities of the project, dictated rapid construction on an extremely restricted site. The bank also emphasized a series of issues related to context, mainly sensitivity to ways of doing business in Hong Kong and respect for its special character. Finally, rather than specify any sort of budget constraints, the client merely established a high standard of quality and architectural merit. Its final instructions were simple and direct: This was to be the best bank building in the world.

Another series of issues surrounded the tradition of the bank itself. The institution and its existing facility had become something of an icon in Hong Kong, a symbol of its continued success and a cultural good luck charm. Great faith was vested in its maintained status and posi-

tion. Because the redevelopment might disrupt such continuity, it was important to observe traditional restraint and local customs. One of these was the practice of feng shui, the art of arrangement in response to concerns for health and prosperity. Although such practices seldom had a direct bearing on the work of the design team, they are emblematic of the sort of sensitivities the bank was looking for.

The actual development of a refined brief was never agreed on by the bank, though Foster's office worked on one from the inception of the competition. For Foster, the design had to grow from a good definition of the problem, from an understanding of the bank's operations and growth. As late as January 1981, eight months into design development, the architect's brief was not completely satisfactory to the bank. Demolition was already fast

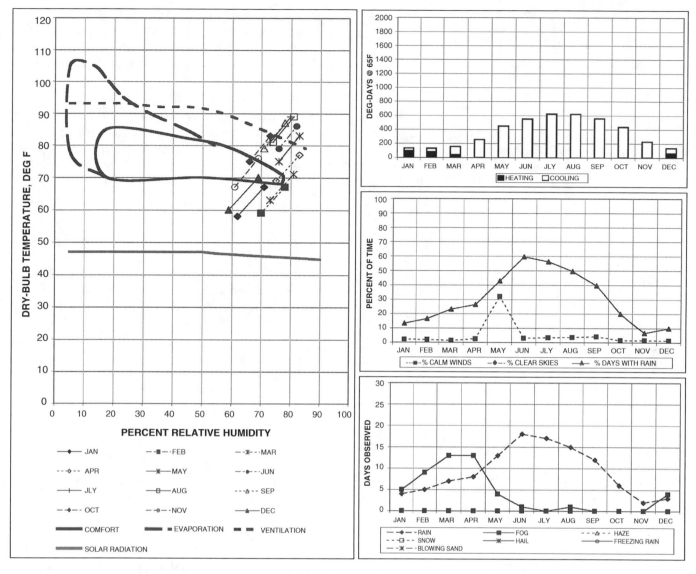

Figure 10.28 Climate analysis graphics.

approaching and the bank's various departments were being scattered across the city, making it increasingly difficult to collect good information. Further, the client was making ever more changes in its requirements and increasing pressures to complete the bank within a shorter and shorter timeframe with more and more program footage. As late as July 1983, HSBC decided to occupy the entire building rather than only 80 percent of it. Eventually, space requirements grew to twice what was proposed in Foster's competition scheme.

Site

Number 1 Queen's Road Central lies at the northern base of Victoria Peak and at the southern end of an open pedestrian mall leading up from the Star Ferry landing. The mall originally terminated on the northeast side of the bank at Statue Square, one of the only open civic spaces in central Hong Kong. The site slopes 6.6 ft (2 m) from south to north. To the south of the bank site is a series of low-rise government buildings, St John's Cathedral, and Battery Path, leading pedestrians uphill to Hong Kong Park. Competitor institutions, namely Standard and Charter Bank to the northwest and Bank of China to the east, made up the surrounding blocks. The pedestrian and infrastructure features were likely more significant to design influences than were the flanking buildings. Hong Kong economics dictated that the low scale of these buildings would make them candidates for redevelopment as well within a few years. I. M. Pei's design for the Bank of China Tower, for example, was located a little farther to the east not long after. Along Statue Square, however, there were some significant colonial era buildings: the Supreme Court (1904) and the Hong Kong Club (1897) to the east and the newer Princess Building (1963) to the west.

Kowloon, Hong Kong

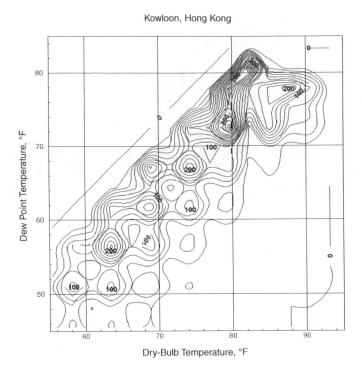

Figure 10.29 Bin data distribution for Hong Kong. Concentric areas of graph indicate the number of hours per year that weather conditions normally occur in this climate. Similar to elevation readings on topographic maps, highest frequency occurrences of weather are at the center peaks of the graph. (Data sources: *Engineering Weather Data, typical meteorological year (TMY) data from the National Climatic Data Center, and the ASHRAE Weather Data Viewer from the American Society of Heating, Refrigerating and Air-Conditioning Engineers.*)

Views from the site are spectacular. Just 1300 ft (400 m) to the north and northeast is Victoria Harbor; to the west-southwest are the 1800 ft (550 m) prominence of Victoria Peak and the ritzy residential neighborhoods that scale its height according to levels of personal wealth.

Climate

Hong Kong is a tropical hot-humid climate with almost 4000 degree-days cooling and just over 300 degree-days heating. Seasonally, there is a monsoon rhythm, with hot-humid rainy summers and drier and cooler conditions during the rest of the year. The average daily high in July is 89°F with a low of 81°F and humidity ranges narrowly from 70 to 81 percent. Even in January, the normal temperature range is 58°F to 67°F, with relative humidity between 62 and 71 percent. Freezes occur only at higher elevations. Environmentally, the problem is straightforward—cooling loads and moisture problems dominate Hong Kong design solutions. Shading and other heat-prevention strategies are essential to mitigating such problems, but year-round air-conditioning is a given in buildings with any sort of internal loads. Proper daylight-

ing strategies and efficient artificial illumination are the best measures toward reducing internal heat gain.

Solar geometry at this low latitude is characterized by high sun and seasonally uniform length of day. Solar noon profile angles on a south window vary from 44.3 in December to directly overhead in June. At the summer solstice, the noonday sun actually grazes the north sides of buildings. At the summer solstice the length of day is 13.4 hours from sunrise to sunset, and the winter solstice day is 10.7 hours long. Although daylighting is extremely valuable in reducing the use of artificial lighting in tropical climates, it must be carefully balanced with solar shading strategies. Solar heat gain is never useful in Hong Kong.

The tall buildings of Hong Kong are also subjected to typhoons, or tropical cyclones, on the average about three times per year. These events bring dangerously high winds and torrential rains. The most destructive forces, however, lie in the narrow center of the cyclone's extremely low air pressure.

INTENTION

Design Team

The client, wishing to assure itself of a quality result, stipulated that the competition winner would work with its own selection of consultants. Accordingly, the bank appointed Ove Arup & Partners as structural engineers. Levett & Bailey, a local and successful quantity surveying firm, was selected to serve that role, and another Hong Kong enterprise, J. Roger Preston & Partners, was named as services engineer. The bank also turned to Palmer & Turner, who had continued as architects for the bank's interim needs, to provide in-house local expertise and help with the initial feasibility study for a new design.

This is the fourth case study in this text covering the work of Norman Foster and one of many buildings discussed that have High Tech underpinnings. To avoid redundancy in this case study, the discussion of architectural philosophy and intention is imbedded in the following expanded sections on critical technical issues.

CRITICAL TECHNICAL ISSUES

Inherent

Modern banking institutions are powerful agencies of a free-enterprise culture—they handle the money. Along with its churches, city hall, and museum buildings, banks are icons of a city's financial and cultural wealth. As agencies of financial trust, bank buildings have always fostered images of solidarity and monumental permanence. In the introduction to *Money Matters: A Critical Look at Bank Architecture*, Brenda Gil (1990) calls this image "an impregnable fiscal integrity."

The first sort of packaging given to this impregnable image relied on classic motifs of monumentality and formal authority. Greek, Roman, Renaissance, and Beaux-Arts banks are still abundant. Later however, classicism was replaced with Modernist models of transparency that were intended to convey honesty through openness and inspire confidence through progressive attitudes about efficiency and technology.

Within their public exteriors, banks are organized around their intrinsic pragmatic issues; security being the most omnipresent background factor and customer interface the most obvious foreground issue. Departmentalization is also important, as banks work with every aspect of finance from personal banking to corporate accounts to international transactions, with architecturally important aspects like mortgage lending and construction finance mixed in. Add to that the internal departments of banking management and the role of a bank as a trading exchange for its own profit. No wonder banks have so many vice presidents.

The Hong Kong and Shanghai Bank was originally organized to finance regional trade. It later grew become one of two money-issuing banks on the island and even had the image of its previous building printed on the hundred dollar note. The optimism that led to its expansion was generated by the waves of banking deregulation and economic boom of the 1980s.

Contextual

Strict height and plot ratio limitations were imposed by local building ordinances for all new construction. More restraints on size and shape were dictated by shadow line regulations, similar to the Right to Light laws that governed the envelope at Lloyd's of London. Building very high or extending broadly across the site held little promise for maximizing the HSBC redevelopment. Building down was also a problem; excavation in the Hong Kong area is difficult because of the poor soil composition of decomposed granite. This problem is exaggerated on the HSBC site by the liability of damage to nearby buildings and below-grade metro lines immediately adjacent to the site.

The high cost of land, however, provides a strong stimulus for maximizing the use of the site. In 1980 estimates placed the value of the one acre bank site at a staggering US $288 million, which is about HK $2250 million or $532 million in 1995 US$. The final cost of the new facility, including the entire fitting out required for a world-class bank, was about US $670 million (HK $5227 million or $1.2 billion in 1995 US$). It would be a very poor investment to place an undersized building on such a premium site. The challenge was to determine how much could be built and where the resources would go.

Furthermore, the bank's intention of operating on the site during construction posed several difficulties with the control of dust, noise, and vibration. The unwillingness of authorities to move the new underground metro line more than a meter from the HSBC basement wall added a long-term vibration problem. To some extent, the continuation of business operations on the site during construction was helpful—it convinced the neighboring buildings that disturbances would be kept to a minimum.

Once the building was under construction, Foster and his team would have to rely, to a large degree, on prefabricated materials from outside Hong Kong. Local craftsmanship was inadequate for the job at hand, and appropriate materials were not to be found in the tiny island state. Furthermore, the client's demand for rapid and clean construction dictated a kit-of-parts approach. Prefabrication, in turn, posed new problems. How would the different components fit together? What if they would not fit on-site? Where would pieces be stored on the cramped site? How would shipping and weather and packaging affect the design of building components and their costs? Clearly, the kit-of-parts strategy would shift a great burden onto the architect. There would be no adjustment on-site, no wet construction to bridge gaps and fill holes. If Foster was going to design everything, he would have to be responsible for everything. All problems would have to be anticipated in design development. There would be no opportunity for change later.

The challenges of prefabrication were compounded by the short project time line. When Foster presented his final schematic design to the bank in January 1981, he promised to deliver the completed building in November 1986. In the interim, the bank would continue operations in its existing building, huddled beneath a construction project suspended bridge-like 40 stories over their heads. The bank would then gradually take occupancy of the new building as successive blocks of floors were completed. How would the security, air-conditioning, building controls, and other systems be coordinated to operate in partial capacity? How would the code officials approve occupancy of an unfinished building? Most important, because construction of the framework would commence before the design of interior spaces was completed, or even the programming of their actual use was decided, how would the design of finished portions of the project affect later design decisions? Again, responsibility was diverted from the construction phase to increase the burden on design activity. All decisions had to be made in advance for this design-build scheme to work, even in the face of incomplete knowledge.

Another structural challenge was a factor of climate, namely, the typhoons and high winds that sweep across Hong Kong an average of three times a year. In addition to available records of local storm events, Arup & Partners needed a detailed topographical description of the island to arrive at a specific solution for wind loading at the bank site. In cooperation with the project's American cladding contractor, a wind engineering study of Hong Kong was undertaken at the Boundary Layer Wind Tunnel Laboratory at the University of Western Ontario in Canada. The study, based on a tennis-court-sized 1:2500 model of the entire island of Hong Kong and adjoining Kowloon, took nearly two years to complete. Other pressure-instrumented model studies were done at 1:500 to investigate the immediate site within a 2000 ft (600 m) radius. In the end, Hong Kong building codes were proven to be adequate for the design of the building, and much was learned about the dynamic loads on its structural steel frame.

Intentional

Foster persuaded the bank to commission him, based in part on his scheme to redevelop the entire site quickly while business operations continued on the same site. The strategic design for the project was just as important as the architectural merit of the finished product. Any of the competitors for the project could have satisfied programmatic and aesthetic requirements; Foster was awarded the commission because his strategic design was superior even to the bank's own feasibility study. His reputation for delivering innovative projects on time proved to be a critical factor in his selection. Basically, Foster proposed to span over the existing banking hall and build above it until new quarters were ready. At that point, bank operations would move into the new building, the old one would be demolished, and four basement levels would be constructed beneath the old foundations. He further convinced the bank that this scheme allowed continuous operations at the same location without the shortcomings of their own feasibility studies, which he identified for them. Foster believed that saving part of a building, as proposed by the bank's first scheme, would never do justice to either the old or the new phase. On the other hand, he reminded the client that a phased redevelopment of the entire site, per the bank's second scheme, would require moving its operations around three times and would end up costing more in time and productivity than it was worth. He called his own scheme for moving into the new building in stages "phased regeneration."

TABLE 10.10 Cost Data for HKSB

Item	HK $1000	% of total
Walkway	8,252	0.16%
Refuge terraces and plaza	21,960	0.43%
Substructure	341,437	6.66%
Steelwork	1,203,228	23.46%
Corrosion protection	69,279	1.35%
Fire protection	141,343	2.76%
External cladding and glazing	1,112,874	21.69%
Sunscoop	9,023	0.18%
Seawater intake system	140,786	2.74%
Basement plant	179,004	3.49%
Subfloor services	229,975	4.48%
Modules and risers	632,397	12.33%
Lifts and escalators	143,291	2.79%
Fire detection and supression	41,482	0.81%
Toilets and utility room fitout	14,372	0.28%
Telephone system	8,545	0.17%
Computer room plant	7,563	0.15%
Partitions and doors	323,864	6.31%
Floors	178,796	3.49%
Ceilings and lighting	102,389	2.00%
Furniture	69,636	1.36%
Signage	12,275	0.24%
Banking hall fitout	34,600	0.67%
Security systems	33,119	0.65%
Safe deposit boxes	20,485	0.40%
Building management system	41,303	0.81%
Public address system	1,998	0.04%
Document handling system	6,392	0.12%
Total	5,129,668	
Site	30,212	0.59%
Structure	1,755,287	34.22%
Envelope	1,121,897	21.87%
Mechanical	1,397,415	27.24%
Interior	721,560	14.07%
Specialties	103,297	2.01%

There was no initial budget for the project, but when Foster presented his first design for a suspended structure hung from a chevron style frame between two rows of concrete towers, the cost was estimated at over HK $2 billion. The conversion rate at that time was about HK $7.8 to US $1. This cost was about seven times the cost of an

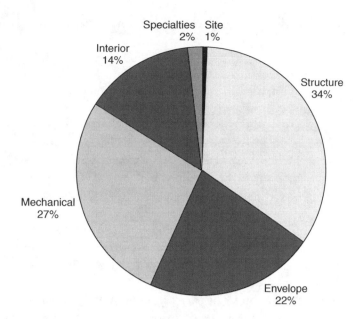

Figure 10.30 Cost data graphic by system.

average speculative 40-story building in the same market and more than three times that of the most expensive building standing in Hong Kong. Following a board meeting of November 23, 1980, the bank imposed a budget of HK $1.3 billion for the building shell. Foster and his group retained the German planning and management consultant firm, Quickborner Team, to do a cost-in-use study to determine the comparative value of Foster's scheme to the conventional one the bank was using for comparison. In late December 1980, Foster used the Quickborner report to convince the bank that his scheme delivered fair value when its expandability, flexibility, and efficiency were accounted for. Despite the obvious fact that it could not be built for less than HK $2 billion, the bank was reluctant to give up on the scheme its architect had laid out. Coupled with a rise in real estate values that added value to the entire project, the client reasoned that some cost savings could be achieved and the project brought into line with a realistic sum. Foster set out to refine his ideas, but the chevron scheme was rejected.

APPROPRIATE SYSTEMS

Precedent

The most fundamental roots for Foster's design of the HSBC building are found in his own solution for the Willis Faber Dumas (WFD) headquarters of 1975 (see case study #7). Completed four years before the Hong Kong competition began, the WFD building portrays many of the ideas consistent and evolving in Foster's work. The

general notion of pushing technical possibilities to the limit in service to building occupants would be important in this instance. His standards of craft, finish, and detail would also come into play at HSBC, as would his egalitarian ideals concerning the workplace. One of the conceptual underpinnings of WFD is found in Foster's use of a bank of escalators as a central open space in place of closed elevator cores. This would be an equally important feature in Hong Kong, as would the raised service floor system and integrated ceiling. The challenge would be to apply all these ideas at a much larger scale to a building site in a different culture located halfway around the world.

The Lloyd's of London headquarters (see case study #24) was undergoing redevelopment on a time line about one year ahead of HSBC's. The bank actually sent a representative to visit Courtenay Blackmore, the person at Lloyd's overseeing its new building. Although Lloyd's new building was one-half the floor area and one-third the height of HKSB, there were important connections. Aside from the High-Tech similarities of the two building strategies, their total redevelopment of sites among existing historical structures offers an interesting parallel. As technical coprecedents, the modularized service towers, permanent service gantries, and prefabricated toilet pods of Lloyd's are features with the most striking resemblance to those of the new Hong Kong Bank tower.

Site

An integral part of Foster's strategy for the bank was to utilize the space under the suspended floor of the Level 3 banking hall as an open pedestrian plaza. His early analysis of the site revealed that the existing bank building abruptly terminated a pedestrian axis extending from the Star Ferry up to Statue Square. Opening up the ground level of the bank site would connect this axis with the Battery Path walking route north of the central district and open circulation to civic buildings, the cathedral, and Hong Kong Park.

More to the point of the design strategy, dedicating the ground level to pedestrians raised the code-allowable plot ratio from 15:1 to 18:1. This meant that 3 more square feet of floor space could be provided for each square foot of site area, a 200,000 ft^2 or 20 percent increase. Without this extra allowance, the design would simply not meet the bank's need for future expansion. As the existing bank structures beneath the floating villages would be demolished during Foster's phased regeneration of the site anyway, the pedestrian plaza was a logical solution to maximizing the use of the site.

Daylight is reflected down onto the plaza from a huge periscope of mirrors positioned on the south exterior at Level 12 and at the top of an interior 170 ft (51.8 m) high atrium. It is possible to use the periscope in reverse by looking up into the atrium to see a reflected view of the sky mysteriously beaming down from midlevel of a high-rise building. The interior mirror is also fitted with artificial downlighting to illuminate the plaza at night. Originally, Foster developed a complementary translucent glass floor for the plaza. This glass floor was to allow light from the daylit atrium above to flow into the lower-level banking hall in the basement. At night, the pedestrian plaza would glow underfoot from artificial uplighting in the basement. This feature was one of the casualties of cost cutting that occurred during early pricing of the design scheme.

Typhoon screens are hung at both ends of the plaza where it passes under the edge of the building. These can be lowered during storms to reduce the venturi effect produced by the plaza's low height relative to the air dam effect of the tall building. Flanking the covered area of the 39.4 ft (12 m) high plaza to the west are elevator lobbies opening behind 16 structural columns. Two fire stairs land at the northwest and southwest corners. The east wall is formed behind another row of columns by stairways, service elevator shafts, and mechanical risers. Two escalators carry customers from the plaza through the glass underbelly up to the banking hall. An open-sky plaza is situated on the southern site boundary beyond the footprint of the building. Another escalator runs from the southwest corner of the open plaza up to a banking hall entrance lobby on the west face of the building.

Structure

After the bank rejected his multichevron idea, Foster explored several alternatives for delivering his phased redevelopment scheme. He explored the structural possibilities with Arup & Partners: a triple chevron and a staggered organ pipe, to mention a couple. By the autumn of 1980 they arrived at a suspension scheme later termed the "coat hanger." Pairs of two-story coat hangers would span between steel mast towers and cantilever beyond them. Central spans would carry suspended floors; the cantilevers would contain all the building services.

Detailed information from the wind engineering study was now available and had to be factored in. Amazingly, the steel frame design for the strongest of typhoons gave the building a structural lifetime rated at 10,000 years, so fatigue should never be a factor. The wind study also made it possible to minimize some of the steel needed in the building through refined design calculations. Earthquake loads were considered but did not offer the extreme limiting factors that potential wind loads did. Further economizing might have been possible if time had allowed for negotiation with the Hong Kong building code

authorities in regard to exactly how the structure would perform.

The building is carried vertically by eight steel masts arranged in two rows of four. These are the only lifting elements of the building and contain more than one-half of the building's total structural steel. The masts rise from the lowest basement foundation level, 115.5 ft (34 m) down, to the top of the building frame, 558 ft (170 m) up. Six of the masts are fitted with permanent service cranes. Foundation support is provided by four 9.8 ft (3 m) diameter concrete piers at the base of each mast column, totally independent of the basement structure. Masts are placed in two rows 110.2 ft (33.6 m) apart and spaced in bays of 36.4 ft (11.1 m) between them. Each consists of four tubular steel columns ranging in diameter from 55 in. (1.4 m) at the base of the building to 31.5 in. (0.8 m) at the top of the building. The corresponding steel wall thickness is 4 in. (100 mm) at the base and 1.6 in. (40 mm) at the top. Center-to-center dimensions of the mast columns are 15.8 ft × 16.7 ft (4.8 m × 5.1 m) in plan. Horizontal bracing at 12.8 ft (3.9 m) vertical intervals produces a vierendeel truss action in both axes of the masts. Diagonal cross bracing across the masts is added in the horizontal plane within each floor slab level.

Two-story-high trusses divide the building into five vertical layers of independently suspended floors. There are 17 pairs of these suspension trusses, spanning 110.2 ft (33.6 m) between the vertical masts and cantilevering 35.4 ft (10.8 m) beyond them. Horizontal truss members are 3.0 ft (900 mm) deep and double as the primary floor beams at the double height levels. Diagonal members are 1.6 ft (500 mm) deep. For aesthetic reasons, the top boom is omitted on trusses exposed to the north and south elevations. Diagonal booms are about 65 ft (20 m) long and attach to gusset plates on the mast columns with pins varying up to 14 in. (350 mm) diameter set into spherical bearings of 0.5 to 2.0 ft (150 to 600 mm). Tubular suspension hangers connect at the center point and end of each two-story truss. There are a total of 102 hangers of about 10 in. (250 mm) diameter to carry the building floors, each hanger being erected in three tapering segments and connected with screwed couplers. All above-grade floor levels are suspended from the hangers, leaving a large column-free area at the ground floor level. Occupied floor space is carried between the rows of masts. Service modules and prefabricated stair units are suspended outside the masts to the east and west orientations and act as cantilevers to balance against occupied floor loads.

North-to-south cross bracing occurs at each of the suspension truss levels across the inner two columns of each mast. In the atrium, from Levels 5 to 8, a larger cross brace is exposed to view from the banking hall.

At the fabrication yards, every piece of the masts had to be built to within 0.08 in. (2 mm) of true. There was also little repetition of elements, because less steel was needed as the structure went higher and proportionally smaller members were used. More than 3400 drawings were needed for steel fabrication and some 700 more for field construction. Full-scale prototypes of the system were tested at the Britannia Works in Middlesborough, England, where they were first subjected to the design building loads and then loaded to destruction. Prefabricated mast sections were delivered to the site as two-story corner assemblies, with connections made on-site at the middle of each horizontal beam.

Floors are built on 15.8 in. (400 mm) secondary beams at 7.9 ft (2.4 m) spacing and act compositely with the 4 in. (100 mm) concrete slab poured on 2.0 in. (54 mm) deep profiled metal deck. These secondary floor beams span 36.4 ft (11.1 m) from north to south and rest on 3.0 ft (900 mm) deep primary beams. In turn, the primary beams span 55.1 ft (16.8 m) between the mast and the central hangers suspended from double height trusses above. The assembly was designed to carry a live load 20 percent greater than code required to ensure flexibility of the interior arrangement and to accommodate advanced office technologies of the future.

Initially, the fire protection and corrosion resistance of the structure was intended to consist of water-filled steel sections with a molecularly bonded stainless steel finish. The offshore oil industry was already using this metal fabrication technology for drilling platforms. In drilling applications however, the stainless finish was inside the steel tubes and a separate asphaltic corrosion-protection material was applied above the platform waterline. Further study showed that the stainless finish could be reversed to the outside of the tube, but this made on-site welding assembly almost impossible. At any rate, the quality of steel used in this process was not adequate for the vertical loads of a 40-story building, so the idea was abandoned. Consequently, corrosion protection, fire protection, and then a finish material would have to be applied in three separate processes. Aluminum was a clear choice for the finish material; it could even be finished to match the aluminum-skinned wall cladding.

Corrosion protection of the steel structure is a cementitious barrier coat (CBC). This is a gunite material consisting of three parts sand to one part cement, mixed with aggregate, a polymer, water, and 5 percent by weight of reinforcing of stainless steel fibers. The alkaline content of the cement ensures protection from rust. CBC was applied in two 0.25 in. (6 mm) layers after the steel was sandblasted clean. Because of delays in the delivery of steel, treatment had to be applied on-site rather than at the factory.

This led to considerable problems of quality control and cleanup during construction. Inevitably, it affected nearby work on other phases of the construction.

Application of two-hour fire protection for the steel followed the CBC. Stainless steel mesh was wrapped around the corrosion protection, and strands of the mesh were bent back to secure a thin ceramic blanket. This was followed with a wrapping of reinforced aluminum foil. Not only did the foil protect the ceramic blanket from construction activity damage, it also sealed it from the air space inside the column cladding that was to be used as a return air plenum.

The four basement levels were formed within a 3.1 ft (1.0 m) thick perimeter wall that extends down to bedrock. The perimeter wall was supported by reinforced concrete slab floors poured over a column grid of 23.6 ft × 26.6 ft (7.2 m × 8.1 m). The columns in turn were supported on 6.6 ft (2.0 m) diameter piers. Basement walls were finished with a concrete mixture combining Japanese cement with washed Pearl River sand and Hong Kong aggregate. The mix was poured into Finish beechwood formwork that had been coated with resin for smoothness and consistency.

Envelope

Aluminum second-skin cladding for the structure was developed with a 6 in. (152 mm) space allowance around the steel members for fire protection and moistureproofing. This void is also used for some HVAC return air paths. Detailing of the cladding joints had to be both waterproof and visually thin, and their finish would have to stand up to the hot-humid climate for at least 50 years. The final solution was a 0.2 in. (5 mm) thick aluminum skin with a nine-step fluoropolymer paint finish that is baked onto the metal at 500°F (260°C). Tolerances for installation were on the order of ± 0.125 in. (3 mm).

Cladding for the opaque exterior surfaces was made from honeycomb reinforced aluminum panels. The technology for this material was developed for aircraft and aerospace applications—it is lightweight and strong enough to be used for helicopter rotors. Panels for the bank are 1.0 in. (25 mm) thick and finished with the same silver-gray coating as the structural cladding.

Glazing for the office areas is 0.5 in. (12 mm) thick insulated glass with a silver reflective coating. An outer sheet of 9 mm glass is clear, the inner 5 mm pane is coated. Between them are perforated aluminum blinds sealed in the air space and controlled by recessed levers in the window mullions. Blinds were omitted on the north elevation to preserve the view of Victoria Harbor. The curtain wall uses full-height glass set in a sill resting below slab level so that the glass appears to disappear into the floor. Vertical framing consists of circular hollow-section aluminum mullions at 48 in. (1.2 m) centers. The glass is set against the mullions in structural silicone sealant. An integral perforated web flange on each mullion provides wind bracing. At the double-height level, an external truss at each window mullion braces the glass wall against wind loads. A special condition occurs at the east end of the banking hall atrium from Level 3 to 12. This has been named the "cathedral wall" and consists of widely spaced double glazing with service walkways carried between the two layers.

The glass is shaded by an aluminum sunscreen extending 5.9 ft (1.8 m) beyond the curtain wall. It consists of an inward-louvered grille and an outer set of four louvers, both resting on perforated support brackets. The mounting bracket's outer edge aligns with the center of the outer mast column. These shades are used on the north side of the building as well as the south, primarily because they also provide a maintenance walkway. Glass panels at each end of the walkway open for access and double as code-required smoke vents. The true solar orientation of the building is about 16 degrees east of north anyway, so the waterfront orientation does receive direct sun until late morning from March through September.

The sunscoop daylighting system is also an element of the envelope. As a periscope, it is composed of two sets of mirrors. On the south exterior of the building, at Level 12, is a bank of 4 in. (100 mm) wide mirrors that track the sun's altitude angle by moving on a horizontal axis. Movement is very slow to prevent distracting flashes of light to the interior. The assembly is supported on a steel space frame bracketed to the vertical masts. An interior reflector assembly is made of steel tube framework. It covers the top of the atrium space with pure aluminum convex reflectors clipped between the tubes. The tubes also support artificial lighting connected directly to them.

A suspended glass canopy at the floor of Level 3 separates the main bank hall and its atrium from the pedestrian plaza below. The form of the canopy is determined by the catenary contour of draped steel V-sections 10.2 in. (260 mm) deep that hold it in tension, like a rope bridge, across the 69 ft (21 m) span and resist wind uplift. An aluminum framing system acts as a stabilizing compression frame to receive insulated panels of 0.4 in. (10 mm) tempered over 0.5 in. (12 mm) laminated glass construction. The strength of the glazing is sufficient to prevent a 1 kg steel ball, falling from the top of the fourth floor, from penetrating through to the pedestrian plaza below. This strength also allows a cleaning crew to simply walk across the glass floor. The canopy is penetrated by two off-axis escalators carrying customers from the plaza up to the main banking hall.

Mechanical

All the air-conditioning, electrical, and plumbing distribution for the building was pushed to the east and west walls, and services are delivered under a raised floor system. Along with elevators and fire-stairs, the mechanical systems are used as buffers to the undesirable orientation. A heavy mechanical equipment plant and electrical gear are deployed in the basement. This scheme has the intended effect of freeing the occupied floor plates, leaving view and flexibility completely uninterrupted. An automated building control system monitors performance from the 27th floor.

Requirements for phased building occupancy and rapid construction led the designers to opt for a modularized service plant that incorporated primary HVAC distribution, toilets, and storage. These modules are similar to those simultaneously planned for Richard Rogers's design at Lloyd's, but the London building's service pods did not include air-conditioning nor had they gone out to a manufacturer for fabrication yet. At HSBC, the service modules were eventually installed at the rate of two per day, always after midnight when the streets could be cleared for large deliveries and the cargo lifted carefully into place. Structurally, the pods are independent of the main building frame, but they do provide cantilever weight to offset the occupied floor span between the main masts. They were covered in stainless steel skin at the factory and clad on-site with aluminum honeycomb panels. Distribution of service mains from the basement cooling plant to the modules occurs at the corners of the building, through prefabricated two- and three-story-high vertical stacks concealed behind layers of exterior cladding. There are 160 total service modules, weighing between 30 and 55 tons apiece and measuring up to 39.4 ft × 11.8 ft in plan and 12.8 ft high (12.0 m × 3.6 m × 3.9 m).

Delivery of air to the occupants is via air terminal units beneath the floor. A constant volume system feeds conditioned air from the service modules to strip louvers along the window walls where thermal loads are consistent. Variable-air-volume fans supply air from the same source to floor registers distributed throughout the interior. Some 80 percent of return air is taken through the floor plenum. The remaining 20 percent is returned through fluorescent light fixtures to remove the waste heat they generate before it is distributed into the room. This air is drawn through the hollow space behind the mast column cladding and then ducted to the service modules.

Heat collected from the building by the HVAC plant is rejected to a seawater cooling system instead of conventional cooling towers. This saves potable water, mechanical equipment, and the space in which towers are placed. The original 1935 building used the same system by pumping water from the bay 1312 ft (400 m) to the building through two 1.3 ft diameter (400 mm) mains laid in a trench just below Statue Square. Local authorities suggested that an expansion of this system might be allowed if it would also service some of their buildings and surrounding businesses. In December 1981, Foster's team proposed to excavate a 23 ft (7 m) diameter tunnel 197 ft (60 m) below Statue Square in bedrock granite for a community sized seawater system. The deep setting of the tunnel was dictated by the depth of the decomposed granite soils that would flood continuously with the ocean tides. Drilling deeper in solid granite allowed for faster completion and avoided requirements for primary support. The tunnel depth was also set to avoid the existing Charter Station metro line that extends 115 ft (35 m) below grade.

Six 40 in. (1.0 m) diameter pipes would carry seawater through the tunnel to the new development's cooling plant; two of them were to provide supply and return for the bank, two of them would be shared with neighboring buildings, and the last two were for back-up in case of repair. A pumping station at the Star Ferry was designed to deliver 1057 gal/sec (4000 l/sec), of which 75 percent was intended for other buildings. After negotiations about shared costs broke down during a brief economic recession, the project was approved out of sheer expediency and implemented in time to allow for an August 1984 completion date. Redesign, after withdrawal of the community partners, resulted in an 18.0 ft (5.5 m) tunnel size and piping in three 28 in. (700 mm) mains.

Electrical service capacity is 21,000 kva, or 21 megavolt amperes, about one-third of which is dedicated to air-conditioning. There are also 6 megawatts of standby generation. More than 3,600 km (11,881,000 ft) of cabling was used in the building.

Interior

Vertically, the building is divided into eight zones plus the street level pedestrian plaza. Basements constitute the sub-level Zones 7 and 8. The remaining six layers are organized as vertical blocks divided by double-height sky lobbies in a scheme that has been compared to a stack of five midrise buildings. The number and placement of these divisions are based on interior requirements; they are not structural load distributions. The lowest of the six villages, as Foster calls them, is the double-height main banking hall, which is reached by escalator from the pedestrian plaza. Each of the upper four villages is accessed by elevators stopping only at the double-height spaces of the suspension trusses. The double-height spaces, which become the focus of the interior by their being positioned as reception areas, include the grander spaces. The restricted access they provide to upper floors also ensures security and compartmentalizes the various departments of the bank into discrete areas. Circulation in and among villages is by open escalator rather than by crowded elevators.

- Zone 1—Level 3/4 is the double-height public banking hall and is accessed by escalator through the glass underbelly of the atrium or by an elevator rising along the west side of the building from Queens Road. There is no suspension truss at this level; the floor is suspended from above. The block of floors extends up through the suspension truss at Level 11 and is united by a central atrium space measuring 36.4 ft × 212.6 ft (11.1 m × 64.8 m). A huge periscope arrangement of mirrors brings daylight from the south façade into the atrium, down its length, and through the glass underbelly to illuminate the pedestrian plaza. Floors above the banking hall in this atrium zone are for the area management department. Floor area is about 176 ft × 213 ft (53.7 m × 64.8 m) overall. Three fire stairs and five mechanical modules serve each level in this zone.

- Zone 2—Level 11/12 is a suspension truss level. It contains the reception area for office floors 13 through 19. This village houses retail banking and various offices. The double-height level contains offices for senior management. Like all of the suspension truss double-height floors above Level 11, substantial east- and west-facing terraces provide amenity and code-required refuge in the event of fire. Setbacks are chiseled into each zone of the east façade providing a successively smaller profile as dictated by shadow line regulations. The setbacks are not visible on the north or south because of fire stair corridors that complete the elevations on those sides. These floor plates are based on a plan area of roughly 176 ft × 176 ft (53.7 m × 53.7 m). Four fire stairs and four mechanical modules serve each floor in this zone.

- Zone 3—Level 20/21 is a suspension truss double-height space for staff amenities, a conference center, and meeting halls. The floors above, Levels 22 through 27, are dedicated to data processing and related departments. These floor plates measure roughly 176 ft × 176 ft (53.7 m × 53.7 m). Four fire stairs and four mechanical modules serve each floor in this zone.

- Zone 4—Level 28/29 is another suspension truss level space, this one for bank officers' dining and recreation facilities. Above it are the floors for the bank's head offices on Levels 30 through 34. These floor levels are cut back in plan by stepping back one mast bay on the south as well as the progressive chiseling into the east elevation above Level 13. Each floor is still roughly 176 ft × 176 ft (53.7 m × 53.7 m). Three fire stairs and three mechanical modules serve each floor in this zone.

- Zone 5—Level 35/36 is the next suspension truss level. The executive dining level is located here. Circulation from this level is more restricted, and it appears to communicate more with the spaces below it than with those above. Levels 37 through 40 actually make the next vertical zone and are dedicated to senior executive boardrooms. The floor plate measures about 123 ft × 123 ft (37.5 m × 37.5 m). Three fire stairs and three mechanical modules serve each floor in this zone.

- Zone 6—Level 41/42 is the highest suspension truss —this is the chairman's apartment with two levels above. The floor plate is roughly 70 ft × 118 ft (21.3 m × 36.0 m). Two fire stairs and two mechanical modules serve each floor in this zone. A visitor's gallery is located on Level 43, separating the chairman's quarters from a rooftop helicopter landing pad.

In plan, the horizontal organization of the bank reflects a concern for views, solar orientation, and daylighting, not unlike that of Lockheed Building 157 (see case study #9). The north and south (NNE and SSW solar orientations) façades are fully glazed, and the interior is largely free of internal obstructions. The east and west (ESE and WNW) walls are used for the mechanical and toilet modules as well as for fire stairs. All of the passenger elevators are located on the west wall. Service elevators are located in the foyer of each fire stair. Small refuge areas are located at the suspension truss levels along the west wall between the passenger elevator lobbies, supplementing the primary terraces provided on the east side.

Expansion of the interior floor space was planned in by oversizing the structure to allow for mezzanines to be constructed in the double-height spaces and for all of the shadow setbacks of the building to be in-filled. If code restrictions are ever relaxed to allow these plans to be realized, interior floor space could be increased by as much as 30 percent.

Floor, Ceiling, and Partitions

A 48 in. (1.2 m) grid was established as the planning module of the interior. Honeycomb reinforced aluminum panels, similar to those used to clad the building, were fabricated to cover a 2.0 ft (600 mm) deep raised floor system over most of the building services. At the center of one-quarter of each panel a hole was drilled to provide either air distribution or service connections. By rotating the panel, services can be located at any center location of a 24 in. grid. The panels are covered in carpet in for office

areas, with a gray metal trim that accentuates the floor pattern.

The ceiling is suspended from dovetail slots in the metal floor deck. It is made of gypsum plasterboard panels in-filling between the cladding of the primary and secondary floor beams to reveal the structural grid and maintain maximum ceiling heights in between. At the perimeter, outside the main floor beam, the ceiling slopes upward to meet the window head and maximize light and view. Fluorescent ambient light and aimable tungsten-halogen task light fixtures are recessed in the suspended ceiling panels, as are fire detection, sprinkler, and public address systems.

Partitions are custom-made to hang from the ceilings and can be rapidly demounted. Accommodation of floor deflections of up to 2.4 in. (60 mm) and lateral swaying of the building frame led to the provision of slip joints at the floor and at vertical joints. Door frames rest on the floor and slide up and down in their mountings. Metal and glass are the materials of choice, with aluminum mullions and transom. Blank panels are made from galvanized sheet steel with gypsum lining to decrease sound transmission. The doors are heavy steel with recessed hinges.

Furniture

Occupancy densities for office areas were established at a level between Eastern and Western workplace standards. Workstations were paired to further recognize the cultural preference for working in close quarters. This arrangement also promised the highest flexibility for various layouts. Desks were logically aligned perpendicular to windows for better daylight quality and reduced glare from bright windows. This alignment also prevents anyone from monopolizing the view. After about 150 suppliers were qualified, a Dutch firm was chosen to provide desk systems. This company's 45 degree linking module seemed to provide the best combinations of possible arrangements. Ergonomic adjustments were made to provide better working conditions for the Asian physique.

Elevators and Stairs

Elevator lift cabs are translucent, and the elevators having exterior shafts are transparent. There are 23 high-speed passenger elevators running at 20 ft/sec (6 m/sec) and 5 freight elevators. Distributed through the building are 62 escalators. Prefabricated stair modules fit into the east and west façades in the same way as mechanical service modules do. Stairs are stacked directly outside the structural masts to form complete towers. Stair modules are located at the outside corners of the west elevation and the two inside bays of the east elevation. Mechanical service modules are located in the opposite manner in the other four slots beside the masts.

Basements

The lower banking hall and safety deposit boxes are located in the first basement level, just below the pedestrian plaza. Some parking is also located at this level. Beneath that are three levels of basements for the heavy mechanical systems' plant and electrical gear.

INTEGRATION HIGHLIGHTS

Physical

- The organization of the site maximizes the redevelopment strategy and establishes a pedestrian mall between major footpath arteries.

- The high degree of prefabrication meant close tolerances for construction. Although accurate tolerances in factory assembly were usually attained, there were several problems with field assembly allowances for dynamic loading under differing construction loads and some difficulties with materials that relaxed or warped during transit to Hong Kong.

- The distribution of mechanical services to modular pods avoids the necessity of locating mechanical floors at high levels of the building. This preserves the premiums of daylighting and view for occupied floor spaces. It also avoids the necessity of an interior mechanical core that would obstruct the open plan of the bank floors and their flexible use.

Visual

- The division of the building into pagoda-like sections corresponds to the interior village organization and structural scheme. It also breaks down the mass of the building into a legible scale. To some extent, this imitates the regional vernacular of stacked spaces frequently found in Hong Kong, whereby restaurants and offices and apartments are successively stacked over street level retail volumes.

- Perimeter air-diffuser strips visually continue the louvers of the external sunscreen. At the upper room level, the outer 9.8 ft (3.0 m) of the ceiling slopes upward to meet the bottom of the sunscreen bracket where it meets the 24 in. (600 mm) deep air diffuser plenum.

Performance

- Sunscreens double as maintenance walkways and are also designed to allow views down to the street. This trio of performances is accomplished without adding a significant structural load at the outside edge of the curtain wall. As a bonus, they are used to decorate the building for seasonal celebrations, saving untold weeks of constructing bamboo scaffolding.

- The high-speed elevator and connecting escalator circulation scheme reduces travel time and manages security. As in the trading room of the Lloyd's building, this has the effect of creating an interconnected single-floor space.

- Open floor planning yields 75 percent useful floor area, versus the usual 60 to 65 percent found in office towers.

- The air space between the aluminum cladding over mast columns and the fireproofing is used as a return air plenum.

DISCUSSION

This bank is nothing less than a new prototype, an example of how to design and construct a building. Nothing about the design of HSBC was taken as a given of standard practice. None of its components were chosen from a catalog. Given the client's mandate to deliver "the best bank in the world," Foster did not set out to select the best available components, but to custom-design every piece of it. The result is a crowning masterwork of High Tech design, which hints about where the evolution of High Tech is leading, what the next step might be.

It is worrisome in some regard that it took a billion-dollar bank building on a half-billion-dollar site to realize this advanced project, but perhaps that is the cost of such an invention. The fact that there are so few components or construction techniques to take from here and apply to other designs may also seem to be a failure of sorts, but new products, however well designed, are not the greatest contribution of this building. Instead, the foremost advance made by the architecture of the Hong Kong and Shanghai Bank is the method used to develop its design and realize its construction. The many successes of its built form not withstanding, HSBC is a lesson in how commodification of technology can lead the practice of architecture, even more than it is the exemplary result of a singular project.

Foster's strategy involved manufacturing and fabrication specialists in the design process. Commonplace adoption of this approach would require ongoing two-way communication between designer and product supplier. Ideally, it would also lead to interactive discussions between all of the design and building team members as decisions made in one area affected others. Communication would pool the expertise of architectural

Figure 10.31   View of the Hong Kong and Shanghai Bank and the Hong Kong skyline from the bay. *(Photograph courtesy of David Chan.)*

generalists and commercial specialists. Idealism, practicality, and coordination would be optimized.

Realization of this strategy at HSBC was less than perfect, of course; there were many failings and cultural differences to sort out along the way. In the more stressful moments, Foster's office and the rest of the building team even joked about moving to Paraguay. Many of the discussions were heated and contentious, both between the design team and the suppliers as well as with the client. The project was large enough, however, to attract the attention of product fabricators around the world, and that helped to ensure its success. There was a sufficient amount of business in this one building to allow for the use of new technologies and the design, testing, and refinement of new products. It hardly mattered whether none of the products would ever be sold again.

Foster has always demonstrated an inclination toward industrial design in his architecture. The suspended glass curtain wall at the Willis Faber Dumas headquarters (see case study #7) is a good example. This component was developed in his office for one project; Foster traded the design rights to Pilkington Glass in exchange for the product liability of the curtain wall's performance on the project. In Hong Kong, Foster began by deciding that every

product in the building would be designed along the same lines of customization. This is the kind of exploration and refinement process that modernists like Eero Saarinen have been leading toward for a long time (see case studies #6 and #10).

The ultimate goal of this process dates back to the Bauhaus ideal of industrial production. The new term for this goal is even more ambitious: *mass customization*—the one-off manufacture of components specifically designed for a single application, achieved at economies made possible by design simulation, virtual performance modeling, and automated precision manufacturing, and able to adapt to subtle variations in production for differing conditions.

At HSBC the elements of this process are all in place. The list of innovative procedures engaged is far removed from the passive selection of building products from catalogs of standardized components that Modernists might have surrendered to. In the twilight years of High-Tech design, HSBC marks a transition from glamorized technology and expressive servicing in the design of buildings to a more complete commodification of technology in the service of architecture.

The following are some of the salient aspects of the design process for HSBC:

- There were 2500 sketch assembly drawings by the architect.
- More than 100,000 shop drawings and 50,000 architectural drawings were eventually produced.
- There were 12 principal contracts and 80 subcontracts.
- Mock-ups and prototypes were refined and tested for the architect's approval in factories all over the world.
- The mechanical contractor sent 50 people to work at Foster's office in London for three months.
- None of the mechanical pods are completely identical, because of complications and variations introduced as the design progressed.
- Fabrication of custom cladding began long before other design decisions were made.
- The construction manager was removed from construction activity.
- The cladding contractor built a robot-controlled assembly operation for the project, and the elevator contractor developed lift technology for the building in conjunction with the NASA space program.

The First Consortium on Advanced Technology in Architecture was held at the Harvard Graduate School of Design in 2000. The discussions and presentations focused on the merging of three computer fields: architectural design as computer-aided design (CAD), engineering modeling as computer-aided engineering (CAE), and fabrication control as computer-aided manufacture (CAM). An example of their integration was given as a component design being exchanged between the three respective parties until it was refined to its essence and to the satisfaction of all concerned—without ever risking time and resources for physical testing and development. Other marvels were also present at the conference: a three-dimensional copier in the lobby for replicating small objects, and a Web site that would bid on fabrication of any object from a three-dimensional CAD model in 15 minutes. Architects spoke about the design possibilities; contractors addressed the cost control and coordination involved; manufacturers touted their six-axis milling machines and 100,000 psi water-jet saws. Boat makers assured one and all that CADCAM was old hat to their success in making watercraft both more economically and of higher performance. Boeing maintained that the 777 could not have been built without it. Car makers spoke of a new car requiring new robotic assembly design, requiring in turn a new factory. All in all, advanced technology seemed like the next step in High-Tech Modernism. It was easy enough to imagine a project like the Hong Kong and Shanghai Bank that would take the next step.

11

Green Architecture

Described as solar, passive, ecological, sustainable, regenerative, or just plain green—environmentally aligned approaches to architecture are guided by both scientific principles and a worshipful romance with nature. Consequently, green buildings are part method, part philosophy, and part ethic.

Ethic

The 2000–2001 traveling exhibit Ten Shades of Green, curated by Peter Buchanan and designed by Tsurumaki Lewis, depicted the Ten Commandments of environmental design. It included the customary variety of notable buildings by prominent architects, but those details are not the present point of this discussion. The exhibition title by itself, taken out of the context of the exemplary work it promotes, provokes a divergent idea. It suggests that there are, in fact, relative shades of greenness, different levels of commitment to environmental principles, that perhaps some buildings are just a deeper tint of green than others. This notion is reminiscent of a frequent assertion first made by Arthur Bowen (personal communication, 1975) that "all buildings are passive, some are just more passive than others." (Arthur Bowen was a cofounder of PLEA, the international organization for

Passive and Low Energy Architecture.) He meant by this that all buildings provide some level of environmental comfort and amenities of light and air by virtue of the designed interactions between building and environment. Obviously enough, and to the point of Bowen's comment, some architects make environmental response the focus of design thinking and others leave it to standard practice. The relative level of environmental ambition and the ultimate ecological result is always somewhere along the ecospectrum, a selective shade of green. Fundamentally, the specific hue and brightness achieved are predetermined by value decisions declared in the building program. This declaration is the ethical context of ecological architecture. As in regard to political issues, there are zealots and ideologues at both extremes of environmental issues. Taken in their entirety, the ranges of opinion form a wide expanse of belief systems, moral stances, and shades of green.

Part of this ethical diversity arises from issues of scope. Given the traditional realm and domain of architectural accomplishment, the newcomer determinants like solar geometry, aerodynamic form, and thermal zoning may appear to usurp some more accepted concerns such as materiality, progression of space, and formal expression. Furthermore, environmental benefits like energy savings and reduced ecological footprint are often difficult to transform directly into architectural features. These challenges lead to separations between the two poles of commitment to green architecture. The pioneering and radically unself-conscious solar designs of the 1960s for example, often seemed rather like quirky science fair projects to many architects and their public audience. It didn't help that green precedents were so hard to pinpoint. If solar buildings at first seemed like things unto themselves, it is probably because there was so little to go by. The commonly quoted indigenous architectural examples were noble enough, but did not employ modern building physics or the latest in high-performance components. And all the epochs of architecture since the preindustrial builders had been dominated more by structural challenges, and therefore more by issues of construction and materiality, than by environmental ones. It has taken the most recent generation or two of architects to refine this issue of scope.

Because of this lack of clear evolution from precedents within the continuum of architectural progression, the exact origins of green design will never be marked by a distinct building or series of works that herald its birth. There is no Crystal Palace of Solar, no Notre Dame de l'Ecology, and no Acropolis of Sustainability. As Butti and Perlin's book, *A Golden Thread: 2500 Years of Solar Architecture and Technology,* so notably documents, the pioneers of green design have been many and their works are diffused throughout every stage of architectural history.

The time has arrived, however, when the demonstrated environmental responsiveness of any building has become a golden measure of its merit as architecture. The professional status of ecological design and the celebration of its cultural value is now status quo. Recent winners of the Pritzker Prize and other international awards are more often recognized and self-proclaimed green advocates than not. The Ten Shades of Green exhibit marks an impressive recognition of this ascendant ethic.

Romance

A second distinguishing ethical factor of green architecture is the humble submission to nature, or at the very least a proactive cooperation with its inevitable forces. Entropy, landscape, weathering, heat transfer, resource consumption, even the eventual reuse or destruction of the building, are all seen as programmatic truths beyond resistance or denial. More important, natural factors are perceived by green advocates to embody what John Keats phrased in the closing lines of "Ode on a Grecian Urn": "'Beauty is truth, truth beauty,'—that is all/Ye know on earth, and all ye need to know."

In ecological ethics, Keats's vision of self-evident beauty is magnified by the inescapable verity of natural events, ecological processes, and environmental limits. What gravity is to structure and materiality, ecology now is to Green. Through all the Ages of Gravity, architectural thinking venerated the tenets of constructability as a vital means of endowing built form with meaning. Moving into the ethic of ecology, design looks to other laws of nature and the romantic ennoblement of servicibility.

Scale of Impact

A final principle of the environmental ethic concerns limits on the boundaries of influence that a design is obligated to consider. Here too there are shades of green determined by the extent of scale. The spectrum crosses between what Norwegian ecophilosopher Arne Naess terms "shallow ecology" and "deep ecology," designating respective degrees of local versus global concern. Local-scale thinking deals with efficiency, economy, and direct benefit to the building user over a finite project life span. Global-scale "deep ecology," on the other hand, frames the question in terms of ecological "footprint" and accounts for environmental origins of construction, embodied energy content of materials, resources used in the occupied life span of buildings, and the eventual reuse or reabsorption of a building into natural processes as it decays. Deep ecology means that a building is providing for everywhere and for all time.

Scale of impact is also a question of social equity. The 10 percent of the world's population that uses 80 percent of its resources and produces 90 percent of its pollution is in an advantaged position to afford the broader long-term ecological view. Propagating the shorter perspective of shallow ecology ensures the prosperity of the affluent few at the expense of the world's many peoples today and of future generations tomorrow. In the deepest shades of green, design is not the activity of satisfying wants and needs—it seeks instead to configure places where humanity and nature can co-prosper in sustainable harmony.

Science

Science fiction author Larry Niven once said, "Any sufficiently advanced technology is indistinguishable from magic." Green architecture captures Niven's sense of alchemy and mystical fascination in its romance with nature.

With that transcendence as a departure point, the sciences of ecology have attained an avid following of techno-design subscribers. They find architectural meaning in the expression of these scientific methods, just as structural expressionism involved the technics of construction method. The new element in green architecture is the embodiment of process, or more exactly, of flow. Flow is precisely what ecological design is about: flows of energy, flows of air, flows of light, flows of water, nutrients, wastes, materials—and of course, of people.

Science and its close cousin, technology, are important dividing points between the ambitions of High Tech Style and those of green architecture. These distinctions are instructive. The similarities are evident in their use of minimalist resources and ethic of efficiency. The departures, however, are more defining. First, there is a difference in what each would treat as optimal levels of technology. For High Tech the goal is unfettered expression—design may be visually minimalist but it is sometimes exaggerated by exuberance. Green buildings, on the other hand, use restrained technologies that satisfy function and work within a regulated cycle of flows while producing the lowest ecological impact. The green goal is one of fit: appropriate technology. The two approaches are not incompatible, but neither are they synonymous.

Second, and perhaps more fundamental, High Tech is based on an ideal of universal flexibility: the kit of precision parts from an anonymous factory that can be configured to suit and reconfigured later almost anywhere. Green-Tech is just the opposite, embracing local materials, site-specific conditions, and complex interactions between occupant, architecture, site, and climate. If High Tech is the universal industrial shed, then Green-Tech is the vernacular hut.

26

THE GREGORY BATESON BUILDING, 1977–1981

Sacramento, California
SIM VAN DER RYN, STATE ARCHITECT

DESCRIPTION

The Gregory Bateson Building was the flagship building of a series of state office projects. These buildings were intended to transform the State of California's building administration practices. The aim was to move state agencies from scattered leased office spaces to more amenable workplaces the state would build to its own higher standards. The Bateson Building was also part of two other programs initiated by then-Governor Jerry Brown to establish new energy performance standards and to revitalize the state capital office area of Sacramento. It was the first of 13 buildings in what was called the Capitol Plan.

The result is a pleasing contradiction in terms: a publicly inviting state office building. It is also remarkably efficient and well tuned to its climate, providing at least 70 percent of its own energy through daylighting, integrated passive design, and intelligent controls. Furthermore, completed construction costs were only $62/ft^2$, a figure within $0.50/ft^2$ of conventional office buildings.

Figure 11.1 The Bateson Building.

TABLE 11.1 Fact Sheet

Project	**Building Name**	The Gregory Bateson Building (GBB)
	Client	State of California, Department of General Services, Governor Jerry Brown
	City	Sacramento, California
	Lat/Long/Elev	38.58N 121.50W, 7 m or 22 ft above sea level
Team	**Architect**	Sim Van der Ryn, State Architect, and the California Energy-Efficient State Building Program
	Other Team Members	Peter Calthorpe, Bruce Corson, Scott Mathews, Glenn Hezmalhalch, Jim Barnett, Ed Street
	Structural Engineer	Karl Stricker
	Mechanical Engineer	Vern Thornburg and Russ Ahrnsbrak
	Civil Engineer	Ben Shook
	Electrical Engineer	Doug Yee and Angleo Spataro
	Construction	Continental Heller Corporation
General	**Time Line**	1977–March 1981.
	Floor Area	267,000 ft^2 (24,793 m^2) gross, not including the enclosed atrium.
	Occupancy	Government offices, mostly in health care area, about 1200 office workers or 22 occupants per 1000 ft^2.
	Cost	$20 million (1978 dollars), $62/ft^2.
	Cost in 1995 US$	46.7 million or $175/ft^2.
Site	**Site Description**	GBB occupies a full 2.5 acre block in downtown Sacramento's Capitol Area. This district was undergoing revitalization as a mixed-use, low-rise, and urban-village-scale pattern of development.
	Parking, Cars	None.
Structure	**Stories**	Four.
	Plan	Rectangular plan with central atrium.
	Foundation	Not determined.
	Vertical Members	Precast concrete ladder frame on concrete piers.
	Horizontal Spans	Cast-in-place concrete beams with precast concrete double-tee spans and concrete topping.
Envelope	**Glass and Glazing**	Automated window shading with translucent rolling fabric.
	Skylights	Skylit atrium of 150 ft (45.7 m) by 144 ft (43.9 m) with 75 ft (22.9 m) height.
	Cladding	Laminated wood timber infill and aluminum-framed glass, R-19 cavity insulation.
	Roof	R-19 insulation.
HVAC	**Equipment**	Central plant steam and chilled water.
	Cooling Type	Two supplementary 660-ton rock beds are located below the atrium floor and insulated with R-19 expanded polystyrene.
	Distribution	Variable air volume.
	Duct Type	Exposed metal.
	Vertical Chases	Flanking the atrium.
Interior	**Partitions**	Glazed to atrium.
	Finishes	Acoustical baffles in exposed concrete ceilings.
	Vertical Circulation	Atrium stairs wrapped around elevator shafts.
	Furniture	Open office.
	Lighting	Fluorescent and task lighting.

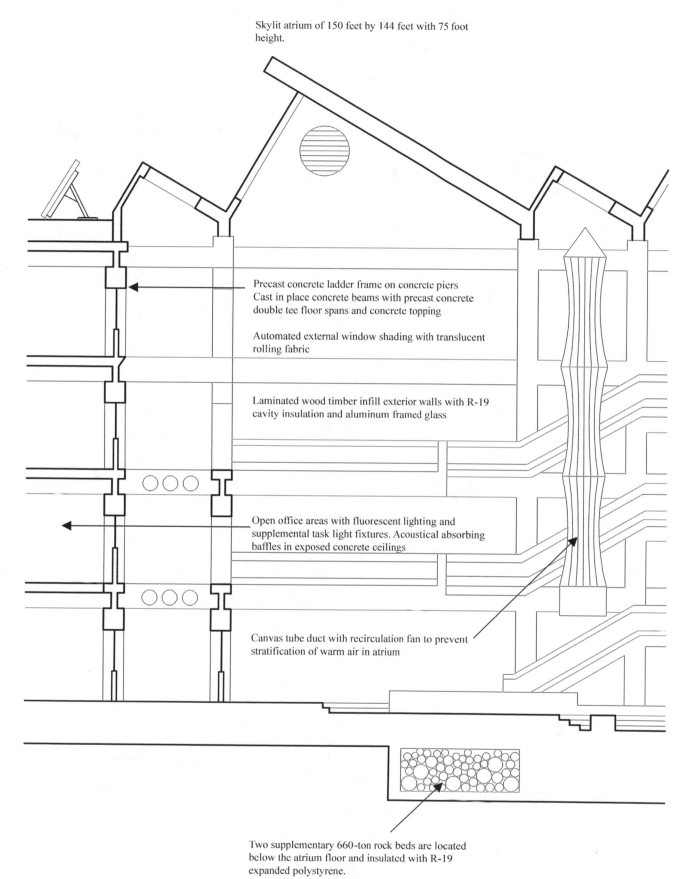

Skylit atrium of 150 feet by 144 feet with 75 foot
height.

Precast concrete ladder frame on concrete piers
Cast in place concrete beams with precast concrete
double tee floor spans and concrete topping

Automated external window shading with translucent
rolling fabric

Laminated wood timber infill exterior walls with R-19
cavity insulation and aluminum framed glass

Open office areas with fluorescent lighting and
supplemental task light fixtures. Acoustical absorbing
baffles in exposed concrete ceilings

Canvas tube duct with recirculation fan to prevent
stratification of warm air in atrium

Two supplementary 660-ton rock beds are located
below the atrium floor and insulated with R-19
expanded polystyrene.

Figure 11.2   Anatomical section.

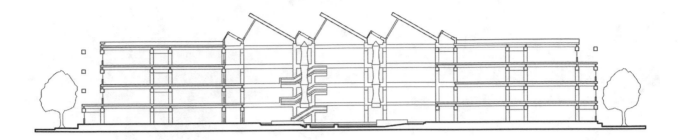

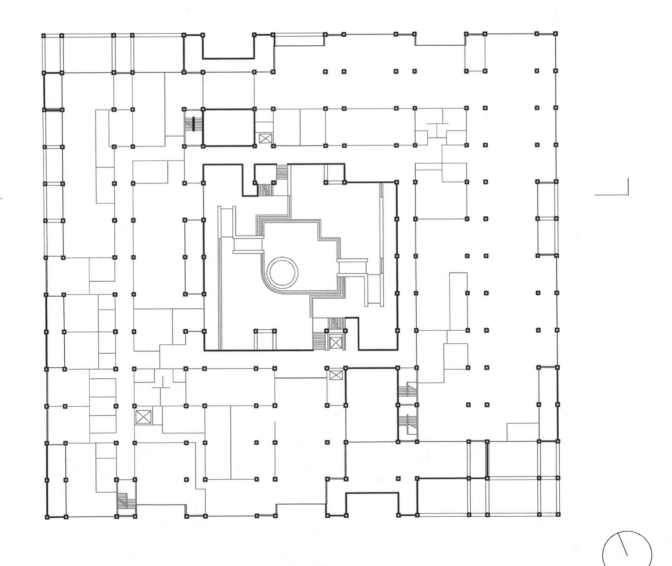

Figure 11.3 Plan and section.

PROGRAM

Client

In the early 1970s, the State of California decided that owning its own office buildings would be more practical than its old policy of leasing space. This decision had to recognize that ownership enabled better control of both operating costs and the working environment. Ownership also meant risks, however—risks associated with poorly designed and potentially unmanageable buildings that California taxpayers would be burdened with fixing or abandoning. The problem of realizing the benefits of ownership without assuming unreasonable risk fell to the state architect, Sim Van der Ryn.

Brief

The Capitol Plan was originally drafted in 1960, years before Brown and Van der Ryn stepped in. The idea at that time was to purchase land south of L Street between the capitol and the Sacramento River for development of new high-rise office buildings. Commercial development had moved farther east of the river, and the area around the capitol mall had gradually become a slum. The need for "Old Town" redevelopment and California's huge postwar appetite for government office space set the plan in motion. Two towers were erected on the west side of the Bateson site, and a central energy plant was constructed. In the early 1960s the California state architect's office grew in size to be something comparable with the largest architectural firms in the world. When Ronald Reagan became governor, however, cutbacks ensued; building construction programs were halted and office space for state agencies was leased instead. In 1975, when Brown took office, a revised Capitol Plan reported that 1.2 million ft^2 of space was being leased in 55 Sacramento locations. The pendulum had swung too far, and consolidation was in order. This is when incoming governor Brown, only 34 years old at the time, appointed Sim Van der Ryn as state architect to institute the multifaceted new building program.

The new-generation Capitol Plan, presented to the California legislature in 1977, was prepared by representatives of broad constituencies. Van der Ryn formed a staff to provide technical assistance. A series of guidelines were then established to transform the compound of day-use office buildings into a 24-hour multiuse campus:

- Clusters of activity centers with cafés and services
- Mixed-use buildings, with residential units included
- Revitalized urban infill to reduce suburban sprawl

- Development of a series of pedestrian and bicycle streets
- Designation of mass transit corridors
- Building height restrictions of 50 ft (15.2 m), or about four stories
- Building entrances that adjoin mass transit stops
- Networking of public and private open space into pedestrian streetscapes
- Reduction of urban "heat island" summer temperatures by planting trees
- Provision of mass transit downtown and connection to the suburbs
- Parking lots or garages located on the edge of the capitol area only
- Parking under fringe area freeways with shuttle bus links to the capitol

Site

The capitol district of downtown Sacramento is just east of the Sacramento River. The specific site for the Bateson project, then called "Site 1A," was a 2.5 acre city block located on Sacramento's grid coordinates bounded by P to Q, and Eighth to Ninth Streets. It is a short three blocks south of the capitol building and the L Street pedestrian mall that runs from the capitol to the Sacramento River. Immediately east of the Bateson site is a one square block park. On the west side is a paved urban plaza with the two 1960s office towers from the old Capitol Plan occupying opposite corners of that block.

Climate

Sacramento is 90 miles northeast of San Francisco and 70 miles east of the Sierra Nevada. The city lies between the Sierra Nevada and the softer Coastal Range in the long central California valley that begins at about Red Bluff and then stretches 500 miles south to Bakersfield. Köppen's classification defines the region as BSk, Cold Mid-Latitude Steppe, placing Sacramento in the same category as San Diego; Roswell, New Mexico; Monterey, Mexico; Jaipur, India; and Cordoba, Argentina. These are dry climates with an annual average temperature below 65°F. Conditions are temperate but sunny and arid. Normal degree-day data reflects the overall mildness: 2679 heating and 1213 cooling degree-days. Because degree-days are taken from daily average temperatures, however, they disguise the magnitude of Sacramento's daily temperature extremes. Characteristically, in dry climates earning Köppen's "B" designation, intense sun and low humidity introduce large swings between day and night tempera-

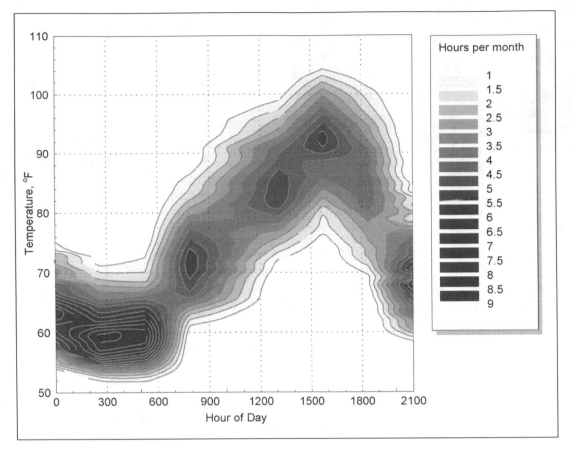

Figure 11.4 Distribution of July temperatures in Sacramento, California.

tures in the same 24-hour period. July highs in Sacramento, for example, average 93°F and the normal daily low is 58°F, so the average daily temperature of 76°F can be quite misleading.

About 75 percent of the meager 17 in. of annual rainfall occurs during the five cooler months of November through March. Water supply for the warm dry season comes from snowmelt in the Sierra Nevada that feeds the Sacramento and San Joaquin Rivers before they turn west into San Francisco Bay. The north-south axis river valley also channels winds along its 500 mile course, keeping them predominantly from the south every month but November, when the wind comes from the north. The flanking mountains protect Sacramento from more severe winter storms, but sometimes severe rain or snowfall on the western face of the Sierra Nevada leads to river floodings, which have plagued the Sacramento area since 1850.

Patterns of June through October weather are sometimes dominated by high-pressure cells that bring a few days of very hot desert air and gusty winds into Sacramento. Other times, a gap in the coastal mountain range at Carquinez Strait occasionally allows cool ocean breezes to travel up the river delta from the San Francisco Bay and bring unseasonably comfortable summer temperatures to the capital city.

Winter patterns between November and April feature rainstorms from the Pacific. They are usually accompanied by mild temperatures but can include gusty winds from the south. Fog occurs during any long absence of the winter rainstorms, when stable air masses tend to lie stagnant in the valley. These fog events are distinctly uncomfortable and can blanket the city for days.

INTENTION

Design Team

The Bateson Building was designed by a team under the direction of State Architect Sim Van der Ryn. One of the lead designers was Peter Calthorpe, who later formed a partnership with Van der Ryn in private practice. Barry Wasserman was deputy state architect and later succeeded Van der Ryn as state architect to complete the building.

Sim Van der Ryn was born in Holland. His family moved to New York City in the early days of World War II, but some of his extended family perished in Nazi concentration camps. At an early age, Van der Ryn took refuge in nearby beaches and marshes, a trait common to the childhood of many environmentalists. Though he grew up wanting to be an artist, his parents persuaded him to earn a degree in architecture at the University of Michigan, Ann

TABLE 11.2   Normal Climate Data for Sacramento

		Jan.	Feb.	Mar.	Apr.	May	June	July	Aug.	Sept.	Oct.	Nov.	Dec.	Year
Temperature	Degree-Days Heating	599	401	347	198	74	11	0	0	7	80	345	595	2679
	Degree-Days Cooling	0	0	0	13	82	206	330	303	212	58	0	0	1213
	Extreme High	70	76	88	93	105	115	114	109	108	101	87	72	115
	Normal High	53	60	64	71	80	87	93	91	88	78	64	53	74
	Normal Average	46	51	54	59	65	71	76	75	72	64	53	46	61
	Normal Low	38	41	43	46	50	55	58	58	56	50	43	38	48
	Extreme Low	20	23	26	32	34	41	48	48	43	35	26	18	18
Humidity	Dew Point	39	42	43	44	47	50	53	53	51	47	43	39	46
	Max % RH	91	89	85	78	72	67	69	74	75	81	87	91	80
	Min % RH	70	59	52	43	36	31	29	29	31	38	56	70	45
	% Days with Rain	42	39	36	24	13	6	2	3	7	15	30	39	21
	Rain Inches	3	2	2	1	0	0	0	0	0	1	2	2	17
Sky	% Overcast Days	58	50	39	27	16	10	3	3	7	19	43	55	27
	% Clear Days	22	28	34	39	49	61	78	75	71	56	34	22	48
Wind	Prevailing Direction	SE	SE	SW	SW	SW	SW	SSW	SSW	SSW	NNW	NNW	SE	SW
	Speed, Knots	8	8	9	9	10	11	9	9	9	9	8	8	9
	Percent Calm	17	15	10	8	6	4	3	5	11	19	23	20	12
Days Observed	Rain	12	11	11	7	4	2	0	1	2	4	9	11	79
	Fog	21	15	8	3	1	0	0	0	1	6	16	22	98
	Haze	17	15	8	4	4	2	4	4	9	15	19	17	123
	Snow	0	0	0	0	0	0	0	0	0	0	0	0	0
	Hail	0	0	0	0	0	0	0	0	0	0	0	0	0
	Freezing Rain	0	0	0	0	0	0	0	0	0	0	0	0	0
	Blowing Sand	0	0	0	0	0	0	0	0	0	0	0	0	0

Arbor. While there, he was inspired by a visit from Buckminster Fuller, who opened his eyes "to the power of intelligent design." After Ann Arbor, Gordon Bunschaft hired him at Skidmore, Owings and Merrill back in New York, but the large office environment had no appeal for young Van der Ryn. He left immediately for California. "Follow your bliss," he quotes from the popular author and historian Joseph Campbell.

After landing a teaching position at Berkeley he was to hold for 33 years, Van der Ryn began building experimental structures with his students. In 1968 he founded the Farallones Institute with a group of hands-on biologists, engineers, builders, and architects. Its mission was to conduct research and education in appropriate technology and address concerns about the deteriorating world environment. When Governor Edmund G. "Jerry" Brown

named him to the post of state architect in 1975, Van der Ryn launched the Energy Efficient State Building Program. Later, in 1978, he formed a private practice with Peter Calthorpe, his teammate at the state office. Scott Matthews, another of the Bateson team, went with them.

Farallones became the Ecological Design Institute (EDI) in 1995. EDI continues the multidisciplinary teamwork principle. The institute designs buildings, building systems, site and community planning, infrastructure design, and educational programs. The central goal of EDI is to bring beauty and ecology into everyday living.

In his private architectural practice, Van der Ryn has fostered connections with groups of people whose vision was consistent with sustainable design practices. Working with these communities, he has designed a number of "Eco-villages" including the San Francisco Zen Center, the

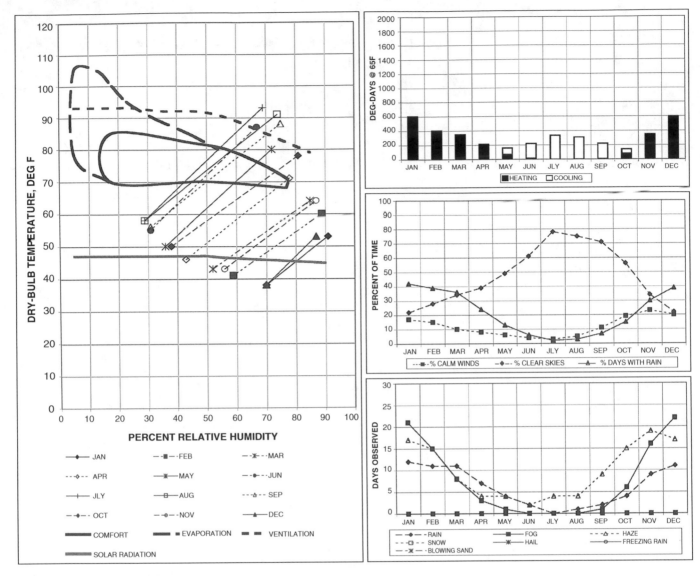

Figure 11.5 Climate analysis graphics.

Lindisfarne Association, and the Ojai Foundation school. The Real Goods Trading Corporation showroom north of San Francisco, the Klein Residence, and an educational program for San Domenico School are among EDI's latest accomplishments. Sim Van der Ryn is the author or coauthor of five books, including *Sustainable Communities* (with Peter Calthorpe) and *Ecological Design* (with Stuart Cowan).

Peter Calthorpe was born in England and grew up in Coral Gables, Florida. He studied at the Yale Graduate School of Architecture but left the program to pursue his personal interests in ecology and community planning. In 1968, Calthorpe became director of design at the Farallones Institute. Moving on with Van der Ryn, he was a primary designer on the California State Office team for the Bateson Building and in 1978 formed a private prac-

tice partnership with Van der Ryn. Calthorpe Associates was established in 1983 to focus primarily on planning issues. His work now includes diverse projects in various-scale settings and many countries. Calthorpe is the author of several books, including the aforementioned *Ecological Design* (1986, with Sim Van der Ryn) and *The Next American Metropolis: Ecology, Community, and the American Dream* (1993).

Philosophy

Anthropologist and philosopher Gregory Bateson (1904–1980) had become a close friend and influential mentor of Sim Van der Ryn while both were teaching at the University of California at Berkeley. At the 1981 commemoration of the building in Bateson's name one year after his death, Van der Ryn spoke at length about the

Sacramento, California

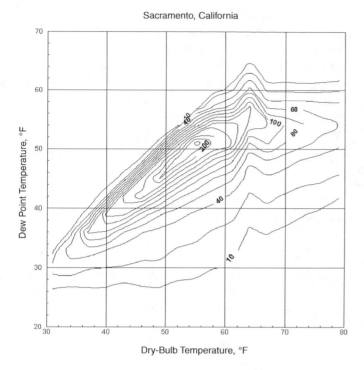

Figure 11.6 Bin data distribution for Sacramento. Concentric areas of graph indicate the number of hours per year that weather conditions normally occur in this climate. Similar to elevation readings on topographic maps, highest frequency occurrences of weather are at the center peaks of the graph. (Data sources: *Engineering Weather Data, typical meteorological year (TMY) data from the National Climatic Data Center, and the* ASHRAE Weather Data Viewer *from the American Society of Heating, Refrigerating and Air-Conditioning Engineers.*).

important influences of his friend's work. The thinking behind the Bateson Building deserves a slight detour through some of Gregory Bateson's contributions.

Gregory Bateson pioneered the field of visual anthropology with Margaret Mead. He taught at several institutions and eventually became a regent of the University of California. Along the way he became accomplished as a philosopher, naturalist, and writer. His work incorporated cybernetics, systems theory, psychiatry, evolution, genetics, communication, and meta-thinking: the science of science, thinking about thinking, and the nature of nature. His books include *Steps to an Ecology of Mind* (1971) and *Mind and Nature* (1979).

Bateson was concerned with systems as patterns and with meta-patterns, the patterns that connect other patterns. He saw a need to shift from outdated old world views, from first-order knowledge about things to a new understanding about the interconnectedness of all things, from parts to the whole, from structure to process, from entities to networks, and from rigid truths to inclusive approximation. Above all, Gregory Bateson wished to illu-

minate the idea that everything is whole and that humanity is the "pattern that connects."

Intent

Sim Van der Ryn interpreted one of Bateson's last personal comments to him as inspirational to the design of the state office building. The comment had to do with "sensitivity to differences." To Van der Ryn, these differences are what produce flow, and in architecture this flow is about the connectedness between buildings and people in a natural environment. The Bateson Building would be a container of flows and a network of connections.

Beyond the philosophical directive, this stated intention gave the design team some tangible goals. All of them are statements about systems integration, mirroring Bateson's assertions about connected systems in a literal but equally idealistic way. Public space, for example, would be the building focus and would connect it to the public network of the campus. Flows of energy, light, and sound were given clarity, and their management was to be tuned to occupant comfort, health, and productivity. Interconnectedness became a theme for both connecting systems of the building together and for meshing the building into a coherent Sacramento capitol campus.

CRITICAL TECHNICAL ISSUES

Inherent

Office workplaces are discussed as a typology in the introduction to Chapter 6. The Bateson Building's specific requirements reflect the practicalities of a state-owned facility. Flexibility was especially important to the Department of General Services because the users of the building were likely to change several times and require adaptation to their specific agency's incoming workforce. Most changes of occupancy occur only with a new owner, but not so here with state ownership.

Other concerns mention the preference for stairs and tie this to the four-story limit on building height. On-site parking was prohibited. A ratio of 20 percent fixed partition space to 80 percent flexible open office plan was suggested. Enclosure and security, clarity of circulation, and other typical requirements generated the criteria.

Finally, the state wanted a building that addressed long-term costs. An estimate placed the building cost over its life cycle at only 8 percent of the total expense. Personnel salaries were pegged at more than 90 percent. The state wanted this equation optimized by provision of worker-friendly offices with amenities like natural light and view, individual environmental controls, and acoustical planning for privacy and quiet. This level of occupant comfort also meant that energy systems would somehow have to be both satisfyingly generous and efficiently stingy.

Contextual

California's Title 24 state energy standards were established for the Office Building Program after 1975. These set an energy reduction goal of 50 percent (down to 19,900 Btu/ft^2 yr or 6042-W/m^2 yr) for state office buildings. These guidelines were included in the 1977 program document, "A Competition for the Design of an Energy Efficient Office Building," as a separate document entitled "Building Value: Energy Design Guidelines for State Buildings," dated January 12, 1976. Interestingly, both documents included forewords signed by Sim Van der Ryn while he was still state architect. Stage I entries for the competition were due May 27, 1977, and Stage II entries were due in July 1977. In fact, Van der Ryn was listed as a member of the competition jury along with Director of General Services Leonard Grimes, California Energy Commissioner Alan Pasternak, architect William Caudill of CRS, and no less than Fred Dubin of Dubin-Bloome engineers, who was Louis Kahn's mechanical consultant for so many years.

Figure 11.7 Exterior view.

The 105-page competition booklet included major sections on the competition rules (18 pages), existing conditions (16 pages), climate (interestingly, the largest section, at 22 pages), the Capitol Area (6 pages), and the energy program (10 pages). It specified not only the format of entry drawings, but also the inclusion of cost estimates and energy conservation schemes. The Building Value reference supplement, in contrast, dealt more with state-of-the-art energy conservation design methods, the cost value of worker productivity, life cycle cost analysis, and categories of energy use in buildings.

Intentional

Van der Ryn's commitment to interconnected flow and sensitivity to differences established metaphysical goals for how the building would connect with nature and the laws of physics. The program guidelines set up a decidedly more humanistic and experiential approach to networks by weaving the office-building program into a pedestrian format for the capitol campus.

APPROPRIATE SYSTEMS

Precedent

Deep-plan atrium buildings evolved from the first attempts to crowd large buildings together in dense urban settings where meandering plans and extended forms were impractical. Before the advent of mechanical services, the atrium was needed to provide light and air to interior rooms of a building. Later, the atrium became a social focus in highly serviced buildings. Hotels frequently use atriums to unite vertical circulation and servicing with aesthetic grandeur. The energy crisis of the early 1970s brought back the atrium as a thermal buffer space and daylighting strategy.

Site

"Site" at the Bateson Building happens at the campus or village scale. The building itself reaches curb to curb, except for important entry courts on the east and west sides. At the street periphery, trees and landscape elements are used to soften the face of the giant block and blend in with the capitol campus scheme. Inside, offices form a rectangular donut, 80 ft (24.4 m) thick around the central court. At the core is the skylit atrium, serving as public space, lunchroom, employee lounge, and passageway connecting a city park on the east to an urban plaza on the west.

Capturing the residual area of the site within the donut enclosure of program space is the raison d'être of the Bateson Building. This strategy secures a comfortable space for people to gather and move through, provides a high level of passive climate control, and contains some of the mechanical system components. Most significant perhaps, the giant atrium acts as an outdoor room, weaving the Bateson Building into the village scale plan for the capitol area's redevelopment.

Two entryways are staggered pinwheel fashion toward the southwest and northeast corners of the atrium. Outside, small courtyards on those corners of the site meet the crosswalks and lead into the walk-up lobbies through skeletal extensions of the building's open concrete frame. Up and down the building are several terraces, including a large dining deck at the second level that dominates the northeast entry court below.

Structure

The desire for a massive concrete structure grew from the intention of capturing cold night air in Sacramento's desertlike climate and harvesting it as cooling energy during occupied hours. Resisting the notion of mass was the need for daylight to flow into and through the building. Resolution was achieved by restricting the vertical structure to an open frame and using double-tee concrete beam floor spans.

The building rests on concrete piers designed for soft soil. The poor load-bearing quality of soil on the site is related to the town's history of flooding. After a devastating flood in 1862, thousands of cubic yards of soil were brought into "Old Town" Sacramento in an effort to raise grade elevations by 12 ft (3.7 m) and avoid future washouts. This soil was mostly dredged from the river and is formed from decomposed river rock and granites. It generally consists of silt, sand, and expansive clays.

Precast concrete columns are set on the piers, and beams are poured in place to produce fixed connections. The floors are double-tee concrete beams with a finish concrete topping. The structure is left exposed to both the interior and the exterior.

The geometry of the structure is set by the establishment of a grid of "ladders," acting as a three-dimensional portal frame, about 14 ft (4.3 m) wide. This ladder frame provides lateral bracing and rigidity. Eight sets of these ladders run from east to west through the structure. They start at the outside walls, divide the office space, and border the atrium. Between the ladder frames are seven bays of approximately 35.5 ft (10.8 m) spanned by the concrete tees. Across the structure from east to west, the building is divided into 12 spans of about 24.25 ft (7.4 m).

Envelope

Daylighting and shading were the keys to envelope design. Insulated glass in aluminum framing covers all four façades from the bottom of the concrete tee structure to a short laminated-wood knee wall. To avoid intense direct solar gain in the dry climate and still maximize indirect daylighting, operable exterior canvas shades are used on the east and west elevations. These bright orange translucent shades are motorized and held in place with steel cables fixed at their bases. A computer-based automation system controls their positions. Interior metal blinds on all four orientations allow for occupant control and act as small-scale light shelves to reflect light off the white painted concrete ceilings and move it deeper into the interior areas. The south elevation is protected by having the glass pulled back one bay inside the ladder frames and covering the outside frames with a trellis of concrete beams. North elevation glass is left unshaded and faces a taller building. In addition, all four borders of the site are planted with trees to provide pedestrian shade and some solar protection for the building envelope.

Exterior wall areas behind the 3 ft (914 mm) high laminated-wood spandrels are framed in steel studs and filled with R-19 insulation. The roof is also insulated to R-19.

Numerous setbacks and terraces are carved into the city-block-sized structural grid. This allows for pedestrian-friendly entries on the northeast and southwest corners. It also softens the form of the building and adds human-scale spaces for both occupants and downtown pedestrians.

The roof of the atrium is clustered with numerous components. First, there are the grand south-facing skylights, equipped with operating vertical louvers that can track toward the sun in winter and shade away from it in summer. Next are the north-sloped skylights to provide smaller apertures and cooler light. These are most effective in the clear-sky Sacramento summers, when light is more abundant and smaller daylight apertures will capture plenty of light without introducing direct solar gain. Completing the sawtoothed arrangement of the atrium roof are 2000 ft^2 (185 m^2) of active solar water heating collectors. All of these components are pushed to the visibly hidden center of the roof area and do nothing to increase the apparent height of the building above the four-story offices. Around the edges of the skylights are airshafts and fans for ventilation.

Mechanical

In organizing the comfort systems in this building, priority is appropriately given to passive systems. Mechanical HVAC systems are, however, integrated with the overall energy scheme by using mechanical ventilation modes to strategically capture, store, and distribute passive heating and cooling. The environment provides most of the energy needed; the mechanical systems are set up to channel the energy flows.

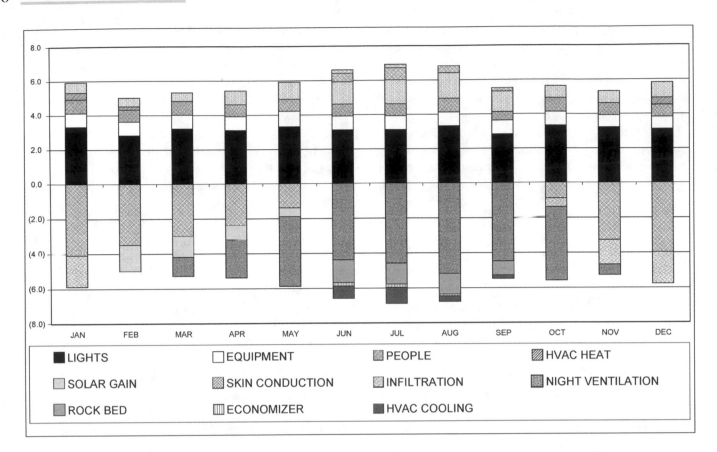

Figure 11.8 Monthly performance estimates for the Bateson Building. (*Adapted from Stein and Reynolds,* Mechanical and Electrical Equipment for Buildings, *8th ed.*)

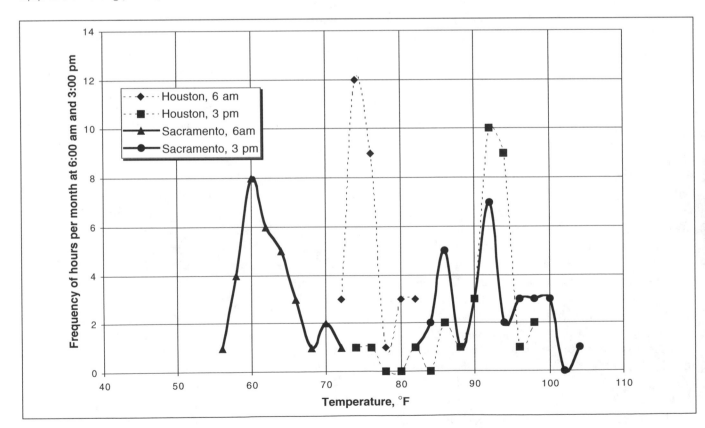

Figure 11.9 July temperatures in Sacramento and Houston.

Cooling of the building relies primarily on night ventilation. This passive strategy provides about 90 percent of the annual cooling required. Figure 11.9 shows temperatures for the coolest and warmest hours of an average July day in Sacramento and corresponding July data for Houston, Texas. In Sacramento the arid climate reradiates accumulated daytime heat very quickly to the clear night sky. Consequently, there are 250 hours per month of nighttime temperature below 65°F versus 494 hours per month of daytime temperatures over 65°F. If temperature is accounted for, as well as hours of occurrence, there are 1235 degree-hours below 65°F and 7754 degree-hours above 65°F. This degree-hour data predicts heating and cooling requirements from temperature loads just as degree-days data does, but at a finer level of detail that does not disguise daily temperature fluctuations. Degree-hour data is used predominantly in calculating cooling loads. Notice that in humid climates like Houston, where there are no July hours below 65°F, nighttime ventilation cooling is ineffective.

By using the mechanical system to flush the building interior with cooler night air for those 250 Sacramento hours below 65°F, enough heat can be absorbed by the exposed concrete floors and ceilings to carry the building through the following day. This can be visualized as a battery that is charged with heat by day and discharged by cooling it at night. One cubic foot of concrete will store about 30 Btu of sensible heat for every degree it is cooled or warmed relative to room temperature. The exposed double-tee ceiling and concrete deck floors at the Bateson Building continually exchange this energy with the indoor air and its occupants. Two 660-ton rock beds in insulated basements below the atrium floor serve as additional remote thermal storage that can be either charged or harvested by circulating air directly through them. If the rock beds alone were charged to 10°F below room temperature, they would store about 400 ton-hours of cooling capacity. Figure 11.8 shows that nighttime ventilation, along with the rock bed storage system and some daytime ventilation on cool days, provides an estimated 95 percent of the annual cooling needs.

Direct-gain passive heating is a much less important concern because of the unavoidable high levels of heat produced inside the compact building by people, lights, and equipment. These internal gains offset most temperature-driven heat loss from the offices through the envelope and by ventilation, even in the coldest months. Mechanical heat in the occupied offices is required only for cold morning start-up. The nonconditioned atrium is another matter, however. As a transitional space, its primary source of heat is solar gain through the three rows of south-facing clerestory skylights. Warm air is kept at floor level by several canvas tubes with fans at the bottom to pull strati-

Figure 11.10 View of the atrium.

fied heat down from the atrium ceiling. Exposed mass in the atrium floor helps stabilize temperatures, and from November to February the rock beds can be utilized to store heat for long periods of time.

Steam and chilled water for backup mechanical servicing come from a capitol district energy plant nearby. Variable-air-volume distribution fans are used for cooling in tandem with hydronic reheat coils at each zone for heating. Outside air for ventilation can be moistened and precooled by evaporative spray air washers. Domestic hot water is provided primarily by 2000 ft^2 (185 m^2) of solar collectors on the atrium roof. Finally, operation of the entire building is coordinated by a computerized automation system.

Interior

Interior space is organized around the structural frame as a series of four rings. At the outermost edge are rooms with exposure to daylight. These are entered through the second ring, a double-loaded circulation corridor defined by the structural ladder frame. An interior ring of office space comes next, with daylight exposure to the atrium skylights. Circulation makes up the innermost fourth ring, aligning a continuous walkway balcony with elevators hidden behind suggestively prominent stairways. Finally, there is the central atrium court.

The basic scheme is interrupted at the ground floor by generous entries on the east and west. Wide lobbies connect the atrium to exterior canopy extensions of the concrete building frame. These two-story open frames clearly identify the passageway into and through the building. Inside the atrium, finishes match the exterior landscaping. Brick tile floors and wood benches are set with bright orange destratification tubes and deep blue mechanical shafts. Balcony railings are made of 3 ft (914 mm) high solid laminated-wood panels identical to the exterior wall infill spandrels.

Finishes in the office space include acoustical baffles suspended in the precast double-tee ceilings. Most of the partitions between offices and the atrium are glazed to admit illumination from the skylights.

INTEGRATION HIGHLIGHTS

Physical

- The atrium serves both as a common space and for protected but unconditioned circulation.
- The double-loaded corridor is also a mechanical service spine for the conditioned spaces.

Visual

- The atrium is treated as an outdoor space to visually establish it as a public link between the park and the urban plaza.
- Landscape elements and tree plantings are shared with surrounding blocks to create a pedestrian campus atmosphere.
- Repetition of natural materials and bright colors lends an informal atmosphere to outdoor and atrium spaces.

Performance

- Exposing the concrete tee structure provides internal thermal mass and allows for 10.5 ft (3.2 m) ceilings without increasing the height of the building.
- Open-frame concrete column and beam elements allow free flow of daylight.

- The total integration of mechanical and passive systems provides, harvests, and controls natural energy flows.
- The active shading systems and personal control of window blinds integrates the benefits of light, shade, privacy, and view without sacrificing performance.

DISCUSSION

The Bateson Building was among the first of a generation of structures designed in response to the 1970s energy crisis. Like so many similar buildings that explored new combinations of technology, it has had its problems. A year or so after occupancy, complaints about the indoor air quality and claims of sickness caused by working in the building led to an in-depth investigation. About 80 percent of the variable-air-volume control boxes proved to be malfunctioning. Consequently, insufficient air was being delivered to the occupants and indoor pollutant concentrations could have affected their health. The problem was apparently made worse by a rushed completion schedule that moved people in before some of the volatile chemicals in the new materials and installation work had time to air out. Formaldehyde, for example, a principal irritant found in many fabrics and plastics, was reportedly introduced at the last minute by an indiscrimate choice of office partition systems.

The integrated passive schemes could not be blamed for these problems. In fact, as long as the building was in the night-ventilation summer mode, indoor air quality problems did not become critical. When the building was sealed up for its first season of cool weather, however, the reduced outdoor air quantity became all too apparent. The problems encountered were attributable to the conventional mechanical system and the rushed final completion for occupancy.

The first generation of Green architecture began with ideas about energy conservation, passive systems, and economic benefits. The Bateson Building is one of the predecessors of the second Green generation, a bridge from the first experiments. Founded on the ideals stimulated by Gregory Bateson himself, as well as the principles and goals of its chief designers, the building is a prominent example of systems thinking, of interconnectedness, of mindful intentions, and thus of integration in the greenest sense.

27

NEDERLANDSCHE MIDDENSTANDSBANK, 1979–1987

Amsterdam, The Netherlands
ALBERTS & VAN HUUT

DESCRIPTION

Organic functionalism is the key to this large banking complex in south Amsterdam. The building is intended to provide a friendly and healthy working environment full of light, water, sun, plants, and art. Not incidentally, Nederlansche Middenstandbank (NMB) was the world's most energy-efficient building at the time of its comple-

tion. The complex consumes less than one-tenth the energy of its old headquarters and one-fifth that of another new bank in the same neighborhood. A few years after its completion, the new home had transformed the institution's image from stuffy to progressive and allegedly doubled its business. It also captured and maintained the 2500-person workforce's hearty endorsement and lowered absenteeism by 15 percent. All this was accomplished at a cost of just 3 percent over conventional examples of other contemporary buildings in Holland.

Ten rambling, medieval-style office towers slope inward from the street. Their brick walls and operable windows surround small interconnected floor plates. Visual scale is reduced by varying the height of each mini-tower. The narrow depth and fragmented shape of the office floors allow for full penetration of daylight. At the towers' base is a 301,280 ft² (27,976 m²) compound of parking garages and storefronts surrounded by pedestrian plazas and gardens. Circulation is organized along a midlevel corridor resting 16.4 ft (5 m) high on top of the podium. This marble-floored corridor, an interior street, meanders 1066 ft (325 m) across the 10.8 acre (4.3 hectare) site, connecting the office blocks, opening into their full-height skylit atriums, and tying together their open stairwells.

Figure 11.11 Overview of NMB. (*Photograph courtesy of Gary J. Coates.*)

TABLE 11.3   Fact Sheet

Project	**Building Name**	Nederlandsche Middenstandsbank
	Client	NMB, now International Netherlands Group (ING) Bank
	City	South Amsterdam, The Netherlands
	Lat/Long/Elev	52.3 N 4.8 E / 7 ft (2.1 m)
Team	**Architect**	Alberts & Van Huut
	Structure	Raadgevend Ingenieutsboreau Aronsohn
	Services	Technisch Adviesbureau Treffers Baarn
	Interiors	Theo Crosby, Pentagram Design Ltd.
	Building Physics	Adviesbureau Peutz & Associes
	Contractor	Bouwcombinatie
General	**Time Line**	1979–1982 design phase, August 1983 construction begins, April 1987 completion.
	Floor Area	538,193 ft² (49,975 m²).
	Cost	Total Costs for green technologies: $865,200 (1996). Total Costs: $53.8 million (1996). Cost/SF: $100 (1996) ($200/SF with furniture, fixtures, and equipment 1996). Site Acquisition Costs: $4.9 million (1996). Site and Building Construction Costs: $49 million (1996) average.
Site	**Site**	10.75 acres (43,500 m²), of which 7.2 acres (29,000 m²), or 67%, are built on.
	Parking	750 cars, 300,000 ft² (28,000 m²).
Structure	**Stories**	Six to nine floors of 9.1 ft (2.8 m) typical height above two parking/service levels.
	Plan	Ten pentagram plan towers connected by a 1066 ft (325 m) long S-shaped pedestrian street, all resting above a two-level podium of parking and service spaces. Each of the ten slanted wall towers is organized around a central light well.
	Foundation	Not published.
	Vertical Members	Precast concrete panels of 7.1 in. (180 mm) thickness.
	Horizontal Spans	Poured-in-place concrete slabs of 11.8 in. (300 mm) thickness.
Envelope	**Glass and Glazing**	Double glazing with automatic external louver sun blind and interior roller blind. Transom windows are operable by occupant.
	Skylights	Pyramidal glass.
	Cladding	4.3 in. (110 mm) molded brick exterior on precast concrete lintels, 3.4 in. (8.5 mm) rock wool, 7.1 in. (180 mm) precast concrete.
	Roof	Seamed metal.
HVAC	**Equipment**	Two gas/diesel-driven 450 kW generators produce electricity and heat.
	Cooling Type	Two 206-ton absorption cooling systems running on heat from electrical generators. One electrically driven 267-ton chiller provides backup.
	Distribution	Vertical shafts.
	Duct Type	Not determined.
	Vertical Chases	Located in core of each tower.
Interior	**Partitions**	Open plan office spaces.
	Finishes	Artwork and crafted installations.
	Vertical Circulation	21 elevators in total complex.
	Furniture	By client.
	Lighting	Custom accent lighting and ambient lighting in public zones.

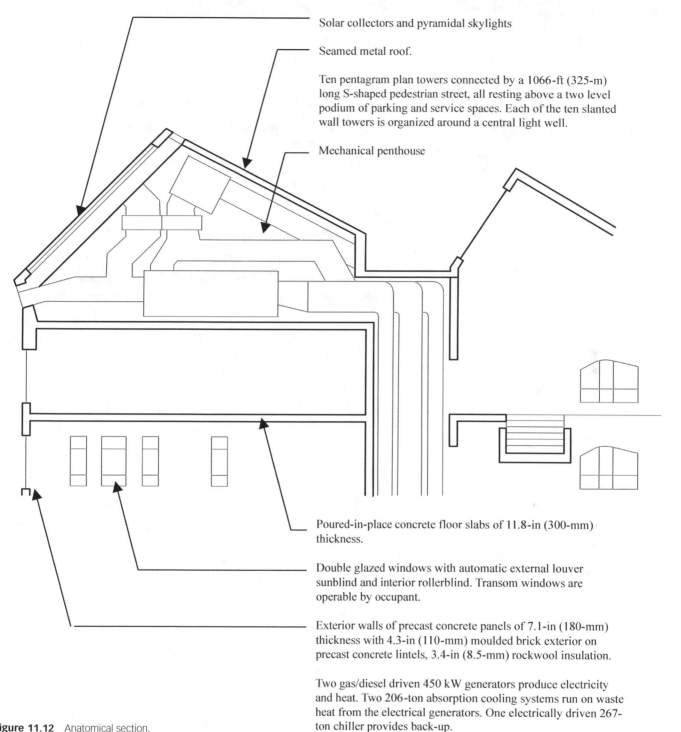

Solar collectors and pyramidal skylights

Seamed metal roof.

Ten pentagram plan towers connected by a 1066-ft (325-m) long S-shaped pedestrian street, all resting above a two level podium of parking and service spaces. Each of the ten slanted wall towers is organized around a central light well.

Mechanical penthouse

Poured-in-place concrete floor slabs of 11.8-in (300-mm) thickness.

Double glazed windows with automatic external louver sunblind and interior rollerblind. Transom windows are operable by occupant.

Exterior walls of precast concrete panels of 7.1-in (180-mm) thickness with 4.3-in (110-mm) moulded brick exterior on precast concrete lintels, 3.4-in (8.5-mm) rockwool insulation.

Two gas/diesel driven 450 kW generators produce electricity and heat. Two 206-ton absorption cooling systems run on waste heat from the electrical generators. One electrically driven 267-ton chiller provides back-up.

Figure 11.12 Anatomical section.

A walk along this pedestrian avenue passes theaters, large conference rooms, shops, a library, and four restaurants. Works of art are designed and built into the public spaces at every turn, along with plants and "flow sculpture" channels of water streaming through the building from the rainwater collection system.

At the top of each office tower is a combined skylight, mechanical room, and solar water heating system. The mechanical services work with the open shaft of the atrium towers to provide heat recovery ventilation in the winter and stack-effect exhaust in the summer with a cooling assist from night ventilation.

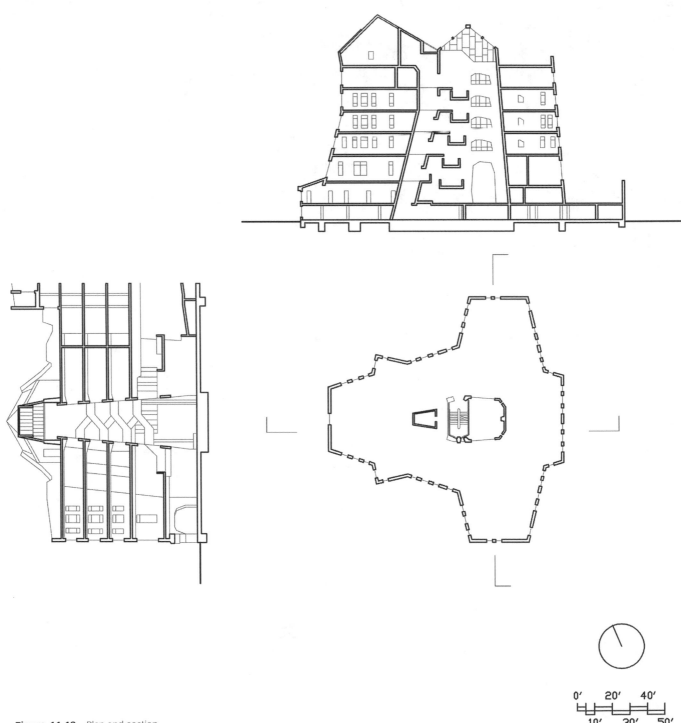

Figure 11.13 Plan and section.

0'   20'   40'
10'   30'   50'

PROGRAM

Client

At the beginning of this project in 1978, Nederlandsche Middenstandsbank (NMB) was the fourth largest bank in Holland. Having outgrown its old headquarters, the NMB executive board appointed an internal working group from within its real estate development subsidiary, MOB, to oversee the design and construction of a new complex.

The MOB committee worked in tandem with a strongly empowered workers' council. In the Netherlands and several other European countries, such worker groups have authority to vote on many managerial decisions. Furthermore, building codes are written to enhance the quality of the working environment—amenities such as daylight and natural ventilation are mandated. The council's oversight even included a voice in the selection of the bank's architect and design team, the new bank location, and details of all design decisions affecting the work environment.

Brief

Collectively, the bank team laid out its aspirations for the building with intentions of both changing the bank's public image and providing a progressive workplace. Beyond elevated standards of efficiency and flexibility, the new headquarters would integrate art, natural materials, sunlight, water, and quiet ambience. The workers' council had its own set of criteria. Its members principally asked for inclusion of health considerations, such as favoring pleasant, open stairways and fewer elevators. They also emphasized contact with the outdoors and abundant interior daylight.

After interviewing and receiving proposals also from Herman Hertzberger, Haans van Beck, and Ton Alberts, NMB and its workers' council decided on Alberts & Van Huut. They agreed that a collaborative multidisciplinary team would be formed and required that all design decisions be understood and processed unanimously. As the team was brought together with the usual expertise of engineering consultants and construction management, it was to include two special elements. The first was a building physics consultant. The second, surprisingly enough, was a group of 22 artists who were to collaborate in all phases of the design and construction.

Site

A location 10 km south of central Amsterdam was chosen for the project. The vicinity, known as the "Bijlmermeer" district, was dominated by 1960s high-density mid-rise housing, and many of the bank's staff lived nearby. The Amsterdam Poort shopping center is located on the immediate south side of the site. Most of the other surrounding structures are office buildings. In general, the area had acquired a mediocre reputation and was in deterioration. Finally, as one might expect in Holland, the building site had to be reclaimed from rising water. For NMB, this was accomplished by filling an existing lake.

Climate

The cool, wet climate of Amsterdam affects a large office building like NMB differently than it does a small structure like Benthem & Crouwel's Experimental House at Almere (See Chapter 9 for case study #20 and climate synopsis). Heat gain from internal loads in buildings like NMB are apt to require mechanical cooling in some zones, even during periods of very cold weather. On the other hand, it is unlikely that small buildings in Amsterdam would ever need more cooling than an open window would provide. Refer to the section on surface-load-dominated versus internal-load-dominated buildings and their respective balance points in Chapter 3.

With extreme temperatures below 10°F (−12°C), there are periods of the year when all areas with perimeter exposure in any Amsterdam building will need heat (see the discussion of thermal zoning in Chapter 3). Especially where generous areas of glass are used to achieve high daylighting levels, the outside perimeter of the building will loose more heat than is being produced by people, lights and equipment located in the same general floor area. Deep-plan buildings, however, often have interior zones away from outside walls and thus have no envelope exposure. The only thermal sensitivity these internal zones have is the load incurred by replacing exhausted indoor air with outside ventilation air. Consequently, deep-plan buildings frequently have some thermal zones that require cooling regardless of outdoor temperature or internal loads.

Deep-plan buildings sometimes have perimeter zones in the heating mode and interior zones in the cooling mode at the same time. Heating and cooling can also happen simultaneously in large surface-load-dominated buildings—for example, if solar radiation is overheating the sunlit orientation while the shaded side of the building is still underheated.

INTENTION

Design Team

Ton Alberts (1927–1999) was born in Belgium and studied at the Higher Technical School and then at the Ecole des Beaux-Arts, Paris. He finished his education at the

Academy of Architecture in Amsterdam and taught there for more than 20 years. In 1963 he established his architectural practice, Alberts Architectenbureau. In the fall of 1993, Alberts was appointed to the Erasmus Chair of Dutch Civilization and Culture at Harvard.

Max Van Huut was born in Indonesia in 1947. He moved to Holland at the age of ten and, like Alberts, later studied at the Higher Technical School before attending the Academy of Architecture in Amsterdam. Van Huut became a partner in Alberts's practice in 1987. Together, Alberts and Van Huut completed some 40 town planning projects and about 50 multifamily residential works including more than 10,000 units. Their work also included hundreds of individual houses and several office buildings, as well as some 30 retail and institutional facilities.

Philosophy

Ton Alberts suffered from poor health in his early adult years and eventually turned to alternative and esoteric practices in search of a cure. This experience led him to a nature-centered principle of beliefs and ultimately to his life pursuit in design. Both Alberts and his partner, Van Huut, labeled their ultimate goal "organic functionalism." Elements of the organic philosophical stance have been reinstituted through popular culture in recent years by revitalized interest in alternative medicine and "New Age" thinking. Although the success of Alberts & van Huut's theories as applied to architectural practice are undeniable, the particulars of their fringe attitudes frequently invited criticism.

TABLE 11.4 Normal Climate Data for Amsterdam

		Jan.	Feb.	Mar.	Apr.	May	June	July	Aug.	Sept.	Oct.	Nov.	Dec.	Year
Temperature	Degree-Days Heating	840	778	695	548	342	197	117	106	215	421	628	768	5663
	Degree-Days Cooling	0	0	0	0	6	19	32	28	3	0	0	0	83
	Extreme High	57	61	70	80	84	90	90	93	83	77	64	59	93
	Normal High	41	42	48	53	61	66	69	70	64	57	48	44	55
	Normal Average	38	37	43	47	54	59	62	62	58	51	44	40	50
	Normal Low	34	32	37	40	46	52	55	55	51	46	39	36	44
	Extreme Low	3	6	18	25	30	37	39	32	36	30	20	7	3
Humidity	Dew Point	35	33	38	40	46	52	56	56	53	47	41	37	44
	Max % RH	91	91	92	90	87	89	90	91	93	93	92	92	91
	Min % RH	86	79	74	66	62	66	68	65	72	78	85	88	74
	% Days With Rain	73	56	71	64	64	66	65	62	68	72	75	77	67
	Rain Inches	3	2	4	2	2	2	3	2	3	4	3	3	32
Sky	% Overcast Days	42	36	35	25	21	23	19	15	21	27	35	41	28
	% Clear Days	7	12	9	10	8	6	6	9	8	7	6	5	8
Wind	Prevailing Direction	S	E	WSW	N	N	W	W	W	SSW	S	SSW	SSW	W
	Speed, Knots	11	11	15	10	9	9	10	10	10	9	13	12	11
	Percent Calm	0	1	1	1	1	1	1	1	1	1	1	1	1
Days Observed	Rain	22	17	21	19	19	20	20	19	21	22	23	23	245
	Fog	18	19	19	17	18	18	17	20	20	20	19	20	225
	Haze	13	17	17	17	18	17	15	16	16	15	11	12	185
	Snow	6	7	4	2	0	0	0	0	0	0	3	5	27
	Hail	1	1	1	0	0	0	0	0	0	1	1	1	7
	Freezing Rain	1	0	0	0	0	0	0	0	0	0	0	1	2
	Blowing Sand	0	0	0	0	0	0	0	0	0	0	0	0	1

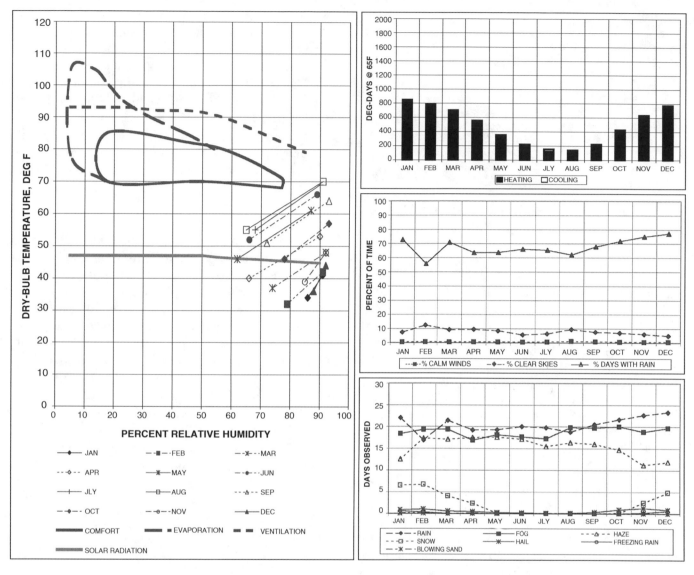

Figure 11.14 Climate analysis graphics.

Intent

Alberts believed that NMB, like other banks, should exist to serve society. He worked to provide for both the public and the individual through "friendliness, warmth, and aesthetics." The notions of organic functionalism he adopted from Rudolf Steiner emphasized the personal experience of space through its geometry and materials. Right angles are not part of this naturalistic expressionism. Nor is the total separation between indoor environment and natural surroundings. These morphogenic principles of organic design give precedence to discovering form in nature. The idea is that natural solutions will always produce an effective result through participation in the environment. Artificial solutions, on the other hand, will always require more and more maintenance for an ever-diminishing

return. The common example cited is organic farming versus intensive agricultural practices.

Starting perhaps with D'Arcy Wentworth Thompson (1860–1948) and his book, *On Growth and Form* (1945), morphological thinking gained modern followers through the growth of environmental movements. In the work of Alberts and Van Huut, the imitation of nature is used to determine and configure the functional systems of a building. In their case, however, organic functionalism goes beyond employing biological processes to produce spontaneous form. Their design for NMB is certainly a statement about their social program of placing people at the center of design. But it also ventures into sacred geometry, number magic and mystical assertions about the curative powers of architectural form. References to the pentangle

Amsterdan, Netherlands

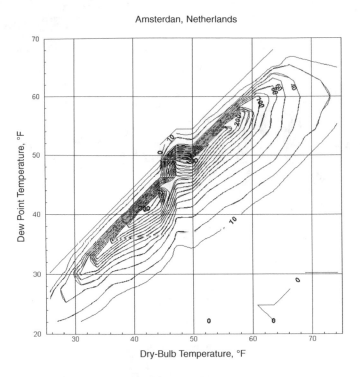

Figure 11.15   Bin data distribution for Amsterdam. Concentric areas of graph indicate the number of hours per year that weather conditions normally occur in this climate. Similar to elevation readings on topographic maps, highest frequency occurrences of weather are at the center peaks of the graph. (Data sources: *Engineering Weather Data, typical meteorological year (TMY) data from the National Climatic Data Center, and the* ASHRAE *Weather Data Viewer from the American Society of Heating, Refrigerating and Air-Conditioning Engineers.*)

for example, border on the occult or at least the intrigue of alchemy. The five-sided figure and its internal corners of nine degrees are repeated in the complex wherever possible. On the other hand, similar fascinations with the pentagon can be found in the drawings of Leonardo da Vinci and Tyco Brae, in which an extended human figure is circumscribed by a pentangle with the planets at the five points and the moon centered anthropocentrically on the genitalia.

CRITICAL TECHNICAL ISSUES

Inherent

The project brief was cooperatively established by the corporate client and the bank staff, so both a top-down and a bottom-up philosophy were ingrained in the program. Such duality may pose questions about the potential differences between an energy-efficient building and one where worker comfort is top priority. This issue often becomes a choice between compact, efficient boxes that are introverted from the environment and rambling,

extroverted surface forms that open to light and air. Image also comes into the conversation. Would this design present a corporate image of a large and powerful institution, or would it be a human-scale village of office suites?

The new NMB complex would not only have to answer these internal questions, but would also have to provide its own service infrastructure. The existing parking and local amenities were insufficient to service the business of a large modern banking institution. Restaurants, shops, and other support services would have to be created.

Contextual

The ambitious scope of the program and its site on the fringe of Amsterdam's mid-rise urban fabric suggest that the bank would have a strong impact on the community. More than an infill project, the complex of new buildings would be a centerpiece among the existing nondescript structures. A strong social statement would be unavoidable.

NMB was shaping up as a small self-contained city. Given the size of the banking complex and its location among neighborhoods where many of the NMB staff lived, important questions of context arose. How would the development fit into the gray mid-rise neighborhood? How could it elevate the urban environment it was to occupy? Finally, with Alberts & Van Huut's organic expressionist ambitions, how would the resulting forms blend with the existing background structures?

Intentional

Alberts's intention of creating a warm and friendly, yet progressive, environment meshed well with the bank's desire to change its public image. But it created challenges as well. How could the scale of the large building program be broken down to a human level? How would organic form be compatible with program and technical requirements? Further, how would the design balance societal and individual friendliness with the needs and organization of a large corporate client?

APPROPRIATE SYSTEMS

Precedent

Although Alberts toured the Berlin Philharmonica with his client, and despite the visual resemblance of NMB to Antonio Gaudi's organic ultrabaroque examples like Casa Batlo, the precedents for this project are elsewhere. As a formal model, Alberts turned to the origins of his naturalistic beliefs and based the design directly on Rudolph Steiner's Goetheanum. There is a very close correspondence between the pentangle plan of the Goetheanum and that of the typical NMB office plate.

Rudolph Steiner (1861–1925) studied at the Vienna Technical College, where he absorbed the philosophies of Goethe and Nietzche. He was the founder of Anthroposophism, a belief founded on the of knowledge of human nature and the central role of humanity in the cosmos. Steiner later developed an architecture based on the alignment of science and nature. He produced few buildings, but is recognized for his design of the Goetheanum in Basel, Switzerland, and the campus of structures that still make up the anthroposoph compound there. Connections to the Goetheanum are strengthened by the fact that Alberts and Van Huut were practicing anthroposophs, as was the chairman of NMB and much of his staff.

Site

A great deal of design effort was invested in capturing private garden space off the main circulation spine. This was achieved by developing terraces above the parking garages and on the roofs of ground-level retail shops. There were also two large terrace-level gardens captured as centerpieces between groups of towers. They are covered with different soil types appropriate to the variety of gardens maintained. The east office blocks wrap around the Japanese Garden and the west towers make a corner at the Winter Garden. Similar attention is given to the one-third

of the site left as open space and devoted to public plazas surrounding the building.

The S-shaped internal corridor that connects all ten of the office blocks crosses over a small street off the main entrance façade from Hoogoorddreef Street. At this point the complex and its podium are divided into two halves. The five east side towers are connected 16.4 ft (5 m) above grade to the five west side towers by a three-level walkway bridging across the 65 ft (19.8 m) span. The walkway is an extension of the principal interior street and the interconnected stairways between the office blocks. Executive and employee entrances are located at the southwest corner of the complex. Parking for about 750 cars is buried within the large podium base.

Structure

From the ground up through the internal pedestrian street the building is supported on concrete columns. Vertical structure above the grand corridor level consists primarily of 7.1 in. (180 mm) precast concrete panel exterior walls. Internally, three continuous columns run up the open tower atriums to carry spans of the floor. The towers, elevator shafts, and fire stairs act as independent rigid structures. Floor spans are of 11.8 in. (300 mm) poured-in-place concrete slabs. They unite the vertical concrete panel boxes laterally into a stable structure.

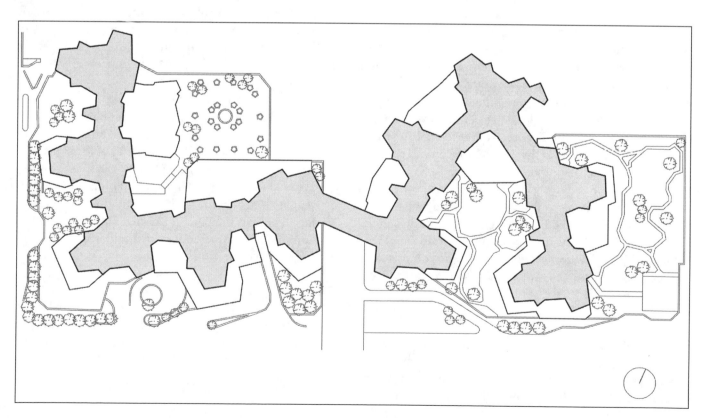

Figure 11.16 Site plan of the NMB complex.

A special condition occurs where the sloping exterior walls, with angles up to 14 degrees from vertical, produce a horizontal thrust at their base. The transition takes place at a point where loads change from uniformly distributed concrete panel walls above to point load columns below. This is nicely resolved by a forest of tapered and angled columns positioned below the load-bearing concrete panels and canting visibly through much of the public and open lobby space.

Envelope

The overall configuration of the complex is broken up to reduce its scale and to provide easy penetration of daylight. This strategy also aids the diffusion of noise and wind. Most exterior walls are fragmented, chamfered, and sloping. Two larger façades facing the main street are set at angles to deflect sound laterally rather than allow it to bounce back and forth in an urban noise canyon between buildings.

The bank's exterior cladding consists of 600,000 custom bricks in 59 different shapes and more t han 2 million standard bricks. Precast concrete lintels above the windows create horizontal banding patterns across all elevations. These bands are accentuated by carrying their lines through the brick coursing.

Each of the ten towers is capped by a glass roof that covers its air-handling equipment and atrium. The mechanical penthouse scheme is similar to the one used at Briarcliff House by Arup Associates (see case study # 8). The feature element is a repeated 1400 ft^2 (130 m^2) sloped skylight in the form of a pentagram-shaped window. Most of these skylights manage to face generally into the south sun, but a few are oriented more to the north.

Insulated glass windows are punched through 25 percent of the brick façade in a regular pattern. Each opening is spanned by a structural precast concrete lintel. Typically, windows are divided into three panels or "lites." The lower lites and the interior blinds are operable by office occupants. Metal louvers acting as small light shelves are located outside the upper transom lite. Shading of the two lower panels is handled by metal blinds suspended on the exterior of the window from below the top transom. These blinds are raised and lowered by automatic controls from a metal housing for the motor that also covers the blades of the sunshade until they are lowered.

Mechanical

Conservation at NMB begins with a total energy system. Two 450 kW generators are driven by engines that can run on either natural gas or fuel oil to produce electricity on-site. Typically, about 90 percent of the energy used by fuel-burning engines ends up as waste heat in the exhaust flue and only 10 percent is delivered as usable horsepower. But the waste heat can be recovered by cooling the engines with circulating water and then storing it in large hot water tanks. In Amsterdam's cool climate, there are plenty of opportunities to recycle the "total" energy consumed by the engines.

Thermal storage of waste heat is held in four 6,605 gal (25,000 l) water tanks of heavily insulated concrete buried beneath the main thermal plant. The 26,420 total gallons of water are charged primarily by cooling the generator engines, but also by recycling heat rejected from air-conditioning chillers and even elevator motors. Hydronic radiators located along the perimeter of the office spaces warm the rooms with hot water circulated from the storage tanks. Backup heating is provided by a 1000 kWh gas-fired boiler but is required only during repairs to the main system and in extremely cold weather.

Two 206 ton (730 kW) absorption cooling systems convert the high-temperature waste heat from cogeneration engines into cooling energy for summer days and for computer rooms. A conventional electrically driven 267 ton (940 kW) chiller provides emergency backup. Under Holland's 1980s building code, conventional cooling equipment could be provided only if it was required to offset heat gain from equipment loads.

Ceramic heat wheels are used to recover heat from exhaust air and simultaneously preheat incoming ventilation makeup air. Such systems usually save 90 percent of the energy normally lost to ventilation during cold weather. Vertical distribution of ventilation air is handled in each tower by a continuous chase at the center of the floor plate aligned against one narrow edge of the atrium.

Primary energy consumption for the office complex is 28,031 Btu/ft^2 (96 kWh/m^2). Another 4,380 Btu/ft^2 (15 kWh/m^2) is used by retail and residential buildings located across the plaza. The Dutch Research Establishment certified total NMB energy consumption levels at 32,411 Btu/ft^2 per year (111 kW/m^2 or 400 MJ/m^2). This is more than 90 percent below that of the bank's previous headquarters and slightly less than the 33,287 Btu/ft^2 (114kW/m^2) annual consumption of the previous record holder for energy efficiency, the Obayashi Gumi building in Japan.

Interior

The organizing principle of the individually small office floors is based on the bank's operational program. It provides for five work groups per floor. Each group includes a team of 8 to 10 people, so there are approximately 40 or 50 occupants on each typical office floor.

The marble floor pedestrian street is the connecting element of the complex. The winding pathway is filled with artworks designed for their special place in the

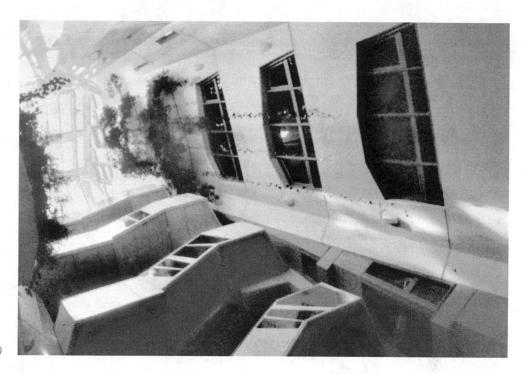

Figure 11.17 Interior view.
(Photograph courtesy of Gary J. Coates.)

building. Light sculptures and stained glass windows activate the penetration of light through the glass-roofed atrium at each office tower. Water runs through the space in "flow-form" sculptures and pools of collected rainwater for the interior plantscaping. Even the stair handrails are used as small streams and fountains. Plants are located in the public spaces to regulate humidity and cleanse the air. The greenery is part of the rainwater filtration system that cascades through the interior of the building. Open stairways are given more visual presence than elevators as an invitation to walk through the space rather than ride up and down. There are only 21 elevators in the entire complex.

Natural materials are used wherever hands touch the building and wherever finish surfaces are needed. Suspended ceilings, for example, are made of wood slats. Textured paints of different colors are used on concrete surfaces to give a sense of individual identity in each office tower. The shades of color are subtly varied according to exposure: cool tints for the sunny sides and warmer tints in shade.

TECHNICAL INTEGRATION HIGHLIGHTS

Physical

- Circulation space also serves requirements for public space.
- Garage roof terraces separate the public plaza from circulation routes of the bank staff.

- Removable wood slat ceilings are suspended below ductwork and services.

Visual

- Rainwater filtration and daylighting systems are treated as objects of art.
- Interior landscaping, terrace gardens, and roofscapes break down the distinctions between inside and out.
- The rich arrangement of space tends to encourage people to use stairs rather than elevators.
- Exposed raked-angle columns in the banking hall express the horizontal thrust of the angled tower walls and enhance the organic expression of space.

Performance

- Small-area floor plates ensure that no one is more than 24 ft from an operable window and the daylight and natural ventilation it affords.
- The atriums serve multiple functions as public spaces, vertical circulation cores, and providers of a variety of environmental services: daylight, wind tower, vertical duct shaft, water filter, and so forth.
- Interior plants and waterscaping control humidity and cleanse indoor air.
- Waterscape flow-forms cleanse rainwater and produce white-noise background sounds.
- Prefabricated structural concrete panels provide thermal storage for winter heat and night-flush ventilation cooling in summer.

- The total energy system uses site energy effectively by sharing waste heat among all its processes of heating, cooling, and servicing.
- The sloping exterior wall configuration aids in deflecting noise and winter winds.

DISCUSSION

In 1980, Malcolm Wells published a collection of thoughts titled *Notes from the Energy Underground.* Presenting a number of perspectives about energy and environment, the book has a particular essay repeating, "Why, why, why?" Why do we have to leave home to have a vacation? Why do we have to go to museums to experience art? Why do we have to go to a park to commune with nature? The list goes on, but the underlying suggestion is that we too often go about life separated from the things we hold most dear and unintentionally tolerate a daily routine that is alienated from beauty, always dividing the sacred from the profane. To Malcolm Wells, this is not the natural condition. He gives us questions to ponder.

Norman Foster had expressed the spirit of this deliberation through a dramatic reversal of conventional office building features and finishes in his Willis Faber Dumas headquarters (1973; see case study # 7). By focusing attention on workspace rather than on high-profile public and executive features, Foster chartered new priorities for daily life in the office world. In 1979, Ton Alberts and Max Van Huut continued the assertion with their headquarters for the NMB Bank (now ING Bank).

In 1989, three years after moving in, the bank commissioned a worker satisfaction survey and compared it with a similar study conducted thirteen years earlier in NMB's previous headquarters. The findings showed a dramatic increase in satisfaction, both with the working environment and with NMB as an employer. People preferred their new open office spaces to the old partitioned ones. Eighty percent of them expressed pride in the building, and 70 percent mentioned the qualities of the meandering public corridor. Seven percent claimed they used only stairs, and 20 percent said they used only elevators.

The profits of these successes clearly outweigh the costs and the risks involved. The green technologies at NMB represent a 2 percent increase in total project cost. In 1995 dollars, that was about $900 thousand. The energy savings alone were determined to pay back more than $2.4 million per year.

Much could be said about the multidisciplinary team members who integrated their specialties. The benefits realized by NMB were, however, clearly the result of the architect's intentions, rather than despite them. There was a particularly fortunate correspondence between Alberts's organic inclinations toward design and the principles employed by the building's physics consultants.

28

EMERALD PEOPLE'S UTILITY DISTRICT HEADQUARTERS, 1987–1988

Eugene, Oregon
EQUINOX DESIGN AND WEGROUP ARCHITECTS AND PLANNERS

DESCRIPTION

The Emerald People's Utility District (EPUD) Headquarters, an office and warehouse complex, was built for a small public utility company in the cool and rainy climate of Eugene, Oregon, in the Pacific Northwest United States. The design vigorously incorporates daylighting and passive strategies for heating and cooling. The site arrangement was governed by ecological sensitivity to the surrounding wetlands and neighboring small industries. The complex is united by a desire to highlight the qualities of both the outdoor and indoor environments.

Figure 11.18 South elevation of EPUD Headquarters. Note the elongated axis, the clerestory windows, and the deciduous shading. (*Photograph courtesy of John Reynolds.*)

TABLE 11.5 Fact Sheet

Project	Building Name	Emerald People's Utility District Headquarters
	Client	Emerald People's Public Utility District
	City	Eugene, Oregon
	Lat/Long/Elev	44.01N 123.02W, 460 ft (140 m)
Team	Architects	John Reynolds (Equinox Design) and Dick Williams (WEGROUP Architects and Planners)
	Mechanical Engineer	Dave Rogers
	Daylighting	Virginia Cartwright
General	Time Line	1987–1988.
	Floor Area	24,255 ft^2 (2252 m^2) (office only).
	Occupants	40.
	Cost	$4,123,600 (entire complex).
	1995 Cost in US$	$5,313,918.
	Stories	One- and two-story office buildings with warehouse and vehicle storage.
	Plan	Courtyard footprint. Two story wing is 122 ft by 60 ft, east-west one-story wing is 98 ft. by 60 ft. Overall plan including courtyard is 167 ft. by 160 ft.
Site	Site Description	A former horse pasture located just outside Eugene near the Willamette River and bordered by paved roads and light industry. Buildings are elongated along the east-to-west axis and sited to preserve the existing small creek and bordering wetlands.
	Parking, Cars	104 cars, plus utility vehicles.
Structure	Foundation	Slab on grade.
	Vertical Members	Load-bearing concrete block exterior fin walls and interior bearing walls at 24 ft on center.
	Horizontal Spans	Precast concrete beam on 24 ft bays running north to south. Hollow-core concrete slab floor and roof spans.
Envelope	Glass and Glazing	Clear double-glazed, ⅜ in. airspace, non-thermal break aluminum, overall U = 0.74.
	Skylights	None.
	Cladding	4 in. concrete block outside, 1 in. airspace, R-19 batt insulation in metal studs at 24 in. o.c., gypsum board inside, corrected R = 11.9, therefore U = 0.084.
	Roof	R-40 insulation over concrete slab, corrected U = 0.028.
HVAC	Equipment	Split system.
	Cooling Type	Direct expansion.
	Distribution	Main system is variable air volume (VAV). A separate 2 ton heat pump serves the computer room and a 1.2 ton heat pump serves the dispatch room because of their longer hours of occupancy schedule. Individually operated electrical resistance heating units are under windows.
	Duct Type	Rectangular ducts furred above circulation paths.
	Vertical Chases	None.
Interior	Partitions	Load-bearing concrete block in 24 ft wide bays spanning horizontally east to west
	Finishes	Carpeted floors, exposed concrete ceilings, gypsum walls.
	Vertical Circulation	One central elevator plus stairs at east and west ends.
	Furniture	Each workstation is located within 20 feet of a perimeter window.
	Lighting	North and south daylighting and indirect fluorescent artificial lighting.

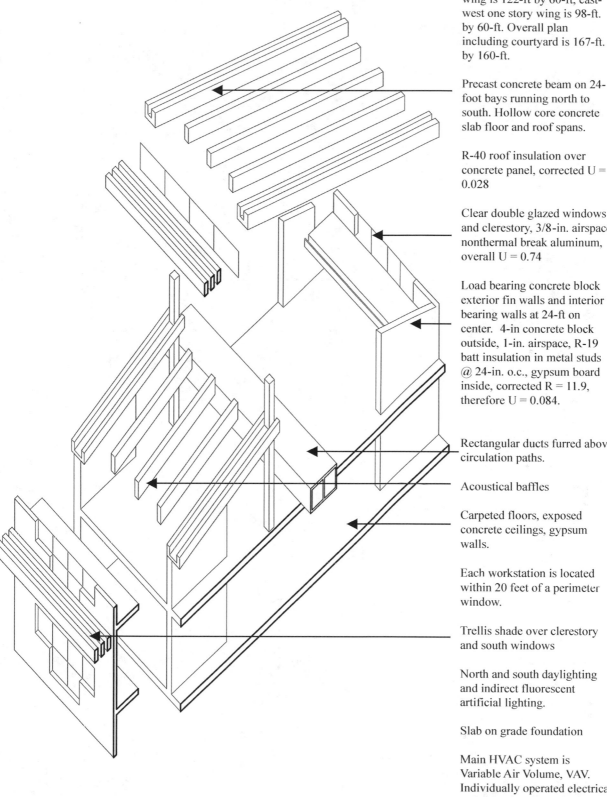

Courtyard footprint. Two story wing is 122-ft by 60-ft, east-west one story wing is 98-ft. by 60-ft. Overall plan including courtyard is 167-ft. by 160-ft.

Precast concrete beam on 24-foot bays running north to south. Hollow core concrete slab floor and roof spans.

R-40 roof insulation over concrete panel, corrected U = 0.028

Clear double glazed windows and clerestory, 3/8-in. airspace, nonthermal break aluminum, overall U = 0.74

Load bearing concrete block exterior fin walls and interior bearing walls at 24-ft on center. 4-in concrete block outside, 1-in. airspace, R-19 batt insulation in metal studs @ 24-in. o.c., gypsum board inside, corrected R = 11.9, therefore U = 0.084.

Rectangular ducts furred above circulation paths.

Acoustical baffles

Carpeted floors, exposed concrete ceilings, gypsum walls.

Each workstation is located within 20 feet of a perimeter window.

Trellis shade over clerestory and south windows

North and south daylighting and indirect fluorescent artificial lighting.

Slab on grade foundation

Main HVAC system is Variable Air Volume, VAV. Individually operated electrical resistance heating units are under windows.

Figure 11.19   Anatomical secction.

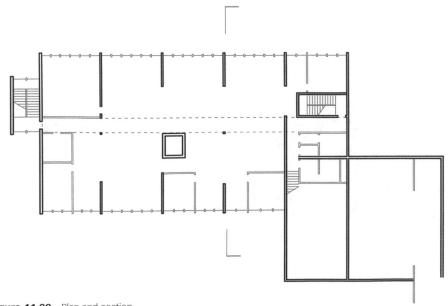

Figure 11.20 Plan and section.

PROGRAM

Client

In October 1970 a small group of rural Eugene residents were brought together by their concern over rising electrical rates. The price of energy from their investor-owned utility company was close to double that of surrounding areas served by publicly owned utilities. Discussions led to further meetings with state officials, and the effort to create their own public utility district was initiated.

It was to be a long struggle. But after 13 years and 14 court cases, the time-consuming and expensive battle was won. The group set out to raise $49 million in bond revenues and purchased the local facilities of the investor utility. The switchover from private investor utility to publicly owned Emerald People's Utility District was celebrated victoriously on November 17, 1983.

Institutionally, EPUD fashions itself as a public service organization, working for the benefit of its service area. Customers are thought of as co-op members of the EPUD community more than as ratepayers. The utility now hosts luncheon tours of its facility, contracts youth groups to wash its service trucks weekly, hosts community functions free of charge, and runs a number of energy information and conservation programs. There is even an EPUD Internet provider service.

EPUD's operating budget includes about 33 percent power purchasing, 22 percent operations and maintenance, 23 percent for debt service, and 20 percent for construction, equipment, and conservation programs. Although 80 percent of the power it purchases still comes from the utility it bought out, EPUD can now resell it at cost to its "members." The remaining power comes from increasingly green sources: 6 percent from certified green power producers and 5 percent from EPUD's own Short Mountain methane power plant, which operates on gas produced from waste in a landfill.

Brief

Several rounds of meetings and group discussions were held between the design team and the client group to jointly develop a program for the new headquarters building. Several points were established:

- Sensitivity to the site, its trees, and nearby streams
- Attractiveness to customers coming to the center to pay bills and attend functions
- Use of the building by customer organizations as a public facility
- Group spirit among staff members and in the workplace
- Prudent use of energy and promotion of energy conservation
- Use of renewable resources to minimize energy consumption

Site

A location for the building was selected along a highway south of Eugene and Springfield. The site is east of the road and separated from it by railroad tracks and feeder streets, a roughly football-shaped area between two existing highway feeder roads. Open pastureland and a small creek lie further to the east, bordering a large wetlands area. The EPUD plot was formerly a horse pasture in an immediate neighborhood consisting of sparse light industry and residences.

Climate

The Willamette River Valley of western Oregon is bounded by the Cascade Mountains to the east and the Coast Range to the west. The state's three largest cities are located in the valley: Portland, Eugene, and Salem. North of Eugene the valley broadens, but to the south it is almost closed in by low hills. This southern end of the valley is where EPUD and its service district are located, the sharp end of a V opening up all the way to Seattle. The region's landscape is one of mixed grassland savanna and open woodland consisting of Douglas fir, oaks, broadleaf deciduous species, incense cedar, and a few remaining stands of ponderosa pine.

The Coastal Range blocks off most of the fog from the Pacific, but storms cross it easily. Three openings to the ocean bring cool air into the Willamette Valley: the Van Duzer corridor from Lincoln City on the coast to Salem in the valley, one from Newport to Corvallis, and one from Florence to Eugene. The Cascade Range, on the other hand, fends off all but the strongest continental air masses from the east. When air does flow into the valley over the Cascades, it brings hot, dry summer weather or clear winter days with frosty nights. Numerous small creeks and low-lying areas of moisture produce considerable fog.

The climate is generally moderated by maritime Pacific air. Its cool, wet winter and mild, dry summer climate is favorable to wine growing, particularly the early ripening Pinot noir grape. There are currently more than 210 wineries in the Willamette Valley, cultivating 6300 acres of vineyard. Summer growing seasons are enhanced by long sunlight hours, up to 15.3 hours at the solstice, and cool nights. The weather is similar to that in the Mediterranean climates of California, but Oregon winters last longer and are colder. Long periods of severe heat or cold, however, are uncommon here. Not surprisingly, normal temperature ranges are narrow. The daily averages in January are a 67°F high and a 33°F low, in July 82°F and 51°F. Overall, temperatures are generally on the cool side; there are 4701 degree-days heating to only 248 cooling. Bin data of hourly temperature observations shows that 1.7 percent of the annual hours in Eugene are hot (above 85°F), 4.8 percent are warm, 10.1 percent comfortable (65°F to 75°F), 22.3 percent are cool, and 61.1 percent are cold (below 55°F). Less than 5 percent of all hours are below freezing.

Rainfall distribution follows a cyclical curve that peaks in December and January and bottoms out in July and August. The winter months have 20 or so rain days and about 8 in. (200 mm) of rain each, whereas the summer months have almost no rain at all. About 50 percent of the annual rainfall occurs in December and January. Regionally, rainfall increases with elevation and with proximity to the coast. Portland, at 21 ft above sea level, receives 37.4 in., and Salem (196 ft) gets 40.4 in. Eugene (359 ft) receives 46.0 in. The EPUD site, in the hills south of Eugene, is at 460 ft elevation.

In regard to daylighting objectives, sky cover data shows marked differences in seasonal availability of natural light. Overcast conditions are prevalent November through February, whereas June through September skies are mostly clear. Equally important, winter days at this latitude are only 8.7 hours long at the solstice, and summers days last up to 13.5 hours.

INTENTION

Design Team
Collaborators on the Emerald project included architect John Reynolds, principal of Equinox Design and known as

TABLE 11.6   Normal Climate Data for Eugene, Oregon

		Jan.	Feb.	Mar.	Apr.	May	June	July	Aug.	Sept.	Oct.	Nov.	Dec.	Year
Temperature	Degree-Days Heating	777.4	602.6	574.4	442.3	295.2	134.9	36.9	32.7	111.5	360.5	585.6	747.6	4701.4
	Degree-Days Cooling	0	0	0	0.1	4.5	28.4	95.1	87.3	32.1	1	0	0	248.5
	Extreme High	67	72	77	86	93	102	105	108	103	94	76	68	108.0
	Normal High	46.0	51.0	56.0	61.0	67.0	74.0	82.0	82.0	77.0	64.0	53.0	47.0	63.0
	Normal Average	40.0	43.0	46.0	50.0	56.0	61.0	67.0	67.0	62.0	53.0	45.0	41.0	53.0
	Normal Low	33.0	35.0	37.0	39.0	43.0	48.0	51.0	51.0	48.0	42.0	38.0	35.0	42.0
	Extreme Low	-4.0	-3.0	20.0	27.0	28.0	32.0	39.0	38.0	32.0	19.0	12.0	−12.0	−12.0
Humidity	Dew Point	36	38	39	42	46	50	52	52	49	46	41	37	44.0
	Max % RH	91	92	91	88	84	81	78	82	89	94	93	92	88.0
	Min % RH	80	72	64	58	54	49	38	39	44	61	79	84	60.0
	% Days with Rain	66.0	65.3	67.4	60.7	47.5	36.6	16.8	21.4	30.3	46.7	69.0	69.7	49.5
	Rain Inches	7.9	5.5	5.3	3.1	2.3	1.4	0.5	0.9	1.4	3.6	7.5	8.3	47.8
Sky	% Overcast Days	69.7	62.9	56.3	50.2	41.9	37.7	21.4	23.8	27.4	46.3	66.6	72.8	48.1
	% Clear Days	8.9	10.5	11.6	13.5	17.6	23.7	41.1	38.1	21.0	7.5	5.9	20.7	18.3
Wind	Prevailing Direction	S	S	S	S	N	N	N	N	N	S	S	S	N
	Speed, Knots	9	9	9	8	8	9	9	9	9	7	9	9	9.0
	Percent Calm	10.9	10.6	7.6	8	9.2	8.9	8.6	10.6	11.6	13.8	11.8	11.8	10.3
Days Observed	Rain	19.9	19.7	20.3	18.3	14.3	11.0	5.0	6.4	9.1	14.1	20.8	21.0	180.7
	Fog	17.7	16.2	10.8	7.4	5.7	4.6	2.4	4.7	10.4	19.6	20.8	19.7	140.7
	Haze	7.0	7.3	4.7	3.1	2.0	1.6	1.6	4.5	9.8	12.7	8.7	6.3	69.9
	Snow	4.5	2.6	2.2	0.7	0.06	0	0	0	0	0.06	0.9	2.8	14.1
	Hail	0	0	0.031	0.1	0.03	0.09	0	0.03	0	0.03	0	0	0.3
	Freezing Rain	0.24	0.06	0	0	0	0	0	0	0	0	0	0.1	0.5
	Blowing Sand	0	0.03	0	0	0	0	0	0	0	0	0	0	0.0

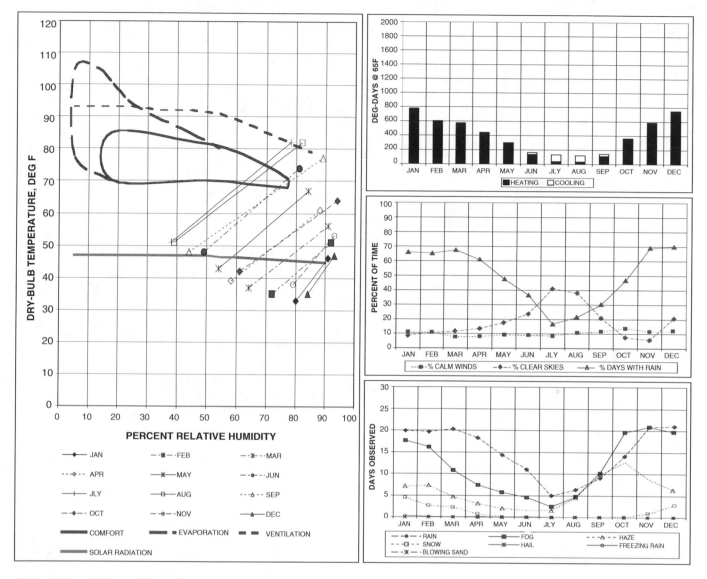

Figure 11.21   Climate analysis graphics.

the coauthor of *Mechanical and Electrical Systems for Buildings*. He is also professor emeritus of the architecture faculty at the University of Oregon. Rounding out the design team was Dick Williams of WEGROUP Architects and Planners. Virginia Cartwright served as daylighting consultant.

Philosophy

In sympathy with EPUD's grassroots ideals and publicly operated enterprise, the philosophy of the project team included a large measure of environmental and social consciousness. Given their collective background, the designers and consultants were well suited to EPUD's mission.

Intent

This headquarters and operations facility would be a clear statement about EPUD's commitment to energy conservation and prudent use of resources. This goal was already programmatic, based on the client's brief and the developmental meetings. So the design team set out to optimize the use of the site and its relationships with the building. One objective, for example, was to provide a prolonged pleasant walk across the site from the parking areas. Another was to make it possible for the occupants to appreciate the site from the working environment. Finally, and perhaps most important, there was the intention of using passive energy systems to provide for interior comfort levels.

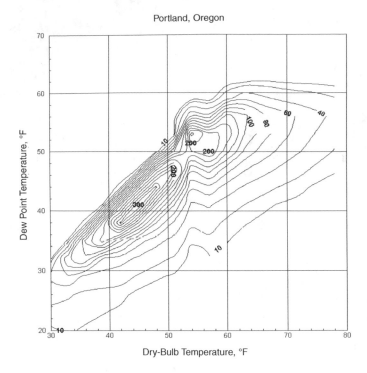

Portland, Oregon

Figure 11.22 Bin data distribution for Eugene. Concentric areas of graph indicate the number of hours per year that weather conditions normally occur in this climate. Similar to elevation readings on topographic maps, highest frequency occurrences of weather are at the center peaks of the graph. (Data sources: *Engineering Weather Data, typical meteorological year (TMY) data from the National Climatic Data Center, and the* ASHRAE *Weather Data Viewer from the American Society of Heating, Refrigerating and Air-Conditioning Engineers.*)

CRITICAL TECHNICAL ISSUES

Inherent

- Aside from the office headquarters, the new facility would also need a warehouse, truck storage, and parking for customers, staff, and administration.

- Part of the office building would be used 24 hours per day for emergency response dispatching.

Contextual

- Although the building was to reflect a corporate image of responsibility, it also needed to have a low-key, grassroots character.

- The site was to provide a natural setting for the building, despite the surrounding highway, light industry, and railroad tracks.

- Wetlands to the east of the site were to be respected.

Intentional

- The design problem centered on the unity of site and building, climate, and environment.

- This building, like other open-envelope, highly glazed buildings that visually unify the interior with the exterior, was also thermally weak in terms of insulation value.

- The cool and gray Eugene winter days and the long, dry summer days made opposite demands on the design.

APPROPRIATE SYSTEMS

It soon became evident to the team that daylighting combined with passive solar heating strategies would be essential to the environmental scheme of the building. Lighting requirements would be substantial in the office workspaces, which suggested natural daylighting. The Oregon winter dictated passive solar heating. What was not certain was exactly how the need for extensive daylight apertures, in relation to winter heat loss, would be met. Further, how would summer solar heat gain be warded off? Careful orientation proved to be the solution for most of these questions, with a well-integrated use of thermal mass for both heating and cooling. The design, as built, now uses 50 percent of the energy consumed by comparable buildings in the same climate.

Precedent

For precedents, the architects relied most on the compilation of previous works that are represented in the standard text of Benjamin Stein and John S. Reynolds, *Mechanical and Electrical Equipment for Buildings.* Making use of precedent begins with scrutinizing work that is simultaneously general to the field and pertinent to the architect's own progress of works. The architects cite one particularly influential reference, elementary school classroom wings of the 1950s with daylighting from both sides and cross ventilation.

The team also took inspiration from the traditional courtyard as an organizing theme for the EPUD headquarters. Reynolds says of his most recent book, *Courtyards: Aesthetic, Social, and Thermal Delight* (2001), "It's my homage to 'firmness, commodity, and delight.'"

Site

The 167 ft x 160 ft (50.9 m x 48.8 m) footprint of the headquarters building was broken into two wings to provide extra wall exposure to the north and south. A smaller one-story structure, the engineering wing, sits to the south, with

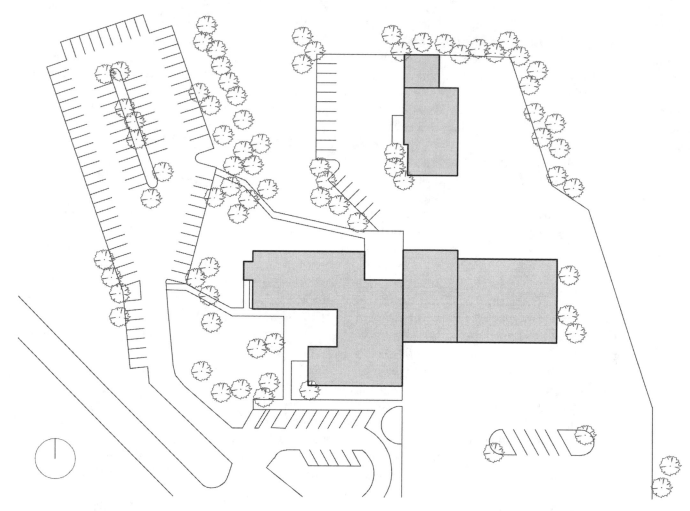

Figure 11.23 Site plan of EPUD.

a roof sloping down northward into the courtyard at an angle calculated to admit the winter sun to the open space. A two-story customer services wing forms the north side of the court. The two wings are connected by a central meeting hall and a smaller north-to-south block of the building. Between them is a semiprotected courtyard that provides views from the interior and a last step in the entry sequence.

Parking is intentionally pulled away from the building to extend this entry sequence. Customer parking is closest, but still isolated from the entry doors by the depth of the courtyard, the single story wing, and landscaping. Staff parking is at the far northwest end of the site. From either location, a short jaunt across the site is meant to accentuate the natural setting. In inclement weather it also allows appreciation of the differences between inside and out. A covered walkway along the west side of the courtyard offers protection and a semienclosed stage of the entry sequence.

The east half of the site is dedicated to EPUD's industrial services. These are pressed against the east side of the offices and pushed away to the northeast. The utility

buildings are screened from direct sight of the offices and the entry sequence. Strategic plantings between the two halves of the site and between the offices and the parking areas reinforce the visual separation.

Structure

A slab-on-grade foundation was used for simplicity. Load-bearing concrete block walls were constructed on the slab running from north to south at 24 ft (7.3 m) intervals. This frame leaves the north and south solar orientations open for light and sun. A precast double beam with a U-shaped profile forms a lintel at the top of the block walls. Hollow-core concrete slabs were used across the 24 ft span to complete the building structure. To integrate airflow for thermal performance, the end cores of the concrete slabs were left open to the crossing channel of the U-beam.

Envelope

Sections of the building show how the north-south profile was configured to admit direct south light and to provide a high clerestory window for illumination deep into the interior. This scheme is used on both wings as well as the connecting meeting hall. Several moderating elements are added to this profile to control solar heat gain and direct glare. On the interior, for both north and south windows, a deep light shelf blocks the view of the sky and reflects light off the ceiling and into the interior. This strategy is supplemented on the south elevation by an open trellis outside the lightshelf and a matching trellis at the ceiling line. Yet another trellis protects the south-facing clerestory. In a subtle integration with site landscaping, these trellises are covered with Virginia creeper vines that shade the windows during the warm summer season. Because Virginia creeper is deciduous, it loses its leaves in time to allow the low angles of winter sun into the building. Characteristically, the vine bears small black berries in the winter and chartreuse, translucent young leaves in spring. By summer it has large dark green leaves, which turn red and translucent again by October.

The north and south wall openings are in-filled with 4 in. (102 mm) concrete block and backed up on the interior with metal stud walls, R–19 insulation, and gypsum board. With a 1 in. air space between the concrete block and the insulation, this assembly yields a corrected thermal resistance of R–11.9. North and south glazing, as well as the clerestory window, uses the same aluminum framed, double-glazed glass units with a ⅜ in. air space between the glazings. The insulation value of the glass is R-1.4. To balance light distribution, more high windows were used above the lightshelf than view windows beneath them. This gives each bay an H-shaped window divided by the trellis and light shelf. The entire assembly was pushed up so that the window head is at the ceiling line and daylight is given the greatest opportunity to infiltrate the space.

Above the hollow-core roof slabs, R-40 batt insulation is loose laid between steel channels and covered with a seamed metal roof. Correcting for thermal bridging, the conductance of the steel channels gives an R-35 thermal resistance for the roof. The east and west exterior walls are finished to match the north and south infill walls.

Mechanical

An air-cooled direct expansion air conditioner sits in a courtyard between the north juncture of the office and the warehouse. It serves a VAV fan distribution system packaged in the mechanical room adjacent to it in the northeast corner of the building. This system serves most of the EPUD offices, with conventional cooling delivered to fan distribution boxes in each zone. The large fan associated with the main air handler in the mechanical room operates at a variable volume to match the total requirements of all the zone boxes.

The VAV fan is also used to provide night-flush ventilation during cool summer night hours. Rather than recirculating a mix of return air and outside air as it normally does, the fan switches to 100 percent outside air and delivers it through the same ducts it uses during the day. Three additional makeup air fans blow filtered outside air into the second floor, ground floor, and engineering wing. Three exhaust fans then remove air from the building by extracting it through the hollow-core concrete floor and ceiling slabs. By morning the mass of the building is charged with "coolth," or more technically, discharged of its heat accumulation from the previous day. Because the temperature of surrounding surfaces is so important to thermal comfort, this operation accomplishes a great deal of the next day's cooling requirements in advance. Another cooling strategy is used on the hottest afternoons:

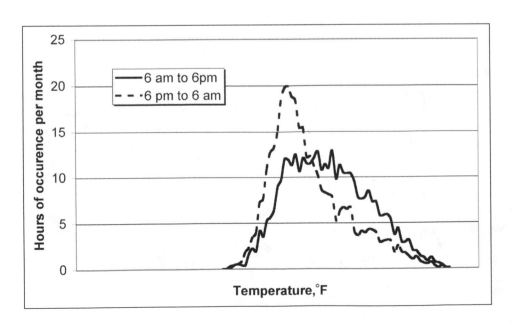

Figure 11.24
Distribution of July temperatures in Eugene for day and night hours.

Figure 11.25 Interior of the EPUD offices. *(Photograph courtesy of John Reynolds.)*

Return air is switched-over from conventional ducts to the hollow slab cores. This harvests the previous night's cooling that remains in its heavy mass and precools the room air before it is conditioned by the VAV system.

In winter, the core slabs are allowed to warm as heat from lights, sun, and activity in the building naturally stratify to ceiling height. Before the staff arrives on a cool morning, return air is taken through the warm slabs rather than through its conventional ductwork. This harvests heat stored from the previous day. In either the heating or the cooling mode, for return air or exhaust, the mass of the slabs is used to store heat when it is generated and give it up during cooler parts of the day. Having hollow-core air channels makes integrating the structure with the mechanical system direct and practical. Remember that the supporting concrete lintels were precast as U-shaped beams for just this purpose—picture them as manifolds feeding into and from the slab cores.

There is no central heating system in the building. Studies showed that it would be more efficient to forgo a heating plant or some form of perimeter zone reheat of the VAV system. Instead, spot heating is provided at each desk by a personally controlled electric resistance unit. By making the passive heating aspect of the building so important, the need for a central heating plant was eliminated completely.

Two special rooms had to have independent HVAC systems. The computer room operated 24 hours per day and could not be set back to less comfortable levels at night with the rest of the building. It is served by a 2 ton heat pump in the northwest corner of the second floor. For the same reason, the 24-hour dispatch room in the northeast corner of

the engineering wing has a 1.5 ton heat pump. Finally, an electrical submetering system was installed to monitor monthly energy use in various parts of the building.

Interior

Interior spaces are defined by the 24 ft structural bays plus the north, south, and clerestory daylight apertures. The central long axis of the typical plan is left open for circulation, access, and the routing of services. Most conspicuous is the long VAV distribution duct containing separate compartments for the supply air and return air streams. On the second floor of the customer services wing this duct acts as another light shelf to scatter sky light from the clerestory.

The concrete structure is left exposed to the interior, providing a durable surface and the thermal benefits of internal mass. With so many hard surfaces in the room however, acoustical absorption had to be provided somewhere or the space would be excessively noisy. This problem was resolved by hanging acoustically absorptive baffles vertically from the ceiling, perpendicular to the windows in each bay. The baffles not only quiet the space, they also help to diffuse light and cut off direct view of the bright sky.

Daylighting design kept all the workstations within 20 ft of a window—at a ratio of less than 2.5 times the height of the window head. Bilateral lighting makes this low ratio possible in the first place, and the central clerestory provides fill light throughout the spaces below. Balancing the distribution of light in the space was also accomplished by the proportion of windows above and below the light shelves so that it is not unduly bright beside the windows and dark in the middle of the room. Overall, the glass area amounts to about 20 percent of the floor area.

Supplemental artificial lighting is provided by indirect fluorescent fixtures with auto-dimming in response to available daylight. These were selected to provide soft light and friendly illumination patterns that would not be reflected in computer screens. One row each is integrated into the inside edges of the north and south light shelves. Another row is mounted as a valence across the bottom edge of the VAV duct, and still another faces the corridor across from the ductwork. All of these fixtures run parallel to the window plane so they can be dimmed progressively.

TECHNICAL INTEGRATION HIGHLIGHTS

Physical

- Passive systems, envelope, interior, and structure are all merged in the hollow-core concrete slabs.

Visual

- Exposed fluted-block concrete walls are finished interior surfaces.
- The interior is visually ordered by the structural grid of 24 ft spans.
- Connection between interior and site is maintained.
- Exposed ductwork defines the circulation corridor through the open plan.
- The entry sequence features the natural setting, and warehouses are kept screened.

Performance

- The Virginia creeper trellises on the south wall can be trimmed or trained to fine tune shade and daylight. Meanwhile, they operate automatically, as Reynolds puts it, "like the iris of an eye," wincing when the sun is bright.
- The thermal mass of the structure is functionally integrated into passive and mechanical performance.
- Daylighting and passive heating are accomplished without excessive heat loss in winter or solar gain in summer.

DISCUSSION

The EPUD Headquarters is distinguished by the use of passive design components that become architectural elements. Overall, the space is thermally comfortable, has high-quality natural and electric lighting, and has proven attractive to staff and customers. This improved comfort and commodity are achieved through passive design fea-

tures without sacrifice. Furthermore, they provide these benefits at a 60 percent energy savings, as compared with typical office buildings in the same region. Annual energy consumption at EPUD is reported as 6.1 kWh/ft^2 (66 kWh/m^2) as opposed to the standard 14.8 kWh/ft^2 (160 kWh/m^2). Several other performance levels can be derived from the examples given in the 9th edition of *Mechanical and Electrical Equipment for Buildings*, as follows:

Calculations for Typical Second-Story Bay	
Heat loss including ΣuA and ACH	5.2 Btu/degree-day ft^2
Estimated solar savings fraction	24.70%
Summer heat gain for one bay	12.87 Btu/ ft^2 hr
Summer heat gain for one bay	117 Btu/ ft^2 day
Natural cross ventilation cooling rate	50 Btu/hr ft^2
Night ventilation cooling rate	16 Btu/hr ft^2
Night ventilation storage capacity	135 Btu/ ft^2 day
Night ventilation forced air change	4.47 ACH
Calculated balance point temperature	50.2°F
Building loss coefficient (BLC), typical bay	7512 Btu/degree-day
Load collector ratio (LCR)	32.8
Solar saving fraction (SSF) based on LCR	25%
SSF with superior performance glass	39.67%
Typical clear day Jan. temperature swing	8.9°F, from 68.4 to 77.3
Detailed night ventilation storage capacity	16,573 Btu/°F
Detailed total mass cooling	212,933 Btu
Detailed calculation, final mass temperature	67.2°F
Detailed calculation, total night ventilation cooling	223,301 Btu/bay
Equivalent total tons of night ventilation cooling	18.6 tons/night/bay
Detailed calculation, required night ventilation air change	5.5 air changes/hour

A postoccupancy evaluation was performed by architecture students from the University of Oregon in the winter of 1999 under the direction of Alison Kwok. Using a set of portable data loggers, they measured temperature, humidity, and light levels in the building. They also surveyed staff members to gather impressions about the comfort levels and how they operated their workstations in response to sun and light.

It was gratifying that the detailed study turned up few problems and several satisfactory results. Occupants were generally pleased with thermal and lighting conditions, glare was not perceived to be a problem, and only one group of occupants thought their space was too cold. Objectively, measured daylighting and thermal performance matched design expectations, but the lighting controls needed fine-tuning.

29

ADAM JOSEPH LEWIS CENTER FOR ENVIRONMENTAL STUDIES, 1996–2000

Oberlin, Ohio
WILLIAM MCDONOUGH + PARTNERS

DESCRIPTION

Imagine entering a building through its waste treatment plant. Now forget everything you ever knew about waste treatment plants and imagine entering a building through something called its "Living Machine," something that looks like a cross between a translucent water sculpture and a hydroponic garden. You have just entered the Adam Joseph Lewis Center for Environmental Studies (CES).

The transition from sewage plants to Living Machines typifies the CES. The facility and the program it houses exemplify a step beyond stopgap industrial measures for saving the environment through conservation and recycling. Features of this project collectively demonstrate the vitality of a postindustrial mindset whereby nature is simultaneously celebrated for its abundance and respected through our dual roles as its stewards and beneficiaries.

McDonough's realization of this "reimaging" fits politely into the mixed fabric of the Oberlin campus. The building is sited away from the curb, bermed up its north wall, fronting a south-facing Sun Plaza, and landscaped by an orchard, a pond, a restored stand of native hardwood trees, and a vegetable garden. The vocabulary is calm and visually appropriate, fitting what its architect calls the suitable resolution between "state-of-the-shelf" material selection and "state-of-the-art" technology. From the outside the structure is glass and brick. Inside is the two-story atrium commons, a high arched wood ceiling, and an abundance of natural light. Every one of the building's features is also a part of the CES curriculum, a hands-on learning laboratory.

Figure 11.26 General view of the CES. *(3-D rendering by Travis Hughs.)*

TABLE 11.7 Fact Sheet

Project	Building Name	Adam Joseph Lewis Center for Environmental Studies
	City	Oberlin, Ohio
	Lat/Long/Elev	41.29 N 82.23 W, 815 ft (248 m)
Team	Design	William McDonough + Partners
	Structural Engineers	Lev Zetlin Associates
	Mechanical Engineers	Lev Zetlin Associates
	Energy Consultants	Steven Winter Associates, Rocky Mountain Institute, and NASA/Lewis Space Center
	Living Machine	Living Technologies
	Wastewater Advisor	John Todd & Michael Shaw, Living Technologies
	Landscape	John Lyle Andropogon, Inc.
	General Contractor	Mosser Construction
General	Time Line	Design: begun early 1996, construction: September 1998 to September 2000 (dedication).
	Floor Area	13,600 ft^2 (1263 m^2).
	Occupants	Not determined.
	Cost	$6.0 million.
	Stories	Two stories with open atrium and high-ceiling auditorium.
	Plan	Classroom and auditorium wings joined by atrium.
Site	Site Description	Campus.
	Parking, Cars	Campus lots.
Structure	Foundation	Concrete piers.
	Vertical Members	Steel frame.
	Horizontal Spans	Steel frame with laminated Douglas fir beams in atrium.
Envelope	Glass and Glazing	Argon-filled triple-glazed units with an R-8.3 performance.
	Skylights	None.
	Cladding	Brick over concrete block.
	Roof	Recycled aluminum-seamed panels with provision for photovoltaic panels above.
HVAC	Equipment	Geothermal heat pumps on closed-loop water source in each space plus two large heat pumps for treatment of ventilation air. An electric boiler is used for backup when the water loop falls below 35°F.
	Cooling Type	Water-to-air heat pump.
	Distribution	Several one-room zones are created by use of many small heat pumps with individual controls.
	Duct Type	Minimal use of ducts, with multiple heat pumps displacing need for duct runs.
	Vertical Chases	Most distribution is under the floor.
Interior	Partitions	Gypsum board on metal stud.
	Finishes	Maple was used for trim in most corridors and classrooms and for auditorium seat armrests and aisle side panels. Hem fir was used throughout the building and for the stage structure in the auditorium.
	Vertical Circulation	Stairs in atrium around one elevator, fire stair at southwest corner.
	Furniture	Various.
	Lighting	0.9 W/ft^2 with occupancy sensor controls.

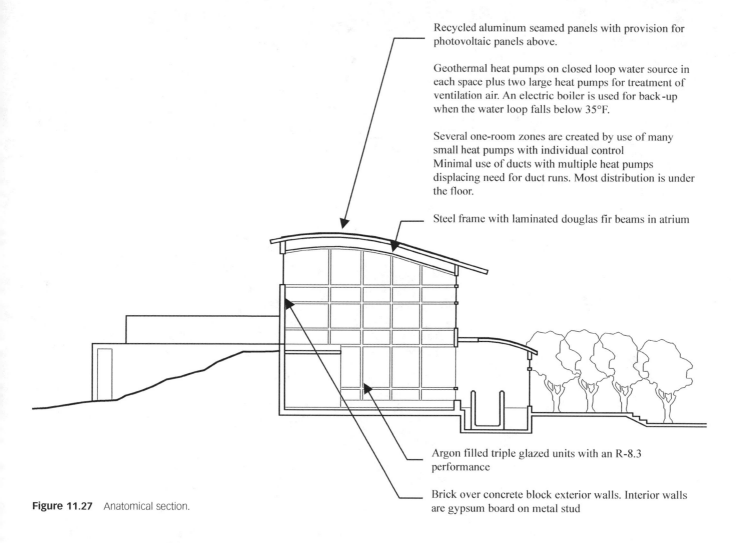

Recycled aluminum seamed panels with provision for photovoltaic panels above.

Geothermal heat pumps on closed loop water source in each space plus two large heat pumps for treatment of ventilation air. An electric boiler is used for back-up when the water loop falls below 35°F.

Several one-room zones are created by use of many small heat pumps with individual control Minimal use of ducts with multiple heat pumps displacing need for duct runs. Most distribution is under the floor.

Steel frame with laminated douglas fir beams in atrium

Argon filled triple glazed units with an R-8.3 performance

Brick over concrete block exterior walls. Interior walls are gypsum board on metal stud

Figure 11.27   Anatomical section.

PROGRAM

Client

Oberlin College, founded in 1833, is 45 minutes' travel time southwest of Cleveland, Ohio. The institution can be described as a relatively small independent college in a very small town; the student population numbers less than 3000 and the entire town population less than 9000. Oberlin College is, however, noted for grand ideologies. It was the first coeducational college in the United States and among the first to admit African-Americans, in 1835. Admission is very selective, as indicated by Oberlin's number one ranking among undergraduate programs whose students go on to complete doctoral degrees. The college motto is adopted from mathematician Alfred North Whitehead's dictum, "Direct knowledge is the foundation of intellectual life." The motto frames the context of the CES program: hands-on, pragmatic, rigorous, multidisciplined, and interactive. The 2000 edition of the Environmental Studies catalog listed 36 courses in 14 dis-

ciplines with more than a third of all Oberlin students were taking at least one course in this curriculum.

Brief

The Oberlin Center for Environmental Studies was established in 1981. In the 17 years leading to the construction of a new building, the Center had become something of a focus for the Oberlin campus. David W. Orr is the director of the Center and author of two books, *Earth in Mind* (1994) and *Ecological Literacy* (1993). As the Environmental Studies program grew in size, popularity, and focus, he began a determined campaign to build an appropriate home for it. His vision was twofold. First, the building would produce zero waste, both on site and off, now and in the future. Second, the building would be integral with the curriculum, part of the learning experience.

In the 1992–93 academic year, Orr offered a course on ecological architecture and brought a series of green design experts to the college. Twenty-five students and a dozen architects participated. Their assigned task was to

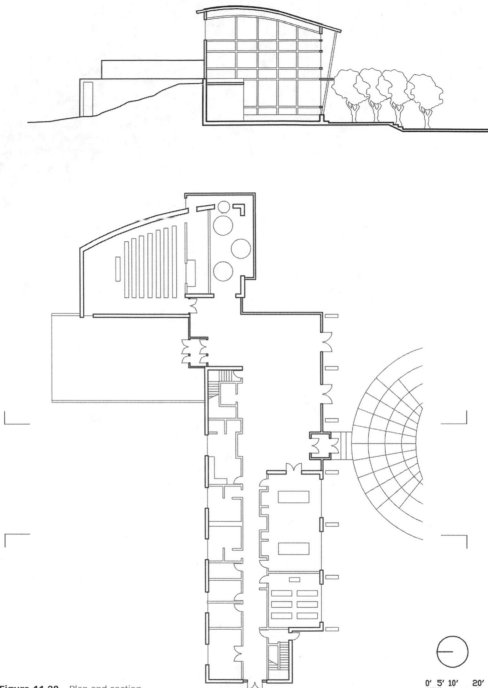

Figure 11.28 Plan and section.

develop architectural criteria for a new Center for Environmental Sciences. The product of their efforts set very high environmental priorities:

- Discharge wastewater and storm water as clean as it came in.
- Generate more electricity than used; become a net energy producer.
- Incorporate no materials with known negative health impacts.

- Use energy and materials with great efficiency.
- Use products that are harvested or manufactured sustainably.
- Participate in a landscape that promotes biological diversity.
- Be cost-effective by full internal and external accounting, achieving a net zero ecological impact.
- Cause no ugliness, for humans or for the environment, now or any time in the future.

By autumn 1995, there were about 60 students majoring in Environmental Science at Oberlin and more than 750 students overall taking courses in this curriculum. Prompted by this growth and encouraged by incoming Oberlin College president Nancy Dye, the first of 13 design charrettes was held to establish the Center's strategies for the proposed landmark building. President Dye has spoken about Oberlin's transition from a liberal arts college and from a curriculum based on the domination of nature to one vested in environmental caretaking. Her charge to CES was to raise monies from new donors without tapping Oberlin's existing development funds, and to complete the design and construction permit processes within two years.

The first planning event and the subsequent 12, attended by faculty and students, were in the style of an open town meeting. Practitioners who took part in these initial stages included two students from David Orr's 1992 class experiment to preprogram the building. Architect John Lyle, author of *Regenerative Design for Sustainable Development* (1994), was hired to conduct the remaining design charrettes. The first agenda for the new Center described a 10,000 ft^2 building with a $2.5 million budget ($250/ft^2). All of the 1992 goals were captured in the brief.

Design charrettes began in the fall of 1995. Some 250 participants were involved, including students, faculty, and community members. Advertising the project brought professional services proposals from 26 architectural firms; 5 were chosen for interview. In January of 1996, William McDonough + Partners was announced as the final selection.

By early 1996, Orr and his program had raised $900,000. In December of that year, businessman Peter Lewis and his son, Adam Joseph Lewis, made a gift of $3 million to the project. The visionary project instantly became a reality. A project budget of $5 million was reported in December 1996 and a construction cost of $6 million was published in December 1998.

Site

The Center for Environmental Studies is located on the southeast corner of the Oberlin campus, a campus that largely constitutes the east side of town. Originally the school was developed around a treeless town square named College Park. The square remains to this day, though fully landscaped and renamed Tappan Square by students after one of the college's abolitionist era patrons. CES is two blocks southwest of the park, skirted by lovely nineteenth-century buildings to the east. Residential areas meet the western edge of the site. Dormitory buildings lie south of the site, a student center and library to the north. Access is from the south side off a campus street. Farther to the east is the Oberlin Conservatory Complex, by Minoru Yamasaki in 1964, along with Gunner Birkert's Conservatory Library addition of 1988.

Climate

Oberlin is close enough to weather stations in Cleveland to share that city's climate data. Their mutual proximity to the south shores of Lake Erie also validates the usefulness of Cleveland measurements. The regional climate most resembles that of Chicago, or Moline, Illinois. Cleveland/Oberlin has annual totals of 6059 degree-days heating and 755 degree-days cooling—very close to the totals of Chicago and Moline.

The continentality of Oberlin is offset to some degree by the lake. Although winds are generally from the south and southwest most of the year, the lake tends to reverse the flow during warmer afternoons. This occurs when the lake is cooler than the bordering land areas, causing the atmosphere to cool over the lake and warm over the land, and so breezes come off the water and onto the land to equalize the flow. They bring with them a temperature moderating effect but also introduce higher levels of summer humidity. August normal daily highs of 81°F are accompanied by 58 percent relative humidity, and the normal daily low of 61°F is matched to 85 percent relative humidity. Only 940 hours per year (11 percent) are expected to exceed 75°F, however, and of those only 150 or so will exceed 85°F (2 percent of all hours).

The larger concern in Oberlin is the heating season. Normal daily lows in December average 25°F. A full 20 percent of annual hours are below freezing, with the frost season spanning from October to April. Snowfall normally totals about 84 in. over the same period. Prevailing winter winds are from the southwest at 11 knots.

The cool portion of the year, covering temperatures between 32°F and 65°F, occupies 52 percent of the weather, or 4530 hours per year. This leaves 1556 hours, or an 18 percent comfortable outdoor climate period.

Rainfall and fog are common occurrences in Oberlin. About 165 days (45 percent) have measurable rainfall, and an equal number of days experience fog. There is no dry season, as the 37.2 in. of annual rainfall are almost evenly distributed through the year. Spring is the wettest season, and most of the clear weather days occur from May to October.

INTENTION

Design Team

William McDonough was born in 1951 in Japan. His childhood was influenced by a contrast of environments —he grew up in crowded and water-starved Hong Kong and spent summers in the lush old-growth forests surrounding his grandparent's cabin on Puget Sound, Washington. He was graduated from Dartmouth in 1973 and later studied at Yale under James Stirling. In 1981 he founded William McDonough + Partners in New York. Among his first major works was the headquarters for the Environmental Defense Fund in Warsaw, Poland. When he was appointed dean of architecture at the University of Virginia in 1994, the firm moved to Charlottesville, Virginia. Among McDonough's corporate clients are an impressive list of mainstream businesses: BASF, Ford, The Gap, Herman Miller, IBM, Palm, Inc., S. C. Johnson, Steelcase, and Wal-Mart.

The other participants in the project complete a surprisingly diverse interdisciplinary team (see the Fact Sheet for a complete list). Their inclusion demonstrates the complexity of the ecological problems addressed despite the relatively small scale of the building program.

Collaborations among specialists like these at Oberlin, or on the NMB Bank projects, are likely to escalate as the model of their design becomes more widely imitated. These new teams also have a remarkable likeness to the natural processes their buildings imitate. Rather than following the old linear model of handing off design development tasks to each successive specialist for work to be done in isolation, green building teams operate as interactive and interdependent organizations. This is a deliberate step, which Director David Orr describes as "intended to maximize the integration of building systems and technologies and the relationship between the building and the landscape."

Philosophy
William McDonough wants to "reimagine the future" by "redesigning design." And, for McDonough, the future is

TABLE 11.8   Normal Climate Data for the Cleveland and Oberlin Region

		Jan.	Feb.	Mar.	Apr.	May	June	July	Aug.	Sept.	Oct.	Nov.	Dec.	Year
Temperature	Degree-Days Heating	1191	1022	859	499	227	50	8	14	106	362	675	1033	6059
	Degree-Days Cooling	0	0	1	9	43	152	249	207	88	12	1	0	755
	Extreme High	73	69	82	88	92	104	100	102	101	89	82	77	104
	Normal High	34	36	46	58	69	79	83	81	74	63	50	38	59
	Normal Average	27	29	37	49	59	68	73	71	64	54	43	32	51
	Normal Low	19	21	28	38	48	58	62	61	54	44	35	25	41
	Extreme Low	-20	-15	-5	10	25	31	41	38	34	19	3	-15	-20
Humidity	Dew Point	19	21	27	37	47	57	61	61	54	43	33	24	40
	Max % RH	79	79	79	76	77	79	81	85	84	81	78	78	80
	Min % RH	70	67	62	56	54	55	55	58	58	58	65	70	61
	% Days with Rain	33	30	43	56	56	50	46	46	46	50	50	40	45
	Rain Inches	3	2	3	3	4	4	4	3	3	3	3	3	37
Sky	% Overcast Days	74	71	65	57	48	40	35	35	37	45	70	74	54
	% Clear Days	10	13	14	18	20	20	23	23	22	23	11	9	17
Wind	Prevailing Direction	SW	SW	SW	S	N	SSW	SW	SW	S	SSW	SW	SW	SW
	Speed, Knots	11	11	12	11	8	9	8	7	8	9	11	11	10
	Percent Calm	1	2	2	3	4	4	4	5	4	3	1	1	3
Days Observed	Rain	10	9	13	17	17	15	14	14	14	15	15	12	165
	Fog	13	12	13	12	13	11	12	14	12	11	12	13	48
	Haze	14	14	13	11	13	15	17	19	14	11	11	12	164
	Snow	21	17	14	5	#	0	0	0	0	1	9	17	84
	Hail	0	0	#	#	#	#	#	#	#	#	#	#	1
	Freezing Rain	1	1	#	#	0	0	0	0	0	0	#	#	2
	Blowing Sand	#	0	#	#	#	#	#	#	#	#	0	0	#

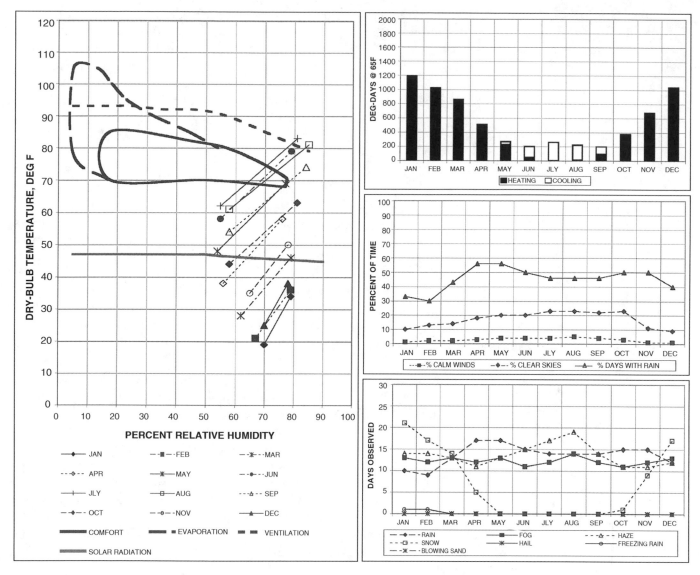

Figure 11.29 Climate analysis graphics.

now. "Conserve, recycle, and reuse" is only a slower dead-end alleyway off the high-speed industrial autobahn into tomorrow. The linear "eco-efficient" measures apply a necessary brake to current patterns of consumption, but they lead only more slowly to the same horizon. "Eco-resource" design, based on the sophistication and abundant vitality of nature, requires a completely different road map, one in which nature is mimicked rather than strip-mined. This path leads to both mechanical simplicity and biological complexity. McDonough sees the new road as something like a parkway.

McDonough's writings are full of these logics. Articles like "The Next Industrial Revolution," "A Declaration of Independence for the Twin Cities," "Securing a Sustainable Future," and "Design, Ecology, Ethics and the Making of Things" (delivered as a sermon, February 7, 1993, at St.

John the Divine in New York City) all convey an insistent message. They reiterate visionary themes of reimaging, of redesigning, and of doing it now. The best-known publication on his vitae is probably still *The Hanover Principles: Design for Sustainability* (1992) wherein he lays out the basic objectives toward achieving sustainability with such precepts as "Waste is food."

Intent
The CES agenda began with goals that included the extensive use of sustainable materials and employment of state-of-the art technology. The mission to house the center's activities was further set by targeting minimal use of nonrenewable energy and other environmental resources. Accounting for the measures of and trade-offs among these elusively complicated terms proved to be a major design activity.

Cleveland, Ohio

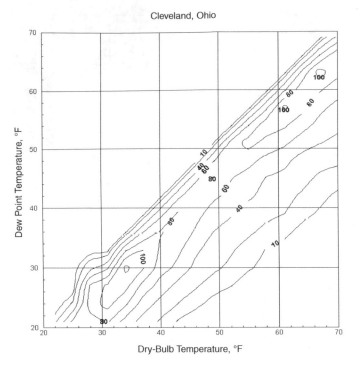

Figure 11.30 Bin data distribution for Cleveland. Concentric areas of graph indicate the number of hours per year that weather conditions normally occur in this climate. Similar to elevation readings on topographic maps, highest frequency occurrences of weather are at the center peaks of the graph. (Data sources: *Engineering Weather Data, typical meteorological year (TMY) data from the National Climatic Data Center, and the* ASHRAE Weather Data Viewer *from the American Society of Heating, Refrigerating and Air-Conditioning Engineers.*

Most formative, however, was McDonough's interpretation of the pedagogical role of the CES building. Each component of the building would be an intentional illustration of his environmental principles. Working dynamics among the systems would be exposed and expressed, even digitally monitored in plain view of students and passersby. Design decisions would have to be so visibly obvious that they would become nothing less than instructive.

Another organizing strategy formulated by McDonough was the distinction between two different metabolisms, or "nutrients," at work in the building. The first was organic; eventually such components would decompose and become food for other organic life. The second category is composed of industrial nutrients that would become recycled feedstock for other products at the end of their useful life. Of course, the pedigrees of both figurative nutrients are as important as their legacies — where they came from was just as much an ecological decision as where they would eventually go. This upstream value system accounted for such things as the embodied energy required to make a construction product, the

amount of pollution produced by its manufacture and transportation, the renewable or destructive nature of its harvesting, and so forth. The downstream consequences relied on choices as well, such as using biodegradable or recyclable materials versus producing toxic waste by dumping industrial nutrients into the organic food chain.

CRITICAL TECHNICAL ISSUES

Inherent
Given the specific character of the brief and the unique requirements of a center for environmental studies, McDonough was faced with some interesting challenges. Programmatically, the Center was simple enough, but the cold, wet climate and the desire for direct connections of interior and exterior spaces were in conflict. Resolving issues like the use of extensive glass areas to break down indoor-to-outdoor separations would be difficult.

Contextual
Collaboration and division of responsibilities also posed a challenge. When a multidisciplinary project team is melded together to achieve an integrated design, the chain of decision making and assignment of specialty tasks is muddled. The only one who can clearly be responsible for the coherence of the project is the architect. Although McDonough + Partners worked with a distinguished and like-minded group of professionals on this project, it is worth noting that the extra burden of integration was the architect's — and the technologies of the Oberlin Center were not trifles.

APPROPRIATE SYSTEMS

Precedent
One of the historical examples of designing and programmatically integrating technical systems for their pedagogical value is the Florida A&M College of Architecture. This college building has three wings. Each has a vented-skin thermal chimney covering the south side of the building wall and roof up to an oversized ridge vent. All interior systems are exposed and color coded for identification: Air handlers, dampers, ducts, and structure are laid out like laboratory lessons.

Site
The long axis of the main building faces south, as does the glazed façade of the Living Machine. There is an unobstructed view to the south and ample solar access across the Solar Plaza sundial and Elm Street. Views to the east

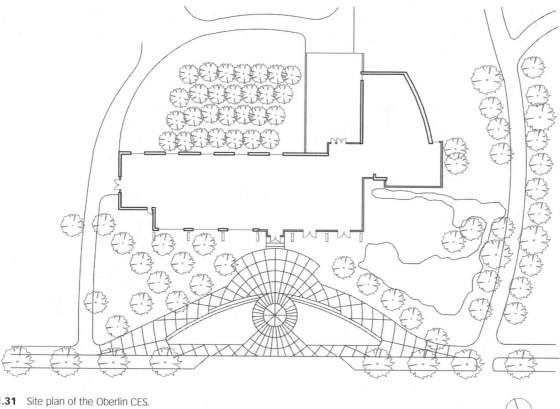

Figure 11.31 Site plan of the Oberlin CES.

encompass the Music Conservatory across Professor Street and part of the nearby 1887 Baldwin Cottage. The auditorium wing acts as a large shading fin to protect east-facing glass from early morning sun in summer months. Native hardwood trees are planted along these elevations facing the street. At the north side of the building earth is bermed up to the second-floor level, and an orchard is planted on the raised ground between the main building and the auditorium. The placement of CES in this particular setting has strategic value: Its atrium straddles a primary walkway between the campus library and student center to the north, and a large block of dormitories to the south.

All storm water on the site and nearby ground drains to a pond at the southeast junction of the main building and the Living Machine. The pond acts as a miniature wetlands ecosystem to filter and purify the water naturally, imitating the large wetlands that used to cover this entire region. This condition is greatly facilitated by the absence of on-site parking area accumulations of motor oil and gasoline that would have to be separated before reaching the pond. The flat roof areas above north facing rooms on the second floor are sod covered to slow runoff to the wetlands pond.

Structure

Vertical support is framed in 70 tons of steel with recycled content. This support is supplemented by load-bearing concrete block walls on the north and west ends of the main building and all of the auditorium except where it faces the Living Machine.

The roof of the two-story gathering space is spanned by laminated Douglas fir arched beams and decked in fir. All wood materials in the building come from sustainably harvested timber. Intermediate flooring is concrete on metal deck over bar joists.

Envelope

The roof of the CES is clad in seamed panels of recycled aluminum. The roof of the main building is then covered with photovoltaic panels that clip to the aluminum seams. North-facing rooms on the second floor have a grass-sod-covered flat roof that provides additional shade and insulation and slow storm water runoff to the wetlands pond below.

Daylighting requirements and a desire for contact with outdoor areas dictated a high ratio of glazing. This is satisfied in the atrium by two full-height walls of triple-layer glass units filled with argon gas. The R-value is an impressive 8.3. At half-height of the atrium's south wall, a trellis of deciduous vines provides solar protection in summer. A roof overhang protects the upper half of the atrium glazing. East-facing glass is protected from low summer sun by the tall mass of the auditorium building. Clear insulated glass with an R-value of 3.4 is used around the Living Machine and in other window areas. A continuous 4 ft high clerestory window separates the north wall from the arching roof, allowing glare-free indirect light to filter down into the main building.

The glazing system also permits natural ventilation. There are operable windows in every space and motorized openers for the north clerestory glazing. Breezes come predominantly from the southwest and are inlet at the atrium floor level and exhausted at a high level through the north clerestory. Computational fluid dynamics modeling was used to study the aerodynamic form of the roof and optimize the system of air pressures around the building that drive the natural airflow.

A tan-colored brick veneer exterior covers the structural concrete block walls. The cavity between the two masonry constructions is filled with insulation, yielding an assembly rating of R-21.

Mechanical

Each space in the CES is served by an individual heat pump for heating and cooling. Having multiple units usually creates a disadvantage because it increases the total system installed capacity in tons of cooling and Btu's of heating—each zone's heat pump unit must be sized to that room's peak load, and capacity cannot be shifted from space to space as it is with a central plant system. The advantages in this case outweigh the increased capacity problem because individual units allow for better control; a unit is used only when the room is occupied. The heat pumps used are water-to-air configurations. In the cooling mode they absorb heat from room air at the evaporator coil and reject it to the condensing coil by the standard vapor-compression freon refrigerant cycle. In the heating mode the freon flow is reversed so that the heat pumps absorb heat from a water stream and reject the same heat to room air.

Aside from efficiency and localized control, there are a few additional advantages to this system. First, the heat pumps can be piped, in parallel, to the same water loop. This connection allows one heat pump in the cooling mode to add heat to the water loop while another heat pump on the opposite side of the building takes heat back out of the same water. Strategically, heat is thus shared between the two heat pump zones with great efficiency. A second major benefit is realized by coupling the heat pumps to geothermal energy for harvesting the immense heat storage capacity and stable temperatures 100 ft below grade. This geothermal connection is made by circulating the heat pump water loop piping through a series of small borings into the earth. Other benefits include the total absence of cluttered outdoor mechanical equipment, independence of each zone for servicing, and avoidance of potential problems related to direct combustion heating with natural gas, such as toxic air quality resulting from

broken heat exchangers. A small electric boiler backs up the water loop for extreme periods of cold weather. Because the building produces its own electricity, there is no pollution debt at a remote generating plant of unseen environmental circumstances.

Ventilation air is provided by two larger heat pumps operating at 100 percent outside air. These units take room air and exhaust it through air-to-air heat exchangers in order to preheat the incoming ventilation air. The atrium has its own separate heating system with circulating hot water pipes embedded in the exposed floor slab.

Photovoltaic (PV) collectors on the roof currently provide most of the CES electrical needs. Advancements in PV system efficiency are expected to make the building a net energy exporter within five years. The existing 3,700 ft^2 (344 m^2) of panels are arrayed across the south sloping section of the roof, an exposure that had to be interfaced with the building's aerodynamic profile required to promote natural ventilation. Steven Winter Associates, energy consultants to the project, estimate that a typical new classroom building in this climate would use 75,000 Btu/ft^2 each year. They project the energy use at CES to be only 23,000 Btu/ft^2/yr, a 73 percent savings. Presently, the PV system provides about 13,000 Btu/ft^2/yr.

Artificial lighting in the Center is held to a power density of 0.9 W/ft^2, less than half of what most new classroom buildings use. The lighting is controlled by occupancy sensors. Along with the high levels of daylight in the building and its daytime-dominated occupancy, the low power density makes the task of providing all of the building's own energy more viable. In many buildings lighting accounts for half of the total energy used, and frequently about half of that is wasted by poor lighting design and lack of controls. The CES succeeds first in reducing the amount of supplemental artificial light needed, then makes certain it is used only as needed. This illustrates the green building principles of first using natural energy to replace nonrenewable energy and then using intelligence to replace resources.

Although the Living Machine does not literally form the entrance to the building, components of it do occupy the auditorium entryway, also called the Living Machine Atrium. As much as 2000 gallons per day of wastewater is first carried to an anaerobic digester tank and then to a closed aerobic digester where the water is cleansed of wastes by bacteria. Both of these closed digester tanks are buried outside the building. In the building and exposed to view, open aerobic digesters cleanse the water stream further with nitrate-absorbing plants and then deliver it to a clarifying tank. From there, the relatively pure water is polished in a constructed wetlands biofilter of plants and snails that surrounds the base of the open aerobic digesters. Then, the water is stored in a holding tank where it is ready for reuse as flush water.

Linking all of the systems together in this advanced-technology building required an integrated control system. Constant performance monitoring and adjustments to provide optimal control and interaction of its various mechanisms could probably not be done without automation. Integrated controls also include alarm functions that alert users if failures occur or are even anticipated. The digital control system designed for CES combines controls for mechanical, security, fire, and the Living Machine systems into one package. Interestingly, the constant monitoring also empowers learning through a continually updated exhibit located in the atrium. It displays data on energy use, photovoltaic power production, water consumption, and other measures of environmental performance.

Interior

Wood from sustainably managed forests was used for the roof beams and roof deck and left exposed for its natural warmth. Maple wood trim was selected according to the same criteria. Flooring is either finished concrete or interchangeable carpet squares, which are essentially leased from the manufacturer, rearranged for uniform wear, and exchanged with the manufacturer for recycling at the end of their useful life.

TECHNICAL INTEGRATION HIGHLIGHTS

Physical

- The raised floor contains electrical, plumbing, and heat pump systems.
- Leased carpet squares incorporate a maintenance program.
- The attachment detail of PV collectors facilitates replacement for technology upgrading.

Visual

- Exposed systems and metered performance features mesh with the CES teaching mission.
- The roof deck is exposed as an interior finish
- The location of CES on the north-south axis of the campus between the library/university center to the north and the largest compound of dormitories to the south ensures foot traffic through building.

Performance

- Efficient building design promotes downsizing of alternative energy systems, thus making both the

basic design improvements and the photovoltaic system cost-effective.

- PV panels shade the roof and are cooled in turn by air circulating between them and the aluminum roof deck.

DISCUSSION

Meta-design, to put William McDonough's approach in the context of Gregory Bateson's steps to an *Ecology of Mind* (1972), can be thought of as "the redesign of design." This means that the ideals of ecological design have to be taken to a logical extreme, through thinking that is considerably different from that by which we got into our current predicaments.

Arup & Partner's Alistair McGregor has stated (personal communication, 2001), "If the ideas of efficiency and alternative solutions are pushed far enough, then conventional systems are greatly diminished or disappear completely." Suddenly, very different kinds of cost-effectiveness can evolve as compared with conventional economic scenarios based solely on long-term energy savings. At Oberlin, for example, the photovoltaic system is feasible because the rest of the building pushes efficiency to the extreme. This principle was demonstrated in a conventional sense many years ago when winning examples of energy-efficient building competitions were analyzed on a first-cost basis. It turned out that the additional costs of increased insulation and higher-quality construction were totally offset by the reduced costs of smaller air-conditioning systems. More insulation means smaller systems and less space to put them in, equals reduced first cost and increased efficiency. What McGregor suggests is the same thing McDonough contends: We should add a design intelligence factor to that equation, finding radical ways to get rid of some conventional systems entirely or replace them with something that does the same thing in a radically different way.

How widespread are programs like the Oberlin Center for Environmental Studies? Judging solely by Internet Web sites in early 2001, there were more than 65 university-based programs in Environmental Studies in the United States, at least 7 in Canada, and more than a few in the United Kingdom. Counted along with education programs in sustainable design in architecture and other colleges, the intellectual momentum is growing. Like green parkland patches on a city map, the greening of universities can be plotted beside the green parkways, the green corporations, and the growing number of green buildings. As they multiply, their footprints spread and touch—small green patches sewn together into a larger and larger quilt.

Bibliography

General

Banham, Reyner. *Theory and Design in the First Machine Age.* London: Architectural Press,1960.

Bednar, Michael J. *The New Atrium.* New York: McGraw-Hill, 1986.

Bouman, Ole, and Roemer van Toorn, eds. *The Invisible in Architecture.* London: Academy Editions, 1994.

Brookes, Alan. *Cladding of Buildings.* 3d ed. London: E & FN Spon, 1998.

Brookes, Alan, and Chris Grech. *The Building Envelope: Applications of New Technology Cladding.* London: Butterworth, 1990.

Brookes, Alan, and Chris Grech. *Connections: Studies in Building Assembly.* New York: Whitney, 1994.

Brookes, Alan, and Chris Grech. *The Building Envelope and Connections.* Boston: Architecture Press, 1996.

Compagno, Andrea. *Intelligente Glasfassaden: Material, Anwendung, Gestaltung* (Intelligent glass façades: Material, practice, design [trans., Ingrid Taylor]). 4th ed. Basel, Switzerland: Birkhauser, 1999.

Davies, Collin. *High Tech Architecture.* New York: Rizzoli, 1988.

Ehrenkrantz, Ezra. *Architectural Systems: A Needs, Resources, and Design Approach.* New York: McGraw-Hill, 1989.

Ford, Edward R. *The Details of Modern Architecture,* Vol. 2, *1928 to 1988.* Cambridge: MIT Press, 1996.

Foster, Michael, ed. *The Principles of Architecture: Style, Structure and Design.* Oxford, U.K.: Quill Publishing, Ltd., 1983.

Frampton, Kenneth. *Studies in Tectonic Culture: The Poetics of Construction in Nineteenth and Twentieth Century Architecture.* Cambridge, MA: MIT Press, 1995.

Groák, Steven. *The Idea of Building: Thought and Action in the Design and Production of Buildings.* London and New York: E & FN Spon, 1992.

McGuinness, William J., Benjamin Stein, and John S. Reynolds. *Mechanical and Electrical Equipment for Buildings.* 7th ed. New York: John Wiley & Sons, Inc., 1986.

Moore, Fuller. *Understanding Structures.* Boston: McGraw-Hill, 1999.

Orton, Andrew. *The Way We Build Now: Form, Scale and Technique.* Wokingham, U.K.: Van Nostrand Reinhold, 1988.

Papadakis, Andreas. *The End of Innovation in Architecture.* Berks, U.K.: Windsor, 1998.

Pawley, Martin. *Theory and Design in the Second Machine Age.* Oxford, U.K., and Cambridge, MA: B. Blackwell, 1990.

Rush, Richard, ed. *The Building Systems Integration Handbook.* New York: John Wiley & Sons, Inc., 1986.

Sandaker, Bjørn Normann, and Arne Petter Eggen. *The Structural Basis of Architecture.* New York: Whitney, 1992.

Saxon, Richard. *Atrium Comes of Age.* U.K.: Harlow: Longman Group, 1993.

Stein, Benjamin, and John S. Reynolds. *Mechanical and Electrical Equipment for Buildings.* 8th ed. New York: John Wiley & Sons, Inc., 1992.

Stein, Benjamin, and John S. Reynolds. *Mechanical and Electrical Equipment for Buildings.* 9th ed. New York: John Wiley & Sons, Inc., 2000.

Wilkinson, Chris. *Supersheds: The Architecture of Long-Span, Large Volume Buildings.* Boston: Butterworth Architecture, 1996.

Zalewski, Waclaw, and Edward Allen. *Shaping Structures: Statics.* New York: John Wiley & Sons, Inc., 1998.

Preface

Rush, Richard, ed. *The Building Systems Integration Handbook.* New York: John Wiley & Sons, Inc., 1986.

Venturi, Robert. *Complexity and Contradiction in Architecture* (with an introduction by Vincent Scully). New York: Museum of Modern Art, 1966.

Part I: Methods

CHAPTER 1

Alexander, Christopher. *Notes on the Synthesis of Form.* Cambridge: Harvard University Press, 1964, p. 73.

Bell, Daniel. *The Coming of Post Industrial Society.* New York: Basic Books, 1973.

Beranek, Leo. *Music, Acoustics and Architecture.* New York: John Wiley & Sons, Inc., 1962.

Bohm, David. *Wholeness and the Implicate Order.* London: Routledge and Kegan Paul, 1980.

Bohm, David. *The Holographic Paradigm and Other Paradoxes.* Boulder, CO: Shambala, 1985.

Capra, Fritjov. *The Turning Point: Science, Society, and the Rising Culture.* Toronto: Bantam Books, 1988.

Csikszentmihalyi, Mihaly. *Creativity: Flow and the Psychology of Discovery and Invention.* New York: HarperCollins, 1996.

Davies, Colin. *High Tech Architecture.* New York: Rizzoli International Publications, 1988.

Hurwitz, Adams Elisabeth. *Design: A Search for Essentials.* Scranton: International Textbook Company, 1964.

Jencks, Charles. *The Architecture of the Jumping Universe: A Polemic: How Complexity Science Is Changing Architecture and Culture.* London: Academy Editions,1995.

Kuhn, Thomas S. *The Structure of Scientific Revolutions.* Chicago: University of Chicago Press, 1962.

Lawson, Bryan. *How Designers Think.* 2d ed. London: Butterworth Architecture, 1990.

Lyle, John Tillman. *Regenerative Design for Sustainable Development.* New York: John Wiley & Sons, Inc., 1994. p. 42.

Margolin, Victor, and Richard Buchanan, eds. *The Idea of Design: A Design Issues Reader.* Cambridge: MIT Press, 1995

Mazria, Edward. "Number Magic." Paper presented at the Annual Meeting of the American Solar Energy Society, Cocoa Beach, Florida, July 1992. Boulder, CO: American Solar Energy Society, 1992.

Nadeau, Robert, and Menas Kafatos. *The Non-local Universe: The New Physics and Matters of the Mind.* Oxford: University Press, 1999.

Pérez Gómez, Alberto. *Génesis y Superación del Funcionalismo en Arquitectura* (Architecture and the crisis of modern science). Cambridge, MA: MIT Press, 1983.

Prawley, Martin. *Theory and Design in the Second Machine Age.* Oxford: Basel Blackwell, Ltd., 1990.

Rowe, Peter. G. *Design Thinking.* Cambridge: MIT Press, 1987.

Rush, Richard. *The Building Systems Integration Handbook.* New York: John Wiley & Sons, Inc., 1986.

Sabine, Wallace Clement. *Collected Papers on Acoustics.* Cambridge, MA: Harvard University Press, 1922.

Stevens, Garry. *The Reasoning Architect.* New York: McGraw-Hill, 1990.

Thompson, D'Arcy Wentworth. *On Growth and Form.* Cambridge, U.K.: Cambridge University Press; New York: Macmillan, 1945.

Whiteman, John, Jeffrey Kipnis, and Richard Burdett, ed.s *Strategies in Architectural Thinking.* Cambridge: MIT Press, 1992.

Willis, Daniel. *The Emerald City and Other Essays on Architecture,* New York: Princeton Architectural Press, 1999.

CHAPTER 2

Aguilar, Rodolfo J. *Systems Analysis and Design: In Engineering, Construction, and Planning.* Englewood Cliffs, NJ: Prentice-Hall, 1973.

Alexander, Christopher. *Notes on the Synthesis of Form.* Cambridge, MA: Harvard University Press, 1964.

Banham, Reyner Peter. *L'Architecttura.* (February 1959):

Banham, Reyner Peter. *L'Espresso* (March 1958):

Banham, Reyner Peter. *The Architecture of the Well-Tempered Environment.* Chicago: University of Chicago Press, and London: Architectural Press, 1969.

Banham, Reyner Peter. *The New Brutalism: Ethic or Aesthetic?* London: Architectural Press, 1966.

Barrow, John D. *The Artful Universe.* Oxford: Oxford University Press, 1995.

Drew, Philip. *Third Generation: The Changing Meaning of Architecture.* New York: Praeger Publishers, 1972.

Fitch, James Marston. *American Building: The Environmental Forces That Shape It.* Boston: Houghton Mifflin, 1966.

Forgacs, Eva. *The Bauhaus Idea and Bauhaus Politics.* Budapest: Central European University Press, 1995.

Geddes, Patrick, Sir. *Cities in Evolution.* Edited by the Outlook Tower Association, Edinburgh, and the Association for Planning and Regional Reconstruction, London. New York: Oxford University Press, 1950.

Gleick, James. *Making a New Science.* New York: Penguin Books, 1988.

Groák, Steven. *The Idea of Building: Thought and Action in the Design and Production of Buildings.* London: E & FN Spon, 1992.

Gropius, Walter. *The New Architecture and the Bauhaus.* Cambridge: MIT Press, 1965.

Kelso, J. A. Scott. *Dynamic Patterns: The Self-Organization of Brain and Behavior.* Cambridge: MIT Press, 1995.

Kepes, Gyorgy. *Structure in Art and in Science.* New York: G. Braziller, 1965.

Lyle, John Tillman. *Regenerative Design For Sustainable Development.* New York: John Wiley & Sons, Inc. 1994.

Margolin, Victor, and Richard Buchanan, eds. *The Idea of Design: A Design Issues Reader.* Cambridge: MIT Press, 1995.

Mueller, Robert E. *The Science of Art: The Cybernetics of Creative Communication.* New York: John Day, 1967.

Mumford, Lewis. *Architecture.* Chicago: American Library Association, 1926.

Norberg-Schultz, Christian. *Intentions in Architecture.* Cambridge: MIT Press, 1965.

Pawley, Martin. *Theory and Design in the Second Machine Age.* Oxford, U.K., and Cambridge, MA: B. Blackwell, 1990.

Pfammatter, Ulrich. *The Making of the Modern Architect and Engineer: The Origins and Development of a Scientific and Industrially Oriented Education.* Basel: Birkhauser, 2000.

Rybczynski, Witold. *Home: A Short History of an Idea.* New York: Viking, 1986.

Serving the World: The New Lloyd's Building. London: Lloyd's List, Lloyd's of London Press, 1986.

Stein, Benjamin, and John Reynolds. *Mechanical and Electrical Equipment for Buildings.* 8th ed. New York: John Wiley & Sons, Inc., 1992.

Stevens, Garry. *The Reasoning Architect: Mathematics and Science in Design.* New York: McGraw-Hill, 1990.

Thompson, D'Arcy Wentworth. *On Growth and Form.* Cambridge, U.K.: Cambridge University Press; New York: Macmillan, 1945.

Whitford, Frank. *Bauhaus.* New York: Thames and Hudson, 1984.

CHAPTER 3

Egan, M. David. *Concepts in Architectural Acoustics*. New York: McGraw-Hill, 1972.

Engle, Heino. *Structure Systems*. Stüttgart, Germany: Gerd Hatje Publishers.

Frampton, Kenneth. *Studies in Tectonic Culture: The Poetics of Construction in Nineteenth and Twentieth Century Architecture*. Cambridge, MA: MIT Press, 1995.

Givoni, B. *Man, Climate, and Architecture*. 2d ed. London: Applied Science Publishers, 1976.

Groák, Steven. *The Idea of Building: Thought and Action in the Design and Production of Buildings*. London and New York: E & FN Spon, 1992.

Hunt, Tony. *Tony Hunt's Structure Notebook*. Oxford: Butterworth-Heinemann, 1997.

Knowles, Ralph L. *Sun Rhythm Form*. Cambridge: MIT Press, 1981.

Lyle, John Tillman. *Regenerative Design for Sustainable Development*. New York: John Wiley & Sons, Inc., 1994.

Macdonald, Angus J. *Structure and Architecture*. Oxford: Butterworth- Heinemann, 1994.

Mostafavi, Mohsen, and David Leatherbarrow. *On Weathering: The Life of Buildings in Time*. Cambridge: MIT Press, 1993.

Norberg-Schulz, Christian. *Intentions in Architecture*. Cambridge, MA.: MIT Press, 1965.

Olgyay, Victor, *Design with Climate: Bioclimatic Approach to Architectural Regionalism*. (Some chapters based on cooperative research with Aladar Olgyay.) Princeton, NJ Princeton University Press, 1963.

Papadakis, Andreas. *The End of Innovation in Architecture*. Berks, U.K.: Windsor: 1998.

Sandaker, Bjorn Norman, and Arne Petter Eggen. *The Structural Basis of Architecture*. New York: Whitney Library of Design, 1992.

Stein, Benjamin, and John S. Reynolds. *Mechanical and Electrical Equipment for Buildings*. 9th ed.. New York: John Wiley & Sons, Inc., 2000.

Wilson, Forrest. "A Time of Relentless Technological Change: Chronicling How It Has Revolutionized Building During the 75 Years." *AIA Journal* 76(12) (December 1987): 115–119.

Zalewski, Waclaw, and Edward Allen. *Shaping Structures: Statics*. New York: John Wiley & Sons, Inc., 1998.

CHAPTER 4

Athanasopulos, Christos G. *Contemporary Theater: Evolution and Design*. New York: John Wiley & Sons, Inc., 1983.

Bazjanac, Vladimir, and Frederick Winkelmann. "Daylighting Design for the Pacific Museum of Flight: Energy Impacts." *Energy and Buildings* 13 (1989): 187–199.

Churchman, C. West. *The Systems Approach*. New York: Delacorte Press, 1968.

Collins, Peter. *Architectural Judgement*. London: Faber, 1971.

"The Crystal Cathedral: Embodiment of Light and Nature." *Architectural Record* 11 (1980): 82.

Csikszentmihalyi, Mihaly. *Creativity: Flow and the Psychology of Discovery and Invention*. New York: HarperCollins, 1996.

Dürckheim, Karlfried Graf. *Hara, the Vital Centre of Man*. London: G. Allen & Unwin, 1962.

Griffiths, John F., and Dennis M. Driscoll. *Survey of Climatology*. Columbus, OH: Merrill Publishing, 1982.

Gropius, Walter. *The New Architecture and the Bauhaus*. Translated from the German by P. Morton Shand, with an introduction by Frank Pick. London: Faber and Faber, 1935.

Harries, Karsten. "Thoughts on a Non-Arbitrary Architecture." *Perspecta* 20 (1983): 9–20.

Hawkes, Dean, ed. *Models and Systems in Architecture and Building*. Hornby, U.K.: Construction Press, Ltd., 1975.

Heidegger, Martin. *Existence and Being*. Chicago: H. Regnery, 1949.

Maslow, Abraham H. *Motivation and Personality*. New York: Harper, 1954.

Milne, Murray, and Barauch Givoni. "Architectural Design Based on Climate." In *Energy Conservation in Building Design*, edited by Donald Watson. New York: McGraw-Hill, 1979.

Mueller, Robert E. *The Science of Art: The Cybernetics of Creative Communication*. New York: John Day, 1967.

Norberg-Schulz, Christian. *Intentions in Architecture*. Cambridge, MA: MIT Press 1965.

Pena, William. *Problem Seeking: An Architectural Programming Primer* (with William Caudill and John Focke). Boston: Cahners Books, 1977.

Olgyay, Aladar, and Victor Olgyay. *Solar Control and Shading Devices*. Princeton: Princeton University Press, 1957.

Olgyay, Victor. *Design with Climate*. Princeton: Princeton University Press, 1963.

Rapoport, Amos. *House Form and Culture*. Englewood Cliffs, NJ: Prentice-Hall, 1969.

Sabine, Wallace Clement. *Collected Papers on Acoustics*. Cambridge, MA: Harvard University Press, 1922.

Sobin, Harris J. "Le Corbusier in North Africa: The Birth of the Brise Soleil." In *Desert Housing*, edited by K. N. Clark and Patricia Paylore. Tucson: Office of Arid Land Studies, University of Arizona, (1980), 153–173.

Steadman, Phillip. "Models in Our Head, Models in the Material World, and Models of Objective Knowledge." In *Models and Systems in Architecture and Building: Proceedings of the Second Annual Conference on Land Use and Built Forms Studies*, edited by Dean Hawkes. Cambridge, U.K.: University of Cambridge, 2000.

U.S. Air Force, Air Weather Service (AWS), Environmental Technical Applications Center. *Facility Design and Planning, Engineering Weather Data*. AF Manual 88–29. Washington DC: U.S. Department of Defense, 1994.

Venturi, Robert. *Complexity and Contradiction in Architecture*. (With an introduction by Vincent Scully.) New York: Museum of Modern Art, 1966.

Willis, Daniel. *The Emerald City and Other Essays on the Architectural Imagination*. New York: Princeton Architectural Press, 1999.

The Pacific Museum of Flight

Bazjanac, Vladimir, and Frederick Winkelmann. "Daylighting Design for the Pacific Museum of Flight: Energy Impacts." *Energy and Buildings* 13(3) (1989): 187–199.

Lin, Charles. "Museum of Flight: A Flight into Light." *Architectural Lighting* 11 (1987):23–29.

Garden Grove Crystal Cathedral

Heyer, Paul. *American Architecture: Ideas and Ideologies in the Late Twentieth Century.* New York: Van Nostrand Reinhold, 1993.

Hubeli, Ernst. "The Church Which Is 'Higher, Wider and Longer than Notre-Dame.'" *Aktuelles Bauen* 16(12) (1980): 7–13.

Johnson, Philip. *Johnson/Burgee, Architecture.* Text by Nory Miller ; photographs by Richard Payne. New York: Random House, 1979.

Knight, Carleton. *Philip Johnson/John Burgee Architecture 1979–1985.* New York: Rizzoli International Publications, 1985.

Pastier, John. "An Evangelist of Unusual Architectural Aspirations: Twenty Years in a Neutra Church [the Garden Grove Community Church], Dr. Robert Schuller is Building a Johnson/Burgee." *AIA Journal* 68(5) (1979): 48–55.

Walden, Russell. "Californian Dream Star." *New Zealand Architect* 6 (1983): 33–40.

Walden, Russell. "Californian Monument to the Power of Televangelism." *Institute for the Study of Worship & Religious Architecture* (1984): 24–32.

Part II: Case Studies

CHAPTER 5: LABORATORIES

"A Moving Target." *Architectural Record* 2 (February 1991): 97–109.

Banham, Reyner. *The Architecture of the Well-Tempered Environment.* Chicago: University of Chicago Press, 1969.

McHarg, Ian L. *Design with Nature.* Garden City, NY: Natural History Press, 1969.

Richards Medical Laboratories

Allison, David. "Places for Research." *International Science and Technology* (September 1962): 23.

"Arcasismo Technologico." *L'Architecturra* VI (October 1960): 410–11.

"Art Serves Science: Alfred Newton Richards Medical Research Building, University of Pennsylvania, Philadelphia, Pa." *Architectural Record* CXXVIII (August 1960): 147–156.

Banham, Reyner Peter. *The Architecture of the Well-Tempered Environment.* Chicago: University of Chicago Press, 1969.

"Shapes of Tomorrow, Two Buildings in Diverging Directions." *Interiors* CXX (July 1961): 41.

Fitch, James Marston. "A Building of Rugged Fundamentals." *Architectural Forum* CXIII (July 1960): 82–87, 185.

Ford, Edward R. *The Details of Modern Architecture.* Vol. 2, 1928 to 1988. Cambridge, MA: MIT Press, 1996.

Fratelli, Enzo. "Louis Kahn." *Zodiac* VIII(1961): 14–17.

Green, Wilder. "Louis Kahn, Architect: Alfred Newton Richards Medical Research Building, University of Pennsylvania." *Museum of Modern Art Bulletin* XXVII(1)(1961):1–24.

Guise, David. *Design and Technology in Architecture.* New York: John Wiley & Sons, Inc., 1985.

Gutman, Robert, ed. *People and Buildings.* New York: Basic Books, 1972.

Gutman, Robert. *Architectural Practice: A Critical View.* Princeton: Princeton Architectural Press, 1988.

Jordy, William H. "Medical Research Building for Pennsylvania University, Philadelphia." *Architectural Review* CXXIX (February 1961): 98–106.

Komendant, August E, *18 Years with Architect Louis I. Kahn.* Englewood, NJ: Aloray, 1975.

"Kahn's Medical Science Building Dedicated at University of Pennsylvania." *Progressive Architecture* XXXXI (June 1960): 49–53.

"Laboratoires de recherches médicales Alfred Newton à l'Université de Pennsylvanie." *L'Architecture d'Aujourd'hui* (35) (February 1962): 76–86.

Latour, Alessandra, ed. *Louis I. Kahn: Writing, Lectures, Interviews.* New York: Rizzoli International Publications, Inc, 1991.

"Louis Kahn." *Kokusai Kentiku* 34(January 1967): 9–98.

"Louis Kahn." *L'Architecture d'Aujourd'Hui* 33(105)(1962–1963): LXXX–39.

"Louis Kahn, Laboratoires à l'Université de Pennsylvanie, tats-Unis." *L'Architecture d'Aujourd'hui* (91–92) (September/October/November 1960): 66–67.

Onobayashi, Hiroki. "Louis Kahn and Alfred Newton Richards Medical Research building." *Kokusai Kentiku* XXVIII (March 1961): 64–69.

Scully, Vincent. "Kahn: Solidity and Silence: Vincent Scully's Talk on Louis Kahn at the RIBA." *Building Design* 449(6) (1979): 2.

Scully, Vincent. *Louis I. Kahn.* New York: Braziller, 1962.

Scully, Vincent. "Light, Form and Power." *Architectural Forum* (August-September 1964): 162–170.

Tyng, Alexandra. *Beginnings: Louis I. Kahn's Philosophy of Architecture.* New York: John Wiley & Sons, Inc., 1984.

Ueli, Roth. "Louis Kahn und die medical towers in Philadelphia." *Werk* (January 1962): 22–25.

Salk Institute for Biological Studies

"Laboratory 1: Procession of Massive Forms." *Architectural Forum* 122(2) (May 1965): 36–45.

"L'Institute Salk à San Diego en Californie." *L'Architecture d'Aujourd'Hui* 55–56 (January 1967): 4–10.

"Louis Kahn." *Kokusai Kentiku* 34 (January 1967): 9–98.

"Louis Kahn." *L'Architecture d'Aujourd'Hui* 40(142) (1969): complete issue.

McCoy, Esther. "Dr. Salk Talks About His Institute." *Architecture Forum* (5) December (1967): 27–35.

McCoy, Esther. "Salk Research Laboratories." *Lotus* (1967–68): 15–123.

"The Mind of Louis Kahn." *Architectural Forum* 137(1) (1972): complete issue.

"Not for the Faint-Hearted." *AIA Journal* 55 (June 1971): :25–31.

"Provocative Setting for an Endless Search." *Engineering News Record* 176(4) (1966): 78–80, 83–84.

"Recent Projects." *Progressive Architecture* 42 (April 1961): 130–149.

"Recent Work of Louis Kahn." *Zodiak* 17 (1967): 58–117.

Rowan, Jan C. "Wanting To Be: The Philadelphia School." *Progressive Architecture* XLII(April 1961): 130–149.

"Salk Institute, La Jolla." *World Architecture* 4 (1967): 40–47.

The Salk Institute. A brochure for visitors distributed at the Institute, February 1992.

Stoller, Ezra. *The Salk Institute*. New York: Princeton Architectural Press, 1999.

"Ten Buildings That Point the Future." *Fortune Magazine* LXXII(6) (1965): 174–8.

"Zwei forrschungalaboratorien." *Werk* 54 (April 1967): 193–204.

Schlumberger Research Laboratory

"British Arch." *Architecture Movement Continuie* 9(10) (1985): 45.

Brookes, Alan, and Chris Grech. *The Building Envelope and Connections*. Boston: Architecture Press, 1996.

Brookes, Alan, and Chris Grech. *The Building Envelope: Applications of New Technology Cladding* London: Butterworth, 1990.

"Centre de Recherche Schlumberger." *L'Architecture d'Aujourd'hui* (2) (1985): 33, 38.

Croak, S. "Appraisal: Schlumberger Research Ltd., Cambridge." *Architects' Journal* 182(38) (1985): 4359.

Davies, Collin. *High Tech Architecture*. New York: Rizzoli, 1988.

Dietsch, Deborah. "Ties that Bind: Schlumberger Cambridge Research Center." *Architectural Record* 174(4) (1986): 136–147.

Hannay, Patrick. "A Glimpse of Tomorrow." *Architects' Journal* 181(20) (1985): 28–31.

Harpin, P. "Zirkus Schlumberger: Forschungsgebaude." *Deutsche Bauzeitung* 120(2) (1986): 24–29.

Haward, Birkin. "Hopkins at Cambridge." *Architects' Journal* 179(5) (1984): 40–47.

Hernberg, H. "High Flyer." *Architects' Journal* 180(43) (1984): 43–63.

Hunt, Anthony. "An Architecturally Minded Builder." *Techniques & Architecture* 356(10–11)(1986): 128–138.

Jenkins, David. *Schlumberger Cambridge Research Centre: Michael Hopkins and Partners*. London: Phaidon, 1993.

"Lightweight Structures." *Building* 10 (June 10, 1983): 28–35.

"Merchandise Seen in a Bright New Light." *Architectural Record* 2 (1982): 106–111.

"Michael Hopkins Architects, Projects and Realizations." *L'Architecture d'Aujourd'hui*. 237(2) (February 1985): 18–58

Moseley, Peter. "Sails on the Cam." *Building Services* 16(2) (1994): 13–16.

Sandaker, Bjørn Normann, and Arne Petter Eggen. *The Structural Basis of Architecture*. New York: Whitney, 1992.

"Schlumberger Cambridge Research." *Tubular Structures* 38(8) (1985): 16–17.

"Schlumberger Cambridge Research Center: Architects: Michael Hopkins & Partners." *A&U* 9(192) (September 1986): 13–22.

"Schlumberger-Forschung in Cambridge." *Baumeister* 83(11) (1986): 34–39.

Winter, John, and Sarah Jackson. "Technology Stretching High-Tech." *Architects' Journal* 196(17) (1992): 31–42.

PA Technology Laboratory

Allen, Edward. *Shaping Structures*. New York: John Wiley & Sons, Inc., 1998.

Blackwell, Lewis. "Princeton Palace." *Building Design*. (September 1985): 10.

Boles, Daralice D. "Roger's U.S. Debut." *Progressive Architecture* 66(8) (August 1985): 67–74.

Brookes, Alan. *The Building Envelope: Applications of New Technology Cladding*. London: Butterworth Architecture, 1990.

Brookes, Alan, and Chris Grech. *The Building Envelope and Connections*. Boston: Architecture Press, 1996.

Buchanan, Peter." Patscenter, Princeton, New Jersey, USA." *Architectural Review* 174(1037) (July 1983): 43–47.

Carstairs, Eileen. "PA Targets Princeton for High Tech: British Consulting Firm PA Technology's Flexible New U.S. Headquarters Could Set a Pattern For Future R & D Facilities." *Corporate Design & Realty* 5(5) (May 1986): 30–35.

Davies, Collin. *High Tech Architecture*. New York: Rizzoli, 1988.

DiBerardinis, Louis J, Janet S. Baum, Melvin W. First, Gari T. Gatwood, and Anand K. Seth. *Guidelines for Laboratory Design: Health and Safety Considerations*. New York: John Wiley & Sons, Inc.,1987.

Ford, Edward R. *The Details of Modern Architecture*. Vol. 2, 1928 to 1988. Cambridge, MA: MIT Press, 1996.

Gardner, Ian. "Patscenter." *Arup Journal* 21(2) (Summer 1986): 8–16.

Moore, Fuller. *Understanding Structures*. Boston: McGraw-Hill, 1999.

Nakamura, Toshio, ed. "Richard Rogers 1978–1988." *Architecture and Urbanism* (extra edition) 12 (December 1988): 1–312.

Powell, Kenneth. *Richard Rogers*. London: Artemis, 1994.

Rogers, Richard. "Richard Rogers—1978–1988." *A&U* 12 (suppl.) (1988): 8–312.

Russell, Frank, ed. *Richard Rogers + Architects*. With an introduction by Peter Cook. New York: St. Martin's Press, 1985.

Sherratt, Alan. *Air Conditioning: Impact on the Built Environment*. New York: Nichols Publishing, 1987.

Sudjic, David. *The Architecture of Richard Rogers*. London: Fourth Estate and Wordsearch, 1994.

Wilkinson, Chris. *Supersheds: The Architecture of Long-Span, Large Volume Buildings*. Boston: Butterworth Architecture, 1996.

Zalewski, Waclaw, and Edward Allen. *Shaping Structures: Statics*. New York: John Wiley & Sons, Inc., 1998.

Wallace Earth Sciences Laboratory

Clarke, Andrew. "Professionalism in the Prairies." *Canadian Architect* 29(1) (1984): 32, 41.

"Not Just Another Glass Box." *Architectural Record* 171(4) (April 1983): 146–149.

Oppenheimer, Andrea Dean. "Sixth Annual Review of Recent World Architecture." *Architecture (AIA)* 76(9) (September 1987): 45–95.

"Research Buildings 1: Scientific Barn." *Canadian Architect* 41(6) (June 1996): 20–21.

Sachner, Paul. "Heavy Metal." *Architectural Record* 175 (6) (May 1987): 126–135.

Wilson, Forrest. "Industrialized Buildings: Our Theories and Techniques." *Architectural Technology (AIA)* 2(2) (fall 1984): 6–19.

Wilson, Forrest. 'The Logic Of Industrial Assembly." *Architecture (AIA)* 76 (3) (March 1987): 50–57.

Wilson, Forrest, Ron Keenberg, and William Loerke. *Architecture: Fundamental Issues*. New York: Van Nostrand Reinhold, 1990

CHAPTER 6: OFFICES

Hartkopf, Wolker, Vivian Loftness, Pleasantine Drake, Fred Dubin, Peter Mill, and George Ziga. *Designing the Office of the Future: The Japanese Approach to Tomorrow's Workplace*. New York: John Wiley & Sons, Inc., 1993.

Heathcote, Edwin. *Bank Builders*. New York: John Wiley & Sons, Inc., 2000.

Laing, Andrew, Francis Duffy, Denice Jaunzens, and Steve Willis. *New Environments for Working: The Redesign of Offices and Environmental Systems for New Ways of Working*. London: BRE & DEGW, 1998.

Parnassus Foundation and Museum of Fine Arts, Houston. *Money Matters: A Critical Look at Bank Architecture*. New York: McGraw-Hill, 1990.

John Deere Headquarters

"Bold and Direct, Using Metal in a Strong, Basic Way." *Architectural Record* 136(7) (1964): 135–142.

Canty, Donald. "Evaluation: The Wonders and the Workings of Saarinen's Deere & Co. Headquarters." *AIA Journal* 65(8): 18–21.

Carter, Brian. "Material Culture: Eero Saarinen and Operational Thoroughness: A Way of Working." Dimensions 14 (2000): 32–39.

Carter, Brian. "Material Culture: Eero Saarinen and Operational Thoroughness." *Ptah* 1 (2001): 20–26.

Cheek, Lawrence. W. *Eero Saarinen: Architect, Sculptor, Visionary*. St. Louis: JNEHA, 1998.

Dean, Andrea O. "Eero Saarinen in Perspective: A Generation After His Loss, a Discussion of His Work and Influence." *AIA Journal* 70(13) (November 1981): 36–51.

"Deere and Co., USA." *Architectural Design* 35 (1965): 404–409.

"Eero Saarinen." *Architecture and Urbanism* (April 1984 extra ed.): 1–240.

Fitch, James Marston. *American Building: The Environmental Forces That Shape It*. Boston: Houghton Mifflin, 1966.

Ford, Edward R. *The Details of Modern Architecture*. Vol. 2, 1928 to 1988. Cambridge, MA: MIT Press, 1996.

Hall, Edward T. *The Hidden Dimension*. New York: Doubleday, 1951.

Hall, Edward T., and Mildred Reed Hall. *The Fourth Dimension in Architecture: The Impact of Building on Behavior: Eero Saarinen's Administrative Center for Deere & Company, Moline, Illinois*. Santa Fe: Sunstone Press, 1975.

Hewitt, William. "The Genesis of a Great Building—And of an Unusual Friendship." *AIA Journal* 56(8): 36–37.

Jacobus, John. "Criticism: John Deere Office Building." *Architectural Review* 137 (May 1965): 364–371.

"John Deere's Sticks of Steel." *Architectural Forum* 121(7) (1964): 76–84.

Lessing, Lawrence. "The Diversity of Eero Saarinen." *Architectural Forum* 113(1) (July 1960): 94–103.

Manser, Michael. "Building Favorites." *The Architects' Journal* (1): 43.

Pelli, Cesar. "Eero Saarinen—His Immediate Influence." *Architecture and Urbanism* 105(6) (1979): 15–18.

Saarinen, Eero. *Eero Saarinen on his Work*. New Haven: Yale University Press, 1968.

Temko, Allan. *Eero Saarinen*. New York: George Braziller, 1962.

Willis Faber Dumas Insurance Headquarters

"*Achitects' Journal* Action Saves Modern Classic. *Architects' Journal* 193(8) (1991): 11.

Banham, R. Foster, Associates. *RIBA Publications Ltd* (1979): 46–47.

Barrie, Giles. *Building Design* 1154 (December 1993): 1.

Bramante, Gabriele. *Willis Faber & Dumas Building: Foster Associates*. London: Phaidon, 1993.

Brookes, Alan. *Cladding of Buildings*. 3d ed. London: E & FN Spon, 1998.

"Cladding: Offices: Foster Associates." *Architects' Journal* 191(19) (1990): 63–65.

Cruickshank, Dan. "Masterclass, Willis Faber & Dumas, Ipswich 1975–1997." *RIBA Journal* 104(7) (1997): 44–51.

Davies, Collin. *High Tech Architecture*. New York: Rizzoli, 1988.

Dawson, Susan. "Glass Evolution" *Architectural Review* 210(1254) (August 2001): 94–97.

Eddy, David Hamilton. "Dreams of the Corporate Man." *RIBA Journal* 97(9) (September 1990): 60–62.

"Federated Skills: In June, Insurance Broker Willis Faber & Dumas Decentralised to Ipswich." *Design* 321(September 1975): 42–49.

"Foster in Ipswich." *Architects' Journal* 161(23) (1975): 1160–2.

Foster, Norman. "Foster Associates: Buildings and Projects. *Architectural Design* 47(9/10) (1977): 614–625.

"Foster Listing Plan Springs a Leak." *Architects' Journal* 194(6) (1991): 10.

Foster, Norman. *Foster Associates Buildings and Projects*. Vol. 2. London: Watermark, 1989.

Foster, Norman. "The Design Philosophy of the Willis Faber & Dumas Building in Ipswich." *ERA* 45(8) (1977): 52–54.

"Foster's Ipswich Classic Doomed." *Architects' Journal* 193(10) (1991): 11.

Hannay, Patrick. "Gläserne Amöbe: Hauptverwaltung Willis Faber & Dumas in Ipswich von Foster Associates, 1973–75." (Glass amoeba: Headquarters). Deutsche Bauzeitung 131(4) (April 1997): 100–104.

Hewitt, John. *Willis Faber & Dumas Building*. New York: Anglian, 1988.

"Hollow Victory at Willis Faber." *Architects' Journal* 196(5) (1992): 7.

"Ipswich Centre." *Architectural Design* 45(7) (1975): 418–19.

"Ipswich Reflections." *Architectural Review* 158 (suppl.) (1975): 130–154.

"Ipswich Headquarters." *RIBA Journal* 84(8) (1977): 330–354.

Kirkwood, Ken. *Construction Methods*. London: Watts, 1991.

LeCuyer, Annette. "Evaluation: A Building that Succeeds in Losing Itself: The Willis Faber Offices." *AIA Journal* 70(4) (1981): 58–67.

"Main Office for Willis Faber and Dumas Ltd. Ipswich." *Architectural Design* 42(11) (1972): 686–701.

"New in England: Uffici (Offices)." *Domus* 552 (November 1975): 30–32 (yellow pages 1–2).

Papademetriou, Peter. "Coming of Age: Eero Saarinen and Modern American Architecture." *Perspecta* 21 (1984): 116–143.

"The Past and Future History of the Willis Faber Dumas Building." *RSA Journal* 143(5463) (1995): 63–76.

"Recent Works of Foster Associates." *Architecture and Urbanism* 125(2) (1981): 43–111.

"RIBA Medal Winner Pulls in the Praise." *Architects' Journal* 191(17) (1990): 11.

Sainz, Jorge. "Un Constructor de Altura, Norman Foster: las Dos Primeras Décadas" (A builder of height, Norman Foster: The first two decades). *A & V* 38 (1992): 6–8.

Sandaker, Bjørn Normann, and Arne Petter Eggen. *The Structural Basis of Architecture.* New York: Whitney, 1992.

Serviens, Stephen. "Willis Faber & Dumas: Roof Gardens." *Architects' Journal* 172(38) (1920): 569–573.

Silva, Donat. *Willis Faber & Dumas Building.* New York: Woodman, 1990.

"Through the Looking Glass." *Concrete Quarterly* 115(10–12) (1977): 10–11.

Wigginton, Michael. "Bossom Lectures on the Making of Great Architecture: 3. Legacies: the Glass Wall and Other Stories." *RSA Journal* 143(5463) (October 1995): 63–76.

Wilkinson, Chris. *Supersheds: The Architecture of Long-Span, Large Volume Buildings.* Boston: Butterworth Architecture, 1996.

"Willis Faber & Dumas: Ipswich 1975–1977." *RIBA Journal* 104(7) (1997): 44–51.

"Willis Faber and Dumas Head Office, Ipswich (England), 1975." *Architecture and Urbanism* 5 (May, extra ed., 1988): 88–101.

"Willis Faber Pool under Threat." *Architects' Journal* 195(3) (1992): 6.

"Working Details Revisit: Cladding: Offices." *Architects' Journal* 191(19) (1990): 63–65.

Briarcliff House

Bonner, Mike, and Terry Raggett. "Leslie & Godwin, Farnborough." *Arup Journal* 20(2) (1985): 2–8.

"Briarcliff House." *A&U* 192(9) (1986): 34–40.

"Briarcliff House." *Tubular Structures* 38(8) (1985): 9.

Hanny, Patrick, and Gordon Nelson. "Farnborough Salute: Briarcliff House; The Glass of '84." *Architects' Journal* 180(36) (1984): 63–82.

Nelson, Gordon. "Energy Revisit: Briarcliff House." *Architects' Journal* 183(7) (1986): 53–56.

Lockheed Building 157

Bednar, Michael J. *The New Atrium.* New York: McGraw-Hill, 1986.

Benton, Charles C., and Marc Fountain. "Successfully Daylighting a Large Commercial Building: A Case Study of Lockheed Building 157." (Details, graphs, photographs, plan, sections, bibliography.) *Progressive Architecture* 71(12) (November 1990): 119–121.

Gardner, James B. "Daylighting Cuts Energy Use to 19,600 Btu per sq ft per Year." (Photographs, plans, sections.) *Architectural Record* 172(1) (January 1984): 138–143.

Lam, William C. *Sunlighting as a Formgiver for Architecture.* New York: Van Nostrand Reinhold, 1986.

McNicholl, Ann. "Daylighting in Perspective." *Architects' Journal* 201(7) (February 16, 1995): 35–37,

Newman, Elizabeth. "Lockheed Building 157: Progettare con modelli e simulazioni" [Lockheed Building 157: The use

of modelling to shape building form]. *Arca* 26(4) (1989): 30–37.

Pilar, Viladas. "Through a Glass Brightly." *Progressive Architecture* 11 (1981): 138.

Saxon, Richard. *Atrium Comes of Age.* Harlow, U.K.: Longman Group, 1993.

Shanus, Michael D. "Going Beyond the Perimeter with Daylight," *Lighting Design and Application* (March 1984): 40.

Smith, Fran Kellog, and Fred J. Bertolone. *Bringing Interiors to Light.* New York: Whitney Library of Design, 1986, 142–147.

CHAPTER 7: AIRPORT TERMINALS

Airports Buildings and Aprons. (3rd ed.). *A reference document of principles and guidance material.* Montreal: International Air Transport Association, 1962.

"Airports." *Domus (1),* 1993.

Zukowsky, John, ed. *Building for Air Travel: Architecture and Design for Commercial Aviation.* Munich and New York: The Art Institute of Chicago and Prestel-Verlag, 1996.

Washington Dulles International

"Airport Development Planning." *Progressive Architecture* 42 (November 1961): 158–163.

Allen, Edward, and Waclaw Zalewski. *Shaping Structures.* New York: John Wiley & Sons, Inc., 1998.

Begde, Prabhakar. "Aviation Architecture." *Architecture & Design* 16(1) (1999): 18–41.

Blake, P. J. "Save Dulles Airport!" *Interior Design* 14(S) (1988): 300–301.

Booth Conroy, Sarah. "The Washington Post Dulles' Soaring Design: After 20 Years, It's Still a Model of Efficiency." *Washington Post,* 24 June 1984, Book World, 10.

Carter, Brian. "Material Culture: Eero Saarinen and Operational Thoroughness." *Ptah* 1 (2001): 20–26.

Carter, Brian. "Material Culture: Eero Saarinen and Operational Thoroughness: A Way of Working." *Dimensions* 14 (2000): 32–39.

Dean, Andrea O. "Eero Saarinen in Perspective: A Generation After His Loss, a Discussion of His Work and Influence." *AIA Journal* 70(13) (November 1981): 36–51.

"Design for the Jet Ages: Dulles International Airport." *Time,* November 30, 1962.

"Dulles International Airport." *Architectural Record* 134 (July 1963): 103–104.

"Dulles International Airport." *Progressive Architecture* 44 (1963): 90–100.

"Dulles International Airport." *Architectural Record* (July 1963): 101–110.

"Dulles International Airport Terminal Building, Chantilly, Virginia." *Architecture and Urbanism* 4 (April 1984 extra ed.): 146–161.

Eero Saarinen: Dulles International Airport. Tokyo: Global Architecture, 1974.

"Eero Saarinen." *Architecture and Urbanism* (April 1984 extra ed.): 1–240.

"Eero Saarinen: International Airport for Washington D.C. (1958–1962)." *Casabella* 65(695–696) (December 2001):36–45.

Fisher, Thomas. "Landmarks: TWA Terminal." *Progressive Architecture* 73(5) (1992): 96–109.

Fitch, James Marston. *American Building: The Environmental Forces That Shape It.* Boston: Houghton Mifflin, 1966.

Ford, Edward R. *The Details of Modern Architecture.* Vol. 2, 1928 to 1988. Cambridge, MA: MIT Press, 1996.

"Four Great Pours." *Architectural Forum* 115 (September 1961): 104–115.

Freman, Allen. "The World's Most Beautiful Airport." *AIA Journal* 69(13) (November 1980): 46–51.

Freeman, Allen. "SOM's Addition to Dulles International Airport: Respects Eero Saarinen's 'Modern Masterpiece'." *Architectural Record* 185(3) (March 1997): 62–67.

Gössel, G., and G. Leuthäuser. *Architektur des 20 Jahrhunderts.* Köln: Taschen Verlag, 1990.

Greer, N. R. "Eero Saarinen's Dulles Airport Wins AIA 25-Year Award: Architecture." *AIA Journal* 5 (1988): S 38–38, 43.

Lessing, Lawrence. "The Diversity of Eero Saarinen." *Architectural Forum* 113(1) (July 1960): 94–103.

McQuade, Walter. "The Birth of an Airport." *Fortune* (March 1962).

McQuade, Walter. "Eero Saarinen, A Complete Architect." *Architectural Forum* (4) (1962): 102–119.

Moore, Fuller. *Understanding Structures.* Boston: McGraw-Hill, 1999.

Oishi, Masato. *Eero Saarinen* Tokyo: A & U Publishing, 1984.

Papademetriou, Peter. "Coming of Age: Eero Saarinen and Modern American Architecture." *Perspecta* 21 (1984): 116–143.

Papademetriou, Peter C. "Eero Saarinen: Il Calcolo e L'invenzion." (The calculation and the invention of the form: Flight of fantasy). *Casabella* 65(695–696) (December 2001): 21–33.

"Saarinen: Terminal Building, Dulles International Airport." *Architectural Forum* 9 (1961): 111–113.

Sandaker, Bjørn Normann, and Arne Petter Eggen. *The Structural Basis of Architecture.* New York: Whitney, 1992.

Spade, Rupert. *Library of Contemporary Architects — Eero Saarinen.* New York: Simon & Schuster, 1971.

Temko, Allan. *Eero Saarinen.* New York: George Braziller, 1962.

"TWA Terminal Gains Landmark Status." *Progressive Architecture* 75(9) (1994): 17.

"Whither Dulles? Cold War Landmark." *Progressive Architecture* 3(S28) (1978): 28.

Wilkinson, Chris. *Supersheds: The Architecture of Long-Span, Large Volume Buildings.* Boston: Butterworth Architecture, 1996

Zalewski, Waclaw and Edward Allen. *Shaping Structures: Statics.* New York: John Wiley & Sons, Inc., 1998.

Stansted International

"Aeroport de Stansted, GB". *Techniques et Architecture* 398(10/11) (1991): 134–141.

"Bewegung als Zeichen." *Werk, Bauen & Wohnen* 10 (1988): 24–39.

Brawne, Michael. "Frontis." *RIBA Journal* 98(5) (1991): 4–5, 8, 10, 12.

Breheny, Michael, and Douglas Hart. "Conflicting Attitudes on the Expansion of Stansted Airport." *Town and Country Planning* 58 (February 1989): 46–48.

Brookes, Alan, and Chris Grech. *The Building Envelope and Connections.* Boston: Architecture Press, 1996.

Brookes, Alan, and Chris Grech. *The Building Envelope: Applications of New Technology Cladding* London: Butterworth, 1990.

Bunn, Roderic. "Flight of Fancy." *Building Services* 13(6) (1991): 21–24.

Cervera, Jaime. "Un aeropuerto amistoso: Foster amplia Stansted" (A friendly airport: Foster enlarges Stansted). *Arquitectura Viva* 12(5/6) (1990): 19–21.

Compagno, Andrea. *Intelligente Glasfassaden: Material, Anwendung, Gestaltung* (Intelligent glass façades: Material, practice, design [trans., Ingrid Taylor]). 4th ed. Basel, Switzerland: Birkhauser, 1999.

"Countryside Airport Checks In." *Landscape Design* 200(5) (1991): 9.

Davies, Collin. *High Tech Architecture.* New York: Rizzoli, 1988.

Dirckinck-Holmfeld, Kim. "Stansted lufthaven" (Stansted airport). *Arkitekten* (Copenhagen) 97(15) (1995): 524–527.

Dubois, Marc. "Een negentiende-eeuwse luchthaven: Stansted Airport van Norman Foster" (A nineteenth-century airport: Stansted Airport by Norman Foster)." *Archis* 10 (1991): 54–59.

Evamy, Michael. "Back to Basics: The Stansted Story." *Design* 507 (1991): 35–40.

Fisher, Thomas. "Against Entropy." *Progressive Architecture* 72(12) (1991): 54–63.

"Flughafenterminal in Stansted" (Air terminal, Stansted). *Baumeister* 88(7) (1991): 14–23, 54–55.

"Flughafenterminal Stansted (GB)" (Airport terminal at Stansted). *Glasforum* 41(5) (1991): 15–28.

"Flughefengebäude in Stansted." (Airport in Stansted). *Deutsche Bauzeitung* 124(11) (1990): 14–27.

Hagen-Hodgson, Petra. "Neuer Air Terminal fur Stansted, London, 1991" (A new air terminal for Stansted Airport)." *Werk, Bauen & Wohnen.* 78/45(9) (1991): 2–11, 77.

Hannay, Patrick, " Flight of Fancy." *Architects' Journal* 193(22) (1991): 24–31, 34–41.

"LeNuove Porte della Città" (The new gates of the city). *Arbitare* 305(3) (1992): 210–235, 308.

"Les lumières de Stansted" (The lighting at Stansted). *Techniques et Architecture* 382(2/3) (1989): 44–51.

"Norman Foster Interview." *Architecture d'Aujourd'hui* 276(9) (1991): 66–76.

Owens, Ruth. "Fit for Take-off: Architects: Foster Associates." *Architects' Journal* 193(13) (1991): 24–27.

Pawley, Martin. "A New Departure." *Blueprint* 76(4) (1991): 36–39.

Pawley, Martin. "L'aeroporto di Stansted a Londra di Foster Associates" (Stansted Airport, London, by Foster Associates). *Casabella* 55(580) (1991): 4–22, 59–60.

Pawley, Martin. "Stansted Airport." *Building* 256(7696) (19) (1991): 49–60.

Pawley, Martin. "Third London Airport, Stansted-Terminal Zone." *A&U* 10(253) (1991): 46–128.

Powell, Kenneth. "Stansted Revisited." *Architects' Journal* 204(7) (1996): 25–31.

Scalbert, Irenee. "Un palais du voyage" (A travel palace). *Moniteur Architecture AMC* 22(6) (1991): 26–31.

"Stansted Airport New Terminal Building." *Tubular Structures* 3 (1992): 1–10.

"Stansted havaalani terminali" (Stansted Airport). *Tasarim* 23(4) (1992): 68–74.

Wilkinson, Chris. *Supersheds: The Architecture of Long-Span, Large Volume Buildings.* Boston: Butterworth Architecture, 1996.

Wislocki, Peter. "Trzecie Londynskie Lotnisko" (Stansted Airport). *Architektura Murator* 5(8) (1995): 32–37.

Wooley, David. "Stansted's Remarkably Simple New Terminal Opened." *Airport Forum* 21(2) (1991): 39–40, 42.

Zung, Jack. "Stansted Airport Terminal." *Arup Journal* 25(1) (1990): 7–15.

United Airlines Terminal at O'Hare

Aldersey-Williams, Hugh. "New Departures." *Designers' Journal* 42(11) (1988): 96–100.

Blackwell, Lewis. "Jahn Unveils Airport Extension." *Building Design* 726(2) (1985): 6.

Bruegmann, Robert. "High flight: United Gambles and Wins at O'Hare." *Inland Architect* 32(5) (1988): 32–41.

Caminada, C. F. "United Airlines Terminal, Chicago." *International Lighting Review* 39(4) (1988): 141–145.

Davidson-Powers, Cynthia. "The O'Hare Station: Last Link to the Loop." *Inland Architect* 29(4) (1985): 28–30.

Dietsch, Deborah. "High-Tech Expansion: Chicago O'Hare International Airport Development Program." *Architectural Record* 173(6/5) (1985): 132–139.

Dona, Claudia. "Cattedrale del volo" (Cathedral of flight). *Modo* 10(102) (1987): 38–39.

"Flughafen O'Hare in Chicago Terminal 1." *Architektur* (Berlin) 40(7) (1991): 16–21.

Jahn, Helmut. "Biography of Helmut Jahn: The first 20 Years." *A+U* 6 (June 1986):1–268.

Joedick, Joachim Andreas. *Helmut Jahn: Design of a New Architecture.* New York: Nichols Publishing, 1987.

"Licht und Luft" (Light and air). *AIT* 97(7/8) (1989): 8–16.

Murphy, Jim. "A Grand Gateway." *Progressive Architecture* 68(11) (1987): 95–105.

Sandaker, Bjørn Normann and Eggen, Arne Petter. *The Structural Basis of Architecture.* New York: Whitney, 1992.

Schwartz, Adele C. "Chicago Spending 2 Billion Dollars to Expand, Modernize O'Hare Airport." *Airport Forum* 18(6) (1988): 41–46.

Shemitz, Sylvan R. "Lighting the Way." *Architectural Record* 175(13) (November 1987): 148–155.

Stucchi, Silvano. "Terminal dell'Aeroporto O'Hare di Chicago" (United Airlines Terminal, O'Hare International Airport, Chicago). *Industria delle Costruzioni* 22(204) (1988): 32–41.

"Um terminal para o futuro" (A terminal for the future). *Projeto* 172(3) (1994): 62–63.

"Underground Station as Shining Example." *Bauwelt* 76(11) (1985): 386–387.

Walters, Brian. "Boeing Places." *Building Design* 858(10) (1987): 30–33.

Kansai International Airport

Beever, Paula. "Burning Questions." *Architecture Today* 56(3) (1995): 45–46.

Buchanan, Peter. "Kansai." *Architectural Review* 196(1173) (1994): 4–7, 31–81.

Buchanan, Peter. "Organiczna maszyna" (Kansai International Airport passenger terminal). *Architektura Murator* 9(12) (1995): 34–41.

Buchanan, Reyner Peter. "Plane Geometry: Architecture." *AIA Journal* 84(1) (1995): 84–93, 97–103.

Compagno, Andrea. *Intelligente Glasfassaden: Material, Anwendung, Gestaltung* (Intelligent glass façades: Material, practice, design [trans., Ingrid Taylor]). 4th ed. Basel, Switzerland: Birkhauser, 1999.

Dilley, Philip. "Kansai Airport Terminal, Osaka, Japan." *Arup Journal* 29(2) (1994): 17.

Dilley, Philip. "Kansai International Airport Terminal Building." *Arup Journal* 30(1) (1995): 14–23.

Fernandez-Galiano, Luis. "Gran escala" (Grand scale). *Arquitectura Viva* 39(11/12) (1994): 17–67.

Gazzaniga, Luca. "Aeroporto Internazionale Kansai, Osaka, Giappone" (Kansai International Airport, Osaka, Japan). *Domus* 764(10) (1994): 7–19.

"Kansai Airport's Artificial Landscape." *Progressive Architecture* 75(9) (1994): 22.

"Kansai International Airport Passenger Terminal." *GA* no. 41 (1994): 66–85.

"Kansai International Airport." *Albenaa* 14(81) (1994): 104–110.

Kazuhiko Nanba. "Design and Construction of Kansai International Airport Passenger Terminal Building." *SD* 12 (1993): 57–80.

Keiser, Robert. "Flugzeugtrager: Der Kansai International Airport in Osaka vor der Vollendung" (Airport expansion: Kansai International Airport in Osaka at the completion). *Werk, Bauen & Wohnen* 4 (1994): 49–53.

Magnago Lampugnani, Vittorio. "Terminal de la isla: concurso del aeropuerto de Kansai" (Terminal on the Island: Competition for Kansai airport). *Arquitectura Viva* 12(5/6) (1990): 14–18.

Miyake, Riichi. "Kansai International Airport Passenger Terminal Building." *Architect* 15 (3) (1994): 4–241.

Moore, Fuller. *Understanding Structures.* Boston: McGraw-Hill, 1999.

Normile, Dennis. "Two-Part Osaka Saga." *World Architecture* 84 (2000): 28.

O'Connor, Mickey. "Is Renzo Piano's Kansai Airport Sinking?" *Architecture* 89(11) (2000): 45.

On a Wing and a Layer. *RIBA Journal* 101(7) (1994): 22–29.

Refiti Shopland, Alice. "Hi-Tech Harmonisation." *Architecture New Zealand* (November 1994): 24–26.

Rush, Richard D. "Buy Now, Fly Later." *Progressive Architecture* 76(4) (1995): 70–75.

Sandaker, Bjørn Normann, and Arne Petter Eggen. *The Structural Basis of Architecture.* New York: Whitney, 1992.

Steed, Peter. "Neuland" (New land). *Bauwelt* 85(34) (1994): 1818–1839.

Sudjic, Deyan. "Airport Architecture as the Nexus of the City." *SD* 362(11) (1994): 5–176.

Suzuki, Hiroyuki et al. "Kansai International Airport Passenger Terminal Building." *Process Architecture* 122 (1994): 6–201.

Walters, Brian. "Boeing Places." *Building Design* 858(10) (1987): 30–33.

Wilkinson, Chris. *Supersheds: The Architecture of Long-Span, Large Volume Buildings.* Boston: Butterworth Architecture, 1996.

Zalewski, Waclaw, and Edward Allen. *Shaping Structures: Statics*. New York: John Wiley & Sons, Inc., 1998.

Zanardi, Bruno. "Kansai International Airport Passenger Terminal Building." *Archis* 2 (1995): 26–37.

CHAPTER 8: PAVILIONS

Allwood, John. *The Great Exhibitions*. London: Studio Vista, 1977.

Cudaky, Brain J. *Cash, Tokens, and Transfers: A History of Urban Mass Transit in North America*. New York: Fordham University Press, 1990.

Friebe, Wolfgang. *Buildings of the World Exhibitions."* (translated from the German by Jenny Vowles and Paul Roper; illustrations Manfred Kahlert]. Leipzig: Edition Leipzig, 1985.

Mattie, Erik. *World's Fairs*. New York: Princeton Architectural Press, 1998.

Rydell, Robert W. *All the World's a Fair: Visions of Empire at American International Expositions*. Chicago: University of Chicago Press, 1984.

Rydell, Robert W. *World of Fairs: The Century of Progress Expositions*. Chicago: University of Chicago Press, 1993.

Munich Olympic Stadium

Picon, Antoine. *L'art de l'ingénieur* (The Art of the engineer). Paris: Éditions du Centre Georges Pompidou, 1997, 311–2.

Behnisch & Partners, Architects. *Arbeiten aus den Jahren 1952–1987*. (Work from the years 1952–1987). Stuttgart: Behnisch & Partner, 1987.

Berger, Horst. *Light Structures: Structures of Light*. Basel: Berkhauser, 1996.

Berger, Horst. "The Evolving Design Vocabulary of Fabric Structures." *Architectural Record* 3 (1985): 152–156.

Birdair, Inc. *Tensioned Membrane Structures*. Amherst, NY: Birdair, Inc., 1995.

"Die Bauten für die Spiele der XX. Olympiade in München und die Stadt" (The buildings for the XXth Olympic Games in Munich and the city). *Baumeister* 69 (August 1972): 837–880.

Drew, Philip. *Tensile Architecture*. Boulder, CO: Westview Press, 1979.

Gauzin-Müller, Dominique. *Fifty Years of Architecture*. Berlin: Academy Editions, 1997.

Geriant, John, and Rod Sheard. *Stadia: A Design and Development Guide*. London: Architectural Press, 1997.

Hamm, Oliver G., and Knut Gabriel. "Heiter: Olympiapark München" (Cheerful Olympiapark, Munich). *Deutsche Bauzeitung* 125(5) (May 1991): 107–109, 112, 116–118, 120, 121.

Hapold, Edmund, and Michael Dickson. "The Story of Munich: Zodiac 21." *Architectural Design* 44(6) (1974): 339–344.

Hunt, Tony. "Building Favourites." *Architects' Journal* 207(21) (May 28,1998): 49.

Ishii, Kazuo. *Membrane Designs and Structures in the World*. Tokyo: Shinkenchiku-sha Co. Ltd, 1999, 124–127.

Kretschmer, Winfried. *Geschichte der Weltausstellungen*. Frankfurt: Campus-Verlag, 1999, 246–247.

Krishna Prem, Swami. *Cable-Suspended Roofs*. New York: McGraw-Hill, 1978.

Leonhardt, Fritz. *Baumeister in einer umwälzenden Zeit* (Building in uncertain times). Stuttgart: Deutsche Verlags-Anstalt, 1984, 218–220.

Leonhardt, F., and J. Schlaich. "Structural Design of Roof over the Sports Arenas for the 1972 Olympic Games: Some Problems of Prestressed Cable Nets." *Structural Engineer* 50(3) (1972).

Linkwitz, Klaus. "New Methods for the Determination of Cutting Pattern of Prestressed Cable Nets and Their Application to the Olympic Roof, Munich." *Zodiac* 21 (1972): entire issue.

Middleton, Robin. "Munich 1972." *Architectural Design* 42 (August 1972): 477–489.

"Munich '72." *Building* 223(30) (July 1972): 35–42.

"Munich Olympics." *Design* 285 (September 1972): 29–59.

"Munich's Olympic Games Site Topped by Cable-Suspended Roof." *Engineering News Record* 11 (1971): 24–25.

Otto, Frei, ed. *Zugbeanspruchte Konstruktionen* (Tensile structures). Cambridge, MA: MIT Press, 1969.

Perrin, Gerald A. *Sport Halls and Swimming Pools*. London: E. & F. N. Spon, 1980.

Roland, Conrad. *Frei Otto — Spannweiten*. (Frei Otto — spanning). Berlin: Ullstein, 1965.

Schlaich, J. "Cable Suspended Roof for Munich Olympic." *Civil Engineer* 52(7) (1972).

Sebastian, Stephanie. "Zeitgeist: Interview mit Günter Behnisch" (Spirit of the time: Interview with Günter Behnisch). *Architektur, Innenarchitektur, Technischer Ausbau* 104(7) (July–August 1996): 70–71.

"Tent Structures Designed to Endure." *Architectural Record* 1 (1979): 141–143.

Thiem, Walter R. "Olympic Games, Munich." *Progressive Architecture* 53(8) (1972): 58–69.

Thompson, P. D., J. A. A. Tolloczko, and J. N. Clarke. *Stadia, Areans & Grandstands: Design, Construction and Operation*. London: Concrete Society, 1998.

Wilkinson, Chris. *Supersheds: The Architecture of Long-Span, Large Volume Buildings*. Boston: Butterworth Architecture, 1996.

Wimmer, Martin. *Olympic Buildings*. Leipzig: Edition Leipzig, 1976.

Institut du Monde Arabe

Anargyros-Intramuros, S. T. "Jean Nouvel, vers une nouvelle architecture" (Jean Nouvel, towards a new architecture). *Maison Française* 403 (1987): S. 28–30.

Auer, G. "Buntes Rauschen: Jean Nouvels mediale Fassaden" (Colored noise: Jean Nouvel's medial façades). *Daidalos* 40 (1991): S, 118–125.

Baroni, Marta. "Come una macchina fotografica" (Like a photo camera). *Frames, Porte & Finestre* 23 (1989): S. 60–65.

Bergeron, C. "L'homme du mois: Jean Nouvel" (Man of the month). *Maison Française* 427 (1989): 17–18.

Boissière, Olivier. "L'Institut du Monde Arabe a Paris." *Arca* (May 1987): 28–35.

Boissière, Olivier. "L'Institut du monde arabe di parigi. *Arca* 15 S (1988): 12–23.

Boissière, Olivier. "La consagracion de Nouvel: El Instituto del Mundo Arabe en Paris" (The consecration of Nouvel: The Institut du Monde Arabe in Paris). *Arquitectura Viva* 4 (1989): 19–21.

Boissière. O. *Jean Nouvel, Emmanuel Cattani und Partner.* Basel: Birkhauser Verlag, 1992.

Boissière, Olivier. *Jean Nouvel.* Basel: Birkhauser Verlag, 1996.

Boles, Daralice D. "Modernism in the City." *Progressive Architecture* 7 (1987): S. 72–79.

Bosoni, Giampiero, and Jean Nouvel. *Jean Nouvel: Una lezione in Italia.* (Jean Nouvel: A lesson in Italian). Milano: Skira Editore, 1996.

Colin, C. "Architettura francese: le case manifesto: L'opera di Jean Nouvel" (French architecture: The manifesto: Jean Nouvel's opera). *Modo* 109 (1988): 50–53.

Compagno, Andrea. *Intelligente Glasfassaden: Material, Anwendung, Gestaltung* (Intelligent glass façades: Material, practice, design [trans., Ingrid Taylor]). 4th ed. Basel, Switzerland: Birkhauser, 1999.

"Concours pour l'Institut du Monde Arabe, Paris" (Competition for the Arab Institue, Paris). *L'Architecture d'Aujourd'hui* 219(S) (1982): 81–90.

Dannatt, Adrian. "A Nouvel Way with Buildings." *Architect's Journal* 9 (1988): 109.

Dannatt, Adrian. "A Nouvel Way with Buildings." *The Architects' Journal* 38 (1988): S, 109.

"Détails: architectes et industriels: quel enjeu?" (Details: Architects and industry: What is at stake?). *AMC-Architecture, Mouvement, Continuité* 12 (1990): S. 47–51.

"Een Arabische sluitsteen voor Parijs" (An Arabian keystone for Paris). *Archis* 2 (1988): S 14–20.

Ellis, Charlotte. "Nouvel Masterpiece." *Blueprint* (October 1987): 38–40.

Ellis, Charlotte. "Split on the Seine." *Architectural Review* 7 (1987): 46–51.

Ellis, Charlotte. "The AIA Journal: France: A Composition of Window Wall Above the Seine." *Architecture* 9 (1988): 92–93.

Emery, M., and M. Brausch. "Nouvel et après" (Nouvel and after). *Architecture Intérieure Créé* 245 (1991): S. 82–103.

Fessy, Georges, Jean Nouvel, and Hubert Tonka. *Institut du monde arabe: Une architecture de Jean Nouvel, Gilbert Lezénés, Pierre Soria Architecture studio* (Arab Institute: A Jean Nouvel architecture). 2d ed. Paris: Demi-Cercle, 1989.

Ford, Edward R. *The Details of Modern Architecture, Vol. 2, 1928 to 1988.* Cambridge: MIT Press, 1996.

Garcias, J., and M. Meade. "Unique Nouvel." *Architectural Review* 1032 (1983): S. 44–49.

Goulet, Patrice. "Portrait: Jean Nouvel." *Architecture Intérieure CREE* 179 (1980): S. 96–105.

Goulet, Patrice. "Le grand jeu" (The big league). *Architecture Intérieure CREE* 222 (1988): S. 104–119.

Goulet, Patrice. "Works of Jean Nouvel." *A+U* 214 (1988): 47–134.

Holden, Richard. "Distilling the Essence of Diverse Cultures." *Planning* (Johannesburg) N. 145(5) (1996): 8–10.

Hondelatte, J., and J. Nouvel. "Lycée polyvalent, Pessac, France." *L'Architecture d'Aujourd'hui* 235 (1984): S. 14–17.

Huet, Bernard. "Architecture mouvement continuite" (Architecture in motion). *Citation* 18(12) (1987): 50–65.

"Institut du Monde Arabe, Paris" (Arab Institute, Paris). *DBZ* 12 (1988): S. 1645–1650.

"Institut du Monde Arabe, Paris" (Arab Institute, Paris). *Glasforum* 38(3) (1988): 28–36.

"Institut du Monde Arabe, Paris"(Arab Institute, Paris). *Bauzeitschrift* 36(12) (1988): 1645–1650.

"Institut du Monde Arabe, Paris. (Arab Institute, Paris). *The Architectural Review* 1113 (1989): S. 104–105.

"Institut du Monde Arabe, Quai Saint-Bernard, Paris." (Arab Institute, Paris). *A+U* 9 (1990): S. 216–237, 263.

"Jean Nouvel. Emmanuel Cattani et Associes." Zurich: Artemis Verlags Ag., 1992.

"Jean Nouvel: Instituto do Mundo Arabe, Paris, França. *Projeto* 124 (1989): S. 81–87.

"Jean Nouvel." (Special Issue). *L'Architecture d'Aujourd'hui* 231 (1984): S. 1–82.

Joffroy, P. "Cinq projets à l'Equerre" (Five T-square projects). *Architectes Architecture* 182 (1987): S. 16–17.

Knapp, G. "Neuer Hit am Seineufer"(New hit on the banks of the Seine). *Architektur & Wohnen* 1 (1989): S. 122–127.

"Konstruktive Intelligenz." *Arch+* 102 (1990): S. 42–52.

Lefaivre, L., and A. Tzonis. *Architektur in Europa seit 196.* (Architecture in Europe since 1968). Frankfurt am Main: Campus Verlag, 1992.

"Le grand jeu" (The big league). *Architecture Interieure CREE. Citation* 222 (February/March 1988): 104–119.

"L'Institut du Monde Arabe" (Arab Institute). *Luminata Sabau. Jahrbuch fur Architektur* (Luminata Sabau: Architecture Yearbook). (1987/1988): 156–158.

"L'Institut du Monde Arabe" (Arab Institute). *Archithese* 18(4) (1988): 30–31.

"L'Institut du Monde Arabe" (Arab Institute). *Kenchiku Bunka* 513 (1989): S. 57–68.

Loach, J. "Parisian Arabesque." *Building Design* 894 (1988): S. 24–29.

Loriers, Marie Christine. "Through the Looking Glass." *Progressive Architecture* 69(5) (1988): 94–97.

Lucan, S. "Jean Nouvel: Presentació de l'obra" (Jean Nouvel: presentation of his works). *Quaderns d'Arquitectura i Urbanisme* 181–182 (1989): S. 170–191.

Mandrelli, D. O. "Una estrella de la excentricidad: Conversación con Jean Nouvel" (A star of eccentricity: conversation with Jean Nouvel). *A & V* 31 (1991): S. 6–9, 80.

Marra, Alfonso, and F. Javier Soto. "Diafragmas para la luz: Centro islamico en Paris" (Diaphragms for light: Islamic center in Paris). *Arquitectura viva Citation* 2(9) (1988): 45.

Millier, J., J. Nouvel, B. Suner, and F. D. Gravelaine. "Nouvel: la Tour sans Fins" (Nouvel: the endless tower). *L'Architecture d'Aujourd'hui* 281 (1992): S. 117–133.

"Modernism in the City." *Progressive Architecture* 7 (1987): 72–76.

Möllring, F. "Architekturportrait Jean Nouvel: Moment der Fantasie"(Architectural portrait of Jean Nouvel: fantasy moment). *Schweizer Baumarkt-Aktuelles Bauen Plan* (1988): S. II–IX.

Montaner, Josep. *New Museums.* London: Architecture and Technology Press, 1990.

Morgan, Conway Lloyd. *Jean Nouvel: The Elements of Architecture.* New York: Universe Publishing, 1998.

Murray, Peter. *The Architecture of the Italian Renaissance.* New York: Schocken Books, 1963.

Nouvel, J. "Sul progetto di architettura" (On designing a work of architecture). *Domus* 742 (1992): S. 17–28.

Nouvel, J. "Schönheit der Effektivität: Eine Erläuterung des Architekten" (The beauty of efficiency: architect's remarks). *Bauwelt* 21 (1992): S. 1177–1179.

Nouvel, J. "Fragmentos de realidad: la mirada del cine" (Fragments of reality). *Arquitectura Viva* 7 (1989): S. 7–9.

Nouvel, J. "Cinéma, architecture: Une envie de déserter" (Cinema, architecture: a wish to desert). *L'Architecture d'Aujourd'hui* 254 (1987): 23–24, 28.

Nouvel, J. "Mit Charme und Kleinen Fehlern: statement" (With charm and small mistakes: a report). *Archithese* 6 (1990): S. 52–53.

Nouvel, J. "Banlieue" (Suburbs). *Toshi Jutaku* 212 (1985): S. 3–61.

Nouvel. J. "Statement Jean Nouvels zu seiner Ausstellung an der ETH Zürich." (Comments on Jean Nouvel's exhibit at ETH in Zurhich). *Schweizer Baumarkt-Aktuelles Bauen Plan* 14 (1990): S. I–III.

Nouvel et Associés. "Les façades de l'IMA [Institut du Monde Arabe, Paris]." *L'Architecture d'Aujourd'hui* 247 (October 1986): XLII–XLV.

Nouvel, J., P. Goulet, and P. Virilio. "Äesthetik des Verschwindens: Jean Nouvel im Gespräch mit Patrice Goulet und Paul Virilio" (Esthetic of evanescence: Jean Nouvel's dialog with Goulet and Virilio). *Arch + Fassaden* 108 (1991): S. 32–40.

Pélissier, Alain. "Transmoderne: L'Institute du Monde Arabe." *Technique et Architecture* 3 (1988) 124–137.

Pélissier, A. "Une architecture d'auteur avec Jean Nouvel" (Architecture interview with Jean Nouvel). *Techniques & Architecture* 366 (1986): S. 72–79.

Peterson, Steven. "Idealized Space: Mies — Conception or Realized Truth?" *Inland Architect* 21(5) (May 1977).

Pisani, Mario. "Body Building." *Artforum* 26(8) (1988).

Poisay, C. "Instituto del mundo arabe, Paris, 1987: Jean Nouvel" (Arab Institute, Paris). *Arquitectura* 275–276 (1988): S 50–65

Ragon, M. "L'année Nouvel" (The Nouvel year). *Connaissance des Arts* 419 (1987): S. 60–65.

Robert, J., and J. Nouvel. "Jean Nouvel." *L'Architecture d'Aujourd'hui* 276 (1991): S. 58–65.

Ryan, C. J. "Jean Nouvel." *L. A. Architect* 3 (1989): S. 6–7.

Sallé, A. "L'Institut du Monde Arabe a un an" (The Arab Institute is one year old). *Archéologia* 242 (1989): S. 4.

"Simbolismo hipertecnológico: El Instituto del Mundo Arabe." *A&V* 17 S. (1989): 48–53.

Skriver, P. E. "Institut du monde arabe"(Arab Institute). *Arkitekten* 23 (1989): S. 592–595.

Soria, P., and J. Nouvel. "Saint-Ouen, Anselme-Hermet." *L'Architecture d'Aujourd'hui* 252 (1987): S, 11–15.

"Split on the Seine: Arab Culture Centre, Paris." *The Architectural Review* 1088 (S) (1987): 46–51 .

Vonier, Thomas. "Culture Clash." *Progressive Architecture Citation* 76(9) (1995): 62–67.

Williams, Stephanie. "L'Institut du monde Arabe, Paris" (Arab Institute, Paris). *Apollo* 331 S. (1989): 189–191.

Zwoch, F. "Institut du monde Srabe, Paris." (Arab Institute, Paris). *Bauwelt* 1–2 (S) (1988): 60–65.

Linz Design Center

Dawson, Layla. "Voluminous Vault." *Architectural Review* 194(1167) 1994: 58–63.

"The Design Center Linz," *Architectural Record* (November 1998): 131.

Herzog, Thomas. *1978–1992 Buildings: A Working Report.* Stuttgart: Germany: Verlag Gerd Hatje.1992

Herzog, Thomas. "Design Center in Linz." *Deutsche Bauzeitschrift* 42(9) (1994): 49–56.

Herzog, Thomas. "Design Center Linz." *Glasforum* 44(4) (1994): 33–40.

Herzog, Thomas. *Design Center, Linz.* Stuttgart: Gerd Hatje, 1994.

Herzog, Thomas. *Design Center Linz.* Stuttgart, Germany: Verlag Gerd Hatje, 1994.

Herzog,Thomas, Gernot Minke, and Hans Eggers. *Pneumatic Structures: A Handbook of Inflatable Architecture.* New York: Oxford University Press, 1976.

"Progetto per il design center di Linz" (Project for the design centre in Linz). *Domus* 709(10) (1989): 8–9.

Thiis-Evensen, Thomas. *Arkitektureus Uttrykksformer* (Archetypes in architecture). Oslo: Norwegian University Press; Oxford: Oxford University Press, 1987.

Ulama, Margit. "High-Tech-Architektur fur Linz" (High-tech architecture for Linz). *Architektur und Bauforum.* 27(161) (1994): 46–50.

Wilkinson, Chris. *Supersheds: The Architecture of Long-Span, Large Volume Buildings.* Boston: Butterworth Architecture, 1996.

Zschokke, Walter. "Design Center Linz, Austria." *Domus* 759(4) (1994): 26–34.

British Pavilion

Arcidi, Philip. "Seville's Expo 92-Modernism on Stage." *Progressive Architecture* 5 (1992):89–91.

"Asiansky Smiles on Grimshaw's Seville Pavilion, Brought Home to North London." *Building* 258(7810) (1993): 10.

"Bid to Bring U.K. Pavilion Home." *Architects' Journal* 195(25) (1992): 5.

"Britain Versus Rest of the World." *Architects' Journal,* 8 (1990).

"Britanniques à Seville" (The British at Seville). *L'Architecture d'Aujourd'hui* 9 (1991).

"British Pavilion May Become a Car Showroom." *Architects' Journal* 196(10) (1992): 5.

"British Pavilion May Come Home." *Building* 257(7769) (45) (1992): 9.

Brookes, Alan. "British Cool." *Architects' Journal* 195(24) (1992): 28–35, 38–43.

Buxton, Pamela. "Expo Pavilion to Become Asian Cultural Center." *Building* 1127 (1993): 3.

Buxton, Pamela. "Government Offers 6 Million Pounds to Expo Pavilion Scheme." *Building Design,* 1209 (1995): 4.

Buxton, Pamela. "Grimshaw's Pavilion at Risk as Asian Project Stalls." *Building Design* 1180 (1994): 4.

"Bye-Bye Blue Sky for Expo Pavilion." *Design* 532 (1993): 8.

Chevin, Denise. "The Gain in Spain." *Building* 10 (1990): 58–59.

Chevin, Denise. "Expo '92 Seville." *Building* 256 (7720)(45) (1991): 42–51.

Cooper, Peter, and Denise Chevin. "Expo 92, Seville — Best of British and the Spanish Acquisition." *Building* 256(45) (November 8, 1991): 17–19.

Coomber, Matthew. "Light Refreshment: British Pavilion Expo '92, Seville." *Building* 257 (7743)(18) (1992): 44–47.

Davies, Colin. "British Racing Green." *Architectural Review* 6 (1992): 24–32.

"Der Britische Pavillon auf der Expo '92 in Sevilla" (The British Pavilion at Expo '92 in Seville). *Detail* 32(6) (December–January 1992): SI-SIV.

Dixon, John Morris. " World on a Platter." *Progressive Architecture*, 73(7) (July 1992): 86–95.

"Expo '92 British Pavilion to Be Moved to London." *Architects' Journal* 197(10) (1993): 9.

Finch, Paul. "Designers' Ingenuity for Seville." *Building Design* 930 (March 31, 1989): 6–7.

Ford, Brian, and Marcus Grant. "Seville: Expo 92 Will Be the Last Universal Exposition of the Twentieth Century." *Architecture Today* 23 (November 1991): 12–14.

Ford, Edward R. *The Details of Modern Architecture*, Vol. 2, *1928 to 1988*. Cambridge: MIT Press, 1996.

Gardner, Ian, and David Hadden. "U.K. Pavilion, Expo '92, Seville." *Arup Journal* 27(3) (1992): 3–7.

"Grimshaw Pavilion in Zoo Rescue Bid." *Building* 257 (7754) (29) (1992): 11.

Grimshaw, Nicolas. "Solar-Powered Pavilion." *RIBA Journal* 99(10) (1992): 32–36, 38.

Harris, Tom. "Seville Service." *Building Services* 14 (7) (1992): 38–40.

"Im Einklang mit den elementen" (In harmony with the elements). *Arch + 7* (1990): 32–33.

"Indian Takeaway." *Building* 1114 (1993): 3.

McCoy, Esther. "Arts & Architecture Case Study Houses." *Perspecta* 15 (1976): 54–73.

Melhuish, Clare. "Team Performance." *Building* 1085 (1992): 2.

Moore, Rowan, ed. *Structure, Space and Skin — The Work of Nicholas Grimshaw & Partner*. London: Phaidon Press, 1993.

Murray, Callum. "Britain Versus Rest of World." *Architects' Journal* 192(7–8) (August 22–29, 1990): 14–15.

"Nicholas Grimshaw: British Pavilion, Expo 92, Seville." *Architectural Design* 65(1–2) (January–February 1995): 36–39.

"No Strategy for Seville." *Architects' Journal* 3 (1989).

"Pavilion Decision Soon." *Building Design* 1108 (1993): 24.

Pavilions of Splendour. New Civil Engineer, 12 March 1992.

Pawley, Martin. "White Knight of Technology." *World Architecture* 14 (1991): 64–71.

Russell, James S., and David Cohn. "Expo '92 Seville" *Architectural Record* 180(8) (August 1992): 114–125.

Stungo, Naomi. "Expo Pavilion Resited in Brent." *Building* 258 (7784)(10) (1993): 13.

Sudjic, Deyan. "Cool Tech in a Hot Climate." *Blueprint* 86 (1992): 26–29.

"The British Pavilion at Expo: Some Missing Labels for the Showcase." *AJ Focus* 6(5) (1992): 5, 7.

"Two for Seville." *Architects' Journal* 189(14) (April 5, 1989): 24–25, 27.

Welsh, John. "Ole: Cool Quality." *Building Design* 1058 (1991): 1, 56.

Welsh, John. "Profiting from the Elements." *Building Design* 955 (October 29, 1989): 14–15.

"Working Details. Internal Structure: Exhibition Building." *Architects' Journal* 195(24) (1992): 45–47.

CHAPTER 9: RESIDENTIAL ARCHITECTURE

Eames House and Studio

"Charles and Ray Eames: Designers of the Twentieth Century: The Work of Charles and Ray Eames: A Legacy of Invention." *Journal of the Society of Architectural Historians* 58(1) (1999): 100–103.

"Charles and Ray Eames' Neutra Apartment: Living with Twin Legacies of California Design." *Architectural Digest* 54(12) (1997): 84.

Colomina, Beatriz. "Reflections on the Eames House." *Blueprint* September 1998.

Gossel, Peter, and Gabriele Leuthauser. *Architecture in the Twentieth Century*. Köhn, Germany: Benedikt Taschen Verlag, 1991.

Heyer, Paul. *American Architecture: Ideas and Ideologies in the Late Twentieth Century*. New York: Van Nostrand Reinhold, 1993.

"Humanizing Modernism: The Crafts, 'Functioning Decoration' and the Eameses." *Journal of Design History* 11(1) (1998): 15–29.

Jestico, Tom. "Favourite Buildings." *Architects' Journal* 206(11) (1997): 63.

McCoy, Esther. *Case Study Houses, 1945–1962*. 2d ed.. Los Angeles: Hennessey and Ingalls, 1977.

McCoy, Esther. "On Attaining a Certain Age." *Progressive Architecture* (October 1977): 80–83.

"Reflections on the Eames House." *Blueprint* 153(9) (1998): 41–45.

Smithson, Peter and Allison. *Without Rhetoric: An Architectural Aesthetic 1955–1972*. Cambridge: MIT Press, 1973.

Smithson, Peter and Allison. *Changing the Art of Inhabitation*. London: Artemis London, Ltd, 1994.

Steele, James. *Eames House: Charles and Ray Eames*. London: Phaidon Press, 1994.

Whiffen, Marcus, and Frederick Koeper. *American Architecture*. Vol. 1. Cambridge: MIT Press, 1984.

Wilkinson, Chris. *Supersheds: The Architecture of Long-Span, Large Volume Buildings*. Boston: Butterworth Architecture, 1996.

Magney House

Bureau of Meteorology. "Climatic Atlas of Australia. Map Set 5, Rainfall — Melbourne, 1975 Drought." *Review Australia*, 1983.

Buttner, Ulrich. "Refugium in den Blue-Mountains" (Refuge in the Blue Mountains). *MD* 42(6) (1996): 48–53.

Blundell Jones, Peter. "Houses. " *Architectural Review* 200(1196) (1996): 4–5, 37–80.

"Country House by the Timber and Tin Miesian." *Architecture* 74(9) (1985): 123–125.

Dovey, Kim, and Denis McDonald. "Architecture for Aborigines." *Architecture Australia* 85(4) (1996): 98–105.

Dovey, Kim. "Myth and Media: Constructing Aboriginal Architecture." *Journal of Architectural Education* 54(1) (2000): 2–6.

Drew, Philip. *Veranda: Embracing Place*. North Ryde, NSW, Australia: Angus & Robertson, 1992.

Drew, Philip. "Aboriginal Shelter." *Architecture* 83(9) (1994): 60–63.

Drew, Philip. "Aboriginal Shelter: Marika House, Yirrkala, Australia." *Architectur* 83(9) 1994): 60–64.

Drew, Philip. *Leaves of Iron: Glenn Murcutt, Pioneer of an Australian Architectural Form.* North Ryde, NSW, Australia: Angus & Robertson, 1991.

Drew, Philip. "Outback Refinement." *Architecture* 84(9) (1995): 147–151.

Drew, Philip. "Arthur's Metaphor." *Architecture Australia* 88(3) (1999): 42–49.

Farrelly, E. M. *Three Houses (Architecture in Detail).* London: Phaidon Press, 1993.

Ferrara, Maddalena. "'Tocca questa terra con leggerezza': Note sul lavoro di Glenn Murcutt" ('Touch this earth lightly": Notes on the work of Glenn Murcutt). *Spazio e Societa* 18(75) (1996): 10–27.

Flaubert, G. "Francesco Dal Co and Others." *Casabella* 63(671) (1999): 4–67, 82–88.

Ford, Edward R. *The Details of Modern Architecture,* Vol. 2, *1928 to 1988.* Cambridge: MIT Press, 1996.

Fromonot, Françoise. "Glenn Murcutt: Architecte solo en Australie" (Glenn Murcutt: Lone architect in Australia). *Moniteur Architecture AMC* 38 (1993): 26–29.

Fromonot, Françoise. "Glenn Murcutt's Ecological Eloquence." *Progressive Architecture* 75(4) (1994): 66–73.

Fromonot, Françoise. "Glenn Murcutt. Della sottile leggerezza: Kangaroo Valley—Una casa" (Glenn Murcutt. The subtle lightness: Kangaroo Valley—A house). *Casabella* 64(684/685) (2000/2001): 106–121, 173–174.

Leben auf dem Land" (Living off the land]. *MD* 40(4) (1994): 62–67.

"Lichtdurchflutet" (Flooded with light); *MD* 40(6) (1994): 76–81.

Melhuish, Clare. "AD Profile 124: Architecture and Anthropology." *Architectural Design* 66(11/12) (1996): 6–96.

"Metal pionero: Refugio para artistas en Sidney" (Metal pioneer: Refuge for artists in Sydney]. *Arquitectura Viva* 31 (1993): 54–57.

Plestina, Lenko. "Kuce za sretne ljude" (Houses for happy people). *Covjek i prostor* 45(5/6) (528/529) (1998): 14–17.

Powell, Kenneth. "Touching the Ground Lightly." *Perspectives on Architecture* 22 (1996): 36–41.

Rambert, Francis. "Glenn Murcutt: L'artisan de Sydney (Glenn Murcutt: Sydney craftsman). House in the Adelaide Hills, South Australia." *UME* 7 (1998): 2–9.

Rodermond, Janny. "Hedengaagse Villas" (Recent houses). *Architect* 2 (March 1997): 10–17, 72–74.

Schoeller, Walter. "Glenn Murcutt.: Pionier einer australischen Architektur" (Glenn Murcutt. Pioneer of an Australian Architecture). *Bauwelt* 85(37((1994): 2027.

Slessor, Catherine. "Touching the Earth Lightly." *Architectural Review* 205(1224) (February 1999): 28–29.

Spence, Rory. "At Bingle Point: House, Moruya, New South Wales." *Architectural Review* 179(1068) (1986): 70–75.

Spence, Rory. "Antipodean Pavilion: Mosman House, Sydney, Australia." *The Architectural Review,* 191(1149) (1992): 46–50.

Susskind, Anne. "It's Quiet Architecture." *World Architecture* 91(2000): 29.

"Von extremem Klima geprägt" (Holiday home). *MD* 41(4) (1995): 64–69.

Watkins, Tony. "Glen Murcutt: Architect of Integrity." *Home & Building* 10/11 (1994): 144–149.

Wislocki, Pter. "Country Report: Australia." *World Architecture* 49(9) (1996): 42–71.

Experimental House at Almere

Brookes, Alan, and Chris Grech. *The Building Envelope: Applications of New Technology Cladding.* London: Butterworth, 1990.

Brookes, Alan, and Chris Grech. *The Building Envelope and Connections.* Boston: Architecture Press, 1996.

Davies, Collin. *High Tech Architecture.* New York: Rizzoli, 1988.

"Dutch Courage." *Architects' Journal* 82(32) (1985): 28–34.

"A House as Laboratory." *Architecture d'Aujourd'hui* 236 (1984): 16–17.

"House in Almere-Stad." *Bouw* 40(21) (1985): 35–37.

Krewinkel, Heinz W. "Experiment: Glashaus auf Zeit in Almere/Niederlande" (Experiment: Temporary glasshouse in Almere). *Glasforum* 37(6) (1987): 21–24.

"Two Customhouses on the Border." *Architecture & Urbanism* 9(204) (1987): 73.

Two-Family House at Pullach

"Batiments economes en energie" (Energy-conserving buildings]. *Techniques & Architecture* 398 (1991): 18–25.

Bodenbach, Christof. "Energiekonzepte" (Energy concepts). *Deutsche Bauzeitung* 134(10) (2000): 67–124.

Cuadra, Manuel. "El orden aleman. De la geometria de Ungers al expresionismo de Behnisch" (From the geometry of Ungers to the expressionism of Behnisch). *Arquitectura Viva* 47 (1996): 17–59.

Dammand Lund, Lene. "Aestetik og okologi" (Aesthetics and ecology). *Arkitekten* (Copenhagen) 100(11) (1998): 2–17.

"Doppelwohnhaus in Pullach, 1986–1989" (Semidetached houses in Pullach). *Werk, Bauen & Wohnen* 77(6) (1990): 8–11.

"Doppelwohnhaus in Pullach, Oberbayern" (Two-family house in Pullach, Oberbayern). *Glasforum* 44(5) (1994): 9–12.

Habermann, Karl J. "Experimentelles Bauen" (Experimental Building). *Detail* 32(6) (1992/1993):552–556.

Haefele, Gottfried. "Solaranlagen und ihre Integration in die Architektur" (Solar energy systems and their architectural integration). *Architekt* 7 (1997): 499–503.

Herzog, Thomas. "Doppelwohnhaus in Pullach/Obb" (Two-family house in Pullach). *Deutsche Bauzeitschrift* 39(12) (1991): 1749–1756.

Herzog, Thomas. "System einer Tonfassade" (Earthenware façade system). *DAM Architektur Jahrbuch* (1993): 110–115.

Herzog, Thomas. "'Dämmkaviar' im Prototypi erste Realisierung einer Fassadenkonstruktion mit Aerogel-Granult en einem Atelierhaus" (Insulating cladding prototype, first realization in façade construction). *Deutsche Bauzeitschrift* 42(11) (November 1994): 125–127.

Herzog, Thomas, ed. *Solar Energy in Architecture and Urban Planning.* Munich: Prestel, 1996.

Herzog, Thomas, Nikolaus Lang Bildhauer, Rainer Wittenborn Maler, Norbert Huse, und Winfried Nerdinger. *Joint works 1972 to 1996: A Discussion with*

Norbert Huse und Winfried Nerdinger. Stuttgart: Hatje, 1996.

Jodidio, Philip: *Contemporary European Architects.* Koln: Taschen, 1998.

Kaltenbach, Frank. "Solares Bauen" (Solar architecture). *Detail* 39(3) (1999): 358–368, 381–438, 445–460.

Labouze, Eric. "Architecture et défi écologique" (Architecture and the ecological challenge). *Architecture Interieure CREE* 268 (1995): 40–149.

Lederer, Arno. "Okochonder" (Eco-chonder). *Architekt* 5 (1999): 21–47.

Magnago Lampugnani, Vittorio. "Casa per abitazione, Pullach" (Two-Family House, Pullach). *Domus* 724 (1991): 40–45.

Marschall, Werner. "Dacher" (Roofs). *Baumeister* 91(4) (1994): S. 3–82.

Pepchinski, Mary. "The Intelligent Exterior." *Architectural Record* 183(10) (1995): 70–85.

Pfeifer, Gunter. " Energieeffizientes Bauen" (Energy efficient building). *Architekt* 2 (2001): 19–52.

"Pioneer of the Sun: Thomas Herzog Interview." *World Architecture* 27 (1993): 22–23.

Schittich, Christian. "Bauen mit Glas" (Glass construction). *Detail* 40(3) (2000): 340–536.

Slessor, Catherine. *Eco-tech: Sustainable Architecture and High Technology.* London: Thames and Hudson, 1997.

Thomas Herzog: Bauten, 1978–1992: Ein Werkbericht (Thomas Herzog: Buildings, 1978–1992: a working report). Catalog of an exhibition held at the Architecture Gallery, Munich, October 1992–January 1993. Translated by Peter Green. Stuttgart: G. Hatje, 1992.

Zschokke, Walter. "Unter grossen Dachern" (Under huge roofs). *Bauwelt* 85(23) (1994): 1256–1279.

CHAPTER 10: HIGH TECH ARCHITECTURE

Appleyard, Bryan. *Richard Rogers: A Biography.* London: Faber & Faber, Ltd, 1986.

Burdett, Richard, ed. *Richard Rogers Partnership: Works and Projects.* New York: Monacelli Press, 1995.

Cole, Barbie Campbell, and Ruth Elias Rogers, eds. *Richard Rogers + Architects.* London: Academy Editions; New York: St. Martin's Press, 1985.

Davies, Colin. *High Tech Architecture.* New York: Rizzoli International Publications, 1988.

Foster Associates. London: RIBA Publication, Ltd., 1979.

Foster, Norman, 1964–1987. May extra edition. Tokyo: A&U Publishing Co., Ltd., 1988.

Pawley, Martin. *Norman Foster: A Global Architecture.* New York: Universe Publishing, 1999.

Ove Arup & Partners. *Engineering the Built Environment.* Basel: Birkhauser Verlag, 1994.

Quantrill, Malcolm. *The Norman Foster Studio: Consistency Through Diversity.* London: E&FN Spon, 1999.

Rice, Peter. *An Engineer Imagines.* London: Artemis, 1993.

Robbin, Tony. *Engineering a New Architecture.* New Haven, CT: Yale University Press, 1996.

Rogers, Richard. *Architecture: A Modern View.* New York: Thames and Hudson, Inc, 1990.

Sudjic, Deyan. *The Architecture of Richard Rogers.* London: Fourth Estate and Wordsearch, 1994.

Treiber, Daniel. *Norman Foster.* London: E & FN Spon, 1995.

Centre Georges Pompidou

"Beaubourg." *Tubular Structures* (32) (1979): 16–17.

Berg, Erik, Lennart Grut, and Ole Vanggaard. "Centre Pompidou in Paris." *Arkitekten* (Copenhagen) 80(1) (1978): 2–13.

Bub, Jochen. "Centre Georges-Pompidou in Paris." *Bauwelt* 69(7) (1978): 254–260.

Campbell Cole, Barbie, and Ruth Elias Rogers, eds. *Richard Rogers + Architects.* London: Academy Editions, 1985.

"Centre Beaubourg Pompidou." *Informes de la Construccion* 30(299) (1978): 13–23.

"Centre culturel du Plateau Beaubourg, Paris: Interview de R. Rogers et R. Piano" (The Plateau Beaubourg Cultural Center: Interview with R. Rogers and R. Piano). *Architecture d'Aujourd'hui* 168 (July–August 1973): 34–43.

"Centre Georges Pompidou." *Piano + Rogers: A Statement.* New York: Rizzoli International Publications, Inc, 1977.

"Centre National d'Art et de Culture Georges Pompidou" (National Center for Art and Culture). *Domus* 566 (January 1977):1–37.

"Centre National d'Art et de Culture Georges Pompidou, Paris" (National Center for Art and Culture). *Architecture d'Aaujourd'hui* 213 (February, 1981): 92–95.

"Centre Pompidou." *RIBA Journal* 84 (January 1977): 13–18.

"Centre Pompidou." *Architectural Design* 47(2) (February 1977): entire issue.

"Centre Pompidou." *Architectural Review* 161(693) (May 1977): 270–294.

"Concours du Plateau Beaubourg (Competition for Plateau Beaubourg)." *Architecture d'Aujourd'hui* 43(158) (October-November 1971): 13–18.

"Concours International du Plateau Beaubourg" (International competition for Plateau Beaubourg). *Architecture d'Aujourd'hui* 43(157) (August-September 1971): 6–10

Corbett, Anne. "A Year of Beaubourg." *New Society* 43(800) (1978): 262–263.

Cruickshank, Dan. "Centre Pompidou: Paris 1977–1997." *RIBA Journal* 104(4) (April 1997): 56–63.

De Bure, Gilles. "Centre Pompidou." *Contract Interiors* 137(1) (8) (1977): 76–80.

Demoraine, Hélène, and François Barré. "Beaubourg: Le C.N.A.C. Georges Pompidou" (Beaubourg: The National Center for Art and Culture). *Architecture d'Aujourd'hui* 189 (February 1977): 40–81.

Ford, Edward R. *The Details of Modern Architecture,* Vol. 2, *1928 to 1988.* Cambridge: MIT Press, 1996.

Giedion, S. *Mechanization Takes Command: A Contribution to Anonymous History.* New York: Oxford University Press, 1948.

Marlin, William. "A Building of Paris." *Architectural Record* 163(2) (1978): 103–114.

Moore, Fuller. *Understanding Structures.* Boston: McGraw-Hill, 1999.

"Parigi: Loggetto Funziona!" *Domus* 575 (October 1977): 1–16.

"Piano + Rogers, Architectural Method." *A+U* 66 (June 1976): 63–122.

"Piano & Rogers, Beaubourg." *Domus* 503 (October 1971): 1–7.

"Piano & Rogers: Centre Beaubourg." *Architectural Design* 42 (July 1972): 407–410.

Sandaker, Bjørn Normann, and Arne Petter Eggen. *The Structural Basis of Architecture*. New York: Whitney, 1992.

Saxon, Richard. *Atrium Comes of Age*. Harlow, U.K.: Longman Group, 1993.

Stewart, Ian. "France's Cultural Power House: The Pompidou National Centre." *Country Life* 166(4287) (1979): 678–680.

Volkwin, Marg. "Centre Pompidou—Monument of a Fixed Idea." *Architekt* 2 (1978): 91–94.

Wassenaar, Stephen. "De Beaubourg: Van utopie tot monument" (Beaubourg: From utopia to monument). *Archis* 5 (2000): 28–35.

Wilkinson, Chris. *Supersheds: The Architecture of Long-Span, Large Volume Buildings*. Boston: Butterworth Architecture, 1996.

Wolfe, Shawn. "Yesterday's Tomorrow: Historical Futurism at the Henry." *The Stranger* 8(46). (electronic journal, cited 1 May 1999; available at http://www.thestranger.com).

Zalewski, Waclaw, and Edward Allen. *Shaping Structures: Statics*. New York: John Wiley & Sons, Inc., 1998.

Sainsbury Centre for Visual Arts

Brookes, Alan. *Cladding of Buildings*. 3d ed. London: E & FN Spon, 1998.

Compagno, Andrea. *Intelligente Glasfassaden: Material, Anwendung, Gestaltung* (Intelligent glass façades: Material, practice, design [trans., Ingrid Taylor]). 4th ed. Basel, Switzerland: Birkhauser, 1999.

Davies, Colin. *High Tech Architecture*. New York: Rizzoli, 1988.

"Fostering the Arts." *Architects' Journal* 167(14) (1978): 622–625.

"Informal Touch—Sainsbury Centre for the Visual Arts at the University of East Anglia."

Moore, Fuller. *Understanding Structures*. Boston: McGraw-Hill, 1999.

Orton, Andrew. *The Way We Build Now: Form, Scale and Technique*. Wokingham, U.K.: Van Nostrand Reinhold, 1988.

"Preview '78. Centre for the Visual Arts, University of East Anglia, Norwich." *Architectural Review* 163(971) (1978): 55.

"Sainsbury Centre for the Visual Arts, University of East Anglia." *Baumeister* 76(9) (1979): 875–880.

"Sainsbury Centre for the Visual Arts, University of East Anglia, Norwich." *Architectural Review* 164(982) (December 1978): 345–362.

Spring, Martin. "Art Shed: The Sainsbury Centre for the Visual Arts at the University of East Anglia, Norwich." *Building* 234(7031)(14) (1978): 52–53.

"The Sainsbury Centre for Visual Arts." *Burlington Magazine* 120(906) (1978): 565, 567.

Wilkinson, Chris. *Supersheds: The Architecture of Long-Span, Large Volume Buildings*. Boston: Butterworth Architecture, 1996.

Williams, Stephanie. "Architects: Foster Associates." *Building Design* 381 (1978): 14–15.

Zalewski, Waclaw, and Edward Allen. *Shaping Structures: Statics*. New York: John Wiley & Sons, Inc., 1998.

Lloyd's of London

Baillieu, Amanda. "Faulty Pipes Don't Inhibit Sale of Lloyd's Building." *Architects' Journal* 203(1) (1996): 11.

"Bovis Tries to Buck Lloyd's." *Building Design* 1311 (1997): 3.

Brookes, Alan, and Chris Grech. *The Building Envelope and Connections*. Boston: Architecture Press, 1996.

Brookes, Alan, and Chris Grech. *The Building Envelope: Applications of New Technology Cladding*. London: Butterworth, 1990.

Catt, Richard. "Lloyd's and the QS Factor." *Chartered Quantity Surveyor* 12(1) (1989): 14–15.

Chevin, Denise. "Lloyd's Bidders Face 'Contentious' Form." *Building* 261(7947) (26) (1996): 11.

Compagno, Andrea. *Intelligente Glasfassaden: Material, Anwendung, Gestaltung* (Intelligent glass façades: Material, practice, design [trans., Ingrid Taylor]). 4th ed. Basel, Switzerland: Birkhauser, 1999.

Davies, C. "Lloyd's: Putting It Together." *Architectural Review* (1986): 69.

"Fine Art Praise for 'Brilliant' New Lloyd's." *Building Design* 449 (1979): 3.

Ford, Edward R. *The Details of Modern Architecture*, Vol. 2, *1928 to 1988*. Cambridge: MIT Press, 1996.

Freiman, Ziva. "Critique: The Price of Hubris." *Progressive Architecture* 75(8) (1994): 66–71.

Hagan, Susan. "Lloyd's Assured." *Architects' Journal* 169(23) (1979): 1144–1146.

Knutt, Elaine. "Lloyd's Leaks Costed at 9 Million Pounds." *Building* 261(7935) (14) (1996): 7.

"Lloyd's of London." *Glass Age* 22(4) (1979): 24–25.

Russel, F. *Richard Rogers, Architects*. London: Academy Editions, 1985.

Sandaker, Bjørn Normann, and Arne Petter Eggen. *The Structural Basis of Architecture*. New York: Whitney, 1992.

Sandori, Paul. "From Coffee House to Espresso Machine." *Canadian Architect* 34(11) (1989): 32–33.

Serving the World: The New Lloyd's Building. London: Lloyd's List, Lloyd's of London Press, 1986.Spring, Martin. "Buildings Revisited: Dealing Flaws: Lloyd's Building." *Building* 262(8007) (37) (1997): 52–58.

"'Two Engineered Solutions." *Architects' Journal* 10 (1986): 7994.

Zein Verde, Ruth. "Concreto e aco high-tech na Londres tradicional" (High-tech concrete and steel in traditional London). *Projeto* 126 (1989): 64–76.

Hong Kong and Shanghai Bank

Brookes, Alan, and Chris Grech. *The Building Envelope and Connections*. Boston: Architecture Press, 1996.

Brookes, Alan, and Chris Grech. *The Building Envelope: Applications of New Technology Cladding* London: Butterworth, 1990.

Compagno, Andrea. *Intelligente Glasfassaden: Material, Anwendung, Gestaltung* (Intelligent glass façades: Material, practice, design [trans., Ingrid Taylor]). 4th ed. Basel, Switzerland: Birkhauser, 1999.

Davies, Collin. *High Tech Architecture*. New York: Rizzoli, 1988.

Ford, Edward R. *The Details of Modern Architecture Volume 2: 1928 to 1988*. Cambridge: MIT Press, 1996.

Foster, Andy. "Hong Kong Airport Core Projects." *Arup Journal* 34(1) (1999): 3–60.

Moore, Fuller. *Understanding Structures.* Boston: McGraw Hill Companies Inc., 1999.

Murray, Simon. "The Seawater Intake System for the New Headquarters of the Hong Kong and Shanghai Banking Corporation." *Arup Journal* 18(4) (1983): 2–7.

Orton, Andrew. *The Way We Build Now: Form, Scale and Technique.* Wokingham: Van Nostrand Reinhold, 1988.

Sandaker, Bjørn Normann and Eggen, Arne Petter. *The Structural Basis of Architecture.* New York: Whitney, 1992

Wilkinson, Chris. *Supersheds: The Architecture of Long-Span, Large Volume Buildings.* Boston: Butterworth Architecture, 1996

Williams, Stephanie. *Monument to Mammon — Hong Kong Bank: The Building of Norman Foster's Masterpiece.* London: Cape, 1989.

Zalewski, Waclaw and Allen, Edward. *Shaping Structures: Statics.* New York: John Wiley & Sons, Inc., 1998.

Zunz, Jack. "The Hong Kong Bank: The New Headquarters." *Arup Journal* 20(4) (1985): 2–43.

Zunz, Jack, and Mike Glover. "The Hong Kong and Shanghai Bank." *Arup Journal* 7(4) (1982): 2–10.

CHAPTER 11: GREEN ARCHITECTURE

Butti, Ken, and John Perlin. *A Golden Thread: 2500 Years of Solar Architecture and Technology.* Palo Alto: Cheshire Books; New York: Van Nostrand Reinhold,1980.

Fitzgerald, Eiuleen, and J. Owen Lewis, eds. *European Solar Architecture: Proceedings of a Solar House Contractors' Meeting, Barcelona, 1995.* Dublin: Energy Research Group, 1996.

Lyle, John Tillman. *Regenerative Design for Sustainable Development.* New York: John Wiley & Sons, Inc., 1994.

The Gregory Bateson Building

"A Milestone Takes Shape in California." *AIA Journal* 70(1981): 58–60.

Ashley, Beth. "A Life Spent Thinking Green." *Marin Independent Journal* 8 (February 2000).

Bednar, Michael J. *Interior Pedestrian Places.* New York: Whitney Library of Design, 1989.

Bednar, Michael J. *The New Atrium.* New York: McGraw-Hill, 1986.

Brown, G. Z. *Architectural Design Strategies.* John Wiley & Sons, 1985.

California Energy Resources Conservation and Development Commission. *A Competition for an Energy Efficient Office Building.* Sacramento: Office of the State Architect, 1976.

California Office of the State Architect. *Building Value: Energy Design Guidelines for State Buildings.* Sacramento: Office of the State Architect, 1976.

Calthorpe, Peter. *The Next American Metropolis: Ecology, Community, and the American Dream.* New York: Princeton Architectural Press, 1993.

Fisher, Thomas. "Architects and the Environment." *Progressive Architecture* 72(3) (1991): 69–105.

Goldstein, Barbara. "Would You Let This Man Be Your State Architect." *Building Design* 395 (1978): 20–21.

Jourda, Françoise. "Climatic Architecture." *Techniques et Architecture* 354 (1984): 49–131.

Lechner, Norbert. *Heating, Cooling and Lighting.* New York: John Wiley & Sons, Inc., 1991.

McIntyre, David. "New Health Hazards in Sealed Buildings." *AIA Journal* 72(4) (1983): 64–67.

Niebanck, Paul L. "Symposium: Dilemmas in Growth Management." *American Planning Association. Journal* 50(4) (1984): 403–469.

Pastier, John. "Energy, Frugality, and Humanism." *AIA Journal* 73(1) (1984): 55–97, 106.

Pearson, David, ed. *Seeing Differently: Insights on Innovation.* Boston: Harvard Business School Press, 1997.

Pearson, David. *New Organic Architecture: The Breaking Wave.* Berkeley: University of California, 2001.

"Practicing What They Preach." California State Office Building Competition Gives Energy Efficiency Top Priority for the Building in Sacramento. *Progressive Architecture* 59(2) (1978): 70–73.

Saxon, Richard. *Atrium Buildings: Development and Design.* London: Architectural Press; New York: Van Nostrand Reinhold, 1987.

Scofield Wilson, David. "Old Sacramento: Place as Presence, Palimpsest, and Performance." *Places* 5(2) (1988): 54–63.

"Ship of State on a Solar Course: Sacramento's Bateson Building Is the Flagship in California's Planned Flotilla of Energy Efficient Big Buildings." *Solar Age* 10 (1981): 49–47.

"State Intentions: State Office Building, Sacramento, California." *Progressive Architecture* 62(8) (1981): 76–81.

"State Office Building, Sacramento, California." *Architecture and Urbanism* 5(140) (1982): 57–64.

Stein, Benjamin, and John S. Reynolds. *Mechanical and Electrical Equipment for Buildings.* 8th ed. New York: John Wiley & Sons, Inc., 1992.

Van der Ryn, Sim. "Thoughts on Sacred Landscape and the Geometry of Hope." *BIO-City* 16 (1999).

Van der Ryn, Sim. "Form Follows Flow." *BIO-City* 6 (1995).

Van der Ryn, Sim. "Eco-Village: Toward Sustainable Design." *Progressive Architecture* (1991): 88–89.

Van der Ryn, Sim, and Peter Calthorpe. *Sustainable Communities: A New Design Synthesis for Cities, Suburbs, and Towns.* San Francisco: Sierra Club Books, 1986.

Van der Ryn, Sim. "Integral Design." In *The Design Connection: Energy and Technology in Architecture,* edited by Ralph W. Crump and Martin J. Harms. New York: Van Nostrand Reinhold, 1981.

Van der Ryn, Sim, and Stuart Cowan. *Ecological Design.* Washington, DC: Island Press, 1996.

Van der Ryn, Sim, et al. "Air Quality Problems Plague California State Building." *AIA Journal.* 71(11) (1982): 18, 22.

Woodbridge, Sally. Governing Energy: California State Office Buildings. *Progressive Architecture* 65(4) (1984): 86–91.

Worsley, John C. Structural Upgrading: Managing Construction on the California Capitol. *APT Bulletin* 20(1) (1988): 17–31.

NMB Bank

Alberts, Anton and Manfred Speidel. "The Essence of a Bank Is the Rendering of Service." *A+U* 12(219) (December 1988): 7–46.

Anzivino, Gino. "Sede centrale della NMB Bank, Amsterdam" (Headquarters building of the NMB Bank, Amsterdam). *Domus* 714 (1990): 33–41.

"Bankgebouw te Amsterdam-Zuidoost" (Bank building in Amsterdam). *Bouw* 43(21) (1988): 35–41.

Bouman, Ole, and Roemer van Toorn, eds. *The Invisible in Architecture*. London: Academy Editions, 1994.

Browning, William. "NMB Bank Headquarters." *Urban Land* 51(6) (1992): 23–25.

Canty, Donald. "Holland: Seemingly Sculpted but Highly Rational Bank Headquarters." *AIA Journal* 77(9) (September 1988): 76–79

Coffin, Christie Johnson. "Thick Buildings." *Places* 9(3) (winter 1995): 70–75.

"Designing the Future." *Arkitekten* 94(15) (1992): 442–449.

"Dialogue: Anton Alberts." *Design Book Review* 20(5) (1991): 12–14.

"Dienstbarkeit: Die Nederlandsche Middenstandsbank in Amsterdam" (Subservience: the NMB Bank). *Deutsche Bauzeitung* 122(10) (1988): 37–43.

Duffy, Francis. "The European Challenge." *Architects' Journal* 187(33) (1988): 30–43.

"Expressionnisme revisté" (Expressionism revisited). *Architecture Mouvement Continuité* 21 (1988): 86–89.

Furness, Janine. "Bank to the Future." *Interior Design* 7/8 (1991): 38–40.

Holdsworth, Bill. "Organic Services." *Building Services* 11(3) (1989): 20–24.

Jesberg, Paulgerd. "Anthroposophische Architektur" (Anthroposophic architecture). *Deutsches Architektenblatt* 22(8) (August 1, 1990): 199–200.

"Knock on Brick." *Progressive Architecture* 27(259): 80–81.

Koster, Egbert, and Joop Niesten. "Hoofdkantoor Nederlandse Middenstandsbank Amsterdam: De techniek van een sprooljesburcht" (Headquarters for the Nederlandse Middenstandsbank, Amsterdam: The technique for a fairy-tale castle). *Architect* (The Hague) 18(7/8) (1987): 30–43.

Lambert, Donald. "Trois Villes: Plus Autonomes que Solidaires Amsterdam, La Haye et Rotterdam" (Three cities: More autonomous than solitary). *Architecture d'Aujourd'hui* 257 (July 1988): 2–47.

Lawlor, Robert. *Sacred Geometry: Philosophy and Practice*. New York: Thames and Hudson, 1989.

Lyall, Sutherland. "Dutch Treat." *Building* 252(7521)(45) (1987): 52–56.

McLean, Richard. "Dutch Courage." *Building Design* 855 (1987): 22–25.

"Mensch und Architektur" (People and architecture). *Deutsche Bauzeitschrift* 39(4) (1991): 467–469.

"Netherlands Merchant Bank." *Interior Design* 11(1986): 40–41.

"NMB Bank, Amsterdam." *Architect & Builder* 2 (1991): 22–27.

"NMB Bank, Amsterdam." *Brick Bulletin* (summer 1991): 9.

"Projects: NMB Bank New Head Office, Amsterdam, Netherlands." *Architecture and Urbanism* 2(185) (February 1986): 14–15.

Speidel, Manfred. "NMB bank head office." *A&U* 12(219) (1988): 7–46.

Tetlow, Karin. "Corporate Humanism." *Interiors* 150(16) (1991): 72–73.

Thompson, D'Arcy Wentworth (1860–1948). *On Growth and Form*. Cambridge, U.K.: Cambridge University Press, 1945.

Towndrow, Jenny. "Organic Bank." *RIBA Journal* 95(7) (1988): 51–55.

Treffers, W. M. "Bouwen aan humane werkomgeving" (Building on humane work environment). *Bouw* 42(6) (1987): 46–49.

van Dijk, Hans. "Pinkstervuur op een laag pitje" (Nederlands Middenstandsbank, Amsterdam). *Archis* 1 (1988): 36–45.

Wells, Malcolm. *Notes from the Energy Underground*. New York: Van Nostrand Reinhold, 1980.

Wood, David. "Sickening for Air." *Atrium* (London) 35 (1990): 9–14.

Wyatt, Graham. "Bank Headquarters, Amsterdam Style." *Progressive Architecture* 69(4) (1988): 27–28.

EPUD Headquarters

Ander, Gregg. D. *Daylighting: Performance and Design*. New York: Van Nostrand Reinhold, 1995.

Novitski, Barabara-Jo. "Northwest Office Building Breaks Through the Clouds to Successful Daylighting." *Architectural Lighting* 3(8) (August 1989): 18–25.

Reynolds, John S. *Courtyards: Aesthetic, Social, and Thermal Delight*. New York: John Wiley & Sons, Inc., 2001

Stein, Benjamin, and John S. Reynolds. *Mechanical and Electrical Equipment for Buildings*. 9th ed). New York: John Wiley & Sons, Inc., 2000.

Stein, Benjamin, and John S. Reynolds. *Mechanical and Electrical Equipment for Buildings*. 8th ed.. New York: John Wiley & Sons, Inc., 1992.

Willoughby, John. "Flush of Success: An Energy-Saving Development in Ecologically Minded Oregon." *Building Design* (July 1988): 6–7.

Adam Joseph Lewis Center for Environmental Studies

Blodgett, Geoffrey. *Oberlin Architecture, College and Town: A Guide to Its Social History*. Oberlin, OH: Oberlin College Press, 1985.

Cook, Jeffrey. "Passive and Low Energy Architecture." *Process: Architecture* 98 (1991): 117–159.

Fisher, Thomas. "Architects and the Environment. " *Progressive Architecture* 72(3) (1991): 69–105.

Green Building's Clean Air Could Help Set Indoor Standards. *Environmental Science and Technology* 34(9)(2000): 201A–217A

Iannacci, Anthony. "Immagine USA" (Imagine USA). *Arca* 127 (June 1998): 2–88.

Lassar, Terry Jill. "Sick Building Syndrome." *Urban Land* 49(6) (1990): 34–35.

McDonough, William. "Redesigning Design Itself." *Whole Earth*, Winter, 1988.

McKee, Bradford. "Sustainable Design." *Architecture* 84(7) (1995): 61–141, 168.

Meadows, Donella. "A Building Can be a Teacher." *The Global Citizen*, October 20, 1997.

"Oberlin to Get Cutting-Edge Environmental Studies Building." *Architectural Record* 185(6) (1997): 42–43.

Orr, David W. Architecture as Pedagogy II

Russell, James S. "Building Types Study: 744. Knowledge-Based Production Facilities." *Architectural Record* 184(12) (1996): 23–53, 147.

Shulman, Ken. "*Think Green.*" *Metropolis* 21(1) (August–September 2001): 76–81,102,126.

Tetlow, Karen. "Adam Joseph Lewis Center for Environmental Studies." *Interiors* (January 1999): 110–111.

Truppin, Andrea. "William McDonough, 1999 Designer of the Year." *Interiors* 158(1) (January 1999): 95–117.

Vogliazzo, Maurizio. "Environmental Studies Center, Oberlin College, Ohio." *Arca* 127 (June 1998): 64–67.

Wagner, Michael. "Creative Catalyst." *Interiors* 152(3) (1993): 53–67.

Wagner, Michael. "Socially Conscious Design." *Interiors* 149(5) (1989): 71–99, 110, 116 118.

Table A.1 GENERAL BIBLIOGRAPHY FOR THE CASE STUDIES

Works listed here contain technical case studies on multiple buildings. The table lists page numbers used as reference for case studies in this text. Full citations are listed on page 455.

					Banham, 1964	Fitch, 1972	Guise, 1985	Bednar, 1986	Davies, 1988	Brookes and Grech, 1990	Sandaker and Eggen, 1992	Saxon, 1993	Brookes and Grech, 1994	Brookes and Grech, 1996	Ford, 1996	Brookes, 1998	Zalewski and Allen, 1998	Moore, 1999	Wilkenson, 1996	Compagno, 1999	Stein and Reynolds, 1992, 2000
Laboratory	1	Richards	1961	Louis Kahn	246		185								311				86		
	2	Salk	1965	Louis Kahn											316				86	86	
	3	Schlumberger	1985	Michael Hopkins					108	92	85			92							
	4	PAT	1986	Richard Rogers					32	81				81	388			167		32	32
	5	Wallace	1988	IKOY																	
Office	6	Deere	1963	Eero Saarinen		107									300						
	7	Willis Faber Dumas	1973	Norman Foster					56		55					160					
	8	Briarcliff House	1983	Arup Associates																	
	9	Lockheed	1983	Leo Daly				160													
Airport	10	Dulles	1962	Eero Saarinen		220					180				296			190	128	128	
	11	Stansted	1991	Norman Foster					66	101			101							74
	12	O'Hare	1988	Helmut Jahn							214										
	13	Kansai	1994	Renzo Piano							97						377			53
Pavilion	14	Olympic Stadium	1972	Behnisch/Otto														135	135	
	15	Arab Institute	1988	Jean Nouvell											396					111
	16	Linz Design Center	1988	Thomas Herzog																	
	17	British Pavilion	1992	Nicholas Grimshaw																	
Residence	18	Eames	1949	Charles and Ray Eames									288			112	112		
	19	Magney	1986	Glenn Murcutt											416					
	20	Experimental	1984	Benthem Crouwel					148	5			5							
	21	Two-Family House	1989	Thomas Herzog																
High Tech	22	Pompidou	1975	Piano and Rogers						66	31			386			142	38	38	
	23	Sainsbury	1977	Norman Foster					58							117	113	43	43	21
	24	Lloyd's	1984	Richard Rogers					42	54	35		54	390						76
	25	Hong Kong	1985	Norman Foster					68	122	14		122	392			59	92	92	94
Green	26	Bateson	1981	Sim Van der Ryn				146												
	27	NMB	1987	Alberts & Van Huut																
	28	EPUD	1988	John Reynolds																
	29	Lewis Center	2000	McDonough + Partners																

Index